Dictionary of Literary Biography

1 *The American Renaissance in New England,* edited by Joel Myerson (1978)

2 *American Novelists Since World War II,* edited by Jeffrey Helterman and Richard Layman (1978)

3 *Antebellum Writers in New York and the South,* edited by Joel Myerson (1979)

4 *American Writers in Paris, 1920–1939,* edited by Karen Lane Rood (1980)

5 *American Poets Since World War II,* 2 parts, edited by Donald J. Greiner (1980)

6 *American Novelists Since World War II, Second Series,* edited by James E. Kibler Jr. (1980)

7 *Twentieth-Century American Dramatists,* 2 parts, edited by John MacNicholas (1981)

8 *Twentieth-Century American Science-Fiction Writers,* 2 parts, edited by David Cowart and Thomas L. Wymer (1981)

9 *American Novelists, 1910–1945,* 3 parts, edited by James J. Martine (1981)

10 *Modern British Dramatists, 1900–1945,* 2 parts, edited by Stanley Weintraub (1982)

11 *American Humorists, 1800–1950,* 2 parts, edited by Stanley Trachtenberg (1982)

12 *American Realists and Naturalists,* edited by Donald Pizer and Earl N. Harbert (1982)

13 *British Dramatists Since World War II,* 2 parts, edited by Stanley Weintraub (1982)

14 *British Novelists Since 1960,* 2 parts, edited by Jay L. Halio (1983)

15 *British Novelists, 1930–1959,* 2 parts, edited by Bernard Oldsey (1983)

16 *The Beats: Literary Bohemians in Postwar America,* 2 parts, edited by Ann Charters (1983)

17 *Twentieth-Century American Historians,* edited by Clyde N. Wilson (1983)

18 *Victorian Novelists After 1885,* edited by Ira B. Nadel and William E. Fredeman (1983)

19 *British Poets, 1880–1914,* edited by Donald E. Stanford (1983)

20 *British Poets, 1914–1945,* edited by Donald E. Stanford (1983)

21 *Victorian Novelists Before 1885,* edited by Ira B. Nadel and William E. Fredeman (1983)

22 *American Writers for Children, 1900–1960,* edited by John Cech (1983)

23 *American Newspaper Journalists, 1873–1900,* edited by Perry J. Ashley (1983)

24 *American Colonial Writers, 1606–1734,* edited by Emory Elliott (1984)

25 *American Newspaper Journalists, 1901–1925,* edited by Perry J. Ashley (1984)

26 *American Screenwriters,* edited by Robert E. Morsberger, Stephen O. Lesser, and Randall Clark (1984)

27 *Poets of Great Britain and Ireland, 1945–1960,* edited by Vincent B. Sherry Jr. (1984)

28 *Twentieth-Century American-Jewish Fiction Writers,* edited by Daniel Walden (1984)

29 *American Newspaper Journalists, 1926–1950,* edited by Perry J. Ashley (1984)

30 *American Historians, 1607–1865,* edited by Clyde N. Wilson (1984)

31 *American Colonial Writers, 1735–1781,* edited by Emory Elliott (1984)

32 *Victorian Poets Before 1850,* edited by William E. Fredeman and Ira B. Nadel (1984)

33 *Afro-American Fiction Writers After 1955,* edited by Thadious M. Davis and Trudier Harris (1984)

34 *British Novelists, 1890–1929: Traditionalists,* edited by Thomas F. Staley (1985)

35 *Victorian Poets After 1850,* edited by William E. Fredeman and Ira B. Nadel (1985)

36 *British Novelists, 1890–1929: Modernists,* edited by Thomas F. Staley (1985)

37 *American Writers of the Early Republic,* edited by Emory Elliott (1985)

38 *Afro-American Writers After 1955: Dramatists and Prose Writers,* edited by Thadious M. Davis and Trudier Harris (1985)

39 *British Novelists, 1660–1800,* 2 parts, edited by Martin C. Battestin (1985)

40 *Poets of Great Britain and Ireland Since 1960,* 2 parts, edited by Vincent B. Sherry Jr. (1985)

41 *Afro-American Poets Since 1955,* edited by Trudier Harris and Thadious M. Davis (1985)

42 *American Writers for Children Before 1900,* edited by Glenn E. Estes (1985)

43 *American Newspaper Journalists, 1690–1872,* edited by Perry J. Ashley (1986)

44 *American Screenwriters, Second Series,* edited by Randall Clark, Robert E. Morsberger, and Stephen O. Lesser (1986)

45 *American Poets, 1880–1945, First Series,* edited by Peter Quartermain (1986)

46 *American Literary Publishing Houses, 1900–1980: Trade and Paperback,* edited by Peter Dzwonkoski (1986)

47 *American Historians, 1866–1912,* edited by Clyde N. Wilson (1986)

48 *American Poets, 1880–1945, Second Series,* edited by Peter Quartermain (1986)

49 *American Literary Publishing Houses, 1638–1899,* 2 parts, edited by Peter Dzwonkoski (1986)

50 *Afro-American Writers Before the Harlem Renaissance,* edited by Trudier Harris (1986)

51 *Afro-American Writers from the Harlem Renaissance to 1940,* edited by Trudier Harris (1987)

52 *American Writers for Children Since 1960: Fiction,* edited by Glenn E. Estes (1986)

53 *Canadian Writers Since 1960, First Series,* edited by W. H. New (1986)

54 *American Poets, 1880–1945, Third Series,* 2 parts, edited by Peter Quartermain (1987)

55 *Victorian Prose Writers Before 1867,* edited by William B. Thesing (1987)

56 *German Fiction Writers, 1914–1945,* edited by James Hardin (1987)

57 *Victorian Prose Writers After 1867,* edited by William B. Thesing (1987)

58 *Jacobean and Caroline Dramatists,* edited by Fredson Bowers (1987)

59 *American Literary Critics and Scholars, 1800–1850,* edited by John W. Rathbun and Monica M. Grecu (1987)

60 *Canadian Writers Since 1960, Second Series,* edited by W. H. New (1987)

61 *American Writers for Children Since 1960: Poets, Illustrators, and Nonfiction Authors,* edited by Glenn E. Estes (1987)

62 *Elizabethan Dramatists,* edited by Fredson Bowers (1987)

63 *Modern American Critics, 1920–1955,* edited by Gregory S. Jay (1988)

64 *American Literary Critics and Scholars, 1850–1880,* edited by John W. Rathbun and Monica M. Grecu (1988)

65 *French Novelists, 1900–1930,* edited by Catharine Savage Brosman (1988)

66 *German Fiction Writers, 1885–1913,* 2 parts, edited by James Hardin (1988)

67 *Modern American Critics Since 1955,* edited by Gregory S. Jay (1988)

68 *Canadian Writers, 1920–1959, First Series,* edited by W. H. New (1988)

69 *Contemporary German Fiction Writers, First Series,* edited by Wolfgang D. Elfe and James Hardin (1988)

70 *British Mystery Writers, 1860–1919,* edited by Bernard Benstock and Thomas F. Staley (1988)

71 *American Literary Critics and Scholars, 1880–1900,* edited by John W. Rathbun and Monica M. Grecu (1988)

72 *French Novelists, 1930–1960,* edited by Catharine Savage Brosman (1988)

73 *American Magazine Journalists, 1741–1850,* edited by Sam G. Riley (1988)

74 *American Short-Story Writers Before 1880,* edited by Bobby Ellen Kimbel, with the assistance of William E. Grant (1988)

75 *Contemporary German Fiction Writers, Second Series,* edited by Wolfgang D. Elfe and James Hardin (1988)

76 *Afro-American Writers, 1940–1955,* edited by Trudier Harris (1988)

77 *British Mystery Writers, 1920–1939,* edited by Bernard Benstock and Thomas F. Staley (1988)

78 *American Short-Story Writers, 1880–1910,* edited by Bobby Ellen Kimbel, with the assistance of William E. Grant (1988)

79 *American Magazine Journalists, 1850–1900,* edited by Sam G. Riley (1988)

80 *Restoration and Eighteenth-Century Dramatists, First Series,* edited by Paula R. Backscheider (1989)

81 *Austrian Fiction Writers, 1875–1913,* edited by James Hardin and Donald G. Daviau (1989)

82 *Chicano Writers, First Series,* edited by Francisco A. Lomelí and Carl R. Shirley (1989)

83 *French Novelists Since 1960,* edited by Catharine Savage Brosman (1989)

84 *Restoration and Eighteenth-Century Dramatists, Second Series,* edited by Paula R. Backscheider (1989)

85 *Austrian Fiction Writers After 1914,* edited by James Hardin and Donald G. Daviau (1989)

86 *American Short-Story Writers, 1910–1945, First Series,* edited by Bobby Ellen Kimbel (1989)

87 *British Mystery and Thriller Writers Since 1940, First Series,* edited by Bernard Benstock and Thomas F. Staley (1989)

88 *Canadian Writers, 1920–1959, Second Series,* edited by W. H. New (1989)

89 *Restoration and Eighteenth-Century Dramatists, Third Series,* edited by Paula R. Backscheider (1989)

90 *German Writers in the Age of Goethe, 1789–1832,* edited by James Hardin and Christoph E. Schweitzer (1989)

91 *American Magazine Journalists, 1900–1960, First Series,* edited by Sam G. Riley (1990)

92 *Canadian Writers, 1890–1920,* edited by W. H. New (1990)

93 *British Romantic Poets, 1789–1832, First Series,* edited by John R. Greenfield (1990)

94 *German Writers in the Age of Goethe: Sturm und Drang to Classicism,* edited by James Hardin and Christoph E. Schweitzer (1990)

95 *Eighteenth-Century British Poets, First Series,* edited by John Sitter (1990)

96 *British Romantic Poets, 1789–1832, Second Series,* edited by John R. Greenfield (1990)

97 *German Writers from the Enlightenment to Sturm und Drang, 1720–1764,* edited by James Hardin and Christoph E. Schweitzer (1990)

98 *Modern British Essayists, First Series,* edited by Robert Beum (1990)

99 *Canadian Writers Before 1890,* edited by W. H. New (1990)

100 *Modern British Essayists, Second Series,* edited by Robert Beum (1990)

101 *British Prose Writers, 1660–1800, First Series,* edited by Donald T. Siebert (1991)

102 *American Short-Story Writers, 1910–1945, Second Series,* edited by Bobby Ellen Kimbel (1991)

103 *American Literary Biographers, First Series,* edited by Steven Serafin (1991)

104 *British Prose Writers, 1660–1800, Second Series,* edited by Donald T. Siebert (1991)

105 *American Poets Since World War II, Second Series,* edited by R. S. Gwynn (1991)

106 *British Literary Publishing Houses, 1820–1880,* edited by Patricia J. Anderson and Jonathan Rose (1991)

107 *British Romantic Prose Writers, 1789–1832, First Series,* edited by John R. Greenfield (1991)

108 *Twentieth-Century Spanish Poets, First Series,* edited by Michael L. Perna (1991)

109 *Eighteenth-Century British Poets, Second Series,* edited by John Sitter (1991)

110 *British Romantic Prose Writers, 1789–1832, Second Series,* edited by John R. Greenfield (1991)

111 *American Literary Biographers, Second Series,* edited by Steven Serafin (1991)

112 *British Literary Publishing Houses, 1881–1965,* edited by Jonathan Rose and Patricia J. Anderson (1991)

113 *Modern Latin-American Fiction Writers, First Series,* edited by William Luis (1992)

114 *Twentieth-Century Italian Poets, First Series,* edited by Giovanna Wedel De Stasio, Glauco Cambon, and Antonio Illiano (1992)

115 *Medieval Philosophers,* edited by Jeremiah Hackett (1992)

116 *British Romantic Novelists, 1789–1832,* edited by Bradford K. Mudge (1992)

117 *Twentieth-Century Caribbean and Black African Writers, First Series,* edited by Bernth Lindfors and Reinhard Sander (1992)

118 *Twentieth-Century German Dramatists, 1889–1918,* edited by Wolfgang D. Elfe and James Hardin (1992)

119 *Nineteenth-Century French Fiction Writers: Romanticism and Realism, 1800–1860,* edited by Catharine Savage Brosman (1992)

120 *American Poets Since World War II, Third Series,* edited by R. S. Gwynn (1992)

121 *Seventeenth-Century British Nondramatic Poets, First Series,* edited by M. Thomas Hester (1992)

122 *Chicano Writers, Second Series,* edited by Francisco A. Lomelí and Carl R. Shirley (1992)

123 *Nineteenth-Century French Fiction Writers: Naturalism and Beyond, 1860–1900,* edited by Catharine Savage Brosman (1992)

124 *Twentieth-Century German Dramatists, 1919–1992,* edited by Wolfgang D. Elfe and James Hardin (1992)

125 *Twentieth-Century Caribbean and Black African Writers, Second Series,* edited by Bernth Lindfors and Reinhard Sander (1993)

126 *Seventeenth-Century British Nondramatic Poets, Second Series,* edited by M. Thomas Hester (1993)

127 *American Newspaper Publishers, 1950–1990,* edited by Perry J. Ashley (1993)

128 *Twentieth-Century Italian Poets, Second Series,* edited by Giovanna Wedel De Stasio, Glauco Cambon, and Antonio Illiano (1993)

129 *Nineteenth-Century German Writers, 1841–1900,* edited by James Hardin and Siegfried Mews (1993)

130 *American Short-Story Writers Since World War II,* edited by Patrick Meanor (1993)

131 *Seventeenth-Century British Nondramatic Poets, Third Series,* edited by M. Thomas Hester (1993)

132 *Sixteenth-Century British Nondramatic Writers, First Series,* edited by David A. Richardson (1993)

133 *Nineteenth-Century German Writers to 1840,* edited by James Hardin and Siegfried Mews (1993)

134 *Twentieth-Century Spanish Poets, Second Series,* edited by Jerry Phillips Winfield (1994)

135 *British Short-Fiction Writers, 1880–1914: The Realist Tradition,* edited by William B. Thesing (1994)

136 *Sixteenth-Century British Nondramatic Writers, Second Series,* edited by David A. Richardson (1994)

137 *American Magazine Journalists, 1900–1960, Second Series,* edited by Sam G. Riley (1994)

138 *German Writers and Works of the High Middle Ages: 1170–1280,* edited by James Hardin and Will Hasty (1994)

139 *British Short-Fiction Writers, 1945–1980,* edited by Dean Baldwin (1994)

140 *American Book-Collectors and Bibliographers, First Series,* edited by Joseph Rosenblum (1994)

141 *British Children's Writers, 1880–1914,* edited by Laura M. Zaidman (1994)

142 *Eighteenth-Century British Literary Biographers,* edited by Steven Serafin (1994)

143 *American Novelists Since World War II, Third Series,* edited by James R. Giles and Wanda H. Giles (1994)

144 *Nineteenth-Century British Literary Biographers,* edited by Steven Serafin (1994)

145 *Modern Latin-American Fiction Writers, Second Series,* edited by William Luis and Ann González (1994)

146 *Old and Middle English Literature,* edited by Jeffrey Helterman and Jerome Mitchell (1994)

147 *South Slavic Writers Before World War II,* edited by Vasa D. Mihailovich (1994)

148 *German Writers and Works of the Early Middle Ages: 800–1170,* edited by Will Hasty and James Hardin (1994)

149 *Late Nineteenth- and Early Twentieth-Century British Literary Biographers,* edited by Steven Serafin (1995)

150 *Early Modern Russian Writers, Late Seventeenth and Eighteenth Centuries,* edited by Marcus C. Levitt (1995)

151 *British Prose Writers of the Early Seventeenth Century,* edited by Clayton D. Lein (1995)

152 *American Novelists Since World War II, Fourth Series,* edited by James R. Giles and Wanda H. Giles (1995)

153 *Late-Victorian and Edwardian British Novelists, First Series,* edited by George M. Johnson (1995)

154 *The British Literary Book Trade, 1700–1820,* edited by James K. Bracken and Joel Silver (1995)

155 *Twentieth-Century British Literary Biographers,* edited by Steven Serafin (1995)

156 *British Short-Fiction Writers, 1880–1914: The Romantic Tradition,* edited by William F. Naufftus (1995)

157 *Twentieth-Century Caribbean and Black African Writers, Third Series,* edited by Bernth Lindfors and Reinhard Sander (1995)

158 *British Reform Writers, 1789–1832,* edited by Gary Kelly and Edd Applegate (1995)

159 *British Short-Fiction Writers, 1800–1880,* edited by John R. Greenfield (1996)

160 *British Children's Writers, 1914–1960,* edited by Donald R. Hettinga and Gary D. Schmidt (1996)

161 *British Children's Writers Since 1960, First Series,* edited by Caroline Hunt (1996)

162 *British Short-Fiction Writers, 1915–1945,* edited by John H. Rogers (1996)

163 *British Children's Writers, 1800–1880,* edited by Meena Khorana (1996)

164 *German Baroque Writers, 1580–1660,* edited by James Hardin (1996)

165 *American Poets Since World War II, Fourth Series,* edited by Joseph Conte (1996)

166 *British Travel Writers, 1837–1875,* edited by Barbara Brothers and Julia Gergits (1996)

167 *Sixteenth-Century British Nondramatic Writers, Third Series,* edited by David A. Richardson (1996)

168 *German Baroque Writers, 1661–1730,* edited by James Hardin (1996)

169 *American Poets Since World War II, Fifth Series,* edited by Joseph Conte (1996)

170 *The British Literary Book Trade, 1475–1700,* edited by James K. Bracken and Joel Silver (1996)

171 *Twentieth-Century American Sportswriters,* edited by Richard Orodenker (1996)

172 *Sixteenth-Century British Nondramatic Writers, Fourth Series,* edited by David A. Richardson (1996)

173 *American Novelists Since World War II, Fifth Series,* edited by James R. Giles and Wanda H. Giles (1996)

174 *British Travel Writers, 1876–1909,* edited by Barbara Brothers and Julia Gergits (1997)

175 *Native American Writers of the United States,* edited by Kenneth M. Roemer (1997)

176 *Ancient Greek Authors,* edited by Ward W. Briggs (1997)

177 *Italian Novelists Since World War II, 1945–1965,* edited by Augustus Pallotta (1997)

178 *British Fantasy and Science-Fiction Writers Before World War I,* edited by Darren Harris-Fain (1997)

179 *German Writers of the Renaissance and Reformation, 1280–1580,* edited by James Hardin and Max Reinhart (1997)

180 *Japanese Fiction Writers, 1868–1945,* edited by Van C. Gessel (1997)

181 *South Slavic Writers Since World War II,* edited by Vasa D. Mihailovich (1997)

182 *Japanese Fiction Writers Since World War II,* edited by Van C. Gessel (1997)

183 *American Travel Writers, 1776–1864,* edited by James J. Schramer and Donald Ross (1997)

184 *Nineteenth-Century British Book-Collectors and Bibliographers,* edited by William Baker and Kenneth Womack (1997)

185 *American Literary Journalists, 1945–1995, First Series,* edited by Arthur J. Kaul (1998)

186 *Nineteenth-Century American Western Writers,* edited by Robert L. Gale (1998)

187 *American Book Collectors and Bibliographers, Second Series,* edited by Joseph Rosenblum (1998)

188 *American Book and Magazine Illustrators to 1920,* edited by Steven E. Smith, Catherine A. Hastedt, and Donald H. Dyal (1998)

189 *American Travel Writers, 1850–1915,* edited by Donald Ross and James J. Schramer (1998)

190 *British Reform Writers, 1832–1914,* edited by Gary Kelly and Edd Applegate (1998)

191 *British Novelists Between the Wars,* edited by George M. Johnson (1998)

192 *French Dramatists, 1789–1914,* edited by Barbara T. Cooper (1998)

193 *American Poets Since World War II, Sixth Series,* edited by Joseph Conte (1998)

194 *British Novelists Since 1960, Second Series,* edited by Merritt Moseley (1998)

195 *British Travel Writers, 1910–1939,* edited by Barbara Brothers and Julia Gergits (1998)

196 *Italian Novelists Since World War II, 1965–1995,* edited by Augustus Pallotta (1999)

197 *Late-Victorian and Edwardian British Novelists, Second Series,* edited by George M. Johnson (1999)

198 *Russian Literature in the Age of Pushkin and Gogol: Prose,* edited by Christine A. Rydel (1999)

199 *Victorian Women Poets,* edited by William B. Thesing (1999)

200 *American Women Prose Writers to 1820,* edited by Carla J. Mulford, with Angela Vietto and Amy E. Winans (1999)

201 *Twentieth-Century British Book Collectors and Bibliographers,* edited by William Baker and Kenneth Womack (1999)

202 *Nineteenth-Century American Fiction Writers,* edited by Kent P. Ljungquist (1999)

203 *Medieval Japanese Writers,* edited by Steven D. Carter (1999)

204 *British Travel Writers, 1940–1997,* edited by Barbara Brothers and Julia M. Gergits (1999)

205 *Russian Literature in the Age of Pushkin and Gogol: Poetry and Drama,* edited by Christine A. Rydel (1999)

206 *Twentieth-Century American Western Writers, First Series,* edited by Richard H. Cracroft (1999)

207 *British Novelists Since 1960, Third Series,* edited by Merritt Moseley (1999)

208 *Literature of the French and Occitan Middle Ages: Eleventh to Fifteenth Centuries,* edited by Deborah Sinnreich-Levi and Ian S. Laurie (1999)

209 *Chicano Writers, Third Series,* edited by Francisco A. Lomelí and Carl R. Shirley (1999)

210 *Ernest Hemingway: A Documentary Volume,* edited by Robert W. Trogdon (1999)

211 *Ancient Roman Writers,* edited by Ward W. Briggs (1999)

212 *Twentieth-Century American Western Writers, Second Series,* edited by Richard H. Cracroft (1999)

213 *Pre-Nineteenth-Century British Book Collectors and Bibliographers,* edited by William Baker and Kenneth Womack (1999)

214 *Twentieth-Century Danish Writers,* edited by Marianne Stecher-Hansen (1999)

215 *Twentieth-Century Eastern European Writers, First Series,* edited by Steven Serafin (1999)

216 *British Poets of the Great War: Brooke, Rosenberg, Thomas. A Documentary Volume,* edited by Patrick Quinn (2000)

217 *Nineteenth-Century French Poets,* edited by Robert Beum (2000)

218 *American Short-Story Writers Since World War II, Second Series,* edited by Patrick Meanor and Gwen Crane (2000)

219 *F. Scott Fitzgerald's* The Great Gatsby: *A Documentary Volume,* edited by Matthew J. Bruccoli (2000)

220 *Twentieth-Century Eastern European Writers, Second Series,* edited by Steven Serafin (2000)

221 *American Women Prose Writers, 1870–1920,* edited by Sharon M. Harris, with the assistance of Heidi L. M. Jacobs and Jennifer Putzi (2000)

222 *H. L. Mencken: A Documentary Volume,* edited by Richard J. Schrader (2000)

223 *The American Renaissance in New England, Second Series,* edited by Wesley T. Mott (2000)

224 *Walt Whitman: A Documentary Volume,* edited by Joel Myerson (2000)

225 *South African Writers,* edited by Paul A. Scanlon (2000)

226 *American Hard-Boiled Crime Writers,* edited by George Parker Anderson and Julie B. Anderson (2000)

227 *American Novelists Since World War II, Sixth Series,* edited by James R. Giles and Wanda H. Giles (2000)

228 *Twentieth-Century American Dramatists, Second Series,* edited by Christopher J. Wheatley (2000)

229 *Thomas Wolfe: A Documentary Volume,* edited by Ted Mitchell (2001)

230 *Australian Literature, 1788–1914,* edited by Selina Samuels (2001)

231 *British Novelists Since 1960, Fourth Series,* edited by Merritt Moseley (2001)

232 *Twentieth-Century Eastern European Writers, Third Series,* edited by Steven Serafin (2001)

233 *British and Irish Dramatists Since World War II, Second Series,* edited by John Bull (2001)

234 *American Short-Story Writers Since World War II, Third Series,* edited by Patrick Meanor and Richard E. Lee (2001)

235 *The American Renaissance in New England, Third Series,* edited by Wesley T. Mott (2001)

236 *British Rhetoricians and Logicians, 1500–1660,* edited by Edward A. Malone (2001)

237 *The Beats: A Documentary Volume,* edited by Matt Theado (2001)

238 *Russian Novelists in the Age of Tolstoy and Dostoevsky,* edited by J. Alexander Ogden and Judith E. Kalb (2001)

239 *American Women Prose Writers: 1820–1870,* edited by Amy E. Hudock and Katharine Rodier (2001)

240 *Late Nineteenth- and Early Twentieth-Century British Women Poets,* edited by William B. Thesing (2001)

241 *American Sportswriters and Writers on Sport,* edited by Richard Orodenker (2001)

242 *Twentieth-Century European Cultural Theorists, First Series,* edited by Paul Hansom (2001)

243 *The American Renaissance in New England, Fourth Series,* edited by Wesley T. Mott (2001)

244 *American Short-Story Writers Since World War II, Fourth Series,* edited by Patrick Meanor and Joseph McNicholas (2001)

245 *British and Irish Dramatists Since World War II, Third Series,* edited by John Bull (2001)

246 *Twentieth-Century American Cultural Theorists,* edited by Paul Hansom (2001)

247 *James Joyce: A Documentary Volume,* edited by A. Nicholas Fargnoli (2001)

248 *Antebellum Writers in the South, Second Series,* edited by Kent Ljungquist (2001)

249 *Twentieth-Century American Dramatists, Third Series,* edited by Christopher Wheatley (2002)

250 *Antebellum Writers in New York, Second Series,* edited by Kent Ljungquist (2002)

251 *Canadian Fantasy and Science-Fiction Writers,* edited by Douglas Ivison (2002)

252 *British Philosophers, 1500–1799,* edited by Philip B. Dematteis and Peter S. Fosl (2002)

253 *Raymond Chandler: A Documentary Volume,* edited by Robert Moss (2002)

254 *The House of Putnam, 1837–1872: A Documentary Volume,* edited by Ezra Greenspan (2002)

255 *British Fantasy and Science-Fiction Writers, 1918–1960,* edited by Darren Harris-Fain (2002)

256 *Twentieth-Century American Western Writers, Third Series,* edited by Richard H. Cracroft (2002)

257 *Twentieth-Century Swedish Writers After World War II,* edited by Ann-Charlotte Gavel Adams (2002)

258 *Modern French Poets,* edited by Jean-François Leroux (2002)

259 *Twentieth-Century Swedish Writers Before World War II,* edited by Ann-Charlotte Gavel Adams (2002)

260 *Australian Writers, 1915–1950,* edited by Selina Samuels (2002)

261 *British Fantasy and Science-Fiction Writers Since 1960,* edited by Darren Harris-Fain (2002)

262 *British Philosophers, 1800–2000,* edited by Peter S. Fosl and Leemon B. McHenry (2002)

263 *William Shakespeare: A Documentary Volume,* edited by Catherine Loomis (2002)

264 *Italian Prose Writers, 1900–1945,* edited by Luca Somigli and Rocco Capozzi (2002)

265 *American Song Lyricists, 1920–1960,* edited by Philip Furia (2002)

266 *Twentieth-Century American Dramatists, Fourth Series,* edited by Christopher J. Wheatley (2002)

267 *Twenty-First-Century British and Irish Novelists,* edited by Michael R. Molino (2002)

268 *Seventeenth-Century French Writers,* edited by Françoise Jaouën (2002)

269 *Nathaniel Hawthorne: A Documentary Volume,* edited by Benjamin Franklin V (2002)

270 *American Philosophers Before 1950,* edited by Philip B. Dematteis and Leemon B. McHenry (2002)

271 *British and Irish Novelists Since 1960,* edited by Merritt Moseley (2002)

272 *Russian Prose Writers Between the World Wars,* edited by Christine Rydel (2003)

273 *F. Scott Fitzgerald's* Tender Is the Night: *A Documentary Volume,* edited by Matthew J. Bruccoli and George Parker Anderson (2003)

274 *John Dos Passos's* U.S.A.: *A Documentary Volume,* edited by Donald Pizer (2003)

275 *Twentieth-Century American Nature Writers: Prose,* edited by Roger Thompson and J. Scott Bryson (2003)

276 *British Mystery and Thriller Writers Since 1960,* edited by Gina Macdonald (2003)

277 *Russian Literature in the Age of Realism,* edited by Alyssa Dinega Gillespie (2003)

278 *American Novelists Since World War II, Seventh Series,* edited by James R. Giles and Wanda H. Giles (2003)

279 *American Philosophers, 1950–2000,* edited by Philip B. Dematteis and Leemon B. McHenry (2003)

280 *Dashiell Hammett's* The Maltese Falcon: *A Documentary Volume,* edited by Richard Layman (2003)

281 *British Rhetoricians and Logicians, 1500–1660, Second Series,* edited by Edward A. Malone (2003)

282 *New Formalist Poets,* edited by Jonathan N. Barron and Bruce Meyer (2003)

283 *Modern Spanish American Poets, First Series,* edited by María A. Salgado (2003)

284 *The House of Holt, 1866–1946: A Documentary Volume,* edited by Ellen D. Gilbert (2003)

285 *Russian Writers Since 1980,* edited by Marina Balina and Mark Lipovetsky (2004)

286 *Castilian Writers, 1400–1500,* edited by Frank A. Domínguez and George D. Greenia (2004)

287 *Portuguese Writers,* edited by Monica Rector and Fred M. Clark (2004)

288 *The House of Boni & Liveright, 1917–1933: A Documentary Volume,* edited by Charles Egleston (2004)

289 *Australian Writers, 1950–1975,* edited by Selina Samuels (2004)

290 *Modern Spanish American Poets, Second Series,* edited by María A. Salgado (2004)

291 *The Hoosier House: Bobbs-Merrill and Its Predecessors, 1850–1985: A Documentary Volume,* edited by Richard J. Schrader (2004)

Dictionary of Literary Biography Documentary Series

1 *Sherwood Anderson, Willa Cather, John Dos Passos, Theodore Dreiser, F. Scott Fitzgerald, Ernest Hemingway, Sinclair Lewis,* edited by Margaret A. Van Antwerp (1982)

2 *James Gould Cozzens, James T. Farrell, William Faulkner, John O'Hara, John Steinbeck, Thomas Wolfe, Richard Wright,* edited by Margaret A. Van Antwerp (1982)

3 *Saul Bellow, Jack Kerouac, Norman Mailer, Vladimir Nabokov, John Updike, Kurt Vonnegut,* edited by Mary Bruccoli (1983)

4 *Tennessee Williams,* edited by Margaret A. Van Antwerp and Sally Johns (1984)

5 *American Transcendentalists,* edited by Joel Myerson (1988)

6 *Hardboiled Mystery Writers: Raymond Chandler, Dashiell Hammett, Ross Macdonald,* edited by Matthew J. Bruccoli and Richard Layman (1989)

7 *Modern American Poets: James Dickey, Robert Frost, Marianne Moore,* edited by Karen L. Rood (1989)

8 *The Black Aesthetic Movement,* edited by Jeffrey Louis Decker (1991)

9 *American Writers of the Vietnam War: W. D. Ehrhart, Larry Heinemann, Tim O'Brien, Walter McDonald, John M. Del Vecchio,* edited by Ronald Baughman (1991)

10 *The Bloomsbury Group,* edited by Edward L. Bishop (1992)

11 *American Proletarian Culture: The Twenties and The Thirties,* edited by Jon Christian Suggs (1993)

12 *Southern Women Writers: Flannery O'Connor, Katherine Anne Porter, Eudora Welty,* edited by Mary Ann Wimsatt and Karen L. Rood (1994)

13 *The House of Scribner, 1846–1904,* edited by John Delaney (1996)

14 *Four Women Writers for Children, 1868–1918,* edited by Caroline C. Hunt (1996)

15 *American Expatriate Writers: Paris in the Twenties,* edited by Matthew J. Bruccoli and Robert W. Trogdon (1997)

16 *The House of Scribner, 1905–1930,* edited by John Delaney (1997)

17 *The House of Scribner, 1931–1984,* edited by John Delaney (1998)

18 *British Poets of The Great War: Sassoon, Graves, Owen,* edited by Patrick Quinn (1999)

19 *James Dickey,* edited by Judith S. Baughman (1999)

See also DLB 210, 216, 219, 222, 224, 229, 237, 247, 253, 254, 263, 269, 273, 274, 280, 284, 288, 291

Dictionary of Literary Biography Yearbooks

1980 edited by Karen L. Rood, Jean W. Ross, and Richard Ziegfeld (1981)

1981 edited by Karen L. Rood, Jean W. Ross, and Richard Ziegfeld (1982)

1982 edited by Richard Ziegfeld; associate editors: Jean W. Ross and Lynne C. Zeigler (1983)

1983 edited by Mary Bruccoli and Jean W. Ross; associate editor Richard Ziegfeld (1984)

1984 edited by Jean W. Ross (1985)

1985 edited by Jean W. Ross (1986)

1986 edited by J. M. Brook (1987)

1987 edited by J. M. Brook (1988)

1988 edited by J. M. Brook (1989)

1989 edited by J. M. Brook (1990)

1990 edited by James W. Hipp (1991)

1991 edited by James W. Hipp (1992)

1992 edited by James W. Hipp (1993)

1993 edited by James W. Hipp, contributing editor George Garrett (1994)

1994 edited by James W. Hipp, contributing editor George Garrett (1995)

1995 edited by James W. Hipp, contributing editor George Garrett (1996)

1996 edited by Samuel W. Bruce and L. Kay Webster, contributing editor George Garrett (1997)

1997 edited by Matthew J. Bruccoli and George Garrett, with the assistance of L. Kay Webster (1998)

1998 edited by Matthew J. Bruccoli, contributing editor George Garrett, with the assistance of D. W. Thomas (1999)

1999 edited by Matthew J. Bruccoli, contributing editor George Garrett, with the assistance of D. W. Thomas (2000)

2000 edited by Matthew J. Bruccoli, contributing editor George Garrett, with the assistance of George Parker Anderson (2001)

2001 edited by Matthew J. Bruccoli, contributing editor George Garrett, with the assistance of George Parker Anderson (2002)

2002 edited by Matthew J. Bruccoli and George Garrett; George Parker Anderson, Assistant Editor (2003)

Concise Series

Concise Dictionary of American Literary Biography, 7 volumes (1988–1999): *The New Consciousness, 1941–1968; Colonization to the American Renaissance, 1640–1865; Realism, Naturalism, and Local Color, 1865–1917; The Twenties, 1917–1929; The Age of Maturity, 1929–1941; Broadening Views, 1968–1988; Supplement: Modern Writers, 1900–1998.*

Concise Dictionary of British Literary Biography, 8 volumes (1991–1992): *Writers of the Middle Ages and Renaissance Before 1660; Writers of the Restoration and Eighteenth Century, 1660–1789; Writers of the Romantic Period, 1789–1832; Victorian Writers, 1832–1890; Late-Victorian and Edwardian Writers, 1890–1914; Modern Writers, 1914–1945; Writers After World War II, 1945–1960; Contemporary Writers, 1960 to Present.*

Concise Dictionary of World Literary Biography, 4 volumes (1999–2000): *Ancient Greek and Roman Writers; German Writers; African, Caribbean, and Latin American Writers; South Slavic and Eastern European Writers.*

Dictionary of Literary Biography® • Volume Two Hundred Ninety-One

The Hoosier House: Bobbs-Merrill and Its Predecessors, 1850–1985: A Documentary Volume

Dictionary of Literary Biography® • Volume Two Hundred Ninety-One

The Hoosier House: Bobbs-Merrill and Its Predecessors, 1850–1985: A Documentary Volume

Edited by
Richard J. Schrader
Boston College

A Bruccoli Clark Layman Book

Detroit • New York • San Diego • San Francisco • Cleveland • New Haven, Conn. • Waterville, Maine • London • Munich

Dictionary of Literary Biography
Volume 291: The Hoosier House:
Bobbs-Merrill and Its Predecessors, 1850–1985:
A Documentary Volume
Richard J. Schrader

For more information, contact
The Gale Group, Inc.
27500 Drake Rd.
Farmington Hills, MI 48331-3535
Or you can visit our Internet site at
http://www.gale.com

LIBRARY OF CONGRESS CATALOGING-IN-PUBLICATION DATA

The Hoosier House: Bobbs-Merrill and its predecessors, 1850–1985: a documentary volume / edited by Richard J. Schrader.
p. cm. — (Dictionary of literary biography ; v. 291)
"A Bruccoli Clark Layman book."
Includes bibliographical references and index.
ISBN 0-7876-6828-1
1. Bobbs-Merrill Company—History. 2. Publishers and publishing—Indiana—Indianapolis—History—19th century. 3. Publishers and publishing—Indiana—Indianapolis—History—20th century. I. Schrader, Richard J. II. Series.

Z473.B63H66 2004
070.5'09772'52—dc22

2003022773

Printed in the United States of America
10 9 8 7 6 5 4 3 2 1

For my teachers and friends at Notre Dame, 1959–1963

Though many laud Italia's clime,
And call Helvetia's land sublime,
Tell Gallia's praise in prose or rhyme,
And worship old Hispania;
The winds of Heaven never fanned,
The circling sunlight never spanned
The borders of a better land
Than our own Indiana.

—from "Indiana," in Songs of a Life-Time, *by Sarah T. Bolton (Indianapolis: Bowen-Merrill, 1892)*

Contents

Plan of the Series

. . . Almost the most prodigious asset of a country, and perhaps its most precious possession, is its native literary product–when that product is fine and noble and enduring.

Mark Twain*

The advisory board, the editors, and the publisher of the *Dictionary of Literary Biography* are joined in endorsing Mark Twain's declaration. The literature of a nation provides an inexhaustible resource of permanent worth. Our purpose is to make literature and its creators better understood and more accessible to students and the reading public, while satisfying the needs of teachers and researchers.

To meet these requirements, *literary biography* has been construed in terms of the author's achievement. The most important thing about a writer is his writing. Accordingly, the entries in *DLB* are career biographies, tracing the development of the author's canon and the evolution of his reputation.

The purpose of *DLB* is not only to provide reliable information in a usable format but also to place the figures in the larger perspective of literary history and to offer appraisals of their accomplishments by qualified scholars.

The publication plan for *DLB* resulted from two years of preparation. The project was proposed to Bruccoli Clark by Frederick G. Ruffner, president of the Gale Research Company, in November 1975. After specimen entries were prepared and typeset, an advisory board was formed to refine the entry format and develop the series rationale. In meetings held during 1976, the publisher, series editors, and advisory board approved the scheme for a comprehensive biographical dictionary of persons who contributed to literature. Editorial work on the first volume began in January 1977, and it was published in 1978. In order to make *DLB* more than a dictionary and to compile volumes that individually have claim to status as literary history, it was decided to organize volumes by topic, period, or genre. Each of these freestanding volumes provides a biographical-bibliographical guide and overview for a particular area of literature. We are convinced that this organization–as opposed to a single alphabet method–constitutes a valuable innovation in the presentation of reference material. The volume plan necessarily requires many decisions for the placement and treatment of authors. Certain figures will be included in separate volumes, but with different entries emphasizing the aspect of his career appropriate to each volume. Ernest Hemingway, for example, is represented in *American Writers in Paris, 1920–1939* by an entry focusing on his expatriate apprenticeship; he is also in *American Novelists, 1910–1945* with an entry surveying his entire career, as well as in *American Short-Story Writers, 1910–1945, Second Series* with an entry concentrating on his short fiction. Each volume includes a cumulative index of the subject authors and articles.

Since 1981 the series has been further augmented by the *DLB Yearbooks,* which update published entries, add new entries to keep the *DLB* current with contemporary activity, and provide articles on literary history. There have also been nineteen *DLB Documentary Series* volumes, which provide illustrations, facsimiles, and biographical and critical source materials for figures, works, or groups judged to have particular interest for students. In 1999 the *Documentary Series* was incorporated into the *DLB* volume numbering system beginning with *DLB 210: Ernest Hemingway.*

We define literature as the *intellectual commerce of a nation:* not merely as belles lettres but as that ample and complex process by which ideas are generated, shaped, and transmitted. *DLB* entries are not limited to "creative writers" but extend to other figures who in their time and in their way influenced the mind of a people. Thus the series encompasses historians, journalists, publishers, book collectors, and screenwriters. By this means readers of *DLB* may be aided to perceive literature not as cult scripture in the keeping of intellectual high priests but firmly positioned at the center of a nation's life.

DLB includes the major writers appropriate to each volume and those standing in the ranks behind them. Scholarly and critical counsel has been sought in

**From an unpublished section of Mark Twain's autobiography, copyright by the Mark Twain Company*

deciding which minor figures to include and how full their entries should be. Wherever possible, useful references are made to figures who do not warrant separate entries.

Each *DLB* volume has an expert volume editor responsible for planning the volume, selecting the figures for inclusion, and assigning the entries. Volume editors are also responsible for preparing, where appropriate, appendices surveying the major periodicals and literary and intellectual movements for their volumes, as well as lists of further readings. Work on the series as a whole is coordinated at the Bruccoli Clark Layman editorial center in Columbia, South Carolina, where the editorial staff is responsible for accuracy and utility of the published volumes.

One feature that distinguishes *DLB* is the illustration policy–its concern with the iconography of literature. Just as an author is influenced by his surroundings, so is the reader's understanding of the author enhanced by a knowledge of his environment. Therefore *DLB* volumes include not only drawings, paintings, and photographs of authors, often depicting them at various stages in their careers, but also illustrations of their families and places where they lived. Title pages are regularly reproduced in facsimile along with dust jackets for modern authors. The dust jackets are a special feature of *DLB* because they often document better than anything else the way in which an author's work was perceived in its own time. Specimens of the writers' manuscripts and letters are included when feasible.

Samuel Johnson rightly decreed that "The chief glory of every people arises from its authors." The purpose of the *Dictionary of Literary Biography* is to compile literary history in the surest way available to us–by accurate and comprehensive treatment of the lives and work of those who contributed to it.

The *DLB* Advisory Board

Introduction

This book provides a documentary history of the Bobbs-Merrill Company and its predecessors. Together they developed into a major American publishing firm, the greatest ever to come out of the Midwest. Primary documentation is drawn mostly from the company archives at The Lilly Library, Indiana University, which include a rich collection of business records and promotional artifacts, along with in-house and author correspondence. The collection is strongest from about 1903 to 1960. Other sources fill out the story from 1850 to 1985.

The company was famous for its promotional methods, for the ways it marketed books after acquiring them. The innovative business practices began around the turn of the twentieth century, with the result that Bobbs-Merrill authors, in the trade, legal, and educational departments around which the company organized itself for most of its existence, sold millions of books. Literature fell within the ambit of the trade department, which had only two editors in chief from 1900 to 1958. In that era the "Hoosier House" was conservative in outlook, and many of its once-popular authors are now forgotten, despite having had a large audience in their own time. The archives, however, tell interesting stories about even the obscure figures in their dealings with Bobbs-Merrill. One aim of this book and its wide range of authors and writings is to provide, as Matthew J. Bruccoli remarked to the editor, "the secret history of what Americans really read."

For more-limited audiences, the legal and educational departments also played significant roles in making Bobbs-Merrill a cultural force. Merrill and Company, one of the earlier firms that eventually became Bobbs-Merrill, first attracted notice from publishing volumes in the long series *Reports of Cases Argued and Determined in the Supreme Court of Judicature of the State of Indiana,* beginning in 1855. The law list expanded during the nineteenth century, partly through the acquisition of titles published by other companies but also through the creation of new textbooks used throughout the country. Eight states other than Indiana had entrusted their digests and statutes to the firm by 1923. In 1936 Bobbs-Merrill began publishing the distinguished *Federal Code Annotated* and in 1958 released recordings of courtroom arguments by renowned trial lawyer Melvin Belli.

The Bobbs-Merrill imprint is perhaps best remembered by people of a certain age for the lines of schoolbooks produced by the educational department. It was founded in 1911, largely to promote the Child Classics series, which marked the formal entry of the company into the education field. The department grew strong through the creation of other series over the years and through acquisitions from other firms. A college division was formed in 1960, just before a merger with the Liberal Arts Press. For twenty-five years Bobbs-Merrill published the Library of Liberal Arts series of paperback classics, still familiar to college students.

Generations of young people also encountered the Bobbs-Merrill imprint through such works as Raymond MacDonald Alden's Christmas story *Why the Chimes Rang* (1908), the titles in the Childhood of Famous Americans series, the Raggedy Ann books of Johnny Gruelle, and the first Wizard of Oz book by L. Frank Baum. Like their counterparts in the legal and educational departments, the Baum and Gruelle books were judicious acquisitions from other publishers.

Fiction, nonfiction, poetry, and drama, which were eventually to be the responsibility of the trade department, were all represented among the few nonlegal publications by the business predecessors of Bobbs-Merrill before the advent of James Whitcomb Riley. But the company's first significant contribution to American literary history came in 1883, when Merrill, Meigs reprinted Riley's *"The Old Swimmin' Hole," and 'Leven More Poems,* which had been privately published earlier that same year. For the first time a literary work brought national attention to the company; many other profitable books by the Hoosier poet followed for Bowen-Merrill (renamed Bobbs-Merrill in 1903). Riley died in 1916, the year before T. S. Eliot published the modernist landmark *Prufrock and Other Observations* in England. No Bobbs-Merrill poet of the new era was to achieve a significant reputation until the 1970s.

Another crucial early publication was *When Knighthood Was in Flower* (1898), an historical novel by Charles Major that was the first in a string of best-sellers for Bowen-Merrill and Bobbs-Merrill. These books, along with the opening of an office in New York, established the Indianapolis company as more than a regional publisher. In addition, the aggressive and innovative promotional techniques of John J. Curtis, the New York editorial representative, were a challenge to older, Eastern competitors–and many now-prominent writers with the house, such as Riley and Major, were Midwesterners. The company catered to the popular taste for historical fiction and mysteries, bringing out works by Emerson Hough, Anna Katharine Green, Mary Roberts Rinehart, Meredith Nicholson, and Harold MacGrath. In 1905 Bobbs-Merrill became the first firm to publish "pocket books," cloth-bound reprints priced at 75¢ apiece. At the high end, the company published a popular gift book, Riley's *An Old Sweetheart of Mine* (1902), illustrated by Howard Chandler Christy, and claimed that it revived the gift-book business.

After financial difficulties in the 1910s the trade department found an audience again in the 1920s and crested in 1925. While other houses published F. Scott Fitzgerald's *The Great Gatsby,* Willa Cather's *The Professor's House,* Ernest Hemingway's *In Our Time,* Sherwood Anderson's *Dark Laughter,* John Dos Passos's *Manhattan Transfer,* Theodore Dreiser's *American Tragedy,* and Sinclair Lewis's *Arrowsmith* in that year, Bobbs-Merrill published Bruce Barton's *The Man Nobody Knows,* an account of Jesus as businessman; Richard Halliburton's *The Royal Road to Romance,* a travel memoir; and John Erskine's *The Private Life of Helen of Troy,* a witty historical novel. Like Bobbs-Merrill's first best-sellers, these books suited a broad audience and sold in the hundreds of thousands over time. The one Jazz Age writer in the company's stable who is still highly regarded is Ring Lardner, but he published with Bobbs-Merrill only from 1917 to 1921.

Characteristically, some of the best-remembered Bobbs-Merrill titles came from authors who did not remain with the house. Most notable among these books are Ayn Rand's *The Fountainhead* (1943) and William Styron's *Lie Down in Darkness* (1951). So, too, many editors and other personnel trained by D. Laurance Chambers left the Indianapolis and New York offices and became important figures with other publishers or on their own. Chambers, who rose to become chief trade editor in 1925 and president of Bobbs-Merrill in 1935, thus influenced the course of publishing history in unintended ways. Editor Hiram Haydn was one of those who left in anger and oversaw significant works elsewhere. Carrick and Evans was founded by Bobbs-Merrill editor Lynn Carrick; Coward-McCann, by editor Thomas R. Coward and sales manager James A. McCann.

The conservative taste of the Hoosier House meant that in the years before World War II the company published Earl Derr Biggers's Charlie Chan mysteries and novels by Inglis Fletcher and Alice Tisdale Hobart, but now and then its reputation was belied. Bobbs-Merrill challenged puritanical critics, sometimes after much in-house controversy, with novels such as Emily Hahn's *Affair* (1935) and Pietro di Donato's *Christ in Concrete* (1939). Later lists included works by Styron, Mark Harris, Robert Raynolds, Sam Shepard, Colette, Amiri Baraka, Nikki Giovanni, and Joel Oppenheimer. Important anthologies of contemporary poetry were compiled by Edward Lucie-Smith (*Primer of Experimental Poetry,* 1971) and William Heyen (*American Poets in 1976,* 1976).

The histories, biographies, and other nonfiction published by Bobbs-Merrill during the Chambers years were consistently substantial. Distinguished works came in from Marquis James, Lord David Cecil, Irvin S. Cobb, Joseph Wood Krutch, Elmer Davis, Louis Kronenberger, Glenn Tucker, J. Christopher Herold, Otto Eisenschiml, Harlan Hatcher, J. Saunders Redding, and Paul Goodman. Chambers initiated the American Lakes, American Trails, and Makers of the American Tradition series. Irma S. Rombauer's *The Joy of Cooking* (1931) was the all-time best-selling trade book by Bobbs-Merrill and a lasting contribution to the American kitchen.

The cultural impact of Bobbs-Merrill was particularly strong in the Midwest. A 1954 advertisement in *The Times Literary Supplement (TLS),* directed to an English audience, enunciates a century-old policy: "Our Indianapolis office keeps a special sensitivity and access to regional literature. We know something of the value of regional expression as well as of the ability of a good book to surmount all sectional differences in its address to the larger community." Bobbs-Merrill became the most significant publishing firm in the Midwest, eventually larger and older than any in Chicago. In 1940 it boasted that it was "the only great American general publishing house west of the Alleghenies."

The company asserted further, "The history of Bobbs-Merrill is, with a few exceptions, the history of Indiana literature." This is an important claim: between 1900 and 1939 Indiana produced more authors of best-sellers than every other state but New York, which had four times the population. The availability of a prominent, sympathetic publishing house in the state capital, along with its homegrown promotional methods, must have helped to account for this achievement. By 1957 Bobbs-Merrill had published more than one hundred Hoosier authors, most of these publications dating from the 1890s to the 1920s. Apart from Riley and Major, the list includes Davis, Nicholson, George

Ade, Kin Hubbard, David Graham Phillips, Gene Stratton-Porter, Maurice Thompson, and Paul Wilstach. It does not include Dreiser and Booth Tarkington, but the latter was a friend of the house for years.

As part of his reflections on the death of Bobbs-Merrill president William C. Bobbs in 1926, Tarkington said,

> The significant life of a city is not in its size but in its beauty and cleanliness and in the culture of its citizens. Most of all, a city's significance is in that culture and nowhere has the culture of Indianapolis found a better expression than in the publishing house known as the Bobbs-Merrill Company. It is an old house, founded when our oldest citizens were young men, but the genius of William C. Bobbs made it more than a Hoosier establishment; he made it an institution of national importance, and it stands now a monument to his intelligence, his energy and his faith.

The genius of such executives and editors informs the Bobbs-Merrill story. They aggressively recruited Indianans such as the humorist Hubbard: Chambers wrote to his assistant in 1926, "Of course we want him and we must get together with him." They collected nearby Midwestern stars such as Lardner, Herbert Quick, and Brand Whitlock. Tellers of tales about other regions were gathered in: Cobb, Julia Peterkin, Irving Bacheller, and James O. Curwood, for example. Bobbs-Merrill was the American publisher of at least one work each by Cecil, Colette, Felix Salten, C. S. Forester, Arthur Stringer, Gaston Leroux, Ford Madox Ford, C. P. Snow, and Vladimir Nabokov. (Chambers was instrumental in getting Nabokov out of wartime Europe and into the United States.) It managed to be a regional, national, and international house.

One of Bobbs-Merrill's many novelties was Book Week during December 1924. In a way not possible for the Eastern publishing centers, Indianapolis showed its pride in this institution by displaying Bobbs-Merrill books, manuscripts, and production artifacts in store windows. One sign stated, "The whole world reads the books that Hoosiers write and Hoosiers publish."

–Richard J. Schrader

Acknowledgments

My first debt is to Dr. Matthew J. Bruccoli for suggesting that I compile this book and for overseeing its progress. William Cagle gave it a careful vetting in its first stage and offered advice that considerably improved it.

The work would not have been possible without the staff of The Lilly Library at Indiana University, home of the Bobbs-Merrill archives. I must mention especially the director, Breon Mitchell, along with Rebecca Cape, Sue Presnell, Francis Lapka, Christopher Harter, and Elizabeth Gray, as well as Jennifer Bryan of the Law Library. The Lilly Library also has my thanks for an Everett Helm Visiting Fellowship and the use of an apartment for visiting scholars.

Those who assisted me in acquiring other materials or provided valuable information include the interlibrary loan staff at the O'Neill Library of Boston College; Professor John Limon of Williams College; Martha Wright, Jill Costill, and Barney Thompson of the Indiana State Library; Chris Winters of the University of Chicago Library; Susan Sutton and Glenn L. McMullen of the Indiana Historical Society; the staff of the Mudd Library, Princeton University; Helen Black of the Oberlin College Library; Chazz Means and Dawn Mitchell of *The Indianapolis Star;* Pamela S. Yohler and Gary Yohler of Tiffany Photography Studio; Michael Manz of Babylon Revisited; Professor Susan Williams of Trident Technical College; James Lardner; the staff of the Indiana State Archives; Harry Miller of the Wisconsin Historical Society; Margaret J. Kimball of the Stanford University Libraries; James Birchfield of the University of Kentucky Library; Karen L. Jania of the Bentley Historical Library, University of Michigan; Fred Bauman of the Library of Congress; Bernard R. Crystal of the Rare Book and Manuscript Library, Columbia University; Philip N. Cronenwett of the Dartmouth College Library; Leslie C. Shores of the American Heritage Center, University of Wyoming; Jeniqua Moore of Simon and Schuster, Inc.; Jennifer Lash of Indiana University Press; Margaret Maybury of Greenwood Press; Monika Konwinska of Houghton Mifflin; Florence B. Eichin of Penguin Putnam, Inc.; and Charles Scribner III.

Once more, I have to thank Stephen Vedder and Bradley Olson of the Audiovisual Department, Boston College, for their technical help. J. Kent Calder, Director of Publications, Texas State Historical Society, facilitated my acquisition of D. Laurance Chambers's memoirs and assisted in editing them. Chambers's granddaughter, Diana Chambers Leslie, gave permission to reproduce the memoirs and provided background information. I had the benefit of correspondence with Leo C. Gobin, last president of Bobbs-Merrill. Finally, I am grateful to the agents, repositories, and descendants who are listed in the permissions section.

The pioneering research of Jack W. O'Bar, cited in the bibliography, helped to establish the framework for the chronology section and was a useful guide. Information on literary prizes was drawn from the tenth edition of *Literary and Library Prizes* (1980), by Olga S. Weber and Stephen J. Calvert, which may be consulted for explanations of the awards.

–Richard J. Schrader

This book was produced by Bruccoli Clark Layman, Inc. R. Bland Lawson was the in-house editor.

Production manager is Philip B. Dematteis.

Administrative support was provided by Ann M. Cheschi and Carol A. Cheschi.

Accountant is Ann-Marie Holland.

Copyediting supervisor is Sally R. Evans. The copyediting staff includes Phyllis A. Avant, Caryl Brown, Melissa D. Hinton, Philip I. Jones, Rebecca Mayo, Nadirah Rahimah Shabazz, and Nancy E. Smith.

Editorial associates are Jessica Goudeau, Joshua M. Robinson, and William Mathes Straney.

In-house prevetting is by Catherine M. Polit.

Permissions editor and database manager is Amber L. Coker.

Layout and graphics supervisor is Janet E. Hill. The graphics staff includes Zoe R. Cook and Sydney E. Hammock.

Office manager is Kathy Lawler Merlette.

Photography supervisor is Paul Talbot. Photography editor is Scott Nemzek.

Digital photographic copy work was performed by Joseph M. Bruccoli.

Systems manager is Donald Kevin Starling.

Typesetting supervisor is Kathleen M. Flanagan. The typesetting staff includes Patricia Marie Flanagan, Mark J. McEwan, and Pamela D. Norton.

Walter W. Ross is library researcher. He was assisted by the following librarians at the Thomas Cooper Library of the University of South Carolina: Jo Cottingham, interlibrary loan department; circulation department head Tucker Taylor; reference department head Virginia W. Weathers; reference department staff Laurel Baker, Marilee Birchfield, Kate Boyd, Paul Cammarata, Joshua Garris, Gary Geer, Tom Marcil, Rose Marshall, and Sharon Verba; interlibrary loan department head Marna Hostetler; and interlibrary loan staff Bill Fetty, Nelson Rivera, and Cedric Rose.

Permissions

Materials from the Bobbs-Merrill Collection held at The Lilly Library used by permission of Simon and Schuster and The Lilly Library, Indiana University, Bloomington, Indiana.

Photograph of Harold Odum courtesy of American Sociological Association.

Photograph of Audrey Thomas by Bill Schermbrucker.

Inscribed half-title page of Robert Nathan's *The Bishop's Wife* courtesy of the Boston Public Library.

Photograph of Sam Shepard © Bruce Weber.

Autobiographical sketch of Ford Madox Ford as Ford Madox Hueffer courtesy of Carcanet Press Limited.

Questionnaire filled out by Emily Hahn courtesy of Carola Vecchio of the Emily Hahn Estate.

Lillian Hollowell, A Series in Children's Books, *Wilson Library Bulletin,* 27 (May 1953): 736–738. (Printed by permission of H. W. Wilson Company.)

Photograph of Irma S. Rombauer and Marion Rombauer Becker © Bettmann/CORBIS.

Photograph of Bruce Barton © CORBIS.

Bibliographical questionnaire of Lord David Cecil for Bobbs-Merrill used by permission of David Higham Associates (Reference: Cecil/6/3/03).

Materials of D. Laurance Chambers courtesy of Diane Chambers Leslie of the D. Laurance Chambers Estate.

Photograph of Vladimir Nabokov, 1926, courtesy of the Estate of Vladimir Nabokov. All rights reserved.

Letter from Bertie C. Forbes to Ralph Barton courtesy of Steve Forbes on behalf of *Forbes Magazine*.

Photograph of William Styron © George Rhoads, by permission.

Photograph of Hiram Haydn by Gould Studios.

Excerpts from *Words & Faces* by Hiram Haydn, © 1974 by the Estate of Hiram Haydn, reprinted by permission of Harcourt, Inc.

Portrait of Lord David Cecil by Augustus John, circa 1943, courtesy of Marquess of Salisbury.

Excerpts from *My Story* by Mary Roberts Rinehart. Copyright © 1930, 1931, 1958 by Mary Rinehart. Copyright © 1959 by Stanley Rinehart, Frederick Rinehart, and Alan Rinehart. Reprinted by permission of Henry Holt and Company, LLC.

Materials from the Julia Peterkin Estate by permission of the Peterkin family.

Photographs and articles from *The Indianapolis Star* and *Indianapolis News* by permission of *The Indianapolis Star.*

Materials from the Ring Lardner Estate by permission of James Lardner.

Photograph of Dean Koontz © Jerry Bauer, by permission.

Letters of Kenneth Roberts printed by permission of Key Bank National Association.

Photograph of Jack Vance © MC Valeda.

Letter from Meredith Nicholson to Mr. Howland printed by permission of the Meredith Nicholson Estate.

Article from *The New York Times Book Review* © New York Times Agency. Reprinted with permission.

Photograph of Brand Whitlock by Pirie MacDonald, courtesy of the New York Historical Society.

Articles from *Publishers Weekly* and photograph of Leo C. Gobin by permission of *Publishers Weekly*.

Materials from the Estate of Raymond Alden by permission of Raymond M. Alden Jr.

Letter of Irving Bacheller to D. Laurance Chambers printed by permission of 1) Department of College Archives & Special Collections / Olin Library / Rollins College / Winter Park, Florida 2) "Printed by permission of St. Lawrence University / Canton, New York."

Photograph of Zola Helen Ross courtesy of Ron Miazga and Sharyn Bolton.

Letters of Roy Hoopes used by permission of Roy Hoopes.

Roy Hoopes with Vice President Walter Mondale, 1977 (photograph by Spencer Hoopes, by permission).

Robert Silverberg (photograph by Susanne Lee Houfek).

Articles from *The Times Literary Supplement* printed by permission of *The Times Literary Supplement*.

Photograph of Bonnie Ammer by permission of Travel Weekly/Northstar Travel Media.

Photographs and articles from the *Indianapolis Times* © SCRIPPS HOWARD NEWS SERVICE.

Photograph of Emerson Hough by permission of the Emerson Hough Papers, Special Collections Department, University of Iowa, Iowa City, Iowa.

Cid Ricketts Sumner (courtesy of Special Collections Department, J. Willard Marriott Library, University of Utah).

Dictionary of Literary Biography® • Volume Two Hundred Ninety-One

The Hoosier House: Bobbs-Merrill and Its Predecessors, 1850–1985: A Documentary Volume

Dictionary of Literary Biography

Overview

Significant transactions and publications of the Bobbs-Merrill Company and its predecessors, along with the entrances and exits of important personnel, are detailed in the chronology section. This overview is a brief narrative of the history of the company, from its frontier beginnings in 1850 to its dissolution in 1985.

Two collateral lines of Indianapolis bookseller-publishers merged in 1885 to form the company that survived for another hundred years. The name changes in the early years were as follows:

Merrill line: Hood and Merrill (1850–1851); Merrill and Company (1851–1870); Merrill and Field (1870–1874/1875); Merrill, Hubbard, and Company (1874/1875–1882); Merrill, Meigs, and Company (1882–1884). A unique publication by Merrill and Smith in 1864 probably resulted from an expedient collaboration during the war.

Bowen line: West and Company (1853); West and Stewart (1853–1854); Stewart and Bowen (1854–1860); Bowen, Stewart, and Company (1860–1884).

In January 1885 Merrill, Meigs and Bowen, Stewart joined to form Bowen-Merrill, which was renamed Bobbs-Merrill in 1903.

The company long insisted that the Merrill line began in 1838, which would have made it as old as some of the better-known eastern publishers. No evidence, however, has been found to support this claim. The earliest verified date is 5 September 1850, when the *Indiana State Sentinel* announced the partnership of E. H. Hood and Samuel Merrill as booksellers and stationers in Indianapolis. Hood was out of the picture within nine months. Merrill (1792–1855), a native of Vermont, had been state treasurer of Indiana and possessed one of the largest personal libraries in a city that could boast four bookstores by 1851. At Merrill's death the business passed to Samuel Merrill Jr. (1831–1924) and son-in-law Charles W. Moores, who died at thirty-five in 1864, after serving only twenty days in the Union army. Merrill also served, and while the two were away, company affairs were in the hands of Moores's wife, Julia, and her sister Catharine Merrill (1824–1900), a prominent educator and author. After the war Merrill formed three brief partnerships before the 1885 merger. The last of these was Merrill, Meigs, and Company, created with William H. Elvin and Charles Meigs Jr. Meigs (1847–1920) had started with Merrill and Company as bookkeeper when he was twenty-one.

The Bowen line was begun as a bookstore by Henry F. West (1796–1856) on 4 February 1853. He

(*Bruccoli Clark Layman Archives*)

had arrived in Indianapolis in 1845 and later died in office while serving as mayor. Like Hood's, his name remained with the company he had founded for only a brief time. West's significant partners were Silas T. Bowen (1819–1895), who had just arrived in the city, and William Stewart, after whose death in 1860 Bowen shared partnership with members of the Stewart family and others.

Both lines produced their first publication in 1855. Stewart and Bowen's was *Morse's Map of Indiana,* jointly published with the Chicago firm of Rufus Blanchard. Merrill and Company's contribution (also a joint publication) was more substantial, and it marked the beginning of a long and distinguished series of law books. The fifth volume of Albert G. Porter's *Reports of Cases Argued and Determined in the Supreme Court of Judicature of the State of Indiana* was published by Merrill with the Philadelphia firm of D. B. Canfield. It was a continuation of the highly regarded volumes on the state supreme court's proceedings compiled by Isaac Newton Blackford, a judge of the court from its founding in 1817 until 1853. Merrill's original and reprinted editions in the series helped greatly to establish the name of the publishing house.

Before the 1885 merger Merrill's law books dominated the publications of the two companies. The few other titles, scattered among practical, educational, historical, religious, and literary categories, only hinted at the strong trade (adult fiction and nonfiction) and educational departments that were to develop later on.

By far the most significant title of this era was James Whitcomb Riley's *"The Old Swimmin'-Hole," and 'Leven More Poems,* published under the Merrill, Meigs imprint in 1883, after private publication earlier that same year. Riley reportedly said that with this work the company "put on its literary overalls." The volume brought national attention to the firm shortly before its merger with the Bowen line; their combined resources made possible even bolder steps into literary publication.

By the time of Riley's advent, the companies had hired three men who went on to become famous as executives with Bowen-Merrill and Bobbs-Merrill: John J. Curtis (1857–1931; hired in 1873), William C. Bobbs (1861–1926; hired in 1879), and Charles W. Merrill (1861–1920; hired in 1882), son of Samuel Merrill Jr. Their rise was facilitated by the retirement of the elder Merrill and Charles Meigs in 1890–1891, after a disastrous fire and a reincorporation. For many years the fortunes of the house were in the hands of a small group of such men who started young, stayed long, and developed a loyalty that they tried to instill in their authors.

After the founding of Bowen-Merrill in 1885, the trade department (earlier known as miscellaneous publications) developed its own reputation in the wake of success with the growing Riley list. Other authors, some widely known and some regional favorites, entered the catalogues. The second step toward national prominence was the publication of the historical novel *When Knighthood Was in Flower* (1898), by Charles Major of Shelbyville, Indiana, writing under the pseudonym Edwin Caskoden. This event was recounted many times in company lore. For the next two years *When Knighthood Was in Flower* was a best-seller–the first for the company. Its sales owed more to Curtis's promotional innovations than to the literary qualities of the novel, now forgotten. Among other things, Curtis has been credited with creating the first single-title and full-page advertisements. The next decade was a time of great success for the company because of the taste for similar historical novels and because of flamboyant promotions. Curtis claimed to have invented the illuminated, colored dust jacket, introducing it with Harold MacGrath's *The Lure of the Mask* (1908).

The company gradually divested itself of other interests, such as its paper and notions trade (1896) and the bookstore (1909), but Bobbs and Charles Merrill were partners in a separate local printer-publisher, the Hollenbeck Press. A little-noted Kansas City bookstore, accounting for the location "Indianapolis and Kansas City" given in several Bowen-Merrill imprints, lasted from 1894 to 1902.

The management team that ran things in the first quarter of the twentieth century began forming when Charles Merrill took over his father's interest in 1890 and became treasurer two years later. Although he had some editorial experience, he generally remained in the background when it came to dealing with authors. Between July 1899 and July 1900 Bobbs became president. In 1900 Curtis established the New York office and ran it until 1919, when he moved to California to handle movie rights. Over the years, the New York office and its series of editors kept the Midwest house at the heart of American publishing and advertising. The eastern stars included Thomas R. Coward (who arrived in 1922), Lynn Carrick (1934), and Hiram Haydn (1950).

Nonetheless, the firm was proudly the "Hoosier House." In the early days, its bookstores were Indianapolis cultural centers. By the middle of the twentieth century, it had published more than a hundred Indiana authors, though not the two greatest ones. Booth Tarkington had begun with another company and remained loyal to it; only a posthumously published collection, *Your Amiable Uncle: Letters to His Nephews by*

Booth Tarkington (1949), bore the Bobbs-Merrill imprint. Had the controversial novels of Theodore Dreiser ever been offered to the conservative and sales-minded editors, they would likely have been rejected.

Robert L. Moorhead (1875–1968), future head of the law department, arrived in 1893, and Hewitt H. Howland (1863–1944), a brilliant editor during some of the best years of the firm, in 1898. Howland moved from manuscript reader to editor in the trade department in 1900. The company showed its acumen by two major acquisitions near the turn of the century: the Houghton-Mifflin law list, acquired in 1898, and L. Frank Baum's first book on the Land of Oz, originally published in 1900 by the Chicago firm of George M. Hill as *The Wonderful Wizard of Oz* and republished in 1903 by Bobbs-Merrill as *The New Wizard of Oz.* In contrast, however, Bobbs-Merrill rejected Edgar Rice Burroughs's *Tarzan of the Apes* (1914).

The arrival of David Laurance Chambers (1879–1963) as secretary to Bobbs in 1903 proved more significant than the name change to Bobbs-Merrill that same year. Chambers later served as an editor throughout the period of his rise to the top of the executive ranks. For the time being, the trade department was dominated by Howland, who remained chief editor until 1925 (with a salary generally lower than Chambers's). Bobbs kept a strong presidential hand in this department, like Chambers later on. During Bobbs's tenure he often formed personal relationships with authors, as did Howland. It was a method of encouraging loyalty to the company, one that worked splendidly with Riley but only temporarily with such difficult cases as Emerson Hough.

In the era of Bobbs and Howland the company developed an impressive but costly fiction list, featuring many best-sellers. Among the still-readable titles are those of mystery writers Anna Katharine Green (*The Filigree Ball* [1903] can be called the first Bobbs-Merrill book), Mary Roberts Rinehart, and Earl Derr Biggers. With *Private Peat* (1917), a wartime account by Harold R. Peat, the company finally had a nonfiction best-seller. It was a precursor to the excellent nonfiction list fostered by Chambers when he took charge. In 1911 emerged what proved to be a company mainstay, the educational department, under the leadership of John R. Carr (1878–1940). The creation of this department followed Bobbs-Merrill's decisive entry into the highly competitive field of textbook publication with the Child Classics series in 1909. The firm also offered the Childhood and Youth series (begun in 1914) and the Bobbs-Merrill Readers (1923), both with mixed success.

Bobbs-Merrill also tried magazine publishing, taking over the *Reader* in 1904 and *Home Magazine* in 1906. Magazine publication was a traditional way for a house to promote its own authors, but works by other writers not affiliated with Bobbs-Merrill, such as Jack London, Joseph Conrad, and Sinclair Lewis, also appeared in the *Reader* and *Home Magazine.* After nearly bankrupting the company, the two periodicals were sold, and Bobbs-Merrill reorganized in 1908. Indianapolis bankers helped with the rescue. Following other setbacks, across-the-board pay cuts were ordered in 1914. The trade list had expanded sixfold since 1901, but popular taste for the kind of historical fiction the company promoted was waning, and the market for nonfiction was growing. The expensive practices of Curtis, such as single-title advertising, reached a notorious crescendo with Owen Johnson's *The Salamander* (1914) and were curtailed in 1916. The board of directors even considered abolishing the trade department altogether. Sales of both fiction and nonfiction finally improved in the 1920s. As Howland was leaving for the editorship of *Century* magazine in 1925, to be succeeded by Chambers, the company published three books whose sales were phenomenal: Bruce Barton's *The Man Nobody Knows,* Richard Halliburton's *The Royal Road to Romance,* and John Erskine's *The Private Life of Helen of Troy.*

Bobbs-Merrill was now established among the most prominent publishing houses in the nation. Apart from Barton, Halliburton, and Erskine, the firm could boast Julia Peterkin, whose 1928 novel *Scarlet Sister Mary* won the Pulitzer Prize in 1929 (the first Pulitzer for a Bobbs-Merrill publication); Marquis James, whose *The Raven: A Biography of Sam Houston* (1929) won the 1930 Pulitzer Prize in nonfiction; and Lord David Cecil, whose *The Stricken Deer; or, The Life of Cowper* (1929; Bobbs-Merrill edition, 1930) won the Hawthornden Prize in 1930. Ring Lardner, perhaps the best fiction writer to have published with Bobbs-Merrill up to this time, abandoned the firm for Scribners in 1924.

Bobbs died in 1926. The company was forced to move from its splendid building, erected in 1910 on East Vermont Street in Indianapolis, and rent an impressive former auto dealership on North Meridian Street. Bobbs's successor as president, Curtis, was absent in California much of the time and left the board of directors to run things. The board ran them so well that when Curtis died in 1931 the presidency was left vacant for four years. Joining the company in 1927 was Jessica Brown Mannon, who rose to editorial assistant in 1931, handling both juvenile and adult books. She is representative of the mostly female corps of like-minded editors surrounding Chambers: intelligent, critically competent, and generally conservative in taste. Lowe Berger (1896–1959) joined the educational department in 1928 and in 1937 replaced Carr as head. Chambers became president of Bobbs-Merrill in 1935 but maintained his editorial duties.

Chambers was the most memorable figure in the history of Bobbs-Merrill, surviving there even beyond the merger with Howard W. Sams and Company in 1958. Like his predecessor, Howland, Chambers was a great editor who left a lasting mark on American literary history, both in the books he helped father and in the editors he trained. Chambers's character has been assailed, most strongly by Haydn, but that picture must be placed next to what emerges from the company archives. In the thousands of letters he wrote to authors–dozens per day, polished and decorous–one sees a cultivated man (a former Wilson Fellow at Princeton University) who wanted quality and wanted to sell books. The rhetoric is often that of a coach, if not Dutch uncle. It is folksy when he deals with the Hoosier writer Elmer Davis (Chambers himself was born in Washington, D.C.), witty and allusive in letters to Columbia University professor Erskine. Many authors wrote Chambers to complain that he did not promote their books as heavily as someone else's, and he would patiently explain his philosophy of spending promotion money on likely best-sellers so that their sales could subsidize publication of the rest. In his dealings with Alice Hobart one sees a typical unwillingness to make "literary" judgments but rather a desire to suggest editing that would enhance readability and thus sales. The tone of Chambers's dealings with authors was meant to convey that they were part of an adoptive family. Like Howland, he was always sincerely inviting them to come to Indianapolis or New York for a personal meeting to thrash things out. Given this attitude, his occasional anger at what he considered disloyalty is not surprising. Yet, a departure did not necessarily mean a divorce. Coward left the New York editorship in 1927 to form his own publishing company, Coward-McCann, but he remained Chambers's closest friend in the business. Across two generations, for the people who loved or hated him, Chambers *was* Bobbs-Merrill.

The company reorganized and sold its stock publicly in 1929, just before the Depression began. Bobbs's family members sold their interest at this time. (His son, Julian, an executive and stockholder, was often a minority of one at company meetings.) Salary reductions and other money-saving measures were taken over the next few years, including a cutback in law publishing, but Chambers resisted the allowing of returns and both the closing of the New York office and the relocation of the main office there. Despite these developments, Bobbs-Merrill's best-known law series began appearing in 1936, the *Federal Code Annotated.* Four years earlier the popular Childhood of Famous Americans series began its long life. The educational department added the Curriculum Readers series to its list in 1934. The company's most significant book since *When Knighthood Was in Flower* and *The Wizard of Oz* was another Depression-era production, Irma Rombauer's *The Joy of Cooking* (1936). It eventually became the publisher's all-time trade best-seller. *The Joy of Cooking* and *The Wizard of Oz* are probably the Bobbs-Merrill books that the world knows best.

A few literary stars appeared in the ensuing years, but most did not stay long. Ayn Rand published just one novel with Bobbs-Merrill, *The Fountainhead* (1943), as did William Styron, whose *Lie Down in Darkness* came out in 1951. Styron was brought in by New York editor Haydn, whose short tenure nudged the firm in directions that sometimes antagonized Chambers. Haydn's list is distinguished, including *Lie Down in Darkness,* J. Saunders Redding's *On Being Negro in America* (1951), Mark Harris's *The Southpaw* (1953), and, in a single year (1954), important nonfiction books by Davis *(But We Were Born Free),* Louis Kronenberger *(Company Manners),* and Joseph Wood Krutch *(The Measure of Man).* But Haydn was gone the next year–as was often the case with Chambers's editors, off to a distinguished career elsewhere. Archibald Ogden left under similar circumstances in 1943, after pushing Rand's *The Fountainhead,* a monumental best-seller.

Business fortunes varied during the last years of Bobbs-Merrill's independence. The World War II era was generally profitable, but in 1947 it was felt necessary to negotiate lower royalties with authors. Nonetheless, the educational department remained strong. Ten years later a decent profit for the house was followed by a slight loss in 1958. Chambers was replaced by Berger as president in 1953, but he continued to dominate the trade department and was chairman of the board until 1958, when he, Berger, and Moorhead sold their majority interest. From Chambers's point of view there were no younger members of the firm who could replace the aging team that had guided it for so long.

Bobbs-Merrill became a subsidiary of Howard W. Sams and Company of Indianapolis, with Sams (1897–1974) acting as president until M. Hughes Miller (1913–1989) took over early in 1959. Initially, the new management brought in substantial profits, thanks to carryover and to "new look" titles catering to popular culture. The educational department was further strengthened by the acquisition of two other companies with the same interest, Public School Publishing and Gregory Publishing, in 1959, and the

Scribners elementary-school line the following year. A perennial backlist series, the Childhood of Famous Americans, was updated in 1959, and Raggedy Ann joined the house in 1960. The law department brought out recordings of trial lawyers in action. A new college division, formed in 1960, took over the Library of Liberal Arts series from the Liberal Arts Press, which merged with Bobbs-Merrill in 1961. The 1962 edition of *The Joy of Cooking* was a best-seller.

The final quarter century of Bobbs-Merrill's existence, always as a subsidiary, featured some notable contributions to African American literature. Ed Bullins, Imamu Amiri Baraka, Charles Gordone, Chuck Stone, and Nikki Giovanni all had their first (and, in some cases, only) publication with Bobbs-Merrill between 1968 and 1971, during the editorship of Robert Amussen. Also published by the firm in this last literary flowering were plays by Sam Shepard, poems by Joel Oppenheimer, and translations of Colette's works. Contemporary poetry was briefly highlighted in ways not seen since the days of Riley. After severe reductions in the trade list in 1978, there was an attempt to revive commercial fiction two years later, but none of the novels produced has been elevated to canonical status. Though the company published some quality literature, profits came from reference books and specialty nonfiction works, such as *The Joy of Cooking* and Bernard Clayton Jr.'s *The Breads of France and How to Bake Them in Your Own Kitchen* (1978), as well as from such acquisitions as the I Can Learn to Write series. Payments for paperback rights to *The Joy of Cooking* set record highs in 1973 and 1982. Not much else was considered valuable in the end.

Miller's dynamic and sometimes contentious presidency had ended in 1963. He was followed briefly by Sams–who at this time donated the Bobbs-Merrill archives through about 1960 to The Lilly Library at Indiana University–and then by Leo C. Gobin (1917–) in 1965. ITT acquired Sams's companies the next year, and when Macmillan acquired ITT's publishing group in 1985, it dissolved Bobbs-Merrill. Macmillan added many author files dating from after 1960 to the Sams donation at The Lilly Library.

Chronology

This chronology provides a selective list of important dates and events in the history of Bobbs-Merrill, noting partnerships and changes in organization and location. Significant publications and series—selected for the importance of the author (from a literary or commercial standpoint), the subject, or the publishing achievement itself, such as the number of volumes involved or the winning of a prize—are identified for each year. On a few occasions, when nothing else of significance happened or was published in a given year, a representative volume has been chosen to fill the gap. The records of the firm do not include copyright or publication dates, so all titles have been dated by secondary sources.

The two collateral lines of Indianapolis bookstore-publishers that merged in 1885 as Bowen-Merrill were established in the first decade covered in the chronology, 1850–1860. The general absence of archival material until the merger necessitates gaps in the yearly record. All known publications until 1885 are, however, noted.

A myth arose that the Merrill line began in 1838. Although no facts support it, that date appears frequently in documents from the nineteenth century on.

Many of the documents dating from after the turn of the twentieth century are company correspondence. The Bobbs-Merrill side is almost always represented by carbon copies, and the authors of these letters have been identified from secretarial or filing notations.

The First Merrill Book Store
In the building surmounted by the watch-tower

Samuel Merrill, who founded the Merrill line in 1850; the first Merrill bookstore (courtesy of the Indiana State Library; from The Hoosier House: The Bobbs-Merrill Company, *1923; Indiana State Library)*

The Bowen-Merrill Predecessors: 1850–1884

1850 Partnership of E. H. Hood and Samuel Merrill is announced on 5 September as Hood and Merrill, Booksellers and Stationers, No. 1 Temperance Hall, Indianapolis.

1851 Merrill buys out Hood no later than June to form the Merrill Company.

1853 On 4 February the Bowen line begins with the announcement of the opening of H. F. West and Company, Booksellers and Stationers, "One door west of Craighead's Drug Store" in Indianapolis. The partners are Henry F. West, George H. West, and James W. Brown. Gross sales are $30,000 for this year. With the retirement of Brown and the purchase of a one-third interest by William Stewart, the firm briefly becomes West and Stewart on 18 November.

Silas T. Bowen, a partner in the Bowen line from 1854 on; Samuel Merrill Jr., who succeeded his father in 1855 (courtesy of the Indiana State Library)

1854 After Stewart retires and West and Stewart again becomes H. F. West and Company, Stewart and Silas T. Bowen form a partnership and purchase it. The new firm of Stewart and Bowen is announced on 1 August.

1855 Merrill dies on 24 August. His business passes to Samuel Merrill Jr. and son-in-law Charles W. Moores.

Albert G. Porter, *Reports of Cases Argued and Determined in the Supreme Court of Judicature of the State of Indiana, Being an Official Continuation of Blackford's Reports,* volume 5 (Philadelphia: D. B. Canfield / Indianapolis: Merrill). The Merrill house and its successors go on to reprint both Blackford's and Porter's reports and publish subsequent volumes by other court reporters.

Charles Walker Morse, *Morse's Map of Indiana* (Chicago: Rufus Blanchard / Indianapolis: Stewart & Bowen).

REPORTS

OF

CASES ARGUED AND DETERMINED

IN THE

SUPREME COURT OF JUDICATURE

OF THE

STATE OF INDIANA,

BEING AN OFFICIAL CONTINUATION OF BLACKFORD'S REPORTS,

WITH TABLES OF THE CASES AND PRINCIPAL MATTERS.

BY ALBERT G. PORTER, A. M.,

OFFICIAL REPORTER.

VOL. V.

CONTAINING THE CASES FROM MAY TERM, 1854, TO THE FOURTEENTH DAY OF NOVEMBER TERM, 1854, INCLUSIVE.

PHILADELPHIA, PA.:
D. B. CANFIELD & COMPANY.
INDIANAPOLIS, IND.:
SAMUEL MERRILL.
INDIANAPOLIS:
ELDER & HARKNESS PRINTERS.
1855.

Title page for the first book published by the Merrill Company (Indiana State Library)

Portion of the 1855 map that was the first publication of Stewart and Bowen (courtesy of the University of Chicago Library)

1856 Porter, *Reports of Cases Argued and Determined in the Supreme Court of Judicature of the State of Indiana,* volumes 6–7 (Indianapolis: Merrill).

1857 Gordon Tanner, *Reports of Cases Argued and Determined in the Supreme Court of Judicature of the State of Indiana,* volume 8 (Indianapolis: Merrill).

Introduction to [Uriah] Parke's Farmers' and Mechanics' Practical Arithmetic (Indianapolis: Stewart & Bowen).

1858 Tanner, *Reports of Cases Argued and Determined in the Supreme Court of Judicature of the State of Indiana,* volume 9 (Indianapolis: Merrill).

1859 Tanner, *Reports of Cases Argued and Determined in the Supreme Court of Judicature of the State of Indiana,* volumes 10–12 (Indianapolis: Merrill).

Samuel Elliott Perkins, *Pleading and Practice under the Code of 1852: In Civil and Criminal Actions, in the Courts of Indiana; with References to the Latest Statutory Amendments and Judicial Decisions* (Indianapolis: Merrill).

1860 On 1 August, after the death of Stewart, a new partnership is formed, consisting of his widow, son Charles G. Stewart, Bowen, Alfred D. Clarke, and Darwin G. Eaton. The house becomes Bowen, Stewart, and Company, located at 18 West Washington Street in Indi-

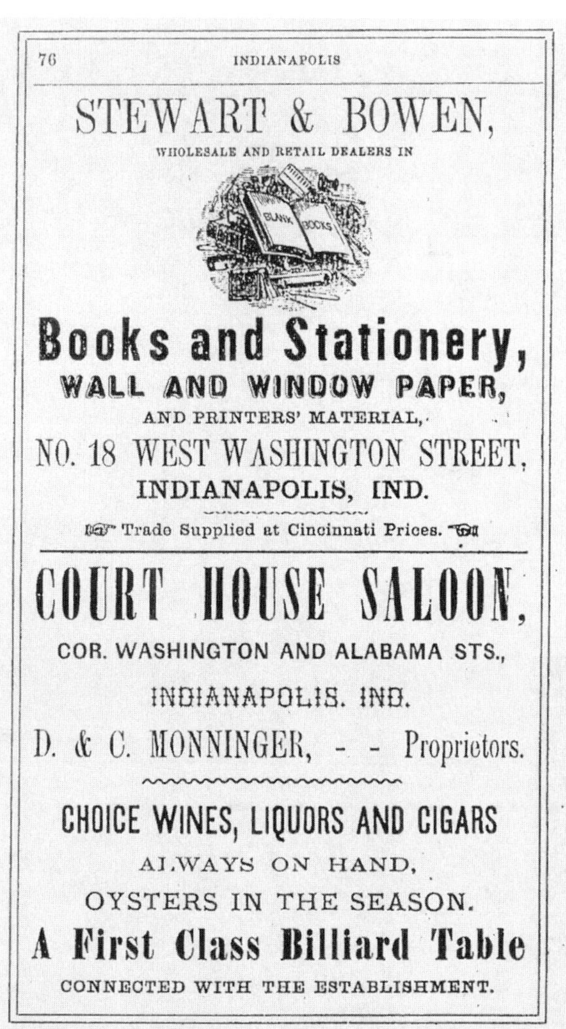

Pages from Sutherland & McEvoy's Indianapolis City Directory *(1860) with advertisements for Merrill and Company and Stewart and Bowen (courtesy of The Lilly Library, Indiana University, Bloomington, Indiana)*

anapolis, and it retains this name until the 1885 merger. This same year, Merrill and Company moves onto Glenn's Block, at 19 East Washington Street.

Tanner, *Reports of Cases Argued and Determined in the Supreme Court of Judicature of the State of Indiana,* volume 13 (Indianapolis: Merrill).

Amos Sutton Hayden, *The Sacred Melodeon* (1849; reprinted, Indianapolis: Bowen, Stewart).

1861 Tanner, *Reports of Cases Argued and Determined in the Supreme Court of Judicature of the State of Indiana,* volume 14 (Indianapolis: Merrill).

Benjamin Harrison, *Reports of Cases Argued and Determined in the Supreme Court of Judicature of the State of Indiana,* volume 15 (Indianapolis: Merrill). Harrison is the future president of the United States (1889–1893).

James Sutherland, *Indianapolis Directory and Business Mirror for 1861* (Indianapolis: Bowen, Stewart).

1862 In the summer Samuel Merrill Jr. is commissioned as a second lieutenant in the 70th Indiana Volunteer Infantry.

Harrison, *Reports of Cases Argued and Determined in the Supreme Court of Judicature of the State of Indiana,* volumes 16–17 (Indianapolis: Merrill).

William Horatio Barnes, *The Drama of Secession; or, Scenes from American History* (Indianapolis: Merrill), a play.

John D. Howland and Lucian Barbour, *A Manual for Executors, Administrators and Guardians* (Indianapolis: Merrill).

1864 The sisters Julia Merrill Moores and Catharine Merrill run the company while Samuel Merrill Jr. and Charles W. Moores are away at war. Moores dies on 10 June, after twenty days of service in the 132nd Indiana Volunteer Infantry. Edward S. Field joins Merrill and Company.

James M. Hiatt, *The Test of Loyalty* (Indianapolis: Merrill & Smith). This Civil War novel was evidently published with J. H. V. Smith, who owned a bookstore at 4 East Washington Street, Indianapolis.

[Catharine Merrill,] *The Soldier of Indiana in the War for the Union* (Indianapolis: Merrill; revised and enlarged in 2 volumes, 1866, 1869).

THE

SOLDIER OF INDIANA

IN THE

WAR FOR THE UNION.

" Let all the ends thou aimst at be thy country's,
Thy God's, and truth's."— SHAKSPEARE.

INDIANAPOLIS:
MERRILL AND COMPANY.
1864.

Catharine Merrill, sister of Samuel Merrill Jr., and the title page for her anonymously published first book (courtesy of the Indiana State Library)

1866 The Merrill and Company address is listed as 35 East Washington Street, Indianapolis.

Hiatt, *The War for the Democratic Succession, Comprising the Great "Battle of Pogue's Run"; the "Battle of Fort Raigins"; the Storming of "Fort Dodd"; the Capture of the "S.O.L." Army at Chicago; The Retreat from Kunkle's Mills; and Many Other Thrilling Engagements between the "Puritans" and "The People"* (Indianapolis: Merrill), a satire.

1867 Merrill and Company is listed at 5 East Washington Street (Blackford's Block) and a connected building at 13 South Meridian Street.

The Store in the Early 'Sixties—The Blackford Block

The Merrill and Company bookstore was located at 5 East Washington Street (Blackford's Block) in 1867 (from The Hoosier House: The Bobbs-Merrill Company, *1923; Indiana State Library)*

1869 Isaac Blackford, *Reports of Cases Argued and Determined in the Supreme Court of Judicature of the State of Indiana,* volume 2, 2nd printing (Indianapolis: Merrill).

1870 In this year Merrill and Company becomes Merrill and Field, Field having been made a partner.

Blackford, *Reports of Cases Argued and Determined in the Supreme Court of Judicature of the State of Indiana,* volumes 3–8, 2nd edition (Indianapolis: Merrill & Field).

Horace E. Carter, *Reports of Cases Argued and Determined in the Supreme Court of Judicature of the State of Indiana,* volume 1, 2nd edition (Indianapolis: Merrill & Field).

Michael C. Kerr, *Reports of Cases Argued and Determined in the Supreme Court of Judicature of the State of Indiana,* volume 20 (Indianapolis: Merrill & Field).

Thomas Clarkson, *A Portraiture of Quakerism: Taken from a View of the Moral Education, Discipline, Peculiar Customs, Religious Principles, Political and Civil Economy, and Character, of the Society of Friends* (1806; reprinted, Indianapolis: Merrill & Field for the Society of Friends).

BOWEN, STEWART & CO.,

16 and 18 West Washington St.,

INDIANAPOLIS, IND.,

BOOK AND PAPER HOUSE.

Orders Filled for all kinds of

BOOKS AND PAPER, SCHOOL BOOKS,
MISCELLANEOUS BOOKS,
ENVELOPES AND BLANK BOOKS,
LETTER, NOTE, AND CAP PAPERS,
WRAPPING PAPER, BONNET BOARDS,

Together with anything and everything usually found in a

First Class Book and Paper Store.

BOWEN, STEWART & CO.,
New Iron Front, 16 & 18 West Washington st., Indianapolis, Indiana.

Illustration and advertisement from W. R. Holloway, Indianapolis: A Historical and Statistical Sketch of the Railroad City *(1870; O'Neill Library, Boston College)*

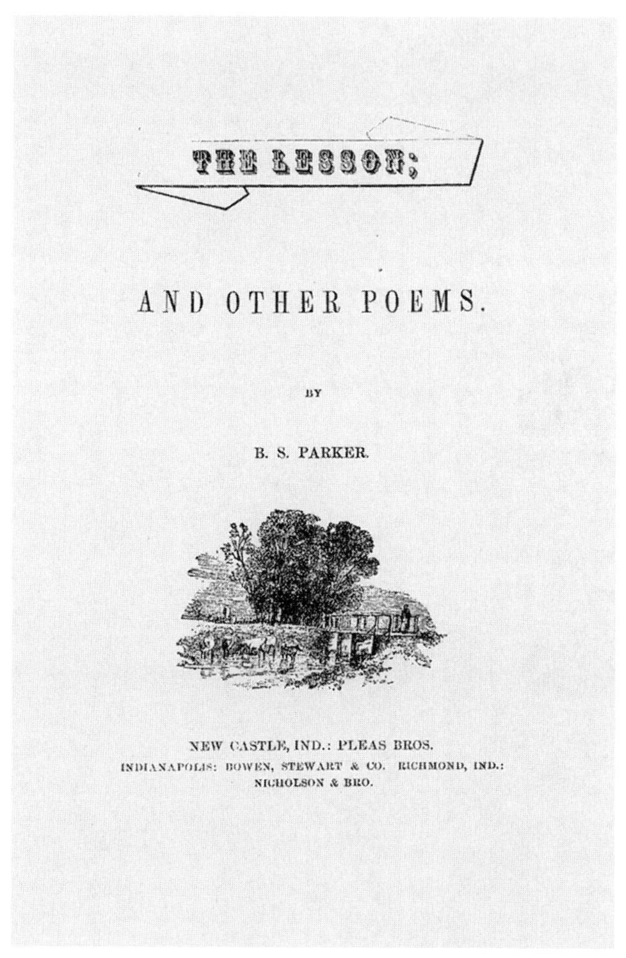

THE LESSON;

AND OTHER POEMS.

BY

B. S. PARKER.

NEW CASTLE, IND.: PLEAS BROS.
INDIANAPOLIS: BOWEN, STEWART & CO. RICHMOND, IND.:
NICHOLSON & BRO.

Title page for an 1871 poetry collection (Indiana University Library)

1871 Harrison, *Reports of Cases Argued and Determined in the Supreme Court of Judicature of the State of Indiana,* volume 23 (Indianapolis: Merrill & Field).

Benjamin Strattan Parker, *The Lesson and Other Poems* (New Castle, Ind.: Pleas / Indianapolis: Bowen, Stewart / Richmond, Ind.: Nicholson).

1872 Harrison, *Reports of Cases Argued and Determined in the Supreme Court of Judicature of the State of Indiana,* volumes 25–26 (Indianapolis: Merrill & Field).

1873 On 13 April, John Jay Curtis is hired at age sixteen by the Bowen, Stewart, and Company bookstore.

1875 Between this and the previous year, Merrill, Hubbard, and Company succeeds Merrill and Field, Samuel Merrill Jr. having entered into partnership with William H. Hubbard and Charles D. Meigs Jr.

1878 Orpheus Everts, *Giles & Co.; or, Views and Interviews Concerning Civilization* (Indianapolis: Bowen, Stewart), fiction.

1879 Eighteen-year-old William C. Bobbs joins Merrill, Hubbard, and Company as a messenger.

Howland and Ferdinand Winter, *A Manual for Executors, Administrators and Guardians* (Indianapolis: Merrill, Hubbard).

1880 Blackford, *Reports of Cases Argued and Determined in the Supreme Court of Judicature of the State of Indiana,* volume 2, 2nd printing (Indianapolis: Merrill, Hubbard).

Indianapolis Board of School Commissioners, *A Manual of Words for Spelling Drill Selected from the Readers, Textbooks and Oral Lessons Used in the Indianapolis Public Schools,* no. 3 (Indianapolis: Merrill, Hubbard; republished, 1881).

Indianapolis Board of School Commissioners, *Speller for Second and Third Years, Indianapolis Public Schools,* no. 2 (Indianapolis: Merrill, Hubbard).

1881 Indianapolis Board of School Commissioners, *Graded Exercises for Practice in the Fundamental Rules: Prepared for the Second Year Pupils of the Indianapolis Public Schools,* no. 1 (Indianapolis: Merrill, Hubbard); revised as *Graded Exercises in Arithmetic,* no. 1 (Indianapolis: Merrill, Meigs, 1883).

Joseph John Mills and Nebraska C. Cropsey, *Graded Exercises in Arithmetic,* nos. 2 and 3 (Indianapolis: Merrill, Hubbard).

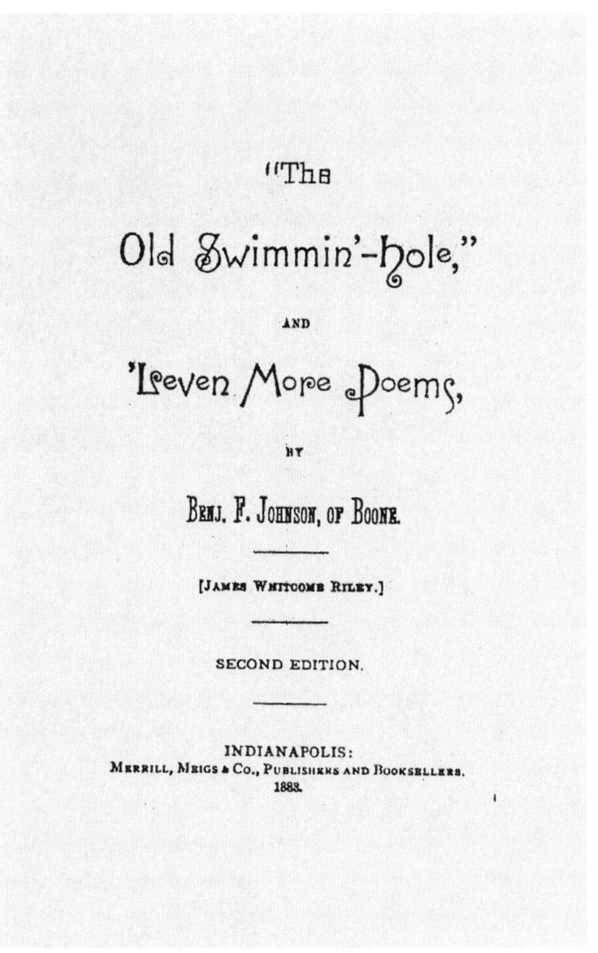

"The

Old Swimmin'-Hole,"

AND

'Leven More Poems,

BY

BENJ. F. JOHNSON, OF BOONE.

[JAMES WHITCOMB RILEY.]

SECOND EDITION.

INDIANAPOLIS:
MERRILL, MEIGS & CO., PUBLISHERS AND BOOKSELLERS.
1883.

Undated photograph of James Whitcomb Riley (seated) with Indiana novelist Meredith Nicholson (left) and editor Hewitt H. Howland, who joined Bowen-Merrill in 1898; title page for the book that brought national attention to Merrill, Meigs, and Company (courtesy of the Indiana State Library; courtesy of The Lilly Library, Indiana University, Bloomington, Indiana)

1882 After Hubbard leaves the firm, Merrill enters a partnership with William H. Elvin and Meigs to form Merrill, Meigs, and Company in March. Merrill's son Charles W. Merrill joins the firm after graduating from Wabash College in Crawfordsville, Indiana.

1883 On 1 October a copy of James Whitcomb Riley's *"The Old Swimmin'-Hole," and 'Leven More Poems* (Indianapolis: Merrill, Meigs) is deposited in the Library of Congress. The book is designated the "second edition" because it has been privately published earlier this year. It is

Where Riley Lived—Lockerbie Street

The Indianapolis house where Riley lived from 1893 until his death in 1916 (from The Hoosier House: The Bobbs-Merrill Company, *1923; Indiana State Library)*

Riley's first book for Merrill, Meigs, and Company and its successors, and a half-million copies will eventually be sold.

Warwick Hawley Ripley, *Digest of Indiana Decisions, from the Organization of the Supreme Court, May Term, 1817, First Blackford, to the Sitting of the Supreme Court Commissioners, May Term, 1881, Seventy-third Indiana* (Indianapolis: Merrill, Meigs, © 1882).

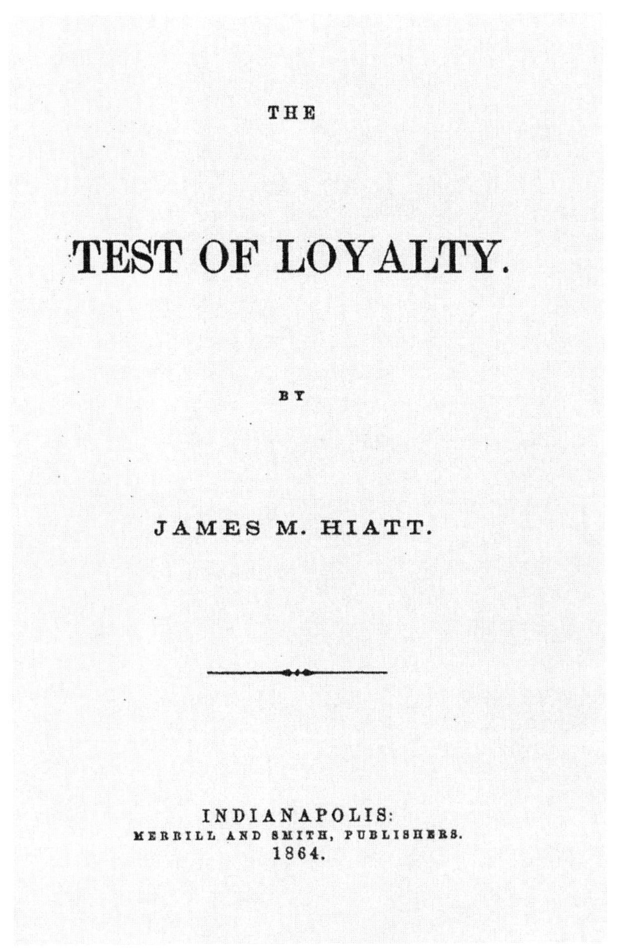
THE

TEST OF LOYALTY.

BY

JAMES M. HIATT.

INDIANAPOLIS:
MERRILL AND SMITH, PUBLISHERS.
1864.

Title page for the wartime novel that Merrill and Company co-published with a nearby bookseller (Brown University Library)

Preface to *The Test of Loyalty*
James M. Hiatt

Some of the forces that led both partners in Merrill and Company, Samuel Merrill Jr. and Charles W. Moores, to volunteer for service during the Civil War, leaving the women in the family to manage the company, are captured in the preface to James M. Hiatt's 1864 novel. It also explains the regional motive behind some of the titles on Merrill's limited list.

It will be remembered by many that, during the year 1862, a number of soldiers belonging to the army of the North-west deserted, and, returning to their homes, were concealed by disaffected partisans. The hero of this story has been selected from a score of these, personally known to the author.

The idea of the work was suggested by a friend, who conceived that such a production, showing, as it necessarily must, the influence, for evil, exerted upon susceptible young men in the army by certain political malcontents, might be productive of good.

The statement that the majority of the characters who figure here are real, their names only being fictitious, is scarcely necessary, as many of them will be readily recognized.

The principal scene has been laid in and about the Hoosier capital, for two reasons: first, because the author is Hoosier, and is partial to Hoosierdom; second, because it is mete that the most gallant of the North-western States should figure in the romance of the present period. She certainly has as much claim to such notoriety as those rebellious States, which have hung so conspicuously hitherto, in the gallery of fiction.

If, in reading this story, any, who have heretofore been blinded by the opaque goggles of party devotion, should have their eyes opened to the great truth that Loyalty admits of no ifs or buts; if any should be convinced that it is the duty of every American to lay party, property, life–all upon the altar of Freedom, then shall my highest hopes be consummated.

To the members of the Metropolitan Literary Institute, who, for eight years, have been to me both schoolmates and teachers, are due my warmest thanks for many kind suggestions.

–*The Test of Loyalty* (Indianapolis: Merrill & Smith, 1864), pp. [5]–6

* * *

Taking Stock

The status and contributions of Merrill, Meigs, and Company and Bowen, Stewart, and Company are described in an 1883 survey of Indianapolis businesses, at a time when the two firms were nearing the end of their independent existence. It was also the year when Merrill, Meigs, and Company achieved national attention because of Riley's "The Old Swimmin'-Hole," and 'Leven More Poems.

MERRILL, MEIGS & CO.,
IMPORTERS AND JOBBERS OF BOOKS, STATIONERY ETC., NO. 5 EAST WASHINGTON AND 13 SOUTH MERIDIAN STS

The leading book and stationery house of Indianapolis, and one of the most extensive establishments of its class west of Philadelphia and New York, is that conducted by the firm of Merrill, Meigs & Co., importers and jobbers and wholesale and retail dealers, whose extensive transactions embrace a wide area of territory throughout Indiana, Illinois and adjacent states. Although the present firm was organized as recently as March, 1882, they are direct successors to a business established as early as 1838, nearly ten years before Indianapolis became a city, or the whistle of the locomotive had resounded through our frontier town. After several removals and changes in the *personel* of its proprietors, the business was established at its present location nearly 20 years ago, where a commodious and conveniently arranged building 22x80 feet in dimensions, with an entrance at No. 5 East Washington St., which connects in the rear with another building 22x60 feet in size fronting on South Meridian St., thus affording ample space for their immense stock, which averages in value about $100,000, comprising a complete and comprehensive assortment of standard and miscellaneous books of both foreign and American publication, stationery and blank books, photograph albums of their own importation, stationers' sundries, and in fact every variety of merchandise pertaining to this special department of commerce, affording a central base of supply for the book trade of the West, whose facilities and advantages will compare favorably with any contemporaneous establishment. Twenty assistants and salesmen are employed in the different departments, and six commercial travelers are constantly on the road in the interests of this house, whose annual transactions range from $200,000 to $250,000. The individual members of the firm as at present organized are Mr. S. Merrill, a native of Indiana, Mr. C. D. Meigs, a native of Pennsylvania, and Mr. W. H. Elvin, a native of Indiana. With an eligible location upon the chief thoroughfare of the city, an inviting establishment, a complete and desirable stock, an established and steadily increasing trade, the enterprise of this representative firm is justly entitled to the consideration and support of the trade and to the liberal notice here accorded among the leading commercial operations which promote the centralization of trade to this metropolis. [. . .]

BOWEN, STEWART & CO.,

BOOKSELLERS, STATIONERS AND PAPER DEALERS, 18 WEST WASHINGTON ST.

This, one of the most prominent business firms of Indianapolis, occupies the same relative position to the book trade of this city that Appleton does to New York and Lippincott to Philadelphia as transacting both a wholesale and retail business. This e[s]tablishment dates its origin to 1854, when under the style of Stewart & Bowen it was organized, with a capital of $10,000, and succeeded to the business previously conducted by H. F. West & Co. In 1860 the present firm name of Bowen, Stewart & Co. was adopted, under which style it has since been conducted, with numerous unimportant changes in the *personel* of the partnership, Mr. Bowen, however, having retained a controling [*sic*] influence as the head of the house for more than a quarter of a century. The premises occupied comprise an elegant and commodious four story business structure 34x120 feet in dimensions, the entire four floors and basement being utilized for the display and storage of their immense stock, consisting of more than 22,000 volumes of standard and miscellaneous literature from the leading publishing houses of Europe and America, together with a general line of school books, legal, commercial and library stationery and fixtures, and every variety of paper and printers' stock in this line. The average valuation of their comprehensive stock is from $60,000 to $75,000, and their trade, which in the wholesale and retail departments extends to various sections of Ohio, Indiana, and Illinois, aggregates a quarter of a million dollars annually. The number of hands employed in the different departments is 22. The individual members of the firm as at present organized are Silas T. Bowen and D. G. Eaton; the latter being a non-resident, the entire management of their extensive business devolves upon Mr. Bowen, who is a native of Otsego County, N. Y., and was born in 1819. Previous to embarking in his present commercial enterprise he occupied the responsible position of teacher and professor in the New York State Normal School for several years and became a resident of Indianapolis in 1853, since which time [h]e has been prominently identified with the business interests of the city and with its growth and development. The establishment over which he has so long presided is the largest of its kind in the state.

–*Manufacturing and Mercantile Resources of Indianapolis, Indiana,* volume 4 (N.p.: Statistical Publishing, 1883), pp. 436–437, 612

Bowen-Merrill: 1885–1902

1885

4 January — Bowen, Stewart, and Company and Merrill, Meigs, and Company merge to form Bowen-Merrill, capitalized at $80,000. The stockholders are Silas T. Bowen, Alfred D. Clarke, James H. Wilson, and Darwin G. Eaton from the former; and Samuel Merrill Jr., Charles D. Meigs Jr., and William H. Elvin from the latter. Bowen is the president, with Merrill, Meigs, Elvin, and Clarke composing the rest of the board of directors. The firm occupies the plant of Bowen, Stewart at 18 West Washington Street, Indianapolis, which includes a bookstore.

21 January — Bowen-Merrill leases 16 and 18 West Washington Street.

19 December — Harrison Burns's *An Index or Abbreviated Digest of the Decisions of the Supreme Court of the State of Indiana Contained in Volumes 78th to 100th Inclusive* appears in the record of new publications in *Publishers' Weekly.* This and the following two items are the only books published by Bowen-Merrill in its first year.

19 December — Joseph Wesley Thompson's *Indiana Citations* (2 volumes) appears in the record of new publications in *Publishers' Weekly.* The second volume includes Burns's *A List of or Reference to the Decisions of the Supreme Court of Indiana,* paginated continuously. From the beginning, Bowen-Merrill (and, later, Bobbs-Merrill) maintains an important list of law titles.

19 December — James Whitcomb Riley's *The Boss Girl, A Christmas Story, and Other Sketches* (with the year 1886 on title page) is published. Riley dominates the Bowen-Merrill trade list for the rest of the century.

1886

8 May — John Worth Kern's *Reports of Cases Argued and Determined in the Supreme Court of Judicature of the State of Indiana* (volume 103) appears in the record of new publications in *Publishers' Weekly.* Bowen-Merrill publishes volumes 104–106 of this ongoing series at intervals later in the year.

1887

16 April — Thomas McIntyre Cooley's *The Acquisition of Louisiana* appears in the record of new publications in *Publishers' Weekly.* It is the text of an address delivered before the Indiana Historical Society on 16 February.

1888

5 June — At the Bowen-Merrill stockholders' meeting, a net profit of $13,672 in the fiscal year is reported. Sales increased $27,566 over the previous year.

10 November — Byron K. Elliot and William F. Elliot's *The Work of the Advocate: A Practical Treatise Containing Suggestions for Preparation and Trial* appears in the record of new publications in *Publishers' Weekly*.

1889

11 June — Bowen-Merrill's fiscal-year sales are reported as $376,391.33, with a net profit of $13,756.02.

19 June — The company leases 24 West Court Street, a two-story brick building.

July — The Indiana State Board of Education awards a contract to Bowen-Merrill for copybooks. After the turn of the century, the company's prominence in education and children's literature will increase significantly. The educational department will form their third important branch, along with the legal and trade departments.

1890

Charles C. Kryter is hired as a messenger boy at age seventeen.

17 March — Fire destroys the Bowen-Merrill building at 16 and 18 West Washington Street. By the time of the 2 June 1891 stockholders' meeting the company has moved to 9 and 11 West Washington Street.

4, 26, 27 August — The stockholders meet at 20 West Maryland Street and reincorporate. Merrill has left the company; his son Charles acquired his interest and was present as a stockholder for the 3 June meeting, the first after the fire.

24 December — Earliest review appears for Meredith Nicholson's first book for the company, *Short Flights,* a collection of poems put together at the instigation of William C. Bobbs. The date on the title page is 1891 (registered for copyright on 8 January 1891).

1891

Meigs's name no longer appears in the company records after this year.

2 June — The treasurer is finally able to give the report for 1890, the year of the fire. He states that "we are not irretrievably ruined," as sales exceeded $420,000 for the fiscal year.

14–19 December — Copies of Sarah T. Bolton's *Songs of a Life-Time* (dated 1892 on title page), edited by John Clark Ridpath, introduced by General Lew Wallace, and with a proem by Riley, are deposited in the Library of Congress for copyright. Bolton was the outstanding Indianapolis literary figure before the Civil War. Wallace's introduction was reused in another Bolton collection, *Paddle Your Own Canoe and Other Poems* (1897), the only appearances by the Indiana author of *Ben-Hur* in Bowen-Merrill titles. (Wallace also supplied data for Catharine Merrill's 1864 volume *The Soldier of Indiana in the War for the Union,* 1864; second edition, 1866–1869).

1892

7 June — The first Bowen-Merrill stockholders' meeting featuring Bobbs and John J. Curtis is held. They are elected directors, along with Elvin (acting president, although Bowen is present) and Charles W. Merrill. Merrill succeeds Elvin as treasurer, a post he holds for most of his remaining years, which are generally spent in the background. Bobbs takes over from Meigs as secretary.

1893

In this year or the next, Robert L. Moorhead, future head of the Law Department, begins working part-time for the firm while still in high school. (The earliest entry for Moorhead in the General Ledger is dated 6 January 1894.)

4 February — By this date Bowen retires as president because of failing health and is succeeded by Elvin.

1894

5 June — The stockholders are informed that Bowen-Merrill has established a branch in Kansas City, Missouri. The bookstore, on 615 Delaware Street, is managed by Daniel S. Pipes. Four law texts are published with both Indianapolis and Kansas City in the imprint this year.

15 December — Harriet Newell Lodge's *A Bit of Finesse: A Story of Fifty Years Ago,* a work of fiction, appears in the record of new publications in *Publishers' Weekly.*

1895

9, 21 December — Two pirated Riley books are entered for copyright by E. A. Weeks of Chicago. They are suppressed after a suit by Bowen-Merrill.

19 December — Bowen dies.

1896

Bowen-Merrill sells its wholesale paper business to the Crescent Paper Company. Its "notions" trade goes to the Indianapolis Book and Stationery Company, two of whose founders were Elvin and Wilson, original incorporators of Bowen-Merrill.

16 October — Journalist and humorist Bill Nye's only Bowen-Merrill book, *A Guest at the Ludlow and Other Stories* (dated 1897 on the title page), is deposited in the Library of Congress for copyright.

1897

The Kansas City store moves to 714 Delaware Street.

27 October — Robert J. Burdette's *Chimes from a Jester's Bells: Stories and Sketches,* illustrated by Louis Braunhold, is deposited in the Library of Congress for copyright.

1898

Bowen-Merrill purchases the Houghton-Mifflin law list and 125 titles from American Publishers Company.

Hewitt H. Howland joins the firm as a part-time manuscript reader. His father, John D. Howland, co-authored legal texts published by Merrill in 1862 and Merrill, Hubbard in 1879.

2 September — *When Knighthood Was in Flower,* by Edwin Caskoden (pseudonym of Charles Major for this novel, his first), is registered for copyright; two copies are deposited in the Library of Congress on 2 November. Ranking second on the *Bookman* top-selling fiction list for 1899 and ninth on the list for 1900, it is Bowen-Merrill's first best-seller but Major's only novel for the firm. Including this book, the company has sixteen best-sellers between 1899 and 1909.

1899

The Kansas City store moves to 725 Wyandotte Street.

Between the 17 July stockholders' meeting and that for 16 July 1900, Elvin, the last of the original Bowen-Merrill incorporators, steps down as president and is replaced by Bobbs. The office of superintendent having been abolished in 1892, Bobbs and his presidential successors exercise managerial control over the company.

1900

Howland becomes editor in the trade department. (The earliest entry for him in the General Ledger is dated 18 May 1901.)

9 April — Charles Frederic Goss's *The Redemption of David Corson,* a religious novel that becomes the seventh-best-selling work of fiction for 1900 (with sales of about 65,000 copies altogether), is registered for copyright.

16 July — A dividend of 25 percent is declared. The stockholders give a vote of thanks to Curtis. He establishes a branch office in New York this year, with himself as eastern editorial representative. Curtis, Bobbs, and Charles Merrill together own 81 percent of the company stock.

16 August — Samuel Merrill Jr.'s *The Seventieth Indiana Volunteer Infantry in the War of the Rebellion,* a history of the regiment he commanded in the Civil War, is registered for copyright.

15 September — Maurice Thompson's *Alice of Old Vincennes* is registered for copyright. It is the first of the firm's best-sellers whose subject was suggested to the author by the editors. Ranking tenth this year on the *Bookman's* best-selling fiction list and second the next year, it sells about 255,000 copies.

1901

13 April — Harold MacGrath's first novel for the company, *The Puppet Crown,* appears in the record of new publications in *Publishers' Weekly.* It is registered for copyright by MacGrath on 20 September 1900 and deposited, in parts, with the Library of Congress between that date and 18 December. *The Puppet Crown* is the 1901 number-seven fiction best-seller.

12 July — Mary Hartwell Catherwood's last novel and her only work published by Bowen-Merrill, *Lazarre,* is registered for copyright.

15 July — A dividend of 40 percent is declared.

15 August — L. Frank Baum's first book for Bowen-Merrill, *The Master Key: An Electrical Fairy Tale,* is registered for copyright; two copies are deposited with the Library of Congress on 29 October. Bowen-Merrill takes over publication of Baum's works from George M. Hill of Chicago.

1902

This year is the last for operation of the Kansas City store, still headed by Pipes.

6 January — The first of John Philip Sousa's two novels for the company, *The Fifth String,* is registered for copyright.

31 January — Frederic S. Isham's first novel for the company, *The Strollers,* is registered for copyright; two copies are deposited in the Library of Congress on 20 March.

31 January	Brand Whitlock's first novel, *The 13th District: A Story of a Candidate,* is registered for copyright; two copies are deposited in the Library of Congress on 7 April.
20 March	Emerson Hough's first novel with the company, *The Mississippi Bubble,* is registered for copyright, and two copies are deposited in the Library of Congress on 22 May. The book becomes the number-four fiction best-seller of the year.
19 May	Hallie Erminie Rives's first novel for the company, *Hearts Courageous,* is registered for copyright.

Formation: Minutes of Bowen-Merrill stockholders' meetings

The minutes of the first stockholders' meeting detail the organization of the new company and, among other things, account for some of the legal books that came over from the Merrill side. In the second meeting, technically the first annual meeting, the bylaws were established.

1st Meeting
Jany 4" 1885

By unanimous agreement the first meeting of the stock holders of the Bowen-Merrill Co. was held at the home of C. D. Meigs Jr. on Saturday Eve Jan 4/85.

Present, in person, Silas T. Bowen, Samuel Merrill, C. D. Meigs Jr., Wm H. Elvin, S. D. Clarke and Jas. H. Wilson. Mr. Darwin G. Eaton was represented by proxy in the hands of Silas T. Bowen, the foregoing comprising all the stockholders of the company.

On motion Mr. Bowen was elected chairman, and C. D. Meigs secty of the meeting.

The Articles of Association of this company, filed in the office of the Recorder of Marion Co. on the 31st day of Dec. 1884–and the Articles of Agreement entered into by the firms of Merrill, Meigs & Co. and Bowen-Stewart & Co. dated on Dec. 26" 1884–were laid before the meeting.

Said Articles of Association, and Articles of Agreement, read respectively as follows–

Articles of Association–or–"Certificate of Incorporation"

Articles of Association
The undersigned, that is to say, Silas T. Bowen, Samuel Merrill, Charles D. Meigs Jr., Wm H. Elvin, and Alfred D. Clarke, for the purpose of forming a corporation under the provision of an Act of the General Assembly of the State of Indiana–approved May 20" 1852–and entitled "An Act for the incorporation of manufacturing & mining companies and companies for mechanical, chemical, & building purposes,["] and under subsequent acts supplemental to said act, or amendatory thereto, or, of parts thereof do make the following certificate of Incorporation, hereby certifying

I Name
That the corporate name of the company to be incorporated by the filing of this certificate shall be and is, The Bowen-Merrill Co.

II Object
The object of the formation of said company shall be and is, the manufacture and sale of blank books, memorandum books, printed books, tablets, and other articles of stationery, and in connection therewith the purchase and sale of books, papers, stationery, school supplies, novelties, and such other articles as are usually kept and sold by wholesale & retail Book and Stationery Houses.

III Capital Stock and Term of Existance. [*sic*]
The amount of the capital stock of said company shall be eighty thousand dollars, and the term of the corporate existance [*sic*] of the company shall be twenty five years.

IV No. & Names of Directors.
The number of the Directors of said company shall be five, and the names of the first board of Directors who shall manage the affairs of the co. for the first year of its existance [*sic*], are, Silas T. Bowen, Samuel Merrill, Charles D. Meigs Jr., William H. Elvin, and Alfred D. Clarke.

V Location.
The Business Operations of said corporation shall be carried on in the city of Indianapolis, in the county of Marion, and state of Indiana.

Executed in duplicate by said corporators this 26" day of Dec. 1884.

Samuel Merrill
Charles D. Meigs Jr.
William H. Elvin
Silas T. Bowen
Alfred D. Clarke

2

1st Meeting

Jany 4" 1885

By unanimous agreement the first meeting of the stockholders of The Bowen-Merrill Co was held at the home of C. D. Meigs Jr on Saturday Eve Jany 4/85

Present, in person, Silas T. Bowen Samuel Merrill, C. D. Meigs Jr. Wm H. Elvin, A. D. Clarke and Jas. H. Wilson. Mr. Darwin G. Eaton was represented by proxy in the hands of Silas T. Bowen: the foregoing comprising all the stockholders of the Company.

On motion Mr. Bowen was Elected Chairman and C. D. Meigs Secty of the meeting.

The articles of Association of this Company, filed in the office of the Recorder of Marion Co. on the 31st day of Dec. 1884, and the articles of Agreement entered into by the firms of Merrill Meigs & Co and Bowen-Stewart & Co dated on Dec. 26" 1884, were laid before the meeting.

Said articles of Association, and articles of Agreement, read respectively as follows:-

Two pages from the minutes of stockholders' meetings, recording the founding of Bowen-Merrill on 4 January 1885 (courtesy of The Lilly Library, Indiana University, Bloomington, Indiana)

3

Articles of ~~Association~~ Incorporation — or —
"Certificate of Incorporation".

Articles of Association

The undersigned that is to say Silas T. Bowen, Samuel Merrill, Charles D. Meigs Jr., Wm H. Elvin, and Alfred [illegible], for the purpose of forming a corporation under the provisions of an act of the General Assembly of the State of Indiana — approved May 20" 1852 — and entitled "An act for the incorporation of Manufacturing & Mining Companies, and companies for mechanical, chemical, & building purposes, and under subsequent acts supplemental to said act, or amendatory thereto, or of parts thereof, do make the following certificate of Incorporation, hereby certifying.

I Name — I That the corporate name of the company to be incorporated by the filing of this certificate shall be and is, The Bowen-Merrill Co.

II Object — II The object of the formation of said company shall be and is, the manufacture and sale of blank books, memorandum books, printed

State of Ind } S.S.
Marion Co }

Certificate of Incorporation

Be it known that on the 31" day of Dec. 1884–Silas T. Bowen, Samuel Merrill, Charles D. Meigs Jr., Wm H. Elvin, and Alfred D. Clarke the corporators within named personally came before the undersigned, a notary public, of said co. at Indpls, in said co. and severally acknowledged the execution of the foregoing certificate of Incorporation by them subscribed. Witness my hand and notorial seal at Indianapolis aforesaid, the day & year last aforesaid.

Merrill Moores

Notary Public [*L.S.* in drawn circle]

Recorded Dec. 31, 1884 at 4½ o'clock P.M. [. . .]

Art 7th Plates

The sterotype [*sic*] & electrotype plates and law books owned by the parties of the first part, and hereinafter named, shall be invoiced to the co. at the following named prices to wit–The plates of 2 vols of Ripleys Ind. Digest at seven hundred dollars ($700.00) per vol. The plates of twenty four (24) vols of Ind. Reports at four hundred dollars ($400.) per vol. The bound vols of Ripleys Ind Digest, of which there shall not be more than two hundred (200) sets, at four and 25/100 dollars ($4.25) per vol. or $8.50 per set. The bound vols of Ind Reports printed from plates, at seventy seven cents (.77¢) per vol. The bound vols of Ind Reports printed from type, of which there are no plates, at two and 50/100 ($2.50) per vol. The unbound vols of Ind. Reports, printed from plates, at twenty nine cents (.29¢) per vol. The numbered vols of Ind. Reports printed from type at two and 05/100 ($2.05) per vol. The bound vols of Thompsons Ind. Citations, at three and 20/100 ($3.20) per vol. and unbound vols of same at two and 75/100 ($2.75) per vol. [. . .]

1st Annual Meeting

2nd Meeting June 2/85

In response to the call of the secretary, made in writing, in accordance with the law, the first Regular Annual Meeting of the stockholders of the Bowen-Merrill Co. was held in the office of the company, on Tuesday June 2nd 1885, at 3.30 o'clock P.M.

There were present Messrs S. T. Bowen, Samuel Merrill, William H. Elvin, A. D. Clarke, James H. Wilson, and Chas. D. Meigs Jr. Mr. Darwin G. Eaton's proxy being in the hands of Mr. S. T. Bowen, the entire stock of the concern was represented.

The minutes of the Special Meeting, held Jany 4" 1885, were read by the Secretary, and approved.

The By Laws of the company, as prepared by their attorneys, Messrs Baker, Hord & Hendricks, were read by the secretary, as follows–

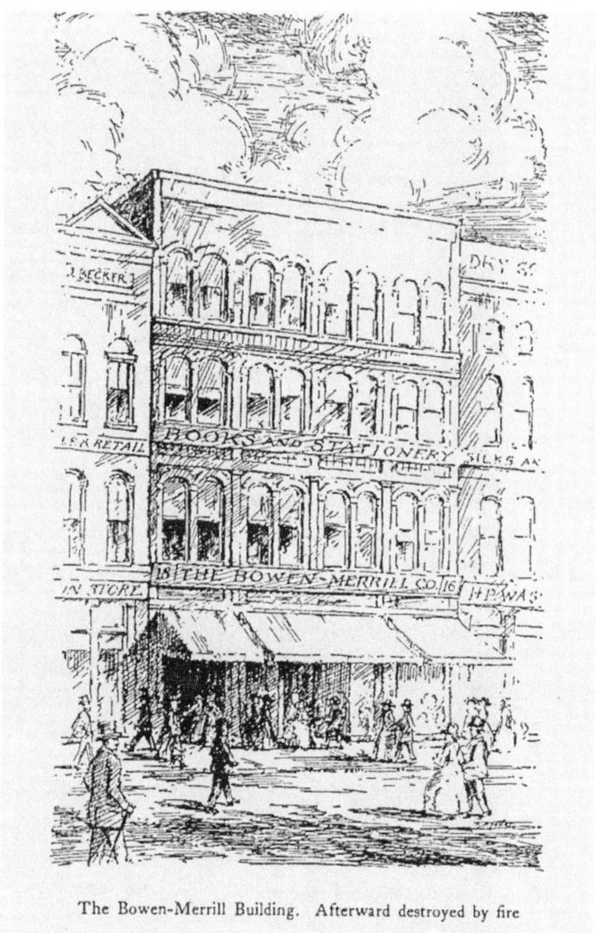

The Bowen-Merrill Building. Afterward destroyed by fire

The store at 16 and 18 West Washington Street, Indianapolis (from The Hoosier House: The Bobbs-Merrill Company, *1923; Indiana State Library)*

By Laws.

By Laws of The Bowen-Merrill Co.

Art. 1st Officers. Sec. 1st Time of Annual Meeting

The Annual Meeting of the stockholders shall be held at the office of the company, on the first Tuesday of June of each year, at which meeting the Directors shall be elected, and such other business transacted as may properly come before the meeting–provided, however, that the Directors to be elected at the Annual Meeting in 1885, shall come into office, upon the expiration of the terms of the present Directors, and shall serve only until the next Annual Meeting.

Sec. 2nd Officers & Time of Their Election

The officers of the company shall consist of a President, a Superintendent, a Secretary and a Treasurer, who shall be elected by the Directors at their first session after each annual meeting, and who shall serve for one year. [. . .]

* * *

*Logo for the company incorporated on the last day of 1884 (*Encyclopedia of Indianapolis, *1994; Indiana State Library)*

CHARACTER SKETCHES

THE BOSS GIRL

A CHRISTMAS STORY

AND

OTHER SKETCHES

BY

JAMES WHITCOMB RILEY

AUTHOR OF "THE OLD SWIMMIN' HOLE," ETC.

INDIANAPOLIS
THE BOWEN-MERRILL CO
1886

Title page for the Indiana poet's second book for the Merrill line of publishers (courtesy of The Lilly Library, Indiana University, Bloomington, Indiana)

Magazine Day
Anton Scherrer

In the late 1880s new magazines arrived at Indianapolis bookstores around the seventh of each month. It was practically a holiday, as Scherrer recalls. Bowen-Merrill's back room was an additional magnet for literati.

> Chronicler Continues His Saga of Magazine Day and Celebrities Who Held Literary Revels in Bookshop.

I didn't have time yesterday to finish what I had to say about Magazine Day. Sidetracked as I was by the intrusion of "Trilby," I didn't get around to proving my thesis, namely, that Magazine Day had the significance of a saint's day.

Well, the reason Magazine Day was like that was because it brought people of similar taste and beliefs together. It was not unlike a church in that respect where a lot of preoccupied souls get together every Sunday to worship at a common shrine. [. . .]

I remember several occasions when the groups were larger and louder than usual. One, of course, was when "Trilby" turned up. It happened again when Paul Leicester Ford brought out "The Honorable Peter Stirling," and had everybody wondering whether Grover Cleveland was the subject of the story. Booth Tarkington's first book, "The Gentleman From Indiana," brought out a big congregation, too.

That was the story with a description of a rain-crow. The groups in the bookshops spent hours, I remember, arguing whether an Indiana rain-crow could possibly make a noise the way Mr. Tarkington described it. The last time I remember anything like an old-fashioned Magazine Day was when Scribners published Edith Wharton's "House of Mirth." It was around the turn of the century.

Book Worms in Huddle

I guess it was Magazine Day that gave the Bowen-Merrill people the idea of the little room in the back of their store. It was a room crammed full of old editions and leather bindings, in charge of Alfred Clarke, and it was here that the book worms from all over the state gathered to unite in worship. On a good day, it was nothing out of the ordinary to see Myron Reed, William Fishback, David Starr Jordan, Barry Sulgrove, Judge Hines and Oscar B. Hord loafing around the place. A little later, James Whitcomb Riley and Oscar McCullough discovered it, too.

Bowen-Merrill's little back room had the merit of bringing the book lovers together everyday instead of once a month the way Magazine Day did, and I suspect that was the reason Ignatius Donnelly didn't get any farther in Indianapolis than he did.

Back in the '80's, Mr. Donnelly wrote a book called "The Great Cryptogram," in the course of which he tried to prove by means of a cute cipher that Francis Bacon wrote the works commonly attributed to Shakespeare.

Well, the thing was fought out in Bowen-Merrill's back room. At one time it looked pretty bad for Mr. Shakespeare. That was the day a youngster by the name of Albert J. Beveridge showed up and said that neither Bacon nor Shakespeare had anything to do with it. It was Sir Walter Raleigh, said Mr. Beveridge, which, of course, complicated matters more than ever.

By this time the champions of Shakespeare were thoroughly aroused and sent for Mrs. Hufford. She came and told Mr. Beveridge where to head in and ever since that day Shakespeare has had everything his own way in Indianapolis.

–"Our Town," *Indianapolis Times,*
15 December 1937, p. 15

* * *

The St. Patrick's Day Fire

The fire that destroyed the Bowen-Merrill building killed thirteen firemen and injured several others. F. Rollin Kautz, an employee who became store manager and stockholder, returned to the flaming building to save the ledgers containing the company's financial records. He had to use one of them to smash a window for his second exit.

About three o'clock in the afternoon of the 17th inst., what seemed to be an insignificant fire broke out near the furnace in the sub basement of the immense establishment of The Bowen-Merrill Co., 16 and 18 West Washington Street, Indianapolis, where they have been housed for nearly forty years. The building is four stories high, with a marble front, facing Wash-

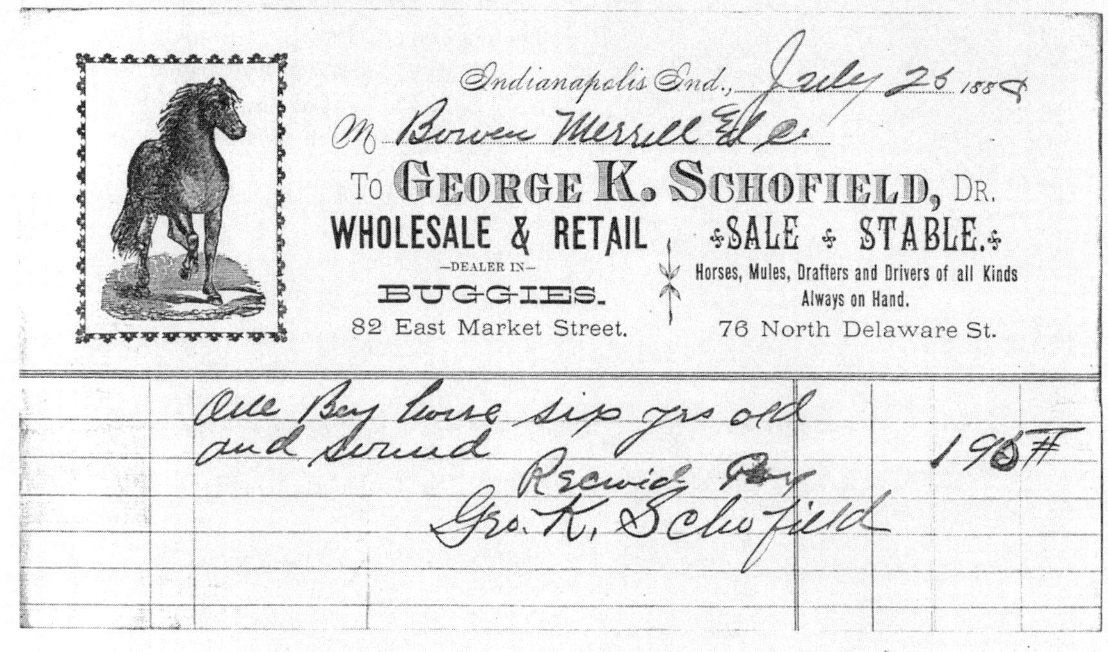

Indianapolis Ind., July 26 1888

Mr Bowen Merrill Co

To George K. Schofield, Dr.

WHOLESALE & RETAIL SALE STABLE.

—DEALER IN—

BUGGIES.

82 East Market Street.

Horses, Mules, Drafters and Drivers of all Kinds Always on Hand.

76 North Delaware St.

One Bay horse six yrs old and sound 198

Received Pay

Geo. K. Schofield

An 1888 Bowen-Merrill business transaction involving the sale of a cart horse (courtesy of The Lilly Library, Indiana University, Bloomington, Indiana)

The Bowen-Merrill fire of 17 March 1890 (Pamela Yoder/Tiffany Studio)

ington Street, just west of Meridian. The Fire Department, when it arrived, seemed at a loss to locate the fire, and began pouring water into the building at the front, when the seat of the trouble was in the rear. For two hours the fight had continued in this way until a majority of the spectators had left, under the impression that the fire was out. About 5:30 o'clock, however, there was a terrible crash, and the entire building, except the front wall, fell inward. A later report announces that this wall has since fallen, injuring several men at work in the ruins. At the time of the fire, a number of firemen, variously estimated at from eight to twenty, were on the roof of the building, and were buried in the débris, which were piled forty feet high within the walls. Ten men were killed outright, and fifteen badly hurt, some fatally, it is feared.

The Bowen-Merrill Company was one of the largest as well as the oldest bookselling concerns in Indiana. The Company was supposed to carry $125,000 worth of stock, very little of which, if any, has been saved. The house was established in 1838, and did business at various times under the following firm-names: Bowen, Stewart & Co., Merrill, Meigs & Co., Merrill, Hubbard & Co., Merrill & Field, Merrill & Co., and, since 1885, The Bowen-Merrill Co. The officers of the Company are President, S. T. Bowen; Secretary, Chas. D. Meigs, Jr.; Treasurer, W. H. Elim [*sic*]; Superintendent, S. Merrill. Col. S. Merrill is colonel of President Harrison's old regiment, and was recently made consul-general at Calcutta, for which post he intended leaving next week. Judging from the proverbial enterprise of this firm, we are confident that they will be on their feet again in a very short time.

–"The Bowen-Merrill Company Fire," *Publishers' Weekly,* no. 947 (22 March 1890): 407–408

Recovery: Minutes of Bowen-Merrill stockholders' meetings

The 1890 annual meeting was brief because of the fire. The quick adjournment led to a series of meetings culminating in reorganization on 26 and 27 August. Treasurer Elvin was unable to make his report until the meeting of 2 June 1891. The 1892 meeting was notable for the prominent roles of Bobbs and Curtis, and for the concentration of managerial duties in the hands of the president. The new treasurer was Charles W. Merrill, who was to hold that office for many years.

5th Annual Meeting
June 3–1890

In response to proper notification the Stock-holders of The Bowen-Merrill Co. met in Annual Meeting, in the Co's office on June 3d 1890, at 3 P.M.

There were present Mr. S. T. Bowen, Mr. C. W. Merrill, Mr. W. H. Elvin, Mr. J. H. Wilson and C. D. Meigs Jr.

Longtime company treasurer Charles W. Merrill (courtesy of The Lilly Library, Indiana University, Bloomington, Indiana)

Mr. D. G. Eaton was represented by Mr. S. T. Bowen, his duly appointed proxy.

The minutes of last Annual Meeting were read and approved.

The Treasurer reported that the fire (of Mch. 19 [*sic*]) had caused so much confusion and delay in office work that the books were not in condition to take the annual statement from, so that he had no report prepared, and he asked for further time in which to make report.

The request was granted, and, there being no further business the meeting adjourned until June 23d at 10 A.M.

C. D. Meigs Jr
Secty

(Read & appv'd June 23d) [. . .]

Stockholders Annual Meeting

1892 June 7
The second [*sic*] annual meeting of the stockholders of The Bowen Merrill Co was held in the Company's building Tuesday June 7, 1892 at 3 P.M. The meeting was called to order by Acting President Mr. Elvin.
There were present Messrs Bowen, Elvin, Merrill, Curtis, Wilson, and Bobbs.
A communication from Mr. F. R. Kautz was read. It appointed Mr. Elvin proxy for May 30 to July 1 for one hundred shares of stock held by Mr. Kautz.
The Minuets [*sic*] of the last anual [*sic*] meeting were read and approved.
The Treasurer submitted the following report which was accepted and ordered spread upon the minuets.

Treasurers Report
To The Stockholders of The Bowen-Merrill Co.}
Gentlemen:
I beg to submit the following report of the affairs of The Bowen-Merrill Co. for the fiscal year ending April 30, 1892.

Assetts [*sic*]

Stock on hand	72 863.35
Plate a/c	19 977.90
Cash on hand	300.67
Cash in banks	3 260.70
Accts receivable	42 225.55
Bills "	10 053.49
Furniture & Fixtures	7 830.63
	156 512.29

Liabilities

Bills Payable	52 494.81
Accts "	20 745.93
Surplus	2 156.02
Capital	79 900.[00]
Net Gain	1 215.53
	156 512.29

The actual gain of the year including the amount used in restoring the capital to par value was 6134.49. [. . .]

A careful analysis of expenses indicates that the ratio of expenses to sales was for the Law Dept. 15.9%
Paper 16
Retail 19
Wholesale 23.6
For the whole business the percentage of expenses to sales was 19.6%. This ratio though .6% lower than last year is yet 3.3% greater than the average of the previous four years.
Respectfully
(sing) C. W. Merrill
Treas The Bowen-Merrill Co.

The following amendment to the By Laws was offered by Mr. Merrill to amend Sec. 1 of Art. 1 to read as follows.
The annual meeting of the stockholders shall be held at the office of the company on the first Tuesday of June of each year, at which meeting four directors

SONGS OF A LIFE-TIME

BY

SARAH T. BOLTON

EDITED BY

JOHN CLARK RIDPATH

With an Introduction by GENERAL LEW WALLACE
and a Proem by JAMES WHITCOMB RILEY

INDIANAPOLIS
THE BOWEN-MERRILL COMPANY
1892

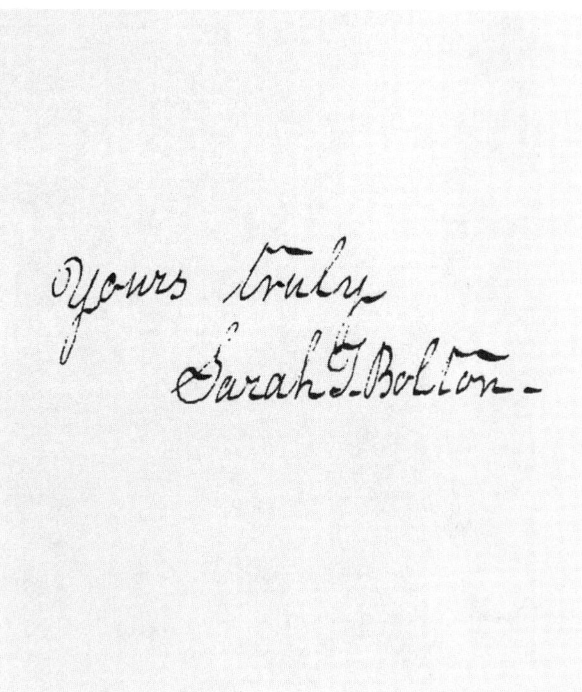

Title page for the poetry collection with an introduction by the author of Ben-Hur *(1880); page inscribed by the author of the collection (courtesy of the Ohio State University Library)*

shall be elected and such other business transacted as may properly come before the meeting.

The following stock was voted upon the amendment

Mrs. Birch 50 shares by Mr. Bowen Proxy

Mr. Bowen 228 "

Mr. Elvin 250 "

Mr. Wilson 80 "

Mr. Kautz 100 " by Mr. Elvin proxy

Mr. Merrill 320 "

Mr. Bobbs 250 "

320 shares held by Mr. Curtis was not voted as it was issued on the day of the meeting.

The Amendment was carried by the following vote

Aff. Elvin, Merrill, Kautz, Bobbs

total 920 shares

Negative Mrs. Birch, Bowen, Wilson

total 358 shares

The following amendments were offered by Mr. Merrill to amend Section 2 of Art. 1 so as to read "The officers of the Company shall consist of a President, a Secretary and a Treasurer["]

To amend Sections 4 and 5 of Art 1 by substituting therefore the following It shall be the duty of the President to exercise a general supervision of the affairs of the Company and to employ the necessary agents and servants and fix salaries all subject to the approval of the board of directors

Both carried unanimously.

The following were unanimously elected directors Messrs Elvin, Merrill, Curtis and Bobbs.

The Treasurer presented a motion that a dividend of 1½% be declared and paid. The motion was unanimously carried.

Adjourned

William C. Bobbs Secy

Read and Approved

June 6, 1893

William C. Bobbs, who joined Merrill, Hubbard in 1879 and became president of Bowen-Merrill twenty years later; John J. Curtis, promotional innovator, founder of the New York office, and president of Bobbs-Merrill from 1926 to 1931 (courtesy of the Indiana State Library; courtesy of The Indianapolis Star*)*

Obituary for Silas T. Bowen

Silas T. Bowen, whose death on December 19 was briefly noted in THE PUBLISHERS' WEEKLY, was born in Cooperstown, N. Y., November 26, 1819. [. . .]

Mr. Bowen's career in Indianapolis, which extended over a period of forty-two years, was eminently successful. For a brief period after his arrival in Indianapolis he held the professorship of natural science and rhetoric in the McLean Female Seminary, at that time the most advanced and most prominent of institutions of it[s] class in the West.

In 1854 he resigned the professorship and formed a partnership with Mr. William Stewart, of Maryland, for the purpose of carrying on the business of publishers and wholesale and retail paper dealers. Under the firm-name of Stewart & Bowen the business at once developed into large proportions. Five years later Mr. Stewart died, and a reorganization followed under the firm-name of Bowen, Stewart & Co. This firm, formed August 1, 1860, was composed of Mr. Bowen, the widow of Mr. Stewart, his son Charles G. Stewart, present managing editor of the Indianapolis *Sentinel,* A. D. Clarke, and D. G. Eaton. Mr. Bowen held the controlling interest. His executive ability and general business management were large factors in the success of the organization. In 1885 Bowen, Stewart & Co. and Merrill, Meigs & Co. (the latter firm having been founded in 1838 by Samuel Merrill, Sr., ex-treasurer of the State of Indiana) consolidated under the firm-name of the Bowen-Merrill Company, and Mr. Bowen was made its first president. This position he held until failing health forced his resignation, in 1893, since which time he took no active part in the business, but retained his stock interest. The firm of the Bowen-Merrill Co., of which W. H. Elvin is president, W. C. Bobbs, secretary, C. W. Merrill treasurer, and J. J. Curtis superintendent, has long ago made for itself a reputation as one of the foremost jobbing houses in the West. In law-books it has a large list of publications, including standard works by the best-known legal authors. It also publishes the works of James Whitcomb Riley, Richard Malcolm Johnston, and Mrs. Sarah T. Bolton, and other minor Western authors.

–"Silas T. Bowen–In Memoriam," *Publishers' Weekly,* no. 1252 (25 January 1896): 192

* * *

IMPORTANT NOTICE TO

THE TRADE!

We shall immediately institute legal proceedings in the U. S. courts against E. A. Weeks & Co.'s "Collection of James Whitcomb Riley's Poems," and shall protect our rights.

THE BOWEN-MERRILL CO.

Indianapolis and Kansas City.

The first Bowen-Merrill notice in Publishers' Weekly *(14 December 1895)*

Charles Major's *When Knighthood Was in Flower*
Hewitt H. Howland

The title of Charles Major's 1898 novel was lifted by Curtis, then with the Bowen-Merrill trade department, from a Leigh Hunt poem. The phrase became proverbial thanks to the popularity of the book. Owing in part to the aggressive advertising campaign launched by Curtis once he had moved to the New York office, about 370,000 copies were sold in ten years. It is sometimes cited as the first nationally marketed best-seller. The story was adapted for the stage in 1907 and for the screen in 1922. Major's historical romance dealt with the affair of Mary Tudor and the duke of Suffolk and was a milestone in a publishing trend described by Howland, writing after the end of his careers as editor at Bobbs-Merrill and Century *magazine. Emerson Hough, Maurice Thompson, and Irving Bacheller were Bowen-Merrill/Bobbs-Merrill authors.*

Speaking not long ago of the trends in fiction, I said to my friend the publisher that literary fashions are made by success, by public acclaim so loud and wide-

Cover for the popular humorist's 1896 book, his only Bowen-Merrill publication; cover for an 1897 book by another humorist (courtesy of The Lilly Library, Indiana University, Bloomington, Indiana)

Hewitt H. Howland joined Bowen-Merrill in 1898 and was chief editor of the trade department from 1900 to 1925 (courtesy of the Indiana State Library)

spread that it cannot be resisted. The trend sets in rather slowly, as a rule. It may extend over several years, a book here and a book there, they may even be successful books, but each stands alone. And then suddenly a novel will appear that catches the universal fancy, that is the talk of all fiction readers as well as of those who never read before. Instantly, it seems, the fashion is set and writers both great and small turn their pens in one direction, establishing a trend that may run a long or short course depending on the health and strength of the popular appeal.

In proof of this rather brash assertion, I recalled the most conspicuous instance of modern times, the phenomenal rise of the romantic-historic novel which began in 1880, reached its height ten years later and passed quietly out of popular favor in 1910. We did not recognize its beginnings at the time, we had no idea what was going on round about us. Not until the flower was in full bloom did we know that a new fashion was upon us. We failed to see the roots from which it sprang, we confused its maturity with its early youth, mistaking the one for the other.

The seed of the Great Revival was sown when, in the shade of his historic elm at Crawfordsville, Indiana, General Lew Wallace wrote the last chapter of "Ben Hur." This was the year that George Eliot died and Garfield was elected President–1880. It was not long after the novel's appearance that people began to stop you on the street to ask if you had read "Ben Hur" and "wasn't the chariot race marvelous?" Preachers preached about it, no literary club's program was perfected without a paper on the Wallace wonder, the sanctimonious put aside their prejudices against novel reading and ballyhooed "Ben Hur" as a Christian duty, while the very air tingled with the book's success. And yet it was seventeen years before the historical trend was established and recognized as a fact.

In 1891, eleven years after "Ben Hur," Conan Doyle gave "The White Company" to a reading world still hungry for romance. Two sterile years followed Doyle's novel of quality and continuing reputation. Then Stanley Weyman and Rider Haggard rode in on the crest of the wave with "Under the Red Robe" and "Montezuma's Daughter," and once more the publishers, rejoicing in their good fortune, were too busy to analyze the public taste, while the public not knowing that it had a taste bought, and bought, and bought!

The following year, 1895, Stephen Crane's "Red Badge of Courage" came to cheer the hearts of the critical, while the great populace rejoiced in Henry Sienkiewicz's "Quo Vadis" and produced for it the largest sale of any novel since "Ben Hur." Its publishers were fully aware of what they had and pushed and publicized the book for all it was worth, possibly more.

Still we did not know that a trend was in the making, though we became suspicious when the turn of the year brought Gilbert Parker and "The Seats of the Mighty." A grand story it was, as I remember it, and certainly a title made to order for a best seller, which it was–the best seller of its year, although Frances Hodgson Burnett gave us "A Lady of Quality" and Robert Louis Stevenson, "Weir of Hermiston."

We are very close now to a full realization of what was going on. The trend was almost in sight. Only one more novel can be said to belong to the preliminary period and that was "The Jessamy Bride" by F. Frankfort Moore, a great success for a little-known writer. This was the opening gun of 1897.

Then the lid was blown off. The distinguished Dr. S. Weir Mitchell of Philadelphia signed his name to "Hugh Wynne" and the historical novel was lifted to a place of eminence such as it had not known since the days of Scott and Thackeray, in spite of the many fine stories that had recently preceded it. "Hugh Wynne" was an immediate success, a literary as well as a popular success that not even James Lane Allen's "The Choir Invisible" could dim, although received with great acclaim in the same year.

These were gala days for the publishers, everybody seemed to be reading novels and, what's more, buying them. Even cash and credit came out of their

WHEN KNIGHTHOOD WAS IN FLOWER

OR

THE LOVE STORY OF
Charles Brandon and Mary Tudor
THE KING'S SISTER, AND HAPPENING IN THE REIGN OF
HIS AUGUST MAJESTY, KING HENRY VIII

REWRITTEN AND RENDERED INTO MODERN ENGLISH FROM
SIR EDWIN CASKODEN'S MEMOIR

BY EDWIN CASKODEN
[CHARLES MAJOR]

225th THOUSAND

INDIANAPOLIS, INDIANA, U. S. A.
THE BOWEN-MERRILL COMPANY
PUBLISHERS

THE great number of requests for portraits, suitable for framing, of the author of "When Knighthood Was in Flower," has led the publishers to present this India proof, copper-plate engraving. It may be removed without defacing the book.

MR CHARLES MAJOR
Author of "When Knighthood Was in Flower"

SOUVENIR OF THE
TWO HUNDRED AND TWENTY-FIFTH THOUSAND

Title page for an undated reprint of the company's first best-seller (1898) and a portrait of the author inserted in the same copy (O'Neill Library, Boston College)

strongholds to hire themselves to would-be book dealers. That day was counted lost in which no new shop was opened.

And so the stage was admirably set for the well-matured plans of a new mid-western publisher. He was "crazy" said his elder brethren of the East. "You can't advertise a book as you can a breakfast food." But they hadn't counted on the trend which, with the coming of 1898, began its spectacular climb to the summit, led by "When Knighthood Was in Flower," the product of Charles Major, a Shelbyville, Indiana, lawyer. What happened to that romance of Mary Tudor and Charles Brandon is too well known to be repeated here. But it was a thrilling experience to any one who lived through it.

Following "Knighthood" and all in the same year were: "Prisoners of Hope" by Mary Johnston; "Red Rock" by Thomas Nelson Page; "The Pride of Jennico" by Agnes and Edgerton Castle; "The Forest Lovers" by Maurice Hewlett, and "Lorraine" by Robert W. Chambers. All of these novels in varying degrees were highly successful, all of them read by tens of thousands, several of them vigorously exploited. The New Publishing Deal was on in full force. What a year!

Eighteen Ninety-nine was not so prolific, but it introduced a new writer who in the grand total of his several books led all others in sales and popularity. This was Winston Churchill with his first novel "Richard Carvel." The other two titles of the year were almost as distinguished as Churchill's: "Janice Meredith" by Paul Leicester Ford, which like "Hugh Wynne" was laid in the time of the Revolution; and "Via Crucis" by F. Marion Crawford, following the lead of "Quo Vadis."

During the first year of the new century the historical novel swept the boards, captured the entire best selling six and made reputations right and left. The first to greet 1900 was "A Friend of Caesar" by William Stearns Davis. That, as you see, was thirty-four years ago, but Caesar's friend is still used in many schools. Even the professors fell for historical fiction. Then came Emerson Hough, famous later for his "Covered Wagon," with "Fifty Four Forty or Fight," one of our early national slogans that almost let us in for a war with Great Britain. Back to the Middle West, Maurice Thompson gave a coming out party for "Alice of Old Vincennes." That this story of Tippecanoe and William Henry Harrison sold into the hundreds of thousands

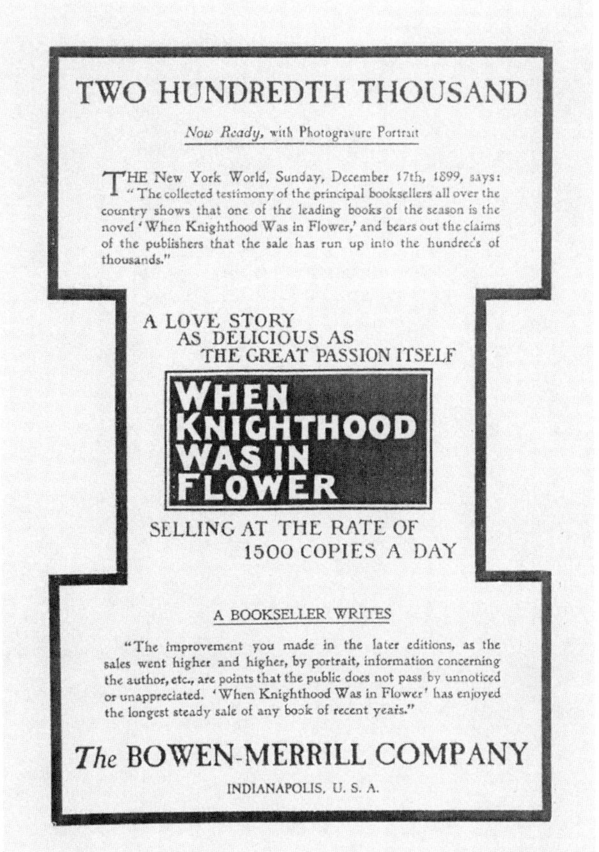

Full-page advertisements in Publishers' Weekly *(5 August 1899; 13 January 1900) for Major's best-selling historical novel*

surprised no one so much as it did the modest author. Thompson was a poet, an essayist, and to find himself the parent of a popular novel and the possessor of a bulging bank balance was almost more than he could bear.

Then the drums beat and the trumpets blew and Mary Johnston returned with "To Have and to Hold," another perfect title playing its part in the making of an almost overwhelming success. Of the last two historical novels of this golden year, one was a return engagement by F. Marion Crawford with "In the Palace of the King." The other introduced a new writer, the now distinguished Irving Bacheller. He came bringing that shrewd philosopher "Eben Holden" out of the Mohawk Valley up to the high hills of popular favor. A fitting climax to a fruitful year.

That 1901 might make a brave beginning Booth Tarkington left "Monsieur Beaucaire" on his publisher's doorstep. He little knew how brave it was to be, for Mr. Tarkington is and always has been genuinely modest about himself and his work. "Beaucaire" won immediate applause not only from the literary experts in the boxes but from the simple readers in the gallery who know what they like, and not much more. In the thirty years that have passed Booth Tarkington's many novels have added to his stature and fixed his place for all time. But "Beaucaire" still lives.

Robert W. Chambers here comes into the list again, this time with what is probably his best work, "Cardigan." And Charles F. Pidgin caught the fancy of American history lovers with his "Blennerhassett," a story of the days and ways of Aaron Burr. But all else was forgotten in the rush to the bookstores of a half million frenzied readers with money in outstretched hands demanding "The Crisis" by Winston Churchill. Everybody fought the Civil War all over again, everybody except the booksellers. They just smiled. Churchill had rung the bell again.

The great days of the American historical novel were from 1897 to 1902–six years. A very definite trend it would seem. Two years after the final outburst, that is in 1904, Churchill came back with "The Crossing," and it was so fine a performance that it still sells. Thomas Dixon stirred up a good deal of dust with his K.K.K. novel, "The Clansman"; Baroness Orczy obliged with "The Scarlet Pimpernel," which I am told is still blooming. And then five years later Jeffery Farnol had the distinction of closing the dwindling era with "The Broad Highway," a very excellent and widely popular novel.

But before the curtain is drawn, I must go back to 1902 long enough to remind you that in this last great up-rush of the historical novel Emerson Hough contributed "The Mississippi Bubble"; Ellen Glasgow, a writer of high distinction but new to the historic field, published "The Battle Ground"; Gertrude Atherton, her novel-biography, "The Conqueror," one of the finest things this brilliant woman has ever written; F. Hopkinson Smith, although long established and popular, could not withstand the pull of the trend and so added to his fame with "The Fortunes of Oliver Horn." And finally Owen Wister stepped into the best-selling class with "The Virginian." Everybody talked about it, everybody enjoyed it hugely, but I never heard anyone call it a historical novel. Yet the catalogs so classify it, and who are we to challenge the catalogs!

Perhaps we are again entering such an era–but with a difference. Looking back over the past few years we may note the steady popularity of such novels as "Arundel," "The Lively Lady," "The Judas Tree," "Eric Water," "Mutiny on the Bounty," coming to a grand climax in "Anthony Adverse," which like "Hugh Wynne" in the earlier era caught the universal fancy. The difference to be noted is that we have exchanged the romantic for the realistic. We still want historical novels, but they must have the flavor of reality.

–"An Historical Revival: Nothing Succeeds Like Success in Setting a Literary Fashion," *Publishers' Weekly*, 125 (9 June 1934): 2135–2137

* * *

The Curtis Revolution: Minutes of Bowen-Merrill stockholders' meeting, 16 July 1900

Innovations attributed to Curtis include full-page newspaper advertisements, illustrated notices for single books rather than lists of the publisher's current offerings, the colored dust jacket, and the blurb. Not all of these attributions can be verified, but his great success, starting with Major's When Knighthood Was in Flower *and Maurice Thompson's* Alice of Old Vincennes *(the original promotional records for which no longer exist), stunned his more conservative Eastern colleagues. Bowen-Merrill's gratitude for his work with the trade department is expressed in these minutes, which are the first signed by Bobbs as president.*

Mr. Buchanan offered the following resolution which was seconded by Mr. Kautz and put upon its passage was unanimously adopted:

Whereas the earnings of the Publication Department during the past year are more than double the total earnings of all the departments of the entire house for any previous year and whereas this result is due most directly to the judgement ability and effort of Mr. John J. Curtis manager of the Publication Department

Therefore: Be it resolved that the stockholders of The Bowen-Merrill Company hereby vote Mr. Curtis this cordial expression of their sincere thanks for his efforts in their behalf and direct the Treasurer of this company to present Mr. Curtis one thousand dollars as a substantial evidence of their genuine appreciation.

Mr. Buchanan moved that the present board of directors be re-elected. Seconded by Mr. Kautz.

The vote upon the election was as follows:

Mr. Bobbs	475 Shares	
Mr. Merrill	475	–
Mr. Curtis	320	–
Mr. Buchanan	200	–
Mr. Kautz	100	–
Total	1570	– in Affirmation

and the following gentlemen were elected Directors for the ensuing year:

Wm C Bobbs, Charles W Merrill Wm H Elvin and John J Curtis

There being no further business the meeting was adjourned by the President

W. C. Bobbs John J. Curtis, Secy
Prest.

* * *

A Reminiscence
Stith Thompson

When an emeritus professor at Indiana University, folklorist Thompson looked far back to his days with the company.

As a high school boy in Indianapolis at the age of sixteen in 1902, I found that my late afternoon and Saturday job in a law office demanded a full-time worker and I was no longer needed. Through J. W. Fessler, a friend of my father and a rising young lawyer, and by means of a phone call to his friend, W. C. Bobbs, I was given work in the Bobbs-Merrill shipping room for all my spare time. Some temporary financial reverses of my father made this place very welcome.

In those days the Bobbs-Merrill Company was already a prestigious publishing house, and I found the two years there very important as a part of my education. The Company occupied a four-story building on Washington Street on part of the present site of the L. S. Ayres Company. The first floor was devoted to a store for retail books and stationery–which years later was taken over by W. K. Stewart. As I recall it, this was an extraordinarily large and well-equipped retail house. On the second floor were the editorial rooms where the

111

1900 Regular Meeting

Mr Buchanan moved and Mr Kantz seconded that a dividend of 25% be declared on all stock of the company and that the balance of the gain be passed to the Surplus account. Unanimously Carried.

Mr Buchanan offered the following resolution which was seconded by Mr Kantz and put upon its passage was unanimously adopted:

Whereas the earnings of the Publication Department during the past year are more than double the total earnings of all the departments of the entire house for any previous year and Whereas this result is due most directly to the judgement ability and effort of Mr John J Curtis manager of the Publication Department Therefore! Be it resolved that the stockholders of The Bowen-Merrill Company hereby vote Mr Curtis this cordial expression of their sincere thanks for his efforts in their behalf and direct the Treasurer of this company to present Mr Curtis one thousand dollars as a

Pages from the minutes of the Bowen-Merrill stockholders' meeting of 16 July 1900, the first to indicate that Bobbs was now president. The stockholders voted their thanks to Curtis (courtesy of The Lilly Library, Indiana University, Bloomington, Indiana).

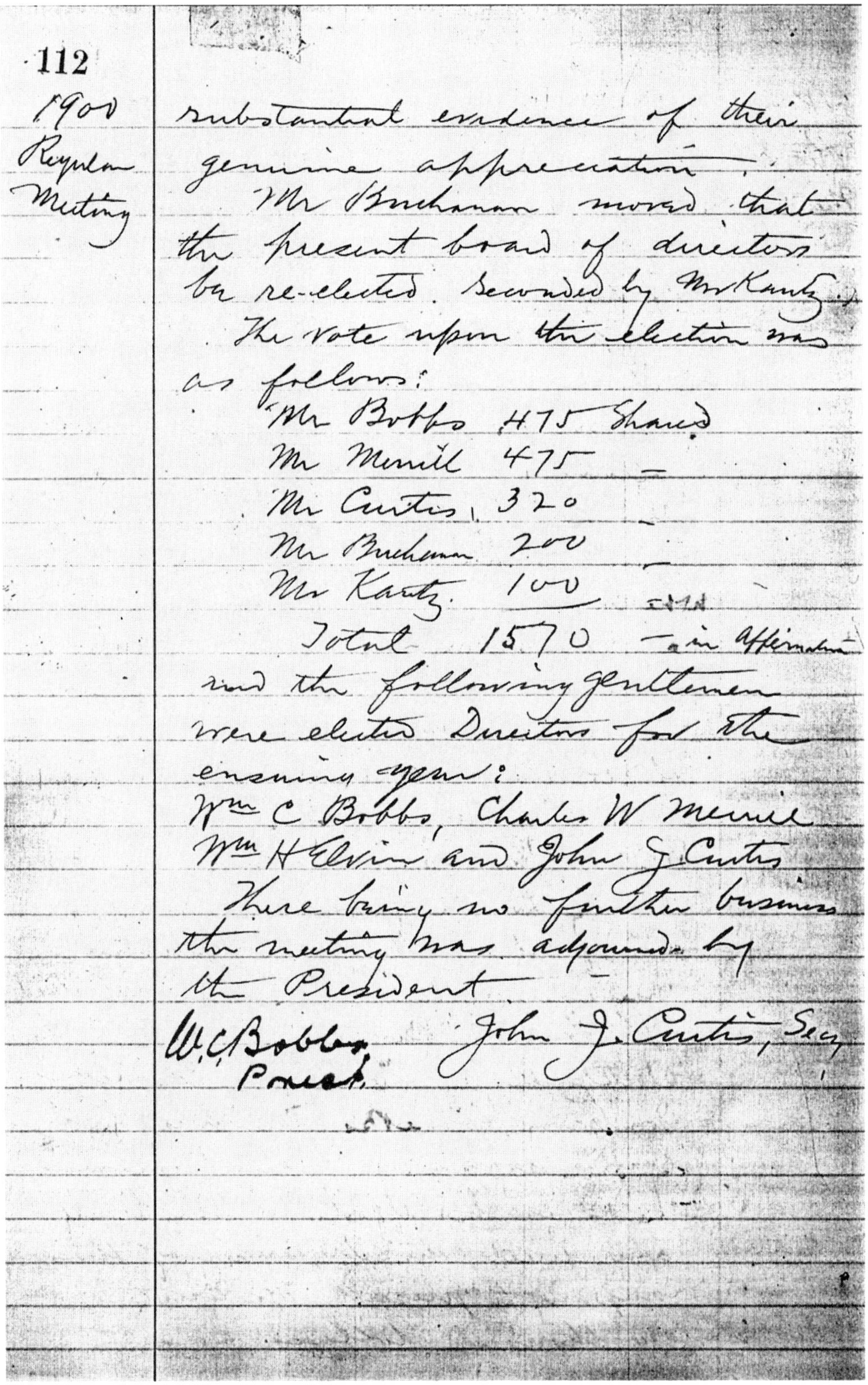

112

1900 Regular Meeting

substantial evidence of their genuine appreciation.

Mr Buchanan moved that the present board of directors be re-elected. Seconded by Mr Kautz.

The vote upon the election was as follows:

Mr Bobbs 475 Shares
Mr Merrill 475 "
Mr Curtis 320 "
Mr Buchanan 200 "
Mr Kautz 100 "
Total 1570 "in Affirmative

and the following gentlemen were elected Directors for the ensuing year:

Wm C Bobbs, Charles W Merrill Wm H Elvin and John J Curtis

There being no further business the meeting was adjourned by the President

W. C. Bobbs Presd. John J. Curtis, Secy

editor, Hewitt Hanson Howland, presided. We knew him, of course privately, as H.H.H. In the rear of that floor was the shipping room. The third floor was the law department, from which the smell of the sheep-bound books penetrated to the regions below. The fourth story I suppose was storage space, though I avoided the upper regions.

In the shipping room were huge bins each filled with one of the titles then in demand. Soon I was initiated into the necessary skills–opening great boxes of books that came in from the printers and binders, packing outgoing boxes economically and efficiently and, above all, wrapping bundles properly for shipment. We unwrapped incoming manuscripts before taking them to H.H.H. Some of these were in longhand, occasionally in pencil, and one of the girls in the office spent her time making fair copies before they went out to the referees.

These were the days of the illustrated novel. We would unwrap the large drawings and admire the lovely ladies of Howard Chandler Christie [*sic*] before they went in to the editor.

In due time I received a promotion, not in salary, which remained at five dollars a week, but in prestige, for Mr. Howland had me copy his letters every evening. These letters, typed with copying ribbon, were entered in large, thin paper books and pressed between damp blotting paper. Eventually I became so skillful that I left only the suspicion of a smear. I had curiosity enough to learn some of the secrets of acceptance or refusal of manuscripts.

And I saw something of the authors themselves–not only the Bobbs-Merrill writers but others who dropped in and chatted with the editor. I am not certain of all these, but I seem to remember Meredith Nicholson, Mrs. Mary Hartwell Catherwood, Charles Major, Booth Tarkington, George Ade, Harry Leon Wilson, and James Whitcomb Riley. I recall taking proofs of *The Main Chance* out to Mr. Nicholson and spending an afternoon setting up sectional bookcases for Mr. Riley at his home on Lockerbie Street. Of course I did not get to know these men, but it was at least educational to see them at close range.

Indianapolis was then a very important center for literature, especially when the Crawfordsville group was added. I heard General Lew Wallace give the dedicatory address for the Soldiers and Sailors Monument. The city felt a most proprietary interest in Riley; and nearly everyone who had any claim to literary taste owned at least one of the special editions of *An Old Sweetheart of Mine* and kept it on the parlor table. At his death in 1916 a line of people two blocks long paid their respects to his remains, which lay in the state house. No one has caught the Indianapolis of my boyhood better than Booth Tarkington–the city of *Seventeen* and *Penrod,* which lay between Meridian and Delaware Streets and Tenth and Sixteenth. But the great ones were moving out, and Mr. Nicholson lived as far away as Thirtieth Street–the Ultima Thule.

Like any great publishing enterprise, Bobbs-Merrill's was a wonderful intellectual stimulus. I read some novels in galley proof, but we could also buy books at a discount–those published by the house at 48 cents and others at 95 cents. And occasionally an unsuccessful edition was dumped into the waste box. I thus acquired a copy of Nicholson's *Short Flights.* But I find to my chagrin that it has disappeared during the moves of sixty-four years.

The career of this great publishing house has been remarkable, for it is one of the very few which has survived the temptation of moving its principal activity to the great Eastern centers. I was especially gratified when I was Dean of the Graduate School to be able to recognize this achievement by the honorary degree we gave to the editor, David Laurance Chambers. His editorship almost spanned the years since I left my duties as office boy.

–"An Office Boy Remembers 1902,"
Indiana University Bookman,
8 (March 1967): 7–9

* * *

Survey

A 1902 editorial in Publishers' Weekly *expresses a low opinion of the kind of fiction and advertising that were earning a great deal of money for Bowen-Merrill at that time. The historical novel outlasted the predicted term.*

Recently the *Record-Herald* of Chicago asked the question: "Are the possibilities of large sales becoming more and more clearly confined to American novels?" Eighteen publishers replied to this query and their opinions are about evenly divided between the affirmative and the negative, the Western publishers leaning towards the affirmative. [. . .] Bowen-Merrill & Co. are of the opinion that any well-written novel well advertised has a chance of achieving large popularity, but also believe "that the pride in things American, which is now so manifest, would probably give some preference to a work by a native author dealing with a subject which concerns us here at home." [. . .]

The impression is general that the phenomenal sales of books are over, and that they were largely due to the generous advertising of the American publishers. It must also be remembered that during the years when

Frontispiece and title page for the posthumously published 1902 essay collection by the daughter of the founder of the Merrill line. She had assisted naturalist John Muir when he was an unknown (Thomas Cooper Library, University of South Carolina).

American historical novels were so popular the English were not publishing so extensively owing to wars and the unusual fascination of newspapers for the average reader. All the world loves a good story, but perhaps the free libraries will little by little educate the people to demand more substantial literature.

Our own opinion, based on interested observation for many years, is that not one novel reader in ten or perhaps twenty has any idea of the nationality of an English-writing author, and that patriotism has nothing whatever to do in the selection of fiction by the average consumer.

–"Popularity of American Fiction," *Publishers' Weekly*, no. 1603 (18 October 1902): 828

* * *

Taking Stock

Bobbs and Charles Merrill had a side interest in the Hollenbeck Press, a printer-publisher. Among other things, the press published the third and final volume (1908) of Ida Husted Harper's The Life and Work of Susan B. Anthony, *which was begun by Bowen-Merrill (1898–1899). The Kansas City "branch house" mentioned in the description of Bowen-Merrill was opened in 1894. In that year Kansas City was included a few times in the imprint; it appeared there regularly until 1901 and never again. The "house" was a retail store that sold law and other books, as well as stationery, until 1902.*

The Hollenbeck Press, one of the most notable printing establishments in the city, was established by C. Hollenbeck, successor to Carlon & Hollenbeck. This is one of the oldest printing establishments in the city and has always enjoyed the distinction of producing fine work, and has had a continued existence since 1864. The line embraces everything in job, book and publication printing, binding and blank-book manufacturing. The character of the work produced by this house is not excelled by any other concern in the country. Many of the well-known illustrated publications published in this city are issued from its press, and are fine examples of first-class printing. About 100 persons are employed in the different departments. The officers of the company are W. C. Bobbs, president; C. W. Merrill, treasurer, and M. B. Barkley, manager.

The Bowen-Merrill Company, publishers, booksellers, stationers and paper dealers, has been in existence for more than half a century, tracing its establishment back to the house founded in 1838 by Samuel Merrill, sr., grandfather of the present treasurer of the firm. In January, 1885, Bowen, Stewart & Co. and Merrill, Meigs & Co. were consolidated and the present house incorporated. The business is located at Nos. 9 and 11 West Washington street, and occupies five floors, running clear through to Pearl street. A branch house is operated in Kansas City. The Indianapolis establishment is one of the largest, most complete and best equipped book stores in the country, and there are only two houses in the United States from which more books are distributed annually. It has been said that Cincinnati is the musical center, St. Louis the art center and Indianapolis the literary center of the west. True it is that Indianapolis buys more books than any other city of four times its size in the United States. In recent years the Bowen-Merrill Company has directed special attention to publishing, building up a list which includes the works of James Whitcomb Riley, Emerson Hough, Mary Hartwell Catherwood, Maurice Thompson, George Horton, Charles Frederic Goss, Robert J. Burdette, Frank L. Stanton, Benjamin Harrison, Edward Dowden, L. Frank Baum and many others of the prominent authors of this country. As law publishers, this house ranks among the very largest in the world. Its publications include some of the most successful law works that have been issued within the last ten years, and its list of authors contains the names of the most prominent legal writers in America, including Judge Byron K. Elliott, Charles Fish Beach, jr., Judge John M. Van Fleet, R. M. Benjamin, W. P. Fishback, Judge Harrison Burns, S. A. Jones, Seymour D. Thompson, Judah R. Benjamin, John H. Gillett. The publications from this department go into every nation in the world where the English language is spoken. Silas T. Bowen, one of the founders of the Bowen-Stewart Company house, retired from active participation in the business in January, 1885 [*sic*], and died in December, 1895. Samuel Merrill, for many years at the head of the house, retired in 1890. The business is now under the management of William C. Bobbs, Charles W. Merrill and John J. Curtis. The history of the house is one which reflects credit upon the city and state, because to maintain and develop a large book establishment requires a community of culture and a population of book readers.

–Max R. Hyman, ed., *The Journal Handbook of Indianapolis: An Outline History* (Indianapolis: Indianapolis Journal Newspaper, 1902), pp. 252–253

An early color dust jacket, illustrated by Harrison Fisher, for Isham's 1902 novel (courtesy of Michael Manz/Babylon Revisited)

Bobbs-Merrill: 1903–1910

1903

17 January — The bridge title, Frederic S. Isham's *Under the Rose,* issued under both the Bowen-Merrill and the Bobbs-Merrill imprints, is registered for copyright (two copies are deposited in the Library of Congress on 6 March). The firm publishes eleven of Isham's books, but none is a best-seller, and he passes into oblivion after his death in 1922.

19 January — The board of directors changes the name of the firm to Bobbs-Merrill.

5 February — Anna Katharine Green's *The Filigree Ball* is registered for copyright (two copies are deposited in the Library of Congress on 2 March). It is Green's first novel with the company and the first book to have only the Bobbs-Merrill imprint. *The Filigree Ball* is still a well-regarded story by the "mother of detective fiction."

6 March — Gene Stratton-Porter's first novel, *The Song of the Cardinal: A Love Story,* is registered for copyright (two copies are deposited in the Library of Congress on 28 May).

15 July — *The New Wizard of Oz,* a republication of L. Frank Baum's classic *The Wonderful Wizard of Oz* (Chicago: George M. Hill, 1900), is registered for copyright. Until Irma Rombauer's *The Joy of Cooking,* it is the company's all-time best-seller.

20 July — After a 7 percent dividend in 1902, a 20 percent dividend is declared for this year. There will be no dividends over the next four years.

September — David Laurance Chambers is hired as personal secretary to President William C. Bobbs.

1904

Robert L. Moorhead becomes manager of the law department.

23 February — The first Bobbs-Merrill copyright is registered for *Reader* magazine (vol. 3, no. 4), which the firm bought from Mitchell Kennerley.

21 March — Miriam Michelson's *In the Bishop's Carriage* is registered for copyright. It becomes the number-four fiction best-seller for this year. Two hundred thousand copies will be sold in the next nine years.

2 May — The first Bobbs-Merrill novel by David Graham Phillips, *The Cost,* is registered for copyright.

18 May — Hallie Erminie Rives's *The Castaway* is registered for copyright. Publication of the novel is the occasion for beginning lawsuits against "undersellers," as the book includes a notice stating that no dealer is licensed to sell the book for less than the stated retail price.

1905

16 January — Bobbs-Merrill opens a lawsuit against Macy's for cutting prices on copyright books.

29 April — Bobbs-Merrill is the first publisher to advertise the trade name Pocket Books.

6 November — Meredith Nicholson's *The House of a Thousand Candles* is registered for copyright. The novel becomes the number-four fiction best-seller of 1906.

1906

15 January — Herbert Quick's first Bobbs-Merrill novel, *Double Trouble,* is registered for copyright.

28 April — The first Bobbs-Merrill copyright is registered for *Home Magazine* (vol. 18, no. 3). Purchased from V. P. Collins of Minneapolis, it absorbs *Madame* and in May becomes a home-and-garden periodical with some literary pretensions.

1 May — The New York office moves from 5 Beekman Street to 34 Union Square, East.

30 August — Raymond M. Alden's first Bobbs-Merrill book, *The Knights of the Silver Shield,* is registered for copyright. Republished in 1908 as *Why the Chimes Rang,* it is a Christmastime favorite for generations.

18 October — Zona Gale's first Bobbs-Merrill novel, *Romance Island,* is registered for copyright.

24 November — Harold MacGrath's *Half a Rogue* is registered for copyright. It becomes the number-ten fiction best-seller of 1907 and sells a total of 160,000 copies.

1907

Chambers joins the executive staff of the firm. He is first listed as a stockholder at the 17 March 1908 meeting.

31 January — Nicholson's *The Port of Missing Men* is registered for copyright. It is the number-three fiction best-seller for this year.

9 March — Gelett Burgess's first Bobbs-Merrill book, *The White Cat,* is registered for copyright.

23 March — Louis J. Vance's first Bobbs-Merrill novel, *The Brass Bowl,* is registered for copyright. It becomes the number-five fiction best-seller for this year and sells perhaps as many as 140,000 copies altogether.

5 April — Humorist Kin Hubbard's first Bobbs-Merrill book, *Abe Martin of Brown County, Indiana,* is registered for copyright. It was first privately published in 1906.

10 May — George Ade's first Bobbs-Merrill book, *The Slim Princess,* is registered for copyright.

15 August — Rives's *Satan Sanderson* is registered for copyright. It becomes the number-six fiction best-seller of the year.

1908

January — Bobbs-Merrill, nearly bankrupted because of losses from magazine publishing, reorganizes. The firm sells *Reader* to Putnam and *Home* to the publishers of *Uncle Remus's Magazine.*

6 January — Vance's *The Black Bag* is registered for copyright; it becomes the number-eight fiction best-seller for the year.

17 March — A special meeting of the stockholders is held to reorganize the firm.

20 March — George R. Chester's first Bobbs-Merrill novel, *Get-Rich-Quick Wallingford,* is registered for copyright (two copies are deposited in the Library of Congress on 14 April). The title of the novel creates a catchphrase.

11 April — Indiana statesman Albert J. Beveridge's first Bobbs-Merrill book, *The Meaning of the Times, and Other Speeches,* is registered for copyright.

29 May — MacGrath's *The Lure of the Mask* is registered for copyright. It becomes the number-four fiction best-seller of the year and goes on to sell seventy-five thousand copies altogether.

1 June — The Macy's lawsuit ends in a loss for Bobbs-Merrill.

10 July — James O. Curwood's first Bobbs-Merrill novel, *The Wolf Hunters,* is registered for copyright.

20 July — At the annual meeting, Bobbs, John J. Curtis, and Charles W. Merrill surrender 2,250 shares of stock to other members of the firm, including Hewitt H. Howland, Moorhead, and Chambers, at an unknown price. Some of Bobbs's losses will be restored to him two years later, and he, Curtis, and Merrill continue to manage the company.

15 August — Mary Roberts Rinehart's first novel, *The Circular Staircase,* is registered for copyright. It is not a best-seller at first but nonetheless sells about eight hundred thousand hardback copies by 1975.

1909

Bobbs-Merrill challenges such textbook giants as Ginn and Company and Scott, Foresman and Company with the Child Classics series, by Grace and Georgia Alexander (no copyright record exists). It is the company's most serious effort at schoolbook publishing to date.

January or February — The on-site bookstore, a part of the company since the 1885 merger, is sold to William K. Stewart.

20 January — Emerson Hough's *54-40 or Fight* is registered for copyright. It becomes the number-seven fiction best-seller for the year.

20 March — Rinehart's *The Man in Lower Ten* is registered for copyright. It becomes the number-four fiction best-seller and the first American detective story to make the list. In five years it sells 129,000 copies.

14 August — MacGrath's *The Goose Girl* is published; it becomes the number-eight fiction best-seller for the year and sells 180,000 copies through 1911.

20 November — Rinehart's *When a Man Marries* is published. It becomes the number-ten fiction best-seller of 1910.

1910

The Washington Street property in Indianapolis is sold, and Bobbs-Merrill builds anew at 18 East Vermont Street, on the north side of University Square. The firm is now exclusively a publisher, except for serving as a sales outlet for other publishers' law books.

29 January — Rives's *The Kingdom of Slender Swords* is published. It becomes the number-five fiction best-seller of the year.

13 August — Rinehart's *The Window at the White Cat* is published. It becomes the number-eight fiction best-seller for the year.

Name Change

Shortly before Bowen-Merrill became Bobbs-Merrill, the firm announced its first book of 1903. It bore in its imprints both the old and the new company names, and it was reviewed under both in March.

THE BOWEN-MERRILL COMPANY announce as their first book of the new year "Under the Rose," a new romance by Frederic S. Isham, author of "The Strollers." The title strikes the keynote of the story, and its implication of secrecy has been carefully maintained by the author in the development of his plot. Howard Chandler Christy has respected the spirit of silence in his illustrations, and in drawing the actors and the scenes he gives no hint of the outcome of the story.

–*Publishers' Weekly,* no. 1616 (17 January 1903): 88

* * *

David Laurance Chambers, who joined the firm as secretary to William C. Bobbs in 1903 and became chief trade editor in 1925 and president in 1935 (Bruccoli Clark Layman Archives)

A TREATISE

ON THE LAW OF THE

EMPLOYERS' LIABILITY ACTS

OF

NEW YORK, MASSACHUSETTS, INDIANA ALABAMA, COLORADO, AND ENGLAND

Second Edition

BY

CONRAD RENO, LL. B.

Author of a Treatise on the Law of Non-Residents and Foreign Corporations
History of the Judicial System of New England, Etc.
and Member of the Boston Bar

INDIANAPOLIS
THE BOWEN-MERRILL COMPANY
1903

Title page for one of the four books published in 1903 under the Bowen-Merrill imprint, before the name change to Bobbs-Merrill (Boston College Law Library)

Stockholders' Meeting

The minutes of the Bowen-Merrill stockholders' meeting for 19 January 1903 record the name change.

1903 Called Meeting Jan 19th

Called stockholders meeting

On January 19th 1903 a special meeting of the stockholders of the Bowen Merrill Co was held in the Company's offices. The meeting was called to order by President Bobbs at 10 A.M. Present Bobbs Buchanan Kautz Merrill owning a majority of stock.

It was moved by Mr. Buchanan seconded by Mr. Kautz that the corporate name of The Bowen Merrill Co be changed to The Bobbs Merrill Co.

Mr. Buchanan took the chair & put the motion which was unanimously carried. It was so ordered–

Adjourned

Charles W. Merrill As Sec

* * *

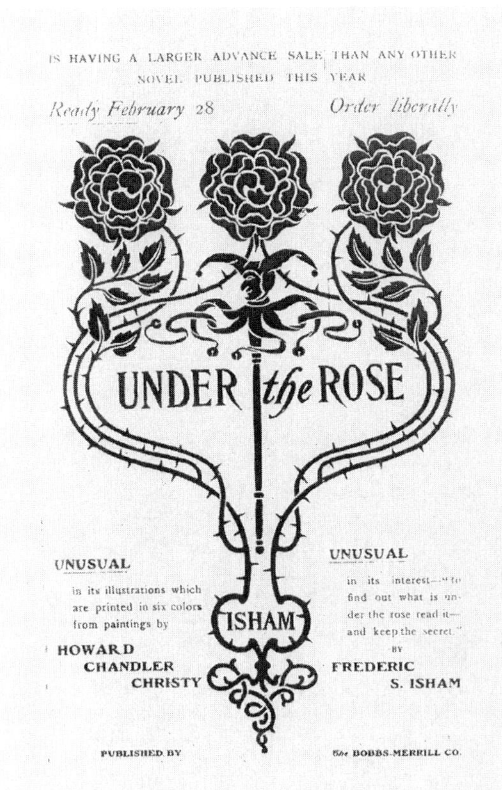

Full-page advertisements from Publishers' Weekly *(21 February, 28 February, and 21 March 1903) for the first book published under both the Bowen-Merrill and Bobbs-Merrill imprints*

118

1903 Called meeting Jan 19th

Called stockholders meeting
On January 19th 1903 a
special meeting of the stockholders
of the Bowen Merrill Co was
held in the company's offices
The meeting was called to order
by President Bobbs at 10 A.M
Present Bobbs Buchanan
Kautz Merrill owning a
majority of stock.
It was moved by Mr Buchanan
seconded by Mr Kautz that
the corporate name of The Bowen
Merrill Co be changed to
The Bobbs Merrill Co.
Mr Buchanan took the chair
& put the motion which was
unanimously carried. It was
so ordered —
Adjourned

Apr 7-1903 date of certificate

Charles Merrill Secy

Page from the minutes of the 19 January 1903 stockholders' meeting, recording the name change to Bobbs-Merrill (courtesy of The Lilly Library, Indiana University, Bloomington, Indiana)

The Bobbs-Merrill Company

The name of the Bowen-Merrill Company, of Indianapolis, Ind., was changed on the 22d of January to the Bobbs-Merrill Company, with William C. Bobbs, Charles W. Merrill and John J. Curtis as the Board of Directors of the concern, there being no change in the ownership, control or policy of the firm. The change in name simply brings into deserved prominence the name of one of the new men who has given this old firm its prestige as publishers.

[. . .] As the older officers retired or died, the younger men who are now in control were admitted to the firm. After Mr. Bowen's retirement from active business life an effort was made to persuade Mr. Bobbs to allow his name to take the place of Mr. Bowen's, but he refused. Another effort was made after Mr. Bowen's death, when the company bought out the interests of the heirs, but still Mr. Bobbs refused. Recently, however, he consented that the change should be made.

–*Publishers' Weekly,* no. 1618 (31 January 1903): 154

Reviews of *Under the Rose*

The nature of popular taste in 1903 is conveyed by this description of Isham's novel issued under the Bowen-Merrill and Bobbs-Merrill imprints.

Another historical novel, but Mrs. [*sic*] Isham has taken us far from America with her heroes and her wars. "Under the Rose" (The Bowen-Merrill Company) has a French setting, and its happenings took place in the court of Francis I. and the camp of Charles VI., with a woodland flight to connect the two.

On the whole, French history lends itself more readily to the novelist's purpose than American history, despite the latter-day fad for the domestic article. A good novel dealing with American history is an uncommonly good thing–witness "The Captain"–but it is exceeding difficult to make the novel a good one. Our spectacular epochs are few and far between. One wearies of fighting Bull Run and Bunker Hill even with the choicest assortment of heroes, but there is so much of French history, and it is all so spectacular! A novelist

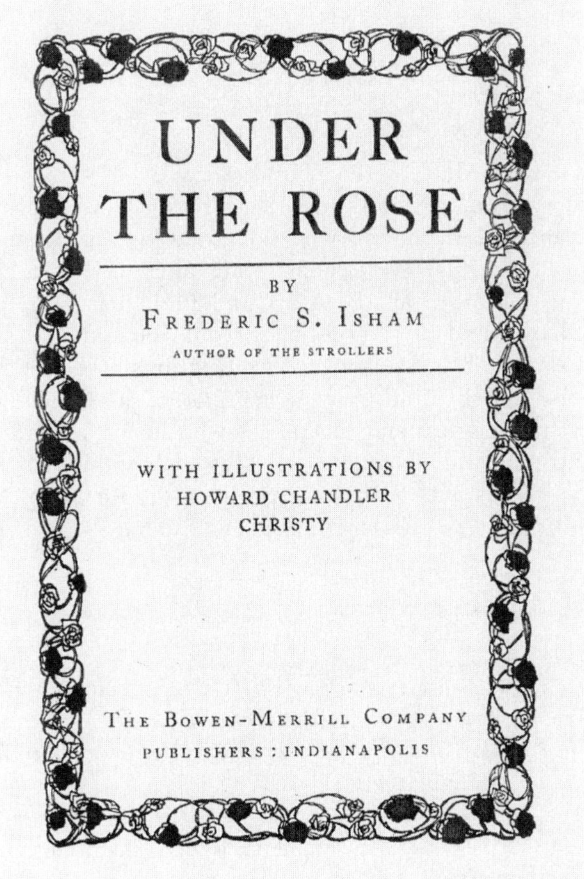

UNDER THE ROSE

BY

FREDERIC S. ISHAM

AUTHOR OF THE STROLLERS

WITH ILLUSTRATIONS BY HOWARD CHANDLER CHRISTY

THE BOWEN-MERRILL COMPANY

PUBLISHERS : INDIANAPOLIS

COPYRIGHT NINETEEN HUNDRED THREE
THE BOWEN-MERRILL COMPANY

JANUARY

PRESS OF
BRAUNWORTH & CO.
BOOKBINDERS AND PRINTERS
BROOKLYN, N. Y.

Title page and copyright page for Isham's 1903 novel bearing the Bowen-Merrill imprint (Providence [R.I.] Public Library)

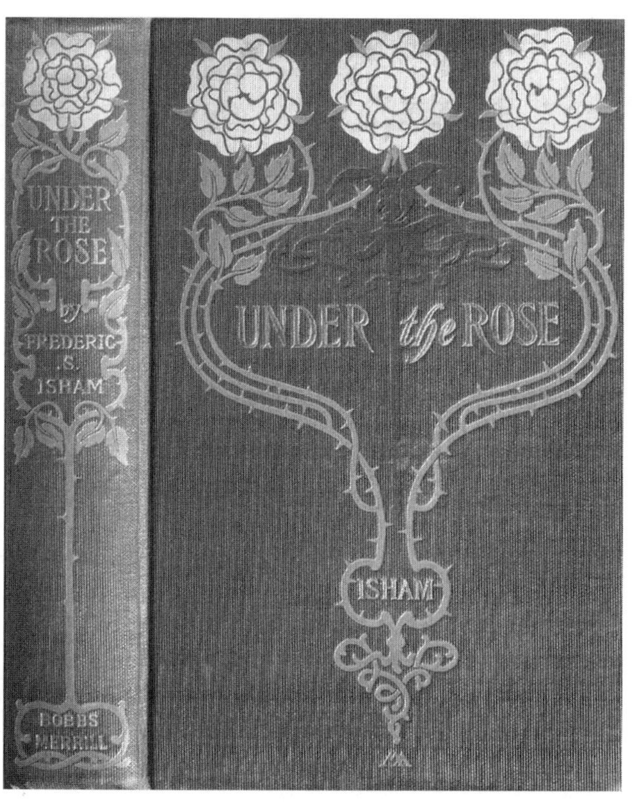

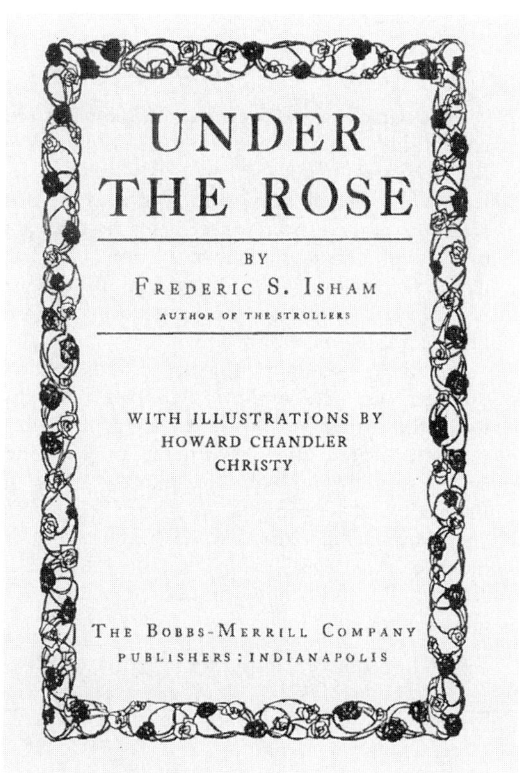
UNDER THE ROSE

BY

FREDERIC S. ISHAM

AUTHOR OF THE STROLLERS

WITH ILLUSTRATIONS BY HOWARD CHANDLER CHRISTY

THE BOBBS-MERRILL COMPANY

PUBLISHERS : INDIANAPOLIS

Cover and title page for Isham's 1903 novel with the Bobbs-Merrill imprint (Mugar Library, Boston University)

may shut his eyes and jump. Wherever he comes to the surface he need but look about him. *Voila son affaire!*

Probably Mr. Isham did not shut his eyes, but he found his affair.

It is an improbable story he tells–a most entertaining story. The court of Francis is brilliant, dissolute, picturesque. Its doors are open to us. From Charles VI. comes the Duke of Friedwald in guise of a jester sent by the Duke to Princess Louise, his betrothed, whom he has never seen. The romantic Duke has visions of winning the beautiful Princess through love's magic, and then, when he has her heart, throwing off his disguise and claiming the promised hand. But princesses are not made upon heroic lines. Louis of Hochfels, bandit baron, comes to the French court masquerading as the Duke of Friedwald, and the real Duke, intent upon his own poetic game, does not denounce him.

The fair Princess smiles upon her jester, and lends an ear to the Duke's suit, and when, too late, the jester would denounce the impostor who has usurped his place, Louis of Hochfels closes his mouth by force.

It is Jacqueline who rescues the unlucky lover–Jacqueline "*la folle*"–who sets her wits at rest against the shrewdest of the court jesters, who joins the merry rout in Fools' Hall, who is lady-in-waiting to Princess Louise, and who flouts the love-sick jester from the first, yet watches him always. Together they escape from the court and find their way to Charles and his army–but it would be a thankless task to tell the story of their adventures. Mr. Isham tells it delightfully, as he tells all of his fanciful, romantic tales; and the reader who loves romance, intrigue, and adventure, love-seasoned, will find "*son affaire,*" as did the author, in "Under the Rose."

–*Lamp,* 26 (March 1903): 161

* * *

The following excerpt is from the first New York Times *review of a Bobbs-Merrill book. Illustrations by Howard Chandler Christy appeared in several Bowen-Merrill and Bobbs-Merrill novels.*

UNDER THE ROSE. By Frederick [*sic*] S. Isham, author of "The Strollers," with illustrations in colors, by Howard Chandler Christy. Indianapolis: Bobbs-Merrill Company.

Anna Katharine Green, the "mother of detective fiction" (Bruccoli Clark Layman Archives), and the cover of her 1903 novel, the first book to bear the Bobbs-Merrill imprint only. Her middle name is misspelled on the cover (courtesy of The Lilly Library, Indiana University, Bloomington, Indiana).

THE FILIGREE BALL: BEING A FULL AND TRUE ACCOUNT OF THE SOLUTION OF THE MYSTERY CONCERNING THE JEFFREY-MOORE AFFAIR

BY

ANNA KATHERINE GREEN

AUTHOR OF
THE LEAVENWORTH CASE

ILLUSTRATED BY C. M. RELYEA

THE BOBBS-MERRILL COMPANY
PUBLISHERS INDIANAPOLIS

Frontispiece and title page for Green's 1903 mystery novel (Thomas Cooper Library, University of South Carolina)

A disguised Duke in fool's motley wooing a Princess proud and beautiful, and winning, not the Princess, but a lady of a noble house of France, also wearing the motley, that is the story of the latest historical novel by the author of "The Strollers." [. . .]

The book is illustrated by Howard Chandler Christy in colors brilliant enough to match the motley which is the garb of the principals. There are pictures of the Princess, golden haired, arrayed in white, with the Duke-jester at her feet, pictures of the lady-jestress, ebon haired, gowned in green, by the side of the golden-haired mistress in red. And there is the Duke again, in his coat of many colors, kneeling and kissing her Highness's hand. Yet again the lady-jestress, still gowned in green, stands between King Francis and the Duke, this time arrayed as the dukes of romance should be.

"Under the Rose" is a good book to take up of an idle evening. There is no moral to it, no lesson of ancient manners hidden in its pages, but you will be apt to keep on reading till the last leaf is turned.

–"Hero and Heroine in Motley," *New York Times,* 14 March 1903, p. 168

* * *

Bobbs-Merrill Publishes a Magazine

In the short run of The Reader *under the ownership of Bobbs-Merrill, the company used the magazine to showcase both its own authors and such others as Jack London, Frank Norris, and Joseph Conrad.*

[. . .] *The Reader,* which two years ago entered the periodical field, has become the property of the Bobbs-Merrill Company, and will hereafter be published from Indianapolis. The Bobbs-Merrill Company, in speaking of the new addition to their

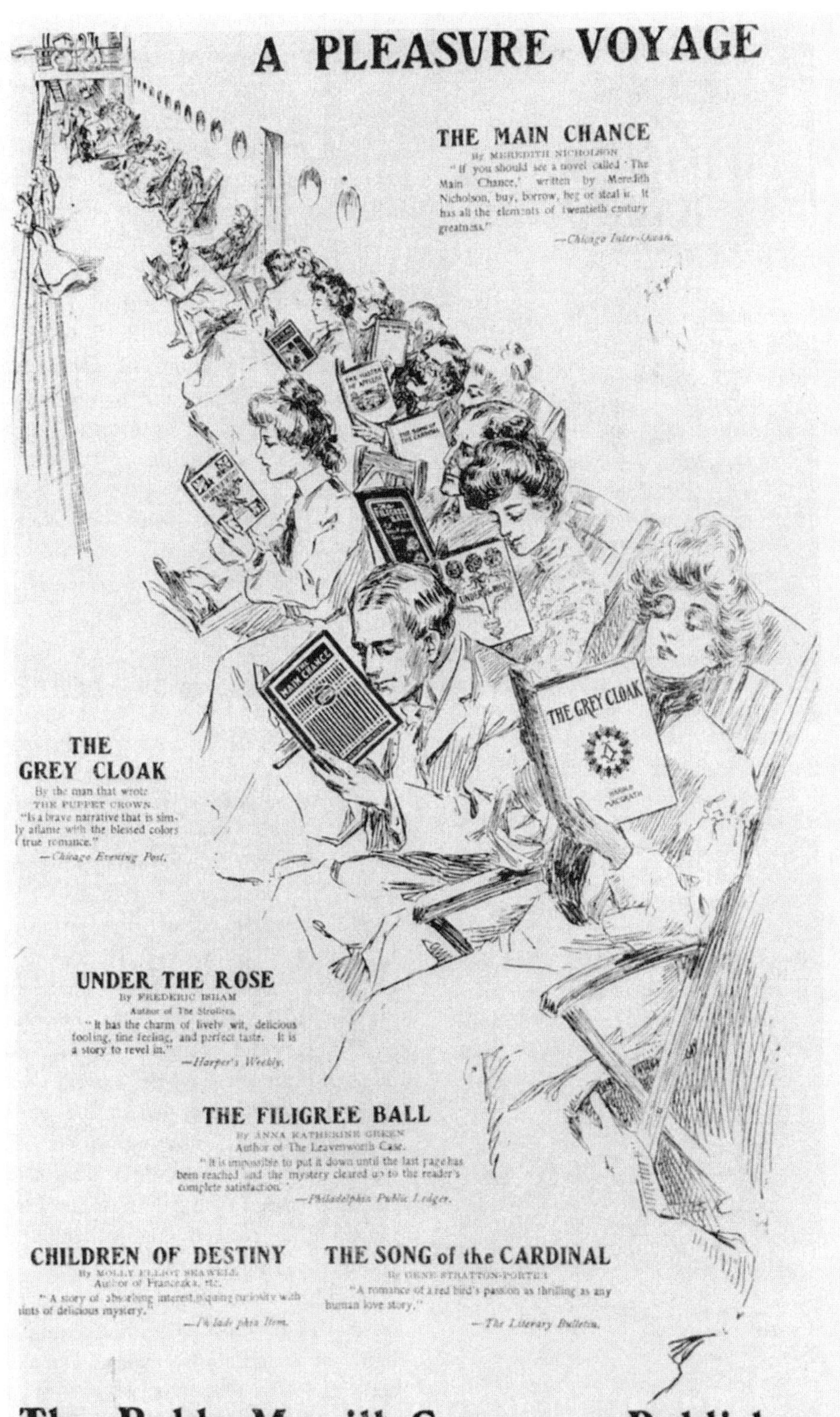

New York Times *advertisement (1903) for Bobbs-Merrill titles (Bruccoli Clark Layman Archives)*

Edited advertising copy for Green's 1903 novel (courtesy of The Lilly Library, Indiana University, Bloomington, Indiana)

The City of the King

What the Child Jesus Saw and Heard

By Mrs. Lew Wallace

Author of
The Storied Sea, The Land of the Pueblos
The Repose in Egypt, Along the Bosphorus

With Illustrations

Indianapolis
The Bobbs-Merrill Company
Publishers

Title page for the 1903 book by Susan Arnold Wallace, wife of the author of the 1880 novel Ben-Hur *(O'Neill Library, Boston College)*

publishing department, say: "It is the ambition of the firm to publish an American magazine–American as typified by the West. *The Reader* is not to be local nor to be bounded by any geographical lines, but will make its appeal and draw its inspiration from the entire country." Mr. Kennerly [*sic*], who has done so much to make the magazine what it is, will remain with it in an editorial capacity and have charge of the New York office. Mr. Hewitt Hanson Howland, who for a number of years has been editor and literary adviser of the Bobbs-Merrill Company, will become the editor of *The Reader,* and Mr. Lee Burns will resign his duties in the publication department to assume the position of manager. He is now in New York arranging for the transfer of the property. [. . .]

–"Journalistic Notes," *Publishers' Weekly,* no. 1669 (23 January 1904): 110

* * *

The Lawsuit against "Undersellers"

Bobbs-Merrill chose a work written by popular novelist Hallie Erminie Rives and illustrated by Christy to take a stand against "undersellers" such as Macy's.

Bobbs-Merrill Company, to whose unconventional and aggressive methods of exploitation the modern "big seller" owes its stimulus, if not origin, have now taken an important step in the direction of placing copyright fiction on the basis of one dollar net, and insisting upon maintaining the price throughout the country. On the *verso* of the title-page of their latest work of fiction, "The Castaway," immediately under the notice of copyright, they have placed the following notice: "The price of this book at retail is One Dollar net. No dealer is licensed to sell it at a less price, and a sale at a less price will be treated as an infringement of the copyright."

This move certainly is in the right direction so far as the principle of bringing the price down to the figure at which all are expected to sell a book is concerned. It has always seemed to us absurd that the price which is used by undersellers as an inducement in the advertising of their other lines of merchandise should be placed on the largest-selling books purposely in advance of the figure at which the publisher and the purchaser know the book is to be retailed. A $1.50 novel, now generally retailed at $1.08, if squarely put out at $1 net would, it has seemed to us,

THE READER MAGAZINE

THE BOBBS-MERRILL COMPANY, PUBLISHERS, INDIANAPOLIS, U S A

CONTENTS FOR JUNE

YEARLY SUBSCRIPTION, $3.00 ISSUED MONTHLY SINGLE COPIES, 25 CENTS

SUBSCRIPTIONS MAY BE TAKEN BY ANY BOOKSELLER OR POSTMASTER

Contents page for the June 1904 issue of the magazine that Bobbs-Merrill took over from Mitchell Kennerley early in the year (Williams College Library)

eliminate the very root of the underselling evil, and would contribute much to conciliating interests now antagonistic to the reform movement–notably those of the library profession.

As to the determination of the Bobbs-Merrill Company to rigidly maintain the price of this book, their action is in line with the decisions so far obtained in patent and copyright cases, and has the support of recent judicial opinion in the cases pending against the American Publishers' Association and its opponents referred to below, all of which give promise that when the suits reach the final stage the courts will grant to the owner of copyright the same protection that it now grants to the patentee. The Bobbs-Merrill Company, indeed, have so much confidence in their plan that in order to test it they have deliberately selected a book which, in the first place, both on account of the attractiveness of its subject and the prominence of the author and illustrator, required no reduction in price to make it popular, and which, in the second place, would be peculiarly tempting to undersellers. Their intention to take action on a specific case of this kind, and the course of Charles Scribner's Sons, who are now taking action against an underseller on the general principle involved, deserve commendation and the

Advertisement from Publishers' Weekly *(29 April 1905) for the first books to bear the trade name "Pocket Books"*

hearty co-operation of all concerned in the sale of copyright books.

–"A Step in the Right Direction," *Publishers' Weekly,* no. 1681 (11 June 1904): 1487

* * *

Suits have been filed by the Bobbs-Merrill Company against undercutters of the dollar price of "The Castaway" in Philadelphia, New York and Detroit. The firm again announces that they are determined to test the principle involved at law so thoroughly that no doubt can remain in regard to it. They are in almost daily receipt of letters from booksellers in all parts of the country assuring them of their hearty co-operation in carrying out their fixed-price plan.

–*Publishers' Weekly,* no. 1694 (16 July 1904): 84

* * *

Argument was heard before Judge Ray, of the United States Circuit Court in New York City, on the 16th and 17th inst., in the suit brought against Macy's by Charles Scribner's Sons for infringing their copyright by cutting prices on their copyright books, and in the suit brought by the Bobbs-Merrill Company, also for infringing their copyright by cutting the price on their copyright novel, "The Castaway." An enormous amount of evidence was presented, owing to which, and the well-known care with which Judge Ray reviews every case brought before him, it is not likely that an early decision will be handed down. Colonel Stephen H. Olin appeared for Charles Scribner's Sons and ex-Attorney-General Miller represented Boardman, Platt & Soley in behalf of the Bobbs-Merrill Company. John D. Carlisle, representing Spiegelberg & Wise, argued the case for Macy's.

–"Arguments Heard in the Suits against Macy's," *Publishers' Weekly,* no. 1721 (21 January 1905): 71

* * *

ABDALLAH

OR

THE FOUR-LEAVED SHAMROCK

BY

EDOUARD RENE LEFEBVRE-LABOULAYE

TRANSLATED BY

MARY L. BOOTH

INDIANAPOLIS U S A
THE BOBBS-MERRILL COMPANY
PUBLISHERS

Representative pages from a holiday edition. Decorative designs by Ralph Fletcher Seymour. A novel use of combinations of punctuation marks, cast on one body, is shown on the fourth page

The illustrations, designs, and typography of Bobbs-Merrill books appeared frequently in Printing Art. *The title page and other pages from this recently published book were tipped in to the November 1905 issue (Widener Library, Harvard University).*

Reorganization

This notice details some measures taken in the face of losses incurred by magazine publishing.

It is announced from Indianapolis that a reorganization has been effected in connection with the Bobbs-Merrill Company which will bring $150,000 new capital into the business and provide for its continuance under the same management. The amount involved in the settlement is, approximately, three-quarters of a million dollars, and most of the merchandise creditors have acceded to the proposition for settlement of 25 per cent. in cash within thirty days and 25 per cent. in one, two and three-year notes, with interest. It is understood that the banks of Indianapolis, which are involved to the extent of about a quarter of a million, have also made arrangements which will insure their continuous support of the concern. The tangible assets, exclusive of plates, are understood to be approximately $650,000, leaving a deficit of $125,000 to be offset by plates, copyright and other intangible assets estimated as high as $300,000, and by the new working capital. The business has not been interrupted during the negotiations for the extension, and will be continued much on the same lines as before, with the possible exception of the periodicals.

The firm made large investments in establishing *The Reader* and the *Home Magazine* and bringing them to the turning point, and to these investments the present situa-

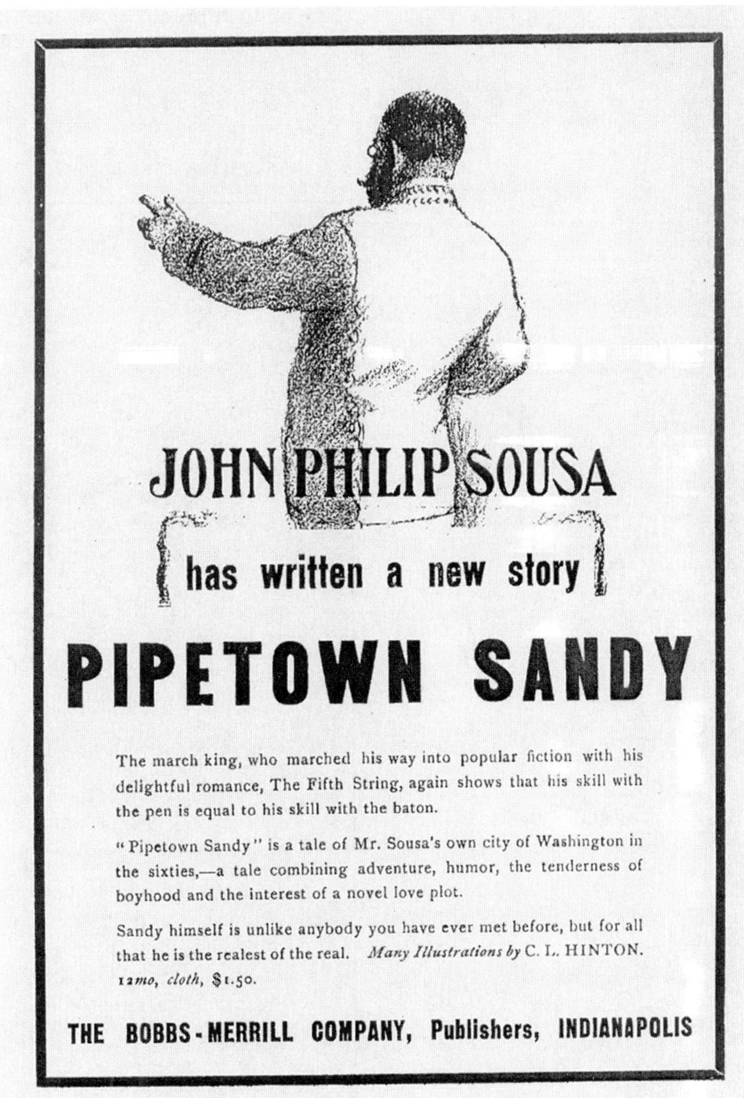

Flier for the second novel by the bandmaster and composer, published in 1905 (courtesy of The Lilly Library, Indiana University, Bloomington, Indiana)

The above advertisement appeared in the *N. Y. Sunday American* with a prize offer for the first answers received. There were over twelve thousand replies. Here is one of them in rhyme:

The best selling novel in America, 'pon my soul
Is Louis Joseph Vance's; It's called The Brass Bowl.

THE BOBBS-MERRILL COMPANY, Publishers, INDIANAPOLIS

Flier for the number-five fiction best-seller of 1907 (courtesy of The Lilly Library, Indiana University, Bloomington, Indiana)

tion is largely attributed. *The Reader,* as announced in full elsewhere, will be combined with *Putnam's Monthly* under an arrangement favorable to both interests. It is understood that the business of the firm, especially in law books and miscellaneous books, has shown a profit approximating on the average $45,000 a year for the past nine years.

A great deal of sympathy and interest is expressed in Indianapolis and throughout Indiana in support of a house which has so notably represented the State in the publishing world.

–"The Bobbs-Merrill Company Reorganization," *Publishers' Weekly,* no. 1877 (18 January 1908): 102

* * *

The End of the Macy's Suit

Bobbs-Merrill failed to establish in law the principle that led it to sue Macy's. Publishers' Weekly *summarized the Supreme Court decisions before printing them in full.*

The text of the decisions of the U. S. Supreme Court in the Macy cases, printed in full elsewhere, confirms the view indicated editorially last week.

In the Bobbs-Merrill suit the pith of the decision can be very simply stated. The court declines to accept the view that copyright cases should follow the precedents of patent law, and incidentally indicates that the question of specific protection of price on a patented article, such as arises in the present cases, has not been passed upon by the Supreme Court in the Cotton Tie case or other cases. It holds that the copyright statute must be construed directly from its own provisions, and that the right "to vend" does not authorize the protection of price beyond the original sale. The right of the Bobbs-Merrill Co. to maintain a stated retail price, as a sequence to the copyright ownership, was denied by the lower courts and this decision is affirmed by the highest authority. [. . .]

–"The Supreme Court Decisions," *Publishers' Weekly,* no. 1898 (13 June 1908): 1922

* * *

Old Tricks

Bobbs-Merrill often practiced advertising gimmicks to promote titles.

The Bobbs-Merrill Company have just brought out a story of adventure entitled "The Coast of Chance," by Esther and Lucia Chamberlain. This extraordinary story of the big game of life played to the utmost with masculine bravado and feminine finesse, turns about a sapphire ring of antique design and immense value which was stolen while on private exhibition in San Francisco, Cal. It then comes into the possession of a wealthy society girl. In spite of herself, and in spite of her fiancé, she falls in love with the man whom she knows to be the thief–a man character among the most striking in recent fiction. As a souvenir to the booktrade the publishers have made a reproduction exactly on the lines of the description of the ring–the "Chatworth Sapphire"–as described in the book. It shows an old gold heathen god curled round himself, with his head between his knees, and a big blue stone on top. The reproduction is an unusual and striking piece of jewelry, and is accompanied by a poster on stiff cardboard to hang up in the show window, calling attention to the fact that it is an exact reproduction of the famous ring, valued at $75,000, told about, etc., in "The Coast of Chance."

–*Publishers' Weekly,* no. 1891 (25 April 1908): 1460–1461

THIS ADVERTISEMENT IS NOW GOING THE ROUNDS OF THE NEWSPAPERS

Best Selling Book in America

As Reported by the Booksellers in April "Bookman"

The New Novel by the Author of

The Brass Bowl

"'The Black Bag' is a winner."—*N. Y. Globe*

Indispensable to the *Tourist—Travels* like a whirlwind—*Holds* the whole family—You can't *Lose* it—*Packed* full of bully stuff—Made of the best *Material*—It never gets *Heavy*—the *Grip* of adventure—Impossible to *Check* it—*Bulging* with excitement. Pictures by Fogarty. $1.50 List.

At All Bookstores **THE BOBBS-MERRILL CO., Publishers**

Full-page advertisement from Publishers' Weekly *(14 March 1908) for Vance's third and last Bobbs-Merrill book*

The Sale of the Bookstore

William K. Stewart was a grandson of the cofounder of Stewart and Bowen, one of the predecessors of Bobbs-Merrill. The bookstore, later renamed the W. K. Stewart Company, continued a close relationship with Bobbs-Merrill.

The Bobbs-Merrill Company have sold their retail book and stationery business in Indianapolis to W. K. Stewart, who has been connected with the business for the last five years, latterly as sales manager of the publication department and member of the firm.

The constantly increasing publication business, which includes a very large line of law books, as well as general literature and particularly popular fiction, has required more and more the personal attention of the heads of the organization in such measure that it became desirable for them to be relieved of the details of the retail business. To this business Mr. Stewart brings a wide acquaintance with the retail book and stationery business over the United States, industry, energy and enthusiasm in a marked degree; and it is the hope both of The Bobbs-Merrill Company and Mr. Stewart that the retail business under his direction will become one of the really model retail book stores of the country. [. . .]

Five years ago, the grandson of William Stewart was employed by The Bobbs-Merrill Company. Subsequently he went on the road and became sales manager of the publishing department. Now he has bought for himself the retail department of a business which his grandfather established, and with which he takes a peculiar pride in again having the Stewart name identified.

While the retail business will be run as The Bobbs-Merrill Bookstore, it will be owned solely and entirely by W. K. Stewart, and will be managed independently of the publishing house in every particular.

–"Bobbs-Merrill Company Sell Retail Business," *Publishers' Weekly,* no. 1932 (6 February 1909): 781

* * *

Building Plans

The plans for new Bobbs-Merrill offices were realized in 1910. Contrary to what is reported here, the company did not continuously occupy the prior building since 1838.

The Hoosier House—University Square

The new Bobbs-Merrill building (1910) at 18 East Vermont Street, Indianapolis, and a detail of the main entrance. The company occupied these headquarters until 1926 (from The Hoosier House: The Bobbs-Merrill Company, *1923; Indiana State Library).*

The Bobbs-Merrill Company has bought the property in East Vermont Street, fronting University Park, Indianapolis. The purpose of the company is to erect on this ground a five-story building for its publishing business. Plans have already been drawn by Foltz & Parker, architects, and work upon the building will begin on March 1, to be ready for occupancy on July 1. The building will front fifty-three feet in Vermont Street and will be 195 feet deep. It will be of fireproof steel construction, with cement floors, the walls to be of colonial brick, trimmed with white marble. Buildings and plans were examined in New York, Boston and Philadelphia, with the view of obtaining an appropriate architectural effect that would accord with the landscape in University Park, and thus definitely avoid evidences of ordinary business architecture.

The basement of the new building will be arranged to carry the unbound sheets of the company's publications. Under the sidewalk will be constructed a plate vault the entire width of the building and the entire depth of the walk. In this vault will be kept the electrotype and stereotype plates from which books are printed. The first floor will contain a salesroom for law and miscellaneous publications of books and the shipping room. The second floor will contain the counting room and general office of the business. The three upper floors will be devoted to the miscellaneous, editorial and art department, to the legal editorial department, and to the library for the use of the editors.

This removal will not in any manner involve either the retail business in Washington Street, which a year ago was sold to the W. K. Stewart Company, nor any change in the printing and binding of the company's books, which is done at the Hollenbeck Press, owned by the company, and located in Indianapolis.

The Bobbs-Merrill Company and its predecessors have been located in Washington Street continuously since 1838, the oldest house in the street. The removal of this business to the north side of University Square will mark the forced extension of the business of the city from the congested district. The property cost $45,000 cash, being at the rate of $850 a foot front, and when the building is completed an investment exceeding $100,000 will be represented. The price paid for this property is regarded by those acquainted with real estate values as exceedingly reasonable.

It is understood that the New York offices of the company, at 34 Union Square, East, will also be enlarged.

–"New Home for the Bobbs-Merrill Company,"
Publishers' Weekly, no. 1986
(19 February 1910): 978

Bobbs-Merrill: 1911–1920

1911

	The educational publishing department is founded; it is organized by John R. Carr.
28 January	The company publishes Gaston Leroux's 1910 novel *The Phantom of the Opera,* the first American edition and Leroux's only Bobbs-Merrill book.
11 March	Vaughan Kester's *The Prodigal Judge* is published. It becomes the number-two fiction best-seller for 1911 and sells 220,000 copies in two years.
30 September	Paul Wilstach's *Thais,* a dramatic adaptation of Anatole France's 1890 novel of the same title, is published; it is Wilstach's first Bobbs-Merrill book.

Front cover for the first American edition (1911) of the novel originally published as Le fantôme de l'opéra *in 1910 (courtesy of Michael Manz/Babylon Revisited)*

1912

30 March	J. Breckenridge Ellis's *Fran* is published; it becomes the number-ten fiction best-seller for the year, although only twenty-five thousand copies are sold.
18 May	Maria Thompson Daviess's *The Melting of Molly* is published and becomes the number-four fiction best-seller for the year. With 107,000 copies sold in six years, it is Daviess's only great success for the company.
25 May	Kester's *The Just and the Unjust* is published posthumously and becomes the number-seven fiction best-seller for the year, selling forty-three thousand copies.
27 November	Hallie Erminie Rives's *The Valiants of Virginia* is published. It becomes the number-nine fiction best-seller of 1913 and eventually sells 121,000 copies.

1913

15 February — Earl Derr Biggers's first novel, *Seven Keys to Baldpate,* is published.

11 October — *Ring for Nancy,* by Ford Madox Hueffer (later Ford Madox Ford) is published. An enlargement of his *The Panel* (1912), it is his only novel for the firm.

12 November — William B. Maxwell's *The Devil's Garden* is published; it becomes the number-nine fiction best-seller of 1914.

1914

9 May — Owen Johnson's *The Salamander* is published and becomes the number-four fiction best-seller of the year. After an intensive advertising campaign, seventy-five thousand copies of the single printing are sold; twenty-five thousand copies are eventually remaindered.

30 June — President William C. Bobbs is authorized to sell 283 shares of the Hollenbeck Press stock for $50,000 in cash.

8 July — The company publishes Winifred S. Stoner's *Natural Education* and Edgar J. Swift's *Learning and Doing,* the first titles in the Childhood and Youth series, edited by Michael V. O'Shea. The aim of the series is to provide guidance to teachers of children.

28 July — Because of losses, the company institutes pay cuts across the board in the trade department. John J. Curtis, Hewitt H. Howland, and D. Laurance Chambers are not excepted.

1915

19 January — Oscar H. Benson and George H. Betts's *Agriculture* is published; it is probably the first textbook published by the company to earn a significant profit.

26 January — Most employees of the firm are given a 10 percent salary reduction.

11 September — William Lyon Phelps's *Robert Browning, How to Know Him* is published as the first volume in the How to Know the Authors series. Eleven other volumes treating famous authors are published in the series from 1915 to 1921.

18 September — Arthur Stringer's first Bobbs-Merrill novel, *The Prairie Wife,* is published.

21 December — The board of directors gives the trade department the responsibility for editing the publications of the educational publishing department, with Howland serving as editor in chief of the latter. He is succeeded by Betts in 1921.

1916

1 January — Julian Bobbs, son of the president, is transferred from New York to the home office.

29 January — Henry Kitchell Webster's first Bobbs-Merrill book, *The Real Adventure,* is published. It becomes the number-six fiction best-seller of the year and sells 48,500 copies in two years.

1 February — The New York office moves from Union Square to 185 Madison Avenue.

18 July — The practice of single-title advertising is ended, and Curtis's authority is curtailed.

18 October	Talbot Mundy's first Bobbs-Merrill book, *King–of the Khyber Rifles,* is published.
15 November	The trade department and the New York office survive the financial crisis, but with a reduced budget.

1917

10 February	Ring Lardner's first Bobbs-Merrill book, *Gullible's Travels, Etc.,* is published.
20 March	An efficiency board is established.
12 April	Irving Bacheller's *The Light in the Clearing* is published and becomes the number-two fiction best-seller for the year. Sales eventually total about one-hundred thousand copies.
16 July	Bobbs-Merrill purchases the "property, assets, good will and business" of the Ohio Law Publishing Company.
5 August	Robert L. Moorhead leaves to join his regiment, and William C. Bobbs takes his desk.
7 November	Harold R. Peat's *Private Peat* is published and ranks fifth among best-selling war books the following year. It is Bobbs-Merrill's first nonfiction best-seller and the firm's only biography to hold that distinction until Irvin S. Cobb's *Exit Laughing* in 1941. In December the company contracts with Peat to manage his lectures. *Private Peat* sells fifty thousand copies in 1917.

1918

14 May	The board of directors authorizes the purchase of a bookkeeping machine for $1,100.
4 December	Louisa Watson Peat's *Mrs. Private Peat, by Herself* is published.

1919

4 February	Moorhead attends his first board of directors' meeting since the onset of the war.
28 July	The title of manager is created for the person in charge of operations of the home office building.
29, 31 July	Curtis attends board meetings in Indianapolis. He moves to Hollywood in semiretirement and looks after the movie interests of the company. Herbert S. Baker will be manager of the New York office.
24 November	Julian Bobbs returns to the New York office.
3 December	Bacheller's *A Man for the Ages* is published and becomes the number-five fiction best-seller of 1920. Sales eventually total two-hundred thousand copies.

1920

13 February	Carr becomes vice president and subsequently chairman of the board.
18 February	Charles W. Merrill dies. After Moorhead fills in as temporary treasurer, Julian Bobbs returns to Indianapolis and assumes the duties of the post.
13 May	Charles D. Meigs dies.

Wire, brier, limber-lock,
Three geese in a flock.
One flew east, one flew west,
And one flew over the cuckoo's nest.

CHILD CLASSICS
THE PRIMER

By
GEORGIA ALEXANDER

With pictures by
FANNY Y. CORY

INDIANAPOLIS
THE BOBBS-MERRILL COMPANY
1920

Frontispiece and title page for a Child Classics volume that was originally published in 1909 (Duke University Library)

Trials of the Educational Publishing Department: Selected Correspondence with the Alexanders, 1911–1924

An early function of the educational publishing department was to market the Child Classics readers, written by the Indianapolis schoolteachers Georgia and Grace Alexander. The series began in 1909 and faced competition from such giants of the field as the American Book Company; Ginn and Company; Scott, Foresman; and, lately, Scribners. John R. Carr was brought in to Bobbs-Merrill to organize the department in 1911 and to secure Indiana's adoption of the readers. In the background the Alexander sisters exchanged letters with President William C. Bobbs that displayed their extreme distrust of Carr, the American Book Company ("A B C"), and school officials. Carr nonetheless sold three million copies of their books, winning five-year state adoptions in 1914 and 1919. In 1924 the Child Classics volumes, having made money for the Alexanders but not for the firm, were replaced by the Bobbs-Merrill Readers.

Georgia Alexander to William C. Bobbs, 28 August 1911

Dear Mr Bobbs,

I send with this Mr K's certificate of character as written by A B C. I thought it might escape you.

Last spring I said to Mr Carr that I thought it might help the books if I got work in the Marion County Institute–he had asked me to work for him two summers ago when he wanted the place with you. His reply was that he and Mr Swails were not very friendly, but that was after he had promised to speak to Mr Swails and I called him up a second time to ask him if he had done so. He said that if I wanted the work I had best apply directly to Mr Swails. I went over to the County Office and found Mr Carr having a confidential talk. Mr Carr introduced me and in a moment I had stated my errand and left them together. You will see that Mr Gordy, the Scribner author has the place.

When I asked Mr Carr why he had never put our books in as the method books in Marion County, he said that he did not have money enough. Yet Marion is certainly not one of the poor counties of the state–and it was estimated that Ward was in a third of the counties when the adoption was on. These things, nor the fact that I saw Robert Hall who told us Mr Carr was so interested in our books during the campaign, arm in arm with Mr Atherton, do not mean anything in themselves. But it is significant that they all point the same way. Personally, I am absolutely convinced. Perhaps if he were shadowed in New York you might get some proof–but even if you found nothing and you might–still I should not be convinced that I am wrong. Mr Lord, the New York man and Mr Cheney the Chicago man for Scribners are absolutely unscrupulous–the letter episode connected with Mr Cooley shows that, and Mr Lord would stop at nothing.

At any rate, mean as I seem in all this, you can but admit that he has done nothing with the books in the eight months. At first he was going to do everything. He volunteered twice that he planned to canvass every county in the state, and said that nine tenths of the men would take the books because of their friendship for him. Now I should be afraid even to have him go out, for he not only would sell no books but he would queer every situation for another man.

You will recall also that he promised Reading Circle business. I saw at Lafayette that Silvers, Scott-Forsman [*sic*] and A B C have a book apiece.

Keep him if you wish–but I have discharged my duty in telling you. I admire you for being slow to believe such a charge. But I haven't played policeman for ten thousand boys without getting somewhat of a detective's characteristics.

Very truly yours,
Georgia Alexander

* * *

Georgia Alexander to Bobbs, 22 October 1911

Dear Mr Bobbs,

I came accidentally upon the fact yesterday that Mr Greathouse had recommended William Wirt, supt of the Gary schools for the place on the program in the Woman's Federation meetings.

I am firmly convinced that any recommendation that Mr Greathouse will make for any position will be an American Book Company person, notwithstanding the relation Mr Greathouse may bear to you. The fact that his choice has already expressed itself in W W Black, Adelaide Baylor, John Carr and John Garber (Philadelphia) is direct proof, for all of these persons have lined up without reserve with A B C.

Mr Wirt is undoubtedly of the same company. His primary supervisor is Annie Klingensmith, author of the primary readers published by A B C and used until the Howe Readers were adopted. The principal of his main building in Gary–the one that is just finished and was written up in the McClur article, is Edward Sargent. Mr Sargent is the second son of the Rev Christopher of this city, as weak a character as his father, but grandson to the former secretary of the American Book Company and heir through his father to a lot of A B C money. Mr Wirt is making a great stir just now, but as I told you before, he is nothing but a new and shiny tin cup. He has had no opposition, no traditions to live down, and a tiny field that he could compass personally. Considering all these things he has done nothing phenomenal.

It was certainly a shame not to have caught Carroll, but I think the situation will be saved if you can persuade Dr Owen of Chicago to come. I enclose an editorial from a Chicago magazine which he wrote.

I cannot see how a friend of Longmans would cut into the Reader adoption, for they will have nothing up at that time. It might affect me later, when Will Howe's Grammar is presented by them at the same time that my spelling book comes up. However I think you are wise to look both men up privately. I mean McGilvrey and Brubacher.

Milo Stuart, principal of Manual Training High School would like to have it, but he is a Mirick man to the finish. Mr Buck would be a far better choice for the schools.

Very truly yours,
Georgia Alexander

* * *

Grace Alexander to Bobbs [27 April 1919]

Dear Mr Bobbs:

The psalmist says it is a good thing to give thanks and to sing praises. [*Marginal inscription by Carr:* "Mr Bobbs,–It is fine to be praiseful as well as prunesful. J.R.C. Apr 29-19."] I am glad of that, for I never felt more thankful and praiseful in my life. The good news of Thursday was a cordial to our hearts. The intensity of the fight makes the keener the flavor of our victory. Please believe that in our rejoicing we are never unmindful of the enterprise and discretion with which the firm handled our books, and that side by side with the pleasure we feel for ourselves in this success is a distinct gladness that at the same time good fortune comes to you and yours.

With congratulations, and fond wishes for a complete rest from the heat and stress of the conflict, I remain,

Yours sincerely,
Grace Alexander

* * *

Bobbs to Grace Alexander, 30 April 1919

Dear Miss Alexander:–

Thank you very much indeed for your extremely pleasant letter in regard to the Reader adoption. It was gratifying in the extreme to win in such a tense fight and, of course, we are thoroughly happy over the outcome. Our pleasure, however, is very greatly enhanced by the satisfaction which you and your sister have in the result and by your cordial appreciation of our work.

It was a case of fine team work where the effort of all of us contributed to the result, and there is glory enough for everybody. But the bright particular credit, of course, goes to John Carr who worked with a zeal and devotion and intensity that I have very rarely had the opportunity of seeing.

Thanking you again for your pleasant letter, I am

Yours very truly,
[William C. Bobbs]

* * *

Bobbs to Grace Alexander, 5 December 1923

Dear Miss Alexander:

Your good letter of October 6th came while I was out of town and was held for my personal attention which I trust will at least explain if it does not excuse the long delay in answering.

The table and graph of the reading tests, which you enclosed, are very interesting indeed and we are glad to have them.

It is gratifying to know that the sales of the books in the last year are as pleasing and encouraging to you as they are to us. We have kept a man at work in the schools over the State and the sales for the present year are due, in some measure at least, to his work.

The manuscripts of the PRIMER and FIRST READER are in our vaults. It would be extremely agreeable to us to make changes not only in the SECOND and THIRD but in all the Readers in whatever particular you think it is desirable to change them for that would give us a talking point and the opportunity for a new copyright.

Concerning the future policy with the Readers we are confronted with some grave problems for which we have not yet been able to work out satisfactory answers. The fundamental difficulty with the Readers, as you know, is that they were bid in 1914 at a very low price for at that time manufacturing costs were at the extreme bottom. We went through that period at a loss to ourselves on account of the increased manufacturing costs and were unable to make a sufficient increase in the price with the new bid.

Now if we submit them again in Indiana we can make only a small increase in the price or the amount of increase will prevent their consideration. If we submit them in Indiana a price on the outside will be controlled by that figure.

Our sales force has been greatly increased in the last year and we are finding new opportunities for selling the Child Classics for supplementary reading. But this sales work can be done only if the price gives us a profit which permits of this expensive solicitation.

It is very clear that we can not get consideration for the Classics in Indiana if the price is put as high as other Readers of the same class.

We are preparing a new set of Readers under the Editorial direction of Dr. Betts which will be submitted at a top price. It might be good business for us to submit your Readers also at a low price, but whether that is the best thing to do remains yet to be seen.

We are making a close house to house canvass of the schools and getting first hand information of just how the books are regarded with a view of knowing what is the best thing to do.

There is a very large asset in the Classics because they have made a good name for themselves everywhere and we would like to realize on that asset with the most profit to us and to you.

If we offer them in Indiana the price will have to be very low. If we get an adequate price for them we will be able to put energetic agency work on them outside of the State but that would bar their fair consideration here.

I shall be glad if you will write me your views on the matter fully. Our interests, I take it, are identical for whatever will make for the greatest profit to us will make for the most royalty to you.

The preparation of the Readers under the direction of Dr. Betts has not yet been announced and I trust you will keep that information quite confidential.

Please let me have an outline also of what you could do by way of revising each of the Classics so that we may be able to change the copyright on the entire series.

Yours sincerely,
[William C. Bobbs]

* * *

CONTENTS

Contents page for The Sixth Reader *(1917), edited by Georgia and Grace Alexander (Duke University Library)*

Grace Alexander to Bobbs, 7 January 1924

Dear Mr Bobbs:

Regarding your letter of recent date: the most interesting sentence it contains seems to us to be "Our interests are identical." To this Georgia and I heartily agree. The only point open to discussion appears, therefore, to be what looks like a failure on the part of the Bobbs-Merrill firm to act in accordance with this statement.

When interests are identical, is it not customary for both parties to the contract to advise with each other fully as to all steps to be taken to advance those interests? You acting for the firm, and Georgia and I acting together as authors, made our last oral contract solely to the effect that the Bobbs-Merrill firm was to offer the Child Classics Readers at the coming state adoption, and, to quote your words, "make an asset of the low price."

If at that time the firm contemplated offering another set of readers, you refrained from mentioning the fact. No mention was made of it to us at any time until you replied to my previous letter: in other words not until within four months of the adoption.

You now urge the idea that to offer our Readers for the Indiana adoption at all will be to lessen their profits to us. Why discuss such an hypothesis when either of the alternatives that the firm offers means that the books cannot be sold at any price anywhere? Failure to offer the books in Indiana would kill all possibilities outside the state; offering them at a lower price than another set marks them as practically discarded by the firm. We cannot see how you have persuaded yourself to take so remarkable a stand.

Of course if you were not offering a rival set of Readers that will kill our books it would have been worth while to take up the question of sales in Indiana and outside. It was quite possible to sell the Child Classics at a low price in Indiana and to have sold a slightly revised edition outside the state at any price the firm desired to ask. Georgia's Spelling Book during its ten years in Indiana, sold thus all over the country at treble the price paid in the state.

Now that you have taken us into your confidence about our identical interests, we take occasion to note that the firm purposes to jeopardize the success of a set of Readers which to quote your letter again "are a valuable asset and have made a good name for themselves everywhere"–books made by trained and well-known educators–by offering at the same time at a price that practically scraps our books another set without tried value and made by persons not identified with the grade schools anywhere.

Yours sincerely,
Grace Alexander

* * *

Bobbs to Grace Alexander, 12 January 1924

Dear Miss Alexander:

Your letter is received and I am very glad to have you write me so frankly. It is evident from what you say that I have not made clear the controlling considerations in regard to the CHILD CLASSICS READERS. And that is, for reasons over which we had no control and could not have foreseen, we have gone through this entire contract of the Indiana adoption at a loss to ourselves. It is a source of satisfaction and pride to be able to say that during this entire time we have made no complaint nor any attempt to cancel or annul the contract nor any suggestion of a reduction in royalties.

If it were true that failure to offer the books in Indiana would kill possibilities outside of the State, or offering them at a lower price than another set would mark them as discarded by the firm, doing either of these things would certainly be both remarkable and inexplicable. It must be evident to you that what we have done is based on a confident disbelief in both statements for it would not be intelligent business to invest a large sum of money in new titles if that course would kill the asset in old titles which have an established value.

Your statement that "Georgia's Spelling Book during its ten years in Indiana sold thus all over the country at treble the price paid in the State" is word that is not only surprising but astounding. It is not my desire to say anything that may be construed as criticism of the policy of another publishing house but I am inclined to think that in our establishment this plain evasion of the law would be considered impossible from the standpoint of business policy even if it were considered permissible from the standpoint of business morals.

While the failure to secure a complete readoption of the Readers five years ago gave us unmistakable warnings consideration of a new set of Readers was taken up with great reluctance and the decision was reached only after careful survey of the entire question and a thorough canvass of the whole field. The investment involved in such an enterprise at the present costs of manufacture is no small matter and could not with prudence be lightly undertaken. One of the controlling reasons for the decision to offer the new Readers at the next adoption was the fact that we could not expect the Board to adopt both Readers and Arithmetics carrying the same author's name. That decision, of course, had not been reached when I last talked to you because at that time we did not know the Arithmetics were going to be offered.

If, after reading this letter, you still feel that your interests are likely to suffer because of our new set of Readers perhaps you might prefer to have us pay you an outright sum as against your future royalties and take over all your interest in the entire set. We are not urging this course but are merely offering it as a possible means of avoiding misunderstandings in the future.

Yours very truly,
[William C. Bobbs]

* * *

Grace and Georgia Alexander to Bobbs, 24 January 1924

Dear Mr Bobbs:

We are glad to have your letter of January 12 continuing the discussion of the Child Classics situation. Of course, Mr Bobbs, we are as desirous as you to avoid misunderstandings, especially as we have been on friendly terms so long.

We are sorry to say, however, that many of the impressions received from your letters of December 5 and January 12 conflict both with one another and with policies actually carried out by the firm. We note one fresh suggestion. You offer in your second letter a cash settlement against all future royalties on the Child Classics. You do not urge this.

Some of the conflicting impressions to which we allude are:

1.

"There is a very large asset in the Classics because they have made a good name for themselves everywhere and we would like to realize on that asset with the most profit to us and to you."

In this statement you tell us you are assured of their value.

"We are making a close house to house canvass of the schools and getting first hand information of just how the books are regarded."

In this statement you are still seeking light on their value.

2.

"Our sales force has been greatly increased in the last year and we are finding new opportunities for selling Child Classics for supplementary reading."

Why do you relegate Child Classics to supplementary use when for fifteen years they "Have made a good name everywhere" as basal readers.

"We are preparing a new set of Readers under the Editorial direction of Dr Betts which will be submitted at a top price."

Why do you propose at the same time you relegate the Child Classics to supplemental use, to submit for basal adoption (books from which the child learns how to read–not merely take exercise) the Betts's Readers–an unknown quantity either as basal or supplementary? [. . .]

The following appears to sum up the attitude of the Bobbs-Merrill firm to the Child Classics Readers.

1909–The firm enthusiastic about the Classics even after non-adoption.
Recall its rapid follow-up campaign of editorials in the News.

1914–The firm enthusiastically enters the field a second time and wins the entire adoption.

1919–The firm enthusiastically enters for a third time and wins 4 out of a possible 9 books. According to Mr Carr, your agent, no house could expect more because the Reader adoption was now so enormous that the business was divided up among several companies. And you voluntarily assured us that at the increased price of the four books, our royalties would be practically undiminished. This has proved true.

Notwithstanding Mr Carr's statement just alluded to, you, Mr Bobbs almost immediately directed us to prepare an enlarged (nine books) series for the 1924 adoption. You will recall that you then offered us a written contract to cover this new edition, the signing of which we mutually agreed to defer until final details were worked out.

(1920) That summer Georgia began the enlargement of the Primer and the First Reader. When they were completed (the work occupied two entire vacation periods) we took the scripts to you and she explained in detail how she worked to save as many of the old plates as possible without lessening the value of the manuscript. You will recall also, Mr Bobbs, that we went so far as to discuss the illustrators; the wisdom of including more patriotic selections; and more Indiana material. The status of Grace's contract with the Wheeler Company of Chicago offered to her by Mr Graff, under which she collected and obtained copyright permissions for practically all desirable material by Indiana authors, except Riley was made a part of the discussion. You proposed farther to re-name the series "The Alexander Readers" because you felt so decidedly the market value of the name Alexander on an educational text.

1921–The firm shows continued faith. According to mutual understanding at the close of the previous interview, we called at your office once more (vacation time again) to conclude final arrangements for the enlargement of the upper books. This time we found to our surprise, that you now thought it best to postpone the enlargement (you retaining the two manuscripts). You explained that you had completely investigated the situation and had concluded that the way for the Classics to win the 1924 adoption was to put them up unaltered. To this we agreed since the adoption of the Classics in 1924 was your whole argument.

CHILD CLASSICS
THE THIRD READER

By
GEORGIA ALEXANDER

With pictures by
ALICE BARBER STEPHENS
SARAH K. SMITH AND
FANNY Y. CORY

INDIANAPOLIS
THE BOBBS-MERRILL COMPANY
1921

Title page for a Child Classics volume that was originally published in 1909 (Duke University Library)

We, therefore, Mr Bobbs, rested in your expressed intention to work and work to win for the Child Classics the Indiana Adoption in 1924. The terms of this oral contract merely reaffirmed the terms of the original contract including the clause which declares that the firm "is to make all reasonable effort to secure the adoption of these readers by State and local boards." [. . .]

How can we avoid feeling that the firm was bound to inform us at once of any later purpose to add fresh terms to our contract (to offer with the Classics a rival set) and to allow us our right to give or to withhold consent? Your remarks (letter January 1924) that as early as 1919 you had received "unmistakable warnings" as to the future of the Classics we cannot reconcile with the fact, as we have shown, that twice since 1919 you voluntarily projected plans by which you hoped to win the adoption for the Classics in 1924.

Apparently you are of a mind to think you may win by first displacing your own property, a tried and successful text, and then convincing the State Board that a new and untried set is better. Do you realize that other publishers will be watching the chair you have occupied so long and that the moment you slip off, they may while you are explaining why you wish to change, slip into your place? Is it not safer to keep your seat continuously?

The Classics have not yet been turned down by the State Board of Education. Why does the Bobbs-Merrill Company propose to turn them down?

In your second letter to Grace you said that you appreciated the frankness with which she wrote. It is in this continued spirit of frankness and with a very earnest desire to come to a friendly settlement that we are writing to you today.

We have two suggestions to make: (1) that you offer the Classics alone and unaltered; or (2) that you offer them in an enlarged edition. The date for the adoption, May 1, is for some reason unusually late. Your letters tell us you are still debating your course of action on that day. We, therefore, call your attention successively to our two plans: [. . .]

The newspaper account of the last State Board meeting contained the following:

> "The Bobbs-Merrill Company has had the contract for the elementary readers for the last two five-year periods. Although they are among the books for compulsory use, it is said some schools have declined to use them. The adoption of these books for continued use in the schools, it is said, will come before the board. It is understood the Bobbs-Merrill Company will offer a new series as well as the old series."

Does this not suggest strongly that our forecast of the situation was correct? Does it not say in effect that you are putting up the Betts's Readers because you find the Classics unsuccessful? Can you read any other construction? If this is so, the presentation of the Betts's Readers by the Bobbs-Merrill Company to the State Board before they have turned down the Child Classics, puts the ruin of the Classics upon the firm.

We shall be glad to hear from you further on this matter.

Very sincerely yours,
Grace Alexander
Georgia Alexander

* * *

Bobbs to Grace and Georgia Alexander, 13 March 1924

Dear Misses Alexander:

On returning home from a tour of the West Indies I find your letter of January 24th and am sorry not to have known about it when I was in New York for I am sure we could arrive at a better understanding through talking things over than we have been able to do by means of writing.

So far as I am able to see there is nothing conflicting in my various statements. As for instance a School House canvass to find out whether the CLASSICS could be readopted does not have any relation to the value of the asset in them or their sale over the country. I should like to answer your letter item by item in detail but confusion seems necessarily to accompany a multitude of words and a brief statement will give you the basis of our judgment and I hope show that our conclusions are reasonable.

Offering the CLASSICS in 1924 involves many intricate questions the most important of which are: first, to get the adoption and second, to if possible avoid investing a fortune in new books. There are three major considerations, however, which seem to control.

First Our survey showed the CLASSICS were not in general favor with the schools of the State.

Second An adequate price on the books in any form would afford such a direct comparison with former prices as to prejudice the Board.

Third Offering two sets of books by the same author for consideration at the same adoption would seriously interfere with the chances of either.

And there was no division of opinion in the House or among the members of the Sales organization that if the books were offered in Indiana and declined for readoption it would hurt their standing everywhere.

There is not only nothing conflicting so far as I can find in my various statements to you but also nothing contradictory in our attitude toward the CLASSICS nor anything inconsistent with that attitude in a decision not to offer them at this time.

From the dark days of defeat of 1909 through the triumphant campaigns of 1914 and 1919 I think we have shared pride and gratification over the record of the CLASSICS. Now I sincerely trust that our position is plain and reasonable and, taking into consideration the age of the books, the time of their use in Indiana, the required price increase, their chances of readoption and the injury from rejection that you approve our course and will find in the future no less cause for satisfaction than you have had in the past.

Yours very truly,
[William C. Bobbs]

* * *

"An Unusual Suit"

This lawsuit was thrown out shortly after it was brought to court.

According to the daily press, William H. Daly, a wealthy mining man, formerly of San Francisco, has brought an unusual suit for $100,000 against the Bobbs-Merrill Company, publishers, and Gelett Burgess, the author of "Heart Line." The plaintiff sues to recover damages for remarks made by the author in his book of fiction about one Dailey, who is described in the book as living at the Palace Hotel, San Francisco, where the plaintiff, Daly, used to live. Daly asserts that the man in the book was meant to represent him. The book tells about "a house of eighteen doors at the foot of Ninth street," and goes on to discuss one Dailey, "the star eater of the Palace Hotel." The story says that this Dailey "used to have four canvasback ducks cooked at once, selecting one and using the juice of the others. He used to eat soup at $1 a plate, and he had a happy way of buying a case of champagne with each meal and drinking only the top glass from each bottle." Dailey says in his suit that these statements are false and defamatory, and hold him up as a curiosity. He says if the things told by the author were true he would be in the category of those who are of unsound mind. The defendants demurred to the complaint, and Justice Davis reserved decision.

–*Publishers' Weekly,* 80 (23 December 1911): 2536

Grace and Georgia Alexander to Bobbs, 5 April 1924

Dear Mr Bobbs:

Replying to your courteous letter of recent date we wish to say that we shall be heartily glad to come to some agreement on the matter now under discussion that will be agreeable to you as well as to us.

In one of your earlier letters you gave the impression that our interests on the Child Classics Readers would be best cared for if in future you promoted them outside of Indiana only. Since you feel convinced of this would it not be a good step toward a possible agreement on this head for you to give us in figures the amount the Readers have earned outside of Indiana in the last five years?

In a later letter you made the interesting suggestion that we accept cash settlement in lieu of all future royalties.

These two suggestions seem to offer a basis of a practical discussion of our relations.

As a distinct issue in the matter you will, we believe, wish to compensate Georgia for the work done on the Primer and the First Reader, the manuscripts of which are now in your vault.

Sincerely yours,
Grace Alexander
Georgia Alexander

Acceptance and Rejection: Selected Readers' Reports and Correspondence, 1913–1915

The favorable reports for Ring for Nancy *(1913), the only Bobbs-Merrill novel by Ford Madox Ford (then still publishing under his original name, Ford Madox Hueffer), show what the house expected of its readers. Ford's* A History of Our Own Times *was rejected by Bobbs-Merrill, and it was not published until 1988 (by Indiana University Press).*

RING FOR NANCY.

There seems one word above all others that precisely suits this story, and this word is "delicious." I haven't read anything so completely diverting in many a day. The book is a charming love story, an original comedy, a clever burlesque all at once, and it is all these without ceasing to be a perfect unit. The idea of having a girl in love with a man who is kept by poverty from asking her to marry him, disguise herself as her own maid, and, by her adroitness, getting rid of a lot of women who are hanging on to him against his will, and bringing him to the point of declaration is certainly novel and delightful. It is a cozy story, with just eight characters of importance, each of them exceptionally interesting and exceptionally well portrayed.

Yet one must not infer that this novel is over-subtle, or that it is for the elect only. In a delicate way it might fairly be described as jolly. The "First Church of Christ, Quietest," is an amusing take-off in the person of one of its leaders who goes about carrying a heavy suitcase stuffed with cheerful statistics. The Major's aunt is a most lovable comedy figure; "she knows as much of evil as an egg knows of aeroplanes." Mrs. Kerr Howe, author of Pink Passion, is a capital burlesque on the modern melodramatic novel writer, and Flossie Delamere, who has six notes in her register, and can kick her back comb out of her hair, is, notwithstanding, a nice little thing.

There is really nothing but praise to be bestowed on anything so thoroughly clever, entertaining and well done. Miss Olympia Peabody, of Boston, who has ensnared the Major, and who is at the head of a Society for the Suppression of Sin, is, of course, slightly exaggerated but nevertheless recognizable, and most laughable. Mr. Foster, the Major's uncle by marriage, who has been always "strictly respectable if not always strictly virtuous", is the quietest member of the octette, but he, too, has his amusing scene when, in the pink chintz room, past midnight, he is suddenly invaded by Olympia.

Ford Madox Hueffer at about the time of his enlistment in the British army, August 1915. He changed his last name to Ford in 1919 (Bruccoli Clark Layman Archives).

Despite the nature of its important scenes, the book is not in the least shocking. Its dramatic possibilities are extraordinary.

G. C. A.

January 21, 1913.

When one has said that the story is a delightful farce, one has said nearly all there is worth remarking; all the rest being merely enlargement and elaboration of that statement. To analyse a farce is about as possible and profitable as chewing soup, yet there must be some reason for the delightfulness of certain farces and the dreariness of others. In this case, one of the reasons is the exceeding agreeableness of the main male figure of this little drama. He has about him everything that attracts and appeals to the sympathy.

In the first place, he is a soldier whose brilliant career has been cut short by a failure of sight, which has been brought about by his over devotion to duty and his ambition to excel in his profession. He has also had, as a motive, the wish to make himself worthy of and to get in a position to marry the girl he has left behind him in England. In spite of the failure of his sight, he has not been a failure, for, before the trouble came, he had won the position of the youngest major in the British army; so, while he appeals to the sympathies of the reader, he is not an object of pity. But beside having his professional career cut short, just at the moment when he seems to have all his wishes within the reach of his hand, he hears that his lady-love, from whom he has been separated by her coming into a fortune and a title, has married. None of all these troubles makes him bitter. He can, as he says, lark with the best, and he keeps sweet-tempered toward women. Indeed, he is phenomenally patient with them, for he bears with wonderful patience the tyranny of the vulgar American to whom he has engaged himself impulsively because she was pitiful when he was knocked over by the news that he had lost the use of his eyes. Brave, chivalrous, ambitious, faithful, gay, impulsive, patient, humorous, handsome, he is all that could be desired in a hero of a serious romance, and so he adds much to the charms of a few days of thorough fooling, and helps one to understand a part of the charm of so much nonsense.

Another good thing to be said of the book is that it has a quite ingenious plot, and just such a one as two women who loved the man and wanted to help him might carry out. The masquerading of the sweetheart is managed with sufficient skill to make the reader believe that it might fool the hero, while the reader is himself rather early in the secret, and yet, at the last, it is a satisfaction to one's sense of the probable to find that the lover is all the time a party to the plot. But there are other very likable people in the book beside Major Brent Foster. His old aunt, who is determined to help him enjoy life, is a delightfully warm-hearted, muddle-headed, sensible, surprising old duck. She has long been a prominent member in a society for the suppression of sin; but she is prepared to do anything, however sinful, to gain happiness for those she loves; she cannot judge harshly the sins into which people are led by the warmth or kindliness of their natures, and she loves beauty and gayety so much that she could even sympathize with her husband when he sought them in other women. She tells him finally that she has long known of his escapades, and that somehow she did not care till he began running after a woman as old as she, far uglier, and hard and underbred. As she puts her feeling, it is perfectly reasonable and understandable, and affords a fine comedy touch to her character. There are two other women, an actress and an author of popular novels, both of whom are likable, and one of whom makes some good fun. Then there is the heroine, who is beautiful, clever, high-minded and daring; altogether, they are a delightful lot of people who live, while we follow their doings, in a charming old house, the atmosphere of which the reader is adroitly made to breathe. There are two absurd men,–the uncle of the hero, who is tyrannical, and is yet always in fear of his wife; and the irrascible [*sic*] head of the Quietist church. This last causes the arrest of the hero for stealing some newspapers from a stand, and thus an excellent opportunity is afforded to make some fun of the administration of justice and of the officers entrusted with that work. Fun is also poked at commerce in the person of a book-seller, of literature in the person of the lady novelist, and by quoting Henry James, whose books the hero uses to "toughen" his brain, and whom he quotes effectively.

There are innumerable amusing situations in the book, and a great many clever observations. These last are not epigrammatic, and so will not bear quoting, apart from the scene into which they are introduced; they are numerous enough, however, to keep one in constant expectation, and clever enough to keep one perpetually amused.

January 16, 1913. Caroline Harrison Howland

* * *

The general company files include correspondence with writers who never became Bobbs-Merrill authors and so did not merit individual files (which also contain rejections). Paul R. Reynolds was a literary agent.

Paul R. Reynolds to Bobbs-Merrill, 10 September 1913

Gentlemen,

I offered you recently a book by Herbert D. Miles entitled "The Eternal Game". The author has asked me if I cannot give him some idea of your reasons for declining the book. Is there anything in your reader's report that you could send me which would be of interest to the author? I shall be very much obliged if you can send me any criticisms of the book that you happen to have.

Very truly yours,
Paul R. Reynolds

* * *

BIOGRAPHICAL SKETCH OF FORD MADOX HUEFFER.

I was born on the 17th of December, 1873. My father Doctor Francis Hueffer was for fifteen years musical editor of the London Times, and, being a remarkable linguist he edited or subedited newspapers in Italian, French, German and Dutch. My grandfather Ford Madox Brown was the celebrated historical painter who was nick named "Father of the Pre Raphaeliti Movement" and I am connected on my mother's side with the Rossetti family so that as a child I was brought up as it were in the centre of the Pre Raphaeliti Movement and in contact with most of the distinguished figures of the Victorian Era in this country. Of these I have written my reminiscences in a book which appeared serially in Harper's Magazine and was published in the United States under the title of "Memories and Impressions". My literary career such as it is owes however very little to the study of English books--my work being almost entirely founded upon French models, and I speak French and German as easily as I speak English. A great part of my time in each year being spent upon the Continent. My first work, a poem written when I was fourteen appeared in a journal called The Speaker; my first book written when I was sixteen, had a very great success, selling twenty thousand copies and selling still at the rate of over a thousand copies a year, so that although it was only a fairy tale it may be said to have become a classic at least of the nursery. My most intimate literary friendships in England have been with Mr. Joseph Conrad and Mr. H. G. Wells, Mr. Henry James, Mr. John Galsworthy and in a lesser degree with Mr. Arnold Bennett. I visited the United States in 1906, not for the purpose of writing a book about them but for amusement and a change--as a rubber neck--and I got amusement and change in large quantities so that, if I had not found the experiences so wildly and hideously expensive I should frequently return to that exciting country. I spent some time in New York, in Boston, in Gloucester, Massachusetts and in Philadelphia and I worked for a short time to oblige a friend upon a farm in West Chester County, Pa. I put up several hundred yards of snake fences, drove the neighbor's sheep out of the corn, stopped up a large number of wasps' nests and cut a good deal of corn which I found the hottest occupation I ever struck, the thermometer standing at something like 120 degrees in the shade and my friend, for whom I was working being somewhat of an agricultural crank. He insisted that the corn must be cut very short in the stalk so that I had to take, if not two bites at a cherry at least three chops at each stalk with an instrument called a machete which my friend had brought from Cuba. He said that that would materially assist his winter ploughing but I lost fourteen pounds in weight in the seven days that it lasted. In Philadelphia shortly afterwards I was the guest of honour of a Clover Club dinner, the only institution in the United States that saw fit to honour me with its notice. On this occasion I wore a velvet coat and when the chairman hauled me to my feet to make a speech which I didn't want to do, the remainder of the audience shouted in unison: "Little Lord Fauntleroy!" (I am a little over six foot in height and weigh 224 pounds). I was clubbed by a policeman during the Brooklyn Rapid Transit Riot and

Undated autobiographical sketch that Hueffer/Ford provided for Bobbs-Merrill (courtesy of The Lilly Library, Indiana University, Bloomington, Indiana)

-2-

I once held the following conversation with the Bar-Tender of a Coney Island steamboat on the way from New York to that agreeable resort. Said I to the Bar-Tender:

"What sort of cigarettesdo you keep?"

Said he to me:

"We don't keep 'em we sell 'em."

F.M.H., "Well, what sort of cigarettes have you got anyhow?"

B. T., "We h'ain't got no cigaretts but we carry a fine juicy line of Colorado Stojies."

F.M.H., "Where do you carry 'em to?"

B.T., "It's up to me now."

I also invented a servicable answer to the gentlemen and ladies who ask one so frequently "What are one's impression of New York, the Adirondacks or Poughkeepsie as the case might be. I found that if one answered:

"Oh, you know, it isn't so much the place as the people! it served all the purposes.

Also when asked one's opinion of any of the handiworks of man-- say a picture, a new coffee machine a special brand of ice cream soda or one of the palaces at Newport, Rhode Island, by the artist, the inventor, the mixer, or the proprietor, I found it a splendid thing to reply: "I don't know how you do it!" These are the chief adventures of a life devoted mostly to conversation when it is not occupied by dictating books to a secretary. Of books I have written 39 and I suppose I have almost as many readers.

Hewitt H. Howland to Reynolds, 12 September 1913

My dear Mr. Reynolds:

I wish I had some adequate report to send you on Mr. Herbert D. Miles' The Eternal Game, but I haven't a word that seems to me in any way helpful or instructive. As a whole, our readers thought the story weak and rather talky. They saw good spots here and there but not enough of them to make further consideration advisable or suggestions to the author feasible.

Very truly yours,
[Hewitt H. Howland]

* * *

Among others never published by Bobbs-Merrill was the son of Nathaniel Hawthorne. Carl Brandt was an agent with Galbraith Welch.

Carl Brandt to Howland, 6 January 1915

Dear Mr. Howland:–

We have lately come in touch with the work of Julian Hawthorne, who has had such hard times recently. We know that he is working on a novel and it strikes me that this might fit in with an opening which you may have. We think Mr. Hawthorne's work needs to be taken with great seriousness and he is a person who could be very well advertised.

If you would be interested in having something from him, won't you let us know and we will take the matter up in detail with you?

Yours sincerely,
Carl Brandt
GALBRAITH WELCH.

* * *

Howland to D. Laurance Chambers, 9 January [1915]

I have a feeling Hawthorne is a good man to let alone. What do you think?

HHH

[subscribed note from Chambers]

Mr Howland

That's my judgment.
DLC
1/9

* * *

Howland to Galbraith Welch, 9 January 1915

My dear Miss Welch:

Thank you for your word about Julian Hawthorne. I don't believe there is any likelihood of our being able to make a place for him on our list. We can use a big book in the late spring but I am afraid, from what I know of Hawthorne's work, that he could not supply it. I am glad, however, that you wrote me about him and hope that you will always let me know whenever any author's work is available.

Very sincerely yours,
[Hewitt H. Howland]

* * *

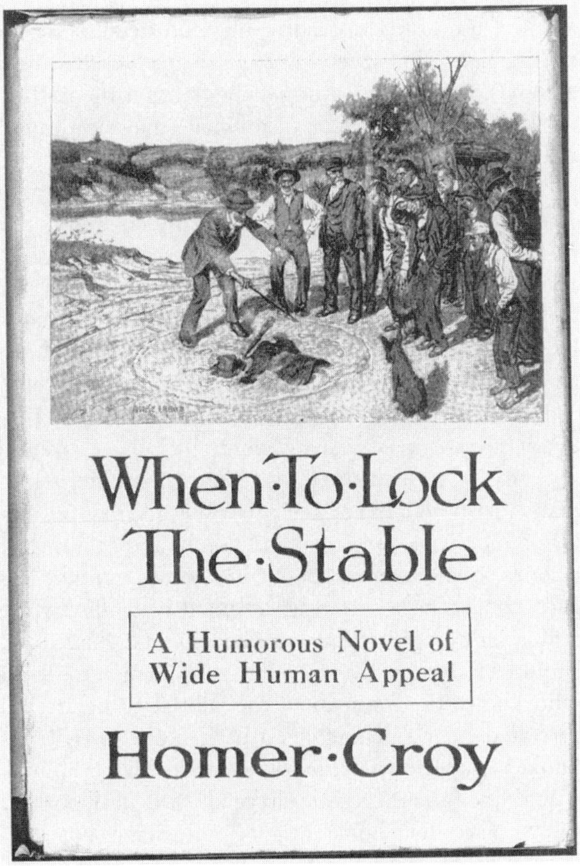

Dust jacket for a 1914 murder mystery (courtesy of Michael Manz/Babylon Revisited)

Childhood and Youth: Selected Correspondence with Michael V. O'Shea, 1913–1915

The series that Michael V. O'Shea, a professor of education at the University of Wisconsin, sold to Bobbs-Merrill was another money-losing educational venture. He proposed about sixty books, five to ten appearing per year, that would together form a key to all knowledge about the training of children. The Century Company ("the New York firm") was also interested in the scheme. After agreeing to terms with Bobbs-Merrill, O'Shea contracted with several authors for individual volumes. Three titles in the series appeared in 1914, and a total of eleven had been published by the end of 1917. The efforts of O'Shea and author Winifred S. Stoner to promote the flagship volume, Natural Education *(1914), did not achieve the desired results.*

Michael V. O'Shea to John R. Carr, 8 March 1913

Dear Mr. Carr:

I should have written you earlier regarding the plan for the series of volumes on "Childhood and Youth" concerning which we have had some correspondence; but a situation has arisen here which I did not anticipate when I first proposed the plan to you. While I am not permitted to mention details just yet, still I can say that several weeks ago a representative of a New York publishing firm came here for the purpose of inducing three or four of my colleagues and myself to become identified with the firm. [. . .]

The plan which I proposed to you in a general way before the Holidays seemed to my colleagues and to the New York firm to be a very good and entirely feasible one. You may remember that in this plan it was my purpose to try to present practically all that is known to-day regarding childhood and youth in such a simple, concrete, and attractive way that it would be of interest and of help to parents, and teachers in their every-day work in training children. I have carefully gone over the whole field, and have consulted all the plans that others have been proposing for that publication of books on childhood and youth, and I think such a series should contain about sixty books, more or less, each containing in the neighborhood of 50,000 words and selling at fifty cents or thereabouts. Each book should be written by the man or woman now living who knows the most about the subject to be treated, provided such a person could be induced to write the book. I am perfectly well aware that the men whom we would like for such a series have all sorts of opportunities to place their books to good advantage; but still I think if we let these people see that we are undertaking a pretty important task, and if we succeed in it, we will get the attention of parents and teachers everywhere, we may be able to attract them. It is entirely possible, of course, that I could not get one-half of the men I have in mind to contribute to this series, because the publishing houses are constantly holding out offers to them. Scarcely a day goes by that the University is not visited by a representative of some publishing firm who wants to get the prominent people to submit their manuscripts to his house. Nevertheless, I think this particular series I have in mind and the method of preparing the books would make a strong appeal to a good many of the leading educational writers in this country and in England.

I have thought this series should be presented under five divisions, as follows:

(a) The Child as Heir of the Past–to include 12 or 13 books each dealing with a special instinct or impulse.

(b) The Physical Welfare of the Child–to include 12 volumes, each dealing with the requirements for healthful physical growth.

(c) Intellectual Training of Childhood and Youth–to include 15 books, each dealing with a particular aspect of intellectual activity, and the best method of dealing with it in the home and the school.

(d) Social and Moral Training–to include 13 volumes, each treating of some one ethical, moral or social trait and its proper training in modern society.

(e) General Characteristics of Childhood–to include 7 volumes relating to such subjects as Individuality, The Exceptional Child, Fatigue, and the like. [. . .]

In respect to the compensation of authors for their work, it has appeared to me that it would be well if the company could pay each author the sum of $350 cash upon the acceptance of his manuscript, and ten percent upon all sales beyond seven thousand copies. It is possible the cash payment would not be necessary in order to attract authors and indicate to them that the company was in earnest about the matter; but still I think it would assist in getting the men and women whom we would want to contribute to the series. The Bobbs-Merrill company is certainly becoming known to educational people. But it has not yet got into the consciousness of some educational writers that the company can do as well for an author in the educational field as some of the companies which have been working in this field for some time. As I say, this may not be a very important item, though I have talked with a number of people regarding the question, and I think it would be of help in interesting authors.

As for the editor of the series, my colleagues who are projecting similar series in their own fields have discussed the matter at considerable length in my presence. The New York firm to which I alluded in the beginning would, if I would permit it, make a definite proposal by which I would become editor or adviser or both with a fixed yearly honorarium. I took no part in the discussion of this, but there seems to have been a practical agreement that the editor should receive from $1,500 to $2,500 yearly, with some allowance for expenses of correspondence, including stenographic aid. In determining what the amount ought to be in my own case, I reached it by a consideration of what I should give up if I should undertake this plan. [. . .]

I would write an introduction to each volume, and of course edit the manuscripts. Needless to say, I would not undertake this sort of thing, if I did not think that I could interest people of such ability that their manuscripts would not need to be modified to any great extent. [. . .]

Well, then, I have given this little outline of the plan so that if the Bobbs-Merrill Company should have time to look over it, we might have a few words regarding it next Thursday. I shall not be surprised if the whole matter is settled in a few words,–to the effect that the company is not particularly interested. But since the matter has been before us for some time, we ought to reach some decision regarding it without further delay.

I wish before closing to say again that what I have said regarding the New York firm should be regarded as confidential for the present. I mentioned the matter to you, because I think it is necessary to have it before us in discussing this plan, which was proposed several weeks before the New York firm appeared on the scene. I referred in a general way to certain of my colleagues, and if you should happen to know whom I have in mind, I am sure that nothing I have said will be used to their discomfort or disadvantage in any way.

Very truly yours,
M. V. O'Shea

* * *

Howland wrote to Bobbs, then at the New York office, with correspondence from O'Shea.

Howland to Bobbs, 11 March 1913

My dear Mr. Bobbs:

With this is enclosed a copy of a letter from Dr. O'Shea which reached us this morning. We are sending it to you in the hope that you will be able to send us a night letter to reach us Thursday morning. Dr. O'Shea is to arrive to-morrow, Wednesday, afternoon and will probably leave Thursday evening. The letter was read at the board meeting this morning and very favorably commented on. Our feeling is that probably there are too many volumes contemplated and that the price per volume is too low. The compensation for the individual author seems to us quite reasonable. As to Dr. O'Shea's compensation, I thought possibly we might discuss with him some such contract as we made with Mr. Haworth. However, I am inclined to think that inasmuch as he will have to give up a number of revenue-producing occupations, he will probably feel that he will have to have a salary or a pretty stiff advancement of royalties with a minimum guarantee. If it comes to a salary or nothing at all, I made the suggestion to the boarding [*sic*] this morning of two thousand dollars out of which Dr. O'Shea would pay his own office and other expenses except traveling. You will notice from the letter that our friend Dr. Ely has evidently been busy. Mr. Merrill, Mr. Chambers and Mr. Moorehead [*sic*] all seemed very favorably impressed, not only with Dr. O'Shea's letter but with the scheme itself.

Hoping to get your suggestions and advice by night letter, I am,

Very truly yours,
H. H. Howland

* * *

Bobbs to O'Shea, 13 April 1915

Dear Doctor O'Shea:

Confirming our conversation in regard to THE CHILDHOOD AND YOUTH SERIES the record of the investment and sales up to the present time is of such character as to make it imperative to us both to decide upon some new basis of operation for the future.

You have performed your part of the enterprise with remarkable zeal and skill. You have succeeded in getting the very best authors in the country for this Series to sign contracts and we have heard no complaint whatever of the books in the Series already published.

On our part we have spent time and energy and money without stint in the effort to sell the books. We have given the best intelligence and the best effort in our office doing whatever we thought could be done effectively to sell the books. Our selling campaigns I believe have had your approval.

The fact that the Series has not had a profitable sale after the efforts which you and we have put into it, seems sufficient reason for prudent considerations to stop any further publication of the Series.

However such a course has its obvious difficulties and embarrassments to both and notwithstanding the loss which we have suffered in the enterprise up to this time, we should be willing to continue the Series if that could be done with proper safeguards against the possibility of future loss.

In our conversation about this matter two courses were suggested as possible:

The first that all authorship and editorial operations on the Series be suspended including the payments under your present contract and advancements to authors until such time as we are able to recover our present loss in the Series. Meanwhile we would publish only such manuscripts as come to us unsolicited and without any effort all ready for the printer without editorial work.

The second course suggested was that we defer authors' advancements until the date of publication, readjust the amounts to cover the advance sales on the titles, and readjust the compensation for your work under the Series from the payments now provided for in the contract to a basis of royalty on the sales of the titles.

Mr. Howland, Mr. Chambers, Mr. Carr and I have gone over the whole matter thoroughly since the talk with you and we are united in the opinion that the first arrangement is the better if we are ultimately to discontinue the publication of the Series, and the second arrangement is better if we shall find it possible to continue the publication of the Series. [. . .]

In submitting this whole matter for consideration I want to repeat what was said in our conversation and that is that we thoroughly appreciate the good work you have done on this Series and the value of your connection with the house and we all hope that nothing may develop out of the present situation which may operate to lessen your interest in this establishment or to relax the close and cordial relationship existing between us.

Yours very truly,
[William C. Bobbs]

* * *

O'Shea to Bobbs, 17 April 1915

Dear Mr. Bobbs:

I have given very careful attention to the contents of your letter of April 13. I wish I felt more confident than I do of my judgment regarding the best course to pursue; but there seem to be some objections to any plan which has been proposed or that I have been able to think out. There is one condition, however, which it seems to me should receive particular consideration in determining what should be done next. I feel we should, if possible, avoid giving the authors of the Series the impression that the Bobbs-Merrill Company has abandoned the Series because the books which have been published have not proved to be successful. Such an impression would, I think, be detrimental to the future welfare of the educational department of the Company, and it would also be a reflection upon the judgment of the editor of the Series, who gave to each author his personal assurance that the Bobbs-Merrill Company would carry out faithfully and efficiently the provisions of any contract which they would make with an author. I may add that I am much more anxious about the good name of the publisher and the editor than I am about realizing the salary which I had planned for in connection with the authorship of the Series.

II.

In view of the matter of chief importance in determining the next step regarding the Series, it has seemed to me it ought to be possible to avoid assuming a further financial burden in publishing new volumes while at the same time not declining to publish the volumes that have been contracted for. [. . .]

V.

In regard to my own remuneration, I regret that the Company does not feel able to continue its contract, and under the circumstances, I shall have to adapt myself to the situation. The plan you propose that I should receive five percent royalty on regular trade sales and two and one-half percent on contract sales and special adoptions of all the titles in the Series, including the other books that have been secured through my influence, will perhaps be the best plan under the changed conditions. This would apply, I presume, to books yet to be published. For those that have been published, how would it do to pay me the rate of royalty mentioned above when the books have earned enough to offset the salary which has already been paid me? Or perhaps you have some other plan which will be more acceptable, and if so, I shall be very glad to consider it.

I may add that I am following up every clue to see if we can make Natural Education the best selling education book of these times. If McClure's Magazine publishes my article on Mrs. Stoner, the book ought to be helped considerably. In addition, I shall presently write up the book for the Mothers Magazine, and a million serious women will read what I write. Don't you think such publicity ought to make the book successful in the highest degree? And if we can get it going, I should think the editor ought in some way or at some time share modestly in the profits to be derived from it, and also from the other books in the Series, if they can be made to yield a profit. [. . .]

I am submitting these matters for your consideration and that of your colleagues, and of course I shall be glad to re-consider any plan herein presented, or one which you may submit, if the various matters I have suggested do not meet with your full approval or cover all the conditions which should be provided for.

Cordially yours,
M. V. O'Shea

* * *

Owen Johnson (courtesy of the John Dixon Library, Lawrenceville School)

The Salamander: Correspondence with Owen Johnson, 1915

Owen Johnson, better known for such works as Stover at Yale *(New York: Stokes, 1912), was the beneficiary of a large first (and only) printing of* The Salamander *(1914), his tale of an emancipated female. Bobbs-Merrill bought the book rights from* McClure's Magazine *to capitalize on the contemporary feminist uproar. Thanks in part to a massive advertising campaign, the book was a best-seller for six months–Johnson's only best-seller, and his only book for the company. The full Bobbs-Merrill arsenal was employed: posters, brochures, gummed stickers, bookmarks, postcards, illustrated handkerchiefs, booksellers' kits, and special company stationery.* The Salamander *inspired a fashion craze, was adapted as a play (staged in October 1914), and was made into a movie. It did not, however, do as much as was hoped to cure the financial woes of the company; a quarter of the one hundred thousand copies were remaindered. For his next book,* Making Money *(1915), Johnson returned to the publisher Frederick A. Stokes.*

Owen Johnson to Bobbs, 1 January 1915

Dear Mr. Bobbs:–

I had intended having a frank talk with you before you left New York but you flitted off before I could get to it.

At present it is necessary for me to see my business engagements clearly ahead and that is why I am writing to you with the utmost directness. In a word then, I have had a growing feeling that your house has not looked upon your arrangement with me with the same enthusiasm as at the beginning, perhaps feeling that my work did not fit into your scheme of publishing. This is not in criticism, but recognizing the situation as it has developed. I myself have begun to wonder if the quality of work I produce is susceptible to your popular handling. Our five year agreement on your part is conditional on your selling one hundred thousand copies in a year. You informed me at The Players that you would not approach that. If this is your experience with a guarantee of $13,500 I can understand that you might hesitate before assuming an obligation of $20,000 a year for five years.

The time has come when I must take up the question of my new novel with Stokes; while I am well disposed to your firm (there are certain clauses we should have to discuss) I should like a declaration of your intentions to guide me. Are you prepared to offer me a five years' contract guaranteeing me $20,000 a book on five books on substantially the lines indicated on the memoranda we hold.

Believe me, I can appreciate your reasons in case the reply is a negative one and whatever happens I should always remember with gratitude the enthusiasm you have put behind The Salamander. You will, I know, understand that it is only fair to me to protect my interests that I should know your intentions, if you have come to consider a five years contract disastrous to your interest.

Will you give me as early an answer to this as possible. With renewed assurances of my personal regard and friendship,

Cordially yours,
Owen Johnson

* * *

L. Nathan to Bobbs, 6 January 1915

Publication date THE SALAMANDER May 9, 1914.

Our guarantee to the Author on THE SALAMANDER provides for an advance payment of $3500.00 and a sale of 100,000 copies within two years; but if that number is not sold within two years from publication date, we are to pay him the royalty for the full 100,000 of the regular edition which amounts to $13,500.

If we sell 100,000 copies within one year <u>from publication date</u>, then he is to sign the 5 year contract. Note this provision is not due until May 9, 1915.

The five year contract provides for an increase in royalty on the five novels of 5%; an advance payment of $2500.00 on signature of each contract and $2500.00 on publication date; and a guarantee of 100,000 sale of the regular edition within 2 years from publication date. This 100,000 guarantee would amount to approximately $20,000. on each title, depending of course on the list price of the book.

Under the 5 year contract, Owen Johnson is free to negotiate with Stokes for the one novel heretofore promised them. Johnson's guarantee under this 5-year arrangement however to give us exclusive publication and secondary serial rights of all his writings for 5 yrs gives the date of such grant as January 1, 1914.

L. Nathan

* * *

Johnson to Bobbs, 8 January 1915

Dear Mr. Bobbs:

On January 1st I send [*sic*] you an important business letter, of which you have not acknowledged receipt.

As the matter is important, will you let me know if the letter has gone astray, so that I may duplicate it.

Cordially yours,

Owen Johnson

Please note this address.

* * *

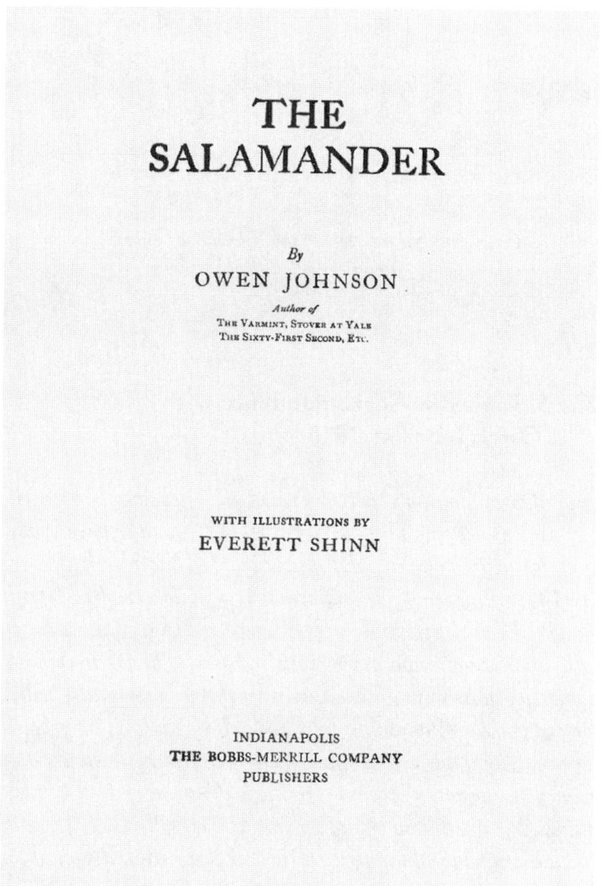

THE SALAMANDER

By

OWEN JOHNSON

Author of

THE VARMINT, STOVER AT YALE

THE SIXTY-FIRST SECOND, ETC.

WITH ILLUSTRATIONS BY

EVERETT SHINN

INDIANAPOLIS

THE BOBBS-MERRILL COMPANY

PUBLISHERS

Cover and title page for the 1914 volume that is the only book Johnson published with Bobbs-Merrill (courtesy of The Lilly Library, Indiana University, Bloomington, Indiana)

A vivid, throbbing, tumultuous portrayal of the mad, lawless, passion-driven life of today. The Salamander is a real woman, one of the few real women in recent American Fiction. —*The Bookman*

Owen Johnson's Great Novel

The Bobbs-Merrill Company. Price $1.35 net, at all stores

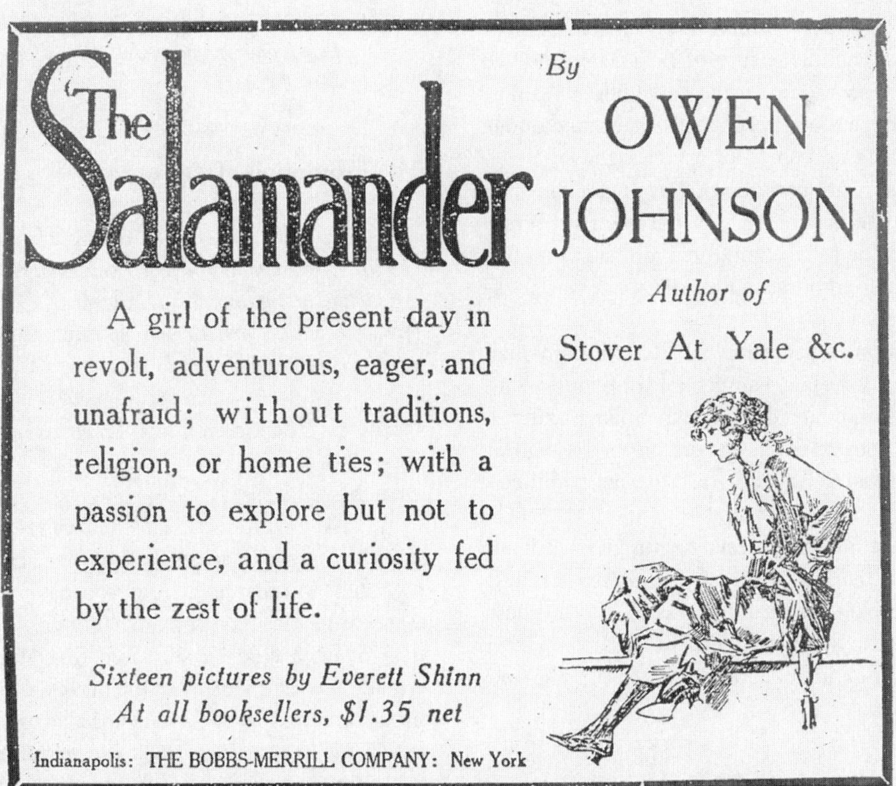

Two fliers promoting Johnson's novel (courtesy of The Lilly Library, Indiana University, Bloomington, Indiana)

Bobbs to Johnson, 9 January 1915

My dear Owen:–

Your letter of January first came promptly but has not been answered because of the pressure of matters requiring my personal attention at the first of the year.

I am extremely sorry to have left New York without seeing you for a last word but was called away from there rather unexpectedly. Of course if I had known that you had something to talk about I would have made it a point to see you.

As regards THE SALAMANDER the sale of the book was satisfactory up to the time of the war. I was delighted with the book, proud of the campaign our organization put on it and am confident that it would have reached our expectations if it had not been for the war.

So far as the future is concerned, this is an extremely difficult time to decide questions. In the present condition of the publishing business it would not be prudent for any publisher to enter into financial obligations of any kind for the future. And with all of the publishers of the country in this state of mind it is not a good time for any author to offer his future manuscripts. Business is likely to turn now almost any time and when it does publishers will want manuscripts and authors can get fair contracts for them.

Our option for undertaking the five-year contract runs one year from the date THE SALAMANDER was published, which was May 9th. A very great deal may happen between this and the first of next May and we should not at this time and under these conditions want to anticipate in any degree what action we might take under the option when the time comes for exercising it.

Our business relations with you have been happy in the extreme and I should be very distressed if I thought we had done anything to give you the impression that our interest in you or our enthusiasm for your work was slackening in any degree.

There is nothing whatever the matter with the quality of your work. It is certainly susceptible of popular handling. But there is something definitely the matter with the times and as you yourself know in such times the highest priced material is most difficult for the publisher and therefore suffers most in immediate value.

Your expressions of appreciation for the work on THE SALAMANDER are gratifying in the extreme and whatever may develop for the future as to our business relations nothing can interfere with the friendship and affection which Ruth and I shall always hold for you and Mrs. Johnson.

Yours very truly,
[William C. Bobbs]

* * *

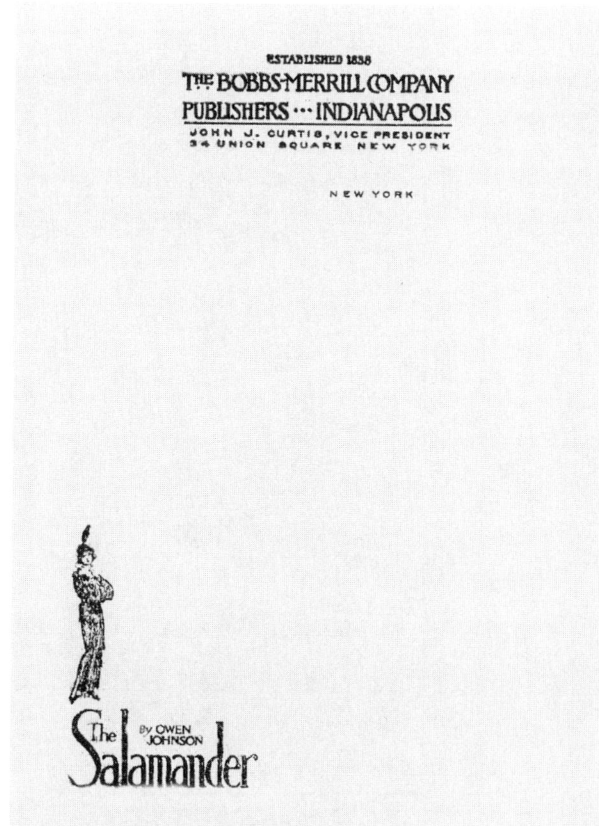

House stationery used to advertise Johnson's novel (courtesy of The Lilly Library, Indiana University, Bloomington, Indiana)

The Promotion of *Agriculture*

Oscar H. Benson and George H. Betts's Agriculture *(1915) was probably the first Bobbs-Merrill textbook to earn a substantial profit from school adoption. The book was heavily promoted by Carr and Benson, an employee of the U.S. Department of Agriculture.*

Oscar H. Benson to Carr, 12 March 1915

Dear Mr. Carr:

I have written special letters to several of the normal school professors at the State Normal School for Iowa, especially to those to whom you have sent copies of the text. I am inclosing a copy of this letter.

I am a little bit surprised that Washington county would give the excuse that the book is too large. The common complaint that I have heard all over the United States is that the average text book on agriculture does not contain enough to make it authentic or to cover the crops in any community. The crime of dealing with the subject in a sort of general and attic arrangement of facts, arousing interest in the subject but not giving instructions for practice has been quite common with the average text. I am not surprised however that they did not select the book. This is one of the counties where I do not even remember knowing personally a single individual. I simply hoped that Dr. Betts was well enough acquainted so that he could pull it through.

I know a few people in the State of Ohio. I am wondering if you have already sent copies to Ray Fife of Van Wert, D. W. Galehouse of Wooster, Lester S. Ivins of the State House, Columbus. Of course there are a number of text books which have been written and prepared by people in the State of Ohio. They and their friends will make a strenuous campaign. I believe, however, that if you have a good agent who knows how to present the book and to show the advantages of pedagogy over those of others that it will go a long way to overcome the local offices.

I hope that you will give me the benefit of all criticisms that come into the field in regard to the book. I have purposely held up the last chapter of the western and southern edition in order to get the criticisms of the book. I have been successful in getting a few that will be mighty valuable.

I believe that you will do well in getting out some of the books on a thinner paper with the idea of reducing the bulk. In case the complaint that the book is too large becomes too general we can very easily cut down the corn chapter and eliminate about 40 pages of it. In other words, use the same amount of material in this chapter that we will use in the western edition.

In answering letters of inquiry about the book in southern and western territory I hope that you will call their attention to the fact that the western and southern edition will be made up on the same general plan but will have a shorter chapter on corn and will have chapters on the following: Southern Agriculture, Western Agriculture, Fruit and Nut Farming, Sugar Farming, Dry Land Farming, and Irrigation, and that some of the other chapters will be revised to meet the conditions of this territory. I have given especial attention to the study of these states by personal visits to every state and will try my best to make the book better than any other book available.

Please let me know by return mail what contract price you are making on the book for county and state adoptions. I have been asked the question a number of times but have never been able to state definitely. All I know is that single copies are selling for $1.25.

Very truly yours,

O. H. Benson

Agriculturist in Charge of Club Work.

* * *

The Return to List Advertising: Minutes of the Board of Directors, 18 July 1916

The trade list had increased sixfold between 1901 and 1915, and John J. Curtis's famous policy of single-title advertising resulted in a growing number of titles that received little or none, given the constraints of the budget in the trade ("publication") department. Curtis's authority in New York was herein made subordinate to that of Bobbs in Indianapolis.

Meeting of July 18, 1916

Called to order by the President at 10:30 am. Present Messrs Bobbs, Merrill, Curtis, Howland, Moorhead, Kryter, Chambers. [. . .]

Mr. Moorhead moved the adoption of the following resolution, which was seconded by Mr. Kryter and carried unanimously:

Meeting adjourned

D. L. Chambers, Sec'y

RESOLUTION

The Board of Directors hereby makes the following appropriation for advertising and promotion for the Publication Department for the last half of the year Nineteen Hundred Sixteen:

1. For Advertising ten percent (10%) of the net book sales of the period, and for Promotion five percent (5%) of the net book sales of the period, said amounts to be expended under the personal direction of the Vice-President, John J. Curtis, to be applied to the particular titles in accordance with the sales of those titles, and not to exceed at the end of any month of the period the total appropriation earned up to that time.
2. Advertising for the period shall be done by groups of titles, having as nearly as practicable uniform space and consideration, and single titles shall be advertised individually only when the sales are sufficient to warrant and a written request for such advertising has been approved by the President.
3. Titles shall be arranged in groups with reference to their subject and appeal by the Indianapolis office, and the advertising shall follow the arrangement of these groups so far as the earning of the individual titles shall justify.
4. Mediums shall be studied by the New York Office with special reference to the various groups of titles, and a list of all mediums to be used shall be submitted to the Indianapolis Office for investigation and approval before being used.
5. Advertisements shall be written, designed, and set up in the New York Office, and submitted to the Indianapolis Office for suggestions at least ten days

before the time the OK'd proofs are required by any medium in which the advertisements are to be run.

6. It is the sense of the Board that ten percent (10%) for advertising and five percent (5%) for promotion is the maximum amount to be expended on any title during this period; that the money earned should be expended on every title the sales of which warrant advertising whether the title be new or old; that money shall not be spent for promotion or advertising until the sales have earned an actual appropriation for that purpose; that advertising for the period shall be group advertising as opposed to individual title advertising, excepting only in the case of those titles the sales of which warrant individual consideration; and that mediums and copy shall have the careful consideration of both offices, and the written approval of the President; that the responsibility for advertising and promotion expenditure shall be in the hands of the Vice-President, Mr. Curtis.

7. The Accounting Department shall furnish the Advertising Department promptly the first week in each month all statistics of sales and expenditures required for the effective operation of this resolution and a list of titles which have earned advertising and promotion appropriation under this resolution[.]

Dust jacket for a 1916 novel of Greenwich Village that was adapted as a movie with the same title the following year (courtesy of Michael Manz/Babylon Revisited)

* * *

Reprieve for the Trade Department: Minutes of the Board of Directors, 14–15 November 1916

The board of directors considered dissolving the trade department and its necessary appendage, the New York office, leaving Bobbs-Merrill with only its legal and educational divisions.

Meeting of Nov 14, 1916

Called to order by the President at 10:30.

Present: Messrs Bobbs, Howland, Moorhead, Kryter, Carr, Chambers. [. . .]

The future of the Publishing Dep't was again informally discussed, and the President appointed Mr. Kryter, Mr. Carr and Mr. Chambers a committee to draft a resolution embodying the conclusions at which the Board had informally arrived.

The Board then adjourned until the next day.

D. L. Chambers, Sec'y

Adjourned Meeting of November 15, 1916

The Board met at the call of the President at 9:45 A.M.

Present:

Mr. Kryter for the committee appointed at the session of the day before introduced a Resolution, which after amendment by general agreement, read as follows:–

Resolved: That we continue to operate the Publishing Department but subject to such a reduction that the total operating expense for the year 1917 shall not exceed the operating expense of the year 1909 (general expense, advertising and promotion being excluded); and that the Advertising and Promotion expense for the year 1917 be not more than 10% and 5% respectively of the net book sales during the same period.

Also, Resolved: that the Department be operated, subject to the above expense arrangement, with a view to its profitable development, and this purpose makes the maintenance of a New York Office desirable.

Mr. Howland moved the adoption of this Resolution. Mr. Moorhead seconded the motion. Carried unanimously.

Mr. Chambers moved and Mr. Kryter seconded the motion: That the President be asked to prepare and submit to the Board a plan for the organization and operation of the Dep't within the prescribed limit of expense and in the meantime to take whatever action seems to him advisable looking to a reduction in expense.

Carried unanimously

Meeting adjourned.

D. L. Chambers, Sec'y

* * *

By
Irving Bacheller
Author of
EBEN HOLDEN

The Light in The Clearing

Now second on its way to the top of the list of six best sellers.

With simplicity and charm; with sympathy and understanding; with humor and wisdom, Irving Bacheller has told this story of the "North Country"—the country of his first great success, "Eben Holden."

In it he has, unconsciously perhaps shown us what patriotism means; has displayed for our inspiration true Americanism, and has given us a dramatic picture of the rugged and simple and honest lives of our ancestors. Illustrated by Arthur I. Keller. 12mo. Cloth, $1.50 net.

HIS OWN COUNTRY

NOT since Judge Tourgee's "Fool's Errand" of a generation ago has there been a Southern romance comparable with this new novel by Paul Kester, HIS OWN COUNTRY, in its mastery of the theme and in its poignant appeal to human interests; while for its peer in the other qualities, dramatic and literary, spiritual and—in the nobler sense—sentimental, we should have to turn back many years more to the primal and perennial work of Harriet Beecher Stowe.—*N. Y. Tribune.*

12mo, Cloth, 692 pages, $1.50 net.

AN AMERICAN NOVEL
By PAUL KESTER

By FREDERIC S. ISHAM

THIS WAY OUT

A sprarkling comedy novel by the author of NOTHING BUT THE TRUTH, the famous novel on which was based the William Collier play now running in New York for over a year. *This Way Out* has the life, the movement, the quick touch, the surprise of a well acted and very funny play.

Illustrated, $1.40 net.

By
Arthur S. Roche
Author of
Plunder and Loot

The Sport of Kings

Three thoroughbreds, a man, a girl, and a horse.

In this novel Mr. Roche handles with skill three factors of popular interest.

In the first place, there is the "turf"—the love of the thoroughbreds, the pride of the jockeys, and the excitement of the race.

Then, there is a love affair which has none of the ear-marks of conventionality.

And of course there is the detective-story element, of which Mr. Roche is a past master, with the lure of mystery and the keen edge of suspense.

Illustrated by Arthur I. Keller. Jacket drawing in full color by Francois Flameng. 12mo, Cloth, $1.40 net.

By SAMUEL MERWIN
Author of THE HONEY BEE

Temperamental Henry

The loves of Henry the Ninth. You'll enjoy it.

"You know every man, woman and child in the story; know that they are real and that if they haven't lived outside the pages of the manuscript they certainly live in them. The humor chuckles in every page and bubbles and overflows to an astonishing extent.

"By all odds this is the best thing the author has yet done."

Illustrated by Stockton Mulford. $1.50 net.

By ETHEL M. KELLEY

Turn About Eleanor

A first novel by a new author with originality and charm.

Half a dozen New Yorkers of the smart and clever class, three men and three girls, all intimate friends, enter into a compact not to marry but adopt a child who shall spend two months with each of them in turn, and for whose welfare and education they shall be collectively responsible, hence "Turn About Eleanor."

Surely no one can read this book without a softening of the heart and an enlightenment of the eyes. Illustrated by F. Graham Cootes. $1.40 net.

New York—THE BOBBS-MERRILL CO., Publishers—Indianapolis

Publishers' Weekly *(21 July 1917) advertisement of summer fiction offerings*

The Efficiency Board: Correspondence with Harper and Brothers, 1918

A flattering request for operational advice from a distinguished older firm was followed by a convoluted rejection of Bobbs-Merrill books. Researchers of Bobbs-Merrill history are the permanent beneficiaries of the simplified filing system that Ornan E. Barker mentions.

Ornan E. Barker to Henry Hoyns, 24 October 1918

Dear Mr. Hoyns:–

Mr. Bobbs has referred to the Efficiency Board your letter of October 9th asking for some information in reference to this Board. The following outline will give you some idea of the objects and methods of this Committee.

The object of this Board is to obtain the best results in operating each Department and in correllating [*sic*] the work of all departments to prevent waste and duplication; to raise the morale of all workers; to devise means to prevent loss from want of punctuality; to investigate and report practicability of new methods of work and to discover and supersede obsolete methods that are inevitable in houses of long standing.

The Efficiency Board is composed of the heads of departments and is organized with a President and Secretary. The meetings are held on Friday afternoon of each week. This committee issues bulletins for government of our employes. It recommends prizes for punctuality, etc.

The results obtained thru the work of the Efficiency Board are as follows. The waste from tardiness has been reduced 50%. The adoption of labor-saving devices in the Accounting Department. The method of interchange of employes of different departments to meet emergencies, etc.

This committee maintains a Suggestion Box and pays a premium for all suggestions of employes found adaptable. It appoints committees to investigate complaints and certifies its action to the Board of Directors.

If there is any further way in which we can help you, kindly command us.

Yours very truly
[Ornan E. Barker]
THE BOBBS MERRILL COMPANY

* * *

Barker to Hoyns, 26 October 1918

Dear Mr. Hoyns:–

Thank you very much for the report you forwarded to us in reference to your Employees' Library.

We are wondering whether or not we could make some sort of an arrangement with you people to exchange books for our House Employees' Libraries. For instance we might exchange new books as issued or we might make an arrangement to ship you 25 or 50 Bobbs-Merrill books against 25 or 50 of your publications.

We believe this idea could be worked out with different publishing houses and of course it would be a much bigger thing for the employes and the expense would be very small.

We would appreciate hearing from you or whoever would have charge of the matter.

Yours very truly,
[Ornan E. Barker]
THE BOBBS MERRILL COMPANY

* * *

Hoyns to Barker, 30 October 1918

Dear Mr. Barker:

Thank you very much for your letter of October 24th, regarding the operations of your Efficiency Board. I hesitate to really bother you very much about this matter, but it is so important and you seem to be so well organized that occasionally, with your permission, I am going to take the liberty of asking you some questions about the operations of that Board.

Mr. Bobbs told me that you have had some trouble with your bookkeeping–if I remember correctly he said not a man was in your Bookkeeping Department at this time who was there over a year ago–and the Board investigated the matter and suggested the use of a bookkeeping machine. Would you be good enough to tell me the name of that machine so that we may have a look at it here?

As to the matter of exchanging books for our libraries. We have gone into that with our people a little bit and found this to be the fact. You see we publish three thousand titles or more, and in order to have that library conducted and not cause too much trouble it is necessary to keep a number of titles down to a working basis; and therefore, we have put in this library only the books we want our people to read, plus the books they want to read. That covers neither our list nor all of our new books; so, we do not feel at this time, at least, that we want to increase our books. A little later on perhaps, when things are running smoothly we may want to take advantage of your suggestion.

In the meanwhile, I beg to remain,

Yours very truly,
Henry Hoyns

* * *

Barker to Hoyns, 2 November 1918

Dear Mr. Hoyns:–

Your very good letter of October 30th is received and we are very glad to know that you are interested in the workings of our Efficiency Board.

Referring to our Bookkeeping Department our Board made a very careful investigation of conditions and decided that the work could be done much more efficiently in every way by the use of a Bookkeeping Machine.

We investigated all of the machines on the market, that is all that we knew anything about, and decided that for our purposes at least the Elliott-Fisher machine would be the most practical.

It is a little hard of course to induct a new system into an office and there is quite a little confusion at first but we are quite well satisfied with the results so far and just as soon as our force is adapted to the machine we are quite sure it will be very much better than anything we have ever had.

Possibly the best results obtained by the Efficiency Board have been manifested in the present filing system. We went over this matter very thoroughly cutting out a whole lot of unnecessary work and simplified the system in every way. We now believe we have one of the best filing systems in any institution. In our different investigations we found that the filing system was a sore spot in a great many concerns.

Another thing we do that we believe will interest you is this. About once a month we devote our afternoon which we give to our board meeting to an investigation of some organization here in the city. We can always get some very good ideas and we have found that all of the business houses are very anxious to co-operate with us.

Regarding the exchange of books for our two libraries we note the conditions you outline but if

Dust jacket for a mystery, published in 1920, that was originally serialized in Argosy *in 1918 (courtesy of Michael Manz/Babylon Revisited)*

you should ever care to take up the matter with us kindly let us know.

Kindly command us if there is any other way in which we can help you.

Yours very truly
[Ornan E. Barker]
THE BOBBS MERRILL COMPANY

* * *

Obituaries

CHARLES W. MERRILL, treasurer of the Bobbs-Merrill Company and president of the Hallenbeck Press, died suddenly on February 18 at his home in Indianapolis. He was born in that city on February 15, 1861. After graduating from Wabash College in 1892, he entered the publishing business founded by his grandfather, Samuel Merrill, in 1838. For a number of years Mr. Merrill held the position of book editor with his firm, Bowen-Merrill Co., afterwards the Bobbs-Merrill Company. He was a close student of literature, especially during the later years of his life, as well as a keen observer of current events. He is survived by his widow, a brother and a sister, and both his parents, who reside at Long Beach, California.

–*Publishers' Weekly,* 97 (6 March 1920): 687

* * *

This obituary for Charles D. Meigs overlooks his place in the company's genealogy prior to the Bowen-Merrill period.

Funeral services for Charles D. Meigs, age seventy-three, who died of heart disease early today, will be held Saturday at 2:30 p. m. at the home, 2243 Central avenue. Burial will be private at Crown Hill cemetery.

Mr. Meigs was born in Philadelphia, but had lived in Indianapolis for more than fifty years, during which time he was associated with publishing houses, being senior member for the last ten years of the Meigs Publishing Company with offices in the Occidental building. This company issues Sunday school and church literature. Mr. Meigs had been ill for more than a year.

A widow, one sister, Miss Sara T. Meigs, and an adopted daughter, Miss Florence Hubbard, survive.

Mr. Meigs came to Indianapolis in 1868 and was bookkeeper for the Merrill bookstore, later becoming commercial traveler and manager of the law department. He afterward became one of the partners of the Bowen-Merrill Company and finally sold his interest to W. C. Bobbs, of Bobbs-Merrill Company. He then engaged in Christian work, was for many years a member of the executive committee of the International Sunday School Association, state superintendent of the Indiana Sunday School Association. He was a member of the Tabernacle Presbyterian church and chaplain of the Indiana Gideons. He was married in 1873 to Anna L. Allen, daughter of the Rev. Archibald C. and Elizabeth Allen.

–"Charles D. Meigs, 73, Dies of Heart Disease," *Indianapolis News,* 13 May 1920, p. 35

Bobbs-Merrill: 1921–1930

1921

19 July — D. Laurance Chambers becomes vice president of the firm, and Julian Bobbs is officially named treasurer.

September — George H. Betts becomes editor in chief of the educational department.

9 November — *Orphant Annie Story Book,* written and illustrated by Johnny Gruelle, is published. It is Gruelle's first Bobbs-Merrill book; the company will acquire the rights to his Raggedy Ann series in 1960.

Front wrapper for the pamphlet that was published in 1923 as a souvenir for the dinner commemorating John J. Curtis's fifty years with the company (Indiana State Library)

1922

Thomas R. Coward joins the firm as the eastern representative.

21 March — Kenneth L. Roberts's first Bobbs-Merrill book, *Why Europe Leaves Home,* is published.

5 December — At a special meeting of the board of directors, the New York office staff is reduced.

19 December — President William C. Bobbs reports to the board the sale of the company's property at 18 East Vermont Street, Indianapolis, to Marion County. Bobbs-Merrill will rent the building until the area is needed for War Memorial Plaza.

1923

The first of the Bobbs-Merrill Readers, edited by Clara Belle Baker, Edna Dean Baker, and Betts, is published. (No copyright record exists.)

1 May — The directors vote $200 to the Bobbs-Merrill Girls Club to assist the group in establishing a summer camp.

31 August — A dinner is held in Indianapolis to celebrate John J. Curtis's fifty years with the firm. The pamphlet *The Hoosier House* is a souvenir of the occasion.

15 September — *Sinners in Heaven,* by Clive Arden (pen name of Lily Clive Nutt), is published. Payments for movie rights to this book and Arden's *Enticement* (1924) are the highest to this time.

21 November — Albert E. Wiggam's *The New Decalogue of Science* is published; it becomes the number-nine nonfiction best-seller of 1924.

18 December — James A. McCann is hired as sales manager of the trade department.

1924

3 September — Samuel Merrill Jr. dies in Long Beach, California, at age ninety-three.

1 December — Bobbs-Merrill Book Week is held in Indianapolis.

1925

In this year in which three "super-sellers" are published, Ross Baker joins the firm.

16 March — Earl Derr Biggers's first Charlie Chan novel, *The House without a Key,* is published.

20 April — Bruce Barton's first Bobbs-Merrill book, *The Man Nobody Knows: A Discovery of Jesus,* is published and becomes the number-four nonfiction best-seller of the year; it is the top-selling nonfiction title of 1926. The book will sell 728,000 copies in forty years. Barton is the son of clergyman William E. Barton, a Bobbs-Merrill author, whose *The Life of Abraham Lincoln* came out in March.

15 September — Hewitt H. Howland formally resigns to assume the editorship of *Century* magazine. Chambers succeeds Howland as editor of the trade department.

12 October — Richard Halliburton's first book, *The Royal Road to Romance,* is published. It becomes the number-seven nonfiction best-seller of 1927 and will sell 795,000 hardback copies by 1975.

23 October — John Erskine's first Bobbs-Merrill book, *The Private Life of Helen of Troy,* is published, becoming the number-one fiction best-seller of 1926. By 1975, 844,000 hardback copies will have been sold.

1926

Owing largely to the Bruce Barton, Erskine, and Halliburton books of the previous year (selling 190,000 copies in 1926 alone), trade receipts double and profits triple.

11 February — William C. Bobbs dies. Until 1929 a majority of the company stock is held by his widow, Ruth, and son, Julian.

8 April — John Barrymore's *Confessions of an Actor* is published.

2 July — Bruce Barton's *The Book Nobody Knows* is published and becomes the number-seven nonfiction best-seller of the year. By 1939 it sells 139,000 copies.

27 July — Curtis succeeds William C. Bobbs as president.

31 August	The company begins the move from University Square, renting 724–730 North Meridian Street (the Parrott Building).
10 September	Biggers's *The Chinese Parrot* is published; it will eventually sell more than eight hundred thousand copies.

1927

22 February	Jessica Brown (later Mannon) joins the firm for $20 a week; she becomes an editorial assistant in 1931.
9 March	Julia Peterkin's first novel, *Black April,* is published.
16 March	C. S. Forester's first Bobbs-Merrill book, *Love Lies Dreaming,* is published.
27 May	Halliburton's *The Glorious Adventure* is published and becomes the number-eight nonfiction best-seller for the year.
19 July	The board grants Chambers $6,500 "for the 1,000,000$^{\underline{oo}}$ record business of the Trade Department" during the fiscal year.
7 October	Robert Nathan's first Bobbs-Merrill novel, *The Woodcutter's House,* is published.
December	Coward and Indianapolis sales manager James A. McCann, having left Bobbs-Merrill, announce the formation of their own publishing company, Coward-McCann. Coward is succeeded in New York by George J. Shively; hired 20 October, he serves as the eastern representative until 1934.

Thomas R. Coward and James A. McCann, who left Bobbs-Merrill in 1927 to form Coward-McCann, photographed in 1938 (Bruccoli Clark Layman Archives)

1928

1 March	Lowe Berger joins the educational department.
2 March	The first volume in Howard Odum's Black Ulysses trilogy, *Rainbow Round My Shoulder,* is published; it is his first Bobbs-Merrill book.
21 March	*Letters from Joseph Conrad, 1895–1924,* edited by Edward Garnett, is published.
19 October	Peterkin's *Scarlet Sister Mary* is published. It becomes the number-nine fiction best-seller of 1929, and Peterkin wins the Pulitzer Prize in fiction for that year. The novel will eventually sell more than a million hardbound copies.

1929

5–7, 22 June	At meetings of the directors and stockholders, the company is reorganized. The stock–formerly three thousand shares, now thirty thousand–is to be sold publicly. Julian Bobbs leaves the firm; the Bobbs family no longer owns shares. Charles C. Kryter takes the new post of vice president in charge of law sales, and Robert L. Moorhead is elected secretary-treasurer. Chambers, John R. Carr, the Kryter family, and Moorhead together own almost half the stock.
14 June	Asher L. Cornelius's *The Cross-Examination of Witnesses* is published; threats of a libel suit arise because the book includes an account of a murder trial involving a conviction that was later overturned.
16 October	Marquis James's first Bobbs-Merrill book, *The Raven: A Biography of Sam Houston,* is published, and James wins the 1930 Pulitzer Prize in biography.

1930

29 March	Lord David Cecil's first Bobbs-Merrill book, *The Stricken Deer,* is published. The biography of William Cowper brings Cecil the 1930 Hawthornden Prize. (He won the James Tait Black Memorial Prize in biography the previous year when *The Stricken Deer* was first published in England.)
25 August	Walter J. Hurley is hired for the New York office.
15 October	Elmer Davis's first Bobbs-Merrill book, *Morals for Moderns,* is published.

Replacing the Child Classics: Letters from George H. Betts to John R. Carr, 1921–1922

George H. Betts, at this time a professor of education at the University of Southern California, was the new editor in chief of Bobbs-Merrill's educational department, a part-time position. He immediately set about looking for a replacement for the Child Classics series by Grace and Georgia Alexander. Eventually the sisters Clara Belle Baker and Edna Dean Baker, collaborating with Betts, produced the Bobbs-Merrill Readers, starting in 1923. Less controversial by design than the prior series, those available were evidently adopted by the State of Indiana in 1924, and sales reached nearly three million copies by 1931.

George H. Betts to John R. Carr, 5 November 1921

Dear Mr. Carr:

I have been thinking between spells about that set of readers which we have in project. So far as I can discover there will not be any authorship help for either reading or language in this immediate vicinity. It may be that I have overlooked talent in my hasty review of the field, but I have not yet discovered any.

The immediate question in my mind now is whether it would be desirable to name the series under some attractive general title, not using either the name of the publisher or of the author, or authors. If this plan were adopted do you think it would then be especially necessary to publish the same authors' names throughout the series for all books especially if an editorial designation was shown on the title page for the whole series?

My own impression is that it is rather doubtful whether it will be possible to find any one person equally skilled throughout the whole range of the readers. Would we not likely find the beginner and primary ability among those highly trained in this field and the elementary grade ability developed among those who specialize in that particular phase? So far as the seventh and eighth grade volumes are concerned it is possible that these could be compiled under my own direction without bothering much about any author to put much time on these two volumes.

You will remember that I had called to your attention last spring Miss Edna Dean Baker and Miss Clara Belle Baker, the former being the president of the National Kindergarten and Elementary College and the other, professor of the elementary curriculum in that institution in Chicago. I had talked in a general way with them over such a project, but had not committed myself on the point of their taking up the enterprise. I do not now see any more promising help than they could probably be in the field of the lowest books. I believe that if it meets with your approval I will definitely raise with them the question of relationship for the first volumes at least without going beyond that at present. I shall be glad to have you write me exactly how you feel about the whole question remembering that I have no specially preconceived notions that must be regarded.

Sincerely,
Geo. H. Betts

* * *

Betts to Carr, 6 January 1922

Dear Mr. Carr:

I think I am going to be able to arrange with the Bakers to join on the Reader project. The only question that is seemingly pending at present is this: They say, and rightly I think, that the services of an illustrator will be necessary in certain of the earlier books and they want to know whether the publishers will see to that expense or whether it will be thrown back on the authors. They seem to feel that the royalties are pretty low and that the authors should not be expected to pay out money for illustration nor possibly for permissions to print copyright material which might be included. Will you kindly write me on this point?

Also, have you and your field men any directions or suggestions of requirements that should enter into the production of these volumes; especially for the first six grades? I think I know your feeling about the seventh and eighth books sufficiently without your troubling with that point again. I have just written Miss Baker a letter in which I

Up To The Minute Text Books

FOR

ELEMENTARY GRADES

BENSON & BETTS' AGRICULTURE—The only text built around the boys' and girls' club idea. 1921 copyright.

Lapp's ELEMENTS OF CIVICS—Teaches patriotism through practice. An extensively used book. 1922 copyright.

Emerson & Betts' HYGIENE & HEALTH series—Their use means a healthy and happy childhood. 1922 copyright.

O'Shea, Holbrook, Cook EVERYDAY SPELLER series—The most effective and economic spelling text in the market.

FAMOUS AMERICANS by Uhrbrock & Owens—A history for fifth grade—A most interesting and teachable text. 1922 edition.

A complete line of commercial texts, reference books, teachers books, library and reading circle books.

Send for complete catalog

THE BOBBS-MERRILL COMPANY Indianapolis, Indiana

Advertisement for educational-department titles from the 22 July 1922 issue of Publishers' Weekly

included the following paragraph dealing with the Reader point of view:

"My own thought is that we want to produce a distinctive series with points of excellence sufficiently marked to attract attention and be beyond controversy. On the other hand we shall have to keep in mind the psychology of school boards, superintendents and other officials. We must have a sufficient ground work of that which is familiar and known to them so that we shall not be classed as faddists and turned down as 'brilliant but eccentric'. It will be somewhat of a guide for us to have in mind that our series is meant to be a basic set of reading texts and that this series will likely be supplemented by various special texts. Indeed we might ourselves later produce special volumes if we choose, but the basic series should I suppose cover a considerable range of materials suited to the various ages in place of specializing heavily in any one particular line in a given text. It is entirely possible that the earlier texts at least should have a teachers' manual to accompany them showing in a simple fashion the general pedagogy of reading while treating more specifically the presentation of the particular volumes of our series. That is a question that will need to be considered".

Will you let me know whether I am on the right track from the point of view of meeting the demands of school boards, superintendents and teachers as you come in practical contact with them?

Miss Baker has promised, if the arrangements can be satisfactorily made for them to take part, that they will have gathered a considerable body of material ready. *[The remainder of the letter is missing.]*

* * *

Working Conditions, 1923

BOBBS-MERRILL CO.

"We contribute liberally to the summer home for the girls in our employ. It is known as the 'Bobbs-Merrilly Inn,' five miles out of town, where life is ideal for its members and living costs very low."

–John A. Holden, "Welfare Work in Publishing Houses: Twenty Firms Tell of Their Various Cooperative Plans," *Publishers' Weekly,* 104 (4 August 1923): 431

Vox Populi: Correspondence with Harriet Clarke, 1924

The company answered, and saved, letters from readers who took the trouble to comment on Bobbs-Merrill books. The Innocents *(1924) was a novel by Henry K. Webster. Winifred S. Stoner wrote* Natural Education *(1914), a contribution to the Childhood and Youth series that failed to sell well; her daughter, also named Winifred, was the author of* Facts in Jingles *(1915), "written between the ages of five and twelve." Albert Wiggam's 1923 nonfiction title* The New Decalogue of Science *was a best-seller in 1924.*

Harriet Clarke to Bobbs-Merrill, 21 September 1924

Dear Sir:

Many years ago when I read "When Knighthood was in Flower["] I came to the conclusion that you were publishers of LIVE LITERATURE and ever since I have been reading your novels with pleasure–until I read your latest INNOCENTS–to me the most unintereasting [*sic*] book that you h[a]ve published. It does not teach a moral so it cannot even find interest in a Sabbath School. It is not my custom to criticize I am only wondering WHY.

In 1914 you published your masterpiece as regards interesting educational matter–in NATURAL EDUCATION. I have been using this book and FACTS IN JINGLES in teaching kiddies for many years. No juvenile book as yet published can compare with Facts IN JINGLES as a book that interests both big and little folks. My music pupils love the jingles about lives of musicians and if you would circularize music teachers I know that every one would feel as I do. Recently since Esperanto have become so popular I have wondered why you did not advertise this book as a help t[o] every listener in. I use it also to teach lessons in religion-NEATH NIAGARA FALLS a great lesson.

Yesterday I was invited to take lunch with a literary frien[d] at National Arts Club and ther[e] I saw Winifred Stoner having a lunch party with Edwin Markham, George Grey Barnard and a number of other noted people. I had heard Miss Stoner previously lecturing in various places and enjoyed her but it was a treat to LISTEN IN at this particular party and the thought came "WHY does not Winifred Stoner write a book on her ideas of real education, quoting opinions of all the celebrities she knows.["] I am sure everyone would read the book.

After lunch I sought the young author and made the suggestion, she laughed and said that publishers published books to sell and educational books do not sell. She said that she had just sold a story to Gloria Swanson's manager for which she received more money than her mother had received for all the educational stuff she had written. Edwin Markham agreed with her but Mr. Barnard, Mrs. David C. Cook of Elhgin [*sic*] and others seemed to think that it is sad that this youn[g] lady will not stick to the work her mother has begun. I am wondering if she would be interested if you would write a letter to her suggesting the writing of a book such as I suggest.

A badly written plea by
Mrs. Harriet Clarke

Your greatest recent book is that of Professor Wiggam. I predict that Natural Education and the Wiggam book will live for all time. They are needed.

* * *

Hewitt H. Howland to Clarke, 25 September 1924

My dear Mrs. Clarke:

Thank you very much for your friendly and interesting letter. We are in correspondence now with Winifred Stoner though not about a book on education. She has mentioned the subject but nothing definite has been done. I am glad to know that you think such a book would sell. Her mother's remarkable NATURAL EDUCATION was financially very disappointing, as are most of the books addressed to parents. Strange isn't it? But we shall not forget your suggestion.

I am sorry you found THE INNOCENTS such dull reading. I confess you are not alone in this feeling, though on the other hand we got many letters praising the book, particularly from child psychologists.

Your praise of THE NEW DECALOGUE OF SCIENCE pleases us greatly. The book has been a wonderful success and undoubtedly exerted wide influence. We shall shortly publish Wiggam's new book THE FRUIT OF THE FAMILY TREE, which I believe you will like fully as much as you do the first.

With many thanks for your interest and courtesy I am

Sincerely yours,
[Hewitt H. Howland]

* * *

Remington Schuyler dust jacket for a 1924 novel of the California gold rush (courtesy of Michael Manz/Babylon Revisited)

Another Innovation

An innovation in the book publishing business was started out in Indianapolis, Dec. 1, when the Bobbs-Merrill Company had a Bobbs-Merrill Book Week. With not an anti-Week person cheeping, the affair was hugely sucessful [*sic*]. Not that every shopper that boarded a homeward-bound car had two or three books under his arm, but Indianapolis became more than ever aware of the Hoosier publishing house in her midst.

The bookstores and book sections of department stores were the drum-majors of the occasion, marshalling their rows of books, their originals of illustrations, photographs of authors, autographed books and original manuscripts into displays aimed to bring to attention the glances of passers-by.

A miscellany of other than bookselling firms joined the ranks and displayed Bobbs-Merrill books in their windows, phalanxed by posters bearing astounding, tho true, phrases:

"More than a million books a year bear the name and fame of Indiana into every corner of the world."

"The name of Hoosier is a title of pride because of the poems of James Whitcomb Riley."

"The whole world reads the books that Hoosiers write and Hoosiers publish."

One of the most interesting windows was arranged by the Indianapolis Bell Telephone Company which for the first time gave its coveted space to an outside firm. This display showed the process in the making of a book from manuscript from [*sic*] a bound copy. The manuscript of Herbert Quick's new novel, "The Invisible Woman," was exhibit A, with the successive stages concretely illustrated by different forms of proof and plates in various degrees of completeness. Books from the law, educational and general departments of the house were scattered in front of background posters bearing pictures of the interior of the Bobbs-Merrill building.

Newspapers carried editorials, features and illustrated articles on the history of the firm and flattering messages of appreciation from Meredith Nicholson, George Ade and John T. McCutcheon. It was related over again how William C. Bobbs, president, secured Riley's first volume of verse, back in 1885 when the company put on its "literary overalls," as Riley said, and how John J. Curtis became one of the leading men in the publishing world by launching "When Knighthood Was in Flower" with a program of nation-wide advertising of a revolutionary character that had never before been attempted and later by putting around Bobbs-Merrill books the first colored jacket ever made.

–"Bobbs-Merrill Has Its Own Book Week," *Publishers' Weekly,* 106 (13 December 1924): 1875

* * *

D. Laurance Chambers Replaces Howland

Contrary to this account of Howland's brilliant career with Bobbs-Merrill, the company had not published a book by Booth Tarkington. This error is found in many accounts, like the myth of the 1838 founding.

Hewitt Hanson Howland, for nearly twenty-five years editor and literary adviser of the Bobbs-Merrill Company, Indianapolis publishers, will become editor of the Century magazine on Oct. 1, succeeding Glenn Frank, who went to Madison, Wis., this week to assume his new duties as president of the University of Wisconsin.

Announcement of the selection of Mr. Howland was authorized by the Century Company at New York yesterday. He expects to take up his residence in that city within two weeks.

The editorship of the Century has long been regarded as carrying with it a peculiar distinction and authority in current American letters. Richard Watson Gilder and Robert Underwood Johnson, the latter an Indianian, were among the earlier editors of the magazine. Friends of Mr. Howland, who learned of his selection yesterday, were unanimous in looking upon it as a high tribute to his personal ability and a merited compliment to his influential part in the literary history of Indiana in the last quarter century.

Happy Over Advancement.

Associates of Mr. Howland at the Bobbs-Merrill Company expressed regret at seeing him leave, but were happy over his advancement to one of the most conspicuous magazine editorships in the country.

"Hewitt Howland has been a member of our organization for nearly twenty-five years," said W. C. Bobbs, president of the company. "In that time he has encouraged many young writers and helped in the development of some of the most popular authors on our list. He has had a very large share in putting forward many best sellers and he enjoys in a marked degree the confidence and respect of a wide circle of literary men and women, not only in America but in England as well. [. . .]

"He goes to his new position with the cordial good wishes of every officer and associate employe in the publishing house and with our sincere and confident expectation that he will make a complete success in it."

Century Announcement.

In its announcement the Century company says in part: [. . .]

"He joined the Bobbs-Merrill Company shortly after the Indiana firm entered the miscellaneous publishing field, with its first success, 'When Knighthood Was In Flower.' Since then he has had a part in all the firm's activities, and, as editor in chief, has passed on thousands of manuscripts, edited many books and met and corresponded with most of the famous writing people of the day.

"As a young man he knew well the first editors of the Century, Richard Watson Gilder and Robert Underwood Johnson, also an Indianian. He recalls with pride that they made overtures for his services, but Mr. Bobbs, to whom they talked, asked them to 'leave him alone.'

"Mr. Howland brings to his new work long experience in every branch of his profession and an exceptionally wide acquaintance with authors in this country and in England."

Philadelphia Appraisal.

The announcement concludes with the following appraisal of Mr. Howland from an issue of the Philadelphia Book News of several years ago:

"He is a unique example of a man without college training or newspaper experience occupying a marked position in the literary world–a position earned by the possession of a genius for literary values that seems almost intuitive, combined with a culture that is fundamental. To these are added charm of manner and a gift for letter writing, the whole superimposed on a vast capacity for hard work."

Mr. Howland, a son of John D. Howland, who in his life was prominent as a lawyer and judge in Indianapolis and Indiana, was born Oct. 8, 1863, and was educated in the elementary schools of the city and in the Indianapolis Classical school, conducted by Theodore L. Sewall. His first employment was in the Yohn book store, on Washington street near Meridian. Then he went for a tour of several European countries and after returning to Indianapolis became a clerk in the freight office of the Monon railroad, rising to chief claim clerk. His next venture was as a merchandise broker, in an office on South Meridian street next to the present Chamber of Commerce building.

While a broker he became a part-time reader of manuscripts for the Bobbs-Merrill Company, and his ability and judgment of literary values was such that Mr. Bobbs persuaded him first to give half his time to the company, and then to relinquish his brokerage business and devote all his time to editorial duties for the company.

Finds Many Writers.

In his long connection with the Bobbs-Merrill Company, Mr. Howland has come into close association with hundreds of writers of America and Europe. He was an intimate of James Whitcomb Riley for many years. Two of Riley's books of verse carry his name on the title page. He had close acquaintance with Henry James and James Lane Allen, and among his friends of today are such writers as Booth Tarkington, Meredith Nicholson, Alexander Black, George Ade, Janet Fairbanks and George Barr McCutcheon. He passed the judgment that gave to the public the first books of Tarkington, Brand Whitlock and Gene Stratton-Porter. Mary Roberts Rinehart gives him credit for having "found her."

"It is a terrible wrench to leave after having spent all my days in Indianapolis," said Mr. Howland. "It hurts to leave old friends, yet there will be some friends in New York."

Mr. Howland is a charter member of the Indianapolis Dramatic Club. He is a member also of the University Club of Indianapolis and the Players Club of New York.

–"Indianapolis Man Selected to Edit Century Magazine," *Indianapolis Star,* 4 September 1925, p. 14

* * *

D. L. Chambers, vice-president of the Bobbs-Merrill Company, has been appointed editor-in-chief of the company, responsible for the acceptance of manuscripts for publication, W. C. Bobbs, president, announced Thursday. He succeeds Hewitt H. Howland, who recently became editor of the Century Magazine.

Charles D. LaFollette, formerly assistant dean of the School of Business Administration of Harvard University, has been appointed assistant to Chambers.

The work Mr. Howland did in the New York office of the company, keeping in touch with authors and the literary market, has been assigned to two members of the company's New York staff, Maxwell Aley, a son of Dr. Robert J. Aley, president of Butler University, and Thomas R. Coward, on the staff of the Yale University Press before coming to the Bobbs-Merrill Company three years ago.

Chambers, a graduate of Princeton University in 1900, was secretary to Dr. Henry Van Dyke, professor of English at Princeton and later American ambassador to the Netherlands. Chambers was assistant to the managing editor of the Ladies Home Journal preceding his alliance with the Bobbs-Merrill Company as assistant to the president in 1903. In 1907 he was made a member of the firm and in 1921 he was elected vice-president. He is vice-president and a director of the National Association of Book Publishers.

Chambers is a son-in-law of Thomas Taggart.

–"Chambers Becomes Bobbs-Merrill Editor," *Indianapolis News,* 3 December 1925, p. 28

* * *

The Death of Bobbs

If the traditional year of his entering the firm is correct, then it must have been Merrill, Hubbard, and Company that William C. Bobbs joined after high school. He became president not in 1895, one of the erroneous dates that became part of company lore, but in 1899 or 1900.

William C. Bobbs, 65 years old, president of the Bobbs-Merrill Company, one of the country's leading publishing houses, close friend of many American writers, vice president of the Riley Memorial Association and for many years associated with the business and social life of Indianapolis, died suddenly at the family home, 1610 North Delaware street, yesterday afternoon of heart disease. [. . .]

Riley's Close Friend.

Mr. Bobbs probably was one of the best known of American publishers, and it was during the years that he served as president of the publishing house that bore his name that almost four score Indiana authors attained fame, and reached the pinnacle in the literary world. He was a close personal friend of James Whitcomb Riley, the "Hoosier Poet," and the Bobbs-Merrill firm now holds the publishing rights on all of Riley's works. [. . .]

High Publishing Position.

Probably no other man in Indiana or the middle West occupied the place in the publishing field that Mr. Bobbs held, and few in the country attained such a position. He is credited with being the man who popularized the popular novel, departing from the old custom of publishers in advertising their publications, and adopted the method of marketing a novel much the same as the modern merchant markets his wares.

First works of many Indiana authors, now famous, were published by the Bobbs-Merrill Company. To this house belonged the distinction of publishing the works of such authors as Riley, Gene Stratton-Porter, Mrs. Mary Hartwell Catherwood, Charles Major, author of "When Knighthood Was in Flower," Maurice Thompson, author of "Alice of Old Vincennes," John T. McCutcheon, Meredith Nicholson of Indianapolis, Albert Edward Wiggam, George Ade of Brook, Miss Anna Nicholas of Indianapolis and many others.

It was during his presidency that the idea was developed of making the Bobbs-Merrill firm a general publishing house. Prior to that time it had been devoted almost entirely to the publication of law books and works on law, but after the advent of Mr. Bobbs as president the firm's attention was turned to general publication and it was through this action that an outlet was provided for Hoosier authors for their works. [. . .]

After leaving the public school, and during that time, he was a newsboy. He became a messenger for Merrill-Meigs & Co., booksellers, located then on the north side of Washington street, between Meridian and Illinois streets, entering their employ in 1879. He grew up in the publishing business, soon after his employment becoming a traveling salesman for the law books published by the firm. In this connection he became acquainted with lawyers of the territory he covered. Soon afterward he was made manager of the law book department.

Shortly afterward the name of the firm was changed to the Bowen-Merrill Company and Mr. Bobbs soon became a director in the firm in 1890. Mr. Bowen retired from the firm, and Mr. Bobbs became president, holding that position until his death. One year after he became president, and over the objection of Mr. Bobbs, the name of the firm was changed to Bobbs-Merrill Company. Charles Merrill, the other partner, died about five years ago. Mr. Bobbs has been president since 1895. [. . .]

Mr. Bobbs's Chief Interest.

Outside the Riley hospital movement, Mr. Bobbs's chief interest was in his publishing work, and in the welfare of those who worked for him. The Bobbs-Merrill Company was one of the first organizations in Indianapolis to establish the Saturday afternoon half-holiday, and under his direction a bonus system for employes was instituted in the firm. He was a devotee of exercise, and often walked from his office to his home, having taken this exercise the evening he became ill and was forced to his bed.

He was always at the front line in literary movements, and was one of the promoters of Book week, the second of which was held in Indianapolis Nov. 28 to Dec. 5, 1925. Bobbs-Merrill books are used nationally, and are known practically to every school pupil, through the publication of text books and works of Riley and other authors.

Describes Firm's Aim.

Mr. Bobb's [*sic*] interest in the publishing world and the interest of his firm in the work is described in an interview with a representative of The Star, published Nov. 30, 1924, during Book week of that year.

Discussing the advent of the firm into the general publishing business, a departure from the law book publication work, Mr. Bobbs said:

"Like most business, we had an aim. Ours was to give people good, clean fiction and corking good tales.

ESTABLISHED 1838
THE BOBBS-MERRILL COMPANY
PUBLISHERS···INDIANAPOLIS

March 26th, 1930.

D. L. CHAMBERS
VICE PRESIDENT

Dear Mr. Barrymore:-

Your kind letter of the 14th is found on my desk on my return from a business trip.

The remaining stock of CONFESSIONS OF AN ACTOR would have to be sold at or less than the cost of manufacture and so there would be no royalty payable. The sales of the book at the regular list price have now reached the disappearing point and you will understand that there is pressure brought on us from our auditors to reduce our inventory on all such items. If you would prefer to buy the plates and stock at cost of manufacture as provided in the contract we shall be glad to give you the cost figures.

Please do—as you wish about this.

no thanks

I enclose a statement of your account showing the sum of $1287.00 unliquidated by royalties from the advancements made to you.

Awaiting your further advice I am, with kind regards

Sincerely yours,

DLC-S

D L Chambers

John Barrymore, Esq.,
Box 694,
Beverly Hills, California.

Actor John Barrymore's 1926 book was not a success, as this letter to him from D. Laurance Chambers indicates (courtesy of The Lilly Library, Indiana University, Bloomington, Indiana).

That is one of the outstanding points of our reputation and we are keeping to it. In this day that is an exacting aim, but a worthy one.

"This year (1924) we published a single edition of a law book, whose total cost exceeded the cost of the erection of this building. The education department shipped thirty carloads of text books to all parts of the United States this fall. All this, strange as it may sound, brings glory back to Indiana." [. . .]

–"W. C. Bobbs, 65, Publisher, Dies at Home Here," *Indianapolis Star,* 12 February 1926, pp. 1, 7

* * *

[. . .] Booth Tarkington, author: "The significant life of a city is not in its size but in its beauty and cleanliness and in the culture of its citizens. Most of all, a city's significance is in that culture and nowhere has the culture of Indianapolis found a better expression than in the publishing house known as the Bobbs-Merrill Company. It is an old house, founded when our oldest citizens were young men, but the genius of William C. Bobbs made it more than a Hoosier establishment; he made it an institution of national importance, and it stands now a monument to his intelligence, his energy and his faith.

Everything for Good.

"It is a public work, in which we all have taken pride, but it is not his only public work. During his whole honorable lifetime his hand had been in everything that was for the public good. Genial and loyal friend, tireless in all charitable and patriotic causes, builder of the best fame that a city can enjoy, we have not his like among us to take his place." [. . .]

–"Friends Unite in Paying Tributes to Memory of William C. Bobbs," *Indianapolis Star,* 12 February 1926, p. 1

* * *

"Century Editor Laments Death"

NEW YORK, Feb. 11.–The shock is too great for me to pay in formal words a just tribute to my old friend and long partner, W. C. Bobbs. His place in the publishing world and in the community to which he gave so splendidly is fixed for all time, high and unalterable. His loss to both is beyond estimate. As for myself, our intimate association for more than a quarter of a century must speak for me now. I am too deeply grieved.

–Howland, *Indianapolis Star,* 12 February 1926, p. 1

William C. Bobbs in his office, holding a copy of Maude Radford Warren's 1923 novel The House of Youth *(*Indianapolis Times *Collection/Tiffany Studio)*

Carr to Betts, 15 February 1926

Dear Dr. Betts:–

Of course by this time you have heard of Mr. Bobbs' death. It was unexpected to us and to his family. His loss is a very personal one to me. However, he left the business in such good condition, so thoroughly organised to the last detail, that I am sure it will go on exactly as it has been going on in the past. There will be no change in the plans of the educational department at least. [. . .]

Sincerely yours,
[John R. Carr]

* * *

Publishers' Weekly Remembers

[. . .] Beside the development of the sale and reputation of Riley, the firm made publishing history by its dramatic entrance into the field of book promotion and advertising. It was John J. Curtis who first suggested to his partners that a popular story might be sold by widespread newspaper advertising, thus creating direct demand in the stores. This was a form of promotion then unheard of. There was little or no advertising of books in newspapers, and the size of the display copy proposed had no precedent. They found a volume suitable to their purpose, Charles Major's "When Knighthood Was in Flower," and the success of this campaign was beyond all expectation. They did not allow this one success to satisfy their ardor, and the campaign was followed by the famous promotion campaigns of "Alice of Old Vincennes," by Maurice Thompson, of "Lazarre" by Mary Hartwell Catherwood, of "The Man on the Box" by Harold McGrath [*sic*], of "The House of A Thousand Candles" by Meredith Nicholson, and of "The Circular Staircase" by Mary Roberts Rinehart, in every case books by then unknown authors, promoted to a notable sale thru every part of the country and even in stores that heretofore had not considered books within their province. This energetic work, for which Mr. Bobbs and Mr. Curtis were largely responsible, changed the whole method of book distribution in the country, and publicity of this kind for titles of popular appeal has now become a commonplace in bookselling.

Of late years, the firm has broadened the character of its publications and has notable successes in the field of biography, science and general literature as well as continued emphasis on fiction.

An important law business was developed, and in 1899 the firm took over the law book list of Houghton Mifflin Company as well as a hundred and twenty-five volumes from the American Publishers Company of Norwalk, Ohio. An educational department has also been part of the program, including such popular series as *Child Classic Readers* by Georgia and Grace Alexander, and the series of books on pedagogy by Dr. M. V. O'Shea of the University of Wisconsin. [. . .]

–"William C. Bobbs, 1861–1926," *Publishers' Weekly,* 109 (20 February 1926): 605–606

* * *

Building at 724–730 North Meridian Street, Indianapolis, which served as company headquarters from 1926 to 1958 (Indianapolis Times *Collection/Tiffany Studio)*

The Move North

After September 1st the Bobbs-Merrill Co. will be located at 724 North Meridian Street, Indianapolis, just a short distance from their present location on East Vermont Street. The state of Indiana, in developing the big war memorial, has taken over the property on which their fine building was located, and the great architectural structure which is the center of the memorial is already rising directly behind the Vermont Street building. They have been fortunate in obtaining a very suitable building which was designed by Herbert M. Foltz, one of Indiana's leading architects. The building is two stories high, but covers so much ground area that they will have more space than before and the location faces the Memorial Plaza, where important public buildings are being erected.

–"New Bobbs-Merrill Building," *Publishers' Weekly,* 109 (12 June 1926): 1919

* * *

The Ascent of Curtis

The correct date of the board meeting at which John Curtis became president is 27 July 1926. As Chambers wrote to author Richard Halliburton on 20 August, "He is the only surviving member of the original Bobbs-Merrill partnership, and his election was quite the obvious thing."

Since the death of William C. Bobbs, in February, the Bobbs-Merrill Company has been without a president, the publishers having waited until the annual directors' meeting before making the selection. On July 26, the board elected J. J. Curtis, one of the three original organizers of the company and long a prominent figure in the book-publishing world. He has been associated with the company for fifty-three years. Mr. Curtis is a Hoosier and lived in Indianapolis for many years. Since 1920 he has lived in Hollywood, California, where he was in charge of the West Coast office, selling the motion picture rights to the novels published by his company.

Mr. Curtis has been known chiefly for his radical departures from merchandising policies. He was the first publisher to adopt colored jackets for books. His original methods of advertising attracted wide attention to the Bobbs-Merrill Company. Shelving the out-worn idea of advertising a number of books together, he began to concentrate on one title at a time, featuring the book–an idea that has since grown to enormous proportions. He believes books to be merchandise and proceeds to sell them as such.

Mr. Curtis proved his theories with two outstanding achievements that broke all records, the exploitation of "When Knighthood was in Flower," whose title was changed by Mr. Curtis from its original innocuous name, and "Alice of Old Vincennes." Due principally to the methods of advertising and marketing, both novels had spectacular sales and established a precedent and a reputation that a quarter of a century of publishing has served only to intensify and augment.

The new president is the only surviving member of a partnership formed years ago. He will spend much of his time in Indianapolis. It is understood that he contemplates no changes in policy or personnel.

The stock of William C. Bobbs was inherited by his widow, Ruth Pratt Bobbs, a well-known portrait painter, and by his son, Julian Bobbs, who was re-elected treasurer of the company. John R. Carr is head of the Educational Book Department, which has grown to be an important factor. The Law Department, in charge of Charles C. Kryter and Colonel Robert L. Moorhead, serves almost every lawyer in the country. The Department of General Literature, comprised of history, biography, science, fiction and poetry is headed by D. Laurance Chambers, who divides his time between Indianapolis and the office in New York where the books are illustrated and printed.

–"Curtis of Bobbs-Merrill Elected President of Old Indianapolis House," *Publishers' Weekly,* 110 (7 August 1926): 531–532

* * *

Promoting *Buccaneers of the Pacific*

Cash prizes to the amount of $200 are being offered by the Bobbs-Merrill Company for the most attractive window displays of George Wycherley's "Buccaneers of the Pacific." Two prizes, $75.00 and $25.00, for windows six feet in length or less and two prizes of the same amounts for windows six feet in length or more are offered. The judges will be Frederic G. Melcher, editor of the *Publishers' Weekly,* M. A. Corrigan of the Baker & Taylor Company and Charles William Taussig.

The contest opened March second, publication day of "Buccaneers of the Pacific" and will close April twentieth at midnight. Awards will be announced June fifteenth. Awards will be made on the basis of photographs submitted by the contestants. Any cards, quotations or ideas developed by contestants which do not win any prize and which the publishers should like to use in their promotion of the book will be purchased from the contestants at a figure to be determined by individual negotiation in each instance. Two dollars will be paid for each photograph of a window devoted exclusively to the book which does not win a prize.

Further particulars may be had on request from the Bobbs-Merrill Company in Indianapolis.

–"Window Display Contest," *Publishers' Weekly,* 113 (10 March 1928): 1088

* * *

This notice accompanied a photograph of the window display at Brentano's bookstore in New York.

The Bobbs-Merrill Company now announces the winners of the Window Display Contest which it held from March 2nd to April 20th of displays of "Buccaneers Of The Pacific" by George Wycherley.

The prizes were divided into two groups, for windows six feet in length or more, and for windows less than six feet in length. Brentano's, New York City, won the first prize of $75 for the large size window. The Methodist Publishing House, Lamar & Whitmore, Agents, Richmond, Virginia, won the second prize of $25 in this group. In the second group, of windows less than six feet in length, The Stamford Bookstore, Stamford, Connecticut, won the first prize of $75 and Dewitt's Bookstore, Oakland, California, won the second prize of $25.

The Judges of the contest were: Frederic G. Melcher, Editor of *Publishers' Weekly;* M. A. Corrigan, The Baker and Taylor Company; and Charles William Taussig, author.

The awards were made on the basis of photographs submitted by the contestants. The Judges selected as winners those which they judged were the most interesting and attractive and which they believed offered the best selling idea. Many effective and novel ideas were carried out in the window displays. Posters, paintings of ships and pirates, skulls and cross bones, treasure chests, jewels, guns and cutlasses, maps and copies of the book artistically arranged, were all used to carry out the idea of "Buccaneers of the Pacific."

–"The Window Display Contest for 'Buccaneers of the Pacific,'" *Publishers' Weekly,* 113 (30 June 1928): 2611

* * *

Reorganization

Despite the public sale of stock after the withdrawal of the Bobbs family, the "collective" control of the insiders was maintained.

Announcement was made last week of the purchase of stock held by the heirs of William C. Bobbs, one of the founders of the Bobbs-Merrill Company, by four of the other stockholders. The shares of the common voting stock were purchased from Mrs. William C. Bobbs, widow of the late president, and his son, Julian Bobbs, treasurer of the company.

The transaction included the sale of more than 1,500 shares of common stock at $100 par value to the present controlling executives and the issuance of a new series of common stock of no par value on the basis of ten to one of the old series. The Meyer-Kiser Bank and the Fletcher American Company of Indianapolis have offered to the public 14,996 shares of the new series. The capital structure of the Bobbs-Merrill Company now provides for $300,000 worth of 6 per cent preferred stock, of which $223,800 is outstanding, and the new issues of 30,000 shares of no par common stock.

Control of the corporation is now held collectively by D. Laurance Chambers, John R. Carr, Charles C. Kryter and Robert L. Moorehead [*sic*]. John Jay Curtis, who has been with the firm over fifty-five years, was re-elected president; Mr. Carr was named vice-president, chairman of the board of directors and head of the education department; Mr. Chambers was re-elected vice-president and manager of the trade department. Mr. Kryter is vice-president and manager of the law department, and Mr. Moorhead is secretary and treasurer. J. J. Kiser of the Meyer-Kiser Bank, and Wendell Sherk of the Fletcher American Company, are members of the board of directors. [. . .]

There will be no change in the management or business policies of the house, the directors state. The principal officers have entered into contracts whereby they will remain in their present capacities in the company for the next five years at least. [. . .]

William C. Bobbs at the time of his death in 1926, was president of the company. After his death, Mr. Curtis was made president. Mr. Curtis lives in Hollywood, California, where he maintains the west coast office at 1730 Vista Street, managing the motion picture interests of the house. At 185 Madison Avenue in New York City, are the advertising, manufacturing and selling offices of the general trade department. The home office of The Bobbs-Merrill Company is at 724 North Meridian Street, Indianapolis, Indiana.

–"Bobbs-Merrill Reorganized," *Publishers' Weekly,* 115 (15 June 1929): 2759

* * *

Dust jacket for the 1929 novel by the author who also published under the pseudonym of Ethel Vance (courtesy of Michael Manz/Babylon Revisited)

Trials of the Law Department: Correspondence with Asher L. Cornelius, 1929

Robert L. Moorhead, the head of the law department, had to intervene in extra-editorial matters. After persuading Asher L. Cornelius that his Cross-Examination of Witnesses *(1929) should be aimed toward lawyers and not a general audience, and after a thousand advance orders had been received, Moorhead was advised that a passage would have to be excised. The murder conviction of Dr. B. Clark Hyde of Kansas City had been overturned, rendering Cornelius's account of his trial libelous, as Hyde's attorney pointed out to Bobbs-Merrill. It proved to be an expensive alteration.*

Robert L. Moorhead to Asher L. Cornelius, 25 June 1929

Dear Mr. Cornelius:

Your letter of June 24th explaining that you secured the Hyde Case from a transcript sent to you from Kansas City attorneys is received.

Upon investigation by our lawyers here we find that this case was reversed in 234 Mo. 200. Our attorneys tell us that there is liability for libel on account of the statement in the first paragraph on Page 408.

Enclosed is a copy of a telegram just received from Frank P. Walsh together with a copy of our response. It is our judgment that you would better go to Kansas City at once and secure an adjustment with Mr. Walsh and Dr. Hyde.

We have by telegraph recalled from the dealers all copies of the book. To destroy these books would entail a large loss which we both want to avoid. The following is suggested for your consideration as a plan for settlement with Dr. Hyde through his attorney–

(1.) That in all books withdrawn from the dealers, that a new page be substituted for Page 408 in which it will state that the case was reversed, re-tried twice, and finally dismissed, and that the matter is given here merely as an example of a well conducted cross-examination.

(2.) That in all future printings and editions of the book that the Hyde Case will be entirely withdrawn, and another case substituted therefor.

It seems to us that you might make this proposal to the parties, and in consideration of our removing the Hyde Case from subsequent printings that they should give to you and to us a full release of all liability in the matter.

To remove the Hyde Case entirely from the books returned is impracticable as a binding possibility. We have already experimented and tried to do this and unless we can correct the present edition by insertion of a page in lieu of the present page 408 it would mean the destruction of the books which would be very costly. Hen[c]e, our suggestion that a modified form of the Hyde Case be allowed to remain in the present printing.

Very truly yours,
[Robert L. Moorhead]
THE BOBBS-MERRILL COMPANY

* * *

In his 25 June letter to Cornelius, Moorhead enclosed a copy of the following telegram of that date from Kansas City, Missouri, lawyer Frank P. Walsh.

AFTER SECURING COPY OF CROSS EXAMINATION OF WITNESSES BY CORNELIUS AND CONSULTATION WITH DR BENNETT CLARK HYDE HE HAS AUTHORIZED ME TO DEMAND THAT YOU IMMEDIATELY RECALL AND SUP-

PRESS THIS BOOK WHICH HE SAYS CONTAINS AND [*sic*] ATROCIOUS AND MALICIOUS LIBEL OF HIM STOP PLEASE WIRE MY EXPENSE 1215 COMMERCE BUILDING KANSASCITY [*sic*] MISSOURI OR DIRECTO [*sic*] TO DR BENNETT CLARK HYDE LEXINGTON MISSOURI WHETHER OR NOT YOU HAVE COMPLIED WITH THIS DEMAND=

FRANK P WALSH.

* * *

Moorhead to Cornelius, 27 June 1929

Dear Mr. Cornelius:

Answering your letter of June 26th, inasmuch as we have notified Mr. Frank P. Walsh that the present printing of CROSS EXAMINATION OF WITNESSES has been withdrawn we do not believe it advisable to ship a copy to Mr. Folsome as requested by you.

One of our newspapers here called on the phone last night to confirm a news item they had from Kansas City that Frank P. Walsh was contemplating libel litigation against us on behalf of his client Dr. Hyde.

It seems to us extremely important that you get in touch with Mr. Walsh at the earliest possible moment. Perhaps it might be well for you to come to Indianapolis enroute [*sic*] to Kansas City.

Very truly yours,
[Robert L. Moorhead]
THE BOBBS-MERRILL COMPANY.

* * *

Cornelius to Bobbs-Merrill, 1 July 1929

WILL FORWARD CORRECTED MATTER IN THE HYDE CASE ALSO COPIES OF CORRESPONDENCE THIS WILL HAVE MY CONTINUOUS ATTENTION UNTIL STRAIGHTENED OUT I SECURED THE TRANSCRIPT IN THE FIRST PLACE FROM FRANK P WALSH OFFICE=

ASHER L CORNELIUS.

* * *

Cornelius to Bobbs-Merrill, 13 July 1929

Gentlemen:–

I received a letter from Frank P. Walsh in New York in regard to the Hyde matter last Monday. He advised me that he was sending you a copy of the enclosure page 408, as revised by him and also a copy of the letter. I assume that you have taken this matter up with him direct and that you are proceeding to follow the lines suggested in my letter to him. If this is the case, I suggest that we communicate with him immediately and ask him to prepare material for inclusion in this chapter for the new edition of the work.

I wish you would advise me of the present status of the matter.

Yours very truly,
Asher L. Cornelius

* * *

A Summing-Up by Curtis

Curtis delivered a speech in California on 24 April 1930, as he was approaching his seventy-fourth and final year. Speaking at the time of the Depression, after the rise of F. Scott Fitzgerald, Ernest Hemingway, and the new realism, Curtis recited the litany of the company's great early successes with historical fiction.

Bobbs-Merrill was organized in 1838. Mr. Merrill often said he he [*sic*] was sorry it wasn't organized a few years earlier because we might then have had Sir Walter Scott on our list.

Along in 1865, my father one day took me by the hand. We walked down the street in Kokomo, Indiana. We went to church. The church was heavily draped in mourning. The preacher gave us an oration. It was "The Death of Abraham."

Going home–I asked my father many questions. He said he would buy me a "Life of Lincoln." That was one of the first books I had. It taught me to love books, and I have loved books ever since.

I finished a short course in college and rolled up my diploma and went down to Indianapolis, to get a job. I saw Mr. Bowen. He said, "I am sorry son. We are full. This is June." "Well," I said, "I want to work in a bookstore. I will work for nothing." So he accepted. He then gave me $6.00 a week.

It was a grand thing in those days, in the '70s, for a young man to get in a bookstore. At that time Dickens was living, and Bulwer Lytton. Wouldn't it be wonderful now to say, "Here is a new book from Charles Dickens–here is a late book from Bulwer Lytton![''] And not only that. We had Longfellow, Tennyson, Whittier, Holmes, Bret Harte, George Eliot. They were all at that time producing books. It was a great thing for a boy to be in a store of that kind. Not only did he meet the best people, but occasionally he met a great author.

In 1880, one day, General Lew Wallace stopped in. He was a pompous old bird, and I hunted around and got a copy of "The Prince of India" and wanted him

TO THE TRADE:

Good times are coming!

The announcement of a new Charlie Chan novel by EARL DERR BIGGERS is gladness for the book world.

SEPTEMBER 15TH is the date. Mark it with a big red circle on your calendar. It stands for good times coming.

CHARLIE CHAN CARRIES ON

is the title--and you'll admit it is a whale of a title.

It keeps up Mr. Biggers' record. It's the best story yet. That's always the way with him, the latest is the best, and each new one outsells its predecessor.

The House Without a Key
The Chinese Parrot
Behind That Curtain
The Black Camel
and now CHARLIE CHAN CARRIES ON

One word betrays the murderer to Charlie. We challenge anybody to spot that word. What will you bet you can find it? If you are as smart as Charlie, you can pat self on back, as he would say.

Of course we shall be behind CHARLIE CHAN CARRIES ON to the limit with advertising, display matter, promotion and publicity, the biggest and best campaign yet.

Good times are coming, with this book that spells entertainment, sells itself, enthralls and delights readers and lifts their thoughts from trouble and days that have been out of joint. Charlie Chan is a national character, an international joy, the favorite of men and women and children the world over.

Price $2.00.

Start taking orders now for CHARLIE CHAN CARRIES ON.

Good times are coming. Carry on!

Cheerfully and Charliechanly yours,

THE BOBBS-MERRILL COMPANY.

D.L.C.-S.

*Announcement drafted by Chambers for the 1930 Charlie Chan novel (*Publishers' Weekly, *30 August 1930)*

to autograph it. He took it and he wrote in "Someone has asked me to autograph this book. Lew Wallace."

In the '80s we began to publish James Whitcomb Riley. He grew to be enormously popular. In the next fifteen years his books had been published in one hundred different ways, separate volumes, lists of poems, combinations of poems, and so forth. This venture in Riley gave us a feeling that we could get farther into publishing, but we did not do this until the '90s. Along in 1895 or 1896, a young lawyer from Shelbyville came in to see us and he brought a manuscript. He called it "Charles Brandon, Duke of Suffolk." We did not like the title, but we liked the book after we read it, and searched for a title. One day at home, one Sunday, I found in Leigh Hunt's poems,–a poem "The Gentle Armour." The first two lines read:

> "There lived a knight when knighthood was in flower,
> He charmed alike the tilt-yard and the bower."

That phrase struck me. The next day I took it to the office. They said it was too long, but I fought for it, and the next year we published "When Knighthood Was in Flower." Some of you may remember the success with which it met. It was afterward made into a play for Julia Marlowe, and made in many editions, and lately, in late years, a picture in which Marion Davies appeared. We followed that with other books. We had tasted blood. We published "Lazarre." Then we published "The Mississippi Bubble," by Emerson Hough, a great friend of mine. One day we had a row about his account and the next Christmas he sent me a telegram reading: "Merry Christmas I have sued you today."

We are now nearly down to nineteen hundred, but I won't go much farther. In nineteen hundred we made an instantaneous success on a novel which we deliberately planned in our own office. We said, we will have a novel on George Rogers Clarke–George Rogers Clarke and the Vincennes Campaign. We said, we will get Maurice Thompson, who lived in Crawfordsville, and he wrote for us under our direction, "Alice of Old Vincennes."

It was an instantaneous success. I took it up to McClurg's and showed it to them. They bought a few and sold them. I went out and took a full news page advertisement in the Chicago papers for this one title, which had never been done before. We got immediate and great returns, and in a short time afterward, A. C. McClurg & Company gave me an order for ten thousand copies to be shipped in one order. I telegraphed the order to Indianapolis. Mr. Bobbs replied "Do you mean ten thousand or one thousand." I said, "Make it ten thousand."

Many of our old friends have passed on. I have lost my old partners, William C. Bobbs and Charles W. Merrill. The young men are now in charge with Laurance Chambers as chief of our trade publishing department.

Our house sends you its warmest greetings.

–Curtis, "Reminiscences of a Publisher," *Publishers' Weekly,* 117 (10 May 1930): 2419–2420

Bobbs-Merrill: 1931–1940

1931

15 January — George Shively is elected to fill the director's term of Herbert S. Baker, who is ill. Baker dies shortly thereafter, having spent more than twenty-five years with the company.

14 March — The company announces the Red Label Reprints, twenty-four religious works to be published on 1 May in conjunction with Harper and Brothers and Henry Holt and Company. Among the titles is one by frequent Bobbs-Merrill author William E. Barton, *My Faith in Immortality* (1926).

15 April — Harlan Hatcher's first Bobbs-Merrill book, *Tunnel Hill,* is published.

25 May — According to the minutes of the board meeting this day, "The matter of the employment of married women in the organization was discussed [by the board of directors] and it was decided that as a house policy in the future the intention would be only to employ unmarried women."

22 July — John J. Curtis dies, and the office of president will remain vacant for four years.

27 July — Jessica Brown Mannon's salary is raised from $30 to $35 a week. She succeeds Anne Johnston as editorial assistant in the trade department.

25 August — Inglis Fletcher's first Bobbs-Merrill novel, *The White Leopard: A Tale of the African Bush,* is published.

12 September — Vash Young's *A Fortune to Share* is published; it becomes the number-three nonfiction best-seller of 1932. This self-help book is an example of the kind that sold well by mail order.

5 October — *The Autobiography of Knute K. Rockne,* edited by Rockne's widow, Bonnie Skiles Rockne, is published.

1932

28 June, 25 July — The company continues to pursue policies of the cost-cutting begun in 1930 because of the Depression, making them effective on 1 September. Most employees are given a 10 percent pay cut.

10 September — Augusta Stevenson's *Abe Lincoln, Frontier Boy,* the first volume in the Childhood of Famous Americans series ("Cofas"), is published. It will be translated into twenty-eight languages. More than two hundred of these embroidered biographies will follow.

1933

28 July — Emily Hahn's first Bobbs-Merrill book, *Congo Solo,* is published.

4 October — Alice Tisdale Hobart's first Bobbs-Merrill novel, *Oil for the Lamps of China,* is published; it becomes the number-nine fiction best-seller of 1934.

18 October — Irvin S. Cobb's first Bobbs-Merrill book, *Murder Day by Day,* is published.

1934

The Curriculum Readers series, by Clara Belle Baker and Edna Dean Baker, is launched. (No copyright record exists.)

1 June — Shively having gone to Frederick A. Stokes and Company, Lynn Carrick leaves G. P. Putnam's Sons to become the Bobbs-Merrill editor in New York.

1 December — The New York office moves to 468 Fourth Avenue.

1935

Lowe Berger becomes a vice president.

16 May — The last meeting of the board of directors is held for which the minutes survive. The board decides on a severe reduction in law publishing.

22 July — D. Laurance Chambers is elected president.

1936

1 May — Irma S. Rombauer's *The Joy of Cooking* (first printed privately in 1931) is published. In all its manifestations, nine million copies of the book will have been sold by 1975. Its sales for Bobbs-Merrill make it the company's most successful trade publication.

31 July — Marjorie Hillis's *Live Alone and Like It: A Guide for the Extra Woman,* the number-eight nonfiction best-seller, is published and has sales totaling one hundred thousand copies this year.

2 September — Andrew Lytle's first Bobbs-Merrill novel, *The Long Night,* is published.

12 October — The first volume of *Federal Code Annotated* is published. The editor in chief is William H. Mason, with John S. O'Brien, Archie McGray, and the Bobbs-Merrill editorial staff assisting. The second volume is published on 18 November. It is the company's best-known law title.

1937

John R. Carr retires as manager of the educational publishing department and is succeeded by Berger.

1 June — Carrick leaves the New York office to form Carrick and Evans. He is eventually succeeded by Lambert Davis.

9 June — Hillis's *Orchids on Your Budget; or, Live Smartly on What Have You* is published and becomes the number-five nonfiction best-seller for the year.

1938

28 February — Dorothy Hewlett's *Adonais: A Life of John Keats* is published. Winner of the Rose Mary Crawshay prize, the biography was first published in England the previous year.

6 May — Vladimir Nabokov's *Laughter in the Dark* is published. A translation by Nabokov of his 1933 novel *Kamera obskura,* it is his first American book and his only Bobbs-Merrill publication.

8 July — Marquis James's *The Life of Andrew Jackson, Complete in One Volume* is published, winning James his second Pulitzer Prize in biography. The book is a dividend selection for the Book-of-the-Month Club.

1939

	Chairman of the board Charles C. Kryter retires but continues to serve as a director until 1945.
13 February	Herbert Krause's first novel, *Wind Without Rain,* is published, bringing Krause the Friends of American Writers Award.
3 May	Pietro di Donato's first book, *Christ in Concrete,* is published and is a Book-of-the-Month Club selection for September.
1 December	*Bambi's Children: The Story of a Forest Family,* by Felix Salten (pen name of Siegmund Salzmann), is published in a translation by Barthold Fles.

1940

	Julius Birge joins the firm as a law-book editor.
1 August	Davis resigns. Guernsey Van Riper Jr. is transferred from Indianapolis to the New York office, which is managed by Walter J. Hurley.
Fall	Ross Baker, sales manager of the trade department since 1936, is elected to the board of directors.
1 October	Archibald Ogden becomes the New York editor.

Obituary: John J. Curtis

As this obituary indicates, it was Curtis's policy to visit the home office only twice a year. He left instructions to the board on 1 September 1926 that matters were not to be referred to him in California unless they were crucial. Because of this autonomy, the board was able to carry on for four years after his death without electing a new president.

John Jay Curtis, president of the Bobbs-Merrill Publishing Company, died Wednesday at the Methodist Hospital.

Although he had lived at Hollywood, Cal., since 1919, his connection with the publishing company and his semi-annual visits to Indianapolis served to maintain his interest in Indianapolis and the publishing world of which he had been a part for nearly sixty years. [. . .]

Mr. Curtis was born in Johnson county on January 21, 1857, and when six years old his family moved to Kokomo and later to Peru. He attended Butler College, then Northwestern Christian University, but the lure of books brought him to the Bowen-Stewart & Co. bookstore in Indianapolis. [. . .]

Mr. Curtis was a man of inventive mind and practically revolutionized the book selling process in America. He took the old covers–dust covers, as the English called them–and blazoned them with colors which today contribute so much to the attractiveness of book displays. He also discarded the old theory of advertising whole lists of books, and concentrated on advertising one copy.

John J. Curtis, successor to William C. Bobbs as president of the firm in 1926 (Bruccoli Clark Layman Archives)

In 1900 Mr. Curtis opened the New York office for Bobbs-Merrill, and from there he contributed greatly to the success of the company. Nineteen years later, wishing to retire, he went to Hollywood, Cal., and there dealt with the company's relations with the motion picture industry. When Mr. Bobbs died, Mr. Curtis was recalled to active service and elevated to the presidency of the company. On August 31, 1923, he was honored in Indianapolis by his associates at a golden anniversary dinner in celebration of his fifty years' association with the house.

Just before he became ill he had written to Chambers, vice-president and general manager of the company, that "next April 13 I shall enter my sixtieth year with the company." [. . .]

On the wall of his Hollywood home, which he called "Dunwandering" in the hopes that the title meant the end of his active career, hung two framed letters from a publishing company. They were acceptances of his two first stories for the sum of $8 each. He always admitted to visitors that he never got over the thrill of those two acceptances and that was why, in later years, he endeavored to encourage young authors. [. . .]

–"Bobbs-Merrill Head, John Jay Curtis, Dies," *Indianapolis News,* 23 July 1931, p. 14

* * *

Resolution of the Board of Directors, 7 August 1931

RESOLVED:

The Board of The Bobbs-Merrill Company records its great sense of loss in the death of President John Jay Curtis.

For nearly sixty years he had served this house with unswerving devotion to the common interest. With the exception of a few years, he had been continuously one of its officers since 1895. He founded and developed first the New York office, and, later, the West Coast office. He was a pioneer in the modern methods of making, merchandizing and advertising books. Many of these methods he himself invented and instituted. He began the selling of dramatic rights for the Company and achieved remarkable success with the sale of motion picture rights.

During his administration as President the house earned large profits and extended its prestige. He was instrumental in guiding it safely through troubled waters and lost no occasion to strengthen the good will of authors, of the Trade, of financial institutions, and of the public toward the organization.

The Secretary is instructed to express to Mrs. Curtis our heartfelt sympathy in her loss and to send her a copy of this minute which inadequately expresses our love and admiration and sorrow for her husband, our President.

R. L. Moorhead
Secretary

* * *

Further Trials of the Law Department

The law department knew as well as the trade department the importance of the title of a book. It was a lesson learned from Charles Major's When Knighthood Was in Flower *(1898) and never forgotten by the institutional memory embodied in the inner circle. The title was one issue with Alfred W. Herzog's* Medical Jurisprudence, *published on 11 May 1931; the other involved the content, style, and punctuation in the book. This letter gives an idea of the extensive and costly editing necessary to make* Medical Jurisprudence *a readable and sellable text for an audience the firm had developed in the course of eighty years and understood better than Herzog did.*

Alfred W. Herzog to Robert L. Moorhead, 8 October 1931

My dear Colonel Moorhead:

Your favor of September 30, stating that you had decided to plate the book and that before plating it you would like me to send you such corrections, typographical or misspelled words, which I may have noted, has come to hand.–

As I wrote to you before, I am so disgusted with the book and the way it has been slashed to pieces, that I do not want to look at it more than I have to.–I have looked at it several times when some inquiry came as to where to find certain matters.–I was able to show that the information was contained in the book, though not in the index, which you preferred to handle in your own way.–

However I will go through as much as I can in the next few days and send you a list of any errors which I may be able to find.–

I will admit that you will most likely be right in your statement that 95% of the book [*sic*] sold will be to lawyers and 5% to physicians.–

In this case you will be right, because you will be the master of the books [*sic*] fate.–I do not know whether you are aware that PHYSICIANS BUY BOOKS much more than lawyers.–Do you know that other publishers send many review copies to medical Journals just for that reason?

I enclose herewith a review of "LEGAL MEDICINE AND TOXICOLOGY by Webster," from the October issue of COLORADO MEDICINE. I send you the review of the same book from the Medico-Legal Journal.–It appeared in my Journal's January-February issue.–

Do you notice the big review the book received? That book does not come [up] to mine, except in the matter of Toxicology.–As a matter of fact, it is not deserving of a very good criticism.–

I do not know whether you have read my review in the Medico-Legal Journal of the book published by you and written by Ralph Brown on Legal Psychology? If this book was published on the advice of your legal staff, I would advise you to do something radical about it.–

Being that I asked for a review copy and received it, I could not say about that book what it deserved, but believe me, I would never have published it under the imprint of the Medico-Legal Journal, except the author paid about twice the cost of publication.–

Since you published my book I have carefully looked for reviews.–I find that only one of my exchanges (I have 102 of them, of which 79 are medical Journals while 23 are Law Reviews published in the United States [)] has reviewed the book (Medical Arts, Indianapolis, Ind.) and that review was spoiled by carrying the ad of the book right under it.–In none of the exchanges have I seen the acknowledgment that the book has been received for review, and in only one legal magazine (The N.Y. University Law Quarterly) have I seen the book advertised.–

I think that your policy is very near sighted.–It surely would not cost you an awful lot to send review copies to twenty or thirty of the largest medical journals in the United States? Then when you saw that there would be returns, you would naturally send them to others.–

However, I am sure that sending review copies to Medical Journals WILL SUBSTANTIALLY INCREASE THE SALE OF MY BOOK TO LAWYERS.

Even though some physicians may not buy the book, they will read the reviews and advertisements.–

Lawyers do ask physicians when they feel that they need to buy a book on Medical Jurisprudence: ["]Say doctor, what is a good book on Medical Jurisprudence to buy?" and generally they buy the book their family physician or the doctor with whom they have a case, recommends.–

Furthermore: You may make my book familiar to Lawyers, but how will they like it, if they should ask in court of a medical witness whether he agrees or disagrees with HERZOG, to receive the answer: "Never heard of him".–

Have just received another book on Medical Jurisprudence for review.–It is "MEDICAL JURISPRUDENCE by Scheffel" published by Blakiston, Philadelphia.–His book is strictly Medical Jurisprudence and he shows that I was right in that I did not wish to call mine "Medical Jurisprudence," but "A HANDBOOK OF MEDICO-LEGAL SCIENCE".

Yours very truly,
A. W. Herzog

* * *

The Legal Market

William H. Kelly was the company's law-school representative, responsible both for selling books and finding authors for Bobbs-Merrill. This report on Harvard Law School shows his extensive connections and also some of the considerations necessary in a department that was finding a diminishing market for these expensive texts during the Depression. "Bohlen" refers to Francis H. Bohlen's Cases on the Law of Torts *(1915), the third edition of which came out in 1930. "Goble" is George W. Goble's* Cases and Other Materials on the Law of Insurance *(1931).*

William H. Kelly to Bobbs-Merrill, 24 March 1932

Gentlemen:–

Wm. F. Walsh has about completed the new edition of his English and American Law. The new book will make around 500 pages, is required at N.Y.U. and Mr. Solomon tells me is quite generally bought by the Fordham Students. I don't know how generally it has been distributed elsewhere. Mr. Walsh would rather we would publish it than anyone else. He insists he must have it by next September.

I saw Basil Pollitt this morning. He has a number of projects in mind. 1st, a series of books, one on each law school subject, in which the local law of New York, New Jersey, Massachusetts and Pennsylvania would be treated.

2nd, a one volume edition of the New Jersey Statutes.

3rd, The revision of most any book in the Agency or Criminal Law field.–or a new book on these subjects.

He also says he could do a book, on Domestic Relations, Torts or Bankruptcy.

Mr. Pollitt has been offered a revision job, I don't know what book by the Harrison Company.

And Mr. Cudahy was in to see him a few days ago, relative to the one volume New Jersey Statutes.

Personally I think Pollitt is available for most any editorial work,–But he has saved enough money to live on for a few years. Dean Pound says he can get him a job with one of the law schools either teaching or doing research work. And he has for some years been doing Remingtons [*sic*] work on his Bankruptcy so he may be overly hard to make an agreement with.

Professor [illegible] is really interested in revising Bishop on Marriage and Divorce, but says he can't possibly get started on it before next January. In the meantime he wishes us to feel free to have someone else undertake it.–I wouldn't depend on him ever doing it overmuch, for I believe he will work with the

American Law Institute and Professor Williston as long as they have anything for him to do.

I am sure that Professor Seavey would rather have us publish his Treatise on Agency than anyone else. He expects to finish his re-statement work this coming Summer, and then start on the treatise.–I expect to see him again tomorrow and may have something farther to report.

There are fifty five graduate students, candidates for the S.J.D. degree at Harvard this year.–I know about thirty of them–teachers in other schools consequently it will take some time to finish out there. However, it's just as profitable to see them at Harvard as at home.–Among today [*sic*] contributions from the visiting Scholars, was an adoption of Bohlen for use in George Washington U. next year by Professor Collier, and an adoption for Goble at Kansas by Professor Leflar.

Very truly yours,
Wm. H. Kelly

* * *

Childhood of Famous Americans Series

The Childhood of Famous Americans series, which began in 1932 with Augusta Stevenson's Abe Lincoln, Frontier Boy, *was a company standby during the Depression and remained such for many years. The army arranged the publication of Stevenson's* Buffalo Bill, Boy of the Plains *(1948) as part of its program to denazify German youth. The strengths and limitations of the volumes in the series are assessed after twenty years by Lillian Hollowell, an expert in children's literature.*

Less than two decades ago, librarians and critics were heartily condemning series in children's books. Lists of not-to-be circulated books were being published which included such familiar names as Horatio Alger, Martha Findley ("Elsie" books), Howard Roger Garis ("Uncle Wiggily"), and many more authors of books by the dozens. We were told that books such as these were a menace to good reading. They were sentimental, unscientific, and lacking in color and vitality. No writer could be more than hackneyed and uninspiring when he carried the same character or a similar theme through twenty or more books. (Horatio Alger had 121 listed to his credit.)

What is the status of series today? Have series changed? [. . .]

In addition to being accurate, admirably written, and well designed, many of the series serve as fascinating introductions to biography and history. Until Bobbs-Merrill started the Childhood of Famous Americans series, there were few books which children could read and learn about their American heritage and those who helped make America great. Many other publishers have followed suit until this business has become a boom.

The formula for writing these fictionalized biographies is to create imaginary episodes which reveal certain characteristics of the person portrayed, and to invent dialogue which enlivens and makes dramatic the narrative. This technique, according to a professor of history, is the same as that used by Parson Weems, who invented the cherry-tree story in his successful life of George Washington. However, Professor Douglas Adair does point out that modern writers have streamlined and improved the Weems formula both in the historical and literary sense for twentieth century children.

Having noted the excellence of some of the series and their superiority over most of those of an earlier date, let us notice some dangers in this trend of children's books. First, too many series are being published. There are too many duplications. At the present rate, the market will soon become so flooded they will lose their identity. Practically every publishing house has several series and more on the way. The success of one series inspires the publisher to add to it or to put out another. An example of the phenomenal growth and sales is the Childhood of Famous Americans, published by Bobbs-Merrill. The first volume, *Abe Lincoln: Frontier Boy,* by Augusta Seaman [*sic*], has sold more than a hundred thousand copies since 1932 when it was published. Recent additions bring this series to about seventy volumes, and the total sales amount to more than two million dollars. [. . .]

Professor Adair addresses a warning to purchasers, principally parents and librarians, to remember that many of these series are not biographies in the strict sense of the term but only introductions. Concerning the "Childhood" biographies, he makes the comment that life in them is always too neat and stereotyped. Here Washington, Wild Bill Hickok, Grant, Boone, Franklin, Lincoln, and Lee all appear as "normal," happy boys with good average parents, playing the right kinds of pranks and dreaming only respectable adolescent dreams, and inevitably they all look very much alike as personalities, no matter what clothes they wear or what age they lived in. [. . .]

–"Series in Children's Books," *Wilson Library Bulletin,* 27 (May 1953): 736–738

* * *

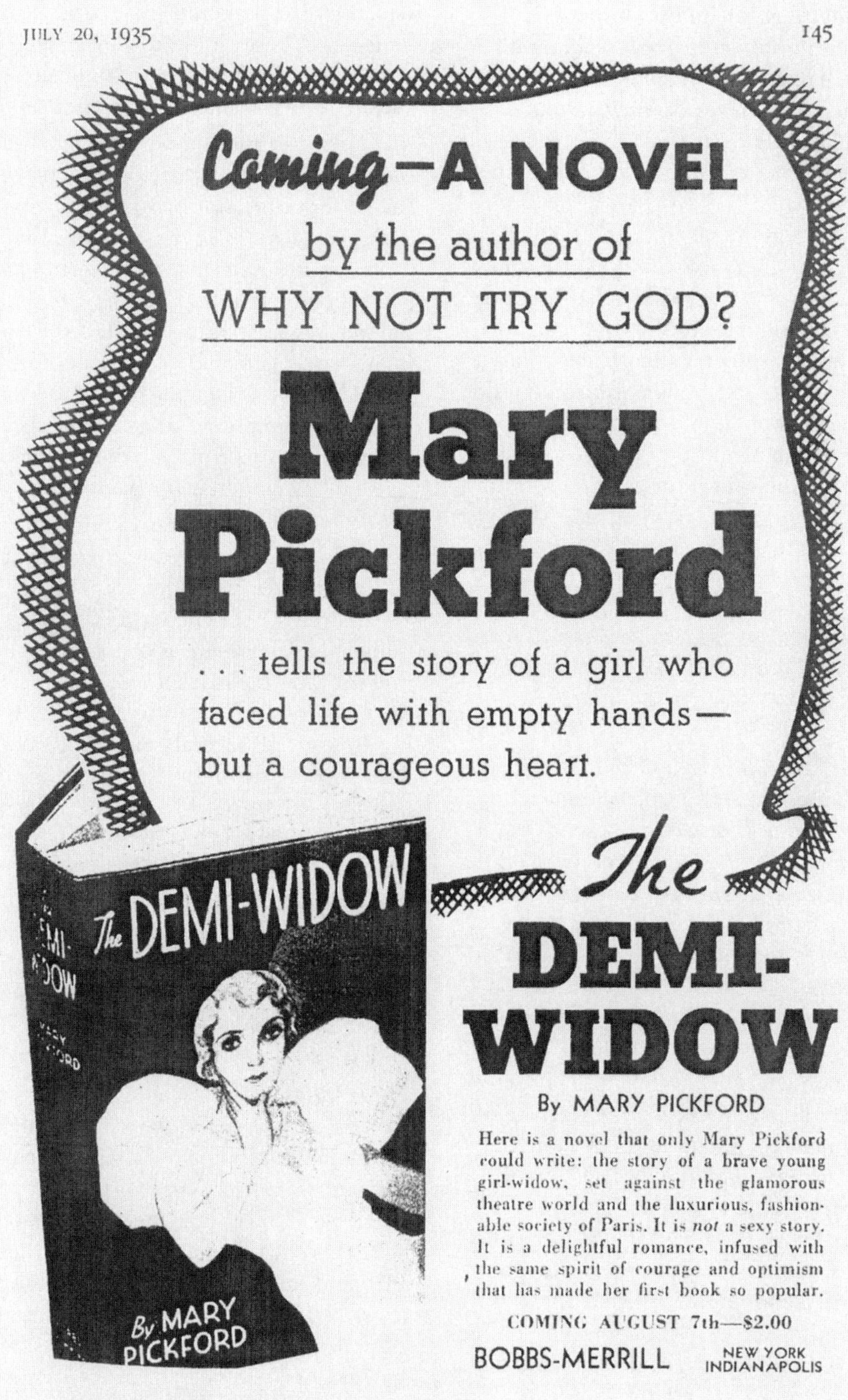

Advertisement from Publishers' Weekly *for the only novel by "America's sweetheart," published in 1935*

Two versions of the dust jacket for the actress's novel (courtesy of Michael Manz/Babylon Revisited)

Depression Measures: Minutes of the Meeting of the Board of Directors, 16 May 1935

In the last surviving minutes of a board meeting, an earlier report recommending reduction of law publications is approved, and other cost-cutting measures are adopted.

May 16, 1935.

The regular meeting of the Board of Directors of The Bobbs-Merrill Company was held in the offices of the company Thursday, May 16, 1935 at 10:30 A.M. Present: Messrs. Carr, Chambers, Kaylor, Kryter and Moorhead.

Mr. Carr presided as chairman of the meeting. [. . .]

Mr. Kryter moved and Mr. Kaylor seconded the motion that the general program for the improvement of the Law Department made by the special committee appointed January 24, 1935 be approved. Carried.

Mr. Moorhead moved and Mr. Kryter seconded the motion that all employees of The Bobbs-Merrill Company who have been in the employ of the house for one year or more be given one week vacation with pay and one or more weeks vacation without pay. The several department managers were authorized to make such changes and exceptions to this rule as may be necessary for the efficient conduct of the business. Carried. [. . .]

* * *

Changes at the Top

D. Laurance Chambers was elected president of the Bobbs-Merrill Company and Charles C. Kryter was elected chairman of the board at the annual meeting of the directors of the company on July 22nd. At the annual meeting of the stockholders previous to the board meeting, J. W. Fesler, the well-known Indianapolis attorney was elected to the board of directors.

Mr. Chambers came to the Bobbs-Merrill Company in 1903 as secretary to W. C. Bobbs, following his graduation from Princeton. He has been vice-president of the firm and manager of the trade book department since 1920. He is first vice-president of the National

D. Laurance Chambers, who became president of the company in 1935, reading a 1947 Bobbs-Merrill publication (courtesy of The Indianapolis Star*)*

Association of Book Publishers and a member of the Council of the Princeton University Press.

Mr. Kryter has been with the company since 1889, serving for years as one of the vice-presidents and manager of the law book department. He has recently served three consecutive terms as president of the American Association of Law Book Publishers, the longest record of service in that capacity in the history of the Association.

Mr. Fesler was an intimate friend of William C. Bobbs, long president of the company. [. . .]

–"D. Laurance Chambers Elected President of Bobbs-Merrill," *Publishers' Weekly,* 128 (3 August 1935): 286

* * *

The Legal Department's "Crown of Thorns": Correspondence with J. R. Bruce, 1937

Bobbs-Merrill's classic Federal Code Annotated *was developed under Richard V. Sipe, who had served the legal department in various capacities for more than twenty years. Two volumes were published at the end of 1936, and the series continued in 1937 with six more of a projected seventeen volumes. The contract was for a joint production with the Mason Publishing Company, and the Bruce Publishing Company was to do the printing (Bruce was also a director of Mason). William H. Mason Sr. was the chief editor; however, he refused to complete the manuscript and committed other violations of the contract, which he hoped to void. The furor caused some subscribers to cancel. Moorhead, in charge of the department, chose not to worsen the situation by legal action until the work was completed. Bobbs-Merrill bought out Mason's interest in 1938.*

Moorhead to J. R. Bruce, 4 January 1937

Dear Mr. Bruce:

Sunday afternoon we received by air mail special delivery from Mr. Rumble a supplementary contract prepared by Mr. Mason which was unacceptable to us in so many ways that we doubted whether we should attempt to reform it. Finally, Mr. Sipe and I redrafted it and sent it to Mr. Rumble with a statement that we would accept it if it was signed immediately.

Mr. Mason has placed the onus of the delay on us and in carrying out the supplementary agreement we would have placed ourselves under the control of Mr. Mason which would have immediately created an impossible situation.

The Mason Publishing Company is in default with us in supplying manuscript and have been so for several months.

If the Mason Publishing Company will sign and accept the supplementary agreement that Mr. Sipe and I left with Mr. Rumble and Mr. Mason we authorize the amount of the cash payment to be changed to $2,500 divided into two payments of $1,250 each, provided it is accepted immediately.

The redraft of the supplementary agreement which we have sent to Mr. Rumble also contains the same provisions for the cash payment.

Mr. Toussaint, the young man formerly of Mr. Mason's editorial staff, reported here this morning and we have also employed an additional editor. We are now proceeding to reconstruct the work from the ground up which is going to be very expensive for the Mason Publishing Company.

We will need some additional copies of the Mason publications and I am enclosing a list addressed to Mr. Sletterdahl which I wish he would secure and send to us without delay. The furnishing of these books from the Mason stock will be a saving to the Mason Publishing Company as otherwise we shall be obliged to go out into the market and buy them.

If either of the supplementary agreements is signed by Mason it should also contain a copy of the approval of the Board of Directors of the Mason Publishing Company.

We instructed Mr. Rumble to give formal notice of our intention to take over the contract January 4 due to the default of the Mason Publishing Company. Personally, in order to save you in your relation to the Mason Publishing Company any expense I shall urge that our people accept the supplementary agreement duly executed and the Mason material if it is received here this week.

Cordially yours,
[Robert L. Moorhead]
THE BOBBS-MERRILL COMPANY

* * *

Moorhead to Bruce, 23 March 1937

Dear Mr. Bruce:

Enclosed is a copy of a letter from W. H. Mason dated March 22.

The supplementary agreement which was executed the first of the year provided that Mr. Mason would read the proof. This was his own election and he insisted upon the inclusion in the provision.

Now he is proposing to charge us $50.00 a week for his services in doing this proof reading. We do not intend to modify the supplementary agreement by a line or a dot and are writing Mr. Mason that we do not propose to modify this agreement.

He writes reams of paper of captious complaints about our editorial work, about our proof reading, about our penuriousness, and is making himself as disagreeable in every way as he can.

The complaints Mr. Mason makes are in almost every instance unfounded or are complaints that anyone could make about a thing that he did not do himself and which he thinks could be done better some other way.

In a letter today Mr. Mason complains about our changing his manuscript. Reference to the manuscript shows that in every instance the changes were made in St. Paul by some of Mr. Mason's editorial force.

All of this is merely to tell you that we are still going along with him but we find the sledding more difficult every day.

Yours very truly,
[Robert L. Moorhead]

* * *

Moorhead to Bruce, 29 November 1937

Dear Mr. Bruce:

Thank you for your letter of November 26. I feel as you do, that the only solution for our mutual crown of thorns is to get rid of the Masons for now and all time. In forty years business experience I have never met with any one like them.

We have tried in every way to get along with them and have made the effort ourselves to do the getting along. When we waive or give in some right that is clearly ours we invariably get a slap back or kick from the Masons as thanks for our effort.

If you can devise a plan for the purchase of their business, we to take the F. C. A., and such deal could be consummated, it would relieve both of us of much future worry. If you were to take over the balance of their law book line we would be glad to cooperate with you should you desire us to do so in helping you both edit and sell the books. By editing I refer to editorial plans and advice rather than to actual work in doing the editing which you would probably want to do. In other words, we would go the full length with you to help make any plan workable.

Very truly yours,
[Robert L. Moorhead]
THE BOBBS-MERRILL COMPANY

* * *

Lynn Carrick Moves On

Lynn Carrick, who has been in charge of the editorial department in the New York office of the Bobbs-Merrill Co., has announced that he will not renew his contract with the firm, when the present contract expires on June 1st. His future plans will be announced at a later date.

Mr. Carrick went to Bobbs-Merrill in June, 1934. Since his connection with the company he has been responsible for a number of successful Bobbs-Merrill books, including, among others, Eleanor Carroll Chilton's "Follow the Furies," Gibbons' "Steel of Empire," James C. Wilson's "Three Wheeling Through Africa," the Mexican prize novel, "El Indio," by G. Lopez y Fuentes, Richard Blaker's "Here Lies a Most Beautiful Lady," and, of course, Marjorie Hillis' "Live Alone and Like It." Before joining Bobbs-Merrill, Mr. Carrick had been editor at G. P. Putnam's Sons.

—"Carrick to Leave Bobbs-Merrill," *Publishers' Weekly,* 131 (13 March 1937): 1240

* * *

D. Laurance Chambers to Hewitt H. Howland, 31 March 1937

Hewitt H. Howland, Indianapolis editor during some of the company's best days and now a literary agent, saw Carrick's imminent departure as a chance to return in his former capacity. Chambers had to turn down his elderly friend and colleague.

Dear Hewitt:–

You ask if I have considered you for the editorial job in New York. You may be sure I have, long and prayerfully, and all the more carefully because of the joy it has been to work side by side with you again, and to find that well-accomplished hand of yours adorning everything it touches.

The fundamental obstacle is that it is now an established policy of the house to employ young men and give them training, even when this means a lack of experience, a loss of motion and considerable temporary difficulty. We all feel that we must have a younger generation coming on to take our places as age reaches out to decrease our energy. You will remember that I referred to this policy in our talk when we lunched at the Vanderbilt. This is all that could stand in the way, but it is a settled policy, and alas, it is enough to prevent the association which otherwise would be so thoroughly satisfactory.

If you can, for a week or two, help me break in a young man, I shall be even more grateful to you than I already am for the friendly help you have given us in an emergency. But, with the demands of your agency work, I can understand that this may be too much to ask.

Affectionately yours,
[D. Laurance Chambers]

Vladimir Nabokov, 1926 (from Ellendra Proffer, ed., Vladimir Nabokov, *1991)*

* * *

Vladimir Nabokov Comes to America: Reader's Report and Correspondence, 1938–1940

In 1938 Laughter in the Dark, *Vladimir Nabokov's only Bobbs-Merrill novel, appeared; it was his first book published in the United States. Chambers was instrumental in helping him escape wartime Europe the next year, but he did not accept any more of his work. Nabokov's biographical questionnaire is reproduced in facsimile in the* DLB Yearbook, 1985, pp. 28–30.

Undated Reader's Report

Laughter In The Dark.

Laughter In The Dark has an elusive, delightful quality about it that sets it apart as a novel that will not fit any given classification. It is as though the story were infused with a drop or two of the fine flavor of parody, as though its scope and depth and meaning were enhanced by a light, magic touch of caricature. It tells a tragic tale and yet one is somehow aware of a faint, lurking echo of wise laughter. It is as though the author said: here is stark, lurid melodrama of the type you often see and perhaps ridicule in the films, but here also is the sad, unadorned truth about a fantastic fate that overtook a respectable, solid citizen; the story is in essence tragic and significant, I grant you, but instead of being too uselessly earnest and serious about it, come and see it with me from the broad humanizing perspective of the comic vein. In this spirit he goes on to achieve a most remarkable feat: he sums up the whole story in the opening paragraph of the novel and then proceeds to tell it in detail in such a fashion that he not only holds the reader's sustained interest but his rapt attention until the very last word. This success may be accounted for in various ways: the story is an engrossing one to start with; it moves swiftly along without pause; it is modern and worldly and is told in a clever, amusing and original manner; and finally it is light, rapid reading of the type that entertains and at the same time commands one's respect.

"Once upon a time"–so the novel begins–"there lived in Berlin, Germany, a man called Albinus. He was rich, respectable, happy; one day he abandoned his wife for the sake of a youthful mistress; he loved; was not loved; and his life ended in disaster."

"This is the whole story"–says the author–"and we might have left it at that had there not been profit and pleasure in the telling; and although there is plenty of space on a gravestone to contain . . . the abridged version of a man's life, detail is always welcome." It seems safe to prophecy that readers of Laughter In The Dark will unanimously and enthusiastically agree with the last.

Abinus [*sic*], although he loved his wife Elizabeth and his little daughter Irma and even his brother-in-law Paul, and though he was sincerely interested in painting about which he often wrote learned articles, was a man who secretly hankered for an amorous adventure of a rather torrid nature. Even as a bachelor he had never managed that sort of thing well and so his hunger for a really erotic experience had never been appeased. He was just ripe for an affair when he fell in love with Margot, the pretty, vulgar little usher at a dingy movie house. And Margot, young as she was, had just the brand of experience and self-confidence that put her in command of the situation. She had been genuinely in love with her first lover, Miller, at sixteen; when he deserted her she had spent a night with two Japanese gentlemen who had underpaid her; then followed an ancient banker who died; and finally she had sunk to this dreary movie job. Now in Albinus she saw a means of improving her fortunes and so, instead of giving in to his urgent entreaties, she first made him thoroughly nervous by visiting his apartment in his wife's absence and then, with a single clever blow, destroyed his domestic peace by sending him a letter which his wife opened. When Albinus returned after his first delirious night with Margot his wife and child and all their belongings had left. Only Paul remained to express himself briefly but forcefully on the subject of his brother-in-law's insane conduct.

Albinus was so completely captivated with his lovely young mistress that he could deny her nothing, not even her demand–on their return from a delightful trip–that they move into the apartment in which he had formerly lived with his wife. He also spent his money freely to finance the production of a motion picture in order to satisfy her long cherished ambition to become a movie star, but the picture, to Margot's great chagrin, proved her a failure as an actress. In answer to his invitations Albinus was not surprised to find that there happened to be 'a remarkable epidemic of headaches among his friends' wives', but men came to his parties and one night there came, among others, that well known cynic and caricaturist, Axel Rex, who was none other than Miller, Margot's first lover. Rex was a thorough going charlatan and a great artist. He loved to watch creatures suffer, to contribute to the torture while adding some aspect of comedy to the tragedy. Finding that the physical attraction between himself and Margot was still strong and mutually felt, he proceeded to deceive Albinus by explaining that he was a homosexual.

It was when Albinus' little girl Irma died that they first betrayed him and then they continued to carry their affair on almost under his nose. Because she was determined that nothing should upset her plan to marry Albinus, Margot was at first annoyed when Axel offered to act as their chauffeur on the trip that was to compensate her for her failure in the movies, but adjoining rooms in a resort hotel and Albinus' obtuseness served not only to mollify her but to make Axel more and more daring. In the end even Albinus learned what was going on but because he could not bear the truth he chose to believe the lies Margot told him, and instead of shooting her as he at first threatened to do, he took her away with him in the car. His lack of skill as a driver resulted in the accident which left him blind.

Then came Axel Rex's great opportunity to indulge his passion for amusing himself while contributing to the suffering of others. Unknown to Albinus he lived in the same house with him and Margot, slept with her, often sat at table with them, and contrived to disturb the otherwise calm atmosphere in various ways which mystified and irritated the blind man. But it was the lovers' greediness which gave them away. An overdrawn check brought Paul who rescued Albinus and took him back to Berlin. But the enraged blind man lived for only one purpose: to kill the little slut who had so cruelly and shamelessly deceived him. When his former doorman telephoned him that she was in the apartment packing up its valuable art pieces he took his revolver and with great difficulty made his way to her. Just as he was on the point of success in the shuffle that ensued his adversary managed to point his gun at himself instead of at her. In a closing, silent scene the author presents: Albinus lying huddled and dead on the drawing room floor, trunks standing about among the upset furnishings, a woman's glove lying on the table, the door standing ajar.

Here is realism indeed, but relieved and given objectivity by a pervasive sort of super humor. The story is concise, direct and dramatic, and it is told with wit and with consummate artistic skill. As an ironic comment, as good light entertainment, as an artistic achievement–Laughter In The Dark is the kind of novel that will be appreciated by different readers for different reasons; but it is also the kind of novel that is sure to prove popular among all classes of readers because of its swift-moving story and the originality of its treatment.

M.S.L. [deleted]

* * *

Dust jacket for the Russian author's only Bobbs-Merrill book, published in 1938 (courtesy of Michael Manz/Babylon Revisited)

Altagracia de Jannelli, a literary agent, wrote Chambers in 1939 with an enclosed letter from Nabokov, who hoped that a note from Bobbs-Merrill would help him obtain a visa from the American consulate in Paris.

Altagracia de Jannelli to Chambers, 15 October 1939

My dear Mr. Chambers:

I am ashamed to bother you in this fashion, however, you will readily understand, in reading the enclosed letter of Nabokoff, whom I and Countess Tolstoy are using our best efforts to bring here, for under the circumstances, being a White Russian, he is now considered an enemy in France, and might be interned or worse.

Having published one book of his, and still having a contract with him, I feel you are the one person to whom I should apply. This letter would mean nothing but a help to him. Of course, I should be very glad that, once here, he wrote you the book, for the man is a grand writer, though his subjects so far haven't been the right ones for America. However, if you should be so kind as to write this letter, I would not mention "Slavonic", but I would say that it would be easier for him to write the books you desire, being here, and that it would be a help to you to have him here.

It is because you have been so very kind to me the several times I saw you in New York that I have taken the liberty of asking you this. Besides, I really think he would write the right kind of a book, if guided on the subject. A word from you would be greatly appreciated. The letter should be addressed to the American Consul in Paris, and should be mailed to me, so that I can in turn mail it by "Clipper" to Nabokoff.

I sincerely hope you will see your way clear to doing this humane thing, which entails nothing for you, but means a very great deal to Nabokoff and his future.

Faithfully yours,
Altagracia de Jannelli

COPY FOR MR. CHAMBERS

September 30, 1939

V. Nabokoff
59, Rue Boileau
Paris, 16 eme

Dear Mrs. de Jannelli,

Thank you for your letter of the 5th of Sept. You have probably got mine so that you know that we are in Paris, the old address.

I also wrote you that we are on the Russian quota, and that our turn ought to come in a few weeks now. As I feel sure you would be ready to help me to come across, I hope you will agree to try and coax Bobbs-Merrill into sending me a letter addressed to the American Consul in Paris, saying something of the following sort:

> . . . . "We should be very grateful if you (that is, the Consul) could help the celebrated Russian author Mr. Vladimir Nabokoff-Sirin to obtain his visa for the U.S., as his presence here would enable us to develop considerably the Russian (or Slavonic) department of our firm". Of course you can word it better than this.

Seeing that Bobbs-Merrill seemed rather desirous to have me come across I do hope that they will find it possible to write this kind of letter,–and, of course, what I chiefly rely upon is your energy and charm. It would be most important to me to have such a letter from them to the Consul, as it would make a lot of difference when I go to see the Consul. Seeing that letters move slowly nowadays and that the thing is extremely urgent for me (if I could get it about the middle of October it would be much better than if I got it at the end of the month), would you be so very, very kind as to mail it by the "Clipper", and, in any case, could you send me a wire–just one word "yes", so that I might know that it is about to be posted. If you can pull it off, I hope to meet you before Christmas, '39, in New York, and apologize de vive voix for all the trouble I am giving you.

And, please, make it quite clear to Bobbs-Merrill that, once in New York, I shall certainly write for them the novel they expect from me.

Yours very truly,
(signed) V. Nabokoff

P.S. I am ashamed of the "celebrated",–but that is what they ought to say.

* * *

Chambers to de Jannelli, 17 October 1939

My dear Mrs. de Jannelli:

Many thanks for your letter of the 15th.

Inclosed is the letter for Mr. Nabokoff, which I hope may serve the purpose. If you do not think it is just right, will you please edit it and return it to me, and I shall then be glad to revise it accordingly? It will be a real satisfaction if we can help Mr. Nabokoff to come over to America.

Sincerely yours,
[D. Laurance Chambers]

* * *

Chambers to the Consul General of the United States, Paris, 6 November 1939

Dear Sir:–

We would be very grateful if you could help the celebrated Russian author, Mr. Vladimir Nabokoff-Sirin, now resident in Paris, to obtain his visa for the United States. He is indeed a writer of extraordinary talent, and his presence here would enable us to guide him in writing books of interest and appeal to Americans and at the same time help us to develop our activity where foreign literature is concerned. His knowledge of that literature is both wide and deep.

Sincerely yours,
[D. Laurance Chambers]

* * *

de Jannelli to Chambers, 1 June 1940

My dear Mr. Chambers:–

Mr. Nabokoff has arrived, and I immediately took him to your New York Office and introduced him to Mr. Davis.

I wonder if you will be in New York in the near future, it would be splendid for Nabokoff to have a talk with you.

Nabokoff told me that your letter had been a good help to him in obtaining his visa, and now that he is here, I hope he will write us THE BOOK.

With all best wishes, I am,

Very sincerely yours,
Altagracia de Jannelli

* * *

In-House Censorship, 1939–1940

Many Bobbs-Merrill novels were published only after lengthy debate. Editors disagreed with readers and among themselves. The house had a well-deserved reputation for conservatism, and a chief bulwark against the excesses of the new realism was Jessica Brown Mannon, who joined the firm in 1927 and became an assistant editor in 1931. Her views on sex and violence were seldom far from those of Chambers.

Jessica Brown Mannon, Reader's Report on Pietro di Donato's *Christ in Concrete*

Pietro di Donato's novel Christ in Concrete *(1939) began as a short story published in the September 1937 issue of* Esquire*; Bobbs-Merrill gave di Donato an advance that let him take a leave of absence from bricklaying and turn the story into a novel. The result, however, was not to the liking of the company. Sipe, editor in chief of the law department, opined that while the book as a whole was not obscene, the language needed editing. Eventually this editing was done, perhaps by Lambert Davis of the New York office.*

CHRIST IN CONCRETE
By Pietro di Donato

It seems strange that so gory and tragic a story should leave a reader completely unmoved. Possibly the fault lies with me. The first few chapters are so fantastic that I felt I was struggling through a foreign language and making a poor job of my attempt at translation. The obscenity made the task of reading the manuscript no more pleasant. As I read I thought of various friends and authors who would be greatly offended by the book and I tried to think what explanation I could offer which would justify in their eyes the publication of such sentences and expressions as "hole of the Virgin whore", "Blood of the Virgin's ass", "if you death-murdered cocks desire not to work then say so and go into the cellar and take down each other's pantaloons". All of these are found on one page (118). There are others equally foul. Lifted from the context this way they are indeed too indecent to quote.

As I analyze the story I can only come to the conclusion that it will never appeal to the ordinary American reader. It may prove a sensation in New York, Chicago and other metropolitan centers where there are Leftists

Editor Jessica Brown Mannon (photo by E. Douglas Holland; courtesy of The Indianapolis Star *and the Indiana State Archives, Indiana Commission on Public Records)*

and protectors-of-the-proletariate-in-theory. Labor Stage ought to go wild about it. All hysterical groups will probably respond and this is an encouraging thought for the publisher. On the other hand readers who prefer subtlety and restraint in an author's style, will never be moved by CHRIST IN CONCRETE. The author does all the "emoting" necessary.

The most serious criticism I have to offer regarding the plot is the scene with the Industrial Board, pages 223 and 224 and 226. The author claims to have written this story from his own life, does he not? I know there are miscarriages of justice every day in the year and that foreigners in industrial centers are cheated of their rights all the time. But in this instance, I think Mr. di Donato instead of gaining sympathy, simply plants a suspicion in the intelligent reader's mind that he either doesn't know what actually took place, or he is making it up out of whole cloth. Industrial Boards were created for the protection of the workmen and carelessness has nothing whatever to do with claims. Most of the accidents which occur are caused through carelessness but the contractor must pay anyway. Furthermore, the collapse of a six story building in which a number of workmen were killed would have attracted the attention of the newspapers. There would have been some sort of an investigation. The fact that the contractor carried no insurance would not have protected him from responsibility or indemnity. And don't tell me they don't have ambulance chasers in New York! I can't conceive of a case where more than half-a-dozen workmen were killed that a lawyer wouldn't have appeared somewhere along the line, though industrial cases are not subjected to the same abuses, perhaps, as ordinary accidents. The author weakens his case by this "phoney" court scene.

Personally, I should like to see some of the worst of the obscenity cut out. Most of it occurs in the earlier part of the book. In comparing the magazine publication with the printed booklet done by Esquire, it seems to me that the expurgated copy is every bit as effective as the unexpurgated.

P. 40. "swollen entrails". Why entrails? Even Italian laborers surely know the difference between entrails and womb.

P. 118. This page is quite too obscene.

P. 133 and 134. The incident of the beer is filthy even if it is realism. The business of urinating is overdone throughout. Why dwell on it through 400 pages?

P. 250-B and p. 252 there is a repetition about Luigi's "callouses disappearing leaving his fingers soft and empty." There are a good many repetitions that are tiring but this is the only one I made a note of.

P. 350 to 382. This wedding supper is the best thing in the book but one wonders where all the food came from, how it was cooked in one small kitchen and how they all managed to crowd into one apartment and still have room to dance.

If any revision is to be done I would recommend that consideration be given to the scene on the train in which the woman assaults Paul–page 294. From there to page 323 there is much agonizing over sex which many readers would find offensive. I hardly know what could be done about it as it is all more or less obscene.

I think the book could very well end on page 393. The subsequent chapter where Paul loses his faith and quarrels with his mother, is I suppose, as well written as the rest but it is an anti-climax and tiresome. I grew so bored with the wallowing and raving I threw it down in disgust, completely fed-up.

I hope the book sells. As far as I can see that would be the only reason for publishing it.

Jessica Mannon

* * *

Unsigned Reader's Report on *Christ in Concrete*

Internal evidence points to Chambers as the author of this report, which is also a statement of "house policy." John was a literary critic for The New York Times. *John L. Lockwood was the company attorney. Davis, George Burford Lorimer, and Angus Cameron were Bobbs-Merrill editors.*

CHRIST IN CONCRETE

1. A book, like a magazine, is free for anyone to buy–and there is no subscription list. No way to label it for a particular audience–men as against women or young people, left-wingers against the conservatives. More people would look for license in a copy of Esquire than in a Bobbs-Merrill book.

2. The manuscript is not now in shape for us to ask either Mr. Chamberlain or Mr. Lockwood or any other outsider to read it–too messed up. Much of it would need to be copied. We can not delegate a question of house policy to an outside literary critic. When we have it in the shape which satisfies us, then it would be fine to get Chamberlain, and perhaps two or three other outstanding critics to read it for us–either recopied or in galleys. If it seems at all likely to us that we will have something to "defend" at law, then before we print we would certainly want the lawyer who would act for us, who would defend us, to read it before the deed was committed rather than after. I believe as a matter of principle that both legal and literary censorships are bad, but the house has no wish to crusade for the sake of the sacred rights of obscenity and would not relish the resultant publicity. The general character of the business of our three departments makes us conservative.

3. The chief responsibility for a matter of house policy rests with me–in whatever consultation with other members of our Board is practical. Three of the five members of our Board are highly conservative. They have high ideals for the house which extreme left-wingers would think outworn.

It would not be fair to ask Mr. Davis to assume this responsibility. He should be left free to say he was overborne by house policy.

4. Of course all proposed changes should be shown to the author. But in this connection refer to the language of the contract as to our rights of revision.

5. The literary fault of the author, not confined to obscenity, is violence. By exhausting emotion himself he numbs the reader instead of arousing the reader's emotion. Some degree of moderation would be much more effective. With less obscenity the outlines of the story emerge more clearly.

6. The prevalence of obscenity, some of it strange and recondite, is a distraction from the story, diverting the reader's attention from its real quality.

7. The profane obscenity relating to the Virgin and her Son is a weakness legally and a detriment to sales.

8. One could not in decency advertise the obscenity; one could hardly in honesty say nothing about it. One would not wish to attract "lewd" readers for a quality which is merely incidental. One would not want to repel readers, because of this incidental feature, from a really fine and significant work. There is a problem of advertising copy. See #1.

9. I read the ending of the novel as an instance of the loss of faith under the horrible blows, accidents, injustice and catastrophes of life–a thing that often happens–and the conflict that results between the child who has lost faith and the parents who hold it. I did not think particularly of the "education" of a paesans into a proletarian–but I can see the force of this intent and interpretation since Paul attributes what happened to his father, godfather and family, to capitalism. It might be made clearer.

I did not comprehend whether Annunziata's death was due to spiritual cause or self-inflicted wound. I was bothered because of this doubt, and thought it, in either case, an instance of the author's excessive violence, though perhaps Ok in a Latin.

10. The editing done by the Esquire staff seems on the whole excellent–not merely from the "decency" point of view, but from the literary point of view and the viewpoint of sales. The progress of the narrative is improved, the outline appears more effectively. It certainly leaves the story "strong" enough in all conscience. It is no meat for babes or spinister [*sic*] schoolmarms. It conveys the realism of the talk of Italian laborers. Such editing certainly can not fairly be called "Bowdlerizing." Some few things Esquire omitted (perhaps just for the sake of space) might be restored, and vice versa. But on the whole, it seems most judicious, observant of the author's peculiar genius, his special style and purpose, and designed to increase his audience.

11. An editing throughout in accordance with the same literary principles would seem in order. D.L.C. would recommend that Mr. Davis do it. He has editing talent of the first caliber. But if this is objectionable to his literary conscience or if his other work prevents, D.L.C. will undertake it, or have it done under his general direction, as fast as may be feasible, and submit to Mr. Davis and Mr. di Donato.

The course of editing is precisely in accord with the attitude of the house since the matter of publication was first broached last year and before the Ms. was signed. Heretofore it would seem to have been the attitude of the N.Y. Office as well as Indianapolis–the understood thing. Letters from Mr. Lorimer and Mr. Cameron would indicate that they expected it and sympathized with it and that the author expected it and agreed to it.

12. In spite of liberalizing tendencies in recent N.Y. decisions, "the law", as the Harvard Law Review says, "in its ponderous generalities, still remains as a weapon of censorship with the only safeguard the mercy of a judge." All states have obscenity laws. No other state is as likely to be as liberal as New York. Massachusetts has shown itself the opposite. We are an Indiana corporation. Action might be lodged against a bookseller anywhere. A complete account of what the book is would need to be given the booksellers before their purchases, and, however they might be assured of protection, it might lead to a limitation on purchases not just to the fine and notable qualities of CHRIST IN CONCRETE. This would certainly be the case in Boston, in the South and in many outlets over the country. The N. Y. State and N. Y. Federal decisions are not controlling decisions.

13. It is my impression that most of the recent books famous for their obscenity have not been large sellers and that the general opinion is that Hemingway's sales, for example, have declined as his obscenity increased–and that booksellers who admire his remarkable talent, think this a pity. The tendency of taste is now away from the Farrells.

14. Since the editing done and remaining to be done is B-M work, the cost of copying the manuscript should be borne by the house.

15. I have on the whole great admiration for CHRIST IN CONCRETE. I would hate to see our ability to make money out of it for the author and ourselves reduced or killed by what seems to me, and others here, both men and women, incidental and unimportant to the author's purpose.

16. Since the work is autobiographical, and written in hatred of capitalism, the author at some stage should be questioned (preferably by Mr. Lockwood) to discover whether he has portrayed in a libelous fashion living persons who may be identified. Cf the GOD'S MAN case.

17. I have great respect for the author's sincerity, though I feel with Mr. Sipe that it has been misled with respect to Paul's sexual developmental experiences. Others have questioned the visit to the priest as far from typical of the normal Catholic treatment of their poor. And others (besides Mr. Sipe) think the visit to Workmen's Compensation Bureau sounds phoney.

* * *

Bobbs-Merrill Publicity Brochure for *Christ in Concrete,* 1939

Early in 1937 Arnold Gingrich, editor of *Esquire,* wired from Chicago to his New York office to get hold of a man named Pietro di Donato. Gingrich had just read the manuscript of a short story entitled CHRIST IN CONCRETE, had pronounced it the most important literary discovery he had made in three years, and wanted to know something about the author at once.

He found out this. Pietro di Donato was born in West Hoboken, New Jersey in 1911, the son of an Italian bricklayer. His father was killed in a construction accident when Pietro was thirteen, leaving him the oldest son of eight children. With his father's trowel he got a job as a bricklayer, moving his family from place to place to avoid the truant officers. At fifteen he was an expert craftsman and at seventeen a foreman on construction in a craft that normally requires its apprentices to be eighteen years old. He supported his mother until her death in 1932, and his seven brothers and sisters through the boom and through the depression. Meanwhile he had found time to take scattered night school courses in engineering, to attempt to run a summer theater, to drift a bit around the country, to read

Front and back cover of the publicity brochure for the writer's first novel, published in 1939 (courtesy of The Lilly Library, Indiana University, Bloomington, Indiana)

a good deal–chiefly the Russian novelists and dramatists. Finally he wrote CHRIST IN CONCRETE, his first short story. He wanted to write a novel with the same title, using the short story as the first chapter.

Mr. Gingrich was right about his discovery. The short story created such interest when published in Esquire that a special reprint in pamphlet form was sold out. It was included in Edward J. O'Brien's Best Short Stories of 1938, and Mr. O'Brien dedicated that volume to Pietro di Donato. And in December 1937 he stopped bricklaying, with a publisher's contract to write the novel. It was completed in January, 1939, and he has returned to bricklaying, at the New York World's Fair and other jobs around New York.

The novel, CHRIST IN CONCRETE, fills every promise of the short story and of the author's extraordinary life. It is not just another labor novel. It is not about labor movements or labor politics at all, but about labor itself. In the lives of his hero Paul, his father and mother, the Italian bricklayers and their wives, di Donato tells what labor is like: its joys and sorrows, its cruelties and its rewards. He tells how work can be a terror of exploitation, how the job can break a body or twist a soul; but he also shows the comradeship of men working and the satisfaction of good craftsmanship. CHRIST IN CONCRETE portrays the lives of the tenement dwellers in all their crises–birth and death, marriage, love of man and woman and love of family, as well as the daily sacrifice of labor–and in every crisis it puts us face to face with humanity in its simplest and most understandable terms.

Nothing in CHRIST IN CONCRETE is more remarkable than the electric style that captures in English the emphatic rhythms of spoken Italian. It is a style that never fails the author in all the varied scenes that fill the book: the death of laborers on the job, the rough and tumble talk of the bricklayers, the rich fiestas of the Italians at play, the vivid sketches of tenement families, the conflicts that bring a sensitive boy to maturity as a man and a bread-winner. The book moves as rapidly as a motion picture thriller; its mood varies from a realism that omits no sight or sound or smell to a poetic insight into the hearts of its characters; but always it has a sincerity and passion that mark it as an important literary achievement.

* * *

Dust jackets illustrated by Carl W. Bertsch for three Bobbs-Merrill novels of the early 1930s (courtesy of Michael Manz/Babylon Revisited)

Within a year, the tale of the acquisition and editing of Christ in Concrete *had become so completely sanitized that it was now an instructive drama fit for the general public. This anecdote led off the first story in a five-part newspaper series on the company by Harry Morrison.*

One of the editors of the Bobbs-Merrill Company was reading a magazine. She came across a short story and went through it not once, but twice. As soon as she got to the office she wrote a letter to the author of that story, one Pietro di Donato.

That letter and ones that followed went unanswered. You might think that a big publishing firm would sooner or later shrug shoulders and let the matter drop. But you don't know publishing houses.

It was discovered that Mr. di Donato lived in New York City. So then the New York office was put on his trail. Fortunately, one of the authors of the house knew him and brought him in for a talk. Mr. di Donato acknowledged that he wanted to write a novel.

But he had no time for writing–he was earning his living laying brick. It was explained that this difficulty could be overcome. The company had sufficient confidence to advance him the money on which to live while he wrote.

A contract was made and money was sent him in installments until the manuscript was completed. The short story made the first chapter.

When the day came for the manuscript to arrive, D. L. Chambers, the president of the company, had the Bobbs-Merrill offices in an uproar. He had set his heart on that book. And he wanted that manuscript.

Time and again the company called the express offices. Nothing had arrived. One of the editors was "sure one of the boys in the stockroom has hidden that package."

Late in the afternoon came a call from downstairs. It was a man from the Post Office, hugging for dear life a huge bunch of straggling white typewritten sheets oozing out of an illwrapped manila paper bundle.

It was "Christ in Concrete"–but not in corrugated paper. It was to go past the 178,000 mark in sales.

"Christ in Concrete," as you probably know, became a Book-of-the-Month Club selection. Most best sellers don't come close to its life on the best selling list. The di Donato book was close to the top for all of six months and is still having a strong sale. [. . .]

–"The Story of Bobbs-Merrill," *Indianapolis Times,* 2 July 1940, p. 13

* * *

Bobbs-Merrill published Bambi's Children: The Story of a Forest Family, *by Felix Salten (the pen name of Siegmund Salzmann), in 1939. Barthold Fles's translation of Salten's book caught Mannon's censorious eye. In this memo to Chambers she also mentions Salten's* Perri, *which the company had published the previous year, and Icelandic writer Gunnar Gunnarsson's* Advent *(1937), which Bobbs-Merrill published in 1940 as* The Good Shepherd *in a translation by Kenneth C. Kaufman.*

Mannon to Chambers, Undated Memo

I have now read these first 59 pages of BAMBI'S CHILDREN. I like the story very much. Personally I like it better than PERRI. The only thing I don't care for is the discussion between Faline and Rollo when they talk about the coming mating season p 12. I don't think children would know what it was all about and to me it sounds overly sentimental. Since the librarians disapprove anyway, I think we should try to persuade Mr. Salten that cutting this out will not spoil the book for adults.

A few expressions puzzled me. Bambi and Faline and the rest of their kind seem to be called "roe-deer". Is this correct? Shouldn't it be simply the "roes" or when speaking of the males "roe-buck"? On p. 54 the translator says the men "mow the corn". That seems a strange thing here in Indiana. Perhaps it is correct for Austria. On pp. 49 and 53 the little Geno and Gurri say: "Who are those?" Should be "Who are they?" But for the most part the translation seems fine. Certainly it is vastly superior to Miss Ramsden's struggle with ADVENT.

One other thing troubled me. On page 14 there is a description of glow worms with wings. Apparently these are fire-flies or what we commonly call lightning bugs. But the author has them flying "high in the sky["] and only those few young venturesome ones come down to the ground and die. My observation of fire-flies is that they rise out of the grass and bushes at night and hover low over the ground. Only occasionally do they fly high in the air. I always see them thicker in the valleys and low meadows than anywhere else. Perhaps this should be checked by an authority.

Jessica.

P.S. Other references to the mating business occur on pp 38, 39 and 34 & 35.

* * *

Dust jackets illustrated by Paul Laune for 1936 and 1938 Bobbs-Merrill novels (courtesy of Michael Manz/Babylon Revisited)

The Values of Chambers and His Editors, 1939–1948

Thomas D. Clark was the author or compiler of five Bobbs-Merrill books from 1939 to 1975, beginning with The Rampaging Frontier: Manners and Humors of Pioneer Days in the South and the Middle West. *He was a professor of history at the University of Kentucky at the time of this 1967 article.*

In the late 1920's I read the sprightly biographies of Sam Houston and Andrew Jackson by Marquis James, Robert Selph Henry's story of reconstruction, and several other titles which had been published by the Bobbs-Merrill Company. When I first joined the University of Kentucky staff, I was especially impressed by a rather handsome book the Company published for William H. Townsend of Lexington, Kentucky. Everybody in Lexington was praising *Lincoln and His Wife's Home Town.* Mr. Townsend was a master storyteller, and his book did not slight the challenge of describing life in ante bellum Lexington at a time when the Lincolns came from Springfield, Illinois, to visit with the haughty Todd family.

I came to know William H. Townsend intimately. Many times I talked with him about his experiences with Bobbs-Merrill. In 1937–39 I was engaged in research and writing a book on frontier humor. By the spring of 1939 I had the manuscript completed and was ready to approach a publisher. Mr. Townsend offered to write a letter on my behalf to Mr. Laurance Chambers, but one night at a dinner party I met an old Bobbs-Merrill salesman who said he would go with me to Indianapolis to see Mr. Chambers.

In the meantime I wrote Mr. Chambers describing my manuscript, and asked if I might bring the manuscript in for him to examine. I will never forget the excitement with which I received his reply, written on his famous fawn-colored stationery and enclosed in a slender executive-type envelope. The letter was brief and pointed: he would look at my manuscript, but he made no commitment in advance about publication. I looked at his almost feminine signature many times trying to guess what kind of man he was. Neither Mr. Townsend nor Virgil Steed had really given me a description of him. Virgil and I left Lexington at four o'clock in the morning for Indianapolis, and I am certain we arrived there before Mr. Chambers came to his office.

The Bobbs-Merrill Company was located on North Meridian Street in a narrow "shotgun" building. The facade of the building, with its muted classic columns, was as impressive as the Company's stationery. On display at either side of the entry were recent Bobbs-Merrill books. Though I gazed at these hoping hungrily that not too far in the future my own book would be there, I was never to know whether it ever was.

Associate editor of the house at that time was Mrs. Jessica Mannion [*sic*], wife of an Indianapolis attorney. Jessica gave my manuscript a hurried perusal, and then said Mr. Chambers was ready to see me. I know now that if she had not seen promise in the manuscript she would have turned me back at that point. I have never been more anxious to make a good impression than at the moment I crossed the threshold of Mr. Chambers' office. I was not, however, prepared for what I saw. Mr. Chambers was a fairly tall, stooped, grey-haired man. He gave me the impression of having stepped fresh out of a Dickens novel. His shirt tail was out, his hair was rumpled, and he looked at me over pince-nez glasses as if I had brought a dead fish into the parlor. He made me sit down across the broad, tousled desk before him and talked in such a low voice that only by the grace of God could I tell what he was saying. The main points I got were that the book business was bad and that he had not worked his shirt tail out in anxiety to publish my book.

He asked me to unwrap the manuscript and hand it to him. When I handed him the manuscript, I slipped off a rubber band. In a nervous fidget, I cocked my pencil on the band, forgot about the pencil, and let go. My missile sailed over Mr. Chambers' head in a perfect arc, just missing him. I do not think he ever noticed what happened. No doubt I came within inches of shooting myself out of a publisher.

A short time after I returned to Lexington I received a contract. It was clear Mr. Chambers did not consider me another Marquis James, but he would publish the book. I worked closely with Jessica Mannion, and two or three times in the process of readying the book for release I talked with Mr. Chambers, always in half-whispered conversations. Once a question arose over whether they would allow me to publish a comic story about a backwoods incident involving a slight matter of miscegenation. Mr. Chambers vetoed the story. It was Jessica who grabbed me by the coat lapels and said, "You can't publish that story!" It was harmless, and today would not be questioned.

A young author could have worked with no finer people than the staff at Bobbs-Merrill. They were not, however, so sentimental about books as their authors were. I was most anxious to see what the *Rampaging Frontier* would look like in final form. So far as I knew, Bobbs-Merrill had closed its doors after I sent the page proofs back to them. One day I was walking across the campus of the University of Kentucky when I met a student with a new book under his arm. I asked to see it, and to my utter amazement it was my book. When I asked Mr. Chambers about this he said he thought it more important to get books on dealers' shelves than into authors' hands.

At this time the Bobbs-Merrill Company was under rather severe pressure. Jessica Mannion told me that the house had advanced $50,000 to Edith Bolling Wilson for her book, *My Memoir*. As a matter of fact, Bobbs-Merrill stationery carried a line of advertising for this book on the flap of the envelope. I think I am correct in saying that *My Memoir* was a disappointment. Mrs. Wilson seemed to me to say little in her book that had real substance.

After the appearance of the *Rampaging Frontier,* which received rather good reviews, I signed a contract for a second book, this time on the role of the country store in modern southern history. Before I had the manuscript of this book ready, Rosemary York became associate editor. I traveled over the South gathering tons of dusty store records as sources for my book. In Chapel Hill, North Carolina, I was told that an old classmate, Bell I. Wiley, was there working in the great Southern collection of the University. He and his wife were living in an old board-and-batten student shack, and I drove around to see them. When I drove into the yard, Bell was standing at a front window stripped to his waist. He yelled for me to come in–I was the very fellow he wanted to see. He told me that Bobbs-Merrill was publishing his *Johnny Reb* and that he was having trouble with Mr. Chambers, Rosemary York, and his wife. He had collected several letters which spelled out in purplish prose the more relaxed phases of soldiering in the Confederate Army. They did not support the image which the Daughters of the Confederacy cherished of the South's brave soldiers. Mr. Chambers and Rosemary would not let Bell publish the letters, and his wife said he should not publish them. A week or two later I was in Indianapolis

Dust jackets for three Bobbs-Merrill novels of the early 1930s that indicate the reading tastes the company tried to serve (courtesy of Michael Manz/Babylon Revisited)

and asked Rosemary about Bell's letters. She told me they were locked up in the Company's vault, where they were going to stay. [. . .]

I never could persuade Mr. Chambers to take advantage of certain potential sales outlets for *Pills, Petticoats, and Plows,* and I still believe these would have proved worth while. Sales had become the Achilles heel of the Bobbs-Merrill Company. Mr. Chambers, no doubt, was hard on his sales managers and promotion people. Too, the depression years were hard on the book business generally. I felt, as perhaps every author has felt from the beginning of time, that the Company did not always push books as effectively as it might have done. [. . .]

I am sure that this Midwestern publishing company had difficult financial sledding. I felt that it was a real asset to this region, and was happy indeed to be one of its authors. When I delivered the manuscript for the *Southern Country Editor,* and after the manuscript had been edited by Harry Platt, Rosemary York asked me one day to come into a back office for a private conversation. I had no idea what we were to talk about, but when we were in the office she said the Company felt it necessary to ask its authors to renegotiate their contracts at lower royalty rates. I agreed to this, even though there ran through my mind some debate on this matter. I could legally stand on my original contract and incur the wrath of some very warm friends, or renegotiate and perhaps help the Company; I did not feel the income from my book would be tremendously important either way. Later I learned that one or two authors proved unruly indeed. I remember one of them afterwards refused to write Mr. Chambers a letter of congratulation on the occasion, I believe, of his eightieth birthday. An appeal had gone out from his friends asking authors to do this. [. . .]

In his later years I had several pleasant visits with, and letters from, Mr. Chambers. Upon occasion when I was in Indianapolis, I stopped by the Bobbs-Merrill office to visit him. He was in retirement but still came to the office. The last time I saw him he asked me to come around the desk and sit by his side. We had a long conversation about authors and books, and when I got up to go he put his arm around my neck and gave me a fatherly pat. I could not help recalling how different that meeting was from that first nervous moment when I came within inches of shooting myself out of a publisher.

–"David Laurance Chambers as I Knew Him," *Indiana University Bookman,* no. 8 (March 1967): 100–106

* * *

Taking Stock

The Hoosier House enjoyed good press in Indianapolis. Its executives had long been involved in the cultural, fraternal, and charitable institutions of the city, and it was a major employer whose activities created other jobs in the ancillary industries needed to supply it. Morrison's Indianapolis Times *series, written as the Depression was coming to a close, provides a look at the workings of the company. (The claim about Earl Derr Biggers has not been verified.)*

[. . .] This world-famous publishing house has a New York office. Important functions are performed there to cover so important a market. The two offices work in close co-operation, as the di Donato story illustrates. But the headquarters of the house are in Indianapolis, and all phases of the work are done right here, from the perusing of manuscripts to the making of plates and engravings, the printing and binding of books.

In reality, Bobbs-Merrill is made up of three distinct divisions:

1. The Trade Department, which each year transforms from 65 to 90 fictional and non-fictional manuscripts into books that go into thousands of homes and hundreds of libraries.

2. The School Book Department, which publishes hundreds of thousands of school books each year. Of the 25 states which have state-controlled school book purchasing, Bobbs-Merrill furnishes school books for 11 of them.

3. The Legal Department, which publishes and sells thousands of law volumes every year. A file in the company's offices here contains the names of more than 50,000 lawyers who buy Bobbs-Merrill law publications. [. . .]

In 1939, a total of 1300 manuscripts was received at the Bobbs-Merrill Publishing Co. here. Every one of them was read, although most of them were unsolicited. In the first 11 days of June, 50 manuscripts came in. One was solicited.

The truth is that in the last three years only six unsolicited manuscripts have been accepted and published. Somewhere in these manuscripts was a touch of fire. And so Bobbs-Merrill introduced a new author.

That is why Bobbs-Merrill keeps going through the manuscripts . . . hunting that touch of fire.

The solicitation method is a complex one. It is done in any number of ways. Besides "friends of the firm," there are the regular literary agents, professors, book sellers, magazine writers, reviewers, all of whom carry on a continual correspondence with officials of the company.

Two young women wield a keen-edged sword on the stacks of unsolicited manuscripts. One of them sits at the desk which Earl Derr Biggers used when he was assistant manuscript editor years ago. You ought to remember Mr. Biggers. He wrote the Charlie Chan stories.

If the two consider a manuscript worth taking a second look at, it goes to other Indianapolis readers who give written reports of their opinion. If the reports are favorable and agree with the editor's estimate of the work, it is then referred to D. Laurance Chambers, president of the firm and head of the company's trade division. [. . .]

"Streamlining" is a modern word, but it is just what the Bobbs-Merrill Co.'s legal department has been doing for years.

As a matter of fact, Bobbs-Merrill prides itself on setting a pioneering pace in what is one of the most difficult of all book-publishing fields. [. . .]

Bobbs-Merrill, in the law publication field, confines itself largely to codes, statutes, textbooks and digests. While there are a number of important law publishing houses in the United States, the Bobbs-Merrill Company's name is found among the first five.

Col. Moorhead's duties as company treasurer keep him busy enough and Mr. Sipe provides the editorial supervision for the department. [. . .]

Well, right now they are working on a new Arizona Code. The last one was compiled, put in book form and passed in toto by the State Legislature. It thus became the last word and any mistake made by the editors was no longer a mistake but the law.

The State was not very well satisfied with what it got and this time selected the Bobbs-Merrill Company to do the work for it. A line by line hunt is now on to discover and explain or correct mistakes in the preceding code. This includes a comparison with the enrolled acts and a check of the opinions of the courts.

The new Arizona code is going to be as near perfection as is humanly possible.

The Indianapolis company started setting the streamlining pace years ago. The old Burns Statutes, first published in 1894, came in three big volumes each as bulky a tome as you ever saw on grandfather's shelf–and just as uninteresting from the outside. But let Mr. Sipe explain it himself:

"In the old days if a lawyer wanted to plead a case that had something to do with insurance he might have to take half a dozen or more volumes to court with him. The law on insurance was scattered all over the statutes. Now we have it in one volume.

"What we have done is to publish 12 volumes instead of the old three. Each of the 12, of course, is much smaller in size, but the set is codified in such a way that a lawyer only needs one volume at a time. [. . .]

In 1933, they hit on making pocket pack additions to the code books as state legislatures made new laws. The books are kept constantly up-to-date in this way. If one of them, through use, wears out, all the lawyer has to do is to buy one new book, not a whole set. [. . .]

Then there was (or is) the Louisiana Blind Tiger Act. In 1915, the Louisiana Legislature made it an offense to sell liquor from premises in the state. When Mr. Sipe came around to editing a new Louisiana Statute after repeal he had to decide whether that act was still in effect. The Legislature hadn't done anything about it and Mr. Sipe decided it was still a State law.

The Supreme Court of Louisiana subsequently decided this was correct. Instances of this kind could be duplicated in other states. [. . .]

In the Law Editorial department of The Bobbs-Merrill Company are about 20 girls whose duties consists [*sic*] of verifying annotations, checking cases against the original reports for accuracy and editing copy for the printer. [. . .]

These girls through long service have become experts and any one of them has read so many cases for so many years she ought to make a crackerjack judge.

At least once almost any week Lowe Berger gets aboard an airplane, bound for almost anywhere in the United States.

His mission: Selling, publicizing, getting ideas for school books.

The significance: Bobbs-Merrill of Indianapolis is one of the leading school book publishers in the world.

Oddly enough, Lowe Berger's school book department, for which Bobbs-Merrill is probably best known in the publishing trade, is the baby of the bunch at 720 N. Meridian St.

It started in 1909 when the company asked the Misses Georgia and Grace Alexander, both Indianapolis school teachers, to get up a set of readers for the primary grades. They were called the "Child Classics" and were illustrated "by the foremost artists of the day." Up to 1923, more than 3,000,000 copies were sold.

After the "Child Classics" came the Bobbs-Merrill Readers, which most of you probably remember. The newest series is the Curriculum Readers.

Some idea of the relative business of the school book and the trade division can be gained when you realize that a trade book is a best-seller when it tops 15,000 and that school books are sold a hundred thousand at a crack. [. . .]

"One of the major problems of school book publishing," says Mr. Berger, "is being constantly on the alert for pertinent social changes that are invariably mirrored in changing school curricula."

He points out that in earlier days there were more "passing over" of certain pertinent facts of history.

Dust jackets for three Bobbs-Merrill novels of the late 1930s (courtesy of Michael Manz/Babylon Revisited)

Newer school books, he declares, do not avoid such facts but present them according to the age of the child expected to read them.

Nor, he says, do publishers avoid the problems of plenty and poverty in the country or that the nation was once at war within itself for logical reasons on both sides. [. . .]

The company has been instrumental in two major advancements in school work publishing technique in recent years. It was the first house to use color engravings for pictures inside the books for grades above the third. And it was the first to use the greenish-tinted paper known as a "sight-saver" for children.

The Bobbs-Merrill "star" right now is Clara Baker. She is a teacher at Evanston, Ill., and she writes her books the same way she teaches her classes. She talks with them–not down to them.

When the company decides it is about time to get out a new series, contacts are made with educators all over the country. They are asked for ideas as to the contents. Then an author–or perhaps two or three–is asked to prepare the manuscript.

When Bobbs-Merrill later issues its trial manuscript, it looks like a New York City telephone directory, except that the covers are red instead of green, and the stories are mimeographed instead of printed. [. . .]

Bobbs-Merrill means more to Indianapolis than just a white-facaded building with huge plate glass windows up on N. Meridian St.

It is "bread and butter" for just about 2000 families. It is one of the "big" customers of local firms selling paper, binding and shipping materials. Its freight bill runs into multiple figures.

Type-setting, plate-making, printing, binding, shipping–all these functions go on in Indianapolis. Bobbs-Merrill is more than a cultural expression. It is one of this city's important industrial concerns.

The center of all these operations is 720 N. Meridian St. It was originally a showroom where electric automobiles were displayed and sold.

That atmosphere is all gone, but you can still see the spots on the floors where the acid dripped from the batteries.

The floor where the old electrics used to stand is still spacious enough for a roller rink. The office that has sold millions of school books is a cubbyhole on the right. On the left is a room used for conferences. The shipping department is in the rear.

A grand staircase, that looks like a part of the "Gone With the Wind" set leads to a long mezzanine, where the rest of the business is conducted. On the right is the manuscript department where the trade department editors wade through the endless hopes of about 1200 would-be authors each year.

In the center is the business department and in the rear the busy law library and law book department.

At the left, up front, is the office of D. Laurance Chambers, president of Bobbs-Merrill. You couldn't miss Mr. Chambers because he looks like a college president and, paradoxically, always works in his shirtsleeves, his collar unbuttoned and an unlighted cigar clamped between his teeth.

Each of the company's three departments is headed by a firm officer. Mr. Chambers handles the trade department. Lowe Berger, vice president of the company, is head of the school book department, and Col. Robert L. Moorhead, treasurer, is responsible for the law book department.

Mr. Chambers is the motivating force of this whole operation. His whole life has been built around books. If you ask his associates what his hobby is they'll reply: "Reading manuscripts."

He likes music. He likes to gather with people. He likes bridge. But he would never think of doing these things if his wife didn't remind him. He rarely takes a vacation. Last year was the first time he was ever seen to go off for a rest without a pile of manuscripts big enough to fill the entire rear seat of an automobile. [. . .]

Directly opposite Mr. Chambers' office is a graphic history of Bobbs-Merrill. It is a square, shelf-lined room. On the shelves are copies of each of the trade books the concern has published. Nobody knows exactly how many books are there. Our guess was 2000. The only other place you can be sure of getting a first edition of a Bobbs-Merrill book is the Library of Congress. [. . .]

Some people talk a great deal about the "soul" of a publishing house. The nearest Mr. Chambers will come to it is to say simply that a publisher has a trust similar to that of a professional man.

"We are constantly in the position of trustee for the work of an author," he says. "We are called upon to give him the benefit of our experience and, in many cases, to help him with his work. If we are unsuccessful in this, we are not good publishers."

Mr. Chambers saw the rise of Bobbs-Merrill as the publisher for outstanding Indiana authors. He deplores the present lack of Hoosier writers, says he doesn't know the reason, hopes still for the miracle that will put Indiana back to the front again as "the" literary state.

–"The Story of Bobbs-Merrill," *Indianapolis Times,* 2 July 1940, p. 13; 3 July, p. 7; 4 July, p. 11; 5 July, p. 15; 6 July, p. 7

Bobbs-Merrill: 1941–1950

1941

17 March — Irvin S. Cobb's *Exit Laughing* is published and becomes the number-nine nonfiction best-seller for the year.

1942

Jessica Brown Mannon leaves the company and is replaced by her assistant, Rosemary B. York.

18 May — Hamilton Cochran's first Bobbs-Merrill novel, *Windward Passage,* is published.

1943

17 February — Channing Pollock's autobiography, *The Harvest of My Years,* is published.

22 March — *By Nature Free,* the first of Hiram Haydn's two Bobbs-Merrill novels, is published.

7 May — Ayn Rand's first Bobbs-Merrill book, *The Fountainhead,* is published. The novel will sell almost three million copies by 1975.

1 September — Archibald Ogden becomes director of the Council on Books in Wartime.

October — Halsey J. Munson replaces Ogden as New York editor.

1944

15 January — Munson enters the navy.

March — John L. B. Williams replaces Munson as New York editor. Harrison G. "Harry" Platt joins the trade department in Indianapolis to perform editorial and promotion work. C. B. Ulery becomes editor of the educational department.

27 March — Fred Landon's *Lake Huron,* the first volume in the American Lakes series, is published.

10 May — Hewitt H. Howland dies.

16 October — Inglis Fletcher's *Lusty Wind for Carolina* is published. The novel will sell a million hardbound copies by 1975.

1945

17 August — Florence Marvyne Bauer's *Behold Your King* is published; it will win the 1947 Friends of Literature Award in fiction.

17 September — Alice T. Hobart's *The Peacock Sheds His Tail* is published. It will sell an estimated 791,000 hardback copies by 1975.

1946

	Leo C. Gobin joins the firm.
July	Patricia Jones becomes the first full-time editor of children's books.
9 August	Zola Ross's first Bobbs-Merrill novel, *Three Down Vulnerable: A Beau and Porgy Mystery,* is published.
3 September	Cid Sumner's first Bobbs-Merrill novel, *Quality,* is published.
30 September	Harriet Torrey Evatt's *The Snow Owl's Secret* is published; it wins the 1947 Ohioana Book Award for a juvenile book.

1947

	Lower royalties are negotiated with authors.
2 April	Robert L. Kincaid's *The Wilderness Road* is published; it is the first volume in the American Trails series, edited by Jay Monaghan.
25 August	The last stockholders' meeting is held for which the minutes survive. In the "Condensed Statement of Financial Conditions at June 30, 1947" there is an earned surplus of $413,588.75.
31 October	*The American Iliad: The Epic Story of the Civil War as Narrated by Eyewitnesses and Contemporaries,* edited by Otto Eisenschiml and Ralph G. Newman, is published.

1948

9 August	The last of Arthur Stringer's thirty-four books for Bobbs-Merrill, *Red Wine of Youth,* is published; it is a biography of Rupert Brooke founded on work begun by Richard Halliburton.
23 August	Hobart's *The Cleft Rock* is published; it will sell 887,000 hardbound copies by 1975.

1949

18 May	A promotional campaign is launched for the movie tie-in with Rand's *The Fountainhead.*
8 August	Robert P. T. Coffin's first Bobbs-Merrill book, *Coast Calendar,* is published.
29 August	Alice Harwood's first Bobbs-Merrill novel, *The Lily and the Leopards,* is published.
9 September	Booth Tarkington's only Bobbs-Merrill book, *Your Amiable Uncle: Letters to His Nephews,* is published.

1950

	Williams leaves Bobbs-Merrill; in October he joins Longmans, Green.
1 July	Haydn joins the firm as editor in the New York office.
21 August	Richard S. Lambert's *Adventure to the Polar Sea: The Story of Sir John Franklin* is published and wins the Canadian Library Association Book of the Year for Children Award.

Promotion in 1943

Hiram Haydn became the New York editor in 1950, but his first experiences with the firm indicate how much things had changed in the trade department since the early days of John J. Curtis.

My earliest experiences with the old Indianapolis firm of Bobbs-Merrill had occurred in the late 1930s. One of their editors had expressed a more than passing interest in one of those unwanted novels of mine that I kept peddling.

Nothing came of this at the time, but in the fall of 1941 I sent Bobbs an outline for a new novel, together with a long opening section. At last, after twelve years of rejections, I received a contract. The president of the firm, David Laurance Chambers, had been persuaded to risk an advance of four hundred dollars on this project.

Never has human hand squeezed a dollar bill tighter than did Mr. Chambers's. A sure thing had to be a sure thing had to be a sure thing before he would give it more than token promotion and backing. My first novel, *By Nature Free,* published in 1943, was supported by inclusion in several "list" advertisements, and went its way to quiet death. The reviews were staggeringly good, but Mr. Chambers's response to my request for more advertising was to assure me that the budget was

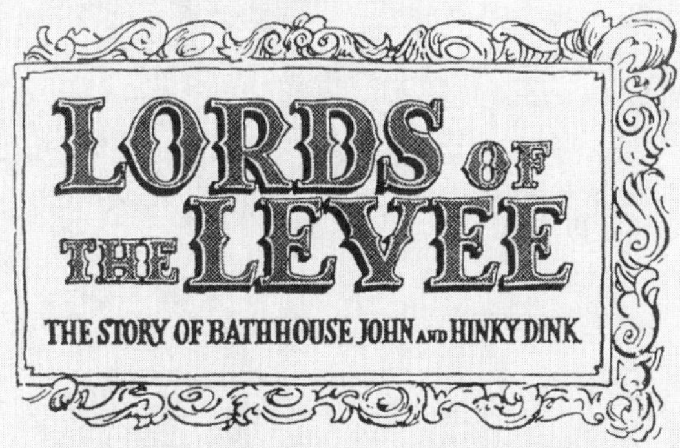

Advertisement from Publishers' Weekly *(16 January 1943) for the 1943 account of two corrupt political bosses of 1890s Chicago*

used up and I should be content with such good reviews. He furthermore sent me now–and only now–a copy of a pre-publication review in one of the trade journals, praising the book as "the best novel about small-town life since Sinclair Lewis's *Main Street,*" and predicting a large sale. Finally, he enclosed a copy of his letter to that reviewer, stating that the praise was welcome, but the prediction way off the mark. "I see no large sales possibility for this book," he wrote, "and we do not intend to promote it in that fashion."

You could call it candor.

A much more startling example of Mr. Chambers's penuriousness and stubbornness involved another novel Bobbs published that year: Ayn Rand's *The Fountainhead.* Despite an unmistakable groundswell of excitement over this book, DLC, as we all knew him, gave it only the most perfunctory advertising support. Solely through "word of mouth" (enthusiasts urging others to read it), *The Fountainhead* became a runaway best seller.

–*Words & Faces* (New York & London: Harcourt Brace Jovanovich, 1974), pp. 32–33

* * *

Obituary: Hewitt H. Howland

Hewitt H. Howland, 80 years old, former editor of Century magazine, and a native of Indianapolis, died in Roosevelt Hospital in New York yesterday after a long illness, according to an Associated Press dispatch from New York.

Mr. Howland was a brother of the late Louis Howland, former editor of the Indianapolis News.

He was born Oct. 8, 1863, in Indianapolis, the son of John D. Howland and Desdemona Howland, member of a pioneer Indianapolis family.

Before going to New York Mr. Howland spent the period from 1900 to 1925 as editor of the Bobbs-Merrill Company here.

D. Laurence [*sic*] Chambers, president of Bobbs-Merrill Company, recalled last night that Mr. Howland was guest of honor at a farewell dinner in the University Club in 1925, when he left Indianapolis to go to New York to take over the editorship of Century magazine.

Mr. Chambers and Meredith Nicholson, Hoosier author, both recalled that Mr. Howland entertained frequently many of the leading literary figures, both of this country and of European countries.

He discovered several authors during his long periods of editorship.

Mr. Howland numbered among his friends all the literary people of Indiana and was an especial friend of James Whitcomb Riley.

Mr. Howland spent several years as editor of Century magazine and then became fiction editor of the Century Publishing Company. In later years he was associated with Jaques [*sic*] J. Chambrun, New York literary agent.

In New York, Mr. Howland was a member of the National Arts and the Town Hall clubs.

Mr. Howland became editor of Century magazine following the resignation of Glenn Frank, who resigned to become president of the University of Wisconsin.

Surviving Mr. Howland is the widow, the former Manie Cobb, sister of the late Irvin S. Cobb.

–"Hewitt Howland Dies In New York," *Indianapolis Star,* 11 May 1944, pp. 1, 9

* * *

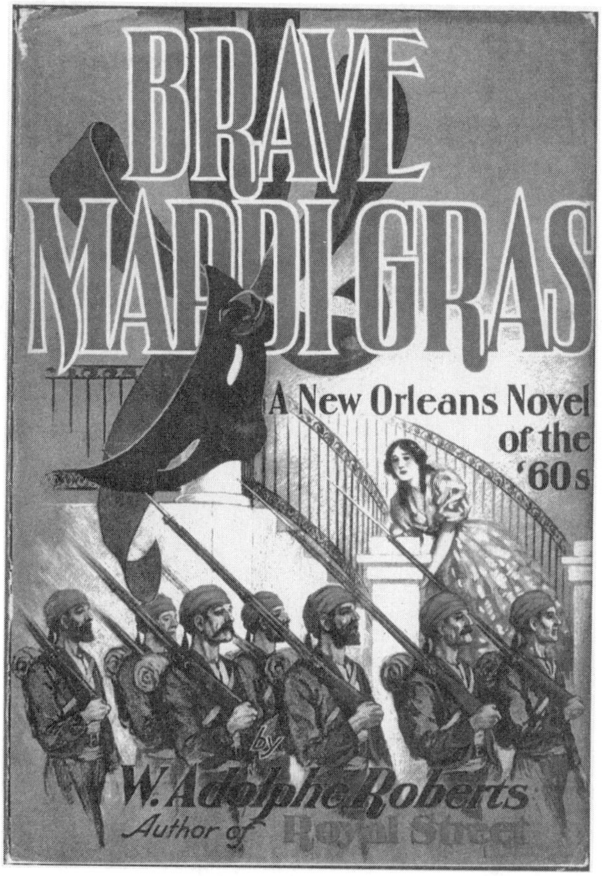

Dust jacket for a 1946 novel by an African American author (courtesy of Michael Manz/Babylon Revisited)

Old Standbys

Bobbs-Merrill says that the new edition of "The Wizard of Oz" by L. Frank Baum which has new color and black and white illustrations has made this famous child's book more popular than ever. The book has been on Bobbs-Merrill's list for almost half a century. The new edition came out in 1944. And speaking of juveniles, Bobbs-Merrill also tells us that the steady sale, year after year, of Richard Halliburton's "The Complete Book of Marvels," which was originally written for children but which many grown-ups have enjoyed has forced the publisher to make new offset plates recently. There are now 33 titles in Bobbs-Merrill's popular *Childhood of Famous Americans* series. A revision of the circular which has been used to promote this series is now being made so that it will include all the titles. A colorful brochure is also being prepared for the sales clerks setting forth the selling factors in this series.

–*Publishers' Weekly,* 151 (8 February 1947): 894

A Wish Fulfilled

Since the Bowen-Merrill era, the house regretted that it had not captured the great Hoosier novelist Booth Tarkington, apart from prefaces to James Whitcomb Riley's The Name of Old Glory: Poems of Patriotism *(1917), May Wright Sewall's* Neither Dead nor Sleeping *(1920), and George C. Tyler's* Whatever Goes Up: The Hazardous Fortunes of a Natural Born Gambler *(1934). This regret was voiced as late as 1940, in Harry Morrison's series of articles on Bobbs-Merrill in* The Indianapolis Times. *Finally, in 1949, the company published a posthumous collection of Tarkington's letters,* Your Amiable Uncle: Letters to His Nephews.

[. . .] One author you'll miss. Booth Tarkington never wrote for Bobbs-Merrill. When he first started writing, he got a couple of stories published in McClure's Magazine. They were "Monsieur Beaucaire" and "The Gentleman from Indiana." It was natural that when they were issued as books, McClure's would do the job. Mr. Tarkington never changed publishers. He always has said that he thought it detrimental for an author to have the bulk of his work done by one publisher and a few outside.

He and Mr. Chambers are warm friends. The two families see much of each other.

Mr. Chambers is a great admirer of Mr. Tarkington and he makes no secret of his desire to publish at least one of the Tarkington books–some day, somehow. [. . .]

–Harry Morrison, "The Story of Bobbs-Merrill,"
Indianapolis Times, 6 July 1940, p. 7

* * *

Booth Tarkington (Gale International Portrait Gallery)

Promotion in 1949

The value of the company's Ayn Rand property was no longer being ignored by the time the motion-picture version of The Fountainhead *came out in 1949. The "hoopla" is reminiscent of Curtis's early promotion work, and the profitable movie rights continued the tradition he founded.*

[. . .] Bobbs-Merrill's campaign to push its best-selling novel, "The Fountainhead," in connection with the Warner Brothers movie scheduled for release late in June, began with an ad which ran in the May 18 *Variety*. Heavy advertising will be continued through the summer months in the book pages, and the Warner Brothers ads will call attention to the book. The publishers are preparing a sticker, designed to fit the triangular space just below the title on the jacket of the book. The copy reads in part, "Read the book. See the magnificent Warner Brothers Production . . ." [. . .]

A spokesman for Warner Brothers reports that his company has rarely had such cooperation from a publisher as from Bobbs-Merrill in connection with the

Attorney and law editor Julius Birge, law-department head Robert L. Moorhead, chief law editor Richard V. Sipe, and vice president Lowe Berger, 1947. Berger served as president of the company from 1953 to 1958 (courtesy of The Indiana Star*).*

film version of "The Fountainhead." Ross Baker of Bobbs returns the compliment. Warners, he says, has not only done a faithful job in transferring the novel to the screen but has worked hand in hand with the publishing house in mapping out an exploitation campaign which should pay handsome dividends for picture and book alike.

In view of the fact that complete mutual satisfaction of this sort is rather rare, the reasons for it may be worth looking into.

One point which stands out is that "The Fountainhead," since its first appearance in 1943, has been a literary phenomenon and is wisely being treated as such in the present context. Without benefit of book clubs and with no departure from its original $3 price, it has gone through 30 printings to date, selling approximately half a million copies. It is hardly surprising under the circumstances that all the advertising for the picture prominently features the book. A typical full-page ad in *Variety* last week depicted Gary Cooper and Patricia Neal, the stars, as figures on a book jacket locked in amorous struggle. Posters announcing the movie and also showing the book, along with quotes from the reviews of the novel, are being sent to

Advertisement from Publishers' Weekly *(31 July 1948) for the revised 1948 edition of a travel narrative first published in 1855*

every public library and every college library and department of English in the country, and practically every bookstore.

Bobbs was busy as long as six months ago laying the groundwork for the current hoopla. At that time the publishers wrote to the nation's booksellers asking them to watch for the picture and advising them not to expect any popular-priced reprint or reduction in the price of the regular trade edition in conjunction with the film's release. Starting June 26 with a full-page ad in the New York *Times Book Review* and others in the Chicago *Tribune* and Los Angeles *Times,* Bobbs will renew large-scale promotion of the novel. Reproductions of the *Times* ad are to be delivered to booksellers along with the posters for window display purposes. A special sticker is being prepared for the "Fountainhead" jacket as a further reminder of the screen transcription. Each dealer will be supplied with the name of the local theatre exhibiting the film, and the theatre managers are being urged to work with the dealers on any additional window display material required.

Already, in private screenings, "The Fountainhead" has stirred up the sort of controversy which has helped keep the novel in the public eye. People tend to

Editors Pat Jones, Guernsey Van Riper Jr., and Rosemary B. York reading Herbert Krause's The Thresher, *published in 1946 (courtesy of* The Indianapolis Star*)*

like it a lot, it seems, or to object strongly to its idea content. Whether for good or ill, most shooting scripts are not written by the authors of the books from which they are derived, but in this instance the tradition was suspended and the results are pure Ayn Rand.

During the period when she was working on "The Fountainhead" as a novel, Miss Rand was supplementing her weekly advance payments from Bobbs by reading for Paramount in New York. Thus the book has been closely bound up with the movies almost from its inception.

–*Publishers' Weekly,* 155 (11 June 1949): 2403, 2405

* * *

The Autumn of D. Laurance Chambers

In 1950 novelist and scholar Haydn came over to Bobbs-Merrill from Crown Publishers, where he had been editor in chief for five years. In his time as New York editor for Bobbs-Merrill he observed the decline of D. Laurance Chambers and left an account that reflects both his distaste and his grudging admiration for the man. Other voices telling of other sides to Chambers are found in the authors section and the appendix, which features his brief memoirs.

In 1945, I finally met DLC, and found him in person a type familiar back in World War I days, with a rather pale soft face, pince-nez and a straw skimmer. [. . .]

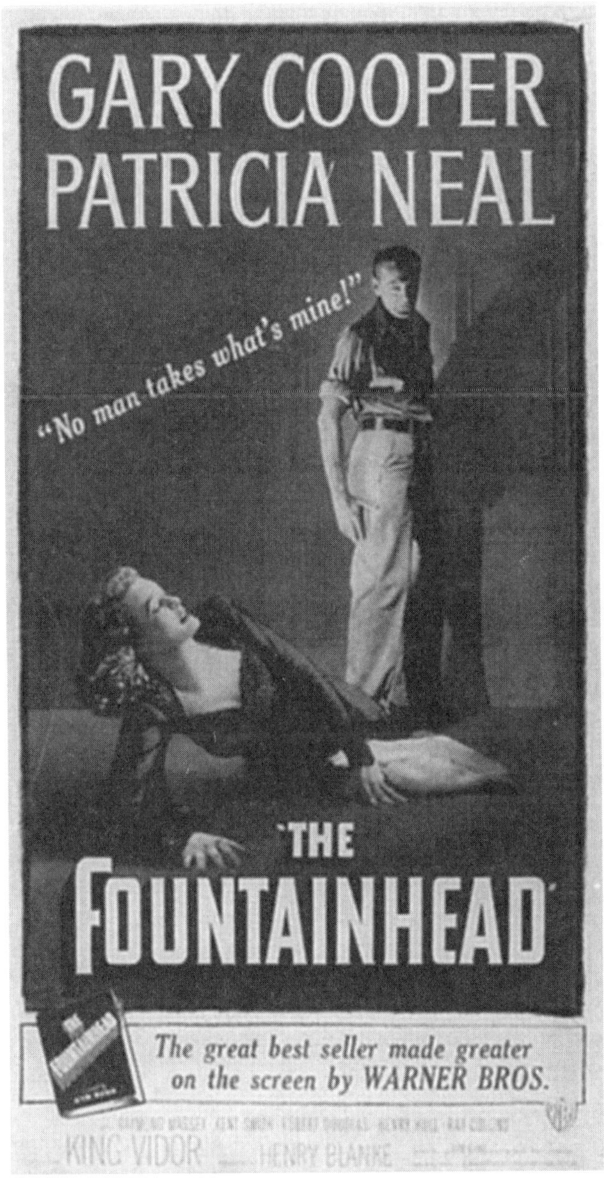

Poster for the 1949 movie version of Ayn Rand's 1943 novel, for which she wrote the screenplay (Bruccoli Clark Layman Archives)

But though he was courteous and cultivated in manner, I had had several bristling letters from him, alternated with gracious assurances of esteem, and should by now have realized that there were steel teeth in this trap.

Indeed, in 1945 and '46 we exchanged unfriendly letters and one phone call during which we both shouted. The issues were lack of advertising for my books and my request to be released from the firm option he held on my next book, through an outdated clause in the Bobbs-Merrill contract. [. . .]

Hence I was surprised to have a phone call, early in 1950, from Ross Baker, the sales manager, who worked in the company's New York offices, only a couple of blocks from Crown. He and I had been friendly, but it had been a long time since we had been in touch with each other.

Our first two lunches mystified me. Ross made cautious references to being on the lookout for a new editor, saying that the present one, John L. B. Williams, a quiet gentleman I knew and liked, and DLC were having trouble, and it was clear that Williams was going to be fired. All this was very confidential. I waited for him to ask me if I would be interested in the job, but he didn't.

[. . .] It was only at the third lunch that he cautiously hinted that Bobbs might be interested in me if I was interested in Bobbs. And it was another month or two before we finally worked it out. I insisted that I would come only if I were given a free hand editorially, with no consultation with DLC required.

Ross had friends at court out at Indianapolis, and it was probably through them that he at last persuaded Mr. Chambers. So, along about July 1, I said good-by to Crown and went to work at Bobbs.

The editorial department was undergoing a clean sweep, and Ross arranged for me to have a series of appointments with applicants for the post of assistant editor. It developed that I needed only one; I appointed the first man I met.

This was Louis Simpson, who was to become one of our finest poets. [. . .]

Before I left, Ross Baker was in charge of the office, but when I arrived in 1950, he and Walter J. Hurley, a ruddy, pleasant man in charge of production, shared responsibilities and to some extent a competitive rivalry. Each had his girl Friday, each his supporters. The gingerly balance of power, however, created the effect of a benign cold war rather than overt friction.

Over us all hung the elongated shadow of DLC, but the threat of a Calvinistic deity six hundred miles away caused only a subdued uneasiness rather than (as I was to discover) the desperation of finding oneself directly under the surveillance of his terrifying Eye. Technology had produced the telephone and the dozens of varieties of memorandum pads, pink, blue, yellow, white and green, that DLC dispensed with an overgenerous hand, but we were spared his Presence.

History was frightening, too. The New York publishing populace would have been drastically reduced had the Bobbs-Merrill alumni been removed from its ranks. Almost every week I encountered yet another highly successful editor, sales manager, production chief, who had been fired by David Laurance Chambers. There was a joke tirelessly repeated: "I owe everything to DLC. If he hadn't fired me . . ."

Section Three
Fourteen Pages

The Indianapolis Times

SUNDAY, MARCH 20, 1949

Editorials ....30 Records 32
Politics .....31 Radio 37
Features ....33 Movies ..40, 41

The House That WORDS Built

Gary Leslie, salesmanager (left), and Richard V. Sipe, editor, take their law by the ton.

Through these doors have passed the magic minds of a literary era . . . the modestly ornate entrance to Bobbs-Merrill Co., Inc.

Miss Mildred Nicholas shows part of the schoolbook line.

D. Laurance Chambers . . . the moving spirit of Bobbs-Merrill.

Up and down these broad stairs walk the literary craftsmen . . . Guernsey Van Riper Jr., editor-author, descends with one of his own books (Lou Gehrig) in hand.

Harrison G. Platt Jr., ex-Brown English professor, is associate editor of the Trade Book Department . . . He's conferring with copy editor Charlott Jeanes.

Col. R. L. Moorehead, treasurer, with the company 54 years . . . he's a young 73, loves his farm next to the law.

Photos by John Spicklemire, Times Staff Photographer.

Miss Jane Throckmorton holds the most hardy perennial of all children's books, "The Wizard of Oz."

This is "Rosemary" . . . more properly Mrs. Rosemary B. York, associate editor of the Trade Book Department.

By HAROLD HARTLEY, Times Business Editor

WORDS did it. Magnolia-scented words of sultry, moist-lipped romance. Leopard-hunting words from orchid-hung jungles. Words glistening in medieval armor. Soft, gentle words read on a mother's knee to her very young.

Then stir in the somber, black-robed words of the law. And schoolbook words for the pig-tailed and corduroy-trousered generation.

These words, spanning the whole spectrum of the emotions, most of the range of jurisprudence and formal learning—frothed with sweet, fragile words and seasoned with the tough, profane blasts of the stevedore—have built the most influential publishing house of the middle west, the Bobbs-Merrill Co., Inc.

❖ ❖ ❖

INSIDE the thick quiet of the Bobbs-Merrill offices at 724-730 N. Meridian St., you feel the presence of a scholarly dignity, a poise born of earned confidence and experience. It is the same rich feeling you get from walking on a thick-piled carpet.

At Bobbs-Merrill, you listen closely for the steady throb of the executive heart. You detect it in many directions. But if you follow it closely, the strongest beat leads to the office and study of D. Laurance Chambers, president.

You find him at a massive desk in an open-throated, soft, blue-gray shirt, an unlit cigar in his curled fingers. At a glance, he is patience and forbearance. But employees assure you that behind his scholarly charm, he is a rigid, insistent perfectionist.

It is a toss-up as to whether Bobbs-Merrill made Indiana authors or the authors made Bobbs-Merrill. It probably was the combination of the smooth-running, fast-flowering enterprise of both.

❖ ❖ ❖

MR. CHAMBERS has the magic touch, the sixth sense which tells a publisher when he has struck

The brittle and yellowed pages of Bobbs-Merrill history reach back 125 years. It was then, in 1824, that Samuel Merrill was treasurer of the state of Indiana and the capital was being moved from Corydon to Indianapolis.

Mr. Merrill brought four wagon loads of belongings to Indianapolis, and in one of these were his precious books, the seed from which the State Library grew.

MR. ZIEGNER begins preparing his sales brochures, pamphlets and news releases. A digest is prepared to be submitted to salesmen some of whom strangely carry the books of several publishing houses. Advertising is prepared in New York in co-operation with Bobbs-Merrill's well-staffed New York office where authors are given all of the help provided by New York publishers.

The book is being set in type, the proofs checked, the cover created, all at the same time. And an elaborate presentation is made to the salesmen at two conferences a year, January and July for spring and fall selling.

Anecdotes pile up in publishing houses. Take Pietro di Doneto. One of the editors noticed one of his stories in a magazine. A letter to him went unanswered. Finally the New York office located him, and found him a poor bricklayer. He said he had a novel to write. The firm made a contract, paid him an advance. When the novel came it was "Christ in Concrete," and sold 175,000 copies.

Scanning the Hoosier horizon, Mr. Curtis found a Shelbyville lawyer named Charles Major. "When Knighthood Was in Flower" sold more than a million copies.

But so did "The Phantom Crown" which became the movie "Juarez," the romance of Carlota and Maximilian. Mrs. Chambers had heard Bertita Harding at a lecture and thought she had literary possibilities.

❖ ❖ ❖

MR. CHAMBERS is probably the foremost living authority on trade books. He has lived through all the cycles. He knows that after a war there is a strong appetite for high emotion. And that the

*First page of a feature story on the company (*Indianapolis Times *Collection/Tiffany Studio, photos by John Spicklemire)*

Lois Stewart Baumgart, D. Laurance Chambers's secretary, in 1967, her fiftieth year with the firm (courtesy of The Indianapolis Star, *photo by William A. Oates)*

It was, then, with something less than exhilaration that I made my first trip to Indianapolis for a conference with Mr. Chambers, an expedition scheduled to recur on a bimonthly basis. [. . .]

That first morning I entered what reminded me of a large old-fashioned department store. Desks and offices were distributed in horrid rows over the first floor, which stretched away from me, it seemed, into that dim distance where parallel lines meet. [. . .]

Up there were executive warrens and, I was to discover, another long vista leading through the mid-floor business offices to the law department. But for the moment I was not looking. To my right, at the head of the stairs, behind a small desk, sat a large, grave woman who was Lois Stewart, Mr. Chambers's secretary. Lois was–is–made of superior stuff: she has survived DLC and is still there.

His office was in marked contrast to that rough workshop shared by Wartels and Simon [at Crown]. It was immaculate, old-fashioned and quietly elegant. And behind a large mahogany desk sat the Great Man. He had removed his jacket and necktie and opened his white, white shirt at his skinny veined neck. His gray hair was very neatly combed to one side, his face, bent over his work (for he did not look up), a small grayish oval. In fact the only living color I saw was a narrow line of pink scalp that marked the part in his thinning hair.

Then he did look up, and I saw where all the color was. In his blue eyes. Pale Alexandrian eyes. Yet I knew, even then, capable of incandescence. [. . .]

But the first hour or so was undeniably pleasant. I had been right in recalling him as a cultivated man, one of good breeding, taste in literature and intellectual competence. Forgotten were the hostile letters, the violent telephone call, Ross Baker's warnings.

The strategy the old man (he was old–at once brittle and pinched–frail, I thought with easy compassion. He was then about seventy-one, and he lasted to over eighty)–the strategy the old man selected was to introduce me to the history of Bobbs-Merrill. Founded in 1838 by Samuel Merrill, the firm was unique: the oldest of the two or three significant publishing houses in the Middle West. I learned of William Conrad Bobbs, and of the Merrills, into whose exalted *ambiance* Mr. Chambers found his way. I heard how he had, step by detailed step, risen to the presidency. All modestly put, in his voice with gravel in it, all in good taste, even a little dry when talking of self.

I was hearing the story of a life, I thought respectfully: the life of a truly dedicated man. I noted the acceleration of pride as he spoke of his relations with Booth Tarkington and Mary Roberts Rinehart, told of the golden list of the twenties, when Richard Halliburton and Bruce Barton and Julia Peterkin were on his roster, and they and John Erskine's *The Private Life of Helen of Troy* made enormous profits.

He did not go on from there. There was a silence, during which I indulged a sentimental fantasy of restoring past glories to the company and winning his enduring gratitude.

"And so," he said at last, "that is the past. We must now speak of the present and the future, of the working relation between you and me."

His voice became soothing, hypnotic. He spoke of his pleasure in securing an editor of my caliber. He stressed the crucial importance of our intimate collaboration, assured me of the priority I would have on his time when, believing I had found a worthy manuscript, I sent it on for his approval.

I was duly mesmerized. [. . .]

Yet I must. I must resist. And I blurted out with awkward assertiveness the conditions under which I had accepted the job. I would not be submitting manuscripts for his approval; the terms of our agreement stipulated that I had the right to accept or reject on my own.

The transformation (which was to prove only the first of hundreds) was devastating. Those eyes took on the deep color of a wild rage; they seemed to me to protrude as though issuing from their sockets on stalks. The palsied hands shook. The voice, grown suddenly

Hiram Haydn, who left Crown Publishers in 1950 to become the New York editor for Bobbs-Merrill (photograph by Gould Studios; from the dust jacket of Haydn, The Hands of Esau, *1962; Richland County Public Library)*

sonorous, must have made the whole building tremble as did the withered, turkey-cock wattles under his chin.

I was an ingrate, an upstart, arrogant and fatuous.

To this I could respond better. Coldly, I told him that these seemed strange charges to fasten on a man guilty only of wanting to stand by an established arrangement and expecting the other party to keep his word as well.

Another instant change. A softening. A pleading note from an old man who had given his life to a task that was now to be stripped from him. [. . .]

"We will talk of this another time," he said coldly. "You are lunching with Mr. Berger and me. We will meet you at the front door. Miss Stewart will show you where the washroom is." [. . .]

I was miserable. In what Halloween farce had I been assigned a victim's role? We walked down North Meridian Street to the Athletic Club, they side by side, hands clasped behind their backs, faces set, attending only the unpropitious prospect before them.

No. Twice, Lowe Berger turned to me and said something. I became aware of *his* eyes (I refuse to mention their color). I became aware in that instant of a man of dignity, sympathy, acute sensitiveness, and self-respect. Above all, a man to trust. And I was right. Never even a shading of the truth as he knew it: constancy, integrity and understanding. I think of him always with love and respect; I mourn his early death. [. . .]

After the return voyage, which they navigated with hands clasped behind their backs, Mr. Chambers left without a word to me.

"Come into my office," Lowe suggested. "Let's get acquainted."

I spent most of the afternoon with him. I learned about the power structure. The law department, with a monopoly on the printing of all state records and documents, provided the company's largest source of revenue. Its head was subordinate to Mr. Chambers, but, since his field was technical, one about which DLC knew little, he was substantially independent. Lowe himself headed the school textbook department, and was vice-president of the company. Without his saying as much, I could see that he had built, in the few years since he had come from Appleton-Century, a department record now rivaling the success of the law department, and thereby entrenched himself in a very strong position.

There was no equivalent executive in the trade department, for that was Mr. Chambers's field. And its profit, as is so often the case, lagged far behind those of the other two divisions. This was a sore point with DLC, and made the task of a trade editor the more onerous. [. . .]

He felt sorry for that old devil, Mr. Chambers. He respected his learning, his achievements, his dedication. But he lunched with him every day, kept fully abreast of "the old sinner's" fantasies, because he knew that he was no longer to be trusted–that ancient griefs and frustrations and hatreds, long pent, had corrupted his judgment. Offering no specific examples, he spoke of the Chambers family in a way reminiscent of the House of Atreus. It was long later that I learned some of the details, most painfully when a son-in-law I knew, Julius Birge, a big, gentle, eager man, went to the basement of his house and blew his head off with a double-barreled shotgun. I was never invited to DLC's home; I am grateful for that.

Lowe told me that one could measure the energy potential of hate by the fact that DLC, suffering acute prostatitis, refused an operation and would, he knew, continue to refuse it so long as he lived, which Lowe predicted would be another decade. Fear could kill, he believed, but it could also engender a hatred that was sustaining, could enable some to live simply for revenge on life.

"And now," he finally said, "I want to make it clear to you that you must not be intimidated by all this. You will never be alone in your fight to build a real trade list."

He commended Ross Baker to me; he assured me that he would himself be constantly vigilant, and see to it that I was forewarned whenever Mr. Chambers mounted an attack.

And that was the way it was. Three times DLC sought to fire me, taking his complaint to his board of directors. Three times Lowe checkmated him, for by now the board, originally in Mr. Chambers's pocket, had come to be aware of, and to distrust, his irrationalities, his vindictive hostilities. They had learned to turn to, and rely upon, Lowe's calm voice, his level scrutiny, and his measured judgments. [. . .]

On such occasions, I would remember again that first afternoon, and Lowe suddenly turning almost severe. "I want you to understand that I am not disloyal to Mr. Chambers. Tomorrow, if I so chose, I could succeed him as president. I never will, so long as he lives and is able to work effectively. I owe him my opportunity, and he has my loyalty. Only now it must take the hard form of opposing him over and over again, protecting him from himself." [. . .]

Oddly enough, the first book I had ready for Bobbs was *The Grand Portage,* by Walter O'Meara, whose *The Trees Went Forth* had been my first at Crown. Walter is an impeccable craftsman; he has always turned in to the copy editor the cleanest "copy" of all the writers I know.

Hence his manuscript made an enormous hit with Mr. Chambers (probably the finest, most precise trainer of copy editors in the country), who assumed that I was responsible for its near perfection. "I can see," he wrote me, "that we have at last a professional editor, who is neither too self-important nor too lazy to deliver a script in its properly finished state."

This alarmed me, and I replied that I could not guarantee such "professionalism" consistently. It was O'Meara who was the unusual professional. My disclaimer was adjudged a case of undue modesty. But not for long. No other manuscript won such praise from him, and the Cold War was resumed. [. . .]

–*Words & Faces,* pp. 33–34, 36, 42–51

Bobbs-Merrill: 1951–1960

1951

Robert L. Moorhead retires as an officer but continues to serve as a director until 1958.

10 September William Styron's first novel and only Bobbs-Merrill book, *Lie Down in Darkness,* is published.

17 October The first of J. Saunders Redding's two books for Bobbs-Merrill, the autobiographical *On Being Negro in America,* is published.

1952

29 February The first volumes in the Notable American Trials series are published. Edited by Francis X. Busch, they are *Prisoners at the Bar: An Account of the Trials of the William Haywood Case, the Sacco-Vanzetti Case, the Loeb-Leopold Case, the Bruno Hauptmann Case* and *Guilty or Not Guilty? An Account of the Trials of the Leo Frank Case, the D. C. Stephenson Case, the Samuel Insull Case, the Alger Hiss Case.*

18 March The first of Mark Harris's two books for Bobbs-Merrill, *City of Discontent: An Interpretive Biography of Vachel Lindsay,* is published.

11 August Robert Raynolds's *The Sinner of Saint Ambrose* is published and is named a Book-of-the-Month Club selection.

24 October Marie McPhedran's *Cargoes on the Great Lakes* is published; the book wins a 1953 Governor General's Literary Award.

1953

13 April Harris's *The Southpaw,* the finest baseball fiction since that of Ring Lardner, is published.

28 September The first three volumes in the Makers of the American Tradition series are published. Edited by Donald Bigelow, they are Harold Syrett's *Andrew Jackson;* Perry Miller's *Roger Williams;* and I. Bernard Cohen's *Benjamin Franklin.*

October D. Laurance Chambers relinquishes the presidency to Lowe Berger, becomes chairman of the board (a position he holds until 1958), and continues to dominate the trade department. Ross Baker becomes vice president. Leland Morgan, manager of the law department, is elected to the board of directors.

1954

15 February Elmer Davis's *But We Were Born Free* is published and becomes the number-nine nonfiction best-seller for the year.

1 March Louis Kronenberger's *Company Manners* is published.

5 April — Joseph Wood Krutch's *The Measure of Man: On Freedom, Human Values, Survival and the Modern Temper* is published. The sequel to his *The Modern Temper: A Study and a Confession* (1929), it wins the National Book Award for nonfiction in 1955.

20 September — Elizabeth Yates's *Rainbow round the World: A Story of UNICEF* is published. The following year it wins the Jane Addams Children's Book Award from the American section of the Women's International League for Peace and Freedom.

1955

1 January — Hiram Haydn leaves Bobbs-Merrill for Random House.

February — Bucklin Moon is appointed New York editor.

7 March — Anne Chamberlain's first Bobbs-Merrill novel, *The Tall Dark Man,* is published.

26 September — Ira Avery's *The Five Fathers of Pepi* is published; it wins a 1956 Christopher Book Award.

1956

31 May — Glenn Tucker's *Tecumseh: Vision of Glory* is published and wins the Mayflower Cup for an outstanding book by a North Carolina writer. This year Tucker also wins the Thomas Wolfe Memorial Award for meritorious writing by a resident or native of western North Carolina.

1957

The company has sales of $2,708,594 and profits before taxes of $115,076.

January — Moon announces his resignation as New York editor.

July — Julius Birge, secretary of Bobbs-Merrill, is appointed manager of the Indianapolis office of the trade department. After World War II he becomes an editor and also house attorney. Stephen Zoll is placed in charge of Eastern promotion and publicity and will perform editorial work in the New York office.

16 September — William F. Steuber Jr.'s *The Landlooker* is published. It wins the 1958 Friends of American Writers Award.

1958

The company moves to 1720 East Thirty-eighth Street (the Williamson Candy Company building), Indianapolis. For this year, sales are $2,375,315, with a loss before taxes of $6,327.

The law department publishes an album of recordings by lawyer Melvin Belli, reproducing some of his opening statements and closing arguments.

24 October — J. Christopher Herold's *Mistress to an Age: A Life of Madame de Staël* is published. The biography wins the 1959 National Book Award for nonfiction and the California Literature Nonfiction Gold Medal.

30 October — Chamberlain's *The Darkest Bough* is published; the novel wins the 1959 Ohioana Book Award for fiction.

11 November — Howard W. Sams announces the purchase of Bobbs-Merrill. At the next board meeting Sams becomes chairman and acting president. Leo C. Gobin is promoted from treasurer to vice president and general manager.

1959

The educational department of Bobbs-Merrill acquires the Public School Publishing Company and the Gregory Publishing Company. The Childhood of Famous Americans series is modernized.

February — M. Hughes Miller becomes president of the subsidiary Bobbs-Merrill Company.

6 April — Jules Dubois's *Fidel Castro: Rebel–Liberator or Dictator?* is published.

May — The New York office moves to 717 Fifth Avenue.

25 May — Paul Goodman's only Bobbs-Merrill book, *The Empire City,* is published.

June — Monroe Stearns becomes managing editor of the trade department, working out of the New York office. William J. Finneran is named sales manager of the department.

August — A farewell luncheon is given for the retiring Baker, formerly vice president in charge of the trade department and sales manager. Walter J. Hurley resigns as production and advertising manager and art director. Zoll retires as editor in chief. Dan Green and James A. Eldridge are named publicity directors of the New York and Indianapolis offices, respectively. Richard Mittenthal is appointed editor in the trade department of the New York office.

8 October — Berger dies.

9 October — The first Bobbs-Merrill copyright is registered for *Education* magazine (volume 80, number 1, September issue), which the company acquired this year. The company will retain it through volume 89, number 4 (April–May 1969 issue).

1960

Editor Harrison Platt leaves early in the year but continues to freelance some projects, notably the revision of Irma S. Rombauer's *The Joy of Cooking* (1931).

June — From the Johnny Gruelle Company, Bobbs-Merrill acquires the rights to twenty-seven Raggedy Ann books and plans to reprint fourteen of them.

June 30 — At the conclusion of the fiscal year Bobbs-Merrill has the greatest total sales volume in its history, exceeding $3,000,000. The law and educational departments have their highest sales ever, while the trade department has its best year out of the last five. Spring sales are 51.4 percent higher than those for the same period in 1959.

July — A college division is created, with Ranald P. Hobbs as executive vice president in charge.

18 October — *Sunny and Gay,* edited by Nila Banton Smith and others, is the first of six volumes published this year in the Best of Children's Literature series.

November — Leo Gans becomes editor in chief of the educational division. Bobbs-Merrill acquires the elementary-school publishing properties of Charles Scribner's Sons.

Rejuvenation under Hiram Haydn

Two of Hiram Haydn's early successes were J. Saunders Redding's On Being a Negro in America *and William Styron's brilliant first novel,* Lie Down in Darkness. *Both books were published over D. Laurance Chambers's objections, and, like Haydn, neither author stayed long with the firm.*

Our next contretemps occurred in his office on one of my early trips to Indianapolis. I had just signed a contract with Saunders Redding, the distinguished scholar and writer, for a book entitled *On Being Negro in America.*

DLC listened in silence to my comments about its possibilities. At last he looked up, pursed his lips, and said, with marked distaste, "Your entire list seems to consist of Jews and Negroes."

I exploded. Standing, I delivered my first real philippic to him. I can remember few other occasions on which I have found without hesitation precisely the words I wanted to express my anger. When I finished, I walked out.

Later, Leo Gobin, Lowe Berger's close friend and the treasurer of the company, sought me out to tell me that DLC had described the incident to him, expressing astonishment at the "degree" of my "fury," and at the way I had "sprung to [my] feet."

Leo chuckled.

"And I said to him, 'And isn't Hiram big?'"

Leo, one of those refreshing redeemers of the Middle West, open, generous and shrewd, is now president of the Bobbs-Merrill Company, and I think of this fact partially as evidence of the persisting influence of Lowe Berger. [. . .]

[. . .] For a long time, I heard frequently, "Oh, you're William Styron's editor." And I suspect that he became infinitely weary over hearing how much I had done for him. Indeed, he said this in the letter in which he told me he was staying with Random House.

What I *had* done was one central thing: I had believed that he was one of the most talented writers, not only of his generation, but of our time–and this when he was as yet wholly unknown. "So what?" as the banality goes. The fact that I literally staked my reputation as an editor on *Lie Down in Darkness* is to me–and I mean every word of this–quite simple, solid evidence that I am moderately intelligent and possessed of reasonably good editorial judgment. Supporting, promoting this book as a really outstanding one was the obvious thing to do; I was filled with joy at having such a work and such a writer walk in and say, "Here we are."

He had been told to come to see me in New York by his teacher at Duke, Bill Blackburn. He signed up at the New School for a fiction course in which he wrote several short stories, and then entered the novel workshop. When he turned in the first twenty pages of *Lie Down in Darkness,* I told him that he was out of place in a class, and took an option on the book for Crown. When I went to Bobbs, he followed, after staging an unusual sit-down strike at Crown until Nat Wartels would see him and release him. I remember that Bill told me he had taken his lunch with him, in case Nat held out until afternoon.

During the several years in which he worked on *Lie Down in Darkness,* the Haydns saw a great deal of him. [. . .]

[. . .] I began work on establishing the novel's quality in the house immediately. I had solid backing from several of its early readers, and especially from Ross Baker. We ordered an unusually large number of bound galleys, and sent them out to critics, hoping for support. Hoping? To me it was a sure thing. Maxwell Geismar, Howard Mumford Jones, Lloyd Morris and others responded handsomely. We began a campaign directed at the bookstores, sending a postcard each week on which was printed extravagant praise for the book, signed by one of these critics.

Hence there was telling support almost immediately, and Mr. Chambers's dour skepticism caused me far less concern than it would have if I had been forced to fight for it alone. That familiar snowballing process that accompanies the establishment of an outstanding new talent had begun, and there was no stopping it. Within a week after the publication of *Lie Down in Darkness,* almost everyone interested in books knew who William Styron was.

–*Words & Faces* (New York & London: Harcourt Brace Jovanovich, 1974), pp. 51, 279–280

* * *

An unsigned, fourteen-page reader's report, by Herman Ziegner (as Styron confirmed to J. Kent Calder) and the only one now in the Bobbs-Merrill archive, is reproduced in facsimile in DLB Yearbook: 1990. *The report anticipates Chambers's objections to* Lie Down in Darkness, *especially to Peyton's soliloquy, which was greatly changed during the editing process.*

Memo from D. Laurance Chambers to Haydn, 23 April 1951

This report from Mr. Ziegner (who has been reading the manuscript without interrupting the proofroom) makes some recommendations on literary grounds which invite your friendly consideration.

To me the report indicates that we are presented with a publishing problem other than how many copies

William Styron (courtesy of George Rhoads; from the dust jacket for Lie Down in Darkness, *1951; Thomas Cooper Library, University of South Carolina)*

we can sell–a problem of possible legal involvements. Mr. Ziegner wishes to make it clear that with this aspect he doesn't feel at all competent to express himself.

Nor am I competent to reckon what the possible involvements might be. I have kept only vague track of the judicial decisions in so-called "obscenity" cases, noting their increasing liberality. Whether Lie Down in Darkness would fall within the precedents that have been established, I do not know. Besides, ignoring precedents is a favorite trick of present procedure, every judge liking to write new law according to his personal view.

At any rate should we not approach this legal problem objectively and seek the best informed opinion, not only for the House's sake but for the author's? What would you think, then, of consulting Melville Cane? He is himself a literary artist and not narrow-minded. He has dealt with such problems for other publishers.

If you approve this suggestion and have not a copy of the script with all corrections in New York, wire us and we will hold up setting type and send you for the purpose the copy we've been working on.

[D. Laurance Chambers]

* * *

Herman Ziegner to Haydn, 27 April 1951

Dear Hi:

Charlotte Jeanes, who has now gone about 450 pages, just came to my desk and said: "I want to tell someone how I feel about this book but I can't put it into words, I can't say it." No one who has read it wants to talk about anything else. This kind of excitement augurs very well, I think. I can't imagine anyone, anywhere being less excited.

One thing I have forgotten to mention to you: I thought the use of the quotation from FINNEGANS WAKE used in the front matter is terrifically effective. It kept returning to me all through my reading and now I've just had pointed to me the excerpt from Urn-Burial in which the title words occur and I'd like to figure out some way to use them in our presentation of the book.

Of course I haven't really had a thing to say here. I told you I couldn't stop talking about this book.

Cordially,
[Herman Ziegner]

* * *

Harrison "Harry" Platt to Chambers, 7 May 1951

This book arouses a strong admiration and liking. I think it comes very nearly up to the encomiums given it by Hiram Haydn and Herman Ziegner. It should enhance our literary position and give us some very fine reviews. On this score the book should outrank From Here to Eternity or any of the other work by new serious novelists. On the score of a heavy sale I think we would all be less sanguine, because the book requires a little greater reader co-operation, a little greater attention and understanding. Even so, the sale should be good and the sale of future Styron's better.

Herman and I have given our best attention to the questionable passages. We were in complete agreement. We both felt, and feel, that we have recommended all the changes that should be made and only those that should be made. The precise wording of the changes is of course up to the author. If all or most of these changes are made, this passage should not receive an undue amount of attention from the critics and should not cause any shock to the moral sense or good taste of intelligent readers. This does not mean that we have asked the author to make the passage sterile. It may still be a little strong for the lower order of Mrs. Grundy's daughters.

As I told you, the book is not necessarily everyone's cup of tea. I might have preferred a conventional chronological development; I don't know. Anyhow, of its kind it is as good as anything I know. Let's have more Styron books.

Harry

* * *

Advertising card for Styron's first novel, published in 1951 (courtesy of The Lilly Library, Indiana University, Bloomington, Indiana)

The note by George Salter that Haydn enclosed with this form letter says in part, "To think that this is the first book of an author only 25 years old seems incredible, incompatible with the display of observation, judgment and compassion. This can hardly be experience, it must then be instinct and might well be genius."

Haydn to Booksellers, 11 May 1951

Dear Bookseller:

On August twentieth we will publish LIE DOWN IN DARKNESS, by William Styron–the finest new American novel that I have read in many years. In the face of his achievement, it seems strange to say "the finest first novel." There is no indication that this is the first book of a young man twenty-five years old. His work reads as though he has been practicing the art with extraordinary ability for many years.

At any rate, I have never, in my experience as an editor, had anything to do with so remarkable a novel as this one. It is my sober and considered opinion that its appearance will mark the most exciting literary event in this country since the advent of Thomas Wolfe.

Each one of us who has read this book has begun it skeptical of the claims of earlier readers. Each in turn has succumbed and joined the chorus of tribute. Perhaps all that this letter will do will be to arouse in turn your skepticism. If so, that seems to me pretty much the way it should be. We are content to wait until you, too, have had an opportunity to discover it for yourself. But in the meantime, we did want to let you know that here is that rare thing, a major novel by a new major novelist.

The enclosed statement by George Salter, the distinguished jacket artist, is sent to you at his request.

Sincerely,
Hiram Haydn

* * *

Taking Stock for an English Audience

On his latest visit to Washington Sir Winston Churchill referred to the interests, concerns–and differences–of the English-speaking nations as "family matters."

Of course, the truth of Sir Winston's happy phrase operates in every cultural or business interchange, but it finds no better application than in the Anglo-American publishing world, where "English-speaking" has significance and importance.

It is this common understanding that encourages the Bobbs-Merrill Company to discuss (if you will permit the phrase) "family matters." In the comfortable assumption of your interest, we propose to tell you something of our House and its current publishing program.

The Bobbs-Merrill Company, Inc. occupies a distinctive position in American publishing. Founded 116 years ago in Indianapolis, Indiana–deep in our Midwest–it now operates through two offices, one in Indianapolis and one in New York. Neither office is in any sense a branch of the other. To a degree true of no other American house, our publishing service depends on both. Our New York staff draws on the great metropolitan literary marketplace. Our Indianapolis staff keeps a special sensitivity and access to regional literature. We know something of the value of regional expression as well as of the ability of a good book to surmount all sectional differences in its address to the larger community.

It follows then that we have the liveliest appreciation of a broader demonstration of these facts–the success in America of English books, the success in England of American books. As is the case with English publishers, most of our books grow from and deal with our own land and people. Yet very many of these have also been published in England, and we are proud indeed to have published in America many distinguished books of English origin.

Of the books that we are publishing in 1954, two come immediately and commandingly to mind. One of these, the leading title on our Spring list, **BUT WE WERE BORN FREE by Elmer Davis** ($2.75), is wholly American and of great and immediate importance to all Americans. It deals with the kind of freedom which America and England have made large sacrifices to preserve. It deals, too, with McCarthyism which may have assumed proportions in the minds of people overseas greater than its actual significance and vitality. The other, which we confidently expect to head our list of publications for Fall, is Lord David Cecil's **MELBOURNE** (***Constable,*** see footnote). [*Footnote:* "English publisher's name in bold face italics designates a book of English origin; regular italics, American origin."] We published the first volume, THE YOUNG MELBOURNE, in 1939 and it is still in print. With the completion and publication this year of the second half of this biography of Lord Melbourne in England, this distinguished work is complete, and in September we are issuing the two in one volume at $5.00.

We are not stressing merely the fact that one of these books is so indigenously American and the other so distinctively British. The two offer another significant study in contrast and complement as well: On the one hand the stirring topical book conceived in the press of momentous national events and designed to be, as it was everywhere heralded, a ringing defense of the rights of man; the other urbane, graceful, scholarly in the best tradition of biography and belles-lettres, conceived and executed in the spirit of all that is designed to last in literature.

Nor is Lord David's work the only distinguished book of this sort to come out of England and find a place on our list in the last several years. Since 1950, we have also published **H. M. Tomlinson's THE FACE OF THE EARTH** and **A MINGLED YARN** (both published in England by ***Gerald Duckworth***) and **Sacheverell Sitwell's SELECTED WORKS,** compiled by the author for an American audience, with a new introduction to that audience.

Two recent American books on our list that combine literary and philosophical appeal with a timely topical interest are **Louis Kronenberger's COMPANY MANNERS: *A Cultural Inquiry into American Life*** ($3.00), and **Joseph Wood Krutch's THE MEASURE OF MAN: *On Freedom, Human Values, Survival and the Modern Temper*** ($3.50). In each case a distinguished observer of the American scene combines with his scholarly attributes his concern about particular tendencies in our present ways of thinking and living. Their two books, together with that of Elmer Davis, gave Bobbs-Merrill three of the top six books in the Spring poll of critics appearing in *The Saturday Review*. [. . .]

Elmer Davis' "ringing challenge to witch-hunters" sold 60,000 copies this Spring. We would like to establish a similar record for a book on an equally urgent subject that we are publishing in September, and we can confidently predict a wide audience for it. **AN AMERICAN IN INDIA: *A Personal Report on the Indian Dilemma and the Nature of Her Conflicts* by Saunders Redding** ($3.50) is an unusually intimate study. The United States Department of State sent Saunders Redding, professor of English at Hampton Institute, Hampton, Virginia, on a special mission to India, perhaps with the persuasion that, beyond Mr. Redding's distinguished attributes, a Negro might have a better opportunity to learn at first hand from Indian government officials, educators and professional men, and indeed this proved to be the case. Mr. Redding was privileged to see and hear much that a white man would not have seen and heard. [. . .]

Two of the most distinguished names on our Fall list are those of **Irwin Edman** and **Henry Steele Commager.** Their books on **JOHN DEWEY** (September, $3.00), and **JOHN MARSHALL** (November, $3.00), respectively are the two newest volumes in the series called ***Makers of the American Tradition,*** initiated in 1953 when volumes on Roger Williams, Benjamin Franklin and Andrew Jackson were published. These books, neither biographies nor anthologies, are a combination of original text and scholarly interpretation. They have been widely received in the United States by scholars, historians and critics as "an extraordinary publishing venture." The fact that such outstanding scholars as Perry Miller, author of THE NEW ENGLAND MIND, and Mr. Edman and Mr. Commager (recently visiting professor at Cambridge University) are contributors to the series attests in itself to its stature. We should also mention that **THE BLUE AND THE GRAY: *The Story of the Civil War as Told by Participants,*** edited by Henry Steele Commager, with a foreword by Douglas Southall Freeman, is being reissued this Fall in a new one-volume edition at $6.50. [. . .]

Within the last few years, we believe it is safe to say that Bobbs-Merrill has introduced as many distinguished new novelists as any other publishing house in the United States. Foremost among these is **William Styron** whose **LIE DOWN IN DARKNESS** *(Hamish Hamilton)* catapulted him to the front rank of living American novelists. Twenty-two thousand copies of this first novel were sold at $3.50 within one year of publication date but its sales were nevertheless secondary to the critical acclaim it received. Any mention of outstanding young novelists today is sure to include his name. Indeed, both in the United States and Europe sober and established critics have indicated their conviction that he is one of the outstanding contemporary American novelists of whatever generation. Space does not permit more than the naming of the others and the titles of their first novels: **A SEED UPON THE WIND** ($3.50) **by William Michelfelder** (referred to by many critics as "an American Graham Greene"), **A GOOD MAN** ($3.00) **by Jefferson Young** *(Constable, "The White House"),* **ALL THE YOUNG SUMMER DAYS** ($3.00) **by Bernice Kavinoky, FLEE THE ANGRY STRANGERS** ($3.75) **by George Mandel, THE SOUTHPAW** ($3.50) **by Mark Harris, DAY OF THE HARVEST** ($3.00) **by Helen Upshaw, THE GATHERING DARKNESS by Thomas Gallagher.** Mr. Styron won the *Prix de Rome,* Mr. Young a Saxton Fellowship. This Fall **GRAND CONCOURSE** (September, $3.75) **by Eliot Wagner, WALKING ON BORROWED LAND** ($3.50) **by William A. Owens** and **LOT'S WIFE** (October, $3.95) **by Maria Ley-Piscator** will be added to this group.

This Fall we shall also be publishing **THE SCOTSWOMAN** (November, $3.95) **by Inglis Fletcher,** who has as good a claim as anyone to the title of dean of American historical novelists. RALEIGH'S EDEN *(Hutchinson),* the first of her Carolina novels, was published in 1940. It is still in print as are her five other Carolina stories, and together they form the record of the development of a state from colonial beginnings to the ratification of the American Constitution. Another distinguished and popular American historical novelist, Shirley Barker, author of RIVERS PARTING *(W. H. Allen),* among others, joins the Bobbs-Merrill list with a novel entitled **TOMORROW THE NEW MOON,** to be published in January, 1955, at $3.50. Of British origin is **Alice Harwood's THE STRANGELING *(John Lane, the Bodley Head)*** which we have just issued in a two-volume set produced appropriately in the physical dress of books published in the Victorian period.

Mrs. Fletcher's highly successful books bring to mind such other Bobbs-Merrill novelists as **Alice Tisdale Hobart** (from **OIL FOR THE LAMPS OF CHINA** to **THE SERPENT-WREATHED STAFF,** published by *Cassell* in England); **Robert Raynolds** whose **THE SINNER OF ST. AMBROSE** *(Secker & Warburg)* was a Book-of-the-Month Club selection in 1952; **Cid Ricketts Sumner** (published by *Macdonald* in England); **Isabella Holt;** and **Ayn Rand.**

THE FOUNTAINHEAD *(Cassell)* by Ayn Rand has indeed had an extraordinary record. A slow starter at first, it is now well past half a million copies in the original $3.00 edition.

We have been primarily concerned with current and recent books, but it is almost impossible not to mention four authors whose books have had enormous followings over a period of years. One of these, **John Erskine,** whose **PRIVATE LIFE OF HELEN OF TROY** Bobbs-Merrill published in 1927 [*sic*], has come freshly to mind to Londoners with the recent success of the stage play THE PRIVATE LIFE OF HELEN. Another is **Richard Halliburton** whose books have sold well over a million copies and whose **THE COMPLETE BOOK OF MARVELS** ($3.49) continues to sell in quantity through the years. The third of these record-breaking authors is **L. Frank Baum. THE WIZARD OF OZ** *(Hutchinson)* is probably the single most popular children's story ever published in the

United States ($2.50). And finally there is **THE JOY OF COOKING by Irma S. Rombauer.** A new and revised edition, **THE NEW JOY OF COOKING** ($3.95) in collaboration with her daughter, was published last year. This "American Mrs. Beeton" has sold 2,500,000 copies since 1932. *Dent* is the English publisher.

Toward the end of BUT WE WERE BORN FREE, Elmer Davis, speaking of democracy, says: "What we have to offer, to the contemporary world and to the future, is a method–and the freedom of the mind that makes that method possible." It seems to us as publishers that in the diversity and broad scope of our publishing lists lies one of the greatest safeguards for that freedom of mind which makes democracy possible.

–"The Bobbs-Merrill Company," *Times Literary Supplement,* 17 September 1954, p. iii

* * *

Chambers Steps Down

Allegedly, one of the episodes that led the board to replace Chambers in October 1953 was the false claim that Haydn was not answering his memos. Haydn offers an assessment based on his four and a half years with the company.

Before I left Bobbs-Merrill, Mr. Chambers retired "upstairs" to the chairmanship of a board he could no longer control, and Lowe Berger was duly installed as president. The incident involving me was only one of a series that had literally forced Lowe's hand and made him take the step he had forestalled as long as he could. Thereafter, working for Bobbs-Merrill became a recognizably realistic proposition.

Looking back, I think I understand better now the course of things at Bobbs. In the twenties and even thirties, the trade department was riding high after the successes of John Erskine and Bruce Barton and Richard Halliburton, that intrepid latter-day Munchausen, and a number of others. Thereafter, for a variety of reasons, the road led downward. Bobbs was unable to compete for leading authors with New York firms as the business became increasingly agent-oriented. True, there was a New York editor in the New York office who had equal access to these agents. But he worked under two heavy disadvantages. He could not negotiate with authority because he had to submit everything to Mr. Chambers, and his competitors either had such authority or at least could confer with their superiors on the spot. Moreover, DLC was unwilling to offer an advance of the size becoming customary in New York.

Another important factor was that he found the work of the new generation distasteful. I do not believe that he would have signed John Dos Passos, Ernest Hemingway, William Faulkner, John Steinbeck or Nelson Algren if he had had the chance. He looked back with painful nostalgia to the genteel tradition in which he and Bobbs had flourished. He never tired of telling about his association with Booth Tarkington. He found what comfort he could in his two consistently best selling authors, Alice Tisdale Hobart and Inglis Fletcher. They wrote decent, inspiring books, *and* they sold. So he continued to insist on his standards. But the other books did not sell. For many years the trade department was primarily supported by a strong children's list (the Childhood of Famous Americans series, in particular) and that hardy perennial, Irma Rombauer's *The Joy of Cooking.*

In rationalization, he fell back on a favorite generalization. "Gross volume," he would say. "That's the answer: gross volume. You can't expect most good books to sell today."

The older he grew the surer he became that he knew the answers, despite staggering evidence to the contrary. And the surer he became, the more tyrannical. It was the old story of a man trusting almost no one else. The more he came to doubt the adequacies of those who worked for him the more he insisted on being in total charge of the list. The less he was able to command the new writers the more he indulged his prejudices. It became DLC against the world, and he would not relinquish the practices that had worked in the past. In my time with Bobbs, he and George Brett of Macmillan were the last two publishers to hold out against selling books on consignment. He would not take books back from the booksellers, and so they were naturally disinclined to place as large orders for Bobbs books as they would with comparable books from other publishers.

I was not aware of all these factors when I went to Bobbs, but I could not remain uninformed for long. And, even more than with Crown, I was confronted with a situation heavily weighted against success. As I look back now, I believe that the list I built at Bobbs, in the face of these odds, represents the best editorial work I have done. But I could never have done it without the generous, unfailing support of Berger and Baker.

The early success of Styron's *Lie Down in Darkness* was of enormous help. The reviews were splendid; the book sold well; the author was established almost overnight. And for Bobbs and me it meant that agents had tangible proof that we could launch successfully a real *contemporary* literary talent. It suggested to reviewers and book-review editors that Bobbs was building a serious, up-to-date literary list that would deserve their scrutiny. [. . .]

[. . .] The two releases I was most happy to secure were from Knopf and William Morrow, to enable, respectively, Louis Kronenberger to write a book on the state of American culture and manners, and Joseph Wood Krutch to write a twenty-five-year-later sequel to his notable *The Modern Temper*. These two books were published in the spring of 1954 as *Company Manners* and *The Measure of Man.*

Both were very well received in every way, and the following spring *The Measure of Man* won the National Book Award for nonfiction. But considerable as their success was, there was another book on the list that far exceeded their records. This was Elmer Davis's *But We Were Born Free.*

Davis, one of our really great journalists, had been a Bobbs author for a long time, but had not written a book for years. Now he had been persuaded by Anne Ross, a part-time editor in the Indianapolis office and an old friend, to put together a book of essays, partly articles he had already published, with a new lead piece that was a frontal attack on Senator Joseph McCarthy's intimidation of America, then at its peak. [. . .]

Joseph Wood Krutch, circa 1961 (Bruccoli Clark Layman Archives)

Our triumvirate of Davis, Krutch and Kronenberger created quite a stir in publishing circles. This was clearly a new Bobbs-Merrill. I had had no real part in securing or editing *But We Were Born Free;* indeed, I did not meet Mr. Davis until a couple of years later. Herman Ziegner, at first in charge of publicity at the Indianapolis office, and thereafter an accomplished editor, both at Bobbs and Atheneum, had collaborated with Anne Ross in the editorial work. But to New York publishing circles, I was *the* Bobbs-Merrill editor, and despite my disclaimers I was given the credit for the Davis as well as for the Kronenberger and Krutch books.

–*Words & Faces,* pp. 56–57, 75–76

* * *

The Sale of Bobbs-Merrill to Howard W. Sams and Company

The company's decline in the later 1950s forced it to surrender the independence it had enjoyed since 1885. According to Publishers' Weekly *(17 November 1958), "Sale of Bobbs-Merrill had been rumored throughout the trade for several months with various prospective purchasers–but not the right one, as it turned out–being mentioned."*

Purchase of the 120-year-old Bobbs-Merrill Co., book publishers, 730 N. Meridian, was completed yesterday by Howard W. Sams, publisher of electronics manufacturing service, and research information.

The purchase price was $1 million which did not include the buildings now being leased.

Howard Sams, who has had phenomenal success in his publishing business, said he would move the book publishing firm to his new building at 62d and Guyon [*sic*] where it will be integrated into his other growing operations.

The Bobbs-Merrill Co., once the shining star of the novel and pleasure reading business, now relies mostly on its law book publishing trade. The company codifies state laws for the legal profession.

It also publishes educational books which Mr. Sams said would tie into the trend for education by television.

"It is one of the finest things that ever happened," Mr. Sams said. "It has given us national recognition in big publishing overnight."

Bobbs-Merrill will retain its present identity and will continue with its educational, legal and trade book departments, Mr. Sams said. He will become chairman of the board.

Lowe Berger, Bobbs-Merrill president; D. Laurance Chambers, who has been with the company for more than 50 years, and Col. Robert L. Moorhead sold the controlling interest to the Sams company.

FICTION

January

Tomorrow the New Moon
By SHIRLEY BARKER $3.75

February

Ceremony of Love
By THOMAS WILLIAMS $3.50

The Tall Dark Man
By ANNE CHAMBERLAIN $3.00

March

The Quality of Quiros
By ROBERT RAYNOLDS $3.75

Watching at the Window
By CHARLOTTE PAYNE JOHNSON $3.00

April

The Scotswoman
By INGLIS FLETCHER $3.95

The Night of Time
By RENÉ FÜLÖP-MILLER $3.75

June

Peace at Bowling Green
By ALFRED LELAND CRABB $3.75

NON-FICTION

January

Easy Home Repairs
By LEE FRANKL. *Illustrated.* $3.00

Sportsman's Workshop
By LARRY KOLLER. *Illustrated.* $2.75

February

Two Minutes Till Midnight
By ELMER DAVIS $2.75

Off to the Right Start
In Choosing Your Household Treasures
By MARJORIE BINFORD WOODS and JUSTINE FEELY. *Illustrated.* $2.95

Complete Book of Kit Boats
By LLOYD MALLAN. *Illustrated.* $2.75

How to Take Better Pictures
By ARTHUR GOLDSMITH. *Illustrated.* $2.75

March

Complete Book of Fishing Tackle
By LARRY KOLLER. *Illustrated.* $2.75

Heroines of Dixie
Confederate Women Tell Their Story of the War
By KATHARINE M. JONES. *Illustrated.* $5.00

The Dawn of Personality
By EMILE CAILLIET $3.00

April

John Dewey By IRWIN EDMAN
(Makers of the American Tradition Series) $3.00

John Marshall By HENRY STEELE COMMAGER
(Makers of the American Tradition Series) $3.00

New Complete Book of Small Boats
By LLOYD MALLAN. *Illustrated.* $2.75

Complete Book of Fishing
By LARRY KOLLER. *Illustrated.* $2.75

June

Complete Book of Camping and the Outdoors
By LARRY KOLLER. *Illustrated.* $2.75

Advertisement for the winter–spring list from the 29 January 1955 issue of Publishers' Weekly

Mr. Chambers will become chairman emeritus and Mr. Moorhead will be honorary secretary-treasurer. [. . .]

Howard W. Sams & Co., Inc., has grown from a 12-man group when it began in 1946 to become the largest technical research and publishing firm in the electronics industry. There are two Indianapolis plants serving 1854 distributors.

The Sams company is associated with The Waldemar Press, Inc.

–Harold Hartley, "Sams Pays $1 Million For Bobbs- Merrill," *Indianapolis Times,* 12 November 1958, p. 3

* * *

Howard W. Sams was elected chairman of the board and president of the Bobbs-Merrill Company at the board's first meeting since Howard W. Sams & Company acquired controlling interest in the 120-year-old publishing house (*PW,* November 17, 24). Lowe Berger, former president, has been granted a leave of absence for reasons of health.

Leo C. Gobin, former treasurer of Bobbs-Merrill, becomes vice-president and general manager. Donald B. Shaw is the new treasurer. Leland C. Morgan, present head of the firm's law division, is secretary of the company.

The new board consists of the officers of the company and the following men: George Brodsky, Chicago advertising executive; John A. Alexander of the Indianapolis law firm of Buschmann, Krieg, DeVault and Alexander; H. H. Bredell of the law firm of Bredell, Cooper and Martin, Indianapolis, and treasurer of the American Bar Association; and William R. Collins of Worthington, Ohio, who was associated for more than 30 years with Macmillan.

D. Laurance Chambers, former chairman of the board, becomes chairman emeritus. Robert L. Moorhead becomes honorary secretary and treasurer.

Howard W. Sams, who purchased Bobbs-Merrill in 1958 (Indianapolis Times *Collection/Tiffany Studio)*

Ross G. Baker remains vice-president in charge of sales of the trade division, with offices in New York City.

Mr. Sams indicated that he will serve as president until the company selects an outstanding figure in the industry to assume that post. "We are determined to make the best use of present Bobbs-Merrill personnel and to attract vigorous, experienced, young executive talent to assure continuous progress for the firm," Mr. Sams stated.

–"Sams Succeeds Berger as Bobbs-Merrill President," *Publishers' Weekly,* 174 (1 December 1958): 23

* * *

M. Hughes Miller Takes Charge

To some, M. Hughes Miller was Chambers redux. Within a few months, Walter J. Hurley and Ross Baker were gone from the New York office, and Miller's editorial judgments were soon to be called into question.

M. HUGHES MILLER has been named president of the Bobbs-Merrill Company. Since December 1956, Mr. Miller has been a vice-president of American Book-Stratford Press (*PW,* September 3, 1956). Previously, he was vice-president and general manager of Charles E. Merrill Books, Inc., and Wesleyan University Press and manager and director of book publications for the American Education Press. Mr. Miller's appointment to the Bobbs-Merrill presidency was announced by Howard W. Sams, chairman of the board, who acquired controlling interest in Bobbs-Merrill last November and who has temporarily filled the office of president of the company (*PW,* November 17, December 1, 1958).

–*Publisher's Weekly,* 175 (9 March 1959): 34

Keeping Current

Jules Dubois's Fidel Castro: Rebel–Liberator or Dictator? *(1959) misread Castro, but the creation and promotion of the book recalled the days of Richard Halliburton's adventures. The project originated in the pre-Miller regime.*

Bobbs-Merrill, in one of the big, rush production jobs of this or any season, sent first copy on "Fidel Castro: Rebel–Liberator or Dictator?" to the typesetter on February 25, received finished books from the bindery March 16, and has rushed them to the stores to meet an April 6 pub date. The idea for a book about Castro was first broached to Chicago *Tribune* reporter Jules Dubois, who has known the Cuban leader since 1947, by Bobbs-Merrill in a telephone call to strife-torn Havana on New Year's Day. It seems that Dubois had been working on an outline of just such a book for some time, saving material, never before published, for many years. The contract was signed February 12, and by February 20 Bobbs-Merrill editor Harrison Platt was en route to Havana to work right along with author Dubois. Mr. Platt had a rough arrival, being whisked off to jail from his plane in a case of mistaken identity that gave him some anxious moments before he was released with apologies.

Bobbs-Merrill's first printing of the Dubois book is 25,000 copies. Circulars and display posters (the latter 12 x 18" in the Cuban revolutionary colors of red and black) have been included in every shipment of books. The initial ad campaign includes the New York *Times Book Review,* Chicago *Tribune,* San Francisco *Chronicle, Newsweek, New Yorker, Saturday Review.* The

National Book Awards ceremony, 3 March 1959, from left: J. Christopher Herold, winner for his 1958 Bobbs-Merrill biography of Madame de Staël; Bernard Malamud; mistress of ceremonies Virginia Peterson; Ken McCormick of Doubleday, standing in for Theodore Roethke; and Daniel Hoffman, who delivered Roethke's acceptance speech (photo by Jay Seymour, courtesy of The Lilly Library, Indiana University, Bloomington, Indiana)

book receives the lead cover review in the April 5 issue of the Chicago *Tribune*.

A letter from Fidel Castro to Jules Dubois, dated February 14, is printed in the front of the book, in which Premier Castro, while withholding any comment on what Mr. Dubois has written until after he has had a chance to read it, does say "Every person in the society of free nations–and even those who are oppressed under the heels of dictators–has a right to express his or her opinion."

Among the Dubois conclusions expressed in the book: Castro "is a sincere idealist who never overlooks any opportunity," and, in answer to the question: "Will Fidel Castro become a dictator?" "Not if he can help it."

Newspaperman Dubois has been on the board of the Inter-American Press Association since 1950 and has often been re-elected chairman of its Committee on Freedom of the Press. Last year, by acclamation, the Association voted him a medal as Hero of Freedom of the Press. He has observed developments in Cuba since the 1930's.

–*Publishers' Weekly,* 175 (30 March 1959): 37–38

* * *

M. Hughes Miller, president of the Bobbs-Merrill division of Howard W. Sams and Company from 1959 to 1963 (Indianapolis Times *Collection/Tiffany Studio)*

Advertising Campaign

One of Miller's first promotions is described in this notice. The stellar books on the 1959 spring list, however, originated with the preceding administration.

Bobbs-Merrill has launched a new, predominantly off-the-book-page advertising campaign for its books that will cost at least $91,000. The campaign is based upon regularity of ad insertion in fixed position in newspapers in major book cities and in national magazines. With certain exceptions, such as the ads scheduled for the New York *Times Book Review* and the Chicago *Tribune Magazine of Books,* the ads will run up near the front of the media or along with or facing first reading, outside of the book page. [. . .]

Four separate ads have been plated and matted for use between now and July, and will run on an alternating basis in the media involved. They are ads for: "Fidel Castro" by Jules Dubois, which now has 30,000 copies in print; "The Trial of Mary Todd Lincoln" by James A. Rhodes and Dean Jauchius; "The New Joy of Cooking" by Irma S. Rombauer and Marion Rombauer Becker; and "Breakdown" by Robert Dahl, which is in a second printing. [. . .]

This advertising campaign is completely separate from any advertising Bobbs-Merrill may do in the daily book review pages or any campaign that may build up for an individual title that seems to be taking off.

–"Bobbs-Merrill's New $91,000-Plus Ad Campaign," *Publishers' Weekly,* 175 (11 May 1959): 37–38

* * *

A New Look in the Atom Age

An old Indiana firm is taking on a new look and a new outlook.

Bobbs-Merrill Co. was publisher for many of the great names of Indiana's golden age of letters. Now, under new ownership and management, it's ready for a fresh go at the atom age.

M. Hughes Miller, new president of Bobbs-Merrill, is the man responsible for the new look. Working a day that starts before 8 a. m. and sometimes lasts until 2 a. m., Mr. Miller gives the impression of a man who intends to make up a lot of time quickly.

It's been a long time since this 120-year-old publishing house was among the leaders in the popular field of the American publishing business. In the period from 1900 to 1930 the works of James Whitcomb Riley, George Ade, Meredith Nicholson, Ring Lardner, John Erskine, Bruce Barton, Richard Halliburton and many others came out under the Bobbs-Merrill name.

One of the men who was greatly responsible for this golden age was D. Laurance Chambers, presently honorary chairman of the board. Mr. Chambers at 82 [*sic*] still puts in his regular day at the office as he has since he joined the firm in 1903.

The first step in the new look came last November when Howard W. Sams Co. purchased the firm. Mr. Sams announced that the old firm would retain its name with its excellent juvenile, legal and trade book departments.

The next step was to find a man to start Bobbs-Merrill back into the popular fiction and nonfiction field. On April 15 [*sic*], Mr. Miller, the 48-year-old executive vice president of American Book-Stratford Press, was picked for the top job.

He has had a long association with writing. He started in the newspaper business, switched to public relations counsel and even wrote two movies: "Gold Is Where You Find It" and "Penrod and His Twin Brother." Mr. Miller said that he had seen one of them on TV recently and that the 25-year contrast was not good.

After working for an Eastern publisher for several years he took the Sams offer and came here. Actually he hasn't arrived permanently as he spends Friday through Monday in the New York office and the middle three days at the E. 38th St. office here. [. . .]

When he returns from the European trip Mrs. Miller and their two sons will move to Indianapolis. For, [un]like the other major publishing firms centered in the East, Howard Sams intends to keep Bobbs-Merrill a Midwestern firm. Eventually the printing offices will be moved back to the city.

On the subject of new books including some not yet in print Mr. Miller mentioned:

– Around the World in 30 Days, the story of three Frenchmen who take a scavenger hunt around the world. Movie rights have already been sold.
– Tonya, the first fiction piece by Gregory (Pappy) Boyington, World War II ace and author of the best-seller Baa Baa Black Sheep. [. . .]
– The Audio Cyclopedia. [. . .]
– God Is a Good God by Oral Roberts, the evangelist.
– An autobiography by Patti Page, the singer.

Mr. Miller also said that the movie rights to Johnny Shiloh, a novel about the youngest soldier in the Civil War, have been sold to Bob and Jack Hope.

On the subject of good literature Mr. Miller said, with regret as an ex-newspaperman, "the greatest source is on the college campus. Only there are thoughts constantly mulled over until they gain permanence."

An Important Announcement
about your best-selling cookbook

ON MARCH 1, 1959
THE NEW PRICE OF
THIS FAST-MOVING
PROFITMAKER
WILL BE $4.95

All orders from booksellers postmarked no later than February 28, 1959, will be billed at the old price of $4.50.

This is your opportunity to add to your earnings on one of your biggest money-makers. Anticipate your needs and order as many as your stockroom can accommodate. Remember. The NEW Joy of Cooking is unique–there's no other cookbook to compare with it.

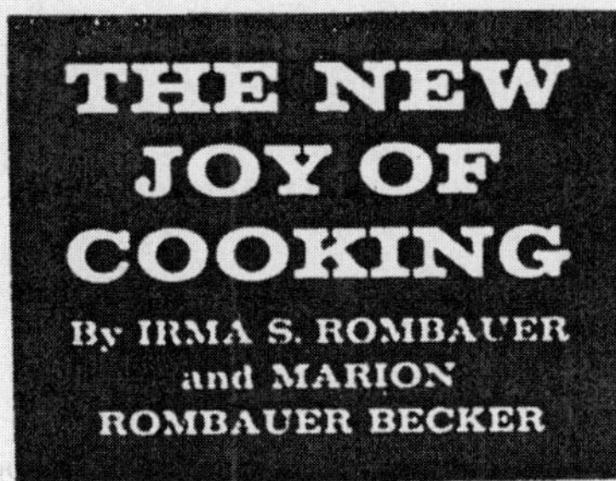

THE NEW
JOY OF COOKING
will now have...

YEAR-ROUND
ADVERTISING
in local and national media

NEW
STATEMENT
ENCLOSURES

CO-OP
ADVERTISING
MATS

Ask your Bobbs traveler to give you full details, or write to

the NEW Bobbs-Merrill
COMPANY, INC.
Indianapolis 6, Indiana

18 PUBLISHERS' WEEKLY

Advertisement for a revised edition of the 1931 cookbook, from the 2 February 1959 issue of Publishers' Weekly

Mr. Miller didn't make any predictions about where Bobbs-Merrill might go under its new head. However, Mr. Chambers said simply, "I hope they make a go of it. It's a great business."

–Gerry LaFollette, "Old Firm in a New Jacket: 18-Hour Literary Toiler Heads Bobbs-Merrill Co.: Hughes Miller Steers Course," *Indianapolis Times,* 28 September 1959, p. 5

* * *

Promotion of the New-Look Products

The titles promised in the Indianapolis News *puff piece of 28 September 1959 appeared on the 1960 spring list and marked a decline in taste from that of the previous year. But the old Chambers policy of no returns had been eliminated, and sales were higher than those of spring 1959. After the success of his first year, Miller stated as the company's five-year objective a sales volume of $12,500,000. According to* Publishers' Weekly *(8 August 1960), "It is Mr. Miller's view that to make money you have to spend it. 'We made a $550,000–$600,000 investment last year,' he says, 'and we increased our business by 50%.'"*

Bobbs-Merrill has announced that it will apply to five top spring books a policy of automatic distribution to booksellers. In another announcement, Bobbs-Merrill outlines a plan for "a new and liberalized cooperative advertising program" for all new titles and the active backlist.

In explaining the automatic distribution plan, M. Hughes Miller, president of the firm, and William Finneran, sales manager, report that salesmen for each account will make up the orders. The books will be shipped fully protected, and will be returnable when the stores consider them no longer salable. Permission for returns will not be required. The five books are: "God Is a Good God" by Oral Roberts (March 21); "Once Upon a Dream" by Patti Page (March 28); "Around the World on a Bet" by Abel Armand and Bertrand D'Oultremont (March 14); "Goddess of the Bullring" by Lola Verrill Cintron (May 2); "Junior Encyclopedia of Sports" by Willard Mullins (April 25). [. . .]

The cooperative ad program, with the largest budget Bobbs has ever put into this kind of advertising, will include mats and a complete kit for each book involved in the program. New titles and active backlist titles, including "The Joy of Cooking" and the Childhood of Famous Americans series, will be promoted in this program. Each kit for a book will contain a glossy photo of the book and one of the author, reproducible copy of other art work, suggested ad copy and a suggested layout. Arrangements with retailers will be worked out by travelers, subject to Mr. Finneran's approval. Payment will be made on receipt of a newspaper invoice with two tear-sheets of the published ad.

–"Automatic Distribution for 5 Bobbs-Merrill Highspots," *Publishers' Weekly,* 177 (25 January 1960): 213–214

Obituary: Lowe Berger

Lowe Berger, 63, former book company president, died last night in St. Vincent's Hospital. He lived at 1321 N. Meridian.

For 18 years he was vice-president and manager of the school book department at the Bobbs-Merrill Co. here. Then, until 1958, he was president of the company.

Born at West Point, Ill., Mr. Berger held an A.B. degree from Columbia University and an M.A. degree from the University of Michigan, where he was at one time an instructor in the economics department.

For a time Mr. Berger was sales manager of the school book department of D. Appleton Co., New York. [. . .]

–"Ex-President of Book Firm Dies at 63," *Indianapolis News,* 9 October 1959, p. 7

Bobbs-Merrill: 1961–1985

1961

January	The Liberal Arts Press merges with the company. Founder Oskar Piest becomes a vice president of Bobbs-Merrill and general editor of the Liberal Arts Press division.
April	The New York office moves to 3 West Fifty-seventh Street.
7 April	A translation of Voltaire's *Philosophical Letters* (1734) is published, the first title in the Library of Liberal Arts series to hold a Bobbs-Merrill copyright.
8 May	Glenn Tucker's *Chickamauga: Bloody Battle in the West* is published; the following year it wins the Fletcher Pratt Award for best nonfiction Civil War book of 1961.
December	Monroe Stearns resigns as managing editor and is replaced by William Raney, who will be in the New York office. Raney is best known for editing Norman Mailer's *The Naked and the Dead* (1948) while at Farrar and Rinehart.
29 December	Johnny Gruelle's *Raggedy Ann and the Golden Ring* and three other titles in the Raggedy Ann series are published, the first with the Bobbs-Merrill copyright.

1962

	William H. Y. Hackett becomes director of the Liberal Arts Press, a part of the college division, upon Piest's retirement.
March	Edward Gorey joins the New York office as production editor and art director of the trade department. His only Bobbs-Merrill book, *The Willowdale Handcar,* is published this year.
April	The Charter Books series is announced, with paperback reprints of backlist titles to go on sale in August.
June	A new plant opens at 4300 East Sixty-second Street and Guion Road, Indianapolis.
20 October	A new edition of Irma S. Rombauer's *The Joy of Cooking* (1931) is published and becomes the number-six nonfiction best-seller for the year.
31 December	Charles Chilton's *The Book of the West* is published; it wins the 1963 Western Heritage Award.

1963

1 January	M. Hughes Miller resigns as president. Howard W. Sams, chairman of the board of the parent company, assumes the presidency. Leo C. Gobin, who is elected executive vice president, takes over the management functions performed by Miller.
12 January	D. Laurance Chambers dies on his eighty-fourth birthday.
8 April	Julia Montgomery Street's *Dulcie's Whale* is published and wins the American Association of University Women, North Carolina Division, Award in Juvenile Literature.

15 July — Tucker's *Dawn Like Thunder* is published. It wins the 1964 Mayflower Cup for an outstanding book by a North Carolina writer.

25 July — Roma Gans's *Common Sense in Teaching Reading: A Practical Guide* is published. The following year it wins the Family Life Book Award and the Delta Kappa Gamma Society Educator's Award.

1964

31 July — Willie Lee Rose's *Rehearsal for Reconstruction: The Port Royal Experiment,* winner of the 1963 Allen Nevins Prize (as a doctoral dissertation), is published. The book goes on to win the 1965 Francis Parkman Prize of the Society of American Historians and the 1966 Charles S. Sydnor Award of the Southern Historical Association.

30 September — Editor in chief William Raney commits suicide.

October — Sams donates Bobbs-Merrill files to The Lilly Library at Indiana University.

November — The company assumes distribution for the publications of Inter-University Case Program, Inc., a nonprofit corporation that develops case studies describing the operations of government.

1965

January — Robert Amussen is named editor in chief.

1 July — Gobin is elected president and serves until his retirement in 1979. Hackett is appointed vice president.

30 August — Jamie Lee Cooper's *Shadow of a Star* is published; it wins the 1966 Friends of American Writers Award.

31 December — Robert Silverberg's first Bobbs-Merrill book, *Antarctic Conquests: The Great Explorers in Their Own Words,* and Tucker's *Zeb Vance: Champion of Personal Freedom* are published. Tucker's biography wins the 1966 Mayflower Cup and Thomas Wolfe Memorial Award.

1966

3 January — Books 1–8 of Ethelyn Davidson's *The New I Learn to Write* are published. Bobbs-Merrill had taken over the rights to the I Learn to Write series from E. C. Seale and Company the previous summer. Originating in 1940, the series had sold more than one million copies in 1964.

14 June — Jack Vance's first Bobbs-Merrill novel, *The Fox Valley Murders,* is published.

11 July — Herbert Wilner's *All the Little Heroes* is published; the novel wins the 1967 California Literature Fiction Gold Medal.

15 July — David Hawke's *The Colonial Experience* is published. It wins the 1967 Society of Colonial Wars in the State of New York Citation of Honour.

9 September — Tana de Gámez's *The Yoke and the Star: A Novel of the Cuban Revolution* is published.

29 September — The International Telephone and Telegraph Corporation (ITT) acquires Howard W. Sams and Company and its subsidiaries, including Bobbs-Merrill.

1967

	Vladimir Markov and Merrill Sparks's *Modern Russian Poetry* is published. (No copyright information exists.) The anthology wins the 1968 PEN Translation Prize.
30 June	Audrey C. Thomas's first Bobbs-Merrill book, *Ten Green Bottles: Short Stories,* is published.
10 November	Sam Shepard's first Bobbs-Merrill book, *Five Plays,* is published.

1968

	Ed Bullins's only Bobbs-Merrill book, *Five Plays,* is published.
15 March	Robert L. Moorhead dies.

1969

21 October	L. Frank Baum's *A Kidnapped Santa Claus* (which originally appeared in the December 1904 issue of the *Delineator*) is published.
18 November	Imamu Amiri Baraka's first two Bobbs-Merrill books, *Black Magic* and *Four Black Revolutionary Plays,* are published.
16 December	Charles Gordone's *No Place to Be Somebody: A Black-Black Comedy in Three Acts* is published, with an introduction by Joseph Papp. The play brings Gordone the 1970 Pulitzer Prize in drama.

1970

28 September	Chuck Stone's only Bobbs-Merrill novel, *King Strut,* is published.

1971

	The first Bobbs-Merrill book by Colette, *Places,* is published in a translation by David Le Vay. (No Bobbs-Merrill copyright information exists.)
30 June	Amussen resigns as director and editor in chief of the Bobbs-Merrill trade division.
July	Eugene Rachlis is appointed to replace Amussen, working out of the New York office.
December	Barbara Norville is appointed senior editor for the trade division, working out of New York to inaugurate a new line of mystery and suspense titles.
30 December	Nikki Giovanni's only Bobbs-Merrill book, *Gemini: An Extended Autobiographical Statement on My First Twenty-Five Years of Being a Black Poet,* is published.

1972

June	The New York editorial, publicity, and subsidiary-rights offices move to 4 West Fifty-eighth Street. Sales and administrative offices remain at the Sixty-second Street plant in Indianapolis.

1973

April	The company receives $1.5 million from New American Library (NAL) for rights to *The Joy of Cooking,* the largest sum ever paid for paperback rights to a single title.
24 August	*The Eye of the Heart: Short Stories from Latin America,* edited by Barbara Howes, is published. The collection wins a 1974 Christopher Book Award.

1974

2 January — Edward H. McKinley's *The Lure of Africa: American Interests in Tropical Africa, 1919–1939,* winner of the 1971 Allen Nevins Prize (as a doctoral dissertation), is published.

12 August — Max Ehrlich's *The Reincarnation of Peter Proud* is published; the novel is named a February 1975 selection of the Contempo and Doubleday book clubs.

6 September — William H. Hallahan's *The Search for Joseph Tully* is published and becomes an alternative selection of the Literary Guild for December.

2 December — Gregory McDonald's *Fletch* is published; the novel wins the 1975 Edgar Allan Poe Award from the Mystery Writers of America for best first mystery, crime, or suspense novel.

1975

10 March — Bjørn Robinson Rye's *The Expatriate* is published. Rye won a 1973 Mary Roberts Rinehart Foundation Award to support completion of the book.

15 May — Helene S. Arnstein's *The Roots of Love: Helping Your Child Learn to Love in the First Three Years of Life* is published. Arnstein's book wins a 1976 Family Life Book Award.

2 October — Marion Davies's *The Times We Had: Life with William Randolph Hearst* is published.

1976

15 December — The first volume of Chaim Grade's *The Yeshiva* is published (and the second volume in 1977) in a translation from the Yiddish by Curt Leviant. The book is the winner of the 1978 William and Janice Epstein Award for Fiction from the JWB Jewish Book Council.

1977

28 January — Leviant's *The Yemenite Girl* is published. The novel wins the 1978 Edward Lewis Wallant Book Award.

1 February — Hallahan's *Catch Me: Kill Me* is published. It wins the 1978 Edgar Allan Poe Award for best mystery, crime, or suspense novel.

March — Daniel Moses becomes editor in chief, and Carol Fein is named managing editor.

1978

28 July — An announcement is made that Moses and eight others are to be dismissed as of 31 August; the trade list is to be severely reduced.

18 August — Bernard Clayton Jr.'s *The Breads of France and How to Bake Them in Your Own Kitchen* is published.

November — James Fisher replaces Rachlis as trade-division publisher, responsible for all the editorial and marketing activities of the division. Rachlis becomes executive editor.

1979

Grace G. Shaw becomes senior editor at Bobbs-Merrill and, later, executive editor.

27 April — An announcement is made that the New York trade office is being reorganized.

1980

February Shaw is appointed executive editor. She replaces Fisher as trade-division publisher.

8 August David S. Reiss's *M*A*S*H: The Exclusive Inside Story of TV's Most Popular Show* is published. The book is updated in 1983 to include an account of the final episode of the program.

November An announcement is made that commercial fiction will be revived in the trade division.

1981

13 May William Bleifuss's *Gold, Where and How to Find It Yourself* is published.

1982

NAL renegotiates the paperback rights to *The Joy of Cooking* for $2.5 million, another record for a single title.

1983

4 March Bernard F. Conners's *Dancehall* is published.

1984

December Bonnie Ammer replaces Shaw as publisher and general manager of Bobbs-Merrill.

1985

March–April Bobbs-Merrill is acquired by Macmillan as part of ITT's publishing group.

May Macmillan dissolves Bobbs-Merrill.

1986–1989

The Bobbs-Merrill imprint appears for the last time on reprints of books about shorthand by Joe M. Pullis, published by the Glencoe Publishing Company, a division of Macmillan.

Merger

The Liberal Arts Press, Inc. has been merged into the Bobbs-Merrill Co., a subsidiary of Howard W. Sams & Co., Inc. Oskar Piest, who founded the Liberal Arts Press in 1948 and has been its president, will become a vice-president of Bobbs-Merrill and general editor of the new Liberal Arts Press Division of Bobbs-Merrill.

The Liberal Arts Press has specialized in publishing, for college courses, classics in the fields of philosophy, political science, history, religion and fine arts. It now has over 180 titles in print largely in paperback editions, but with many also available in cloth editions. Liberal Arts Press books are published in four series: the Library of Liberal Arts, the American Heritage Series, the Library of Religion and Forum Books. They are currently being used in over 2000 courses in some 800-plus colleges and universities. In the past five years over 1,500,000 copies of books published under the Liberal Arts Press imprint have been sold.

As general editor of the Liberal Arts Press Division of Bobbs-Merrill, Mr. Piest will work closely with Ranald P. Hobbs, executive vice-president of Bobbs-Merrill, towards integrating the new division into the overall publishing program of Bobbs-Merrill. Approximately 60 new books are in preparation, including new translations of Boethius' "The Consolations of Philosophy," Plato's "Epistles," Aristotle's "Nichomachean Ethics." [. . .]

–"Liberal Arts Press Merges with Bobbs-Merrill," *Publishers' Weekly,* 179 (16 January 1961): 97–98

* * *

An Essay of Dramatic Poesy

A Defence of an Essay of Dramatic Poesy

Preface to the Fables

JOHN DRYDEN

Edited, with an Introduction and Notes, by

John L. Mahoney

The Library of Liberal Arts

published by

THE BOBBS-MERRILL COMPANY, INC.

INDIANAPOLIS • NEW YORK

Title page for a 1965 volume in the Library of Liberal Arts series, which Bobbs-Merrill acquired from the Liberal Arts Press in 1961 (courtesy of John L. Mahoney)

Paperbacks

Bobbs-Merrill is entering the paperback lists with Charter Books, a line designed, according to M. Hughes Miller, president of Bobbs-Merrill, "to fill the gap between popular mass market paperbacks and the more highly esoteric lines the sales of which depend heavily on the college market." The first 20 titles will go on sale in August. Thereafter, books will be published at the rate of about four a month.

Charter Books will be distributed by the Macfadden-Bartell Corporation. For the first seasons Charter Books will be taken from the Bobbs-Merrill trade and law backlists, the technical backlist of Howard W. Sams & Co., which owns Bobbs-Merrill, and the Liberal Arts Press, another Sams subsidiary. Later, titles from other publishers and original paperbacks will be considered for the list. [. . .]

Among the first Charter Books, all from the Bobbs-Merrill backlist, will be J. Christopher Herold's NBA winner, "Mistress To an Age"; "Melbourne" by David Lord Cecil; John Erskine's "The Private Life of Helen of Troy"; Harry Barnard's biography of John Peter Altgeld, "Eagle Forgotten"; Mark Harris' novel, "The Southpaw"; "Night of Time" by René Fülöp-Miller; Ayn Rand's long-time best seller, "The Fountainhead"; Joseph Wood Krutch's NBA winner, "The Measure of Man"; Louis Kronenberger's "Company Manners"; "On Being Negro in America" by J. Saunders Redding; "The Denatured Novel" by Albert Van Nostrand. [. . .]

–"Bobbs Merrill Enters the Paperback Field," *Publishers' Weekly,* 181 (16 April 1962): 74

* * *

Run-Up to a Best-Seller

After production problems, this new edition of a mainstay of the trade list appeared in October, and its 150,000-copy first printing sold out in only a few weeks.

The "Joy of Cooking" will be published by Bobbs-Merrill on July 25 in its first new edition in 10 years. The initial advertising and promotion budget is $100,000. Since its original publication in 1936 the Irma Rombauer and Marion Rombauer Becker cookbook has sold close to 5,000,000 copies. Since 1943 it has never sold fewer than 80,000 copies a year. Marshall Field's, alone, estimates its sales total at 80,000. Yet the "Joy of Cooking" has never appeared on a national best seller list and only made a local list once, St. Louis in 1943, Mrs. Rombauer's home town. [. . .]

The details of Bobbs-Merrill's $100,000 campaign for the new edition of the "Joy of Cooking" will be featured at the firm's ABA Convention booth, where canapés from the book will be served and lots of prizes offered [. . .]. J. L. Hudson's in Detroit and Farberware are cooperating in a "Joy of Cooking" week from June 3 to 9, in which four times a day one floor of the store will be given over to cooking demonstrations of 100 recipes from the book, and there will be window displays, major advertising and other local promotion. Orders will be taken for the new edition, which will not be ready until late July.

In New York Bobbs-Merrill is planning a most unusual luncheon for 100 top cooking and book page editors. M. Hughes Miller has devised the idea of giving guests a chance to select in advance, from four separate menus from the cookbook, the one they want to be served.

The $50,000 advertising budget will include full-page ads in major newspapers across the country this summer, including *This Week* supplement, plus ads on the radio. There will be magazine and TV coverage. There will be self-mailers, brochures, window streamers, slit-cards, statement enclosures, big posters, giant books. The entire full-page and co-op ad program which starts this summer will be repeated on the same national scale at Thanksgiving and again at Christmas time. Special arrangements and allowances will be made for window, counter and store displays of the new edition of the "Joy of Cooking." And, for the benefit of any bookseller who doesn't already know it, we remind him that, ever since 1936, Bobbs-Merrill has had a standing practice of giving a free copy of the "Joy of Cooking" to any bookseller who requests it.

–"Bobbs-Merrill Spending $100,000 To Launch New 'Joy of Cooking,'" *Publishers' Weekly,* 181 (4 June 1962): 77–78

* * *

Last Triumph of the Miller Era

For the first time since Howard W. Sams & Co., Inc., acquired the Bobbs-Merrill Company as its subsidiary, December 1, 1958, the operations of both firms are housed under one roof. This is Sams' new 2.5 million dollar building consisting of 200,000 sq. ft. in Northwest Indianapolis, 4300 E. 62nd Street at Guion Road, to which the combined firms recently moved. There has been an extensive building program because of the rapid expansion of the two firms, which now include 14 separate divisions as well as two newly acquired subsidiaries, operating in almost every phase of the publishing field. In the process of its growth and expansion, the companies spilled over into four different locations, employing almost 600 persons. In 1961, the management decided to construct a single large building that would provide adequate space for efficient flow of work, from product manufacturing to distribution, as well as house the editorial, accounting and executive offices. The move consolidates the work done not only in the four locations in Indianapolis, but shipping and warehousing in various parts of the country. [. . .]

The rapid growth of the combined firms includes the expanded design and production departments. The traditional concept of the green cover and simple stamping has been scrapped; a new design department under Edward Gorey (*PW,* April 30) has been set up; the complete art department of the Howard W. Sams & Co., as well as outside art agencies in New York and Chicago, have been called in to supply artists for all publications issued by the combined companies. From the Bobbs-Merrill trade backlist many books which once sold very well and have gone out of print have been reissued in new formats with new covers and jackets. An example of the stepped-up design program which has paid off is the Childhood of Famous Americans series which now has 129 titles and was one of the first groups of books on the Bobbs-Merrill list to be repackaged in design, color, new illustrations and new typeface by the George Brodsky Agency of Chicago, with a resultant increase in sales. For both the trade and education editions, the format was completely modernized by opening up pages with more leading and white space, running full-page and double-page illustrations in color, dropping lead lines, setting text in a modern typeface acceptable for the third-grade reading level, adding new jackets and introducing color.

In the education fields, Bobbs-Merrill has brought out three multi-volume projects, among others–the 16-volume "Best of Children's Literature," the 16-volume "Health for Young America" and the 7-volume developmental reading text workbooks. [. . .]

A production control chart is followed very carefully to watch the status of each book in process and to watch inventory. With this new and efficiently planned operation, Sams and Bobbs-Merrill believes that it can keep an even tighter control on inventory in all fields. This control is to be applied to trade books which are kept in sheets or finished books; or to educational books frequently kept in sheets waiting for state adoptions; or law books where sometimes only one-third of a printing, which has been produced to last fifteen years, is bound and the rest kept in folded and gathered signatures to be bound when needed.

–"Sams, Bobbs-Merrill Push-Button Plant is Ready for the Future," *Publishers' Weekly,* 181 (11 June 1962): 70, 74

* * *

Another Banner List from

Bobbs-Merrill

February:	**I AM ONLY ONE** by Myrtie Barker	Inspiration	$2.95
March:	**HUNTING ANYONE?** by Syd Hoff (Illus.)	Humor	$2.95
	FRIENDLY COVE by Irving Brant	Fiction	$4.00
	THINK AND GROW SLIM by Peg Stokes		$3.95
	QUAIL IN ASPIC by Cecil Beaton (Illus.)	Satire	$4.00
	O.E. — HISTORIAN WITHOUT AN ARMCHAIR by Otto Eisenschiml		$4.00
	OUR MAN STANLEY by Philip Hamburger (Illus.)	Intimate History	$4.00
	DEATH OF AN ANGEL by Clay Richards	Mystery	$3.50
	ALL I COULD SEE FROM WHERE I STOOD by George Christy	Fiction	$4.00
	BEYOND CONFLICT by Robert Balzer (Illus.)	Personal History	$6.00
	RUSSIAN FRONTIERS: From Muscovy to Khrushchev by William G. Bray	History	$5.00
	COMMUNIST EDUCATION by Edmund J. King		$4.00
April:	**DAWN LIKE THUNDER** by Glenn Tucker	History	$6.50
	COMEBACK: The Story of My Stroke by Robert E. Van Rosen & Kendell Crossen (Illus.)	Self-help	$3.95
May:	**KENNEDY & McCORMACK: Dynastic Politics in Massachusetts** by Murray B. Levin	Political Science	$5.00
	AUCTION! by James Brough (Illus.)		$7.50
	THE MOON: New World for Men by Martin Caidin (Illus.)		$4.95
	PETTY LARCENY by Bruce Petty	Cartoons	$4.00
June:	**SPECTACULAR ROGUE: Gaston B. Means** by Edwin P. Hoyt, Jr.	Biography	$5.95
	WORLD OF THE DESERT by Slater Brown	Natural History	$4.50
	READING COMMON SENSE by Roma Gans		$2.95
	THE SOUTHERN FRONTIER by John Anthony Caruso	History	$6.50
	THE HAWK IS HUMMING by George Mendoza	Fiction	$3.95
	JUDAH P. BENJAMIN by S. I. Neiman	Biography	$3.95

— AND HIGHBALLING INTO '63
JOY OF COOKING
GET ABOARD!

Write for complete catalogue
THE BOBBS-MERRILL COMPANY, INC.
A SUBSIDIARY OF HOWARD W. SAMS & CO., INC.
4300 WEST 62ND STREET · INDIANAPOLIS 6, INDIANA

Advertisement for the spring list in the 28 January 1963 issue of Publishers' Weekly

The Death of D. Laurance Chambers

D. Laurance Chambers, Indianapolis publisher and a close friend of Indianapolis authors Booth Tarkington and James Whitcomb Riley, died today in his home on his 84th birthday.

Chambers has been chairman emeritus of Bobbs-Merrill Co. since November, 1958, when the controlling interest of the firm was sold to Howard W. Sams & Co.

Mr. Chambers joined Bobbs-Merrill Co. in 1903 as William Bobbs' secretary, shortly after the firm's name was changed from Bowen-Merrill. Prior to that he was on the editorial staff of the Curtis Publishing Co. in Philadelphia.

A magna cum laude graduate of Princeton University in 1900, he became the personal secretary of Dr. Henry van Dyke, Princeton's leading literary figure upon graduation.

During his three-year stay with Dr. van Dyke, Mr. Chambers earned his M. A. degree from Princeton in 1901 on a Charles Scribner Fellowship in English. In 1937 he received an honorary Litt. D. from Wabash College and in 1948 Indiana University awarded him with an honorary L. L. D. degree.

A native of Washington, D. C., Mr. Chambers was graduated from the Columbian Preparatory School in that city.

In 1907 he joined the executive staff of Bobbs-Merrill and became its president in 1935. He was elected chairman of the board in 1953.

Prior to and during his position as president, Mr. Chambers headed the trade book department and was the foremost living authority on trade books. This department published fiction, non-fiction and children's books.

He was a warm friend of James Whitcomb Riley, Mr. Chambers said, "He was the shyest man I ever knew. At the same time he abhorred being alone."

Booth Tarkington also was a warm friend and Mr. Chambers used to visit with Mrs. Tarkington prior to his illness.

An author, he wrote "The Metre of Macbeth" (Princeton University Press, 1903) and "Indiana: A Hoosier History" (Bobbs-Merrill, 1933). He complied [*sic*] with Dr. Van Dyke on "Poems of Tennyson" (Ginn & Co., 1903).

He played a good game of bridge, was an excellent tennis player and had a remarkable collection of more than 14,000 stamps. Mr. Chambers, nicknamed "Dell" at Princeton, was a member of the First Baptist Church of Indianapolis and formerly a member of its board of trustees; Phi Beta Kappa; Indiana Historical Society; Players Club, New York; Civil War Round Table of Chicago, and the Indianapolis Athletic Club. [. . .]

He married Miss Nora Taggart, who survives him, in April of 1910 and they had three children. [. . .]

Mr. Chambers is survived by a daughter, Mrs. Evelyn Birge; a son, David L. Chambers Jr., president of the Indianapolis Stock Yards Co., and seven grandchildren. His other daughter was the late Mrs. Judith C. Test. [. . .]

–"D. L. Chambers, 84, City Publisher, Dies," *Indianapolis Times,* 12 January 1963, p. 11

* * *

Tribute to Chambers

A native of Illinois, who now lives in North Carolina, claims that Indiana has failed to pay proper tribute to "the greatest editor who ever lived."

Inglis Fletcher, whose novels have gained her a long-lasting literary reputation, said in an interview that D. Laurance Chambers, who died earlier this year, was the person most responsible for her career and the careers of many other writers.

"He helped more people than you Hoosiers know," Mrs. Fletcher said. "He was the greatest American editor who ever lived. He taught me everything I know about writing."

Chambers, known to Hoosiers as the former president of Bobbs-Merrill Co., also was a personal friend of Booth Tarkington and James Whitcomb Riley, as well as many other writers.

Mrs. Fletcher said Chambers was too shy and reserved ever to take credit for the help he gave to anyone. She said, however, that he never lost interest in the authors whose careers he had bettered with his blue pencil and advice.

"I think the last letter he wrote before he died may have been to me," Mrs. Fletcher said. She suffered a crippling stroke two years ago, but is now "learning to walk again." [. . .]

She said her chief memory of Indianapolis is of a hotel room in which she shut herself whenever she needed to meet a deadline for publication of a book.

She sent her hand-written sheets to Chambers, who read and criticized them, and sent them back to her to rewrite.

–Hortense Myers, "Chambers Called Greatest Editor," *Indianapolis News,* 8 October 1963, p. 20

*Leo C. Gobin, president of the company from 1965 to 1979 (*Publishers' Weekly, *2 August 1965)*

The Takeover by ITT

The International Telephone and Telegraph Corp., the world's ninth largest industrial employer, announced on May 13 it has agreed to acquire Howard W. Sams & Co. for an exchange of stock valued at about $33.8 million. The acquisition, which would bring about the fourth absorption of a major publisher by an electronics firm within the past year, is subject to approval by Sams stockholders, who will be called to a special meeting later this year. Plans call for Sams to be operated as a wholly owned subsidiary, and an ITT spokesman tells *PW* that for the many firms it has acquired, ITT generally brings no major changes in management or policy. [. . .]

–"ITT Plans to Acquire Howard W. Sams & Co.," *Publishers' Weekly,* 189 (23 May 1966): 54

* * *

Stockholders of Howard W. Sams, at a special meeting on September 29, approved the acquisition of the company's assets by International Telephone and Telegraph Corporation (*PW,* May 23). The acquisition will be effected by the transfer of Sams' assets to a newly formed ITT subsidiary, Howard W. Sams, Inc., through the exchange of Sams stock for ITT common and preferred stock. As previously announced (*PW,* July 11) Sams stock-

Advertisement for the thirty-five-year-old series from the 16 January 1967 issue of Publishers' Weekly

holders will receive .423 shares of ITT common and .236 shares of ITT preferred for each share of Sams common. There are 647,313 outstanding shares of Sams stock.

Howard W. Sams, who founded the company in 1946, and who is chairman and president of Sams, will be chairman, president and chief executive officer of the new corporation.

–"Sams Stockholders Agree on Acquisition by ITT," *Publishers' Weekly,* 190 (10 October 1966): 52

* * *

Obituary: Robert L. Moorhead

Robert L. Moorhead was the last surviving major executive from Bobbs-Merrill's independent salad days.

Robert Lowry Moorhead, 93 years old, long an executive in the old Bobbs-Merrill Company, former state legislator and civic leader, died yesterday in Community Hospital after a short illness.

He was a veteran of the Spanish American War and World War I.

Mr. Moorhead, R.R. 10, Box 405, was associated with the historic publishing firm, now Howard W. Sams Company Inc., from 1893 to 1950. He served as a director, vice-president and treasurer and was in charge of its law publishing.

He retired in 1951, but served as a director until 1958.

Mr. Moorhead was a director and past president of Central Publishing Company, the firm which prints the acts of the Indiana General Assembly.

He began his career with Bobbs-Merrill, then the Bowen-Merrill Company, working afternoons while he attended Indianapolis High School, now Shortridge High School, and Butler University. [. . .]

–"R. L. Moorhead Dies; Publishing Executive," *Indianapolis Star,* 16 March 1968, p. 28

* * *

Taking Stock

Bobbs-Merrill Co.

Although all editorial functions of the Bobbs-Merrill Company were moved from Indianapolis to New York in 1962, four years after its acquisition by the Indianapolis-based technical publisher Howard W. Sams & Company, it is still difficult to think of

Charles Gordone, whose No Place to Be Somebody, *published by Bobbs-Merrill in 1969, won him the 1970 Pulitzer Prize in drama (Bruccoli Clark Layman Archives)*

*Advertisement for the series inaugurated by the new senior editor at Bobbs-Merrill, Barbara Norville (*Publishers Weekly*, 14 August 1972)*

Bobbs as anything but a Hoosier publishing house. It was, after all, the publisher of Indiana poet James Whitcomb Riley and of Charles Major, whose novel "When Knighthood Was in Flower" sold more than a million copies late in the last century. It was Bobbs-Merrill editors who discovered William Styron and published his fine first book "Lie Down in Darkness," and who brought out Ayn Rand's fabulous best seller "The Fountainhead" after it was turned down by many New York publishers.

Despite its longtime tradition as a Midwest house, the company found it necessary, it says, to open a New York office as far back as the early 1900s, "primarily to attract agents." Today all acquisitions and editing are done in New York, where Eugene Rachlis is editor in chief. Production, advertising, billing, shipping and warehousing are still done in Indianapolis, where Leo C. Gobin is president.

Thomas J. Eastwood, who directs advertising and public relations from Indianapolis, reminds us that it was a Midwest author, Irma S. Rombauer, author of "The Joy of Cooking" (12 editions, 31 printings), who this year gave Bobbs-Merrill the largest sale of paperback rights in history, when New American Library shelled out $1,500,000. That ain't exactly peas.

–Van Allen Bradley, "Trade Books: Alive and Kicking," *Publishers Weekly,* 204 (22 October 1973): 61

* * *

The Spirit of John J. Curtis

An imaginative promotion for "The Reincarnation of Peter Proud" by Max Ehrlich and the film to be based on the book gives purchasers of the book the opportunity to see the film free. A coupon has been incorporated on the inside back flap of the book jacket. The reader is invited to clip the coupon and mail it in to Bobbs-Merrill, which will send back a ticket to the film, scheduled to open in early 1975. It stars Michael Sarrazin and Jennifer O'Neill. The Bobbs-Merrill book ($6.95), which has a September 22 pub date, is one of Bobbs' lead titles for fall, and is a full February selection of the Contempo and Doubleday book clubs. [. . .]

–"Bobbs-Merrill Book to Carry Free Coupon to See a Movie," *Publishers Weekly,* 206 (12 August 1974): 45

* * *

How do you attract the attention of the media when your author prefers not to make appearances? Bobbs-Merrill's answer in the case of William H. Hallahan, author of "The Search for Joseph Tully," a novel of "vengeance beyond the grave," was the planting of a gravestone to commemorate the life of Joseph Tully, November 11, 1468–October 15, 1974 (pub date). The stone was set on the grassy island in the middle of New York's heavily travelled Park Avenue, on the corner of 57th Street. [. . .]

–"Bobbs-Merrill Plants Gravestone for Character in New Novel," *Publishers Weekly,* 206 (28 October 1974): 41

* * *

Plans for 1976–1977

[. . .] Sams and Bobbs will produce 190 books in 1976, and plan 213 in 1977. They do half their business with bookstores; about 40% with libraries; and the rest with book clubs and through direct mail. Fiction and juvenile output may be cut back a little, but remain important in a broad list of general nonfiction, crafts, cookbooks, science and technology. The firm has no plans for mass market paperbacks. All-time backlist sellers are "The Joy of Cooking," over five million in print, and the deathless Raggedy Ann and Andy titles.

–*Publishers Weekly,* 209 (21 June 1976): 60

A Late Case: Selected Correspondence with Roy Hoopes, 1977–1978

Author files for the significant Bobbs-Merrill literary figures still working at this time are not in the company archives at The Lilly Library, but among the nonfiction writers represented in the archives is Roy Hoopes. His Cain: The Biography of James M. Cain *(1982), winner of an Edgar Award, was published by Holt, Rinehart, and Winston, not Bobbs-Merrill. Nonetheless, Hoopes thanks Daniel Moses in the acknowledgments for his assistance during the early stages of writing the biography. Moses' stay at Bobbs-Merrill was short (March 1977 to August 1978), and his departure coincided with a reduction in the trade list.*

Roy Hoopes to Daniel Moses, 23 November 1977

Dear Mr. Moses:

At the su[gg]estion of David Madden, I am sending you a proposal for a biography of James M. Cain, who died recently. As you know, David did a literary study of Cain for Twayne publishers, and I have been in touch with him concerning my biography. I am talking seriously with one or two publishers, but also circulating the enclosed proposal in the trade, and David thought you might be interested.

The enclosed material includes:

- A proposal discussing my interest in an approach to a Cain biography;
- An article I wrote about Cain for the Washingtonian magazine;
- The New York Times obituary;
- A chronology of Cain's life and achievements;
- A list of Cain's writings other than his novels;
- My professional resume;
- Some reviews of my recently published book, Americans Remember the Homefront.

If you would like to see a copy of my homefront book or samples of my writing, I would be glad to send them to you. I hope you have some interest in this prop[o]sal.

Sincerely,
Roy Hoopes

* * *

Hoopes to Moses, 24 December 1977

Dear Danny:

Here are the signed Cain contracts. Monday morning I am leaving for Jekyll Island, Georgia, where I will be doing an article for the Washingtonian and spending the week. After Tuesday, you can reach me through Lynn Cheek at the Jekyll Island Promotional Assoc.–(912) 635-2545–if there are any problems with the contract. I will be back in Washington around January 2.

One thing we did not discuss about the Cain biography is photographs. I assume that we will want to include some in the book. I have come across some vintage photos of Cain and will be on the lookout for more, unless you veto photos. I also took several myself during the last couple of years. One of them ran with my article on Washington writers, which was in the December Bookviews. I think you would be interested in the piece if you have not already seen it.

I'll be talking with you when I return
happy holidays
as ever
Roy

* * *

August

AMATEUR HOUR a novel of suspense by ROBERT HARDIN. $7.95 (52255-1)

YOGA AND COMMON SENSE revised edition by INA MARX. Photos by Diana Bryant. $7.95, paper (52269-1)

September

AMERICA'S GREATEST GOLFING RESORTS by DICK MILLER. Foreword by Arnold Palmer. 8½ x 11. Photos. $20 (52133-4)

RUGMAKING: 3 QUICK AND EASY WAYS by JOAN SCOBEY and MARJORIE SABLOW. Cooking and Crafts Club (Book-of-the-Month Club) Main Selection. Better Homes & Gardens Crafts Club Main Selection. Better Homes & Gardens Family Book Service Main Selection. Columbia House Needle Arts Society Alternate. 8½ x 11. Drawings, diagrams, photos. $12.95 (52132-6)

SHELL CRAFT by VIRGINIE FOWLER ELBERT. Better Homes & Gardens Crafts Club Featured Alternate. Better Homes & Gardens Family Book Service Featured Alternate. Drawings and photos. $12.95 (52176-8)

THE NOTRE DAME FOOTBALL SCRAPBOOK by RICHARD M. COHEN, JORDAN A. DEUTSCH, and DAVID S. NEFT. 8½ x 11. Illustrated. $6.95, paper (52335-3)

THE OHIO STATE FOOTBALL SCRAPBOOK by RICHARD M. COHEN, JORDAN A. DEUTSCH, and DAVID S. NEFT. 8½ x 11. Illustrated. $6.95, paper (52334-5)

ELUSIVE VICTORY: The Arab-Israeli Wars, 1947-1974 by COL. T. N. DUPUY, USA, Ret. Photos and maps. $14.95 (51974-7)

THE SPORTS COLLECTORS BIBLE, 2nd Edition by BERT RANDOLPH SUGAR. Foreword by Jim Bouton. Introduction by Roone Arledge. Illustrated. $9.95, paper (52351-5)

FEARLESS AND FREE: The Seminole Indian War, 1835-1842 by GEORGE WALTON. Illustrated. $13.95 (52250-0)

HOW TO MAKE UPSIDE-DOWN DOLLS by JOHN COYNE and JERRY MILLER. Cooking and Crafts Club (Book-of-the-Month Club) Alternate. Better Homes & Gardens Crafts Club Alternate. Better Homes & Gardens Family Book Service Alternate. Columbia House Needle Arts Society Alternate. 8½ x 11. Drawings, diagrams, patterns, photos. $12.95 (52157-1)

ALL ABOUT DOLL HOUSES by BARBARA L. FARLIE with Charlotte L. Clarke. 8½ x 11. Photos and diagrams. $8.95, paper (52367-1), $14.95, cloth (51976-3)

October

MOLLY COMPANION a novel by MAURA STANTON. $8.95 (52353-1)

SECRETS OF THE LOST RACES: New Discoveries of Advanced Technology in Ancient Civilizations by RENE NOORBERGEN. Photos, maps, and drawings. $10 (52289-6)

WEASEL HUNT a novel of suspense by JAMES K. MacDOUGALL. $8.95 (52337-X)

WESTERNS OF THE 40's: Classics From the Great Pulps edited by DAMON KNIGHT. Illustrated. $12.50 (52036-2)

NUMBERS, PREDICTION & WAR: Using History to Evaluate Combat Factors and Predict the Outcome of Battles by COL. T. N. DUPUY, USA, Ret. Illustrated. $12.95 (52131-8)

CARLETON VARNEY DECORATES FROM A TO Z: An Encyclopedia of Home Decoration by CARLETON VARNEY. First Serial: *Good Housekeeping*. 8½ x 11. Drawings and photos. $15 (51863-5)

THE FRANCO YEARS: The Untold Human Story of Life Under Spanish Fascism by JOSE YGLESIAS. A Book-of-the-Month Club Alternate. $10 (52352-3)

November

THE NIRVANA CONTRACTS a novel of suspense by JAMES P. WOHL. $7.95 (52340-X)

THE STAR TREATMENT by DICK STELZER. First Serial: *Ladies' Home Journal*. $7.95 (52290-X)

THE MORELAND LEGACY a romantic novel by DIANA HAVILAND. $10 (52336-1)

THE YESHIVA, Volume II: Masters and Disciples by CHAIM GRADE. Translated from the Yiddish by Curt Leviant. $15 (52344-2)

SELF-MASTERY THROUGH SELF-HYPNOSIS by DR. ROGER BERNHARDT and DAVID MARTIN. $8.95 (52058-3)

WIN OR LOSE: A Social History of Gambling in America by STEPHEN LONGSTREET. Illustrated. $12.50 (52253-5)

December

MAN OF THE WORLD: Herbert Bayard Swope and the Golden Days of American Journalism by ALFRED ALLAN LEWIS. Illustrated. $15 (51858-9)

SWORD OF THE RAJ: The British Army in India, 1747-1947 by ROGER BEAUMONT. Introduction by Robin Higham. Illustrated. $15 (52136-9)

January

THE TAKERS a novel by ROBERT ACKWORTH. $10.95 (52298-5)

Distributed by Bobbs-Merrill

PEEBLES PRESS

INTERNATIONAL PHOTO ALBUM: ATHENS photographs by NICOLAI CANETTI and NICK MANLEY. $12.95 (52358-2) October

THE MEMOIRS OF SARAH BERNHARDT: Early Childhood Through the First American Tour edited and with an introduction by SANDY LESBERG. Illustrated. $12.95 (52355-8) October

FIVE YEARS OF MY LIFE: The Diary of Captain Alfred Dreyfus introduction by NICHOLAS HALASZ. 7 x 10. Illustrated. $12.95 (52356-6) October

THE PEOPLES OF ISRAEL by CARL UNDERHILL QUINN. Photographs by Nicolai Canetti. 8½ x 10⅞. $13.95 (52363-9) November

AMERICAN PHOTO ALBUM: WASHINGTON, D.C. photographs by NICOLAI CANETTI. 8½ x 10⅞. $12.95 (52362-0) November

HAMMER DOWN: The Heavy Truckers' Romance With the Open Road photographs by STEVE LESBERG and NAOMI GOLDBERG. 9 x12. $7.95, paper (52368-X), $14.95, cloth (52361-2) November

COUNTY FAIR photographs and text by STEVE LESBERG and NAOMI GOLDBERG. 9 x 12. Over 200 photos, 16 pages in full color. $7.95, paper (52369-8), $14.95, cloth (52360-4) December

THE RODIN MUSEUM OF PARIS edited by SANDY LESBERG. Photographs by Nicolai Canetti. Introduction by Mme. Monique Laurent, curator. 9 x 12. $25 (52364-7); Collector's Limited Edition $75 (52370-1) November

SAUCY LADIES by RON STIEGLITZ and SANDY LESBERG. 8¼ x 7½. Illustrated. $7.95 (52359-0) Cookbook. October

CYRCO PRESS

POLITICS OF DEFEAT: America's Decline in the Middle East by JOSEPH CHURBA. Introduction by Admiral Elmo R. Zumwalt, Jr., USN, Ret. $8.95 (52371-X) September

LERNER PUBLICATIONS

POLITICS IN ART by JOAN MONDALE. 8 x 10. Illustrated. $3.95, paper (ISBN 0-8225-9950-3) September

THE LIVING WILDERNESS by EARL W. HUNT. Illustrated by George Overlie. Includes pen and wash drawings. $7.95 (ISBN 0-8225-0760-9) August (YA)

THE WILDLIFE ATLAS by SYLVIA A. JOHNSON. Illustrated by Alcuin C. Dornisch. 9⅜ x 8½. Includes 60 full-page watercolor illustrations. $10 (ISBN 0-8225-9951-1) September (YA)

Please add Bobbs-Merrill's prefix, 0-672-, to all code numbers to get full ISBNs.

BOBBS-MERRILL

Publishers since 1838

4300 West 62nd Street
Indianapolis, Indiana 46206

Retailers are free to charge whatever prices they wish for our books. Prices slightly higher in Canada.

Advertisement for the fall list from the 29 August 1977 issue of Publishers Weekly

Contract

The statement is inscribed "R. Evans 1/5".

BOOK UNDER CONTRACT
The Bobbs-Merrill Company, Inc.
Trade Division
Editor: Daniel Moses

Title:	Biography of James M. Cain
Author:	Roy Hoopes
Category:	Non-fiction
Agent:	None
Contract date:	December 22, 1977
Delivery date:	January 1, 1980
Publication date:	Fall 1980
Length:	100,000 words
Probable Price:	$12.50
First year's sales:	10,000 copies

THE BOOK

One of the most popular novelists of the 20th century, James M. Cain was, in all aspects of his life, a writer. Tom Wolfe advised Norman Mailer to read some James M. Cain and learn how to write a novel. Albert Camus thought Cain was one of America's greatest writers and acknowledged that The Stranger was modeled on Cain's The Postman Always Rings Twice. Ross MacDonald called Postman and Double Indemnity "a pair of native American masterpieces."

These two books, with Mildred Pierce, were Cain's greatest successes. But before he even wrote them, he led a professional writer's life. He wrote for H. L. Mencken's The American Mercury, composed editorials for Walter Lippmann on The New York World, and toiled as managing editor of The New Yorker. He then moved to Hollywood, where, for 17 years, he was a scriptwriter. He married four times, suffered through three divorces and several major illnesses, and died, at 85, in 1977.

In this revealing and provocative work, Roy Hoopes, who interviewed Cain, details a life full of success and failure, of a man who started a new career–novel-writing–at 42. And, in addition to this, [h]e became a critic of the America he saw, and published his insights in The Saturday Evening Post, Esquire, The Atlantic Monthly, and the Washington Post. Through all his work is the source of his popularity: an unflinchingly truthful look at his country, and particularly, his fellow

Roy Hoopes with Vice President Walter Mondale, 1977 (photograph by Spencer Hoopes, from Anne Commire, Something About the Author, *1977; Thomas Cooper Library, University of South Carolina)*

Americans. In this book, Roy Hoopes relates the talent, force and truth behind this great writer.

About the author: Roy Hoopes is also an experienced writer. He has worked as an editor for Time-Life International, National Geographic, and Newsday. He has also worked in the Department of Health, Education and Welfare. As a freelance writer he is the author of eighteen books; the most recent one is Americans Remember the Home Front.

THE TERMS

Advance:	$8500.	$1500. on signing $1000. monthly, for 5 months, upon evidence of acceptable progress $2000. on delivery of acceptable manuscript
Royalties:	Cloth	10% on the first 5,000 copies sold 12.5% on the next 5,000 copies sold 15% thereafter
	Paper	7.5% on all copies sold
Rights:	Clause 12: (1–6) Equal division, (7–9) delete Clause 13: Author 100%	

* * *

Susan Suffes to Hoopes, 14 February 1978

Dear Mr. Hoopes:
Enclosed is your check for $1,500, representing the amount due on signing of the contract for the biography of James M. Cain. Also enclosed is a fully executed copy of the contract for your files.

Yours sincerely,
Susan Suffes
Assistant Editor

* * *

Alfred Allan Lewis wrote Man of the World: Herbert Bayard Swope, A Charmed Life of Pulitzer Prizes, Poker and Politics *(Bobbs-Merrill, 1978).*

Hoopes to Moses, 18 May 1978

Dear Danny:

Thanks for the Alfred Allen [*sic*] Lewis address. I have written him.

I have abandoned the Crowell project of a juvenile bio. on Cain. I need the money, but I am uncomfortable about doing anything that Bobbs Merrill might be disturbed about. And in this case, I think there would be some justification. I sent for one of the Crowell biographies (John Steinbeck) and find that it is a much more ambitious job than I had imagined. It is nearly 60,000 words and quite well written, that is, it is sophisticated enough for an adult to enjoy. I think a similar bio. of Cain might well be considered compet[it]ive to our book. So that's that.

I have lined up an apartment for June–at least for a short time. So keep your ears open for something, maybe in July or August. I plan to be in New York for awhile, beginning June 6, so we can get together then.

I have been giving a lot of thought to the kind of book I want to do on Cain and the book I had conceived turns out to be very much like the biography of Raymond Chandler by Frank MacShane (Dutton; Penguin). It is about the right size and written with extensive quotes from Chandler's letters and other autobiographical writings–but no footnotes and no long letters printed in full, single-spaced and indented. I think this is the right approach to biography. He gives the sources for all the Chandler quotes and other factual information in the Chapter "Notes" at the end of the book. I think it is a very good way to handle the documentation. He also has a simple, not annotated, bibliography at the end.

I think the public and the critics have rebelled against these huge, detailed biographies that tell the reader more than he needs to know about the subject and is studded with footnotes and long, single-space letters. They slow a book down considerably. Peter Prescott commented on the trend toward "overlong and graceless" biographies in his Newsweek review of Christopher Sykes' Evelyn Waugh and just about every reviewer reacted negatively to the long, detailed biography of Rex Stout by John McAleer. If you haven't read it already, I suggest you pick up a copy of the MacShane biography and we can talk more about it when I come to New York next month. Incidentally, I like the Swope biography, but it has too many indented letters.

As ever
Roy

* * *

Hoopes to Moses, 28 May 1978

Dear Danny:

Another thing I want to talk about when we get together in early June is photographs in the book. I am running into a lot of good old shots as I go along and expect to find more when I get out to Hollywood and into his publishing files. And then there is the whole business of stills from the movies. I have always preferred integrating photos with the text as it was done in Douglas Day's biography of Malco[l]m Lowry (Oxford) and Bennett Cerf's Autobiography. This of course means using slightly better paper, but I think the result is much much better than the 4- or 8-page inserts of photos which is the usual way photos are handled in biographies. Give it some thought.

The more I become inundated with Cain material, the more I am confronted with the problem of what kind of book to do–the massive literary study (a la Baker's Hemingway, Schorer's Sinclair Lewis, McAleer's Rex Stout, etc.) or to confine it to the neat, long, novel-size (a la M[a]cShane's Raymond Chandler). I have always leaned toward the short book, as you know, but it does mean leaving out a tremendous amount of material, which will open the door for someone else to want to come along and do another one. The Library of Congress material seems inexhaustible, and now I have come up with another Cain Memoir from his agent. It seems that she also had a second 142-page memoir, plus a 63-page self interview, both of which are excellent sources. There is considerable overlap between the first and second memoirs (both of which I have now), but the second one is much better written and much more quotable. We'll talk about all this later.

AS EVER–Roy

* * *

Reality in 1978–1979: Reduction of the Trade Division

Nine employees, including the editor-in-chief, in the New York office of the trade division of Bobbs-Merrill were told July 28 that their jobs would end August 31. The dismissals are part of a "restructuring" in which the number of titles to be published in the coming year will be cut by half, according to Stanley S. Sills, general manager of ITT Publishing and chairman of Bobbs-Merrill.

While acknowledging that the "sales growth of the trade division is not what we hoped, nor is the trade division doing as well as other sections," Sills declared, "Make no mistake. We are enthusiastic about trade publishing."

Publisher Eugene Rachlis also emphasized that the developments did not mean a phasing out of the trade division. Although the number of titles to be released per year will be reduced from over 50 to 25, Rachlis said this was the result of a new strategy. "We are in the trade business and we intend to remain in the trade business. This is simply a regrouping in order to operate in a new way."

Stating that it is better "to invest in 10 good books than many marginal books," Sills said: "We have taken a hard look at what we do well and will do it better. This means cookbooks–we do specialty cookbooks as well as 'Joy of Cooking.' This means nonfiction, particularly books like those of Edwin Newman and biographies and autobiographies like that of Beverly Sills. We will also do some fiction if it has lasting value."

Pointing out that a reduction in titles necessarily results in a reduction in personnel, Rachlis said that the New York office staff was cut from 23 to 14. Those who received a month's notice of the termination of their jobs included editor-in-chief Daniel Moses, who joined Bobbs-Merrill in March 1977, having previously served as editorial director of Link Books/Quick Fox and as a senior editor at Simon & Schuster and Prentice-Hall. Also notified was Barbara Norville, senior editor in suspense novels and nonfiction for seven years, who was mystery editor at Simon & Schuster for 10 years before joining Bobbs-Merrill. Staff cuts also included the art director, three assistant editors, an editorial assistant, an assistant to the art director and production manager and a secretary.

Other sections in the ITT publishing group, according to Sills, are education and law, both "doing extremely well"; licensing operations for Raggedy Ann and other properties in the U.S. and abroad; and motion picture and TV film production, which he termed "a growing business."

–"Bobbs-Merrill Dismisses Nine, to Cut Back Titles," *Publishers Weekly,* 214 (7 August 1978): 17–18

* * *

ITT Publishing announced April 27 that it was consolidating its consumer publishing activities in the New York offices of Bobbs-Merrill as the Consumer Publishing Group. These activities include the Bobbs-Merrill trade division, a newly created consumer direct response division and the ITT character licensing division that licenses the name and image of Raggedy Ann and Andy and other characters.

Reorganization has also taken place within the Trade Division. According to James Fisher, who was appointed trade division publisher last November, in-house advertising and publicity have been discontinued; these functions will be handled by outside agencies on a book by book basis. The sales operation, which in the past had functioned partly through house sales representatives and partly through independent sales people, will now be handled entirely by independent commissioned representatives. Fisher said that Robert Evans, former marketing director, and Kevin Connors, former house sales representative, are now in the process of setting up an organization to represent Bobbs in the field.

Executive editor Eugene Rachlis, Fisher said, "will remain with the organization to work on special projects. His exact title has not yet been designated."

It is understood this arrangement will not prevent Rachlis from doing work with other publishers.

The Bobbs-Merrill trade division, founded 141 years ago, has published such authors as Colette, Niki [*sic*] Giovanni, Mark Harris, Chaim Grade and the first novel by William Styron.

Fisher said the fall list contains 22 titles: four sports, three cookbooks, three military, four children's, one mystery, one nautical, one gardening, two woodworking and three novels. (The novels are "Shoot the Moon" by Jack Page, "Operation Artemis" by Douglas Scott and "Pleasure Dome" by David Madden.)

"The list reflects the redirection of the publishing trade effort that was initiated last fall, in which the center of gravity moves toward service books, family reference books, specialty nonfiction and quality fiction," Fisher said.

–"Bobbs-Merrill Reorganizes New York Trade Office," *Publishers Weekly,* 215 (14 May 1979): 126

* * *

The Last Campaign

When Bobbs-Merrill's trade division underwent a major reorganization in April 1979, an emphasis was placed on "service" and "informational" books by then-publisher James Fisher. Although Fisher said the house would continue to issue "quality fiction," the publication of novels took a back seat to reference volumes and specialty nonfiction.

Now, with the departure of Fisher to Grosset & Dunlap and the recent appointment of Grace G. Shaw as publisher/trade books of Bobbs's consumer publications division, there will be a shift in editorial policy. "We will still be concentrating on nonfiction," Shaw told *PW* in a recent telephone interview, "but we will be considering commercial fiction on a book-by-book basis. We aren't interested in literary fiction so much as we are in what I call 'brand-name' publishing that has some backlist potential." [. . .]

–"Bobbs-Merrill to Revive Commercial Fiction," *Publishers Weekly,* 218 (28 November 1980): 32

Finale: "Just Plain Uneconomic"

The reduction of the trade list mainly to nonfiction, and then to old standbys within that category, took most of the life out of Bobbs-Merrill even before it was extinguished with the absorption of the parent company into Macmillan.

"ITT is a good purchase for us," Edward P. Evans, chairman and chief executive officer of Macmillan, says. "It'll make a good addition to our publishing and information services segments.

"It has legal publishing, including state and city codes," he continues, referring to the Michie Co. He then goes on to discuss some of the other companies that make up ITT Publishing and their lure for Macmillan. "Marquis Who's Who has directories. Bobbs-Merrill does educational publishing and has the *Joy of Cooking.* In G. K. Hall there is large-print publishing and scholarly and professional reference books. Howard W. Sams has technical manuals and computer books and some software. All in all I think it has a fit to the kind of businesses we're in." [. . .]

–John Mutter, "Talk with Edward Evans: Macmillan's Head Discusses ITT Purchase, Other Changes," *Publishers Weekly,* 227 (22 March 1985): 17

* * *

Having grown progressively weaker in the last few years, the 147-year-old Bobbs-Merrill, whose first bestseller was a collection of verse by James Whitcomb Riley and whose last is *The Joy of Cooking,* has finally succumbed.

Jeremiah Kaplan, chairman of Macmillan Publishing Company which acquired Bobbs-Merrill last month when it bought ITT Publishing, said, "Basically, Bobbs-Merrill has a very small publishing list. It has only five cookbooks on the next list and it is just plain uneconomic."

Founded in Indianapolis where the bulk of its employees are located, Bobbs-Merrill had a staff of six in New York City. Three, including publisher Bonnie Ammer, are moving to Macmillan to handle the Bobbs-Merrill backlist and titles that have been contracted. There are just under 100 active backlist titles, Kaplan said, and no decision has been made on whether to continue the Bobbs-Merrill imprint.

Prominent on the backlist are *The Fountainhead, Breads of France,* the Raggedy Ann and Raggedy Andy series and *The Joy of Cooking,* which has sold well over 10 million copies. In addition to Ayn Rand, other writers published by Bobbs-Merrill include Colette, Mary Roberts Rinehart, Richard Halliburton, Robert

The Sheraton World Cookbook
Great Recipes From Great Chefs
Finest chefs from Sheraton hotels offer interpretations of authentic local dishes from their regions. Over 250 recipes. *$15.95 cloth (0-672-52672-7) March*

How To Cash In On The Coming Stock Market Boom
by Myron Kandel While the stock market has been depressed for the past decade, here's specific advice for the growth ahead. *$12.95 cloth (0-672-52690-5) June*

Tasting Good
by Merle Schell Now everyone can savor good food—and good health with 1,000 recipes in 10 cuisines to reduce your salt intake. *$14.95 cloth (0-672-52623-9) May*

The Master Plan
by Bruce Jack Freshman Thriller novel weaves a terrifying tale of the ascendance of Hitler's son to the U.S. Presidency. *$12.95 cloth (0-672-52682-4) March*

Moving Free
by Carol Walter with Lenore Miller The first book to provide women who have had breast cancer surgery with a comprehensive exercise program for total rehabilitation. *$9.95 paper (0-672-52686-7) April*

From Tent to Cabin
by Laurence Gadd With this complete step-by-step guide, you need no special skills to build your own country cabin and live comfortably on the site, too. *$12.95 cloth (0-672-52687-5) June*

Armored Combat in Vietnam
by General Donn A. Starry An exciting survey of the history, nature, development and effect of armored units used during the Vietnam War. *$15.00 cloth (0-672-52673-5) February*

The Complete Book of Basketball—
***New York Times* Scrapbook History**
Fascinating details about college and professional basketball, plus a wonderful history of this relatively young sport. *$14.95 cloth (0-672-52639-5) January*

The Complete Book of Soccer/Hockey—
***New York Times* Scrapbook History**
A comprehensive picture of internationally popular soccer in the U.S. and a portrayal of ice hockey's rapid rise in popularity. *$14.95 cloth (0-672-52642-5) January*

Cater From Your Kitchen
by Marjorie P. Blanchard Learn from a catering expert how to cook for profit. Includes financial advice, menus, shopping, cooking, serving for a variety of occasions. *$8.95 paper (0-672-52688-3) May*

Food and Drink in America
by Richard J. Hooker An exploration of our eating habits over the last 200 years, reflecting our cultural heritages and changing social patterns. *$14.95 cloth (0-672-52681-6) May*

The Art of Picture Framing
by Sherwood & Connie McCall Protect valuable artwork by conservation framing. For anyone who enjoys art and wants it shown at its best. 68 photos; 73 drawings. *$14.95 cloth (0-672-52390-6) May*

The Complete Book of Track and Field—
***New York Times* Scrapbook History**
Legendary exploits of courageous and determined men and women competing in events that demand almost superhuman stamina. *$14.95 cloth (0-672-52640-9) April*

The Complete Book of Horse/Auto Racing—
***New York Times* Scrapbook History**
A chronicle of breathtaking racing events, jockeys, trainers, champion horses and cars. *$14.95 cloth (0-672-52647-6) April*

The Complete Book of Water Sports—
***New York Times* Scrapbook History**
Facts, figures and behind-the-scene information about the Olympic competition water sports. More than 100 photos and stunning drawings. *$14.95 cloth (0-672-52648-4) April*

Bobbs-Merrill
Publishers since 1838
4300 W. 62nd Street,
Indianapolis, Ind. 46206

36 PUBLISHERS WEEKLY

*Advertisements for the spring 1981 and fall 1984 lists (*Publishers Weekly, *6 February 1981, 31 August 1984)*

BOBBS-MERRILL/FALL 1984

BY YOUTH POSSESSED
The Denial of Age in America
By VICTORIA SECUNDA
How and why our culture equates youth with allure and success—and how that view paralyzes people of *all* ages.
October. 52791-X. $15.95 cloth

A.D. 2000
A Book about the End of Time
By RENE NOORBERGEN
Prophets and seers throughout the ages have envisioned the coming of Armageddon. Is that cataclysmic time upon us?
September. 52769-3. $15.95 cloth

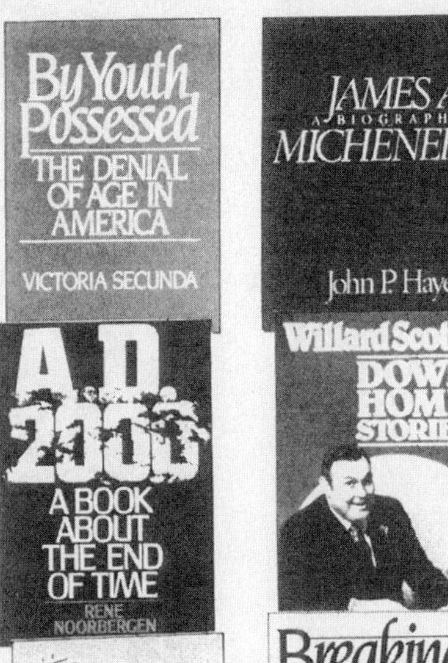

THE CHILDREN'S PHARMACY
Everything You Should Know About Medicine for Your Children
By ANNE CAREY, R.N.
No parent should give a child any medicine without consulting this book.
September. 52727-8. $15.95 cloth

MERLIN AND THE DRAGONS OF ATLANTIS
By RITA and TIM HILDEBRANDT
A fantastic tale of conflict and wizardry in the last days of the lost continent. Included are twenty-five original line illustrations by the master of fantasy art, Tim Hildebrandt.
October. 52704-9. $16.95 cloth

BOY OR GIRL?
Revised Edition
By ELIZABETH M. WHELAN, Sc.D.
The most up-to-date, trustworthy method of selecting the sex of a child at the time of conception.
October. 52811-8. $10.95 cloth

JAMES A. MICHENER
A Biography
By JOHN P. HAYES
The first biography of the man behind such bestsellers as *Sayonara, Hawaii, The Source, Iberia, Centennial, Chesapeake,* and *Space.*
November. 52782-0. $17.95 cloth

WILLARD SCOTT'S DOWN-HOME STORIES
By WILLARD SCOTT
Television's gregarious sage serves up hearty slices of life, chock full of wisdom, wit, and love.
November. 52768-5. $15.95 cloth

BREAKING FREE
From Compulsive Eating
By GENEEN ROTH
A specific how-to program to stop dieting—and start losing weight—for compulsive eaters.
December. 52810-X. $15.95 cloth

THE WOMAN'S DAY CAN'T-FAIL, EAT-ALL-DAY DIET
By SUSAN DUFF and the Editors of *Woman's Day*
Enjoy hearty meals without daily diet cooking; splurge on snacks without counting calories—and *lose ten pounds a month* on the easiest weight-loss plan ever.
November. 52812-6. $15.95 cloth

CENTURY 21's GUIDE TO HOW TO BUY AND SELL REAL ESTATE
All the basics for homeowners from Century 21's own book!
October. 52664-6. $14.95 cloth

AUDEL®
Professional home hobby and do-it-yourself books. Many newly revised editions are now available.

Add ISBN prefix 0-672

BOBBS-MERRILL COMPANY, INC.

630 Third Avenue, New York 10017 / 4300 West 62nd Street, Indianapolis, Indiana 46206

PUBLISHERS WEEKLY

Nathan, Joseph Wood Krutch, Edwin Newman, Mark Harris, Nikki Giovanni and William Styron.

Howard W. Sams, a technical publisher founded in Indianapolis in 1946, acquired Bobbs-Merrill in 1958. Sams was merged with ITT in 1966 during the rash of acquisitions by ITT's Harold Geneen.

Kaplan said that 100 employees of both the Sams and Bobbs-Merrill operations in Indianapolis would lose their jobs. The dismissals would bring Howard W. Sams "back to the size it was before it went off on a computer publishing program that didn't work too well," Kaplan noted. "Its basic business will continue." [. . .]

[. . .] The company was among the first to use colored, pictorial jackets and to display a single title in an advertisement instead of the customary list.

Much of the early vitality dissipated in recent years. The trade division underwent a reorganization in 1979 when the emphasis was placed on service and informational books; a year later, the number of titles was reduced from 50 to 25 per year; and last year the decision was made to emphasize cookbooks.

–"Bobbs-Merrill, 147 Years Old, Being Dissolved," *Publishers Weekly*, 227 (10 May 1985): 116

Bonnie Ammer, the last publisher and general manager of Bobbs-Merrill (from Travel Weekly, *3 May 2001; South Carolina State Library)*

Bowen-Merrill/Bobbs-Merrill Authors: 1885–1960

Best-selling and prize-winning books are described in the Chronology.

George Ade (1866–1944)

See also the Ade entries in *DLB 11: American Humorists, 1800–1950* and *DLB 25: American Newspaper Journalists, 1901–1925.*

Like other great American humorists with an interest in the vernacular (such as Mark Twain, Ring Lardner, and H. L. Mencken), George Ade learned his craft while a newspaperman. The earliest of his five hundred "fables in slang," only half of which have been collected, were written for The Chicago Record. *These comic observations displayed his facility with colloquial speech and brought him national fame. He was an especially keen witness of the rural American encountering the city. Bobbs-Merrill published only three of Ade's many books during his lifetime, and these were not the most characteristic works among his sketches, stories, novels, plays, and essays. (The posthumous 1947 anthology was compiled by his biographer.) Ade was one of the few famous Hoosier writers not to publish with the company while his reputation was being formed, although his regional qualities are what he is most remembered for today.*

BOBBS-MERRILL BOOKS BY ADE: *The Slim Princess,* illustrated by George F. Kerr (Indianapolis: Bobbs-Merrill, 1907);

Verses and Jingles (Indianapolis: Bobbs-Merrill, 1911);

The Permanent Ade: The Living Writings of George Ade, edited by Fred C. Kelly (Indianapolis: Bobbs- Merrill, 1947).

George Ade (Bruccoli Clark Layman Archives)

OTHER: *An Invitation to You and Your Folks from Jim and Some More of the Home Folks,* edited, with an introduction and postscript, by Ade (Indianapolis: Bobbs-Merrill, 1916).

Review: *The Slim Princess* (1907)

Clearly Mr. George Ade, one of the later cryptic school of American humorists, was in his best comic opera mood when he wrote "The Slim Princess" (Bobbs-Merrill.) The scenery suggests the strangely international character of contemporary operetta or "musical comedy," the plot is as unlikely as any of the most expert librettists could invent. The idea that because Oriental beauty is generally associated with plumpness due to inactivity, a slim Turkish girl is necessarily accounted ugly and unmarriageable in her own land, is one of Mr. Ade's choicest humorous fancies. The idea that his heroine's slender proportions are due to the perfidy of a revengeful tutor who has cultivated in her a fondness for physical culture and pickles derives from the storied humor of a full generation of comic opera librettos. Mr. Sydney Rosenfeld is really the father of this kind of American humor. Mr. Ade's story, however, is lively and diverting, and amazingly up to date in its employment of slang and its "topical allusion." It tells of the love of a young steel magnate of Pennsylvania and the Princess Kalora, who is hideous in Turkey but a dazzling beauty in Washington, and as a love story it is quite as convincing as many we are apt to encounter in the more serious fiction of the hour. It is short enough to be read through in one sitting, and Mr. George F. Kerr's yellow and black illustrations catch the spirit of the author's fun.

–*New York Times,* 18 May 1907, p. 320

THE
SLIM PRINCESS

By
GEORGE ADE
Author of
Fables in Slang
In Pastures New, Pink Marsh, etc.

With Illustrations by
GEORGE F. KERR

INDIANAPOLIS
THE BOBBS-MERRILL COMPANY
PUBLISHERS

VERSES AND JINGLES

By
GEORGE ADE

INDIANAPOLIS
THE BOBBS-MERRILL CO.
PUBLISHERS

Title pages for Ade's 1907 and 1911 books (courtesy of The Lilly Library, Indiana University, Bloomington, Indiana)

Related Letters

For An Invitation to You and Your Folks from Jim and Some More of the Home Folks *Ade gathered contributions by Indiana authors and wrote an introduction and "P.S."* The Philistine *was a recently defunct magazine edited by Elbert Hubbard.*

George Ade to William C. Bobbs, 7 March 1916

My dear Bobbs:

As Chairman of the Home-Coming Committee appointed by the Historical Commission to boost the centennial celebration this year I am compiling a little book which we hope to circulate broadcast. It is an invitation to the absent Hoosier–a symposium by the Governor, Tom Marshall, Charlie Fairbanks and the members of the literary colony.

I am sending on a copy for the book to W. C. Woodward of the Commission.

We want permission to use the verses by Riley, "The Hoosier in Exile". Riley has written a letter to be included in the volume and offered to help in any way possible before we appealed to him. I think the little volume will be copyrighted so that the poem will be safe.

I am writing you to ask that you confer with Mr. Woodward regarding the style of this book. I do not suppose your house would care to take this kind of work which will have to be done rather cheaply and in pamphlet form but I want to get full value for our money and make the little book as attractive as possible and you can be of great help to us if you will suggest the proper size for the book and give some instructions regarding typography and make-up.

The plan is to sell these little books in envelopes ready for mailing at a nominal cost and not for profit. I may have to finance the first issue myself.

If you will talk to Mr. Woodward on the telephone and tell him where and how to have the books printed I will be duly grateful to you.

I trust you are well and happy.

Sincerely, George Ade

I think the book should be about the Philistine size as to pages–dignified and not fussy or freaky as to composition.

G.A.

* * *

Hazelden, Ade's house near Brook, Indiana (Bruccoli Clark Layman Archives)

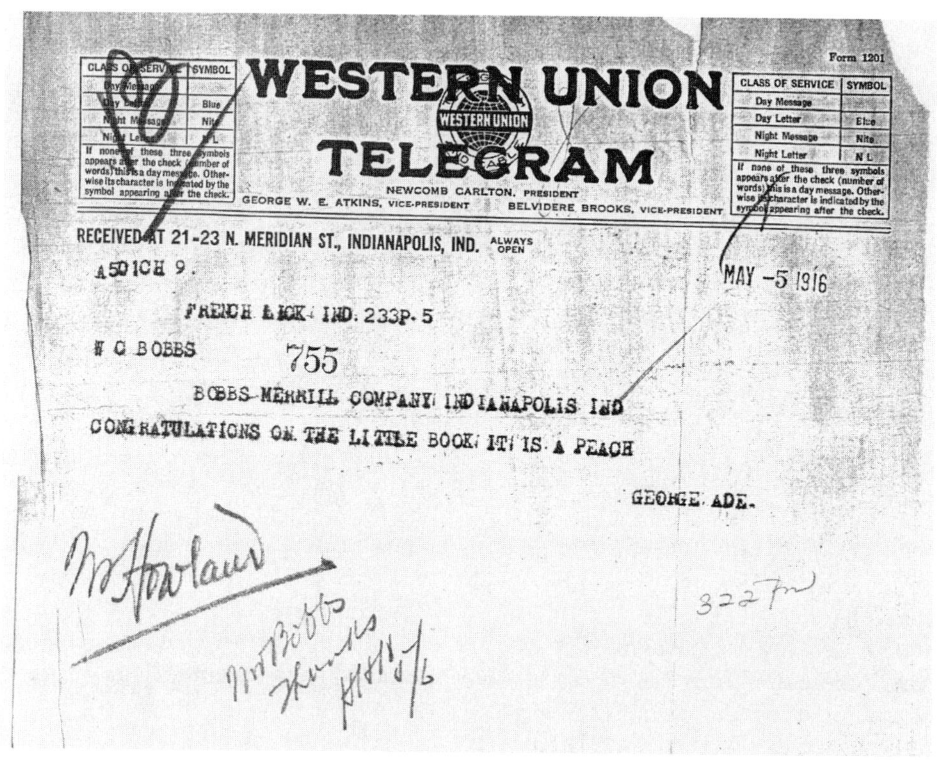

Form 1201

WESTERN UNION TELEGRAM

CLASS OF SERVICE	SYMBOL
Day Message	
Day Letter	Blue
Night Message	Nite
Night Letter	N L

If none of these three symbols appears after the check (number of words) this is a day message. Otherwise its character is indicated by the symbol appearing after the check.

NEWCOMB CARLTON, PRESIDENT
GEORGE W. E. ATKINS, VICE-PRESIDENT BELVIDERE BROOKS, VICE-PRESIDENT

RECEIVED AT 21-23 N. MERIDIAN ST., INDIANAPOLIS, IND. ALWAYS OPEN

A50ICH 9.

MAY -5 1916

FRENCH LICK IND. 233P. 5

W C BOBBS 755

BOBBS-MERRILL COMPANY INDIANAPOLIS IND

CONGRATULATIONS ON THE LITTLE BOOK IT IS A PEACH

GEORGE ADE.

Ade's comment on An Invitation to You and Your Folks *(1916) in a telegram to Bobbs-Merrill president William C. Bobbs (courtesy of The Lilly Library, Indiana University, Bloomington, Indiana)*

Bobbs to Ade, 23 March 1916

"Hewitt" is the editor of the trade department, Hewitt H. Howland. Ade was writing from Belleair Heights, Florida.

My dear George:–

Your letter now fully two weeks old was promptly received and has been held until I could have a talk with W. C. Woodward of the Historical Commission.

He has been in and we have talked over the manuscript and it is now on Hewitt's desk waiting for the final word.

It will give us a good deal of pleasure not only to help in working out the plan and the scheme for the books but also to have our imprint on them.

The details can be worked out with Mr. Woodward and depend largely on what your desire in the matter may be. I explained to him the advantages and disadvantages of the better and the cheaper form and told him that we would undertake to make the book in cost up to the necessary trade price of any list you might decide upon.

He has already written you fully about this I think and is now waiting for your final word to go ahead with the manuscript.

I hope you are having a bully time in the South and will soon be home for the Spring opening at Brook.

Yours very truly,
[William C. Bobbs]

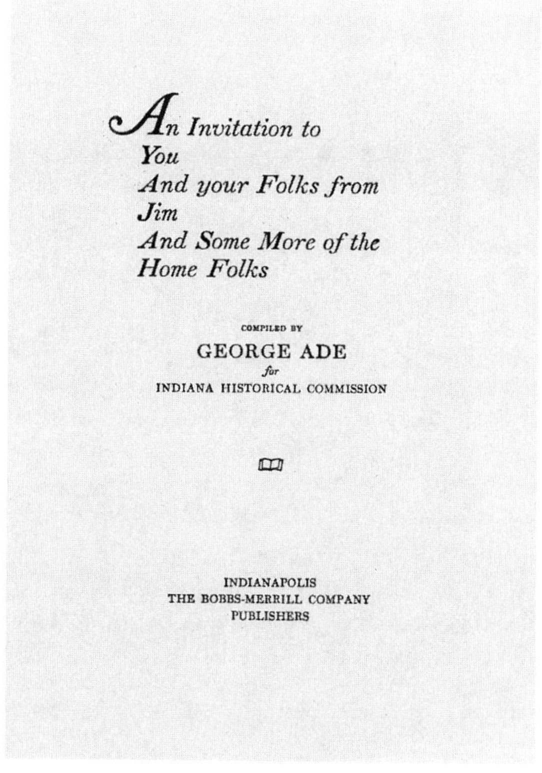

An Invitation to
You
And your Folks from
Jim
And Some More of the
Home Folks

COMPILED BY
GEORGE ADE
for
INDIANA HISTORICAL COMMISSION

INDIANAPOLIS
THE BOBBS-MERRILL COMPANY
PUBLISHERS

Title page for the 1916 collection compiled by Ade (courtesy of The Lilly Library, Indiana University, Bloomington, Indiana)

Raymond Macdonald Alden (1873–1924)

For Bobbs-Merrill, Raymond Macdonald Alden was almost exclusively a children's author, but his primary career was as a literary scholar specializing in the works of William Shakespeare. A notable teacher at the University of Illinois and Stanford University, he tried his hand at many kinds of writing. In creating juvenile literature he was imitating his mother, Isabella Macdonald Alden, whose pen name for her moralistic stories was "Pansy." (On his father's side, Alden was a descendant of Mayflower *pilgrim John Alden.) The 1908 volume* Why the Chimes Rang, *originally published as* The Knights of the Silver Shield *in 1906, sold well as a Christmas story for many years, but no correspondence about it survives in the archives. The company took advantage of Alden's scholarship by calling on him to contribute the Alfred Tennyson volume (1917) to the How to Know the Authors series.*

BOBBS-MERRILL BOOKS BY ALDEN: *The Knights of the Silver Shield,* illustrated by Katharine Hayward Greenland (Indianapolis: Bobbs-Merrill, 1906); republished as *Why the Chimes Rang* (Indianapolis: Bobbs-Merrill, 1908);

The Palace Made by Music, illustrated by Mayo Bunker (Indianapolis: Bobbs-Merrill, 1910);

The Forest Full of Friends, illustrated by Harold Speakman (Indianapolis: Bobbs-Merrill, 1915);

Alfred Tennyson, How to Know Him (Indianapolis: Bobbs-Merrill, 1917);

The Boy Who Found the King: A Tournament of Stories, illustrated by W. H. Lohse (Indianapolis: Bobbs-Merrill, 1922);

The Christmas Tree Forest, illustrated by Rafaello Busoni (Indianapolis: Bobbs-Merrill, 1958).

At the time of this letter D. Laurance Chambers was vice president of the company. Stuart Pratt Sherman's Matthew Arnold, How to Know Him *and William Allan Neilson's* Robert Burns, How to Know Him *were both published in 1917. William Lyon Phelps's* Robert Browning, How to Know Him *was published in 1915.*

Raymond Macdonald Alden (courtesy of Raymond M. Alden Jr.)

Raymond Macdonald Alden to D. Laurance Chambers, 17 May 1917

My dear Chambers:

I have received the copies of Sherman's "Matthew Arnold" and Neilson's "Burns" which you were good enough to send me, and have looked them through pretty carefully. They are both well made books, as was pretty certain to be the case on the part of their writers, and will add distinctly to the standing of the series. I must say that I was a little disappointed that Sherman took his subject as

Study for the title page of the 1908 book first published in 1906 as The Knights of the Silver Shield; *illustration for the book by Katharine Hayward Greenland (courtesy of The Lilly Library, Indiana University, Bloomington, Indiana)*

seriously in all respects as he did, and restrained himself from having a little fun with some of Arnold's foibles–as he is so well qualified to do; but perhaps for the present purpose he was the wiser to keep to the other course.

I cannot say that I see any good prospect of our using these books in some of our courses, as you suggest. So far as my own teaching is concerned, I should feel that what the volumes do is represented by what I bring out in class discussion, and that they would therefore form an admirable aid to students who have been <u>unable</u> to take formal work in the authors concerned. I shall therefore take occasion to recommend them for supplemental and outside reading. But both Phelps and I, for example (in the Browning and Tennyson volumes), give the reader just what I should wish the college student to try to figure out for himself. In other kinds of courses teachers may feel quite differently.

I said to Howe that I should be quite willing to add a short chapter on Tennyson's dramas, as some of you suggested, if you seriously think it desirable. But as they are by far his least interesting material, and as the MS. errs now in the direction of size, I should think it better to follow the example of the Browning volume, and omit them.

Sincerely yours,
Raymond M. Alden

PROOF *from* BOOKS OF THE MONTH

OF YOUR ADVERTISEMENT TO APPEAR IN THE JUL ISSUE

Please read carefully and forward O K or corrections promptly to Herbert S. Browne, 608 S. Dearborn St., Chicago

TWO NEW VOLUMES IN
HOW TO KNOW AUTHORS

Robert Burns. By William Allan Neilson, Professor of English, Harvard University, author of Essentials of Poetry, etc. Burns is the poet in whom there ought now to be a special interest. He hated tyranny, he pitied suffering, he was a patriot in as democratic a nation as the world has ever seen. A clear, vivid, and truthful picture of Burns, the man, is given in a most interesting biographical sketch. There are exceedingly interesting chapters on the language of the poet. Probably the best thing about the book is the happiness of the selections from Burns. There is not an old favorite missing, and there are many good things most readers have overlooked. With portrait. $1.50 net.

Matthew Arnold. By Stuart P. Sherman, Professor of English, University of Illinois. Perhaps no Victorian writer has held his own in these changing times better than Matthew Arnold. Although he was misunderstood in his own day and generation, as we have come to know him more intimately, we have come to admire him more for his unswerving loyalty to the cause of human intelligence in the management of the affairs of the world. This book presents Arnold as poet and critic of books, of men, of education and religion. This presentation is fully illustrated by the quotation of many complete poems and long passages from the prose works. With portrait, $1.50 net.

Other volumes in this Series:
Each with portrait, $1.50

Browning, How to Know Him. By William Lyon Phelps, Lampson Professor of English, Yale University.

Carlyle, How to Know Him. By Bliss Perry, Professor of English, Harvard University.

Wordsworth, How to Know Him. By C. T. Winchester, Professor of English, Wesleyan University.

Dante, How to Know Him. By Alfred M. Brooks, Professor of Fine Arts, Indiana University.

Defoe, How to Know Him. By Wm. P. Trent, Professor of English Literature, Columbia University.

Stevenson, How to Know Him. By Richard Ashley Rice, Professor of English Literature, Smith College.

BUY THESE BOOKS OF YOUR BOOKSELLER

Proof of an advertisement for the Bobbs-Merrill series that later included Alden's 1917 work Alfred Tennyson, How to Know Him *(courtesy of The Lilly Library, Indiana University, Bloomington, Indiana)*

Irving Bacheller (1859–1950)

See also the Bacheller entry in *DLB 202: Nineteenth-Century American Fiction Writers.*

Considered an Upper New York State regionalist (and having the same Mayflower *ancestor as Raymond Macdonald Alden), Irving Bacheller was a best-selling author during the first two decades of the twentieth century. But if he is remembered now, it is usually for his part in the careers of others. From 1885 to 1898 he syndicated fiction to newspapers for serial publication. He made money for many familiar authors, notably Stephen Crane, whose* The Red Badge of Courage *(1895) was published in truncated form in ten newspapers. Bacheller's novel* Eben Holden: A Tale of the North Country *(1900) sold more than a million copies. His work for Bobbs-Merrill often celebrated historical figures, such as Benjamin Franklin, in an uplifting, patriotic spirit. In his long life Bacheller grew to lament the evils of modernity, but his calls for simplicity were made possible by the great wealth that he accrued from his writing.* The Light in the Clearing: A Tale of the North Country in the Time of Silas Wright *(1917) was probably the first title since James Whitcomb Riley's* "The Old Swimmin'-Hole," and 'Leven More Poems *(1883) to earn a 20 percent royalty from the house. The standard rate was 10 to 15 percent, with the money saved going into advertising to create greater sales.*

Irving Bacheller (Bruccoli Clark Layman Archives)

BOBBS-MERRILL BOOKS BY BACHELLER: *The Light in the Clearing: A Tale of the North Country in the Time of Silas Wright* (Indianapolis: Bobbs-Merrill, 1917; London: Collins, 1918);

Keeping Up with William (Indianapolis: Bobbs-Merrill, 1918);

A Man for the Ages: A Story of the Builders of Democracy (Indianapolis: Bobbs-Merrill, 1919; London: Constable, 1920);

The Prodigal Village: A Christmas Tale (Indianapolis: Bobbs-Merrill, 1920);

In the Days of Poor Richard (Indianapolis: Bobbs-Merrill, 1922; London: Hutchinson, 1923);

Father Abraham (Indianapolis: Bobbs-Merrill, 1925; London: Hutchinson, 1925);

Opinions of a Cheerful Yankee (Indianapolis: Bobbs-Merrill, 1926);

Coming Up the Road: Memories of a North Country Boyhood (Indianapolis: Bobbs-Merrill, 1928);

The House of the Three Ganders (Indianapolis: Bobbs-Merrill, 1928; London: Hutchinson, 1929);

A Candle in the Wilderness: A Tale of the Beginning of New England (Indianapolis: Bobbs-Merrill, 1930);

The Master of Chaos (Indianapolis: Bobbs-Merrill, 1932).

Related Letters

President William C. Bobbs wrote an in-house memo to trade-department editor Hewitt H. Howland concerning Bacheller's royalties from The Light in the Clearing.

William C. Bobbs to Hewitt H. Howland, 10 March 1917

The attached letter from Bacheller explains itself.

He agreed to yield 8 cents a copy of his royalty on the first 25,000 in order to help the advertising and promotion campaign, and to accept payment for the quarterly settlements in notes which I understood to be without interest. All of that is covered in a memorandum in the contract files.

WCB

* * *

At the time of this letter D. Laurance Chambers was vice president of the company.

D. Laurance Chambers to Irving Bacheller, 30 March 1917

Dear Mr. Bacheller:–

It gives us pleasure to enclose herewith our check for $3500.00 by way of advancement of royalties on THE LIGHT IN THE CLEARING. The contract provides that this advance is to be paid on publication date. The publication date is April 12th. I trust, however, that there will be no objection to our anticipation.

With kind regards, I am

Cordially yours,

[D. Laurance Chambers]

THE BOBBS-MERRILL COMPANY

* * *

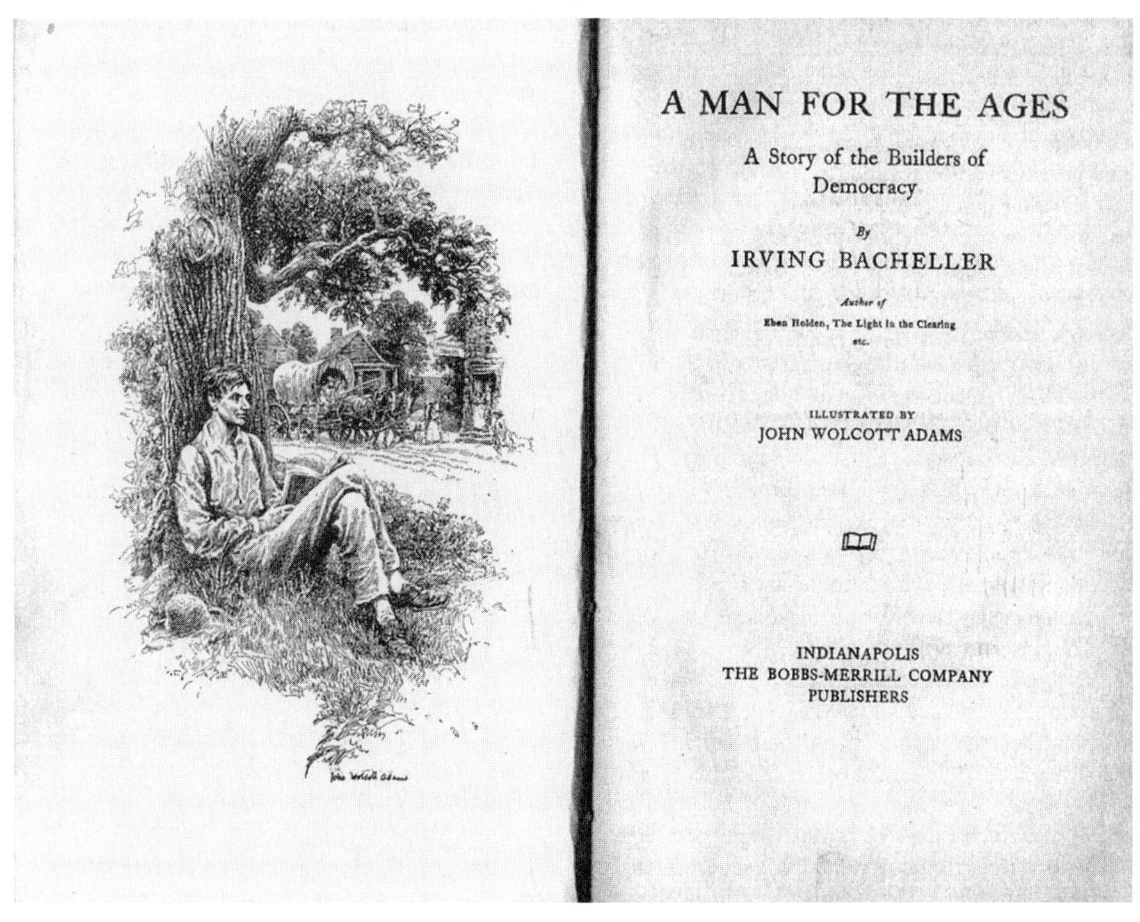

Frontispiece and title page for Bacheller's 1919 novel, the first in a trilogy based on the life of Abraham Lincoln (Thomas Cooper Library, University of South Carolina)

Review: *The Light in the Clearing*

Very different in method and purpose from any of his previous stories, Mr. Bacheller's new novel must be accounted, at the outset, as quite the most important piece of fiction he has put forth. In its own way it is as good as his famous North Country character studies, of which "Eben Holden" was the first, and, perhaps, the best known and as skillfully done as his series of dashing, splashing, story-cartoons of which "Keeping Up With Lizzie" was so widely read as to cause its title to become a national catchword. But its way is so different from either of these lines of story telling that comparison with them is unfair to both the new and the old.

This new story is an interpretation of the rude and simple but high-souled life of the youthful years of this nation and a tribute to its high significance in the making of American ideals–a kind of fiction of which American literature has far too little. Mr. Bacheller has written sympathetically of that life, and understandingly, but without any of that commiserating superiority with which a more cushioned and sophisticated age is too prone to look back upon the life of its grandparents. He is not at all sorry for his toiling farmers of Northern New York three-quarters of a century ago because they did not have steam heat and concrete pavements and strawberries in January and electric lights and a theatre around the corner. Rather, his mental attitude is that of doffed hat and bowed head, because of the power of the spirit that was in them, a power great enough to send the "light in the clearing" on down through generation after generation. His title page bears a line from Proverbs: "The spirit of man is the candle of the Lord." And that, in brief, is the meaning of his tale about these unpretentious men and women who exercised so much fine and noble influence.

But, first and foremost, "The Light in the Clearing" is an interesting story, real and vital in its presentation of character and incident, that moves entertainingly through varied scenes, sometimes with merriment and jollity, sometimes with peaceful happiness, sometimes skirting the coasts of tragedy, and every now and then rising to dramatic scenes and thrilling moments. It is told in the first person and its time covers some fifteen years in the boyhood and young manhood in the thirties and forties of the last century, of the narrator, one Barton Baynes. Mr. Bacheller weaves a bit of curiosity-compelling mystery about this character in his foreword and preface, wherein he says that all the characters except this one and two others are imaginary and that Barton Baynes ended his life "full of honors early in the present century." [. . .]

There is a great variety of characters in the story, men, women, and children, of higher and lower and medium estate–including a glimpse of President Van Buren–but to each one of them the author has given a touch of individuality and outstandingness. All of them, even those that are most thoroughly worked out, are drawn with a few broad, speaking lines. The shadowy "Michael Henry," who is such an efficient member of the household of the jovial Irish school teacher, is a more pleasing aspirant for fame than Sarah Gamp's Mrs. Harris, and quite as humorous.

Mr. Bacheller has written a good story, with skill and heart and fine and true perception. It is as wholesome and tonic as a wind from out of its own North Woods, and, popular as have been his former books, it deserves a wider reading than any of them, because it is a bigger and a better book.

–"Irving Bacheller's Tale of North Country Life Eighty Years Ago [. . .]," *New York Times Book Review,* 8 April 1917, p. 1

* * *

Related Letters

Genevieve Teachout to Bacheller, circa 1925

My dear Mr. Bachellor:

I have just finished your book "Father Abraham" and I think it is great! I am only eleven years old and it is the first grown up book I have read.

It was very clever of you to put in that about the little witch dwarfs. Our little witch dwarf is my brother David Jr. and he was very wise in selecting our mother and daddy.

I except to be an author someday. I have made up lots of storys but they're not all written down. I'm afraid they never will be if I don't "get busy" before school opens.

My favorite author is Louisa May Alcott. I just love her books and I have read most of them. I especially like "Little Men and Little Women.

I like reading about the Civil War. I have just finished a book called "A Yankee Girl at Fort Sumter" The "Yankee Girl" was eleven years old. My grandma was eleven years old also when the civil War began. She lived in Missouri about ten miles from the James brothers those famous bushwackers so I've heard quite a bit about the war from Grandma.

Hoping that I may read another book like "Father Abraham" soon,

I am
Your true friend
Genevieve Teachout

* * *

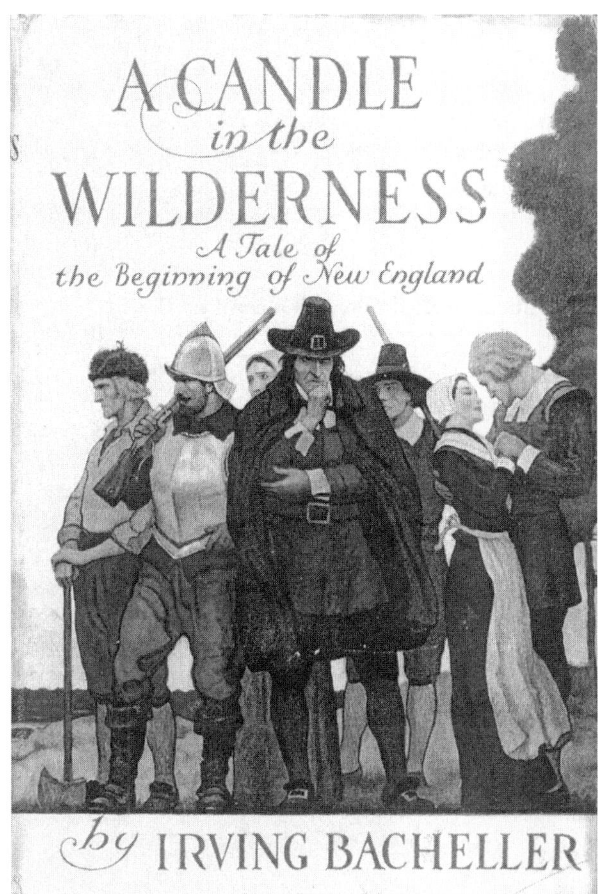

Dust jackets for 1928 and 1930 novels by Bacheller, with art for the latter by N. C. Wyeth (courtesy of Michael Manz/Babylon Revisited)

By the date of this letter Chambers was trade-department editor in chief as well as vice president.

Bacheller to Chambers, 22 June 1929

Dear Laurence [*sic*]: In re yours of June 17 I would like the contract for the Hempen Rope to be the same as those for The Light in the Clearing and A Man for the Ages–the advance to be regulated agreeably with your statement the limit to be $5000. That however is an amount I do not expect to ask for.

The book has begun to grow at the rate of about 800 words a day since I got here. I am in love with it. Before you return I want you to go over with me when shall have been accomplished.

Yours sincerely
Irving Bacheller

* * *

Unsigned letter (from editorial assistant Anne Johnston?) to Bacheller, 25 June 1929

Dear Mr. Bacheller:

As you may have heard by this time, Mr. Chambers has been ordered by the doctor to take a complete rest for several weeks in consequence of a partial collapse from overwork which he suffered here last week. In the meanwhile, I am to carry on in my feeble fashion the things that he usually does.

In regard to your letter of the 22nd, he has instructed me to tell you that we just cannot see our way to publishing books nowadays at a profit when we must pay 20% royalty. So we could not agree to make the contract for "THE HEMPEN ROPE" conform to that for "THE LIGHT IN THE CLEARING" or "A MAN FOR THE AGES" in this one respect. I hope that you will find it possible to agree to the proposition made by Mr. Chambers in his letter to you of June

17th. If you do, please let me have your signed copy for the files.

I am getting more and more anxious to see the actual chapters of "THE HEMPEN ROPE". It sounds like a big historical novel as well as a most interesting psychological study.

* * *

Chambers to Bacheller, 9 December 1929

Dear Mr. Bacheller:

We have checked and rechecked the manuscript and can make it total only 52,000 words. Our most expert counters made the estimate. Now we understand that you are going to bring the total up to 70,000 words even though this imposes some extra work on you because you had considered the manuscript we have as containing 55,000 words. I am sorry for the burden we're putting on your shoulders, but I know you will assume it as you do every fair obligation, and so we are counting on you to do it and to get it to us by Christmas. I think–and I am sure you'll agree with me–that it would be a great mistake to let it run any shorter than the 70,000 words we agreed on. And we have planned a type page on that basis. When we get the balance we shall work at top speed to finish the composition so that we may publish in March at the height of the spring season.

Since I wrote you at the end of last week we have consulted some of the bigger booksellers in Boston about the title and curiously enough they all advise us strongly against THE CANDLE IN BOSTON COVE and in favor of A CANDLE IN THE WILDERNESS. So let's all decide on A CANDLE IN THE WILDERNESS, and I hope you are as enthusiastic about this title as we are.

Faithfully yours,

[D. Laurance Chambers]

Bruce Barton (1886–1967)

Bruce Fairchild Barton was perhaps the greatest adman of the twentieth century, inventing Betty Crocker, a hundred memorable slogans, and the image of Jesus as model businessman. His father was William E. Barton, a Congregationalist minister and a Bobbs-Merrill author. After careers as editor, sales manager, and writer of inspirational articles, the younger Barton helped form the best-known advertising agency in America after a 1928 merger: Batten, Barton, Durstine and Osborn. Taking literally Jesus' statement "I must be about my Father's business," Barton created a sensational nonfiction best-seller, The Man Nobody Knows: A Discovery of Jesus *(1925), which came to Bobbs-Merrill when Scribners rejected it. The book presents not "a weak and sad-faced Savior" but the greatest advertiser and salesman of his time, whose organizational skills started a worldwide religion with just twelve men. Like another 1925 "super-seller" of the house, John Erskine's* The Private Life of Helen of Troy, *Barton's book severely modernized an old story, but without Erskine's self-awareness. The Bible received the same treatment in* The Book Nobody Knows *(1926), with similar success. It was St. Paul's turn in* He Upset the World *(1932), but this Depression-era book did not sell well.*

BOBBS-MERRILL BOOKS BY BARTON: *The Man Nobody Knows: A Discovery of Jesus* (Indianapolis: Bobbs-Merrill, 1925);
The Book Nobody Knows (Indianapolis: Bobbs-Merrill, 1926);
What Can a Man Believe? (Indianapolis: Bobbs-Merrill, 1927);
On the Up and Up (Indianapolis: Bobbs-Merrill, 1929);
He Upset the World (Indianapolis: Bobbs-Merrill, 1932);
The Man and the Book Nobody Knows (Indianapolis: Bobbs-Merrill, 1956).

Related Letters

Trade-department editor Hewitt H. Howland wired Barton prematurely with news of the firm's enthusiastic acceptance of the manuscript of The Man Nobody Knows.

Bruce Barton (© CORBIS)

Hewitt H. Howland to Bruce Barton, 17 January 1924

WE ACCEPT MANUSCRIPT WITH UNBOUNDED CONFIDENCE AND ENTHUSIASM IT IS THE MOST ORIGINAL CONVINCING AND COMPELLING CONTRIBUTION TO THE SUBJECT EVER MADE WE CONGRATULATE OURSELVES ON THE OPPORTUNITY IT OPENS FOR REAL SERVICE LETTER FOLLOWS

BOBBS-MERRILL COMPANY

* * *

Howland to Barton, 18 January 1924

My dear Mr. Barton:

While the fever is on me I want to tell you of my admiration for your manuscript–THE MAN NOBODY KNOWS. I was enthralled by it and tremendously moved. You have done more for the cause of righteousness than all the pulpits in the country have done in a generation. You have taken Jesus out of the stained glass window and made him a man. You have interpreted his motives and his methods and his message and translated them into the terminology of today.

But you know better than anyone else what you have done; I merely want to register my enthusiasm. I was brought up on the New Testament, but my Sunday was a day of feasting; I was not made to go to Sunday school, which institution I intuitively despised; as for Church, to go with my father was a delight. And there I learned of the New Testament, through the lessons and the gospel for the day, but I got only a little more than the conventional portrait of Jesus. Forgive these reminiscences, but they may show you how well prepared was the ground for the seed you have sown.

If properly presented, I believe that even the world's best Babbitt can be induced to read your book, and when he has read it he will be as strong for Jesus as he now is for his local Rotary. For you have made Jesus a hero, a man's hero; so that no one can ever again think of him as the sacrificial lamb, the meek and lowly.

I telegraphed you last night a faint echo of our enthusiasm; its full diapason we hope to make audible by our performance.

Sincerely yours,
[Hewitt H. Howland]

* * *

Writing to company vice president D. Laurance Chambers, Barton had not yet learned the true author of the 17 January telegram. "Mr. Aley" was Maxwell Aley, literary adviser in the New York office.

Barton to D. Laurance Chambers, 19 January 1924

Dear Mr. Chambers:–

On my return from Detroit I found your very gratifying telegram about the manuscript. It is quite flattering to have my hopes about the manuscript reenforced by the judgment of someone who knows so much more about such things than I do.

Frankly though, I am a little bit embarrassed, and have just talked to Miss Lane on the telephone about it. She says that Mr. Aley took the manuscript on the train with him as a purely personal matter, and with the distinct understanding that he was not submitting it formally to you, but only leaving it for your reading as a friend.

I think I said to you at the beginning that this book has been in the back of my mind for several years and that at different times I have–perhaps uncautiously–mentioned it to several friends in the publishing business. The only ones to whom I feel under obligation are Scribners and Ray Long, of the International Book Company. I did promise them, as I have promised you, to give them a chance to read it and talk to me about it. So far I have not done so because I want to rewrite the manuscript considerably before it is published anywhere.

All this does not mean that the book may not be a Bobbs-Merrill book in the end. But it does mean that I feel obliged to let these two friends read it, and then to make for myself the best deal I can, all things being considered.

With best wishes,

Faithfully yours,
Bruce Barton

* * *

It was unusual for either Howland or Chambers to be in the reversed position of trying to sell Bobbs-Merrill to an author.

Howland to Barton, 7 April 1924

My dear Mr. Barton:

I have been in this business twenty-five years and have suffered enough disappointments–I had imagined–to make me hard-boiled. But as the time draws near for your decision, I find myself as nervous as a debutante used to be and as apprehensive as an oil-speculating senator.

If I were only a fatalist I could sleep o' nights. But I'm not. I agitate myself continually, wondering what I can do to tip the scales in our favor. I must publish that book.

What others can give you I don't know, but I don [*sic*] know that it is not greater understanding, enterprise or enthusias [*sic*]. There is no other publisher who could center the force of his drive on one title–your title–as could we; the very length and importance of his non-fiction list would make it impossible.

Our recent success with Sir Harry Johnston's STORY OF MY LIFE, with Wiggam's THE NEW DECALOGUE OF SCIENCE, with Roberts' BLACK MAGIC, has fixed the eyes of the trade on us. There is a new Richmond in the field; expectantly they are watching for his next move. Let us make it with your book. Is there anything I can do or say?

Yours faithfully,
[Hewitt H. Howland]

* * *

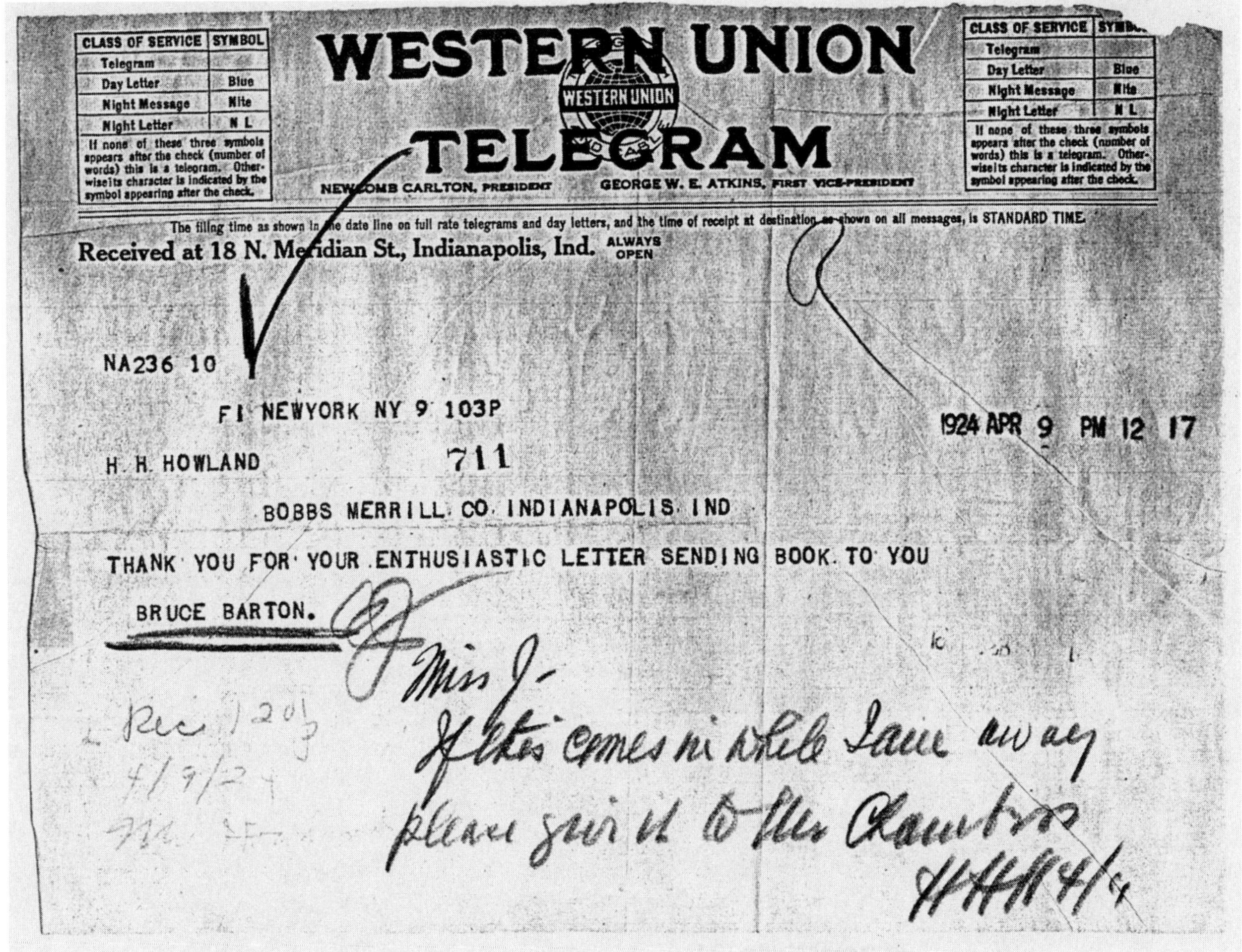

WESTERN UNION TELEGRAM

NEWCOMB CARLTON, PRESIDENT GEORGE W. E. ATKINS, FIRST VICE-PRESIDENT

CLASS OF SERVICE	SYMBOL
Telegram	
Day Letter	Blue
Night Message	Nite
Night Letter	N L

If none of these three symbols appears after the check (number of words) this is a telegram. Otherwise its character is indicated by the symbol appearing after the check.

The filing time as shown in the date line on full rate telegrams and day letters, and the time of receipt at destination as shown on all messages, is STANDARD TIME.

Received at 18 N. Meridian St., Indianapolis, Ind. ALWAYS OPEN

NA236 10

FI NEWYORK NY 9 103P 1924 APR 9 PM 12 17

H. H. HOWLAND 711

BOBBS MERRILL CO INDIANAPOLIS IND

THANK YOU FOR YOUR ENTHUSIASTIC LETTER SENDING BOOK TO YOU

BRUCE BARTON.

Telegram from Barton agreeing to allow Bobbs-Merrill to publish The Man Nobody Knows *(1925), with note by recipient Hewitt H. Howland (courtesy of The Lilly Library, Indiana University, Bloomington, Indiana)*

Bertie Charles Forbes was the founder of Forbes *magazine. Bobbs-Merrill targeted natural audiences when promoting books. As a result,* The Man Nobody Knows *was endorsed by both religious and business figures.*

Bertie C. Forbes to Barton, 30 November 1925

My dear Bruce:

I have just written an editorial for "Forbes" about "The Man Nobody Knows," giving brief extracts calculated to appeal to business executives.

I would like to devote a newspaper column to it and I was wondering whether you would help me out by putting into five hundred words or so your conception of Jesus, along lines which would have an appeal to business men.

I am no good as a book reviewer. Besides, I don't want a review. I want to give the pith of your invigorating message to the several million readers of the forty-five newspapers I have the privilege of writing for daily.

Yesterday I heard a sermon by the Rev. Dr. Knox, Columbia Chaplain, and while he didn't expressly say so, I gathered from the tone of some of his statements that he had been reading your refreshing book.

With kindest regards,

Yours very sincerely,

B. C. Forbes

P.S. I have just ordered a bundle to send out at Christmas.

F.

ESTABLISHED 1838
THE BOBBS-MERRILL COMPANY
PUBLISHERS···INDIANAPOLIS

D. L. CHAMBERS
VICE PRESIDENT

March 26, 1926

Dear Mr. Barton:

Know all men by these presents that THE MAN NOBODY KNOWS is evidently stepping high wide and handsome!

Yours cordially,

D L Chambers

DLC:J

Bruce Barton, Esq.
Barton, Durstine and Osbórn
383 Madison Avenue
New York City

Hooray for our side — B.B.

How about mentioning these in the ads.

Letter from D. Laurance Chambers to Barton, with Barton's response (courtesy of The Lilly Library, Indiana University, Bloomington, Indiana)

L. Frank Baum (1856–1919)

See also the Baum entry in *DLB 22: American Writers for Children, 1900–1960.*

Of the many books that L. Frank Baum wrote for children, the sixteen in the Oz series are the most famous. The Wonderful Wizard of Oz *(1900) was not originally a Bobbs-Merrill publication (and the earliest correspondence with Baum has not survived), but it was a valuable property of the company for many years after republication in 1903 as* The New Wizard of Oz. *In fact, it was the best-selling children's book in America during the period when the firm owned it. A large part of the success of* The Wonderful Wizard of Oz *is owed to the brilliant illustrations by W. W. Denslow, who made it one of the most elaborate children's books produced to that time. Baum's first Bobbs-Merrill work,* The Master Key: An Electrical Fairy Tale *(1901), was innovative in another way, being one of the earliest juvenile science-fiction stories. The company never had exclusive rights to all Baum's works, nor did they have movie rights to* The Wonderful Wizard of Oz *when the 1939 M-G-M motion-picture adaptation was being produced. That financial bonanza fell to Baum's surviving family, which included his widow, Maud, and son Frank J. Baum.*

L. Frank Baum (Gale International Portrait Gallery)

BOWEN-MERRILL/BOBBS-MERRILL BOOKS BY BAUM: *The Master Key: An Electrical Fairy Tale,* illustrated by Fanny Y. Cory (Indianapolis: Bowen-Merrill, 1901; London: Stevens & Brown, 1901);

The Life and Adventures of Santa Claus, illustrated by Mary Cowles Clark (Indianapolis: Bowen-Merrill, 1902; London: Stevens & Brown, 1902);

The Enchanted Island of Yew, illustrated by Cory (Indianapolis: Bobbs-Merrill, 1903);

The New Wizard of Oz, illustrated by W. W. Denslow (Indianapolis: Bobbs-Merrill, 1903; London: Hodder & Stoughton, 1906); **first edition,** *The Wonderful Wizard of Oz* (Chicago: George M. Hill, 1900);

The Surprising Adventures of the Magical Monarch of Mo and His People, illustrated by Frank Verbeck (Indianapolis: Bobbs-Merrill, 1903); **first edition,** *A New Wonderland* (New York: R. H. Russell, 1900);

Baum's American Fairy Tales, revised and enlarged, illustrated by George F. Kerr (Indianapolis: Bobbs-Merrill, 1908); **first edition,** *American Fairy Tales,* illustrated by Ike Morgan, Harry Kennedy, and N. P. Hall (Chicago: George M. Hill, 1901; London: Hutchinson, 1926);

A Kidnapped Santa Claus, illustrated by Richard Rosenblum (Indianapolis: Bobbs-Merrill, 1969)–originally published in the *Delineator* (December 1904).

Illustration by Mary Cowles Clark for The Life and Adventures of Santa Claus *(1902); publicity flier for the book (courtesy of The Lilly Library, Indiana University, Bloomington, Indiana)*

Readers' Reports

Unsigned report on *Baum's American Fairy Tales*, 14 November 1907

AMERICAN FAIRY TALES

I enjoyed this little book of children's tales. The very notion of such a book is so clever that one's attention is caught by it. The idea of fairies in Chicago is an audacious conception, but as the author says, why not? His plea that fairies may be assumed to exist, because it has never been proved that they don't and that there is no reason why they should not inhabit the hills and dales of America as well as those of older lands, as set fourth [*sic*] in his introductory note is very pretty. The author's invention supplies him with attractive conceits; the experiment of trying key after key in the big black chest sent by a long-lost uncle from Africa is certainly a fascinating occupation for a child, and having the pictures in an animal book come suddenly to life and leap from its pages, transforming the room into a menagerie, is a delightful surprise. The very incongruity of connecting fairy mystery–something as old as the race–with the rush and whirl of the twentieth century gives a fresh savor, a relishable sauce piquante. Old devices are furnished up anew or substitutes found for them. Thus when Claribel wishes to be able to sing and play and dance so that she may go on the stage the magician gives her magic bonbons, pink and white and lavender, to eat instead of bitter pills as of old. And the witch whom Mary-Marie visits in order to learn witchcraft isn't ugly and ancient and never rode a broom-stick in her life. The little girls in the story are all highly modern; they are alert, resourceful little heroines, who are capable of extricating themselves from difficulties that would have daunted the little English or Irish girls of the last generation's fairy books. Even the names Martha, Gladys, Marie, etc. suggest a different sort of child from the Sylvias and other etherial [*sic*] little creatures of the old fashioned regime.

The stories have a genial quality, a happy absurdity. The air of naivete with which the utterly impossible is related is delightful,–the three robbers unpacking themselves successively from the carved chest, and Martha's first remark–not one of surprise but a caution not to smoke; the sang froid with which perils and dangers are met, are engaging. The results of the misplacing of the box of magic bonbons, sending a prosaic sober-minded family on the madest [*sic*] sort of larks, is very comical. The stories are peopled with such gay figures as bandits with braided velvet jackets and knee breeches of sky-blue satin, long fierce mustaches and deep, growling voices; with spotted clowns and bears and leopards, all inviting to a child's imagination. And there are some things, too, to tickle the fancy of the grown-up mind, as when the fat robber tenders his regrets to the thin one for having pressed him unduly within the narrow limits of the black chest. Amusing logic is a feature, as when one of the bandits exclaims "Our wickedness has an excuse, for how are we to be bandits unless we are wicked?" And "Are there, then, no bandits in Chicago? Well, we do not call them bandits."

Children so enjoy pretense that these mock bandits should prove ever so many times more delightful than serious ones. Many of the stories have a moral at the end, not a real moral but a burlesque one, such as "This story should teach us to think quickly and clearly upon all occasions; for had Jane Gladys not remembered that she owned the bear he probably would have eaten her before the bell rang."

The three new stories: The Witchcraft of Mary-Marie, Strange Adventures of an Egg and The Ryl do not seem to me so bright and entertaining as some of those in the original collection. In fact, the old material, in my judgement, shows considerable discrepancy in merit. The first three stories,–The Box of Robbers, The Girl Who Owned a Bear and The Magical Bonbons seem to me so much the best as to quite outclass the rest. Still, I mean to make it clear that adverse criticism of the remaining stories is only comparative and I feel that the whole would make an attractive collection. The book is not quite homogeneous both because the American flavor is not present in all of the stories and because the addition of a moral at the end of so many makes one feel that it ought to appear at the end of each and every one. The Box of Robbers seems to me one of the brightest fairy tales for children that I recall,–it seems a delicious stage piece or matinee in story form. The stories for all their modernness are gentle, not flippant, in tone. They seem to me so full of invention, so ingenious in treatment and altogether so jolly that I cordially recommend them.

* * *

In this in-house memo to company president D. Laurance Chambers, associate editor Rosemary B. York opposed publication of a Baum biography by his son Frank. To Please a Child: A Biography of L. Frank Baum, Royal Historian of Oz, *by Frank J. Baum and Russell P. MacFall, was published by Reilly and Lee in 1961.*

Rosemary B. York to D. Laurance Chambers, 8 December 1950

L. FRANK BAUM, The Royal Historian of Oz by F. J. Baum

I do hope we are under no obligation to publish this work! Unfortunately the author did not inherit his father's writing talent, nor has he the faintest notion of modern biographical technique. This is the stodgiest, most amateurish copy I've read in a long time–a eulogy of the funeral-oration kind.

Conceivably there might be a book on L. Frank Baum. I rather expected this would be a "portrait of my father," with some attempt at characterization. Instead the author is trying to write a strictly impersonal biography. He even writes of himself in the third person.

I consider this a hopeless manuscript. The only possible use that might be made of some of the material would be, it seems to me, in a give-away brochure on the author of the WIZARD. Even then it would have to be rewritten (by another hand).

Sample of the style:

"Until the day he sailed away on the Eternal Dream Ship, he was kind, gentle, considerate, thoughtful of others and loving toward all with whom he came in contact, whether it be man, woman or child.

"He was so pure in heart and guileless himself that he could not conceive of any human being acting differently. For this reason he was frequently imposed upon during his life yet he never lost faith in the essential goodness of mankind. As a result, he never had an enemy as long as he lived.

"To know him was to love him for he was one of those chosen few who steadfastly believed in, and lived up to, the very letter of the Ten Commandments and the Golden Rule. He held a firm and fixed belief in his God, his own destiny, and the future greatness of the United States."

On and on and on ad nauseum [*sic*].

Rosemary

* * *

Posthumous Letters and Promotion

Chambers was company vice president and trade-department editor in chief at the time of this letter.

Frank J. Baum to Chambers, 28 July 1933

Dear Mr. Chambers:

I am negotiating for the picture rights to the Wizard of Oz and the producers have asked me to get a "quit claim" from you to show that you will not come in later on and make a claim to the picture rights of this book.

As this is merely a matter of form for their records I trust you will execute same and return to me without delay.

Your attention to this matter will be greatly appreciated.

Cordially yours,
Frank Baum

* * *

Chambers to Frank J. Baum, 12 September 1933

Dear Mr. Baum:–

Your letter of July 28th has just been received. I do not know why it has taken six weeks to reach me.

Judy Garland and Baum's widow, Maud Gage Baum, in 1939, when M-G-M filmed The Wizard of Oz *(courtesy of Metro-Goldwyn-Mayer)*

We have no interest in the dramatic or motion picture rights in THE WIZARD OF OZ, by L. Frank Baum and W. W. Denslow, and you are at full liberty to show this statement to any party at interest with whom you may be dealing.

We could not, however, sign the document which you enclose with your letter. It would entirely incorrect [*sic*] to say that we do not own any interest in the copyright to the literary composition. We own the exclusive publication rights under the contract with Mr. Baum and Mr. Denslow of February 28, 1903.

Yours very truly,
[D. Laurance Chambers]

* * *

Ross G. Baker was the sales manager at the New York office.

Ross G. Baker to salesmen, 21 September 1939

TO THE SALESMEN:

Now when the question of re ordering in quantity on THE WIZARD OF OZ comes up, it might be well to present the following sales argument:

The theatre attendance in second run houses is always much greater than the theatre attendance at first run houses. The bookings in the first run houses on THE WIZARD OF OZ will soon be over and in a very few days they will start booking the picture in second run houses. This means that the audiences for the picture will be doubled in comparison with what it has been up to this point. The second run houses should not be confused with the third run houses. Second run houses attract the suburban audiences and these people can well afford $1.19 for a book.

It will be about five weeks before the picture gets to the third run houses–these are the 15¢ and 10¢ admissions. The second run houses charge between 35¢ and 50¢.

If this information which the moving picture people have given me is true it means a greater sale on THE WIZARD OF OZ in the next month than we had in the preceding month.

Blue Ribbon Books are including THE WIZARD OF OZ in their circular that will be distributed to 1,500,000 homes and it will be included in the full page promotional ads for Blue Ribbon Books. However, as in the past we will retain all of the accounts that were earmarked for our own selling.

Yours–
RGB

* * *

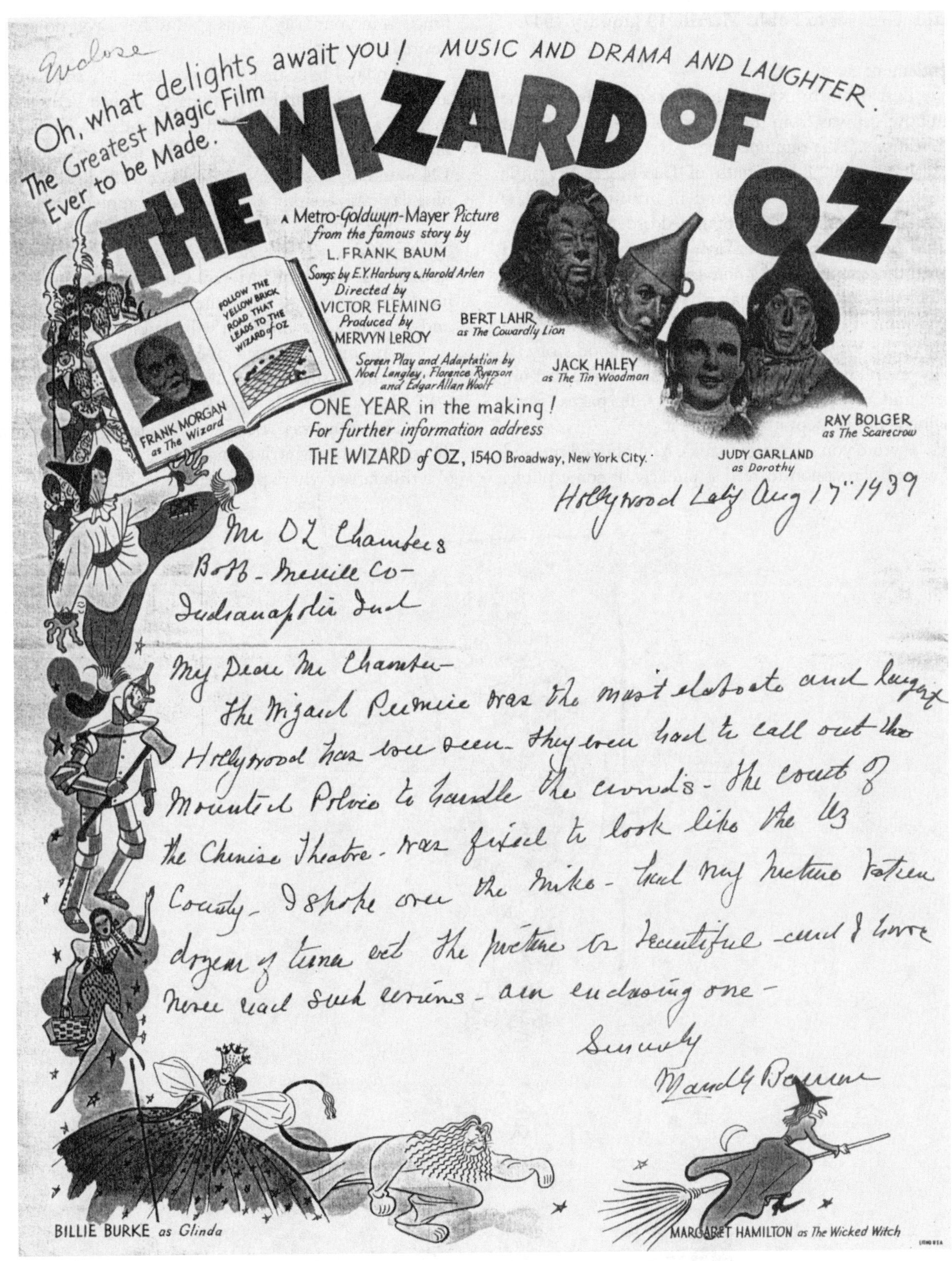

Enclose

Oh, what delights await you! MUSIC AND DRAMA AND LAUGHTER.
The Greatest Magic Film Ever to be Made.
THE WIZARD OF OZ
A Metro-Goldwyn-Mayer Picture from the famous story by L. FRANK BAUM
Songs by E.Y. Harburg & Harold Arlen
Directed by VICTOR FLEMING
Produced by MERVYN LeROY
Screen Play and Adaptation by Noel Langley, Florence Ryerson and Edgar Allan Woolf
FOLLOW THE YELLOW BRICK ROAD THAT LEADS TO THE WIZARD of OZ
FRANK MORGAN as The Wizard
BERT LAHR as The Cowardly Lion
JACK HALEY as The Tin Woodman
RAY BOLGER as The Scarecrow
JUDY GARLAND as Dorothy
ONE YEAR in the making!
For further information address
THE WIZARD of OZ, 1540 Broadway, New York City.

Hollywood Calif Aug 17" 1939

Mr D L Chambers
Bobbs-Merrill Co-
Indianapolis Ind

My Dear Mr Chambers–

The Wizard Premiere was the most elaborate and largest Hollywood has ever seen– they even had to call out the Mounted Police to handle the crowds– The court of the Chinese Theatre– was fixed to look like the Oz Country– I spoke over the mike– had my picture taken dozens of times etc The picture is beautiful– and I have never read such reviews– am enclosing one–

Sincerely
Maud G Baum

BILLIE BURKE as Glinda
MARGARET HAMILTON as The Wicked Witch

Letter from Maud G. Baum to D. Laurance Chambers on the premiere of the movie adaptation of her late husband's 1900 book (courtesy of The Lilly Library, Indiana University, Bloomington, Indiana)

Frank Greaves to Bobbs-Merrill, 13 January 1947

Gentlemen:

Last Night by Radio I heard a song "Beyond the rain-bow"; it was from the Wizard of Oz–(one of your publications. This reminded me–:

It was in 1923–month of December. My little son, then four years old found in my mail your law book advertisement with a Stamped order Card. I was sick in bed at the time but my son–a precocious child copied thereon a part of a note to Santa Clause [*sic*] and scribbled (from copy) his name.

Some days later he received from Bobbs Merrill a copy of the Wizard of Oz–(the only childhood story he really ever loved. His mother read that book to him, over and over. It became loose, the pages came unglued–but he kept it, and loved it.

I wrote you a letter of thanks. You phoned me and requested permission to read it publicly at some public function in your City. I was glad to have you do as you desired with it.

Today I have that book you sent. My son married and left a widow and two little girls named Patricia and Joan. My son went down with 82 of the crew of the submarine "Bull Head" in the Java Sea. It sank August 6 in 1945–and, by coincidence that was his child's (Patricia's) birthday, also the day of my wedding anniversary.

When my son was last home–he found the book "The Wizard of Oz". After perusing it a moment, he said: "Dad–the Bobbs Merrill Company are great people. I was a mere tad when they sent this book. Keep it, and some day Pat and Joan will read it.["]

Last night a Voice over the Radio said "They would sing 3 songs from the show–"The Wizard of Oz." I laid aside my law book and listened.

The song was "Beyond the rain bow." I recalled the gift of Bobbs Merril to my only son; also, I thought–of a distant sea where palms stand sentinel in the moon-

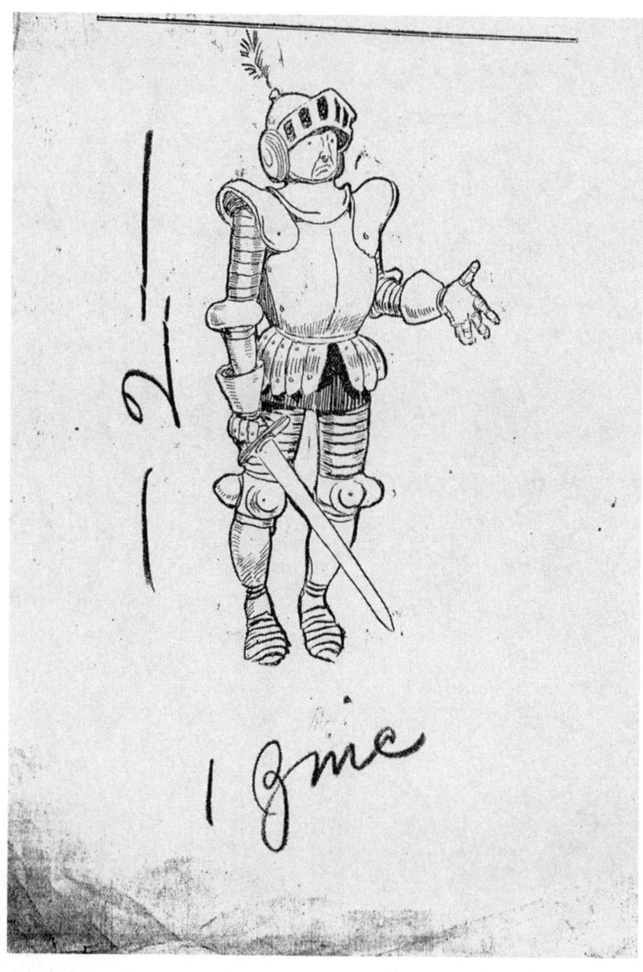

Sketch of an illustration for Baum's 1903 book The Enchanted Island of Yew *(courtesy of The Lilly Library, Indiana University, Bloomington, Indiana)*

light and only the Sea, and stars, and God shall remain when Islands and mountains dissapear [*sic*]–only they will mark some spot beneath a cross of southern Stars the place they sleep. Cradled in the arms of the deep. That spot is unknown to me. The war record merely said 'in the Java Sea,' but as I listened to that song last night I knew it was beyond the rain bow–beyond the fairy land of the Wizard of Oz–but never beyond the touch of memory–never beyond the resurrection of love.

Before me here is the book Bobbs Merril gave him when he was 4 or 5 years old. It's pages stained with his finger prints. He seems to say to me now "Thank Bobbs Merrill again. They are great people of great hearts.["]

So I have written to explain why–I say to you, now, gentlemen–"Thank you, and God bless you["]–for his sake and also such is my sentiment.

At last he is beyond the rain bow, and the beautiful fairy land your gift created in his mind–years ago, when you gave him 'The Wonderful Wizard of Oz.[']

Sincerely yours
Frank Greaves atty

* * *

Chambers to Greaves, 16 January 1947

My dear Mr. Greaves:

Your beautiful letter of the 13th has touched us all deeply. It recalls a happy occasion twenty-three years ago when we had the pleasure of sending your son a copy of THE WIZARD OF OZ, and the charming and delightful letter we received from you in return.

We learn with most sincere regret of your son's heroic death in the service of his country and offer you our deepest sympathy. And yet how proud you must be of his memory!

We are sending you with our compliments a copy of the new edition of THE WIZARD OF OZ with new pictures which we hope Patricia and Joan will enjoy as much as their father enjoyed the former edition with Denslow pictures.

Our most cordial regard to you, our appreciation of a letter which has warmed our hearts, and every good wish to you and yours.

Faithfully yours,
[D. Laurance Chambers]

Earl Derr Biggers (1884–1933)

Before creating the detective Charlie Chan, Earl Derr Biggers was a successful playwright, and his first novel, Seven Keys to Baldpate *(1913), was profitably adapted for the stage by George M. Cohan. Biggers also wrote for magazines and the screen, but today he is remembered for the Chan novels, all serialized before book publication in* The Saturday Evening Post *with illustrations that inspired the makeup for actors starring in the more than forty movie versions.* The House Without a Key *(1925) featured the initial Chan appearance (although in a secondary role), and fan mail (if not sales) indicated that more appearances were required.* Behind That Curtain *(1928) was the first novel in which Chan utters Oriental aphorisms. His behavior in the fiction is not as stereotypical as it is in the movies, and Biggers said that the benevolent sage was a deliberate attempt to counter the conventional image of the "sinister and wicked Chinese."*

Earl Derr Biggers (from Stanley J. Kunitz, ed., Authors: Today and Yesterday, *1931; Thomas Cooper Library, University of South Carolina)*

BOBBS-MERRILL BOOKS BY BIGGERS: *Seven Keys to Baldpate* (Indianapolis: Bobbs-Merrill, 1913; London: Harrap, 1926);

Love Insurance (Indianapolis: Bobbs-Merrill, 1914);

Inside the Lines, by Biggers and Robert Welles Ritchie (Indianapolis: Bobbs-Merrill, 1915; London: Hodder & Stoughton, 1915);

The Agony Column (Indianapolis: Bobbs-Merrill, 1916);

The House Without a Key (Indianapolis: Bobbs-Merrill, 1925; London: Harrap, 1926);

Fifty Candles (Indianapolis: Bobbs-Merrill, 1926);

The Chinese Parrot (Indianapolis: Bobbs-Merrill, 1926; London: Harrap, 1927);

Behind That Curtain (Indianapolis: Bobbs-Merrill, 1928; London: Harrap, 1928);

The Black Camel (Indianapolis: Bobbs-Merrill, 1929; London: Cassell, 1930);

Charlie Chan Carries On (Indianapolis: Bobbs-Merrill, 1930; London: Cassell, 1931);

Keeper of the Keys: A Charlie Chan Story (Indianapolis: Bobbs-Merrill, 1932; London: Cassell, 1932);

Celebrated Cases of Charlie Chan (Indianapolis: Bobbs-Merrill, 1933; London: Cassell, 1933)–comprises *The House Without a Key, The Chinese Parrot, Behind That Curtain, The Black Camel,* and *Charlie Chan Carries On;*

Earl Derr Biggers Tells Ten Stories (Indianapolis: Bobbs-Merrill, 1933).

Review: *Seven Keys to Baldpate*

Baldpate Inn is a Summer hotel on the side of a mountain, and thither, in the early Winter goes the hero of Mr. Biggers's tale, to find the solitude in which to produce a novel of more consequence than the "best sellers" that had brought him much gold, together with the scorn of the critics. One after another several people appear, each with a key to Baldpate, and each seeking solitude. In the first few pages the reader makes their acquaintance, scents mystery and guile in the stories they tell to explain their presence, and without more ado feels himself launched on a novel in which "something happens on every page." It is a gay, saucy story, with a facetious hero, who is never at a loss for something to say and never fails to say it amusingly. There is a pretty girl who, in the words of the hero concerning another damsel, "is scattered tastefully through it" with such good effect that the inevitable love affair between her and the hero comes rapidly to its necessary conclusion.

Mr. Biggers has been for several years editor of the humorous column and the dramatic page of The Boston Traveler. The brilliant way in which he has written this, his first novel, gives promise of excellent things to come in his career as a novelist.

–"The Tale of an Inn," *New York Times,* 23 February 1913, p. 101

* * *

Related Letters

George H. Lorimer was editor of The Saturday Evening Post. *Biggers's frequent references in the following letters to the attractive title of* The Chinese Parrot *reflect an obsession shared with vice president and trade-department editor D. Laurance Chambers, whose first name he consistently misspells.*

Earl Derr Biggers to D. Laurance Chambers, 9 February 1926

Dear Laurence:

I know you will be glad to hear that I completed the first draft of the novel yesterday morning. By an odd chance Lorimer arrived in Los Angeles the night before, and after lunch with him yesterday, he came up to my office, approved of THE CHINESE PARROT title, and held the manuscript affectionately on his knee for a few minutes. I have promised him the completed draft not later than April first, but I am pretty sure it will get to him a week or two sooner than that.

As I am about all in, I am taking a week's rest before starting the next draft. It seems a good idea to take a little jaunt around the route followed by the story, with the hope of picking up some added bits of color. Consequently I am leaving for San Francisco in the morning, and after a few days there, will drop down to Barstow and take another look at the desert country where the major portion of the story takes place. I should be back on the job by February 18th. Usually a second draft is a matter of between three and four weeks, though this one may need a little more.

I am enclosing a royalty report on the popular edition of Baldpate, evidently sent out by some underling. The rate of royalty is not correct–unless the popular edition has gone back to selling for fifty cents. On the recent popular edition of LOVE INSURANCE, which has the same contract as BALDPATE, you paid me five cents a copy, and I am sure it is not unreasonable to ask for the same rate on BALDPATE. In any event, the rate on this statement is obviously incorrect, and I know you will be glad to rectify the matter.

What is the publication date for FIFTY CANDLES? I have been straining my eyes to the East.

Well, I'll be back on the job soon after you get this. With all good wishes,

As ever
Earl Biggers

* * *

SEVEN KEYS TO BALDPATE

By

EARL DERR BIGGERS

ILLUSTRATED BY
FRANK SNAPP

INDIANAPOLIS
THE BOBBS-MERRILL COMPANY
PUBLISHERS

Title page for Biggers's first novel, published in 1913 (courtesy of The Lilly Library, Indiana University, Bloomington, Indiana)

The Chinese Parrot

Elmer Davis says:

"This man Biggers, God bless him,
is the Emily Post of mystery writers.
He does everything as it should be done,
exactly when and as it should be done"

Two promotional pieces for Biggers's 1926 novel (courtesy of The Lilly Library, Indiana University, Bloomington, Indiana)

Chambers to Biggers, 17 February 1926

Dear Earl:

Thank you for telegraphing me about Mr. Bobbs' death. It was an awful shock–struck me all of a heap. But I've picked up the pieces and keep going, and it is good to know that I have your sympathy and understanding. The blow came so suddenly! Of course for his sake I must be grateful that the end was swift and painless; but it is hard for us all, finding us unprepared for such a loss.

I am mighty glad to know that the first draft of THE CHINESE PARROT is done and that Lorimer approves the title. So do I. By the way I just happened to see an English notice of a book by Katharine Newlin Burt called THE GRAY PARROT. I don't know that it's being published under that name in this country and in any case it's not close enough to yours to do our book any harm, do you think? If you get the Post the manuscript by April first it looks like summer publication for us–they seem to be eating stuff up so rapidly there just now–and summer isn't a bad time at all for a mystery story.

Your jaunt around the story's route sounds like a pleasant trip. Are the scenes all laid in California or do you sport again on the beach at Waikiki?

I'm ever so much obliged to you for calling my attention to the royalty report on the popular edition of SEVEN KEYS. It's apparent that our auditor was confused by the fact that the royalty on the original popular edition was figured at two and a half cents, and took that as establishing the rate. But that was when popular editions sold at retail price of fifty cents, and for several years now they have been listed at seventy-five. So you are quite right, and the royalty should be five percent of seventy-five cents, or three and three-quarters cents a copy. The corrected royalty statement is enclosed.

I am somewhat embarrassed on looking into this to find a mistake was made on LOVE INSURANCE too, this time in your favor. According to the contract the same rate of three and three-quarters cents a copy should have applied instead of five cents. I say I am embarrassed because while I am glad to correct an error to your advantage, I hate to seem to turn the tables on you! Let me know what you think fair under the circumstances.

The clause in the contract for THE HOUSE WITHOUT A KEY covering popular editions is drawn in a different way from that of LOVE INSURANCE and SEVEN KEYS. That is, it provides that we are to pay you half the net receipts. That right?

On February tenth I wrote you that your author's copies of FIFTY CANDLES and the new edition of THE AGONY COLUMN had started to you. Get 'em? Like their looks? Publication date was January 30th. We're straining our eyes to the east too now–and north, south, west–watching for reviews.

Yours ever,
[D. Laurance Chambers]

* * *

Olsen is unidentified.

Biggers to Chambers, 9 March 1926

Dear Laurence:

Passed the half way mark in the rewriting this morning. Barring unexpected events it now seems certain that the manauscript [*sic*] will reach Lorimer by April first. Another copy should be in your hands a few days before that.

I have your long letter of recent date, and I am hurrying to take advantage of your kind offer to make changes in the "Agony Column" plates before another printing. One solitary change is all I ask. I feel that at present the first line of the story gets the reader off to a wrong start, and the matter strikes me as serious. At present that line reads: or rather the first sentence reads:

"Two years ago, in July, London was almost unbearably hot."

I should like it changed to read:

"London, that historic summer, was almost unbearably hot."

As you will note, this is practically the same number of letters, and should mean an alteration on the first line only. I will be very grateful if you will make this change before a new printing–which I hope comes soon. After that, the story is O. K. as at present.

The adjustment you suggest on Love Insurance popular royalties is O. K.

I don't know whether I told you, but we are leaving here April tenth–taking a big plunge–the boy out of school for the rest of the term–and sailing for Europe around the first of May. Haven't been over for twelve years, and I feel I have earned the rest–and I always get more than I spend out of any trip. I shall ignore the whole writing business for four blessed months, just opening my mind to ideas for the future. I really haven't done this for years–though there have been long periods when I did nothing, still I was shutting myself up every moring [*sic*] and trying–and getting into a nervous frenzy when the ideas wouldn't come. I believe this will do me worlds of good. I can feel pretty secure financially after this new book. And I expect to bring something good home–last time it was "The

Agony Column" and "Inside the Lines." In the fall we'll probably return here, and I'll do a few short stories and then begin to think about a new novel.

We'll be in New York the last two weeks in April, and I hope I shall see you there. It would be fine if I could have the galleys before I went–but of course if its too soon for you, I can correct them in Paris.

Have you given any thought to a jacket for the new one? The parrot theme ought to provide plenty of promotion material–it's nice when you can fix on something definite like that. Has a parrot ever figured prominently in a mystery story? I don't seem to recall any. He might make a good jacket, too, along with Charlie Chan, perhaps. If you wanted me to I could pick up a few desert pictures for you here–but don't ask it unless your intentions are serious, for they cost a fortune. I thought at one time a desert jacket might be good, but I'm afraid now it would suggest a "western" rather than a mystery story. No doubt you can reply to all this when you have read the book, and if you want desert pictures then, you can pick them up in New York. It would be fine to have a talk with you before sailing. We'll be in a good deal of a hurry, so I'll be in Chicago only a few hours. I have to pause in New York for a long session with my doctor.

I heard from Olsen yesterday, and expect to see him soon.

Well, back to the treadmill. That long cheer you'll hear in a couple of weeks will mean the book is done.

As ever
Biggers

* * *

Paul R. Reynolds was a literary agent. Anne Johnston was an editorial assistant in Indianapolis, while Herbert S. Baker was in the New York office. Leslie Hood was evidently a Pasadena bookseller.

Biggers to Chambers, 31 March 1926

Dear Laurence:

Reynolds wired yesterday that his copy of the manuscript was at hand, and as yours went the same day, I trust you have it long before this, and have read it with some pleasure. I did my best. In some respects it doesn't come up to the "House", but I believe that in the matter of plot it is O. K. I have tried the title on a few intelligent people, and their comments have been amazingly enthusiastic. So at least you have one big selling point–a good title.

I am writing chapter heads and will forward them to Miss Johnston in a few days.

I would like to stop in Indianapolis, but I don't see how I can. I am feeling quite rocky again, and want all the time I can get with my doctor in New York. I'd like to see you, but I don't think there is enough demanding discussion to make it necessary for you to come to New York unless you are coming anyhow. The only thing I would have to talk over would be the jacket, and I can take that up with Baker. As a matter of fact, I haven't a single idea on it. I shall be in Chicago all day April fourteenth, and if you were inspired to come up there we could lunch together. However, as I say, much as I'd enjoy seeing you, there is really nothing to make it imperative. If you should decide to come to Chicago, wire me where to meet you.

I'm sorry to say I had no moment alone with Olsen. Our little friend Hood was right on deck.

The new page for "The Agony Column" is fine, and thank you for troubling. I think it a big improvement. I was glad also to have the review from the London Times. Now that that famous paper has approved the "House" I guess the last word has been spoken. I was particularly pleased they liked Chan. Ought to sell a couple of hundred books in England now.

Reynolds will take care of my mail again this summer, and I think it safest for you to communicate with me through him. Please spread the word through the office not to send any more letters to me out here after you get this, but to send everything to me Care of Paul R. Reynolds, 599 Fifth Avenue, New York. (A new address, you will note.) However, I can be reached by telegraph here until noon of April 10th.

Hope you liked the book, and that we'll have the best sale ever on "The Chinese Parrot." As ever

E.D.B.

We sail from N.Y. on the Lapland, Friday, April 30th.

* * *

Chambers to Biggers, 7 April 1926

Dear Earl:

A number of things interfered with my reading THE CHINESE PARROT until Sunday. Then I got started, and finished it last night. I telegraphed you today how enthusiastic I feel over it. In quality of sheer entertainment I don't think you have ever done anything as good as this. It reads as if you'd had a perfectly bully time writing it, and that adds a lot to the reader's enjoyment. There's a gusto, a constant bubbling humor that makes the book, rather than the mystery part, unusual and air-tight as it is. You have a bully title and a wonderful setting.

I am awfully sorry you can't stop off in Indianapolis for we'd love to have Mrs. Biggers and you with us. But I'm going to make a desperate effort to get to New York before you leave. It is more likely that I can do that than that I can meet you in Chicago on the fourteenth.

Olsen says friend Hood will give us great support on the new book. As soon as you know when the Post is going to run it, will you let us know so that we can make our plans for book release. If by any chance I don't make New York before you sail I'll send the contract to Baker to take up with you. You'll want to see him and he'll want to see you anyhow to talk over the jacket and format of the book.

Yours ever,

[D. Laurance Chambers]

* * *

Thomas P. Costain was an editor at The Saturday Evening Post. *Curtis Brown was a literary agent. George G. Harrap and Company was Biggers's current British publisher.*

Chambers to Biggers, 30 April 1926

Dear Earl:

When your letter came this morning giving your date of sailing I despatched a wire to your boat as a substitute since I couldn't see you off. I am still terribly sorry I was kept here. But I shall hope to be at the dock to meet you when you come back. Be sure and let me know when that is.

I don't give a damn about the option clause. I know I can count on your loyalty as long as we behave ourselves as good publishers should. And if you ever felt like leaving us we shouldn't let an option clause stand in the way.

Congratulations on making the Post come clean with an advance in price. Sorry it wasn't more, if you wanted more. And who doesn't? Wish they'd hurry up and schedule it, but I suppose they have to wait for the illustrations. We'll keep in touch with Brother Costain.

When you're in London, won't you drop in on Pollinger, of Curtis Brown, Ltd., 6 Henrietta Street, Covent Garden? I've told him you were coming and asked him to extend the courtesies of the office. Glad you're going to see Harrap. In Paris I want you to look up Robert Forrest Wilson if he's in town. He lives at 35, rue de la Tombe-Issoire. He's a mighty fine chap and he wrote one of the most delightful books on Paris imaginable in PARIS ON PARADE which we published last fall. I've written him to look out for you too.

Thanks very much for the interesting letter about the HOUSE which I return. And for the suggestion about the portrait sketch, which I shall use. Kindest regards–

Yours,

[D. Laurance Chambers]

* * *

"Miss Kinsey" is presumably Mina Kersey of the Indianapolis editorial staff.

Biggers to Chambers, 3 June 1926

Dear Laurence:

Your letter of May 21st has just got in. I am surprised at the date of June 26th for the Parrot in the Post–they certainly rushed it. As they have it scheduled for six issues that will end it in the issue on sale July 29th and means August publication for you if you hanker for it. Though it seems to an onlooker that early Sept. would be early enough.

I am praying that you get the proofs to me here before June 14th as I go on a six weeks tour on that date. If they have not arrived then I won't get them until July first or thereabouts–if they reach me at all. Mail is slow and uncertain here. I am also hoping Baker reaches me with his sample jackets before the 14th.

I sent a letter from New York to Miss Kinsey with the chief alterations to be made in the copy after reading the Post proofs. If these have been made it is unlikely that I will have any important changes to make–though I shall feel safer if I see the galleys. Page proofs are out of the question this time.

Paris continues cool and rainy but interesting–and marvellously cheap with the franc so fallen. It is the weakness of the franc that has lured me into staying here five weeks. I never saw such pretty hotel bills. However we are off on the fourteenth–Switzerland and the Italian lakes, then Munich and down the Rhine to Holland and Belgium. I have my hotel in London for August first, and we sail from Glasgow on the Cameronia August 28th.

The Equitable Trust will follow me at intervals with the mail and any cables, but there will be a few stretches where I shall be out of reach. I shall fire back the proofs in 24 hours–here's hoping they reach me before I leave Paris.

I am sorry to say that Wilson is out of town and will not return before we go.

ESTABLISHED 1838
THE BOBBS-MERRILL COMPANY
PUBLISHERS ··· INDIANAPOLIS

September, 1926

Dear Customer:

Estimates, on the number of new books published annually, vary from six thousand to ten thousand. It is virtually impossible for the bookbuyer to know what he wants to know about so many books.

Realizing what a task this quantity publication imposes on the bookbuyer, we propose to experiment by sending out letters on important new books. If the experiment has the effect we expect, each of us will profit. Each letter will be short, and the advance information will be of three sorts:

1. A paragraph on the contents.
2. A paragraph on the author.
3. Outstanding sales points.

For example:

THE CHINESE PARROT--September 15.

PLOT: The California desert with its deformed Joshua trees, is the location, and there are glimpses of San Francisco and Hollywood, Charlie Chan, who starred in THE HOUSE WITHOUT A KEY, the self-deprecatory Chinese detective brings the Jordan necklace to the lonely ranch of the great financier, P.J. Madden, A bilingual Chinese parrot shrieks in the night, "Help! Murder!" and then things begin to happen.

AUTHOR: He who wrote SEVEN KEYS TO BALDPATE, THE AGONY COLUMN, THE HOUSE WITHOUT A KEY, FIFTY CANDLES.

Form letter to book buyers plugging The Chinese Parrot *and inviting comments on this kind of advance notice (courtesy of The Lilly Library, Indiana University, Bloomington, Indiana)*

ESTABLISHED 1838

THE BOBBS-MERRILL COMPANY
PUBLISHERS ··· INDIANAPOLIS

Sales points:

1. A corking mystery with the rare combination of humor.

2. Biggers' first full-length novel since THE HOUSE WITHOUT A KEY and a worthy successor to it, as well as SEVEN KEYS TO BALDPATE.

Write us your opinion of the plan, and give any suggestions which occur to you. Would copies of the letters be useful to your salespeople? Your problem of "keeping up" is their problem, too.

Write down the number of copies you'd like to have for distribution to your sales force.

Cordially yours,

THE BOBBS MERRILL COMPANY
C.D. LaFollette

CDL:H

Please send _____________ copies your mimeographed sheets, as issued, on forthcoming books. These are for distribution to our sales force.

Buyers name ______________________________

Firm name and address ______________________________

____

I imagine you are making big plans for the Parrot. Everybody applauds the title and I hope you can find a jacket they'll like–and buy. All good luck.

As ever
Biggers

* * *

"Mr. Curtis" was John J. Curtis, the new president of Bobbs-Merrill and a resident of Hollywood. In time, The Chinese Parrot *sold more than eight hundred thousand copies, despite Biggers's worries.* Galahad *was a book by John Erskine, also published in 1926.*

Biggers to Chambers, 19? October 1926

Dear Laurence:

I meant to write sooner, but have been very busy since my arrival. We have bought a most attractive house from your friend Stevenson, and have found him about as generous a builder as the California sun ever shone on. It is made of remarkably good materials, and is in a section where land values are certain to increase. I am sure it is a good investment. Also, I have rented a very cheerful office in a new building and move in tomorrow. While I am mulling over the possibilities of Chan's next adventure, I hope to do two or three short stories. This is really an excellent place to work, for if you don't, you die of boredom.

Larry perhaps wrote you that Universal finally signed the contract–at five o'clock on the night I was taking a six o'clock train for the west. But they haven't paid me a penny yet, the lowlifes. The only way I could get them to sign that day was to waive the down payment for a few weeks–as the story runs–and I thought it a good idea to at least get their official signature on the contract. Such a business!

I haven't seen Mr. Curtis yet, but he knows I am here and is arranging a grand tour in town some day this coming week.

All the way out here the journey was brightened by the fact that "The Parrot" was everywhere. The best distribution on any book of mine yet, I believe. I want to tell you that I am delighted by the way you have launched it–the work you have done, advertising, etc. Only one fly in the ointment–I am fearful that the results won't be as good as they should be. I may have been wrong, but on my call at the New York office my last day there, I gathered that the thing was not going any too well. If we don't get a good sale, I shall be at a loss to explain it. You have done your part beautifully, and I believe that I have done mine–a good story, and a good title. I ascribe any lull in sales at present to the confusion attending the launching of this terrific flood of new novels. The market is bound to be a whirlpool for a period, and when it clears, some books will be floating on top and many will have sunk forever. And among those latter there will be good books. Let's hope the Parrot can swim!

I note you have added the line "Humor and Mystery" to your smaller ads, and I think it was a good idea. Striking as those ads have been, I do believe that some bit of description is necessary to get the idea over at present. Best of all, to my mind, are brief bits from reviews, but of course you are handicapped there for the moment by the maddening delay in getting reviews–due again to the flood of books. There have been a few in papers worth while–but not many. The N. Y. Evening Post, the Transcript–and a few others. I am hoping the N. Y. Times comes across today. I believe the reviews in any of the good papers are going to be mighty kind and helpful. By the way, did you know that Minot of the Boston Herald, in his weekly book talk over the radio a short while back, announced that the "Parrot" was the best mystery story in years? That ought to help in Boston–and perhaps it has, for I got a couple of clippings yesterday from the Transcript and Globe with best seller lists, and the Parrot was on both–second in one case. Also, it ought to mean we'll have a good review in the Herald some of these days.

Perhaps I am a bit impatient about all this–as I recall, the House was out in Feb. and it was June when it began to really sell. Perhaps, later on, if you don't feel you're getting the House readers it might be a good plan to advertise Charlie Chan a bit–Detective Sergeant Chan of the Honolulu police–it has an alluring sound. Baker told me he was thinking of doing this. Also, it would help with the next book–and if you want any assurance that you're going to have that book, here it is right now–and all the rest of my books as long as the House is as intelligently run and efficient as at present.

None of these suggestions and roaming remarks are in any sense criticism but only an effort to be helpful. I want you to be rewarded by sales commensurate with your efforts, and I'll feel badly, quite aside from any financial angle, if you're not. As a matter of fact, I've made a ridiculous sum of money out of this story now. I'm not greedy for more, but I really take a pride in the Bobbs-Merrill company and like to see you put 'em over. I'd be tickled to see the Parrot trailing along after Galahad this fall.

Well, I won't stretch this out any longer. Don't worry about that book "The House of Seven Keys." There must be some mistake about it. Leslie Hood

AT THIS PAGE IN

Charlie Chan Carries On

YOU HAVE ALL THE EVIDENCE CHARLIE NEEDS

TO SOLVE THE MYSTERY.

IF YOU ARE AS CLEVER AS HE, PLEASE

PAT SELF ON BACK, AS HE WOULD SAY,

AND TELL US ABOUT IT.

The Bobbs-Merrill Company.

Promotional item for Biggers's 1930 novel and a page insert demonstrating Bobbs-Merrill's responsiveness to customer comments (courtesy of The Lilly Library, Indiana University, Bloomington, Indiana)

told my cousin it was out, and my cousin told my wife, and there you are. Probably he saw some reference to the English edition. I'm not going to ask him about it, because he doesn't like to be proved wrong about anything. A regular prima donna, Leslie. A little cool at present–I don't know why. Got a new competitor in Pasadena. And business is simply terrible, as it always is at this season, before the winter crowd rolls in. I think perhaps he bought a little heavily on the Parrot. A book of mine will always sell much better in Pasadena if published in the winter than at other seasons–the regular residents here are not the book buyers. However, I didn't urge him to buy, and Leslie's life will no doubt brighten when the crowd heads this way. I was in the store the other day, and it was a scene of desolation. All the clerks were laid off, and the "stock-holders" were sitting gloomily round on chairs.

I'll be happy to do anything I can for Mr. Curtis out here, and if there is anything I can do to help the book back east, let me know. By the way, if you ever want to write me in a hurry, the Air Mail this year is wonderful. Goes direct to Los Angeles, and you can get a letter to New York in a little over two days.

Good luck, and lots of it.

As ever
Earl Biggers

Gelett Burgess (1866–1951)

See also the Burgess entry in *DLB 11: American Humorists, 1800–1950.*

Beginning as an avant-garde humorist in the Bohemian circles of San Francisco, Gelett Burgess had a long career as a novelist, illustrator, poet, and playwright. The author of dozens of books, he is remembered now only for clever verse trifles, the coinage of "blurb," and the new sense he gave to "bromide." In fact, had Burgess not written the following widely quoted quatrain in 1895, his eclipse might have been complete: "I never saw a purple cow, / I never hope to see one; / But I can tell you anyhow, / I'd rather see than be one." His New York Times *obituary says not a word about his novels; literary histories, which seldom bother even to describe them, offer little to justify the high regard Burgess once received for his abilities in that genre.*

BOBBS-MERRILL BOOKS BY BURGESS: *The White Cat* (Indianapolis: Bobbs-Merrill, 1907);

The Heart Line: A Drama of San Francisco (Indianapolis: Bobbs-Merrill, 1907);

Find the Woman (Indianapolis: Bobbs-Merrill, 1911);

The Master of Mysteries (Indianapolis: Bobbs-Merrill, 1912);

Love in a Hurry (Indianapolis: Bobbs-Merrill, 1913);

Two O'Clock Courage (Indianapolis: Bobbs-Merrill, 1934);

Too Good Looking: The Romance of Flossidoodle Darlo (Indianapolis: Bobbs-Merrill, 1936).

Gelett Burgess (Bruccoli Clark Layman Archives)

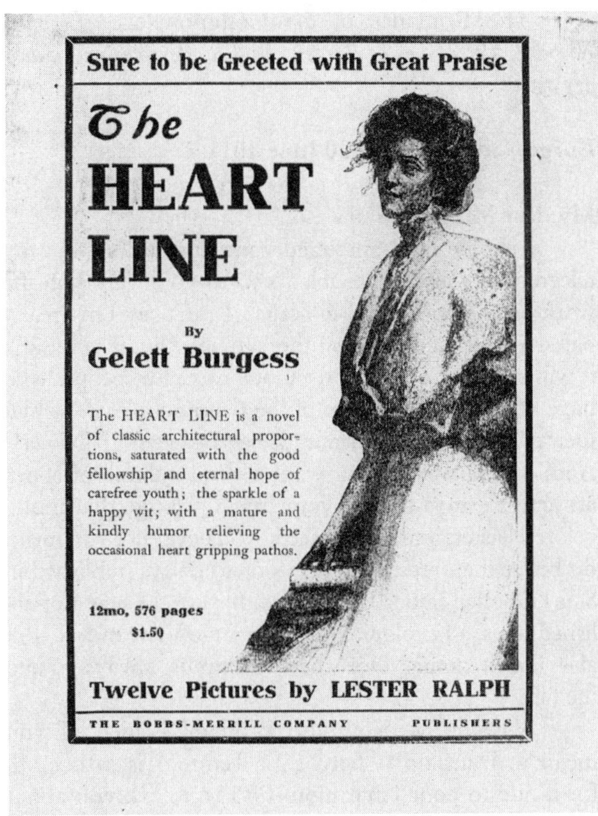

Flier for one of Burgess's 1907 novels (courtesy of The Lilly Library, Indiana University, Bloomington, Indiana)

Related Letters

Ralph Hale was assistant trade-department editor. Bobbs was president at this time.

Gelett Burgess to William C. Bobbs, 11 June 1911

My dear Mr. Bobbs;

I find that in the contracts sent me, you have inserted a new clause, not in previous agreements, or rather a part of a clause binding me to offer you, upon the same terms, my next two books. This I am not willing to do.

I had this subject thrashed out before, with Mr. Hale, I think, with the result that you accepted a sort of moral obligation on my part to give you a chance at my next book. As a result I offered you "Lady Mechante" and "Who was Belle Charmion?" You must let it go at that, in this case, as I do not wish to sign a pledge to that effect. I have no doubt that I shall offer you my next novel, and probably at the same terms as this, but I object very strongly to being forced to. All this business is very objectionable to me. I had thought that, having agreed with you in the matter once, I should not have to fight it out for every subsequent book. I can see very little that your company has done, so far, to increase my good will. To every complaint I have been answered by easy elusions. I cannot feel reassured in any way by anything that has happened. To be sure, nothing serious has occurred; it is mainly a feeling that when it comes to talking business, things will be unpleasant. I am sorry that it is not over, but trust that you will accept this amendment. Also, I would like the deletions initialed as is, I think, usual, though perhaps in this case unnecessary. Then we can go ahead with the book, I hope, with no further discussion.

Yours faithfully,
Gelett Burgess

[Indication to forward to "Mr. Howland"]

* * *

The following letter is presumably from Hewitt H. Howland, editor of the trade department. In response to the request for a title change, Burgess wired his reluctant acceptance.

Hewitt H. Howland to Burgess, 14 June 1911

My dear Mr. Burgess:

Your letter of June eleventh to Mr. Bobbs, together with the amended contracts, has been sent to my desk for reply. We have deleted the next two book clause and have initialed all changes as you request. We have filed one copy of the contract and are returning the other to you herewith. I am sure everything is satisfactory now and we shall put the manuscript into type at once, sending you galley proofs for revision.

I am very enthusiastic over the story and can see no reason why it should not prove widely popular. I do not know whether Mr. Bobbs told you or not but I wrote him that the story was a combination of Robert Louis Stevenson, O. Henry and Gelett Burgess at their best, and that that was a combination pretty hard to beat.

There is only one handicap, as I see it, to the story's successful promotion and that is in its title. Charmion is not an easy name to remember. I can hear the intelligent customer asking the intelligent book clerk for "that new story by Gelett Burgess–Who Was Bell Somebody-or-other". Moreover, the title does not arouse the enthusiasm in our selling and advertising department that makes for the greatest success. Feeling all this and being anxious that no stumbling block should be left in the road that leads to the Six Best Sellers I set about to devise a new title. The result of my efforts has the vociferous approval of every branch of the service, from the man who O. K's. the advertising appropriation to the man who sells the book on the road. Its adoption will clinch the situation and do more to create confidence and stimulate enthusiasm than any one thing that could happen. It is my honest belief that by sending a collect telegram of hearty approval you will add many thousands to the sale of the book. It is

Find The Woman

and I am, as ever,

Sincerely yours,
[Hewitt H. Howland]

* * *

Burgess to Bobbs-Merrill, 16 June 1911

Title scarcely expresses the book or my taste but I Consent for want of a better
Gelet [*sic*] Burgess

* * *

Unsigned letter (Howland?) to Burgess, 20 June 1911

My dear Mr. Burgess:

We are sending you to-day a set of galley proofs of "Find the Woman," although the original title still stands on the galleys. Will you read, correct and return these to us as quickly as possible? You will understand that all this type has been set on machines and that the sub-headings for the various stories will be reset by hand when we come to make up into pages.

I am wondering if it might not be a wise thing not to display these story titles, but to run them right into the body of the text. In this way for instance (see galley six):

"With this preamble she began The Story of the Dead Fare".

What do you think of this suggestion?

Hoping soon to hear from you, I am, as ever,

Faithfully yours,

* * *

The Romance of the Commonplace *(Elder & Shepard, 1902) was by Burgess. Paul R. Reynolds was a literary agent.*

Burgess to Howland, 20 June 1911

My dear Mr. Howland;

I should have answered your letter before, but my telegram has already enabled you to go ahead with the work on the book. As I indicated, I can't say I'm greatly pleased with the title "Find the Woman" but if you think it will sell the book, I don't much care. But people who have read "The Romance of the Commonplace" will lift their eyebrows and murmur "Gelett Burgess?" ["]Never!" And, by the way, if you want a good volume of short, attractive essays to give your lists a prestige that multi-colored jackets and frontispieces won't ever do, you might do better than republish the 18 or so essays published in San Francisco under that title, with some 18 new unpublished ones, all exploiting the Romantic View of Life. But alas, I'm dreaming. One's best work must always go into the bin.

Now as to "Find the Woman"–which, if you mean to translate "Cherchez la Femme" is rather off, for a title to poor Charmion–I'd like to ask you about proper names. The onlm [*sic*] real persons mentioned are Nat Goodwin and Rooseveldt [*sic*], I believe, and we need anticipate no libel suits from them. As to places, I've mentioned Scheffel Hall, a real restaurant, the Cadillac Hotel, the Friars' Club, Hotel Plaza. There is an "Anti-Profanity League" in Brooklyn, an offshoot of the "Holy Name" wherefore perhaps it would be well to change that name, to the "Amalgamated Non-Cursers" as well as the names, especially Roman Catholic organizations represented as being in the league. Shall I do that, and give fancy names, such as the Sons of Jehu? The Story of the Dead Fare resembles a similar true story, told of one of the Belmonts, some years ago in New York, but not near enough to be dangerous, I fancy, and no names are mentioned.

The serial begins in the Asso. Sund. Mags in July, under the title of "Who was Belle Carillon?" I suppose it is too late to change it, even if a change would help the book.

Let me ask you next, if you ever received through Reynolds, a string of 24 detective tales by me, (alias Alan Braghampton) called "The Master of Mysteries"–or, perhaps, "Astro the Seer"?. I have them now, (serial ran in the Ass. sund. Mags. also) for sale, thought [*sic*] I think it would hurt me to put them out under my own name. They are, I think, good detective stories, but hardly have that flavor which I wish to be known as characteristic of my work. The hero is Astro, a clairvoyant, who, while pretending to solve his mysteries by occult means, is really a clever detective. He has an assistant, Valeska Wynne, and there is a frail love-plot meandering through. Let me know if you care to consider such a book.

I am now writing a symbolistic novel–don'T jump, for the symbolism is all hidden in the guise of realistic comedy, and won't hurt. One might describe it as the story of a fairy in New York, who, (somewhat like Undine) through suffering, loses her power, and gradually becomes human. On the other side, the hero, helped by the fairy with magic gifts, becomes rich, and discovers that happiness is not a question of money. It's of course a love story, dramatic, and realistic, with much comedy, though rather ethical in trend. Of that I'm making a play, indeed, the play was done first. If this is the sort of book that would sell, you might try it. I hope to sell it serially this fall. I mention it mainly as an evidence of good faith in regard to certain deleted clauses of my contract. The name is "Justin's Delight[.]" Isn't that provocative? Delight is the name of the sylph. There's a deep symbolism underlying the whole book, an esoteric side that the multitude won't get.

Let me know, at your leisure,
Yours,
Gelett Burgess

* * *

Review: *Find the Woman* (1911)

Hung on the memory of a little boy for a girl is an eventful life of twenty years which reaches its climax in a whirl of excitement and adventure of one night in the streets of New York, into which are crowded, in exactly the time it takes to tell the story, a suicide, a murder, several abductions, robberies, and all sorts of strange and curious happenings, which far surpass in nature and variety anything in the Arabian Nights, and, for logical sequence, the forensic of a Sophomore. Never was fancy more riotous, the phenomena of coincidences more rationally sustained. Never was there a better economy of the reader's attention demonstrated according to the most elusive rule of Spencerian rhetoric. Not a word is wasted; the element of suspense is pushed to the extreme, no more. The reader follows the adventures of the hero about the Great White Way as in a dream, and both finally "find the woman" simultaneously. It is a wonderful moving picture without waits and without broken films; best of all, it appears to be that indefinite thing called "literature." The conservative critic, however he may shudder at the performance, will be obliged to admit that it will bear the most searching rhetorical analysis. The pictures by Mr. Booth will be found to be

Nov. 13—No. 70—Van Cleve—Times

A New Novel

By GELETT BURGESS

Author of *The Heart Line, The White Cat, etc.*

FIND THE WOMAN

Find the woman is in the form of a sort of Arabian Nights' Entertainment comprising adventures in every section of New York from Wall Street to Harlem with widely varying types of metropolitan character. The whole comprises the story of a single night.

Mr. Burgess is known for his satire and wit and in these qualities of writing he has never appeared to better advantage than here. The gaiety, mystery, and adventure of the romance too will add greatly to its reputation.

Pictures by Hanson Booth. At all Booksellers. Price $1.25 net.

UNION SQUARE NEW YORK THE BOBBS-MERRILL COMPANY UNIVERSITY SQUARE INDIANAPOLIS

PROOF FROM
The New York Times
"All the News That's Fit to Print."
Actual net Paid Sales over 1,000,000 Copies a Week.
Monday, Nov. 13, 1911

Proof of an advertisement for the 1911 novel whose title was provided by Hewitt H. Howland (courtesy of The Lilly Library, Indiana University, Bloomington, Indiana)

excellent if the reader can tear himself away from the story long enough to look at them.

–*New York Times,* 3 December 1911, p. 793

* * *

Related Letters

Albert L. Rabb of Thompson, Rabb & Stevenson in Indianapolis supplied the following reader's report on a Burgess manuscript with the working title "The Strange Week." It was published as Two O'Clock Courage *in 1934.*

Albert L. Rabb to Bobbs-Merrill, 11 August 1933

Gentlemen,–

I have read, and return herewith, the manuscript of "The Strange Week" by Gelett Burgess. I have read this with greater interest because of the considerable lapse of time that has followed the publication of his last book, and because of pleasant recollections of his "Master of Mysteries" and "Find the Woman"–his only books that actually are detective stories.

The story is well enough conceived and told, in my opinion, as to negative any impression of lack of novelty in some of the ideas. This is not the first time where the central figure is a man who is suffering from temporary amnesia–as witness that most interesting story, "The Man Without a Shadow" by Oliver Cabot. Nor is it the first appearance of a character who liberally volunteers historical facts and allusions; compare, for example, Wallace's J. G. Reeder, or some of H. S. Keeler's characters. In this connection the reference appendix of historical anecdotes I would certainly omit: it smacks to me either of pride of compilation, or of an educational intent, both of which are out of place in a detective story. The proper names of the characters are typical of Burgess.

Without going into detail, the chief impression and criticism I have is that the story is somewhat slow; its action could well be accelerated; and it does not read as smoothly as it seems to me it should; but, and principally, I do not think this is Burgess at his best. This is not the Burgess of the "Master of Mysteries" or of "Find the Woman". Perhaps even at that, this story would have ranked relatively well twenty years ago. I do not think it is, in its present form, of high rank today. But it was interesting.

Very truly yours,
Albert L. Rabb

* * *

Burgess wrote a four-page letter to D. Laurance Chambers, vice president and trade-department head, responding to the readers' reports. Like Howland, Chambers was always intent on finding a title that would help sell a book.

Burgess to D. Laurance Chambers, 3 September 1933

Dear Mr. Chambers;

On account of business arrangements I had to let my agent, Mr. Sanders negotiate the book rights of my STRANGE WEEK, as I was not in New York. But now that the agreement seems to be satisfactory, I would like to take up with you directly the suggestions which Sanders sent me from your office. It's too bad we can't have a talk together.

I consider that my book has a new form of construction. I have done what some have thought impossible, but which the best critics have advocated, i. e. the combination of a novel with a mystery story. It is a tour de force in technique which, I think, has never been done.

The book is a true novel ("of observation" as the French say) by virtue of its weight, veritability and characterization. It is, strictly, a novel of adventure. But it is also a genuine mystery story in that there is not an incident, hardly a paragraph that is not concerned with the murder, or affected by it. It is a novel about a murder, and the murder is always central and dominant. The "detective story" aspect of it is unique, I think, because the story is told from the inside, that is, by one of the suspects of the crime, who, indeed, suspects himself.

I spent two years on the book, and every page has been written and rewritten many times, and its logic and perspective most carefully considered, with a view to suspense. It does not have the tempo of a thriller, and I think it would be a mistake to class it as such. It is a novel about a murder. If it is a little slower in tempo than a thriller, it has much more verisimilitude, and the characters are, I think alive and authentic. It is more important than a thriller, more vital.

For these reasons I do not agree to your suggestion that the name be changed. True, I did think of calling it Two O'Clock Courage. But to my mind that title is deceptive and would be disappointing to the reader. It over emphasizes the crime at the expense of the adventure and psychological experiences of the teller of the tale. I think, in short, that it would be a mistake to force the book into a class where it does not belong. It cannot compete with these stories of mass murder and impossible crimes. It is in a class by itself, and the nearest book that I can recall resembling its quality (although the technique is quite different) is The Bellamy Trial, where the love interest was frail and entirely disconnected with the murder theme. My heart interest is continually broken into by the murder theme.

I have had many titles in mind, and have tried them on many people. Almost every one chose THE STRANGE WEEK as the most provocative. "What was strange about it?" they said. I tried The Man in Brown which is banal, and Who am I? and many others. I have spent a good deal of time considering it and can find nothing better. It seems to me a good selling title. Will you please think this over carefully and see if you don't agree with me, and meanwhile if I can think of anything better I shall let you know. [. . .]

As to the shortening. I have been over and over the book, and can now see no place to cut it where it wouldn't bleed. But on re-reading one does usually find some short cuts possible. I am so busy finishing my new novel that I can't spare the time now to go over the MSS to try to cut it, but if on reading the galley proofs I can find any opportunity to slash I shall do it, you may be sure. I notice that your reader doesn't suggest any particular places where it drags. Isn't his suggestion merely because he is inclined to think of the book as a thriller, with a tempo that prevents any real verisimilitude?

You will have noticed, I hope, that the book is strictly modern in style. Booth Tarkington once said, "If they ever catch me writing, I'm done for." You will find no "writing" in my novel. There is hardly an adjective or an adverb (except in the speeches of the characters), and the whole story is "reported" as the critics say, in the most direct fashion. The author is never ahead of the reader, he never keeps anything back. I have taken the greatest care to keep this simplicity and directness in order that the story may seem every minute plausible and have a rugged reality, impossible to a thriller. It is this sincerity, rather than an excitement to find out what happens next, that I depend upon to make the book a Best Seller.

As to the suggestion that Gannett must have used an uppercut on Jetland's jaw, instead of an undercut, you may change it if you wish, although the blow was, in fact, just what I said.

Finally let me say that I am sure my character names are the best possible. The title of the book is, I

Sketches by Lester Ralph for The Heart Line *(courtesy of The Lilly Library, Indiana University, Bloomington, Indiana)*

know well, of great importance to the sale. But I don't believe in fooling the purchaser, and masquerading the book for a trashy melodrama. I insist that it is a genuine novel, the first to embody, in an artistic frame, the story of a murder without violating on a single page, the rules of suspense desiderated by every mystery story. And I hope, Mr. Chambers, that you will agree with me, after you have read this letter.

Yours sincerely,
Gelett Burgess

P.S. As to Chap. XXV, Page 9, your reader is right. The name should be Gannet, not Steever.

* * *

Chambers to Burgess, 15 September 1933

My dear Mr. Burgess:

Thank you cordially for your fine and considerate letter of the 3rd. We count ourselves fortunate that we are to publish so unusual and striking a book as THE STRANGE WEEK. Indeed I wish that we might sit down together and talk it over. At this distance all that we can hope and expect is to lay our suggestions before you and have you give them your friendly thought. You have done this and of course we must accept your view as to each point and we do this in the best grace in the world.

We, too, have been delighted with your achievement in answering the prayer of Mr. J. B. Priestly and others for a murder story that approaches in its construction, characterization and atmosphere what is expected of a true novel. The criticism as to length which we offer gently would apply to it as a novel and not particularly to its mystery aspect. I am grateful that in going over the proofs you will keep in mind the possibility of cutting here and there.

Our criticism of the title was inspired by a notion that it is somewhat conventional and reminiscent. There have been a number of book names of this sort. I do not mean to suggest that we ought to adopt a distinctly mystery name. If a title could be found that more directly suggests the psychological experiences of the teller of the tale, a title somewhat more out of the common and more distinctly applicable to the peculiar story, I think it would be a gain. I have nothing at the moment to suggest. If you are wedded to the STRANGE WEEK we shall accept it without further challenge. But perhaps by the time we are ready to make the plates you will think of something better.

To me it would seem that what you gain by way of distinguishing your characters you lose in plausibility by the strain of seeking out such unfamiliar combinations in their names. It is a point which has come up with a number of other books in the past where readers have reported an impression of a loss in the sense of illusion. Jane Swan is not one of the names that have struck us as too eccentric. I see no reason for changing it. Poits and Festril might, I think be changed to advantage and I shall await your definite instructions. You can depend upon our proof readers to get such changes straight in the script before it goes to the printer. And if they overlook them occasionally, to catch them in the proofs.

As for the initials, J. S., let us change Jane Swan to Edna Fish or whatever you wish and let the others stand. It strains credulity to find so many people all at once with the same initials and any reduction in the number would be a gain.

If Gannett used an undercut it should stand. We shall make the correction on Page 9, Chapter 25.

With kindest regards, I am

Sincerely yours,
[D. Laurance Chambers]

Lord David Cecil (1902–1986)

See also the Cecil entry in *DLB 155: Twentieth-Century British Literary Biographers.*

Lord David Cecil came from a distinguished family whose fortunes were founded in Elizabethan times. Bobbs-Merrill was the American publisher for several of his books. Written with literary flair, his biographies–notably of William Cowper, Lord Melbourne, and Max Beerbohm–are famous for their style and depth and for conveying the spirit of the ages in which the subjects lived. A marginal Bloomsbury figure, Cecil's biographical technique is sometimes compared to that of Lytton Strachey, but Cecil was the more accurate of the two. As a critic he was better at appreciation than theory, specializing in eighteenth- and nineteenth-century English literature, and he was also an expert anthologist. Cecil's Hardy the Novelist: An Essay in Criticism *(1943) was crucial in the history of that author's reputation. In 1949 Cecil became the first Goldsmith Professor of English Language and Literature at New College, Oxford.*

BOBBS-MERRILL BOOKS BY CECIL: *The Stricken Deer; or, The Life of Cowper* (Indianapolis: Bobbs-Merrill, 1930; **first edition,** London: Constable, 1929);

Early Victorian Novelists: Essays in Revaluation (Indianapolis: Bobbs-Merrill, 1935; **first edition,** London: Constable, 1934);

The Young Melbourne and the Story of His Marriage with Caroline Lamb (Indianapolis: Bobbs-Merrill, 1939; **first edition,** London: Constable, 1939);

Hardy the Novelist: An Essay in Criticism (Indianapolis: Bobbs-Merrill, 1946; **first edition,** London: Constable, 1943);

Two Quiet Lives: Dorothy Osborne, Thomas Gray (Indianapolis: Bobbs-Merrill, 1948; **first edition,** London: Constable, 1948);

Melbourne (Indianapolis: Bobbs-Merrill, 1954)–comprises *The Young Melbourne and the Story of His Marriage with Caroline Lamb* and *Lord M.; or, The Later Life of Lord Melbourne* (**first edition,** London: Constable, 1954);

The Fine Art of Reading, and Other Literary Studies (Indianapolis: Bobbs-Merrill, 1957; **first edition,** London: Constable, 1957).

Portrait of Lord David Cecil by Augustus John, circa 1943 (Collection of the Marquess of Salisbury, Hatfield House; from David Cecil, The Cecils of Hatfield House, *1973)*

Bobbs-Merrill Biographical Questionnaire

MELBOURNE
FALL, 1954

Name: Lord David Cecil
Date of birth: April 9th, 1902
Place of birth: London
Present address: New College, Oxford
Married to whom: Rachel MacCarthy, daughter of Sir Desmond MacCarthy.

Winner of the Hawthornden Prize

for the best piece of imaginative prose or verse by a British author under forty-one years of age

"Rarely beautiful . . . a great book"

—Stanley Baldwin

Promotional piece, with a quotation from the British prime minister, for Cecil's 1929 biography of William Cowper, published in America by Bobbs-Merrill as The Stricken Deer; or, The Life of Cowper *in 1930 (courtesy of The Lilly Library, Indiana University, Bloomington, Indiana)*

Children: 2 boys, one girl.
Notable ancestors or members of family:

Viscount Melbourne, first Prime Minister of Queen Victoria (great, great, great uncle)
Lord Burleigh, chief minister of Queen Elizabeth I
Robert, Earl of Salisbury, chief minister of James I
Robert, 3rd Marquess of Salisbury, Prime Minister of Queen Victoria

Living Members
Viscount Cecil of Chelwood, statesman (uncle)
Robert, 5th Marquess of Salisbury, President of the Council in the present Government (brother)

Education: Eton
Christ Church, Oxford

Occupation other than writing:

Goldsmith Professor of English Language and Literature in the University of Oxford.

Books or articles previously published:

Biographies: The Stricken Deer or The Life of Cowper
Two Quiet Lives (the lives of Dorothy Osborne and Thomas Gray)

Criticism: Early Victorian Novelists
Hardy the Novelist

Clubs, fraternities, organizations: Poets and Storytellers

My aim in writing this book is to give a picture of a very remarkable and attractive personality. Melbourne is a wonderful subject for a biographer. Not only was he a leading figure alike in the politics and social life of his time; not only was he the man who introduced Queen Victoria to public life; but he was himself a man of distinguished intellect, fascinating manners, and one of the most delightful talkers that England can ever have produced. By a stroke of luck much of his talk has been recorded for us in detail by various of his contemporaries, more particularly by the Queen herself. By assembling this mass of scattered information together it should be possible to recreate his figure far more vividly and intimately than is generally possible with most men who have been dead for more than a hundred years. To do this has been my aim. I have been all the more attracted to this subject by the fact that Melbourne in addition to being brilliant and delightful was also original, independent and odd. No character has more to attract the student of human nature. I seem always to have known about him because he was a relation of whom many stories were told to me by my mother; but it was not till I began to investigate the subject that I discovered how rich a mine I was exploring. I have had the good fortune to be allowed to see many documents never seen before, particularly those in the archives at Windsor Castle; with the result that I have been able to give a more detailed account of his relation to the Queen than previous historians.

Melbourne is, I think, of particular interest today because he is a typical example of one age who survived into another very different one. We who live in a time of transition can enter into his predicament.

* * *

Related Letter

At the time of this letter, D. Laurance Chambers was chairman of the board and editor in chief of the trade department; Walter J. Hurley was production and advertising manager in the New York office. Ross and Hiram are Ross G. Baker, sales manager, and Hiram Haydn, editor. E. B. White's The Second Tree from the Corner *was published by Harper in 1954.*

D. Laurance Chambers to Walter J. Hurley, 2 April 1954

Dear Walter:

This immensely fine work presents a problem and a challenge. How to make the most of it?

Fifteen years ago we published The Young Melbourne with a small type page, following roughly Constable's format in England. 60,000 words.

The sale was by no means equal to the critical acclaim. (We sold 13,648 and the Fiction Book Club distributed 17,477.) The book lingered in the minds of certain readers as a classic. I expect you and others in the New York staff have heard them mention it with admiration through the years.

When we published The Young Melbourne in 1939, Constable expected that we and they would follow it with Lord Melbourne in 1940.

Then the war broke out and Lord David Cecil could not get access to the libraries in the great Whig houses which were closed for the duration. When the war ended he was engaged in other literary tasks.

The plan of publication contemplated in the contract of February 28, 1939, called for 2 volumes to be issued successively and also as a set when the second volume was published; we might, if we wished, issue the two combined in one volume a year after the publication of Lord Melbourne.

Now, after 15 years, we have the manuscript of the second volume, the rest of the biography. It is more than half again longer than The Young Melbourne–94,300 words.

The question is: how has the lapse of time affected the plan of publication?

We may dismiss from our minds the idea of publishing Lord Melbourne with the same type page as The Young Melbourne. It would look obviously padded and require an incongruously high retail price.

What are the other alternatives?

1. We might give Lord Melbourne its own type page, different from that of The Young Melbourne and appropriate to its greater length. Price would be based on cost. (We have not yet received the subjects for illustrations. There were 8 in The Young Melbourne; perhaps there will be 12 for Lord Melbourne.) We would hope to sell off our stock of The Young Melbourne (500 bound; 1800 sheets–all carried at no value.) Presumably the price of Lord Melbourne would be considerably higher than that of The Young Melbourne.

Under this plan, we would have as a boxed set two volumes of strikingly different appearance. It seems far from ideal publishing.

2. When we determine on the type page of Lord Melbourne we could reset The Young Melbourne in the same format. It would make a smallish book and its separate price would be different from its longer companion. (How about bulking?) We would hold the present stock of The Young Melbourne for later remainder sales. The present plates could be melted; they are carried on the books at a valuation of $11.20. The last chapter of The Young Melbourne would be largely duplicated in the Prologue of Lord Melbourne.

Is this ideal?

3. We could seek permission from Constable (which would involve getting Lord David Cecil's permission too) to issue the whole work in one volume now instead of waiting for a year. The argument for this is strong.

It is all one homogeneous literary composition, one biography, all in the same distinguished style. The full impact of Lord Melbourne cannot be felt unless The Young Melbourne is in lively recollection. Readers should be invited and given every opportunity to read the life through from beginning to end. It executes the author's original plan.

He says in a prefatory note to Lord Melbourne:

> "This book was originally intended to form part of a single volume covering the whole course of Melbourne's life, and divided into three sections. The first, extending from childhood into middle life, was to describe the formation of his character; the second was to give an analysis, illustrated by reference both to his earlier and subsequent history, of this character when set into its final form; and the third was to tell how this character exhibited itself in action during his later years. Owing to various untoward circumstances, it was not possible to carry out

this plan to its intended conclusion, and the first and second sections appeared in a single volume. When, some years afterwards, I returned to my task, I found it impossible to make clear my interpretation of Melbourne's later history without recourse to the analysis of his character which concluded the first book. Merely to recapitulate it in different words seemed a futile waste of effort. I have therefore taken the liberty to include a section of the final chapter of The Young Melbourne in the Prologue to the present volume."

We would call the combined one-volume work simply Melbourne (like Guedalla's Palmerston) if approved by the author.

It would be divided into the three sections mentioned by Lord David: Section I, The Young Melbourne; Section II, The Finished Product (this is the slightly rewritten last chapter of The Young Melbourne, made over as the Prologue of Lord Melbourne and would be used once only in its final form, avoiding duplication); Section III, Lord Melbourne. One new prefatory note for the entire work, to be written by the author, one list of Chief Events, one index. (There are now two of each.)

We have been figuring on various type pages for this single-volume publication simply as suggestions for your consideration. It is estimated at 147,000 words (the difference between the combined count of The Young Melbourne and Lord Melbourne being accounted for by the dropping of the last chapter of The Young Melbourne.)

Set in 11-pt Baskerville, 3-pt lead, 24 picas wide, 32 lines, 503 pages.

Set in 11-pt Baskerville, 2-pt lead, 24 picas wide, 34 lines, 475 pages.

Set in 10-pt Electra, 4-pt lead, 24 picas wide, 32 lines, 455 pages. This is the type page of The Second Tree from the Corner. With a 3-pt lead and adding 2 more lines, 431 pages.

Won't you please get out your pencil and do some budgeting?

Price?

Against this plan, it may be urged that present owners or old readers of The Young Melbourne would object to being forced to buy what they already possess or are familiar with. How serious is this objection after 15 years, considering the vagrant habits of Americans and the way their libraries get scattered about? How good are memories after half a generation?

There are two copies at the Indianapolis Public Library; the last date of borrowing was in 1951. The copy in the Indiana State Library has not been borrowed since 1941.

At any rate we would put prospective purchasers on notice by stating clearly on the jacket that the volume includes The Young Melbourne.

We presume Constable plan to follow the original scheme of separate publication of Lord Melbourne but we have not been advised.

A big club, we suppose, would be interested only in a one-volume work. If there is anything pertinent still left in its name it is hard to see how the Book-of-the-Month Club could fail to find Melbourne the book of whatever month it is published in. But of course there is no accounting for judges.

Whatever we do should be elegantly done. That seems the one best word to describe the literary work. It is what the author and his art product deserve.

Will you and Ross and Hiram please go into a huddle and then one of you phone me your advice? We should act promptly when we are agreed on the course we'd like to pursue.

Faithfully yours,
[D. Laurance Chambers]

Crown 8vo would be favored over full 8vo.

Title page for the "immensely fine work" shepherded by D. Laurance Chambers, the 1954 volume that combined The Young Melbourne *(1939) with* Lord M.; or, The Later Life of Lord Melbourne, *first published in England in 1954 (O'Neill Library, Boston College)*

Anne Chamberlain (1917–1988)

Born and educated in Ohio, Anne Chamberlain worked on newspapers in West Virginia and taught creative writing at Marietta (Ohio) College and Parkersburg (West Virginia) Community College. She also contributed to such magazines as The Saturday Evening Post *and* The New York Times Book Review. *Chamberlain wrote just three novels, which she classified as "psychological suspense," and all of them were published by Bobbs-Merrill. From 1939 to 1959 she was married to Clyde E. Brown.*

BOBBS-MERRILL BOOKS BY CHAMBERLAIN: *The Tall Dark Man* (Indianapolis: Bobbs-Merrill, 1955; London: Hart-Davis, 1955);

The Soldier Room (Indianapolis: Bobbs-Merrill, 1956; London: Hart-Davis, 1956);

The Darkest Bough (Indianapolis: Bobbs-Merrill, 1958; London: Hart-Davis, 1959).

Anne Chamberlain (photo by Ellis Studios; courtesy of The Lilly Library, Indiana University, Bloomington, Indiana)

Related Letters

Herman Ziegner was a Bobbs-Merrill editor. This letter was copied to Ross G. Baker, sales manager, and Hiram Haydn, editor in the New York office.

Herman Ziegner to Anne Chamberlain, 19 November 1954

Dear Mrs. Brown:

Within a few days galleys of your book will be coming along and they'll have, as I promised you, a few queries. Meanwhile, we thought you might like to see the title page, the half title and the type page of your book. We think it's very attractive, and of course we hope you will too.

Before the galleys come, you may want to consider the single question which would demand much reflection. Two or three of our readers (and I was among them) confessed to a curious feeling of frustration at the very end of the story they extravagantly admire. It was as if there should have been one or two more pages to turn that would answer questions seemingly left unanswered. Perhaps we wanted to hear the sirens in the street and know that the murderer's capture was imminent. That would be a complete resolution of the immediate drama and would eliminate the slightly disturbing thought that the murderer was still abroad and (though it would be unlikely) still able to endanger Sarah.

But, most of all we wanted a complete resolution of Sarah's other drama. She begins to work toward emotional safety when she makes her stepfather the image of love and security. There is left behind her still the terrible (yet sometimes longed-for) figure of the tall, dark man. At the end of the book she is safe, forgiven, restored to reality. Yet in her mind (and the reader's) the tall, dark man and her father have been possibly identical. Can she be–tomorrow and the next day–really secure until she knows the truth or until she has decided in her mind that there is no identity?

Let me assure you that we do understand and appreciate the symbolical value of the tall, dark man and it may very well be that you prefer to leave the story exactly as it is. We raise the question only for your consideration and only because it's a part of our obligation to report as honestly as we can the reactions of our readers. In any case the adjustment (if you agreed to make it) would involve only a few lines. Whatever you decide to do, you have written a beautiful book, and–for one of the few times in a long blurb-writing career I can say the word truthfully–an enthralling one. It's a privilege to publish it, and we can promise you that we'll work very hard in its interest.

Cordially,
[Herman Ziegner]

* * *

Chamberlain to Ziegner, 22 November 1954

Dear Mr. Ziegner:

Thank you for your splendid letter of Nov. 19th. The title page, the half title and the type page are beautiful. In design and typography, they capture the very spirit of the book. They far surpass anything that I had dared to hope for.

Before I forget: It is not too late (I certainly hope not) to dedicate the novel "To Dud Chamberlain"? I had thought there would be a longer and more formal time before it went to press. And I still haven't the faintest idea when these suggestions should be made. "Dud" is my father, getting along a bit in years now, and the man most responsible for my early literary training.

And: Did Hiram Haydn pass on to you my request that an extra set of proofs be pulled for an author friend of mine, who has watched over my writing since childhood? If such should be too inconvenient or expensive, of course she will understand.

Now for the serious question: Should I add a few more definitive lines to the finish? I appreciate the sympathetic reaction of the readers, and am particularly moved that you all understand so well what I tried to do. I can answer promptly because the same question occurred so often while at work on the book. In fact, I wrote several versions of the ending, one of them including the wail of sirens and a more positive conclusion.

I arrived at this seemingly foreshortened ending by slow and painful degrees. The final arrival was, however, an illumination for me. I did not want to solve, forever, the problem of the tall, dark man. Forever he must lurk in Sarah's life, as indeed he lurks in the lives of all of us. Police sirens do not eliminate him. Discovering for sure that he was not her actual father would not banish him. The tall, dark man, symbol of death and negation, of all in mankind that tends toward self-destruction, toward denial of life, is ever with us. Ever with Sarah, hovering in the outer darkness. She has found not a whole faith (who finds it at her age–or ever?) but a gleam of faith, a strength and a lightness, a will to go on, to love and be loved. That does not abolish the hovering darkness. For that must be ever with us, and we are in constant combat with this shadow. I intended to leave the readers slightly frustrated. Frustration is more honest than complete triumph. Complete triumph does not exist in this world, except in moments of rare emotion, and it should not exist in art. By leaving a question, I feel, most dedicatedly, that I am leaving more answers. There is really not much chance that this particular figure will bother Sarah again. But he or his counterpart will return and return, the ever present challenge, the black grief which is a part of man's and woman's heritage. Next time, though, she will be stronger in her battle. I think, in the long run, she will win out. And when, in the end, she must meet this person face to face, she will be the victor and will emerge into radiant light.

I hope the above does not read too temperamentally. But you will understand that I have thought and fought this question through, and so feel strongly about it. Will not that lurking question have, in the end, more impact than a definitive, detailed finish? Well, who knows? I only hope so.

Meanwhile, my heartfelt thanks for your kind words about the novel. I loved it when I was writing it, and I wrote it over and over without submitting it. At the time I hadn't the faintest idea if anybody would understand what I was attempting. It is, needless to say, most rewarding that people do. Now I'm even crazier about my next novel, already in progress.

It is good to work with you and with Bobbs-Merrill!

Cordially,
Anne Chamberlain Brown

* * *

Ziegner to Chamberlain, 29 November 1954

Dear Anne:

I venture the use of the first name because we should and will be friends and because even now it seems curiously stiff and foolish to be so formal.

Of course it's not too late for the dedication, which will be made as you instruct. And we haven't forgotten the galleys for your friend; they'll be ready in a couple of days.

Well, it's been a long time, really, since I've read so cogent and persuasive a letter as yours. It has to be as you wish. The tall dark man must remain free for the moment and perhaps forever, the actual and immediate fused with the symbolic in his

Advertising proof exploiting the success of Chamberlain's first novel, published in 1955 (courtesy of The Lilly Library, Indiana University, Bloomington, Indiana)

figure. Yet because we covet so much for your book we are still not content with what you very aptly describe as a "foreshortened" ending. Give me one moment more, and I'll forever hold my peace.

Five of us in this office have now read The Tall Dark Man with unanimous enthusiasm and the fostering of high hopes, not only for this book but for your future as a novelist. All of these readers—and they are very acute—felt (as I reported to you) a let-down feeling at the end. Tremendous tension had been built up. It demanded release. It was not released. Hence a sense of frustration.

But—and here is the really important thing—every one of these readers lost that feeling when he had read your letter. The boldness and truth, the dramatic force in your explicit account of the nature of the tall dark man who walks behind Sarah and each of us—this lifts the novel to an even higher level, this makes the ending as you have it strong, commanding, thrilling.

Can you—should you—disclose directly to the reader what you gave us in your letter, perhaps using (briefly) the thoughts and/or words of Rowland Ruth and Sarah's own intuitions? We'd hope you would at least try it out on your typewriter, remembering that five good readers failed to derive all they should have from those last few pages. It's my own conviction that being a little more explicit—only a little more—would not destroy effect but, rather elevate and enhance it.

The rest of the galleys go to you today. And thank you for listening and considering patiently.

Cordially,
[Herman Ziegner]

P.S. Can't you one day come to see us here? We'd like that very much.

* * *

Ziegner to Hiram Haydn, 4 December 1954

The Tall Dark Man

Dear Hi:

It was a fine talk with Anne Brown, who loves us all. The book stands as is. I read her a blurb rough which she likes and which will (I think) take care of a part of what I see as the problem. Details tomorrow.

Cordially,
[Herman Ziegner]

* * *

Ziegner to Ross G. Baker, 15 December 1954

The Tall Dark Man

Dear Ross:

I have just come back from putting Anne Chamberlain Brown on the train. It's been a long time since I have been more impressed with an author as a person. This girl has fine intelligence and a real integrity. She served a long apprenticeship, writing books that she did not intend to publish and for which she has refused publication even when it was offered. She feels that she knows now what she wants to say and how she wants to say it. She convinces me. I think we will have many very fine novels from her, and all this makes us doubly glad that her visit here was a really happy experience. She told me as I left her that she was now completely convinced that we were the publishers for her.

Cordially,
[Herman Ziegner]

George Randolph Chester (1869–1924)

See also the Chester entry in *DLB 78: American Short-Story Writers, 1880–1910.*

George Randolph Chester was perhaps born in Indiana, but the matter is obscure, and his writing career was spent elsewhere. He became a newspaperman after various other jobs and in that capacity developed his tale-telling abilities. Finding that he could invent as well as report, he began publishing fiction in 1905 and then devoted himself to it full-time. Stories in such magazines as Collier's, Cosmopolitan, *and* The Saturday Evening Post *brought Chester great popularity and wealth. His most popular creation was J. R. Wallingford, "an American business buccaneer," who appeared in a series of books. Chester's well-regarded business stories were noted for the accuracy of their satirical portraits. In a short career, his output was prodigious.*

BOBBS-MERRILL BOOKS BY CHESTER: *Get-Rich-Quick Wallingford: A Cheerful Account of the Rise and Fall of an American Business Buccaneer* (Indianapolis: Bobbs-Merrill, 1908; London: Richards, 1908);

The Making of Bobby Burnit (Indianapolis: Bobbs-Merrill, 1909);

The Cash Intrigue: A Fantastic Melodrama of Modern Finance (Indianapolis: Bobbs-Merrill, 1909);

George Randolph Chester (Bruccoli Clark Layman Archives)

GET-RICH-QUICK WALLINGFORD

A CHEERFUL ACCOUNT OF THE RISE AND FALL OF AN AMERICAN BUSINESS BUCCANEER

BY

GEORGE RANDOLPH CHESTER

INDIANAPOLIS
THE BOBBS-MERRILL COMPANY
PUBLISHERS

Title page for Chester's best-selling 1908 story collection (Bruccoli Clark Layman Archives)

The Early Bird: A Business Man's Love Story (Indianapolis: Bobbs-Merrill, 1910);
Young Wallingford (Indianapolis: Bobbs-Merrill, 1910);
Five Thousand an Hour: How Johnny Gamble Won the Heiress (Indianapolis: Bobbs-Merrill, 1912);
The Jingo (Indianapolis: Bobbs-Merrill, 1912);
Wallingford and Blackie Daw (Indianapolis: Bobbs-Merrill, 1913);
Wallingford in His Prime (Indianapolis: Bobbs-Merrill, 1913);
A Tale of Red Roses (Indianapolis: Bobbs-Merrill, 1914).

Related Letters

George H. Lorimer was editor of The Saturday Evening Post *and author of* Letters from a Self-Made Merchant to His Son *(1901). William C. Bobbs was president of Bobbs-Merrill at this time.*

George Randolph Chester to William C. Bobbs, 21 June 1909

My dear Mr. Bobbs:

In looking over my press clippings I see that you have sent out a notice that the BURNIT book was similar in some respects to the LETTERS OF A SELF-MADE MERCHANT TO HIS SON. This has been used by several papers, and one paper, the Rochester New York Advertiser, in its issue of Saturday June 12th, alludes to me as the author of that celebrated bundle of wisdom. I cannot imagine that this will please my friend Lorimer, if he becomes advised of it, as doubtless he will.

The notices that I have received so far run very favorable. I hope the advance sales have been equally so.

Yours cordially,
Chester

* * *

Chester to Bobbs, 15 July 1909

My dear Mr. Bobbs:

I have received a very pleasant letter from Mr. Lorimer which I enclose herewith, and which you will kindly return to me after reading. Clippings still come in misinterpreting your advance notice and giving me credit for THE LETTERS OF A SELF-MADE MERCHANT. All joking aside, I do not like this. I do not feel at all comfortable under it and I do not want the slightest bit of credit–either direct or implied–for anything which I have not done myself. Whether I accomplish much or little, I want distinctly to stand upon my own efforts. BOBBY BURNIT was not even an imitation of the LETTERS OF A SELF-MADE MERCHANT, and was not–even sub-consciously, I am sure–inspired by that excellent work of Lorimer's. Don't you think your publicity man had better get busy with a general denial, which would once more bring to public attention the names of Lorimer, THE SELF-MADE MERCHANT, the Saturday Evening Post, the Bobbs Merrill Company, BOBBY BURNIT and George Randolph Chester. It seems to me several lines of print might be secured on this, hurting nobody and helping everybody.

Yours cordially,
Chester

P.S.–<u>WHEN DO I GET THOSE BOOKS</u>!!! *[three hands drawn pointing to this postscript]*

* * *

George H. Lorimer to Chester, 13 July 1909

My dear Chester:

I received your note of the 23rd. while I was in Colorado, and I asked Collins, who left before I did, to send you a line of acknowledgement, and to say that I hadn't the slightest feeling about the mix up in our identity. I'd be proud if I had written Bobby Burnit, and you, too, should feel a thrill at the thought of having written the Merchant Letters. At the same time, if anybody in the office of Bobbs Merrill and Company has been getting gay–I know that this couldn't be with the consent of those in authority–I think he ought to be called down on general principles, because I may write a book sooner or latter [*sic*] that you would not care to be mixed up with.

I need not say that I was greatly disappointed when I found that no more stories in the series had been received from you during my absence, and I think you will agree with me that we have been getting a little the worst of it this Spring.

Yours very truly,
George H. Lorimer

* * *

Bobbs to Chester, 19 July 1909

Dear Mr. Chester:-

Your very good letters of the 15th together with the letter from Mr. Lorimer of the 13th are all on my desk on my return to the office this morning and I am glad to have them.

Perhaps I answered you a little flippantly when you first called my attention to the confusion of the authorship of Bobby Burnit and the Letters of a Self Made Merchant, because it seemed to me then a more or less isolated exception of the stupidity of the book reviewer. Now that the mistake has been repeated, I want to say to you most emphatically that no one in this organization at any time ever made the slightest attempt to create this confusion or gave out any statement or interview or information that we believed at the time was capable of creating the confusion. It is not our method of doing business; and even if it were, it would be extremely bad policy in this instance.

We shall certainly take immediate steps to correct the mistaken impression.

In regard to the Altemus Company and the contract for Wallingford, your information is com-

THE JINGO

BY
GEORGE RANDOLPH CHESTER

Author of
YOUNG WALLINGFORD, THE MAKING OF BOBBY BURNIT
FIVE THOUSAND AN HOUR, ETC.

With Illustrations By
F. VAUX WILSON

INDIANAPOLIS
THE BOBBS-MERRILL COMPANY
PUBLISHERS

Frontispiece and title page for Chester's 1912 novel, from the 1978 Arno Press facsimile edition (Thomas Cooper Library, University of South Carolina)

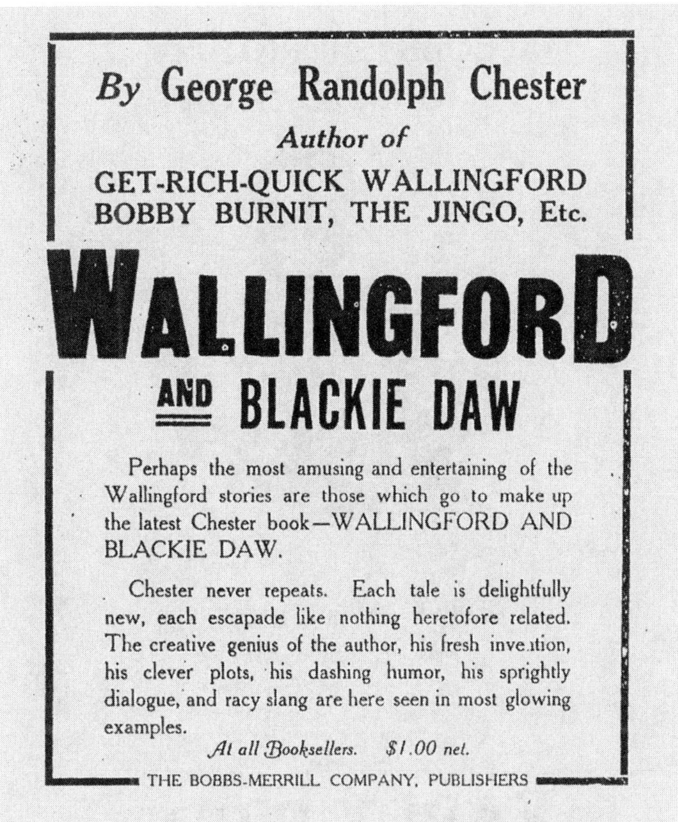
By George Randolph Chester
Author of
GET-RICH-QUICK WALLINGFORD
BOBBY BURNIT, THE JINGO, Etc.

WALLINGFORD AND BLACKIE DAW

Perhaps the most amusing and entertaining of the Wallingford stories are those which go to make up the latest Chester book—WALLINGFORD AND BLACKIE DAW.

Chester never repeats. Each tale is delightfully new, each escapade like nothing heretofore related. The creative genius of the author, his fresh inve.ition, his clever plots, his dashing humor, his sprightly dialogue, and racy slang are here seen in most glowing examples.

At all Booksellers. $1.00 net.

THE BOBBS-MERRILL COMPANY, PUBLISHERS

Flier for the last Bobbs-Merrill book in the Wallingford series, published in 1913 (courtesy of The Lilly Library, Indiana University, Bloomington, Indiana)

plete and satisfactory and we will proceed with that negotiation immediately.

Yours very truly,
[William C. Bobbs]

* * *

Reviews: *The Cash Intrigue* (1909) and *Young Wallingford* (1910)

"The Cash Intrigue," (the Bobbs-Merrill Company,) by George Randolph Chester, author of "The Making of Bobby Burnit," is the most daringly lurid vision of what might result from the combination of unlimited wealth and unlimited ambition that any of the busy young authors of the modern and American picaresque novels has yet indulged in. The author describes it in the sub-title with commendable modesty of statement as "a fantastic melodrama of modern finance." It tells how an enormously rich man, who bears much resemblance to Mr. Rockefeller, drains the country of its currency by demanding cash payments for the bread of whose baking and distribution he has gained a complete monopoly, and locks up gradually millions of money in his vaults. Then he enters into a combination with a young man as greedy for power as he is for wealth, and together they bring about a ghastly state of affairs.

—"Recent Stories of Clever Rogues," *New York Times,* 20 November 1909, p. 721

* * *

"Young Wallingford" (Bobbs-Merrill, $1.50), by George Randolph Chester, is the delightfully cynical story of a good-natured but open-eyed scamp. Wallingford isn't unusual; he likes to spend money, but has no special aptitude for hard work. He knows all the get-rich-quick schemes, and he knows the law. In real life the majority of those who get "touched" are duped through their own cupidity. Wallingford remains something of a hero, because he dupes only those who deserve to be overreached and "touches" them only in the act of overreaching others. The book is a very good guide to Flimflamia and its suburbs.

—*New York Times,* 2 April 1911, p. 186

A BOBBY BURNIT KIND OF STORY

A.W.B.

By GEORGE RANDOLPH CHESTER

Author of BOBBY BURNIT
THE CASH INTRIGUE

THE EARLY BIRD

An ingenious, amiable, blithe, brisk, breezy book, with emphasis on the two practical aims in life: getting on in the world and finding the right person to get on with. The reader's interest is caught up and carried lightly, rapidly forward from incident to incident in a most agreeable fashion with surprises at every turn. Sam Turner, the hero, is a sudden kind of chap, and this story of his exceedingly energetic vacation is irresistible.

Pictures by ARTHUR WILLIAM BROWN. $1.50 Retail

A LIBERAL DISCOUNT TO THE TRADE

The Bobbs-Merrill Company
Indianapolis, Indiana
Please send via__________

__________copies of

THE EARLY BIRD
By GEORGE RANDOLPH CHESTER
At $1.50 Retail

Name__________
Address__________
Date__________

Order form for one of Chester's 1910 books (courtesy of The Lilly Library, Indiana University, Bloomington, Indiana)

Irvin S. Cobb (1876–1944)

See also the Cobb entries in *DLB 11: American Humorists, 1800–1950; DLB 25: American Newspaper Journalists, 1901–1925;* and *DLB 86: American Short-Story Writers, 1910–1945, First Series.*

A man of parts, the Kentucky humorist Irvin S. Cobb even acted in movies. As a public performer and the author of sixty books and three hundred stories, he had the same stature that Mark Twain enjoyed in an earlier generation, although few would compare the two today. In his time, however, Cobb was one of the highest-paid American writers. His best-known creation was Judge Priest, who began his career in The Saturday Evening Post *stories that were first collected in* Back Home *(Doran, 1912). The judge lived in a world of Southern stereotypes, although Cobb's aim was to defend the South. The wise jurist made his first appearance as an amateur detective in a 1936 magazine story. Cobb's best-selling autobiography,* Exit Laughing *(1941), was written in two months when he thought he was dying. He was the brother-in-law of Hewitt H. Howland, until 1925 the Bobbs-Merrill trade-department editor and afterward a literary agent.*

BOBBS-MERRILL BOOKS BY COBB: *Murder Day by Day* (Indianapolis: Bobbs-Merrill, 1933);

Faith, Hope and Charity (Indianapolis: Bobbs-Merrill, 1934);

Judge Priest Turns Detective (Indianapolis: Bobbs-Merrill, 1937);

Exit Laughing (Indianapolis: Bobbs-Merrill, 1941);

Glory, Glory, Hallelujah! (Indianapolis: Bobbs-Merrill, 1941);

Roll Call (Indianapolis: Bobbs-Merrill, 1942).

Irvin S. Cobb (Bruccoli Clark Layman Archives)

Reader's Report

Elisabeth Yager submitted a report on the Cobb manuscript that was published as Murder Day by Day *(1933).*

<u>CRITICAL REPORT ON IRVIN S. COBB'S "BLOOD MONEY"</u>

Gilbert Redd tells us the story, as it unfolds under his eyes, of the search for the murderer of his unsavory half-brother Uncas Cresap, found dead of a gaping wound in his forehead in a room which also held the dead body of Wong Gee, Cresap's Chinese servant, dead apparently of heart failure or apoplexy. Redd was the first called to the scene of the crime, and hastened from the grisly room to reassure Florence Dane, his niece and Cresap's, and the light of Redd's eyes. Under suspicion in the household besides the beautiful Florence, were the cook, chauffeur, outside man, two maids, and the unplesant [*sic*] Cresap's unpleasant croney [*sic*], Sabino, a dwarf of mixed blood. Suspicion first falls on Florence and her fiance, who had come east on her urgency, to try to keep Cresap from cutting Florence out of his will if they married. The fact that the fiance, Thorpe, had been missing ever since the discovery of the crime, made him the logical suspect. Meanwhile Captain Bray, detective and old friend of Redd's in the latter's newspaper days, followed all clues, finding the usual number of persons who quarrelled with the deceased and admitted hating him, including Redd, the town sot, and an Italian rum-runner who was working with Cresap but split with him when Cresap proposed also to run in opium. Discovery that Thorpe had been hurt in a hold-up and in a hospital at the time of the crime, sent Bray looking for new trails, which the dwarf Sabino promptly supplied by blackmailing Florence Dane. When the girl went to the Canadian border to buy him off, Bray acted; arrested her and brought her back to New York in handcuffs. Redd went to meet her, and his heart torn by his darling's plight, secured Bray's promise not to use any third-degree methods in questioning her until he, Redd, had had one night in which to find Sabino. Then Redd, knowing what the reader might have suspected but doesn't, that Sabino is dead in a dog's coffin in a pet cemetery where Redd himself interred him,–Redd then goes home, finishes this manuscript, makes his will and sends a bullet through his own head, as a newspaper clipping attached to his manuscript confirms. So the reader learns in the last chapter that it was Redd who killed Cresap to end his ugly attentions to their niece Florence; also that Wong Gee didnt [*sic*] die of apoplexy, but suffered a mild heart attack when he came upon the scene just after Redd had slain Cresap, which Redd promptly helped along by slinging the Chinese up by the heels till dead, a device he grateful [*sic*] acknowledges reading in "The Omnibus of Crime"! Sabino, suspecting Redd, searched his cottage late at night for evidence, and Redd coming soundlessly upon him, strangled him to death and substituted his body for the corpse of the old dog he had arranged to bury next day!

The idea of having the narrator prove to be the murderer is not absolutely new, but is so rarely used that it is unlooked for, and so Cobb succeeds in keeping the reader guessing right to the end. Unfortunately using this device means that some of the major action–the death of Sabino notably–must be kept back from the reader, and therefore we really dont [*sic*] get our just allotment of gore and thrill and tension. When you analyze the action chapter by chapter there really is not enough. Aside from the introduction of the village sot–and I am inclined to think he takes up more time and attention than he is worth to the reader–the only action is the tracing of Th[o]rpe (whom the reader never sees and therefore isn't so much excited about) and the tracing of the bootleggers which comes to nothing, and finally Sabino's nocturnal visits to the cottage and threats against Florence. The action is all described second-hand in conversation very much cumbered by colloquial dialect; Sabino's sleuthing is the only thing described first hand that has any great tension involved.

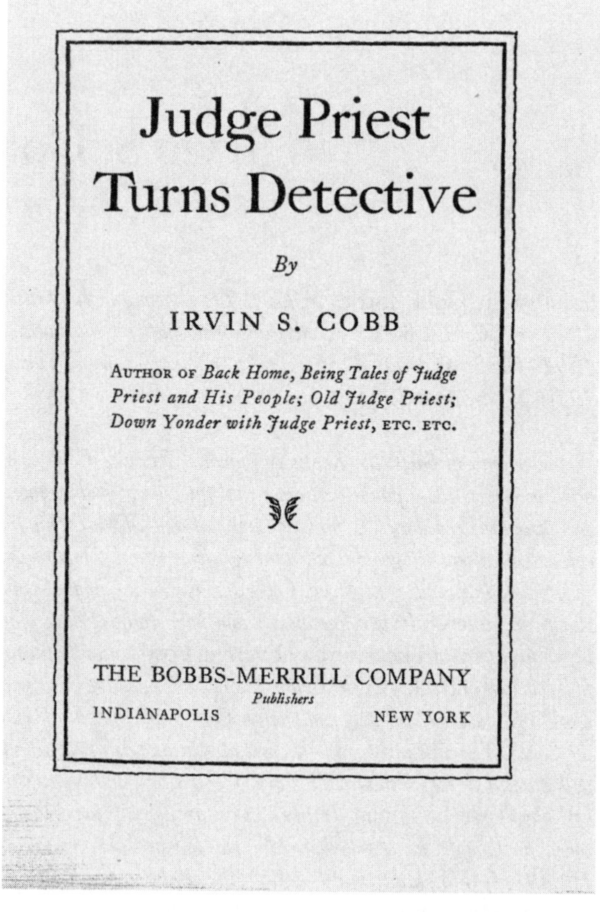
Judge Priest Turns Detective

By

IRVIN S. COBB

AUTHOR OF *Back Home, Being Tales of Judge Priest and His People; Old Judge Priest; Down Yonder with Judge Priest,* ETC. ETC.

THE BOBBS-MERRILL COMPANY
Publishers
INDIANAPOLIS NEW YORK

Title page for Cobb's 1937 story collection (courtesy of The Lilly Library, Indiana University, Bloomington, Indiana)

Moreover, the characters, introduced as they are when our attention has already been focussed on sleuthing out the murderer, do not get the reader's sympathy. Redd, Florence and Thorpe, especially and perhaps Hilda as well, should get the reader's loyal support, if there is to be any real suspense when they are in turn suspected. The author's penchant for sketching quaint characters, reproducing their dialect and mannerisms, is not so well adapted to a mystery story where the fans want a story that marches steadily from the first chapter and lots of suspense and thrills. These chapters even when they come to a climax are apt to go on with several calmer paragraphs to reduce the effect of the suspense.

My suggestion to overcome these two major difficulties is to do quite a bit of revising. As the book

ack

185 Madison Ave.
Mrs Josephine Reynolds

BOBBS-MERRILL AUTHORS' QUESTIONNAIRE

This is our own "Who's Who and Why," because the regular "Who's Who" is most inadequate. The questionnaire when you fill it out is almost invaluable to the publicity department in preparing special news stories about your books, your life and your favorite breakfast food.

Please sign on the dotted lines and return to THE BOBBS-MERRILL COMPANY, INDIANAPOLIS, INDIANA, U. S. A.

*****

Name and pseudonym: Irvin S. Cobb

Date of birth: June 23, 1876

Place of birth: Paducah, Ky

Present address: 830 Park Avenue, N.Y. City

Notable ancestors or members of family:

Descendant of Thomas Chittenden, first governor of Vermont, and Linah Mimms, acting governor of Virginia; nephew of Major Robert Cobb, distinguished Confederate artillery officer; father of Elisabeth Cobb, novelist.

Education:

Common schools until 16. No high school or college training

First attempt at writing:

At 15

List of books, plays, etc.:

See Who's Who in America

Bobbs-Merrill questionnaire filled out by Cobb (courtesy of The Lilly Library, Indiana University, Bloomington, Indiana)

- 2 -

Stories and articles in following magazines:

Practically all the first class ones — probably that's what ails 'em now.

Single or married to whom:

Married to Laura Spencer Baker at Savannah, Ga.,

Children:

One - Elisabeth Cobb Brody.

Occupation other than writing:

Radio - lectures -

Personal experiences I consider remarkable or unusual:

Being born

Idiosyncracies, if any:

Scores of them

Personal preferences:

For the out-o-doors and wholesome people and cornbread without sugar in it

Personal dislikes:

People who get up fool questionaires

Superstitions:

Plenty, having been reared in the South

My aim in life:

To keep on living awhile and while so doing to mix work with play - but not too much work.

The vocation I was advised to follow:

Sketch artist or lawyer or actor. I started out in life to try to draw pictures; my people thought I should follow the law; I have had ~~numerous offers~~ several chances to go on the stage.

-3-

World War service. Army, Navy, Red Cross, etc.:

Served as War Correspondent for Saturday Evening Post.. Colonel on the staffs of three governors, Major, O.R.C., U.S. Army.

Clubs, fraternities, sororities, organizations, etc.:

Lambs - Players - Lotos - Elks - Southern Society in New York, Kentucky Society in New York, French Legion of Honor.

Hobbies, collections, etc.:

I collect Indian relics and trophies,

Favorite outdoor sports:

Hunting - fishing - camping

Favorite indoor sport:

Thinking about hunting and fishing and camping

Favorite book and why:

Huckleberry Finn (I) Treasure Island (II) Book of Job (III)

Favorite author and why:

Kipling - because he is my favorite

How I happened to write that book:

I needed the money

Any other information not particularly specified:

None

Irvin S. Cobb

stands, it would have to sell on the author's reputation, and would not make him a reputation for mystery stories. But there is here the making of a fine murder story if a little more pains and a little more understanding of the mystery reader's needs are applied. I suggest writing a new first chapter–or a new chapter one and two–to precede the present ones, introducing us to the queer Cresap household before the murder, enlisting our sympathies (directly, instead of through Redd) in the cause of Florence and Gregory [Thorpe] and in Redd for backing them so loyally; perhaps also giving us a chance to dislike Cresap and the Chink and to distrust and fear Sabino. Let Redd have his conference with Cresap; perhaps overhear part of what followed. Keep from the reader the other events of the night. Then take up the story where the author now begins it, with the finding of the corpses, and you'll have your reader on his toes, worried about Gregory–whose disappearance would really get us worked up this way–distressed for Florence, loyal to the interests of Redd. In addition, I'd advise cutting out chapter 5 completely, and very completely rewriting chapter 19 which doesn't hold the interest at all. Then it seems to me the dialogue needs very steady pruning. The action is hampered by so many talky characters–Redd goes into his own mental processes too much, Bray–especially when he goes Hibernian–is very talky, and the housekeeper and outside man are the same variety. The result is pages of dialogue which produce only very minor points of evidence. Chapters which would be improved by less talk and more action are 3, 4, 9, 12, 13, 15, 17, and 18.

It seems to me the author's attention should be drawn to the necessity of building up more support for his plot by involving the sympathies of the reader. As the book stands, the reader is only a by-stander, hearing descriptions of developments which he gets second and third hand, involving characters in whose plight he has too little information to be concerned. It is necessary to keep from him Redd's part in the fatal scene certainly, but important to enlist him otherwise in what is being done.

Elisabeth Yager *[name struck out by hand]*

* * *

Related Letters

Joseph Medill Patterson, whose family was connected to the Chicago Tribune, *created the New York* Daily News *in 1919. At the time of this letter, D. Laurance Chambers was vice president and trade-department editor of Bobbs-Merrill.*

D. Laurance Chambers to Irvin S. Cobb, 9 February 1933

My dear Mr. Cobb:

It is delightful of you to have put so promptly the amending touches to the manuscript of BLOOD MONEY. They seem just right. The comments from Redd and Florence at the end give a nice and a different effect. I hope this feature may be reserved for the book and not used in the serial. [*Cobb's note:* "It will be!"] We always like to have some new point to talk about. And I feel sure that the elimination of the bust, accomplished so neatly, will help. [*Cobb's note:* "I'm glad!"]

I am going to have our reader who is such a shark with mystery stories see if she can discover any loose ends. If there are any, she'll find them. But I don't think there are any to be found.

I must tell you again how proud and happy we are to number you in our family of authors, and how eager we are to start publishing for you. [*Cobb's note:* "Thank you!"] Armed with the letter which you have so kindly obtained from Colonel Patterson, I hope Hewitt will be able to persuade the Tribune people to give us a very early release. And I hope you'll be planning other stories for us–stories of that home scene which you have made so distinctively your own.

Sincerely yours,
D. L. Chambers

[*Cobb's note:* "Yours Sincerely
Irvin S Cobb"]

* * *

Cobb to Chambers, 17 June 1933?

For Mr. Chambers' consideration–Immediate!

Suggested alternative titles
for
BLOOD MONEY
viz:

IN COLD BLOOD
MURDER AT KETTLE POND
WILFUL AND PREMEDITATED
HERE'S MURDER FOR YOU
MURDER AT THE MELTING POT
HERE'S CRIME
BLOODIED MONEY
MURDER AND THEN WHAT?
BY VIOLENT MEANS
THE KILLER OF KETTLE POND
YELLOW FOR GOLD AND RED FOR BLOOD
BLOOD ON THESE DOLLARS

MURDER BY ROTE
I'LL TELL YOU NO LIES
THERE'S BLOOD ON THESE DOLLARS
THE BETTER DEAD CLUB
MURDER DAY BY DAY
IN THE MIDST OF LIFE

Respectfully submitted,
Irvin S. Cobb
P.S.–Now you think of one.
C.
BLOOD GUILT [*Possibly in another hand*]

* * *

Unsigned letter (from Chambers?) to Cobb, 19 June 1933

Dear Mr. Cobb:

We do not find that MURDER DAY BY DAY has been previously used. We are going ahead with it, and think it's fine. I suppose you will make sure that the Chicago Tribune uses it too.

Thanks awfully for the questionnaire. [. . .]

* * *

Review: *Murder Day by Day*

As might be expected, Mr. Cobb's first attempt at a full length mystery novel is distinctly worth while. The scene is somewhere toward the eastern end of Long Island, and many of the characters are natives, for the action of the story takes place in the Fall, after the Summer residents have returned to their Winter haunts. Uncas Cresap, a thoroughly despicable old man, is found dead in a room over his boathouse, and near by is the body of his Chinese servant. There is no mark on the Chinese, but Cresap's head has been split with an axe or some such weapon. The narrator is Gilbert Reed, Cresap's stepbrother, who is a retired newspaper man, and who records in his notebook the events of each day, beginning with the discovery of the murder. The sleuth, Patrick Bray, is a retired New York policeman, who has tried his hand at chicken farming but found it so lacking in excitement that he has set up as a private detective. There is no attempt on the part of the author to portray Bray as a superman. He is a good detective, better than the average sleuth in real life, but by no means infallible. While the experienced reader of detective fiction may find no great difficulty in guessing the identity of the murderer, he will still find enough drama in the story to keep him interested to the end. The book has its humorous episodes, presented in Mr. Cobb's best vein, but they are handled with restraint and are never overdone.

–"New Mystery Stories," *New York Times Book Review,* 22 October 1933, p. 23

* * *

Reader's Report

In 1940 Anne Ross reported on Cobb's autobiographical manuscript that was published as Exit Laughing *(1941).*

Critical Report COBB AUTOBIOGRAPHY

I did enjoy this manuscript immensely. It is long even in this unfinished state–but I could read much more of it. And also, I must here admit, less of it too. For instance, I thought the first chapter, the justification for the autobiography, pretty wordy, pretty far-fetched, and pretty dull. I don't see any need for it at all. There is no other material that I remember that I think should be cut out so ruthlessly, but there is a deal of rambling around and store-barrel philosophizing that doesn't amount to much and that certainly could be condensed–"briefened" as Mr. Cobb would say. Isn't it a horrid word? That's another thing. It is astonishing that a man who can write–sometimes–so well, does write so often so ill. I suppose a lot of the mistakes in spelling and proper names (such as ambassador Gerard being called Girard and the town Scituate in Massachusetts called situate) are just typographical errors on the part of his secretary, but there are enough slips in geography–such as calling Jacksonville instead of Danville Joe Cannon's home town–and so forth to make one suspect the manuscript should be very carefully checked. It should also be very carefully edited, for the constructions, grammatical I mean, are frequently something awful! I suppose I should not take the liberty of making such a suggestion, but it does seem as if Mr. Howland would be an ideal person to edit these memoirs without taking any of the meat out of them and straighten out the English with[out] mutilating their casual, Southern, rambling charm.

But as is, they do ramble too much for this reader, I must say. It's pure exasperating to be jumped around all over the world and all over forty years the way he jumps us and just as we're getting really interested in one phase of his experience to be torn ruthlessly away from it and plumped into something entirely different. I just can't see why it's necessary and why the author can't be fairly chronological; not exactly, that isn't necessary but enough not to confuse the reader, I do think we can ask that much.

Oh, and I said I didn't know of anything but the first chapter that needed drastic cutting, but I take that back. I do think a blue pencil would help a lot all thru the chapters about his ancestors. They were some of them right interesting characters, but most of them were much more interesting to him than to any one outside his family.

And if only instead of raving on about being a descendant and all this and that he would tell us more, more, more about his newspaper friends–about Frank O'Malley and Mr. Dooley and all the rest, and more about his experiences as a reporter, and more about his war corresponding–I suppose a lot of this has been covered in previous books and that's why there isn't more in this one; but I wish there were. If I've read the previous books I've forgotten them.

And here is a point that seems to me very important. At the end of every chapter are foot-notes. Now foot-notes are a nuisance even when they are a necessity, and even more of a nuisance when they are not necessary at all. Nobody likes them, Mr. Cobb, nobody! In a book that is almost purely to be read for its entertainment value, why annoy your readers with them? All the stuff that's worth incorporating into the body of the book should be so dealt with and if there are any notes not worth so much, let them be discarded.

Let me say again I have enjoyed this book very much and look forward eagerly to reading the rest of it.

But oh, how I wish he would not say man-child and soldier-man and briefened!

And I should like to pick a little quarrel with him over fried pies which he says is a Northern term. I beg to state I am a Northerner and never heard of fried pies till I married into a Kentucky family which has been in Kentucky longer than his'n; and as a mother of a direct descendant of Daniel Boone, himself, Mr. Cobb, let me state that that descendant's grandmother and great-grandmother, both born in Paducah, have said fried pies all their natural lives–and still say fried pies.

Anne Ross *[name struck out by hand]*

* * *

Related Letters

Howland wrote to Chambers, now president as well as trade-department editor, on the letterhead of the Jacques Chambrun agency.

Hewitt H. Howland to Chambers, 14 August 1940

Dear Lawrence [*sic*]:

I have expressed you the first 28 chapters of I.S.C.'s life story.

Having had some discussion with him as to the method of procedure and having won my point, I feel I must keep my word as to a prompt decision on your part. You will keep the wheels turning, won't you?

Irvin says there will be probably 12 more chapters–a rather long book. He'd prefer it done in one volume, but will yield if you think two better.

Yours in haste,
Hewitt

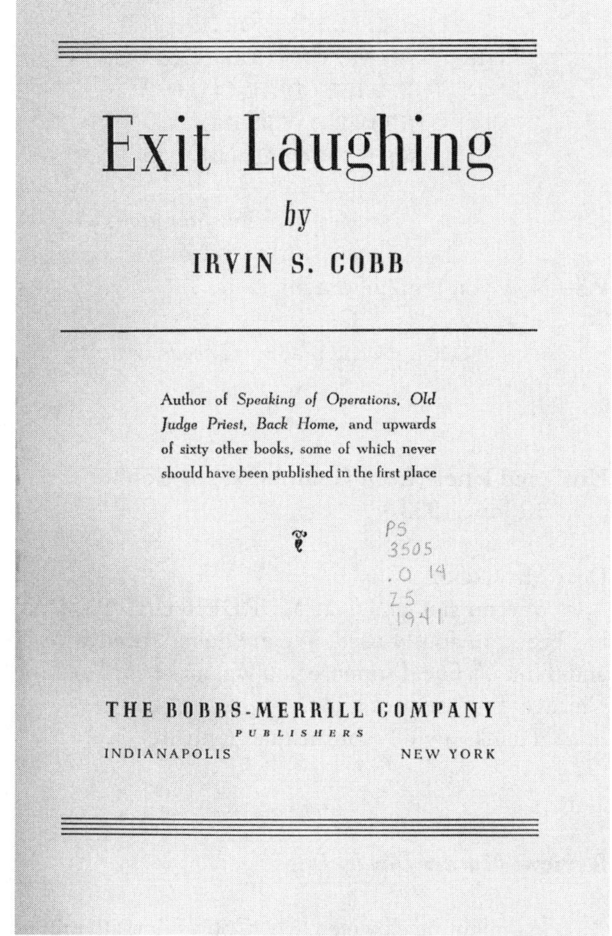

Exit Laughing

by

IRVIN S. COBB

Author of *Speaking of Operations, Old Judge Priest, Back Home*, and upwards of sixty other books, some of which never should have been published in the first place

THE BOBBS-MERRILL COMPANY

PUBLISHERS

INDIANAPOLIS NEW YORK

Title page for Cobb's best-selling 1941 autobiography (Thomas Cooper Library, University of South Carolina)

* * *

Chambers to Howland, 17 August 1940

Dear Hewitt:–

Many thanks for your letter of the 14th.

We shall work just as fast as we possibly can on Mr. Cobb's life story. It is a big book, and it is not possible to treat it casually, or to form an off-hand opinion.

Decidedly I would prefer one long volume to two.

Ever yours,
[D. Laurance Chambers]

THE BOBBS-MERRILL COMPANY

PUBLISHERS  INDIANAPOLIS

CALLING ALL EDITORS - CALLING ALL REVIEWERS!

The green spot above means something important for you. It is a "get ready to go" signal. It means that on or about the 17th of February (just a month before publication) you will receive a bulky green-wrapped package.

Watch for it! Open it at once! Then clear your desk of all other matters for you will find inside the most entertaining, the most delightful, the most superb life story of a great American you have ever read. It is:

EXIT LAUGHING
By Irvin S. Cobb

We've warned you! So stand by. Watch for the green package.

THE BOBBS-MERRILL COMPANY.

Promotional item for Cobb's autobiography (courtesy of The Lilly Library, Indiana University, Bloomington, Indiana)

[Handwritten:] I hear it's grand–some parts better than others, as is natural–but very badly typed with many mistakes in names. There's no doubt about our wanting it.

* * *

Howland to Chambers, 23 August 1940

Dear Lawrence [*sic*]:

I am delighted to have your acceptance of Irvin's autobiography, with the reader's reports for "my eye" only. I have read them with great interest and some apprehension. As you know, Irvin is not disposed, for some strange reason, to listen to suggestions for changes or cuttings. He made it a condition of acceptance that the manuscript as delivered should be the manuscript published–no cuttings, no changes. You understood this, I know. Of course mis-spellings and mis-statements of facts would have to be corrected, but unless his attitude has changed–which is most unlikely–I couldn't suggest myself for any editorial work. In fact I couldn't in any case suggest myself, and feel it would be a mistake for you to offer me up on the editorial altar. What do you say to letting this phase of the situation stand until you have the complete manuscript? Then you can weigh the criticisms and suggestions, pick out the most vital, and write him that you understood the manuscript was to be accepted as submitted and that you had done so gladly and enthusiastically. But as his publisher you felt it a duty to put before him, etc. etc. believing that the changes would add to the book's acclaim, its popularity, its sales and its financial returns. How does this idea strike you? If by good fortune he should consent and consent to your doing it, then you could have the very intelligent and understanding writer of the reports do the gentle job of editing. Let's think it over.

Yours faithfully,
Hewitt

P. S. I have telegraphed Irvin of your enthusiastic acceptance. I think we'd better have a separate contract. Thank you.

H

* * *

Chambers to Howland, 26 August 1940

Dear Hewitt:–

Many thanks for your letter of the 23rd. I don't think you had explained to me before, had you, how strictly averse Mr. Cobb is to any changes in his autobiography? At any rate I understand it now and quite agree with you that the course you propose is the one to take. Is there any possibility of his coming East, so that we might talk things over with him? That is always so much easier than writing letters, and so much less likely to exacerbate an author.

I'll get up a contract ri[g]ht away and send it on to you. I suppose it's all right to use the title EXIT LAUGHINGLY, and to give the retail price as approximately $5.00, though I hope we shall be able to work down the length and get the price lower than that.

Faithfully yours,
[D. Laurance Chambers]

P.S. Here's the contract in duplicate, signed, with an extra copy for your reference. D.L.C.w

"THERE are some veterans who think that the streaming across-the-page headline came in with Yellow Journalism. But when I was in my teens I remember how an ordinarily staid Southern newspaper was moved under emotional enthusiasm to break column rules. I forget now whether it was a Louisville newspaper or a Memphis newspaper. Ben Butler, most hateful to Southerners of all Union generals, having passed on, this paper came out with this screamer: 'Praise God from Whom All Blessings Flow, the Beast Is Dead!'" —*from Irvin S. Cobb's autobiography,* EXIT LAUGHING.

The publishers of a great book by a great reporter take this opportunity to salute a great newspaper.

THE BOBBS-MERRILL COMPANY
Established 1838
INDIANAPOLIS & NEW YORK

Proof of an advertisement for Cobb's autobiography (courtesy of The Lilly Library, Indiana University, Bloomington, Indiana)

Hamilton Cochran (1898–1977)

Hamilton Cochran's primary career was in business, working in sales, marketing, and advertising for a wax-paper company, Standard Oil, and The Saturday Evening Post, *among others. During the 1930s he was commissioner of public welfare for St. Thomas in the Virgin Islands, where he gathered material used in* Captain Ebony *(1943). As his titles for Bobbs-Merrill indicate, Cochran's avocation was sailing, and he served in the Coast Guard during both world wars. Along with novels and historical studies, he wrote poems and magazine articles.*

BOBBS-MERRILL BOOKS BY COCHRAN: *Windward Passage* (Indianapolis: Bobbs-Merrill, 1942; London: Jarrolds, 1946);
Captain Ebony (Indianapolis: Bobbs-Merrill, 1943);
Silver Shoals (Indianapolis: Bobbs-Merrill, 1945);
Blockade Runners of the Confederacy (Indianapolis: Bobbs-Merrill, 1958);
The Dram Tree (Indianapolis: Bobbs-Merrill, 1961);
Freebooters of the Red Sea (Indianapolis: Bobbs-Merrill, 1965).

Hamilton Cochran (courtesy of The Lilly Library, Indiana University, Bloomington, Indiana)

Reader's Report

The following is an unsigned report, circa 1942, on Cochran's Windward Passage.

WINDWARD PASSAGE

The title of the book does not seem particularly appropriate or even as exciting as the book deserves. The first minor action is the only reference to the Windward Passage until Morgan is sent away as a prisoner, when another reference is dragged in rather obviously. Moreover, I find myself confusing it with the Westward Passage of several years ago.

The novel possesses both narrative and dramatic interest and the buccaneer activity furnishes an excellent background for the thwarted romance in the foreground. As for the historical background–the main outlines are all right, but I suspect that the author lacks a very sure grasp of his period. He seems shaky on details and properties of his settings, and his language lacks an authentic flavor. I don't know where the line comes between reasonable and pedantic objections, but the dialogue fails to convey to me any sense of the period. I'm not begging for archaisms, but I think this dialogue depends too much on modern usage and connotations. The narrative is, however, so absorbing that most readers would probably forgive the anachronisms.

The character of Judith puzzles me. She seems rather 19th-century in her reactions, attitudes, morals, and speech, and is vaguely reminiscent of Scarlett O'Hara. I think she is at her best when she is seen and not heard, particularly when she is being coy and clinging for Modyford. The angle of Brokenrood and Judith is not very clearly handled. Is his estimate of her character supposed to be accepted by the reader? And what justifies his first outburst against her–just masculine intuition? The end of the story suggests that Brokenrood really understood her–that she suffers punishment for her sins. But I really can't decide what the author wants the reader to think of her.

Otherwise I think the characterization is good. Morgan, especially, seems well conceived and developed, and Modyford is entirely adequate. Brokenrood is also convincing as the snake in the grass, though the transition from dutiful quartermaster to misanthropic plotter is a little abrupt. Glimpses of the buccaneers and the King are interesting. The author makes good romantic drama of his story, which is clear, interesting and very readable. I think J.D.'s suggestions of inserting flashbacks in Book V would strengthen the story.

* * *

Related Letter

Despite president and trade-department editor D. Laurance Chambers's reservations, and after another decade of work on the book, Bobbs-Merrill published Cochran's The Dram Tree *in 1961.*

D. Laurance Chambers to Cochran, 18 May 1950

My dear Hamilton Cochran:

My interest in THE DRAM TREE during the three years you have been working on it could hardly have been greater if I had been a collaborator with you. I encouraged you to embark on a novel on a grand scale. I know how absorbed in it you have been and how high are your hopes for it–a devotion which I have admired and a hope which I have shared.

Nevertheless I must give you my impressions and conclusions in all honesty, for that is the part of friendship. To be sure they were not eccentric, I had two experienced members of our staff read the manuscript carefully–and quite independently–and give me their advice.

It is not necessary for me to say that you have studied carefully everything that will give THE DRAM TREE authenticity–local scenes, tradition and custom, the economic structure of the slave states, the political situation, the growth of the Confederate Navy, the plans of fortifications, the details of battles, etc., etc.

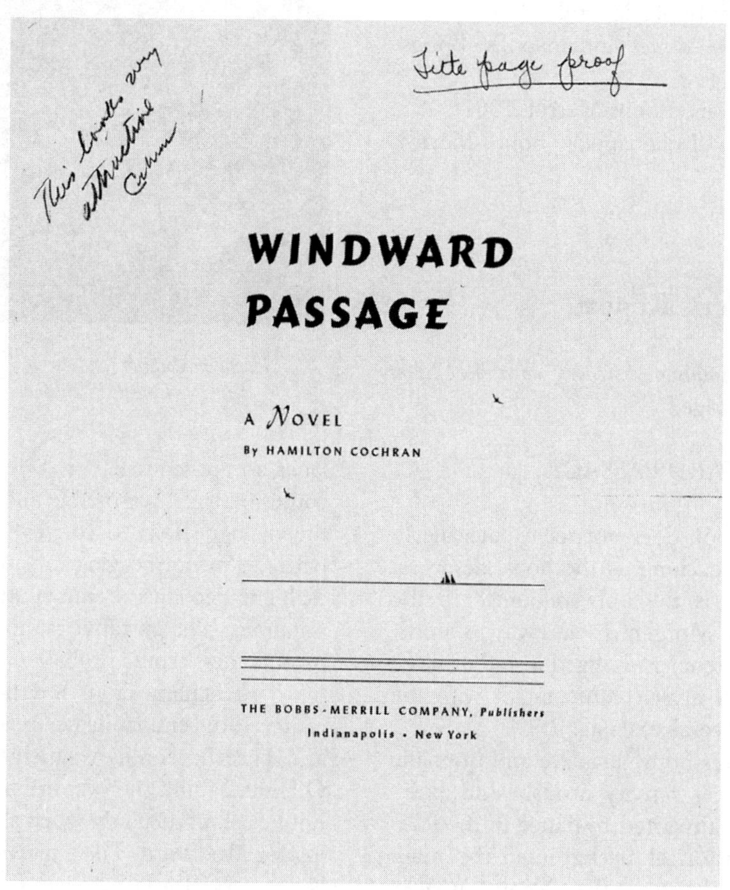

Title page proof

This looks very attractive Cochran

WINDWARD PASSAGE

A NOVEL

By HAMILTON COCHRAN

THE BOBBS-MERRILL COMPANY, Publishers

Indianapolis • New York

Proof for the title page of Cochran's first Bobbs-Merrill novel, published in 1942 (courtesy of The Lilly Library, Indiana University, Bloomington, Indiana)

WINDWARD PASSAGE

As the stormy seventeenth century drew to a climax, a Welsh farm lad who had once been sold into West Indies slavery became the scourge of the Spanish Main. In 1671, Henry Morgan led his buccaneer horde to attack Spain's golden New World city, Panama. Against this dramatic backdrop Hamilton Cochran has set a tempestuous love story, a lusty tale of human hope and conflict, fitting to that volcanic era when the destiny of the Western Hemisphere hung in the balance as England and Spain fought for dominance in the "back yard of the world."

For both scene and character, Mr. Cochran has borrowed boldly from history, enriching fact with an amazing originality to create a rousing novel of a man spurred to reckless valor by a curious admixture of motive: greed of gold, desire for a beautiful and unscrupulous woman, and a patriotism that had been nearly stifled in his ruthless heart.

At this time, across a narrow kink of land joining two great continents, the vast wealth of the Andes streamed out of Panama to waiting galleons. From the brilliant twisted brain of a young English fugitive and buccaneer's quartermaster sprang a wild plan to seize this booty almost beyond reckoning and to break the power of Spain. The desperate wits of a girl condemned by Morgan to be hanged clutched that feverish dream and made her exquisite self the means to its achievement, forcing the one man capable of the *coup* to realize that with her aid it might be done.

But there were two things the lovely, scheming Judith failed to foresee: that the disciplined emotions of bitter, monk-like young Brokenrood would one day waken, and that her own slumbering ardors would stir to

(*Continued on back flap*)

(*Continued from front flap*)

the touch of a hot-blooded rogue. Nor did Henry Morgan, who had wenched from one pillaged Spanish port to the next, ever expect to find a woman whom he could want so much and distrust so greatly that he could scarcely tell love from hate.

Mr. Cochran's superb plot of passionate natures in clash is peopled with striking characters: strange Brokenrood with the face of a youth taking holy orders, yet with the dark genius to frame a devil's own revenge; beautiful Judith Lacy of the selfish heart that love turned piteously vulnerable; Sir Thomas Modyford, primping Governor of Jamaica, too palid a lover for Judith after Henry Morgan's violent arms; Morgan himself, blustering, uncouth but likable, triumphant over his traitors, ironically defeated by himself. Not only will these principals live in the memory, but also sly Charles II, "bawdy Nelly" Gwynn, and Morgan's men: the gaunt old Cockney Oakum; the gorilla-like Dyke, loyal as far as the thumbscrew's torment; the handsome young Galoon; the four deserters from jungle hardship who brought back to Port Royal a premature but fateful tale.

Each character plays his part to the hilt in Mr. Cochran's turbulent story that is briny with the tang of a lawless sea, and vivid with the warfare of a day long past as Henry Morgan's tatterdemalion Brothers of the Coast meet Spain's resplendent dragoons on Panama's savannas.

Windward Passage is a page from history vitalized to top-flight fiction standard — a narrative of high action, high emotion and high crisis centered about a strategically important strip of land to which the deeds of Henry Morgan drew the eyes of the seventeenth century, and upon which, sooner than we wish, the gaze of our own troubled times is turning.

Proof for the dust-jacket flaps of Cochran's 1942 novel (courtesy of The Lilly Library, Indiana University, Bloomington, Indiana)

The wealth of material led you to a grand conception. But with the grand conception has come a loss of focus. The social history impedes the storytelling. Perhaps to some degree it became overextended because of the promotional opportunities you saw in Wilmington and North Carolina generally. But it is an interference, we think, with the first necessity–making THE DRAM TREE interesting from the first word, increasingly interesting all the way, with a growing concern over what will happen to the persons of the story.

The chapters prior to Jeffrey's becoming a blockade-runner are devoted to the very deliberate development of character and situation. Action is subordinated to the close study of a large group of characters as they live while the Civil War impends and begins. Nearly a hundred thousand words are spent in this development. Yet the characters, it seems to us, remain too conventional types here; the situations are not strong enough to keep the reader engrossed. The plot is tenuous, the story element slight. The background swamps it. And the writing often has an old-fashioned tinge in conversation.

In, roughly, the second half of the book, action is very well done–you're always grandly at home on the sea–and the siege of Fort Fisher is a fine and unfamiliar climax, but character development and the conflict of

THE BOBBS-MERRILL COMPANY

PUBLISHERS  INDIANAPOLIS

5-16-42

-----------------:

It seems to us that in the trying months ahead a lot of people are going to want to find solace from the headaches of the war in tales of adventure. Such a story is WINDWARD PASSAGE by Hamilton Cochran, which we have sent you for review.

Against the dramatic backdrop of the Spanish Main during the seventeenth century, Mr. Cochran has set a tempestuous love story, a lusty tale of human hope and conflict. It is appropriate to that volcanic era when the destiny of the Western hemisphere hung in the balance.

We think you will find pure pleasure in reading it, and that perhaps many others who read your review will be led to seek it out. Your review can be released any time after May 18th.

Very truly yours,

THE BOBBS-MERRILL COMPANY

AHH:MH

A. H. Hepburn

Draft of a letter to accompany review copies of Windward Passage *(courtesy of The Lilly Library, Indiana University, Bloomington, Indiana)*

characters seem to stagnate. Here about the same space is devoted to several years as has been given previously to a comparatively few months, but account is not always taken of the effect on personality of the passage of time. The rare meetings of Jeffrey and Ellen resume as though they had been separated for only a few hours. The promising romantic rivalry with Arley Touville is dropped. Julie, by all odds the best of the women characters, is killed off long before the end. The feeling between Jeffrey and Llewelyn Morgan never comes to a head. Jeffrey's antagonism toward and enforced association with Edrick Courtney offer romantic possibilities, not realized.

But I should not attempt an analytic "bill of particulars" without being invited to do so. Long before this you are probably saying, "Chambers doesn't know what he's talking about. He's dead wrong." It would indeed ill become me to suggest that after you have already put in so many, many hours writing THE DRAM TREE you should devote many hours more to revising it. But that is what we think it would need for us to make good–a thorough revision in overall structure and in some detail, though much could be salvaged from the present script.

Nor is it my function to pretend to a literary criticism. The point is that on a commercial judgment we do not feel that we could assure you of a rewarding sale for THE DRAM TREE. It pains and disappoints me greatly to say this. I had counted on it to be a bright star in our fall line. It just doesn't seem, in our reckoning, to have the suspenseful interest to command a wide audience in a highly competitive market.

You have been loyal in your consideration of us and I am grateful. You will no doubt wish now to turn to another publisher, who may be enthusiastic over THE DRAM TREE and give you the fine service that in all fairness we cannot promise. We are old friends. I hate the idea of our parting company, but this should not for one minute stand in the way of your doing what is to your best interest.

Ever faithfully yours,
[D. Laurance Chambers]

Dust jacket for Cochran's 1958 historical work (Chapel Hill Rare Books)

James Oliver Curwood (1878–1927)

Owosso, Michigan, was James Oliver Curwood's birthplace and permanent residence, but he became famous for adventure stories based on his experiences in Alaska and northwest Canada. After success in placing articles and then with the publication of his first two novels by Bobbs-Merrill in 1908, he left the editorship of The Detroit News-Tribune *to write full-time. Also in 1908, the Canadian government paid Curwood to explore and write about undeveloped areas of the Northwest to attract tourists. In time he wrote thirty-three books, mostly about that region, and several of them were widely translated. His tales of Mounties and of heroic animals such as Kazan (part wolf, part husky) were especially well received. (While not a children's book,* Kazan *[1914] remained popular with boys for some time.) Looking for better sales, Curwood left Bobbs-Merrill to publish with Harper, Doubleday, and the Cosmopolitan Book Corporation.*

BOBBS-MERRILL BOOKS BY CURWOOD: *The Wolf Hunters,* illustrated by C. M. Relyea (Indianapolis: Bobbs-Merrill, 1908; London: Cassell, 1917);

The Courage of Captain Plum, illustrated by Frank E. Schoonover (Indianapolis: Bobbs-Merrill, 1908; London: Hodder & Stoughton, 1924);

The Gold Hunters, illustrated by Relyea (Indianapolis: Bobbs-Merrill, 1909);

The Danger Trail, illustrated by Charles Livingston Bull (Indianapolis: Bobbs-Merrill, 1910; London: Hodder & Stoughton, 1924);

The Honor of the Big Snows, illustrated by Bull (Indianapolis: Bobbs-Merrill, 1911); republished as *The Honour of the Big Snows* (London: Hodder & Stoughton, 1924);

Philip Steele of the Royal Northwest Mounted Police, illustrated by Gayle Hoskins (Indianapolis: Bobbs-Merrill, 1911; London: Everett, 1912);

Kazan, illustrated by Hoskins and Frank Hoffman (Indianapolis: Bobbs-Merrill, 1914; London: Cassell, 1914);

Falkner of the Inland Seas, edited by Dorothea A. Bryant (Indianapolis: Bobbs-Merrill, 1931).

James Oliver Curwood (from Stanley J. Kunitz and Howard Haycraft, eds., Twentieth Century Authors, *1942; Richland County Public Library)*

Review: *The Wolf Hunters* (1908)

Two young fellows, one white and the other half Indian, spend an exciting and a profitable Winter in the far northern wilderness in James Oliver Curwood's "The Wolf Hunters" (The Bobbs-Merrill Company.) The book is one unbroken series of adventures from the first chapter to the last–adventures with wild animals, especially with the packs of wolves which they are hunting for the bounty on their scalps, adventures while they are on exploration bent, adventures when they get lost, adventures with outlaw Indians, adventures when they get snowed in at camp. The book shows intimate acquaintance with the Canadian wilderness, enjoyment of its wintry wastes, and sympathy with the spirit of adventure.

–"Wolf Hunting in the North," *New York Times,* 19 December 1908, p. 783

* * *

Cover of Curwood's 1910 novel (Mainly Fiction, Auckland, New Zealand)

Related Letters

Hewitt H. Howland was trade-department editor at this time; John J. Curtis ran the New York office. Curwood was right about the promotion of Vaughan Kester's mystery-adventure The Prodigal Judge *(1911), which became a best-seller for Bobbs-Merrill.*

Curwood to Hewitt H. Howland, 10 March 1911

My dear Mr Howland:–

Your letter of the 9th came to me today, and I am writing to Mr. Curtis, in New York. Thank you for the suggestion.

I suppose that in your editorial work you have some unpleasant things come to you, as well as pleasant; a few knocks, as well as boosts; a few words written now and then, perhaps not too wisely, which reflect something besides hope, charity, and the other things. If I didn't know that you would take what I'm going to say as a gentleman, and feel, perhaps, that it comes from one, I'd tear this page up immediately. But as it is I'm going on, confident that you, as always, will come back with one of those big loads of cheer which you so delightfully contrive to get into a letter. To cut it short, a little bug is working in me–and I don't want to call it Dissatisfaction, and won't. But it stirs me up to write you, anyway. The Bobbs-Merrill Company has published five of my books, they have got them out in splendid style, and yet four of those books have fallen flat–have not been worth the writing. And what I fear just now is that my fifth, "The Honor of the Big Snows," is going the same way. I cannot fail to notice that new writers are coming into your fold almost every year, and that each year one or more of these new writers blooms forth as a success–as, for instance, the author of "The Prodigal Judge," which you are widely advertizing, and which will no doubt be a success. Why is it, I wonder, that I cannot write a book, after five attempts, that really makes a hit with the advertizing end of the business, and at least a small hit with the public? "The Honor of the Big Snows," in which I put my best work, and of which I had highest hopes, is, I am afraid, to be scarcely advertized at all; while books like the "Prodigal Judge"–first books, are pushed to the queen's taste. Tell me wherein I am wrong. Is it because the people do not want out-of-door stuff? Do they like a poodle-dog story better than a story of the North? If that is so, and you people know it, and FEEL it when you push your books, it would be charity to tell me, so that I may try the other end of the game.

I know that you will look at all this like a good Christian. You will remember that my Captain Plum went only 1700 copies, and that my two juveniles were worth nothing. The Danger Trail went better, but I've got an ambition that will never stop at a sale of 10,000 copies. If I thought that was my limit I'd go into the north again for the Government–back to my old job of making pamphlets and gathering material for maps. I want to write stuff that sells, or I don't want to write at all? Do you see anything that is not right in that? And, perhaps, might you not say the same when, after having had five books published by the same firm, you again see a new writer or writers boomed clean ahead of you? My book was published on the 4th, The Prodigal Judge on the 11th; yet in spite of that my book has had no advertizing, and the Prodigal Judge a bunch of it–so much that I already foresee its success, inasmuch as a book that you particularly boom must be a book which you judge the public wants.

Again let me ask you to read this with just as kindly feelings as you can, and assure you, a thousand times, that it isn't in the first degree an expression of dissatisfaction with my publishers; but merely the expression of facts which have, I am sorry to say, brought to me a certain degree of discouragement, for I had hoped that "The Honor of the Big Snows" would prove one of your 'big' books, and I have, perhaps without sufficient reason, brought myself to believe that it is NOT to be–for, if so, it

THE HONOR OF
THE BIG SNOWS

By

JAMES OLIVER CURWOOD

AUTHOR OF
THE DANGER TRAIL
THE COURAGE OF CAPTAIN PLUM

WITH ILLUSTRATIONS BY
CHARLES LIVINGSTON BULL

INDIANAPOLIS
THE BOBBS-MERRILL COMPANY
PUBLISHERS

Title page for Curwood's 1911 novel that he felt was not adequately promoted by his publisher (Ohio State University Library)

would be taking its place along with some of your other widely advertized books. And, after all, this all leads to one question: Am I on the wrong track? If not, it seems to be an endless road, for it brings me nowhere. Even if it was not my book, I'd say the Big Snows is one of the handsomest gotten up volumes that has come into my hands for a long time. I'm delighted with it–but it's the sales and the booming that counts; and when you flood the country with the advertisements of one or two books, doesn't the one NOT included have to suffer?

I feel that if I am wrong you will set me straight on this; and that whatever you say, it will be in a most friendly fashion.

I shall have the Philip Steele story down to you before the first. Am now on the last half of the story.

With all best wishes, I am,

fraternally yours,
James Oliver Curwood

* * *

All Around Magazine *became* Gunter's Magazine; *then, briefly,* The New Magazine *(1910–1911); and, after that,* New Story Magazine.

Howland to Curwood, 14 March 1911

My dear Curwood:–

Your letter of yesterday enclosing one from the editor of the New Magazine is before me. I had just heard from Mr. Halloran and was rather amused at his artful though apparent dodging. "I am sure it will be a successful book but–" etc. We are sending you the galley proofs as you request, although you must not think you have been imposing on us.

We have heard nothing from the Associated Sunday Magazines. I guess we had better investigate them.

Your longer letter of March tenth I have not answered because I wanted to show it first to Mr. Bobbs who has been out of town. He has just returned and as soon as I can have a talk with him I'll write you fully. I do want to say now, however, that I took all you had to say in the spirit that you would have me take it. You have always been most generous and loyal in your attitude toward us and the warm personal friendship that I have always felt for you would be weak indeed if it would not stand the strain of such a letter. I have an author here in town today and I shall probably not be able to write you at the earliest until tomorrow. In the meantime be assured of my understanding and of my abiding friendship.

As ever yours,
[Hewitt H. Howland]

THE NEW CALL OF THE WILD

KAZAN

KAZAN is a study in fundamentals, a bit of vibrant philosophy, and yet a very real dog. He is successful as a story-character because he is both real and absorbing. He embodies all the gentleness and the fidelity of the dog together with the ferocity and the keen instincts of the wolf. The two natures are woven together so cleverly there is no incongruity. If Ouida's Dog of Flanders has the more pathos, KAZAN participates in more adventure. Drama of vigorous, stirring sort is supplied here in abundant measure; the love of mate, of master, of offspring, are by turns the mainspring of action and again it is sheer love of life, or the needs of hunger. There are perils of storm, cold, famine, fire. There is a battle with a blizzard with the rim of the sky touching the earth a mile away. There are short respites in cabin or camp, long days on the trail.

By JAMES OLIVER CURWOOD

Author of The Danger Trail
The Honor of the Big Snows, Philip Steele, Etc.

The setting in such a story must needs play a large part but the life interest remains supreme. Kazan is as real, as sympathetic a personality as any man could be. Yet there is a careful avoidance of undue sentiment and a strict adherence to scientific fact. The loyalty he has inherited is deeply embedded in his nature and he is shown in the noble light of friend, protector and avenger of man. In the end his mate and the wolf blood triumph and he reverts wholly to the wild.

Strikingly Illustrated by GAYLE HOSKINS

Price $1.25 Net

Promotional item for Curwood's 1914 novel inviting comparison with Jack London's 1903 book The Call of the Wild *(courtesy of The Lilly Library, Indiana University, Bloomington, Indiana)*

Elmer Davis (1890–1958)

Elmer Davis began his distinguished journalistic career while still a schoolboy in his native Indiana. After reporting for The New York Times *for ten years, he turned to freelance writing, fiction and nonfiction, with several works published before he came to Bobbs-Merrill. He became nationally famous during World War II as a radio commentator, often working in tandem with overseas broadcaster Edward R. Murrow, and was named director of the government Office of War Information. In the 1950s he used broadcasting and writing to attack Senator Joseph McCarthy's extremism. The citation for his George Foster Peabody Radio Award in 1951 remarked on "the sanity, the horse sense, and the dry Hoosier wit with which Mr. Davis contemplates a troubled world."*

BOBBS-MERRILL BOOKS BY DAVIS: *Morals for Moderns* (Indianapolis: Bobbs-Merrill, 1930);
White Pants Willie (Indianapolis: Bobbs-Merrill, 1932);
Bare Living (Indianapolis: Bobbs-Merrill, 1933);
Love Among the Ruins: Little Novels of Hard Times (Indianapolis: Bobbs-Merrill, 1935);
Not to Mention the War (Indianapolis: Bobbs-Merrill, 1940);
But We Were Born Free (Indianapolis: Bobbs-Merrill, 1954; London: Deutsch, 1955);
Two Minutes Till Midnight (Indianapolis: Bobbs-Merrill, 1955);
By Elmer Davis, edited by Robert Lloyd Davis (Indianapolis: Bobbs-Merrill, 1964).

Elmer Davis (from Stanley J. Kunitz and Howard Haycraft, eds., Twentieth Century Authors, *1942; Thomas Cooper Library, University of South Carolina)*

Related Letters

Davis refers to Walter Lippmann's A Preface to Morals *(1929) in speaking of his first Bobbs-Merrill book. "Holt" is presumably the publisher Henry Holt, who died in 1926. Edwin Balmer was editor of* Red Book *magazine.*

Elmer Davis to Bobbs-Merrill, 18 April 1930

Sir–

Pending the commencement of operations on this novel, regarding which I have done no more as yet than to decide on certain things that aren't going into it, I offer you this thought (which I may have adumbrated the last time you were here)–why not a volume of short stories?

At which you tear your hair and emit a fiendish howl–"In God's name, why a volume of short stories?" Well–such a volume could be ready for October publication; there's no hope of a novel (unless, God forbid, I fail to sell the serial rights) before spring. It will be two years in October since I had a book on the market; and it seemed to me that any book might serve to remind booksellers and publishers of my existence and keep the market alive till a novel comes along.

I may be all mistaken in supposing that the customers are saying to themselves with increasing wonderment, "What has Davis been doing all this time?" But in case anyone has that innocent curiosity, we could satisfy them. I don't want to issue another novel unless it looks good, at least to the biased eye of the author; I let my customers down with GIANT KILLER and even if that was their fault more than mine I can't afford to do it twice in a row. So, while I try to cook up something good, we can give them this for a stopgap.

What the hell kind of stopgap would a volume of short stories be? you well may ask. Well, the point is it would suit that little group of wilful men, the old traditional Davis customers–the people who liked TIMES HAVE CHANGED and SWEENEY and so on. Not much humor in this collection, I fear, but that priceless gift seems to have deserted me so there probably won't be much in the next novel. But out of the last three or four years' output of short stories I could pick ten or twelve that are really good, and that I needn't be ashamed to offer to the people who used to like my novels. If you see any merit in this idea I'd send you a selection of about fifteen, perhaps with a couple of 25,000-word novelettes; out of which you could select a fair-sized bookful of what looks best.

As to sale, I had an idea which the astute Mr Holt thought might make the book sell as many as five or six thousand copies. There has been much argument of late about morals–the new modern rule book replacing the traditional precepts, etc. I do not aspire to the immense sale of Mr Lippmann's book, but there are some loose threads in the argument that Lippmann left out. To Lippmann's naive optimism it seems that a rationalist moral code would work itself, if people once accept it. I think it would probably work better than Christian principles; but there are going to be a lot of individual disasters in cases the new rule book doesn't quite cover.

These stories would all, or almost all, deal with such instances–case histories in modern morals. This could be pointed at in the title or subtitle (I'm afraid Lippmann could claim a cut in the royalties if we called it POSTSCRIPT TO MORALS) and emphasized by a fake quotation from some hypothetical philosopher, following the title page, which would serve as text to the sermon.

As to date, the core of this book would be a batch of short stories I have sold the Red Book, of which only one has been printed as yet. But barring a change in Balmer's schedule the last one will go into the November issue, on the stands October 12th. He would want a spread of two or three weeks after magazine publication, but you could issue the book early in November; or in October, at the sacrifice of one story. And, as I say, I don't see a novel before spring at best. How about it?

As always,
Elmer Davis

* * *

At this time D. Laurance Chambers was vice president and trade-department editor in chief.

D. Laurance Chambers to Davis, 21 April 1930

My dear Elmer Davis:

Generally speaking, yes, when an author approaches me bearing a collection of short stories in one hand and a cup of hemlock in the other, I take the hemlock. The agony is shorter. But you present the case so suavely, with such urbane charm, your reasoning is so lucid, your persuasion so gentle, that I find myself doing what most of us Hoosiers do when we get up against a city slicker who never wrote a story about old Ma Sweeney in his life, and I take the short stories, tickled to death to get 'em! Against my better judgment, if any, I am convinced that you have a swell idea in this collection of case histories. Delighted to do it for fall.

At the same time, however, you will of course allow me to cover my tracks with a firm, if hasty, asseveration that the said collection is not to be held against us. I had hoped to make our take off with a Davis novel that would give us a chance to show our best sales stuff–and you a chance to measure it. Well, you know the old trade prejudice against short stories; you know that mighty few collections go to the five or six thousand copies that the astute Mr. Holt predicts for this one. We shall do our derndest; more I can not say, and what more can an angel do? If we are able to get the sort of sale we'd like to have for our first Davis book, let the credit go where it is due (to the publisher, of course); if we're not, why, whose idea was this, anyhow?

I wonder if you couldn't get Balmer to agree to let us include the last story in the back and make publication October 27th? That's two weeks after the magazine is on the stands.

But first of all, will you get all the stories together right away, arrange them in the preferred order, and shoot 'em out to me? If there are some that don't fit into this case book, I wish you'd send 'em anyhow, novelettes and all, so that we may study them also.

Why wouldn't A POSTSCRIPT TO MORALS make a good subtitle for the book, if you think it looks too much like stealing Lippmann's thunder as a main title? Let me break down and confess here and now that there are two reasons why I don't take poison rather than another book of short stories, and one is that they are by Elmer Davis, and the other is that the book has a theme on which to hang 'em. I wonder it couldn't be emphasized as you put the stories together–perhaps by the use of half titles that would ring the changes on the idea, perhaps by the introduction of a paragraph at the beginning or end of a story, perhaps by a brief foreword. How about this?

Short stories or not, I am rejoiced beyond words that we are to have your name on our fall list. Blow, ye trumpets, sound, ye brasses! Three rousing cheers!

Yours ever,
[D. Laurance Chambers]

P.S. Can you get the material for the book into our hands by the first of May? I should like very much to have it then.

* * *

Davis to Chambers, 23 April 1930

Dear DLC–

It was warming, on this chilliest 23rd of April in the history of our Weather Bureau, to find that you didn't thumb down the idea of a short-story collection. Naturally I feel somewhat apologetic, as if you had asked for bread and I had given you a stone; but there is no bread as yet and maybe the stone is not wholly devoid of nutrition.

I can probably get the stuff to you by May 1st; all the stories have to be rewritten, of course (because I have only the magazine pages in my file) and I figure that while I am at it I had better drain the more obvious magazinishnesses out of them. There are seven or eight short stories that look good (to their author) and are all on this line; also a novelette and two or three other short stories that are not quite so good, but on the same line. . . Then there are other stories that are better, but could be called case histories in modern morals only by a considerable stretching of nouns and adjectives. Maybe I might send you a couple of those as alternate delegates, but I think that the closer we stick to this line of argument the better.

I'm afraid to use a Postscript to Morals even as a subtitle; it would look as if the dogs were trying to eat the crumbs that fell from the children's table. Don't you think "Case Histories in Modern Morals" would serve? As for the title itself, I'd thought of SPARROWS THAT FALL–not so good, maybe. (Too long.) We could always take a title from one of the stories, but none of them has such wide renown that it would have a pull in itself. However, there are two stories with titles that would fit the whole book–COUNT NO MAN HAPPY (the argument of Solon to Croesus that you can't be sure a man is happy till he is dead and nothing more can happen to him) and FREE SOIL, the point of which is that people who have got rid of their inhibitions and the inquisitive neighbors back home feel in New York like Eliza when she had crossed the ice and left the bloodhounds yapping on the Kentucky shore. But I surmise that before long Eliza discovered that even on free soil she was still a nigger. This, to my notion, is only about the third best story in the book; I suppose we ought to lead with the best one, and also with the title story if possible. But the two best are BACHELOR GIRL and AMATEUR, neither of which titles fits the volume at all; and FREE SOIL could I think be stiffened up in revision so that we might lead with it. "FREE SOIL: Case Histories in Modern Morals." How about that? With the fake quote from some synthetic philosopher with a resonant name as text for the sermon.

As always,
Elmer Davis

P.S.–In the name of my not very epistolary son, I thank you for the latest batch of stamps.

* * *

Chambers to Davis, 25 April 1930

Dear Davis:

Many thanks for your letter of the 23rd. I am delighted that you are working the stories over and getting the "magazinishnesses" out of them. Send me all of 'em even if they don't stick to the line of argument. We should like to look them all over.

Yes, I should think CASE HISTORIES IN MODERN MORALS would serve as a subtitle–if it doesn't sound too heavy. As for the title itself I suppose we can tell better about it when we've read the stories. Some of these you mention don't sound much like fiction. I don't think FREE SOIL does, although I like the idea of the story and using it for the headliner.

I expect you'll have a number of new ideas as you go over the stories, and maybe when we see them we'll have something to suggest too. Mighty glad you're going to get the stuff to us by May first–or try to, anyhow.

My devoted regard to the family.

Yours ever,
[D. Laurance Chambers]

* * *

LOVE AMONG THE RUINS:
Little Novels of Hard Times
By Elmer Davis

Some one ought to get up with a trumpet and a loud foofaraw and discover that in Elmer Davis we have, actually, a writer of sophisticated short stories who ~~xxxxxxxxxxxxxxx~~ can and does write plots. Oh, of course, there are plot-writers left in plenty, but they are pretty nearly all doing mystery and adventure and romance. Your smart, sophisticated fiction writer who isthe latest thing, ~~in fiction~~ deals in streams of consciousness and in the allusive and adumbratory--to such an extent that the franker among his readers confess that while we read with admiration and interest we don't quite know what it's all about! Not so with the works of Elmer Davis. ~~Xxxxxxxxxxxx~~ No writer can be smarter, more modern, his characters, his themes, his backgrounds all strike the latest note--but unafraid of fashion trends and fads, he turns his back boldly on the unformed, jellyfish blob style story, and gives us not only ~~xxxxxxxxxxxx~~ brilliant writing and character drawing, but sound, honest plot construction as well. You know what his characters are doing and why they are doing it, and by God ~~that~~ there is the author for me.

This is a volume, as the ~~xxxx~~ subtitle boldly states, of Little Novels of Hard Times. ~~xxxxxxxxxxxxxxxxxxxxxxxxxxxxxxxxxxxxxx~~ It's a dozen love stories of the present era, each one so closely packed with character and incident that it is indeed a little novel rather than a short story. You're getting plenty for your money! There are stories of marriage--an institution of which Mr. Davis ~~is~~ frequently shows us new aspects--of divorce, of courtship, of business; but whatever they're about, they're always full of romance and wit and charm. Mr. Davis simply doesn't know how to be dull. He has always had a delicious gift for turns of phrase and he uses it without stint here.

But to the stories--the first is HELPMEET. This is the story of Frank Crozier, a young financial wizard in 1928 and a successful, if less spectacular, man today. He married the wrong woman, divorced her, married the right one, and spent the rest of his life working his head off to make enough money ~~xxx~~ to support both of them. Camilla, his second wife, is perfect--"a lover and a hostess and a business partner and then the indefinable something more." But even with her help

First two pages of the five-page reader's report by Anne Ross for Davis's Love Among the Ruins, *published in 1935 (courtesy of The Lilly Library, Indiana University, Bloomington, Indiana)*

#2

Frank might never have come through so well if the gold-digger pig of a Marga hadn't been ~~behind~~ there, reminding him of her alimony. "'In the critical moments of his life,' said Marga proudly, 'I've always been his inspiration.'"

Paula Mayhew is the CAGED SONGBIRD of the next story. A music student in New York, she decides to give up her music and marry Gil Mayhew and devote herself to him. She divorces him when she decides to return to her music, and marries a man deeply interested in her career. When the critics don't find her debut worth a slam, she gives up her career and her second husband and returns to the first. Paula had always complained to Gil that he didn't make her diet or stop smoking, as she knew she shuld. So Gil, anxious for her happiness, urged her second husband to manage her, as she desired, and as he never could. Which is how come Paula divorced the second man for cruelty! There are some delicious sidelights in this story on college folk in the big city--but that's the difficulty with reviewing this book, the side issues are so good one is tempted to leave the main ones to describe them.

NEW LEAF is a prodigal son story about Phil Hazen, scion of the knit underwear house, who throws away all his money and then goes home to go to work at knit underwear and turn over a new leaf. So he does till he saves enough money to skip to New York with his brother's fiancee. The poor hard-working, gypped, elder brother threatens to go out and get drunk and paint things red in his turn, but their father shakes his head. "Youre not the type, son,' he said gently. 'You couldn't turn over a new leaf any more than Phil could.'"

In THE ROAD TO JERICHO, a married woman, having an affair with a married man, discovers the stuff he's made of when he refuses to stop his car to investigate an accident for fear they'll be found out. And her struggle to decide whether to shield herself, her lover, her family, and let the wrong man be hanged for murder, makes the story of Janice Blair.

"There's a great moral lesson somewhere in what happened to ~~Siexix~~ Carla Furness if you can only figure it out. . ." Carla didn't like to be on a SURE THING, but she needed money, and her interior decorating business was dead of inanition, and Rex Ainsworth persuaded her to let him buy into a pool for her.

Davis to Chambers, 11 July 1934

Dear DLC–

It seems increasingly probable that I shall never write another novel. BARE LIVING proved that I could still, or again, do it, at least with a collaborator to give me a shove; but it didn't prove anything else. In the circumstances, I don't know that you'd be interested in a volume of short stories. However, I've looked over the files and discover that I have twelve or fifteen which seem to me of suitable quality–six of them as good as the average of the other volume you published. That may not be much recommendation; it all depends on whether you would make enough to pay out on it. If I make $500 and have a few of my good stories embalmed in a form where they can easily be reached, that is as much as I expect.

The last volume was all pre-depression stuff, except for one which enshrined the actual October 1929 collapse; the general theme of this one (perhaps even the title) would be LOVE AMONG THE RUINS–how the broke but not totally indigent middle class manages its romances and its pride in the Hoover epoch. Three or four of them touching recovery so that they would be reasonably up to date. I couldn't get this ready for fall publication as most of them will need revision to take off a few of the more obvious requisites of magazine salability; but I could deliver copy by the end of September. That is, if you regard the idea as anything worth considering at all.

As always,
Elmer Davis

* * *

An in-house memo signed "L.C." was probably written by New York editor Lynne Carrick.

L. C. (Lynne Carrick?) to Chambers, 15 July 1934

I quite agree with you as to the desirability of continuing with Elmer Davis, and I am all for his collection of short stories for Spring. As for his pungent prose pieces, are not most of these decidedly topical in nature? I would advise caution here.

L. C.

* * *

But We Were Born Free

by ELMER DAVIS

THE BOBBS-MERRILL COMPANY, INC.
PUBLISHERS
INDIANAPOLIS NEW YORK

Two Minutes Till Midnight

by ELMER DAVIS

THE BOBBS-MERRILL COMPANY, INC.
PUBLISHERS
INDIANAPOLIS NEW YORK

Title pages for Davis's 1954 book attacking McCarthyism and his 1955 book on the threat of nuclear war (Thomas Cooper Library, University of South Carolina)

Promotional piece for Davis's 1954 book (courtesy of The Lilly Library, Indiana University, Bloomington, Indiana)

Andrew H. Hepburn wrote the following memo in response to a short note from Chambers about the feasibility of publishing another Davis short-story collection.

Andrew H. Hepburn to Chambers, (16?) July 1934

Mr. Chambers: On the basis of MORALS FOR MODERNS (2457 copies all told) I'd say it is no go. On the other hand if the library market ever gets itself back to normal I'd say we ought to be able to sell upward of 4000 copies of a good collection of short stories, over a name as well know [*sic*] as Elmer Davis's. But we'd be taking a terrible gamble under present conditions. AHH

* * *

Anne Johnston Ross was a part-time editor in the Indianapolis office and a friend of Davis. She had been replaced as editorial assistant in 1931 by Jessica Brown Mannon. By "chelah" Chambers probably means the Anglo-Indian chela, *a disciple of a guru.*

Chambers to Davis, 18 July 1934

My dear Elmer:–

Thank you for your letter of the 11th. I delayed answering it until I could see how my colleagues thought about it both here and in New York, and could consult also with your chelah Anne Johnston Ross. Everyone is strong for doing the volume of short stories, and are delighted that we are to have it on our list for the spring. If you can deliver the copy by the first of October that will be fine. LOVE AMONG THE RUINS is a good title, as old Robert Browning discovered, and it has a nice touch for the times. We might consider as a subtitle "Little Novels of America", taking a cue from old Maurice Hewlett.

But you can not think of giving up your career as a novelist. I do feel that as changes come over your mood and thought the novels you will write hereafter may represent a very different approach from your early manner. Your short stories come more at grips with life; are more serious, as is inevitable. Novels in that fashion are indicated. The talk with Anne developed the idea that one of these days you might like to do a Roman Empire story and show up Robert Graves. You could make it a telling satire on modern America. And why not use all that lore with which your mind is richly stored?

I am sending you a copy of TOM TIDDLER'S GROUND, a novel by Edward Shanks, which we publish on the last day of the month. I hope you may enjoy reading it, and if you do that you will let me know. You will recall mentioning his apocalyptic novel in that article you did for the Saturday Review.

My love to the family.

Yours ever,

[D. Laurance Chambers]

John Erskine (1879–1951)

See also the entries on Erskine in *DLB 9: American Novelists, 1910–1945* and *DLB 102: American Short-Story Writers, 1910–1945, Second Series.*

John Erskine made his reputation as a great teacher at Columbia University, numbering Carl Van Doren, Kenneth Burke, Mortimer Adler, and Clifton Fadiman among his students. Erskine produced scholarly works (starting with a dissertation on the Elizabethan lyric), essays, poems, and even music. He could have had a career as a pianist, and in fact performed with major symphony orchestras. In 1925 his first novel, The Private Life of Helen of Troy, *was published, and he became famous in another area of the arts. Like some other of the seventeen novels by Erskine that followed,* The Private Life of Helen of Troy *brought an old story into the new age primarily by means of witty dialogue. Books of various kinds continued to appear, reflecting the many interests of this true Renaissance man and bearing out his pedagogical method, which was to show what could be found in the great works of all disciplines.*

John Erskine (Bruccoli Clark Layman Archives)

BOBBS-MERRILL BOOKS BY ERSKINE: *The Private Life of Helen of Troy* (Indianapolis: Bobbs-Merrill, 1925; London: Nash & Grayson, 1926);

Galahad: Enough of His Life to Explain His Reputation (Indianapolis: Bobbs-Merrill, 1926; London: Nash & Grayson, 1926);

Adam and Eve: Though He Knew Better (Indianapolis: Bobbs-Merrill, 1927; London: Nash & Grayson, 1928);

Prohibition and Christianity, and other Paradoxes of the American Spirit (Indianapolis: Bobbs-Merrill, 1927; London: Nash & Grayson, 1927);

The Delight of Great Books (Indianapolis: Bobbs-Merrill, 1928; London: Nash & Grayson, 1928);

Penelope's Man: The Homing Instinct (Indianapolis: Bobbs-Merrill, 1928; London: Eveleigh, Nash & Grayson, 1929);

Sincerity: A Story of Our Time (Indianapolis: Bobbs-Merrill, 1929); republished as *An Experiment in Sincerity: A Story of Our Time* (London: Putnam, 1930);

Cinderella's Daughter, and Other Sequels and Consequences (Indianapolis: Bobbs-Merrill, 1930; London: Putnam, 1931);

Uncle Sam in the Eyes of His Family (Indianapolis: Bobbs-Merrill, 1930; London: Putnam, 1930);

Jack and the Beanstalk: A Fairy Opera for the Childlike, libretto by Erskine for music by Louis Gruenberg (Indianapolis: Bobbs-Merrill, 1931);

Unfinished Business (Indianapolis: Bobbs-Merrill, 1931);

Tristan and Isolde: Restoring Palamede (Indianapolis: Bobbs-Merrill, 1932; London: John Lane, 1933);

Bachelor–of Arts (Indianapolis: Bobbs-Merrill, 1934);

Helen Retires: An Opera in Three Acts, libretto by Erskine for music by George Antheil (Indianapolis: Bobbs-Merrill, 1934);

Forget if You Can (Indianapolis: Bobbs-Merrill, 1935);
Solomon, My Son! (Indianapolis: Bobbs-Merrill, 1935; London: Joseph, 1936);
The Influence of Women and Its Cure (Indianapolis: Bobbs-Merrill, 1936);
Young Love: Variations on a Theme (Indianapolis: Bobbs-Merrill, 1936);
The Brief Hour of François Villon (Indianapolis: Bobbs-Merrill, 1937; London: Joseph, 1938).

Related Letters

Erskine agreed to a higher price for The Private Life of Helen of Troy, *and the target audience was composed of the sophisticated and learned, who indeed endorsed the book. But both author and D. Laurance Chambers (at this time vice president of Bobbs-Merrill) misjudged the width of the actual readership.*

D. Laurance Chambers to John Erskine, 3 August 1925

My dear Professor Erskine:

This is just a line to tell you how greatly I have enjoyed the last half of THE PRIVATE LIFE OF HELEN OF TROY. I did not have an opportunity to see it until it got into galleys as I remained in the East far longer than I expected. It is just too clever, and wise, and delightful for words.

It seems to me now that so artistic a thing deserves a more attractive format than would be possible with a $2.00 retail price. I do not believe that cultivated people will hesitate to pay $2.50 for it. And it is not for the morons. What do you think about that?

Faithfully yours,
[D. Laurance Chambers]

* * *

JoBy Adams, of the Indianapolis firm JoBy Adams Advertising Service, wrote Chambers (now also editor in chief of the trade department) to thank him for a copy of The Private Life of Helen of Troy.

JoBy Adams to Chambers, 3 November 1925

My dear Mr. Chambers:

There is but one Helen and John Erskine is her prophet.

Mr. Erskine's book will, in my opinion, be accorded the whole-hearted admiration of the self-elected cognoscenti, and, what is more important, gain the approval of the booboisie (who make and unmake profits), even of those who choose this book under the impression that "Private Life" is a euphemism for adulteries exposed and explained.

Thank you ever so much for sending me this remarkable book. I have enshrined its author in my private Pantheon, where, on soft couches, recline Mr. Cabell, Mr. Shaw, Mr. Morand, Mr. Dumas (pere), Mr. Machen, and that versatile and composite being who composed "The Thousand and One Nights".

Sincerely yours,
JoBy Adams

* * *

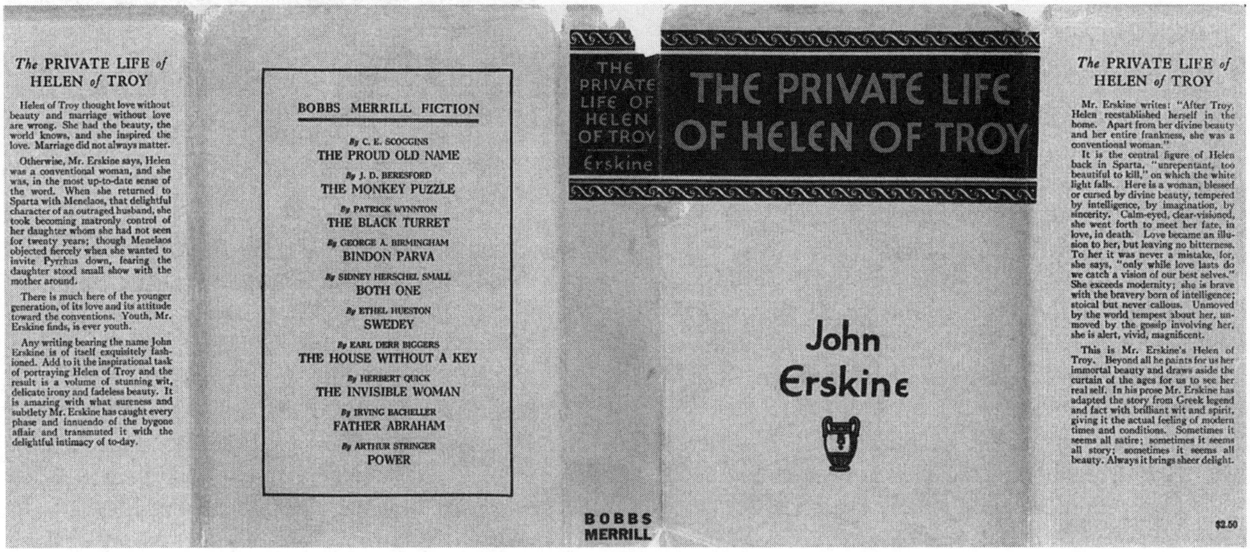

Dust jacket for Erskine's 1925 novel, the number-one fiction best-seller in 1926 (courtesy of The Lilly Library, Indiana University, Bloomington, Indiana)

Chambers to Erskine, 16 December 1925

Dear Mr. Erskine:

Just got back to my desk and found there your delightful letter of November 23rd. I hope that since you wrote you have received your copies of HELEN which we sent long since, and that you like her looks in the dress we gave her. Every one here does. I've been in New York for the last fortnight and find the book catching on there in a highly gratifying way. Every one seems to be reading it or promising himself to read it, and in any case talking about it. It is the talk of many dinner parties, teas and wherever two or three of the sophisticates are gathered together. I think it certainly safe to say it is the hit of New York. Our problem is to spread it over the country, arousing everywhere the same degree of interest. We are working hard on this and are keyed up to the highest enthusiasm for the book. We're going to make it one of the spring best sellers or bust. The reviews, almost without exception, have been very appreciative–here is one we are sending to the trade throughout the country. I only wish you were here to hear all the good things that are being said, and to give us your advice as to what we can do for HELEN's exploitation.

I was pulling wires in New York to have the Paris Herald and Tribune cable stories about you, this under the impression that you've been in Paris. I hope you were and that they caught you.

The news about GALAHAD is great. I'm crazy to see it, and shall be in New York the first of February sure as shootin' to welcome you home and grab the new manuscript. But I quite agree with you that we shouldn't bring it out until fall if HELEN keeps up her gait as we all confidently expect. It looks as if you had struck the richest vein going–one fellow said to me in New York, "You needn't fear competition on that book, because there can't be anything else like it!" And as Mencken said of Conrad (with permission of Doubleday, Page, adv) we might say of HELEN, "There is no one like her, there is no one remotely like her." One suggestion I'll pass along for what it may be worth as you write GALAHAD–a few have found the uninterrupted dialogue somewhat wearying; few they are indeed, still their hint may help you perfect your unique, delightful method.

We're advertising the book every day in the New York papers. And here's something interesting–we have the Neighborhood Playhouse interested in the idea of making a play based on the book. It's a little too early to say how definite the prospect is, and I don't know what it may come to, but they may want your help when you get back to New York.

You must be having a mighty fine time, but I'm selfish enough to wish you were here. In the meantime, however, I wish you'd consider that you're one of those friends by adoption tried we want to grapple to our souls by hoops of steel. We want everything you write if we may have it, fiction or nonfiction. By the beard of Jove and the topless walls of Ilium, in the name of the daughter of the gods, divinely tall and most divinely fair, I adjure you to pay no heed to the blandishments of those wily sons of Laertes, European representatives of American publishers; make no entangling alliances, but be true to us. And I am, I assure you, now and ever

Faithfully yours,
[D. Laurance Chambers]

Advertising copy for Erskine's worldwide success (courtesy of The Lilly Library, Indiana University, Bloomington, Indiana)

* * *

Harriet Comstock was the author of Penelope's Web *(1928).*

Chambers to Erskine, 11 August 1928

Dear John:

Thank you for your wire. It is great to know that we may depend on your sending the rest of the manuscript of PENELOPE'S MAN to Indianapolis by the end of next week. With that assurance, I am beating it for the Hoosier scene, where many things call me, and shall not stick around and act like a goad.

When it arrives, we'll turn handsprings and flip-flops and do a lot of ground and lofty tumbling to put it all in type in a grand rush. And then I'm going to count on you to read the galley proofs a bit faster than you ever read anything. If you can see your way clear to leave the reading of the pages to us, it will help.

For some "stunt" work and short cutting are going to be called for to get PENELOPE'S MAN out by our usual November date, when it should certainly appear, and we shall need your cooperation at every stage.

Have you thought of one of your wonderful subtitles?

I see there's a new novel called PENELOPE'S WEB. Do you think that makes any difference?

If you could manage to have the manuscript complete in our hands at Indianapolis by Saturday, the 18th instead of Monday, the 20th, it would be a distinct gain. The office here can accomplish it if you'll give them the final instalment before five Friday afternoon–by getting it special delivery on the fast train west. Better have Miss Miller send the earlier parts direct as finished.

Devotedly yours,
[D. Laurance Chambers]

* * *

Erskine wrote the following letter on the stationery of the Juilliard School of Music, where he was president from 1928 to 1937. Joseph "Joe" Anthony was presumably the novelist of that name. D. Putnam Brinley illustrated the endpapers for Erskine's Penelope's Man: The Homing Instinct *(1928).*

Erskine to Chambers, 4 September 1928

Dear Lawrence [*sic*]

I am sending to you the "Adam and Eve" and also the proofs of "Penelope's Man," this latter first class special delivery. I am wondering on second thoughts whether "Penelope's Man" isn't sufficient title without anything else. Joe Anthony was here the other day and that was his opinion.

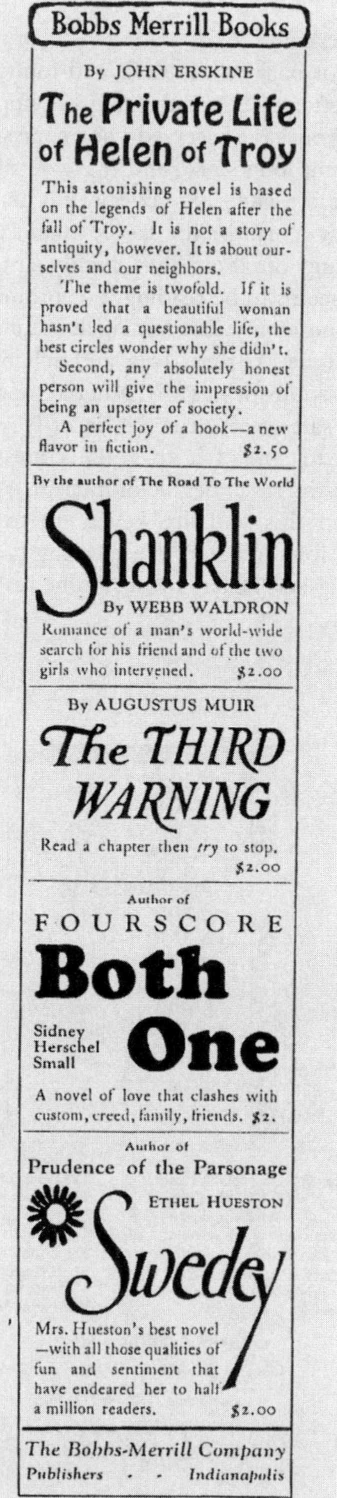

Flier (1925) for Bobbs-Merrill titles, including Erskine's first novel (courtesy of The Lilly Library, Indiana University, Bloomington, Indiana)

Now I have a great idea for the book. Putnam Brinley, who has just finished in my studio a beautiful decoration embodying the characters of the first three books, wants to do a map of the journey of Odysseus, a sort of fantasy after the manner of medieval maps with all the dangers to be portrayed on the way, the whole thing to be done in color. It occurred to me that if you like the result, as I am sure you will, it might be to our advantage to publish it with the book in a flap inside the cover. Perhaps you intended to bring it out at $2.00. With the map I should think you could easily charge $2.50.

Brinley had the idea Sunday afternoon and I imagine that when I go home today I may find a sketch waiting for me. I will submit it to you at the earliest opportunity.

There is a rumor going around that Ziegfeld is going to ask us for permission to put on "Adam and Eve" as a musical comedy!

My regards to the household.

Faithfully
John

* * *

Mina Kersey worked in the Indianapolis office.

Erskine to Mina Kersey, 14 September 1931

Dear Miss Kersey

I am returning galleys 1–19 of "Unfinished Business."

Also the first pages of "Jack and the Beanstalk". Please note that in the list of books on the inside I have changed the description from Juveniles to Opera Libretto. Will you be careful not to let the word Juvenile creep into "Unfinished Business" when you are describing "Jack and the Beanstalk"? It would greatly damage the sale of the libretto if it contained the word Juvenile, since the opera is a full sized libretto, and I hope the book will sell as a libretto.

With cordial regard,
Faithfully yours
John Erskine

* * *

Dust jacket for Erskine's 1934 novel set at Columbia University (courtesy of Michael Manz/Babylon Revisited)

Three years after this letter Erskine decided that Bobbs-Merrill was not interested in promoting his books and left for another publisher.

Chambers to Erskine, 5 March 1934

My dear John:–

Thank you for your letter of the 3rd. We shall plan to do HELEN RETIRES for the next season. That is an excellent suggestion. Meanwhile we will be formulating our ideas about a format, and I will discuss it with you on my next trip East.

UNCLE SAM is the only one of your books, I believe, now on the reprint list. It will be coming back to us in due course. The Grosset & Dunlap contracts are always made for a period of three years, and indeed books do not always remain that long on their list by any means. Of some other novels we have, as you know, sold remainders. But neither of these things should stand in the way of earnings to your "estate" from regular editions if a revived interest comes along. We have all the plates and stock of all titles. Of UNCLE SAM we have a particularly large stock. I can't see that there is anything wrong or unusual in the handling of the property. It has followed the normal course.

I like your ideas about advertising UNCLE SAM. Logically it would seem that they ought to work out. "Experts" and most experience tend to the idea that book advertising does not create sales or make a revival. It operates at best to increase a momentum already under weigh. However, we will chew on it and see if we or Grosset & Dunlap can develop a merchandising program which would help to make advertising profitable. I suppose an advertisement that didn't pull would, apart from the money factor, not be a real contribution to the general cause.

Yours ever,

[D. Laurance Chambers]

Inglis Fletcher (1879–1969)

Inglis Fletcher spent much of her early married life traveling to mining camps with her engineer husband. When nearly fifty, she trekked alone through British Africa for five months, picking up material for lectures, articles, and fiction, as she did during other adventures in her life. Her two earliest novels were based on her African experience, the first for children, the second for adults. After that she moved to North Carolina, where her family had ancient roots. Raleigh's Eden *(1940) became the first of twelve novels in her Carolina Series, each carefully researched for historical accuracy. Her entertaining preservation of history, more than the literary qualities of the works, earned her high praise and good sales among contemporaries. She was always grateful to D. Laurance Chambers, who had a particular interest in historical writings, for guiding her career. He and Jessica Brown Mannon worked with her on* Raleigh's Eden *for five years.*

BOBBS-MERRILL BOOKS BY FLETCHER: *The White Leopard,* illustrated by Kurt Weise (Indianapolis: Bobbs-Merrill, 1931; London: Hodder & Stoughton, 1931);

Red Jasmine: A Novel of Africa (Indianapolis: Bobbs-Merrill, 1932; London: Hutchinson, 1933);

Raleigh's Eden (Indianapolis: Bobbs-Merrill, 1940; London: Hutchinson, 1941);

Men of Albemarle (Indianapolis: Bobbs-Merrill, 1942; London: Hutchinson, 1943);

Lusty Wind for Carolina (Indianapolis: Bobbs-Merrill, 1944; London: Hutchinson, 1947);

Toil of the Brave (Indianapolis: Bobbs-Merrill, 1946; London: Hutchinson, 1948);

Roanoke Hundred (Indianapolis: Bobbs-Merrill, 1948; London: Hutchinson, 1949);

Bennett's Welcome (Indianapolis: Bobbs-Merrill, 1950; London: Hutchinson, 1952);

Queen's Gift (Indianapolis: Bobbs-Merrill, 1952; London: Hutchinson, 1953);

The Scotswoman (Indianapolis: Bobbs-Merrill, 1954; London: Hutchinson, 1956);

The Wind in the Forest (Indianapolis: Bobbs-Merrill, 1957; London: Hutchinson, 1958);

Wicked Lady (Indianapolis: Bobbs-Merrill, 1962);

Rogue's Harbor (Indianapolis: Bobbs-Merrill, 1964).

Portrait of Inglis Fletcher (courtesy of The Lilly Library, Indiana University, Bloomington, Indiana)

Related Letters

Fletcher wrote to Bobbs-Merrill editor Anne Johnston (later Anne Johnston Ross) from San Francisco. Johnston redirected the letter to Jessica Brown Mannon with the notation "Jessica, You take care of her. A."

Inglis Fletcher to Anne Johnston, 15 July 1930

Dear Miss Johnston;

Are you still interested in a book on Africa for children? I am more than half through a book for boys fro[m] twelve to sixteen or seventeen. A series of tales of an administrator in the middle of the continent who

THE BOBBS-MERRILL COMPANY

PUBLISHERS  INDIANAPOLIS

File copy for
Trade Dept.

November 14, 1940

RALEIGH'S EDEN by Inglis Fletcher is now in its 8th edition and is being reported by booksellers all over the country as a best seller. From the first printing we held out 500 sheets with the idea in mind of preparing from these first edition sheets a special limited edition for North Carolina for the Christmas trade. Within a very few days this limited Christmas edition will be ready for shipment. It will be called "The Old North State Edition" and will be signed by the author.

The North Carolina Edition was sold out before publication date and the Albemarle Edition was completely sold out as a result of the mailing announcing it to the North Carolina dealers. None of these limited editions have been sold anywhere except in North Carolina and if you want stock of this limited Christmas edition autographed by the author and prepared from first edition sheets, please let us know by return mail. A self-addressed envelope is enclosed for your convenience in ordering.

Orders will be filled with the idea of giving everyone a fair share of this special edition as we did on the other limited editions, so get your order in promptly.

Sale of this book is being confined to the North Carolina trade and never again will we be able to offer you books prepared from first edition sheets of RALEIGH'S EDEN. This should make an ideal Christmas gift.

Yours very truly,

THE BOBBS-MERRILL COMPANY

RGB:D

Promotional form letter by Ross G. Baker for Fletcher's 1940 historical novel Raleigh's Eden *(courtesy of The Lilly Library, Indiana University, Bloomington, Indiana)*

has to use his wits and skill to get him out of many difficulties for he has no soldiers and his next white neighbor is two hundred miles away.

Tales of witchcraft, of hunting and stalking and the adventures that happen every day. Local color correct. Stories give an idea of the responsibility of the white man who governs natives–or inferior races.

Please let me know if you are interested. I should like to do some of the illustrating myself. My drawings are crude but might be more effective than drawings done by a more skillful illustrator.

Cordially yours,
Inglis Fletcher

* * *

Jessica Brown Mannon to Fletcher, 17 July 1930

Dear Miss Fletcher:

Thank you so much for your letter of the 15th which Miss Johnston has handed to me as I am in charge of our books for boys and girls.

Your manuscript sounds mighty interesting and we shall be glad to have you send it along whenever it is ready.

Cordially yours,
[Jessica Mannon]

* * *

Fletcher had been inspired to travel to Africa by the lectures of Rodney Wood, an agricultural scientist. He told her some of the tales that appeared in The White Leopard *(1931). The illustrations were finally done by Kurt Weise. Company vice president and trade-department editor D. Laurance Chambers wrote with the news that her manuscript had been accepted.*

D. Laurance Chambers to Fletcher, 26 August 1930

Dear Mrs. Fletcher:

It is with the greatest of pleasure that I tell you that we are eager to publish your manuscript, ADVENTURES IN AFRICA. We are all most enthusiastic about it and I would send you a contract by this mail if I were sure of the status of Mr. Rodney Wood. Is the contract to be made with you alone, or with you and Mr. Wood? If with you, only, can you guarantee us against claims from Mr. Woods [*sic*]?

Ordinarily we publish our juvenile books only in the fall, but as this intended [*sic*] for older boys and grown-ups it may be possible to publish in the spring of 1931. We have something of a problem to work out with this book because if it is published as a boys' book, adults will not read it. And if it is published using the title, ADVENTURES IN AFRICA, that will accentuate the fact that it is a collection of short stories and a book of short stories is seldom popular and difficult to sell. We wish to reduce this short story element as far as possible. What would you think of calling the book THE LEOPARD and making each story a chapter? This is really essential, in my estimation, to the success of the volume. I should like for you to go carefully over the entire manuscript keeping this fact in mind–weeding out repetitions, seeing that the stories follow one another chronologically, that as each new character appears he is properly introduced and explained. The end of each chapter should lead the way to the next and the beginning of each chapter should connect up with the one which has preceded it. In this way, with just a little more work, you will have a splendid, unified book, much more desirable than a mere group of adventures.

There is one story, THE SNAKE GOD, which I do not think should be included here. It does not seem at all fitting for a boys' book and even if it were rewritten I do not believe it would meet with the approval of the librarians over the country. In going over the manuscript you will want to keep in mind that this is a boys' book and anything that the librarians and teachers might find objectionable should be eliminated. It is important to have their approval for they can do much to promote the sale and interest in such a book as this. I'm sure they would frown upon too much black magic and I am inclined to think myself that it isn't a good thing for young minds to dwell upon. Your stories have so many superior qualities that I am sure the book will not suffer from the omission of THE SNAKE GOD.

And now as to the illustrations. Your portraits of the various types of natives are good and serve well to give one a clear idea of their appearance. But once again I must repeat that this is a boys' book and we have found that action pictures are practically a necessity. And the more illustrations one uses the more the book will cost. We generally limit ourselves to four or five full page illustrations, for to exceed this number, the book would have to be priced higher than the usual $2.00. And just now with the price-cutting movement of some publishers creating havoc with the market, it would be fatal to price the book at more than $2.00. Nothing would please us better than to have you do the illustrations yourself, but if you are doubtful about your ability, I am sure your sketches would be a great aid to the artist whom we should then select. I shall be glad to have your opinion in regard to this matter.

The manuscript is of sufficient length as it is, so that we need not worry about lengthening it. If SIGNAL FIRES OF PEACE is not too long and would make a strong, fitting end to the book, I think it would be well to include it.

ESTABLISHED 1838

THE BOBBS-MERRILL-COMPANY
PUBLISHERS···INDIANAPOLIS

D. L. CHAMBERS
PRESIDENT

Inglis Fletcher has again dipped her pen into the rich, colorful past of North Carolina and created a novel that, we think, will quicken the blood of all Americans.

She stirs history to life with her enthralling tale of the M E N O F A L B E M A R L E, the women they loved, the liberty under law they died to establish early in the 1700's.

It is, we think, a grand historical romance, an advance even on Raleigh's Eden. It is a boon for times of distraction and depression, a story of love and valor in which one can become completely absorbed, "lost to the world."

So it strikes us. We hope it will strike you the same way. A reading copy has been sent you with our compliments. Does not Men of Albemarle offer a wonderful bookselling opportunity? Please let us know how you size it up. Publication date is October 19th.

We shall give Men of Albemarle the same intensive promotion and advertising that made Raleigh's Eden a best-seller.

Cordially yours,

DLC:MH

Promotional form letter by D. Laurance Chambers for Fletcher's 1942 novel Men of Albemarle, *the second novel in the Carolina Series (courtesy of The Lilly Library, Indiana University, Bloomington, Indiana)*

This Signed Edition
is limited to
________numbered copies
of which this is
Number________

Facsimile reproduction of autograph page for
limited Albemarle Edition of MEN OF ALBEMARLE.
Each copy signed by the author, Inglis Fletcher.
To be published October 19th.

Certificate of limitation for Men of Albemarle, *used as a promotional item (courtesy of The Lilly Library, Indiana University, Bloomington, Indiana)*

I am returning the manuscript to you today and shall await your comment with impatience, for I am eager to get that contract ready for your signature!

With heartiest congratulations on your achievement and very best wishes, I am

Cordially yours,
[D. Laurance Chambers]

* * *

"The Snake God" does not appear as a chapter in The White Leopard, *but the story referred to by Mannon is in chapter 5.*

Mannon to Chambers, 6 October 1930

Mr. C.

I have now finished my reading of THE LEOPARD and I think we can easily fix up the little discrepancies in the manuscript here without returning the manuscript to Mrs. Fletcher. I am preparing a letter to her now for you to sign, telling her what we are doing.

I notice that she has omitted one story that had to do largely with witchcraft. It concerned the death of one of the chiefs and the witchdoctors were trying to incite the deceased chief's wives to commit suicide against Murdock's orders as had formerly been their custom. A white mouse or rat figured in the story but Murdock out-witted them by having one of his boys shoot a cat and after dyeing it white, he used it at an effective moment to scare the witchdoctors out [of] their witchery and the chief's wives were spared. I rather liked the story though it was somewhat gruesome. Omitting it, makes Chuma-chu-pela, the witch-doctor, rather an unimportant person in the story. I would be in favor of putting it back in. What do you think?

Jessica

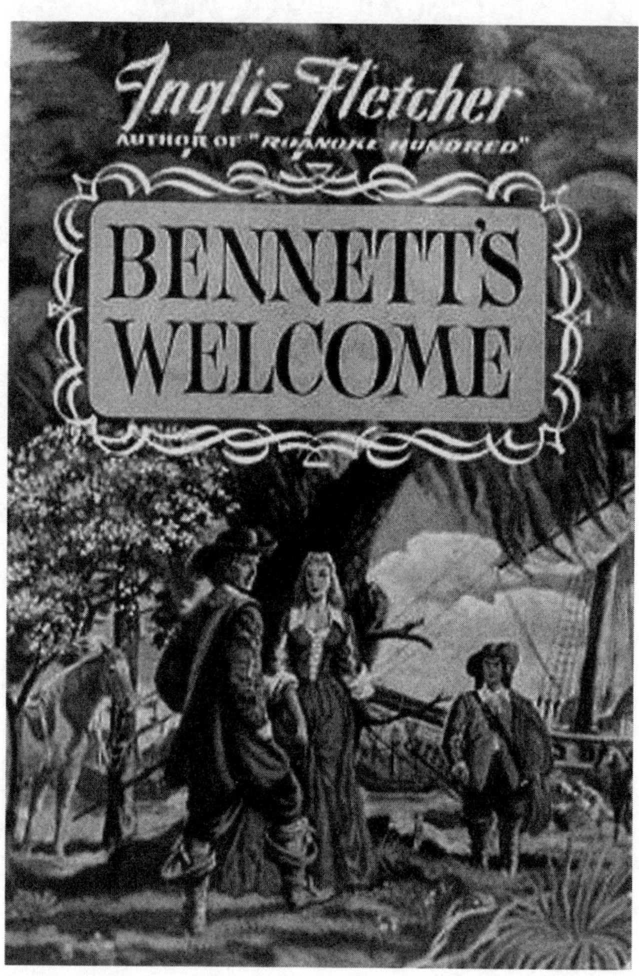

Dust jacket for Fletcher's 1950 novel (Thorn Books, Tucson, Arizona)

C. S. Forester (1899–1966)

See also the Forester entry in *DLB 191: British Novelists Between the Wars.*

After Payment Deferred, *a 1926 thriller by C. S. Forester (the pen name of Cecil Lewis Troughton Smith), was made into a successful play and movie, the author emigrated from his native England to California in 1932 and remained there for the rest of his life. Within five years of the move he had written* The African Queen *(1935)–filmed in 1951 with Humphrey Bogart and Katharine Hepburn–and the first of the eleven Captain Horatio Hornblower novels for which he is best remembered. During an earlier phase of Forester's prolific career,* The Daughter of the Hawk *(1928) became his tenth published book in five years, which partially accounts for the weakness of his Bobbs-Merrill novels, all of which appeared first in England.* Lord Nelson *(1929) was the last of his four biographies.*

BOBBS-MERRILL BOOKS BY FORESTER: *Love Lies Dreaming* (Indianapolis: Bobbs-Merrill, 1927; **first edition,** London: John Lane, 1927);

One Wonderful Week (Indianapolis: Bobbs-Merrill, 1927); **first edition,** *The Wonderful Week* (London: John Lane, 1927);

The Daughter of the Hawk (Indianapolis: Bobbs-Merrill, 1928); **first edition,** *The Shadow of the Hawk* (London: John Lane, 1928);

Lord Nelson (Indianapolis: Bobbs-Merrill, 1929); **first edition,** *Nelson* (London: John Lane, 1929).

C. S. Forester (Bruccoli Clark Layman Archives)

Related Letters

J. H. Crocket was a director of John Lane The Bodley Head Limited, Forester's London publisher. Thomas R. Coward was the New York representative of Bobbs-Merrill.

J. H. Crocket to Thomas R. Coward, 30 March 1927

Dear Mr. Coward,

I am sorry but I must pass on to you the comments Mr. Forester makes about your edition of "LOVE LIES DREAMING", he says:–"the jacket and binding are very good indeed, but the proof reading, (if there was any), is simply vile. I would much prefer the labour of reading the proof myself (should the same firm publish any more of my books), to having such work appear with my name on it, even with the wrong initials".

I am sorry but I have not read your edition myself, so I do not know how far Mr. Forester's criticisms are just, or due to the artistic temperament. In any case if there is anything seriously wrong will you please have it put right in your next edition. I do hope you will find it necessary to print another edition and that you will have a big success with the book.

Yours faithfully,
for JOHN LANE THE BODLEY HEAD LIMITED
J. H. Crocket
Director.

* * *

At the time of this letter, D. Laurance Chambers was vice president and trade-department editor.

D. Laurance Chambers to C. S. Forester, 30 March 1927

Dear Mr. Forester:

No doubt you've received your copies of our edition of LOVE LIES DREAMING which we sent you through John Lane some time ago, and I hope you're pleased with the look of the book. I am sorry a few copies got through with the wrong initials on the jacket and binding. We caught it right away, and had it corrected.

There's already been some interesting comment on the book. Elmer Davis, a well-known and witty American novelist writes us: "It's a delightful book. A publisher was telling me the other day that the need of the times is a novel which makes marital passion as glamorous as sin; which Forester accomplishes in very fair measure." He plans to elaborate this theme in reviewing your book for one of the leading literary papers.

Isn't there a new novel under weigh that we may hope to see soon? I've observed with some jealousy that Dodd, Mead is bringing out your VICTOR EMMANUEL II. I hope you're not letting them tie up any of your future work–I like these Forester books and I should like to have a monopoly on them!

Faithfully yours,
[D. Laurance Chambers]

Title page for the edition of Forester's 1927 novel; he was dissatisfied with the publisher's proofreading (Roger Williams College Library).

* * *

Forester to Bobbs-Merrill, 10 April 1927

Dear Sirs,

I was very pleased indeed to receive your letter of March 30th.

The general appearance, I thought, of 'Love lies Dreaming', was simply charming–we will not say anything more about the printing, as I have already expressed my views on that and have come to the conclusion that either they do things differently in America or else there was some slip in the office. That is more than I meant to say.

With regard to Victor Emmanuel II, the book was written a long time ago, and would have appeared in England and America, had it not been for the general strike last year, some time before I even knew of the existence of the Bobbs Merrill Company.

Methuen and Co., who produce my historical books in England, have, I believe, a very close relation with Dodd Mead and Co. If historical books are at all in your line perhaps it would be better for you to get into touch with them; I am certainly not tied in any way in America for my future work, and I enjoy writing heavy biographies as a pleasant change from novels.

Yours truly,
C. S. Forester

* * *

Dust jacket for the 1928 novel that was originally published that same year in England as The Shadow of the Hawk *(courtesy of The Lilly Library, Indiana University, Bloomington, Indiana)*

Anne Johnston (later Anne Johnston Ross) was a Bobbs-Merrill editor. Julia Peterkin's Scarlet Sister Mary *(1928) was a best-selling Pulitzer Prize–winning novel.* The Bishop's Wife *(1928) was by another Bobbs-Merrill author, Robert Nathan. Forester's* Brown on Resolution *(1929) was published in America as* Single-Handed *by G. P. Putnam's Sons.*

Forester to Anne Johnston, 1 January 1929

Dear Miss Johnston,

Thank you very much indeed for your Christmas wishes and for 'Scarlet Sister Mary'; it is not too late at present (although I suppose it will be by the time you receive this) to wish you a prosperous New Year.

I am very sorry, but Sister Mary did not captivate me; it did not seem very real or intense, in fact it was almost an effort to finish. Perhaps it was only post-Christmas mood, though–that is always rather blighting. I don't know whether you ever see English press cuttings, but I enclose a review of 'The Bishop's Wife' by the man whose opinion I value most of all among English reviewers. It corresponds exactly with what I thought about it.

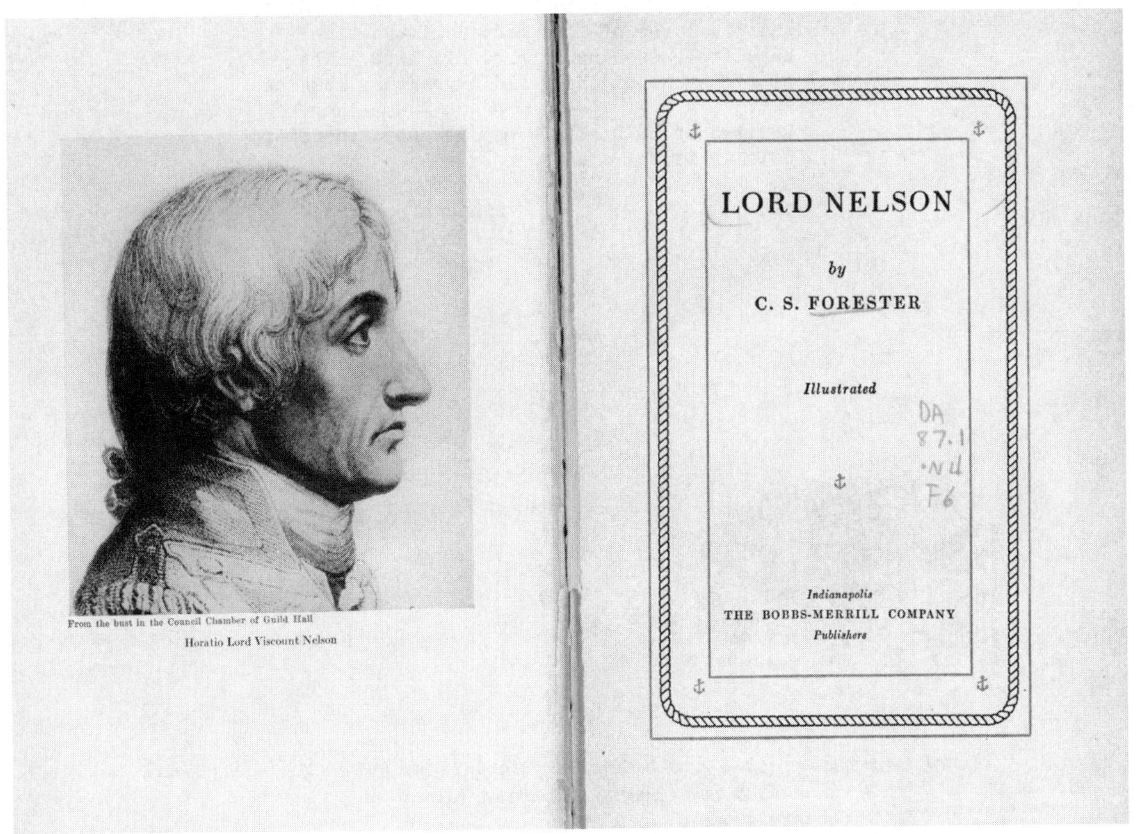

Frontispiece and title page for Forester's 1929 biography (Thomas Cooper Library, University of South Carolina)

ESTABLISHED 1838

THE BOBBS-MERRILL COMPANY
PUBLISHERS ··· INDIANAPOLIS

LORD NELSON

by

C. S. Forester

is sent you for review. There are really two C. S. Foresters though the same person. One is the author of those delightfully humorous novels, "Love Lies Dreaming" and "One Wonderful Week." And the other is the biographer of Louis XIV, Jospehine, Napoleon and the latest, LORD NELSON. This merely shows the versatility of the man.

His LORD NELSON is an intensely human account of the man who could be the hero of the Nile and the lover of Emma Lady Hamilton, the beautiful, dashing love of his life. Their story is one of the world's greatest romances.

Reviews of LORD NELSON may be released after October 24.

Sincerely yours,

MRH:

Form letter accompanying review copies of the 1929 biography by Forester (courtesy of The Lilly Library, Indiana University, Bloomington, Indiana)

It was very, very, good of you to make the offer to John Lane to allow me to try to sell Nelson elsewhere, but I am quite sure John Lane will do nothing of the sort. The book is slowly taking shape–I haven't a thought in my head nowadays except about it. You can't imagine how grateful I am for the suggestion.

Just as a matter of interest (I don't want to irritate a sore point) I must tell you that Lane is making a big push with 'Brown on Resolution'–prizes for the public & the trade & all that sort of thing. I only hope it comes off, as they do deserve some reward for their clairvoyance with regard to me!

Very best wishes,
C. S. Forester.

* * *

Forester's The Voyage of Annie Marble *was published by John Lane in 1929.*

Johnston to Forester, 14 January 1929

Dear C. S. Forester:

Thanks so much for your letter and for the review of THE BISHOP'S WIFE by Gerald Gould. We are sending it along to Mr. Nathan. I know he'll be delighted to see it. But I'm sorry you didn't care about SISTER MARY. I think it's quite wonderful, but I have wondered how it would seem to an English or Continental reader–though to be sure the plantation Afro-Americans are as strange to us northerners as they could be to foreigners.

We are all thrilled that you are so keen about Nelson. I know you'll do a marvelous book.

And I am glad Lane is giving BROWN ON RESOLUTION such a good start. You know I am a great admirer of that book in spite of our decision that we couldn't sell it over here, and I hope it's the best seller of English novels. By the way, do you know that we still have the manuscript, as well as ANNIE MARBLE? We asked John Lane for shipping instructions, as we thought they might like us to send 'em to some other publisher over here, but no word yet. We failed to sell any of the Annie Marble story to a magazine or newspaper, so I am returning you that manuscript–the copy you sent for that purpose, I mean.

The best of luck to you for 1929.

Yours,
[Anne Johnston]

Emily Hahn (1905–1997)

An adventurer all her life, Emily Hahn was the first woman to earn a degree as a mining engineer from the University of Wisconsin. Prevented from advancing in the field because of her sex, she took to traveling and writing. In 1930 she began three years in the Belgian Congo (now the Democratic Republic of the Congo) and then went to China as a correspondent for The New Yorker. *During World War II Hahn saw firsthand the horrors of the Japanese occupation. Her life was distilled into many books, including novels, historical works, children's stories, studies of animals, and autobiographies. Her book about her African adventures and the novel drawn from the same experience had to be toned down because of their frankness about sex and colonial exploitation. The autobiographical novella* Affair *(1935), centering on issues relating to working women in the Depression, was promoted vigorously by Bobbs-Merrill but did not sell well.*

BOBBS-MERRILL BOOKS BY HAHN: *Congo Solo: Misadventures Two Degrees North* (Indianapolis: Bobbs-Merrill, 1933);

With Naked Foot (Indianapolis: Bobbs-Merrill, 1934; London: Transworld, 1952);

Affair (Indianapolis: Bobbs-Merrill, 1935).

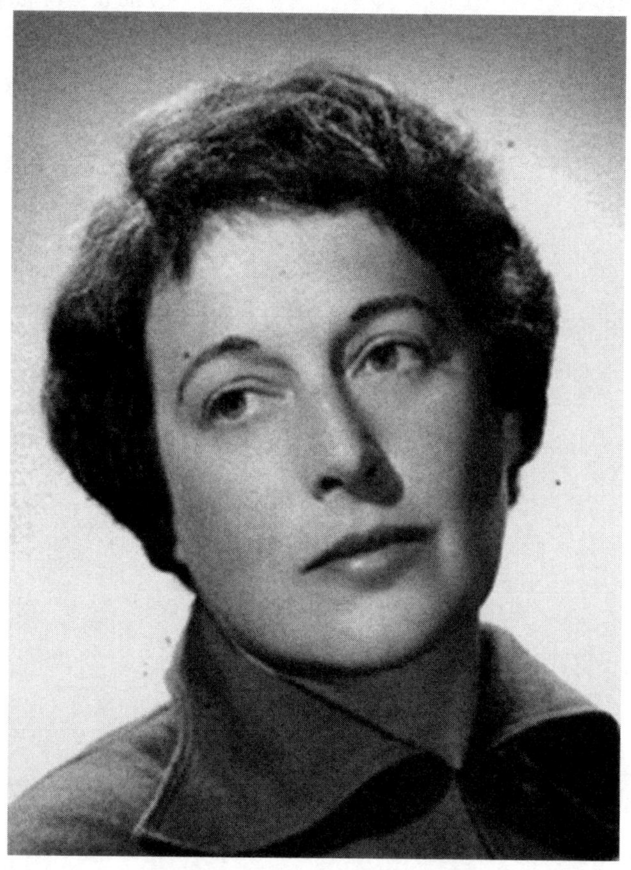

Emily Hahn (H. W. Wilson Company)

BOBBS-MERRILL AUTHORS' QUESTIONNAIRE

This is our own "Who's Who and Why," because the regular "Who's Who" is most inadequate. The questionnaire when you fill it out is almost invaluable to the publicity department in preparing special news stories about your books, your life and your favorite breakfast food.

Please sign on the dotted lines and return to THE BOBBS-MERRILL COMPANY, INDIANAPOLIS, INDIANA, U. S. A.

*****

Name and pseudonym: EMILY HAHN — "Mickey"

Date of birth: January 14, 1905

Place of birth: St Louis, Mo.

Present address: 14 West 74th St, N.Y.C.

Notable ancestors or members of family:

None whatever

Education:

U. of Wisc. – B. Sc. in Mining Engineering
Grad. work in Mineralogy, etc. @ Columbia

First attempt at writing: Story about night-club for old "World"

List of books, plays, etc.:

Seductio ad Absurdum
Beginner's Luck

Hahn's three-page Bobbs-Merrill author questionnaire (courtesy of The Lilly Library, Indiana University, Bloomington, Indiana)

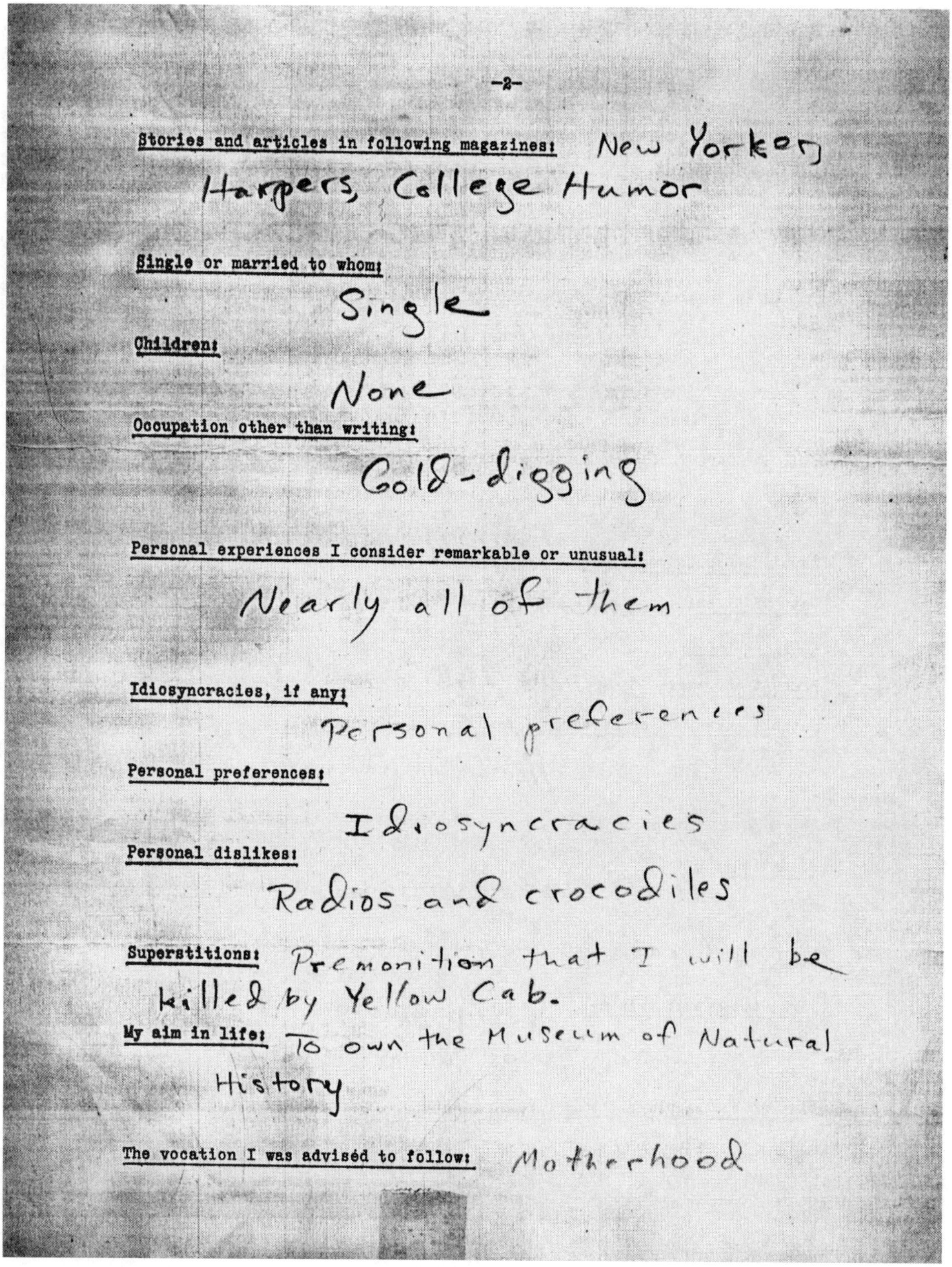

-2-

Stories and articles in following magazines: New Yorker, Harpers, College Humor

Single or married to whom:

Single

Children:

None

Occupation other than writing:

Gold-digging

Personal experiences I consider remarkable or unusual:

Nearly all of them

Idiosyncracies, if any:

Personal preferences

Personal preferences:

Idiosyncracies

Personal dislikes:

Radios and crocodiles

Superstitions: Premonition that I will be killed by Yellow Cab.

My aim in life: To own the Museum of Natural History

The vocation I was advised to follow: Motherhood

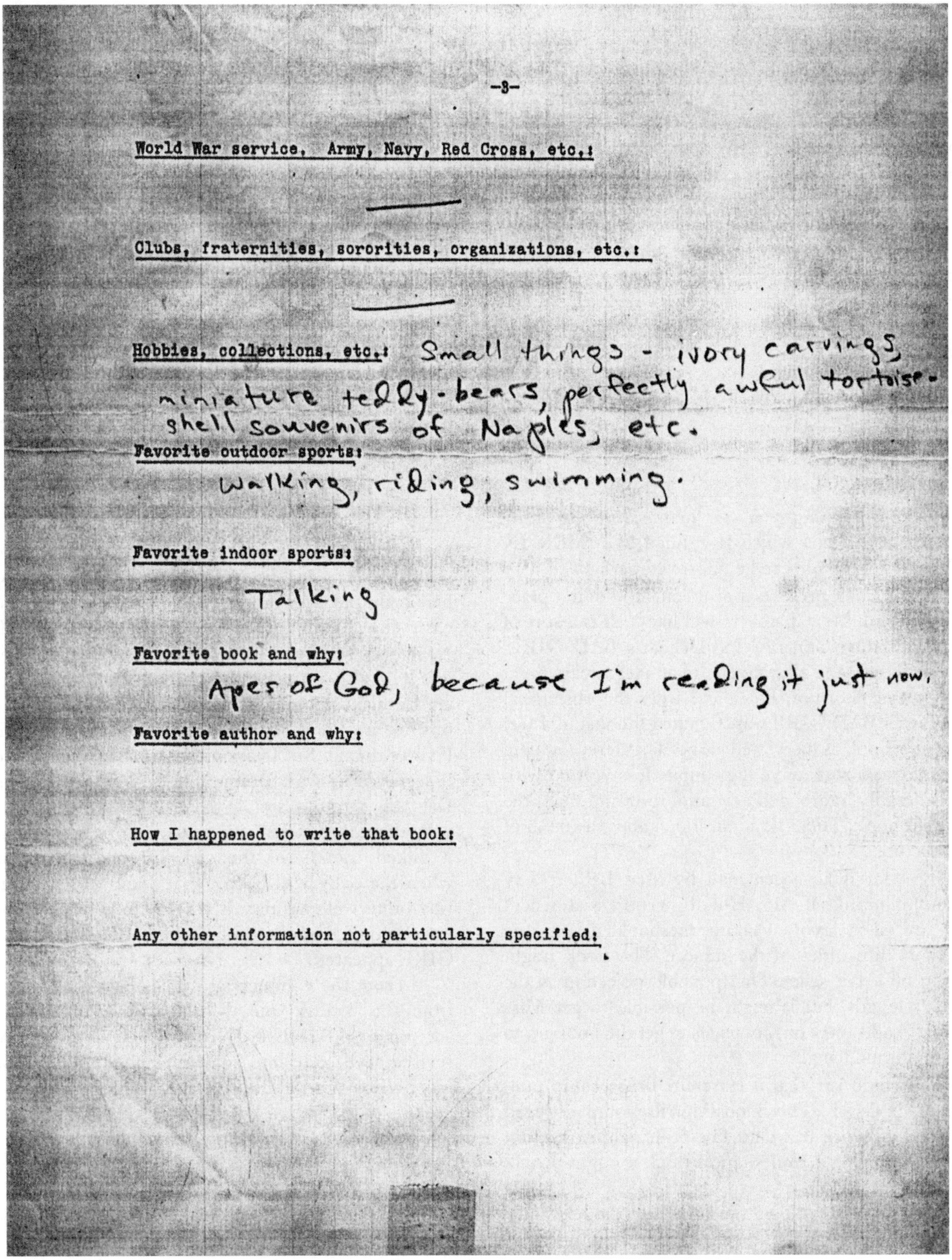

-3-

World War service. Army, Navy, Red Cross, etc.:

—

Clubs, fraternities, sororities, organizations, etc.:

—

Hobbies, collections, etc.: Small things - ivory carvings, miniature teddy-bears, perfectly awful tortoise-shell souvenirs of Naples, etc.

Favorite outdoor sports:

Walking, riding, swimming.

Favorite indoor sports:

Talking

Favorite book and why:

Apes of God, because I'm reading it just now.

Favorite author and why:

How I happened to write that book:

Any other information not particularly specified:

Related Letter

Vice president and trade-department editor D. Laurance Chambers was in charge of a staff that included Dorothy Leffler and Tay Hohoff. (Later, at J. B. Lippincott Company, Hohoff, whose full name was Therese von Hohoff Torrey, edited Harper Lee's To Kill a Mockingbird *[1960].) Jessica Brown Mannon was an editorial assistant with Bobbs-Merrill's Indianapolis office. New York editor Lynn Carrick had good reason to fear Mannon's puritanical tendencies, which she shared to some extent with Chambers. Bernice Baumgarten was with the literary agency Brandt and Brandt. Carrick wrote Mannon regarding the manuscript that became* Affair.

Lynn Carrick to Jessica Brown Mannon, 10 August 1934

Dear Jessica:

I am sending you the manuscript of Emily Hahn's new novel which is entitled SUMMER IN SPRING. (The title can be improved perhaps.)

The book presents a problem. In the first place I don't think Mr. Chambers will like it. It is a sort of modernized version of Vina Delmar's BAD GIRL. The subject is the alluring one of an illegitimate pregnancy and abortion. But it is hardly the obstetrical novel that BAD GIRL was. Granted the theme, I feel that the book is very well done. I suffered acutely with the unfortunate young couple. It is written with considerably more delicacy and restraint than the Delmar book. There is no question about the truth of the picture.

So far it has been read by Miss Leffler, Tay Hohoff and myself. Miss Hohoff's report is attached. We are all in favor of taking the book, despite the obvious difficulties of the subject. The book might easily be a big seller. One possible objection is the book's length, but it might be possible to get Miss Hahn to add forty or fifty pages to get the book up to more normal length.

I would say that if Harcourt Brace could publish BAD GIRL, The Bobbs-Merrill Company need not feel afraid of this one. The principal justification would of course be sales–and I think it ought to sell. Miss Hahn, if I may say so, seems to know her subject. I am not a cynic on the subject of modern morals, but I feel sure that the case described in this book is typical of thousands. Do not allow your puritanical Hoosier background to put you off.

I have had some discussion with Bernice Baumgarten about this book, and you will of course let me handle matters here. And by the way, let's make it a rule that in the case of any book that I send on to you the final disposition is to be made at this end.

Yours,
Lynn

* * *

Reader's Report

Mannon reported on the text of Affair *in 1934.*

SUMMER IN SPRING
By Emily Hahn.

This novel strikes me less as a novel than a case history of an abortion. My "puritanical Hoosier background" is not affronted. I did not feel that this was in any sense a shocking or sensation story. In fact it was all old stuff and has been much better treated in real novels. I am afraid the author does not make her characters real. Surely I am not so hard hearted and narrow that I wouldn't have been moved by Kay and Jimmie's predicament if the story had been told with the skill and insight of a true novelist. This, I maintain, was a coldblooded record of a "case history", if that is the correct term used in clinics. It is also propaganda arguing for birth control and legal abortion. I have always been in favor of birth control and I am quite in sympathy with Miss Hahn's theme. But I cannot see the book as a novel. It seems in no way comparable to BAD GIRL. Vina Del Mar wrote a simple love [*sic*] that appealed to people because it first was a good story and second, it talked frankly of the girl's hospital experience when the baby was born. That angle was new and was quite well written. EX-WIFE and many other novels have described illegal operations since BAD GIRL appeared.

From the commercial point of view as well as from the literary one, I cannot vote in favor of accepting SUMMER IN SPRING. It might be revised and made into something if Miss Hahn put more effort into it, but it is a poor job as it stands.

Jessica Mannon

* * *

Related Letter

Reverend Merle H. Anderson, minister of North Presbyterian Church in New York, wrote Walter J. Hurley, manager of Bobbs-Merrill's New York office, to express his opinion of Hahn's Affair *after Hurley sent him a copy. Hansen was probably the literary critic Harry Hansen.*

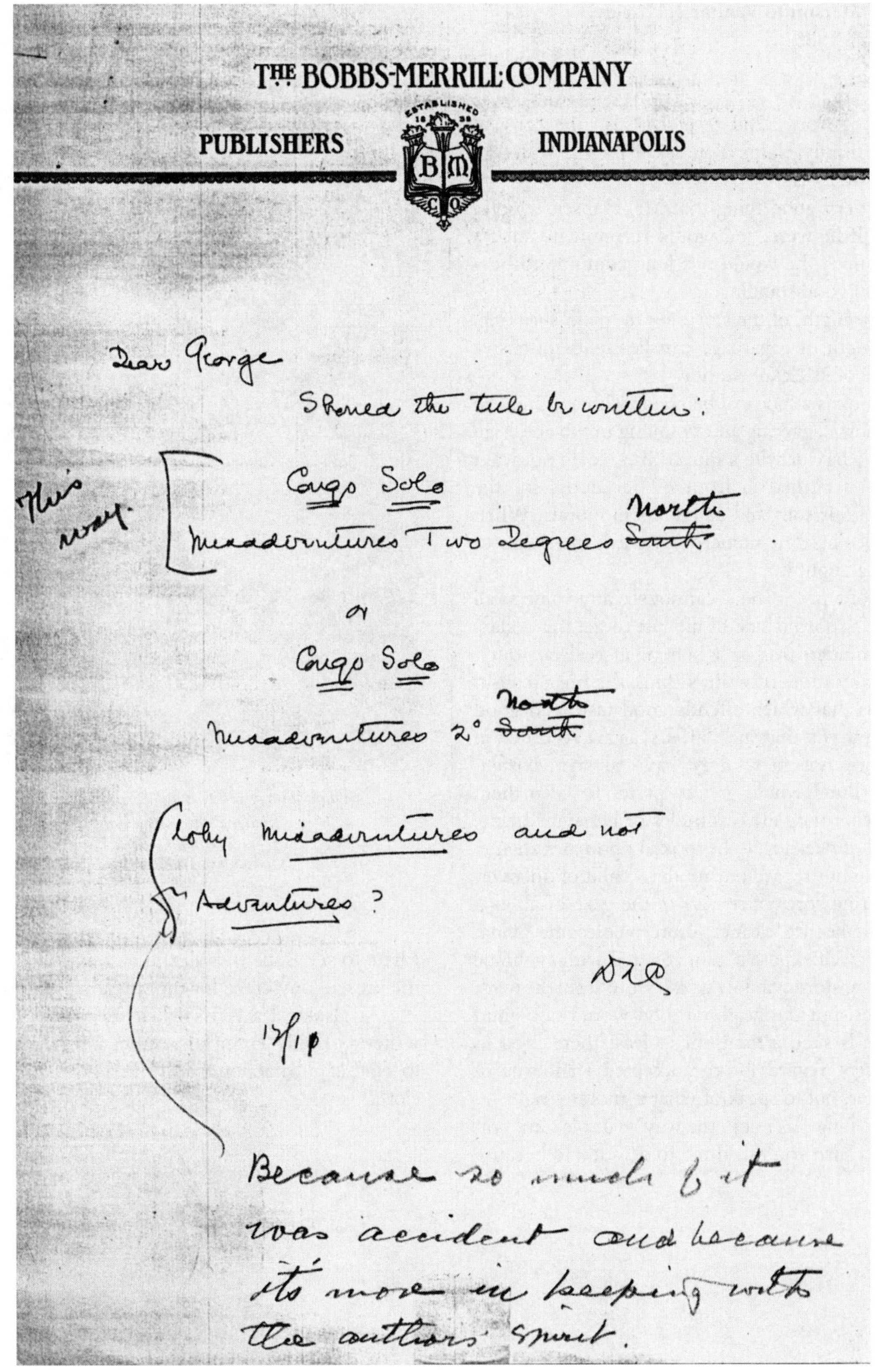
THE BOBBS-MERRILL COMPANY
ESTABLISHED 1838
PUBLISHERS INDIANAPOLIS

Dear George

Showed the title to writer:

This way. Congo Solo
Misadventures Two Degrees ~~South~~ North.

or

Congo Solo
Misadventures 2° ~~South~~ North

Why Misadventures and not
"Adventures?

DLC

12/1?

Because so much of it
was accident and because
it's more in keeping with
the author's spirit.

Mock-up by D. Laurance Chambers of the title page for Hahn's Congo Solo: Misadventures Two Degrees North *(1933), probably advanced to editor George Shively (courtesy of The Lilly Library, Indiana University, Bloomington, Indiana)*

Merle H. Anderson to Walter J. Hurley, 25 April 1935

Dear Sir:

Yours of April 22nd received; also the copy of AFFAIR, by Emily Hahn. You ask if I agree with Mr. Hansen. My reply is:

It is a very good thing that Mr. Hansen is not a churchman. If he were, and would recommend such a book to his flock, he would not long continue to be a churchman in good standing.

The 'strength' of the story lies in 'plain speaking' like the strength of a garbage can lies in its offensive smell in spite of its clean exterior.

The book is a 'book of behavior with a moral'; so is a drunk man staggering and vomiting in the gutter an example of 'behavior with a moral.' But we do not want such examples parked in front of our doors for the instruction of our sons and daughters in morals. When such examples become numerous we ask the police to do something about it.

I am not a prude, but I cannot see any value at all in parading the sordid side of life just to get the dollars of prurient-minded people. I believe in realism; but I cannot see why modern writers think the only realism that is real is that which offends good taste and good morals. I grant you that such 'affairs' as are recorded in this book are not new; they have always existed; always will. But I would greatly prefer to keep them tagged for what they are–examples of behavior below the standard of decency, to be looked upon as a shameful thing. I cannot regard our modern habit of uncovering the festering sores of society to the gaze of all as a policy that makes for cleaner, more wholesome living. Might just as well expose a man covered with syphilitic sores in a drug-store window as a lesson. It might work in some cases, but the neighborhood would not stand for it. There is such a thing–or at least there used to be–as a decent regard for the accepted standards of what is proper, not to speak of what is morally right.

I am writing this not in the way of unpleasant criticism, but because you asked me to do so; and because I hate to see Bobs [*sic*] Merrill add an honored name to the present-day craze for the spreading of filth.

I also feel a sense of shame when so talented a writer as Emily Hahn prostitutes her talent by using it to clothe putrifaction [*sic*] in literary silks and broadcloth.

Very truly yours,
Merle H. Anderson

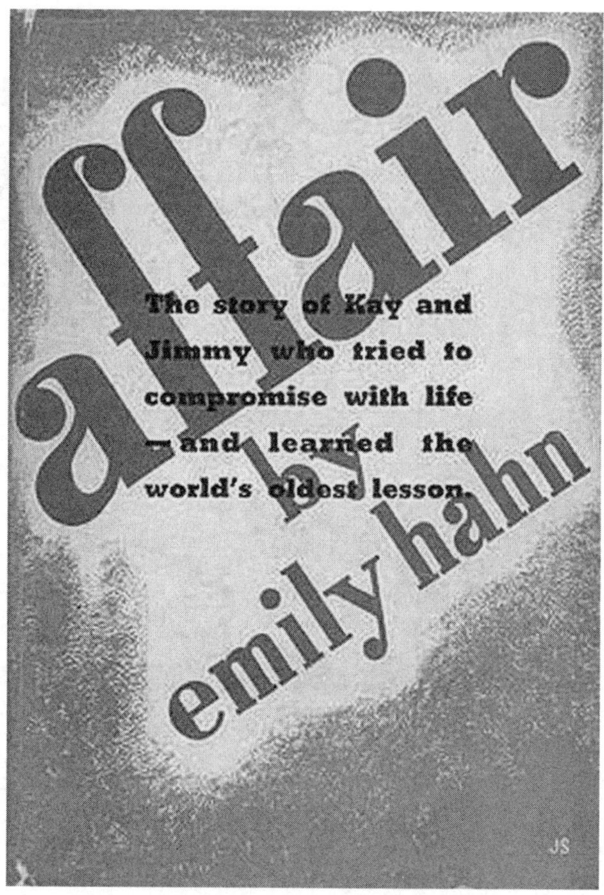

Dust jacket for Hahn's autobiographical 1935 novel (Between the Covers Rare Books, Merchantville, N.J.)

Richard Halliburton (1900–1939)

*Richard Halliburton took "romance" seriously, dedicating his life to one quest after another. He poured his worldwide adventures and stunts into books that usually sold well but were dismissed by critics as juvenile in outlook. With extraordinary courage he followed Ulysses' wanderings (*The Glorious Adventure, *1927) and was the only person to swim the Panama Canal (*New Worlds to Conquer, *1929). He was also a popular, flamboyant speaker, and after one of his performances, fellow Princetonian D. Laurance Chambers, along with editor Thomas R. Coward (later of the publishing firm Coward-McCann), agreed to look at* The Royal Road to Romance *(1925), although it had been rejected by ten publishers. In one of his final tasks, editor Hewitt H. Howland helped lick the book into the shape that made it a best-seller. Halliburton was the kind of author (unlike John Erskine, for example) whose works Bobbs-Merrill sometimes helped plan and write. He was much admired by the company staff, although his posturing and risk taking were worrisome. In 1939 Halliburton set sail from Hong Kong in a Chinese junk, hoping to reach San Francisco, but the ship went down without a trace. In the next twenty-five years his books sold almost a million copies.*

Richard Halliburton (from Stanley J. Kunitz and Howard Haycraft, eds., Twentieth Century Authors, *1942; Thomas Cooper Library, University of South Carolina)*

BOBBS-MERRILL BOOKS BY HALLIBURTON: *The Royal Road to Romance* (Indianapolis: Bobbs-Merrill, 1925; London: G. Bles, 1925);

The Glorious Adventure (Indianapolis: Bobbs-Merrill, 1927; London: G. Bles, 1928);

New Worlds to Conquer (Indianapolis: Bobbs-Merrill, 1929; London: G. Bles, 1929);

The Flying Carpet (Indianapolis: Bobbs-Merrill, 1932; London: G. Bles, 1933);

Seven League Boots (Indianapolis: Bobbs-Merrill, 1935; London: G. Bles, 1936);

Richard Halliburton's Book of Marvels: The Occident (Indianapolis: Bobbs-Merrill, 1937); republished as *A Book of Marvels* (London: G. Bles, 1937);

Richard Halliburton's Second Book of Marvels: The Orient (Indianapolis: Bobbs-Merrill, 1938); republished as *A Book of Marvels of the East* (London: G. Bles, 1938);

Richard Halliburton: His Story of His Life's Adventure as Told in Letters to His Mother and Father (Indianapolis: Bobbs-Merrill, 1940; London: G. Bles, 1941).

Collections: *Richard Halliburton's Complete Book of Marvels* (Indianapolis: Bobbs-Merrill, 1941)–comprises *Richard Halliburton's Book of Marvels: The Occident* and *Richard Halliburton's Second Book of Marvels: The Orient;*

The Famous Adventures of Richard Halliburton (Indianapolis: Bobbs-Merrill, 1947)–comprises *The Flying Carpet, Seven League Boots,* and *Richard Halliburton: His Story of His Life's Adventure as Told in Letters to His Mother and Father;*

The Royal Adventures of Richard Halliburton (Indianapolis: Bobbs-Merrill, 1947)–comprises *The Royal Road to Romance, The Glorious Adventure,* and *New Worlds to Conquer;*

The Romantic World of Richard Halliburton (Indianapolis: Bobbs-Merrill, 1961).

Related Letters

Halliburton welcomed Howland's advice on The Royal Road to Romance, *except in the matter of the title, a traditional concern at Bobbs-Merrill. It was unusual that neither Howland nor Chambers could get him to change it.*

Hewitt H. Howland to Richard Halliburton, 5 May 1925

Dear Mr. Halliburton:

Am sending the first fourteen chapters. I set out to make general recommendations, but became so interested that I got down to cases and did a rough job of both editing and cutting. There's a reason for everything I did, but I'll not bother you with explanations; hope they are not necessary. The last two or three chapters are not so meticulously edited; they seemed to me to need cutting more than anything else; cutting first, at any rate. And for the reason that they are not so interesting, not so romantic, not so adventurous, not so original in the experiences recorded. You have set a high standard and all that doesn't measure up to it, suffers terribly by contrast and in my opinion should come out. You remember Stevenson said that good books are made not by what you put in them, but by what you take out. You have the makings of a good book. I have bracketed the paragraphs that might be dispensed with. The reader, I think, is going to wonder a bit over the rise and fall of your finances. I'd watch out for this. Without waiting to hear from you I'll take the liberty of going ahead with the rest of the manuscript, but an early expression of your approval or disapproval will be greatly appreciated. As I said, I am tremendously interested, and I'm told the story gets better and better as it goes on. With hearty congratulations and all friendly wishes, I am

Sincerely yours,
[Hewitt H. Howland]

* * *

Company vice president Chambers succeeded Howland as chief editor and wrote Halliburton concerning The Glorious Adventure. *Coward was in the New York office.*

D. Laurance Chambers to Halliburton, 8 February 1927

My dear Dick:

I've read the last chapter (proofs of which I enclose) and now I'm swinging back to your first version. Perhaps–to begin at the end–the difficulty is that the attempted parallel between Ulysses and Penelope, and you and Fifi, is so incongruous as to be ridiculous.

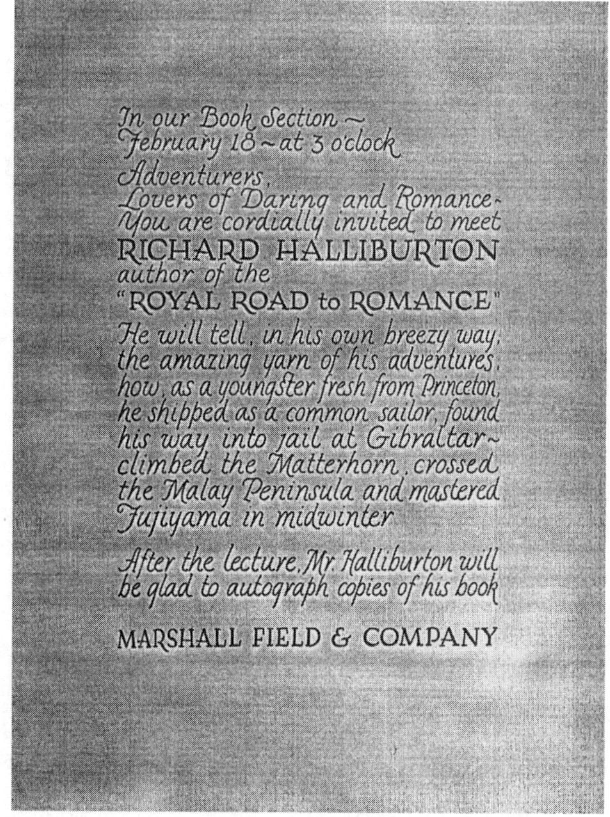

Flier from one of Halliburton's many speaking tours (courtesy of The Lilly Library, Indiana University, Bloomington, Indiana)

Alas, it isn't even funny! It's the failure to establish that kind of parallel that makes one doubt the wisdom of putting Fifi in, at all. Not that you have fallen down in the way you've handled it. But it just can't be done. The material itself is lacking. As long as Fifi was just used for light comedy as in Chapters 19 and 20, I thought we might get by, but from the beginning of 21 where you have an irate husband writing Fifi, and Fifi cabling him for money for you, the fun isn't there. At least your literal-minded readers would never see it as you do. They'd call it bad taste. So we still have a serious problem in the last chapter, and something of a problem in the last three. We shall try to work out some definite ideas of how to fix them and be ready to talk to you when you come on the 20th.

Of course the trouble with the last three chapters, as I think you've recognized from the first, is really that you have very little in them except the Homeric story, and that you have tried to build them up with purely imaginary incident, which I'm very much afraid will be readily recognized as such. Indeed they are so patently manufactured that they may cast doubt on the things you really did: doubt that you swam the Hellespont or climbed Mount Olympus. And that would be calamity.

What is needed, it goes without saying, is more real substance based on your actual experiences. But I gather from your own saying that you didn't have much in the way of actual experience on Gozo, Corfu and Ithaca. If that's the case, I should think compression rather than expansion of this part of the story would be wise. If there's nothing in what happened to you on the island of Ithaca to supply a story, I think we'd better go back to your glowing account of the fight with the suitors.

Coward writes me that in addition to the magazines of which I wrote you previously, the Delineator, Collier's, Pictorial Review and Asia have seen THE GLORIOUS ADVENTURE. All have declined but Asia. And as I'm wiring you today, they can only use the Hellespont story in the April number which is published March 15th. I wish we could do better, but Coward says this is absolutely the last chance of anything. He tells me that he emphasized the illustrations in trying to sell the story, but the magazines are piled high with nonfiction.

I wrote you at Holland and we mailed the pictures you asked for there. Hope you get 'em.

Faithfully yours,
[D. Laurance Chambers]

* * *

The artist mentioned in the following letter was W. H. Lohse, an illustrator of other Bobbs-Merrill books. Evelyn was Chambers's daughter. Baker was either Herbert S. Baker of the New York office or Ross G. Baker, who was in sales in the trade department.

Chambers to Halliburton, 29 October 1927

My dear Dick:

Thank you for your letter. Please keep us advised of your address as best you can so that we may reach you promptly. When you get to New York, better

Frontispiece and title page for Halliburton's first book, published in 1925 (Thomas Cooper Library, University of South Carolina)

speak first to Miss Phillips at the office and make sure it's Lohse who is doing the new jacket. In all probability they will use him, but it's never certain that the artist to whom we apply first is available to do a job immediately, and it's possible that we'll have to use another. Miss Phillips has reported to me that the matter is in hand.

As I told you I think you greatly exaggerate the importance of what criticisms you've heard of the make-up of the book, and the idea that it's been hurt seriously in any way by the jacket blurbs, etc. But there's a chance to use a new jacket for clearing things up and stimulating the sale. However, it's extremely doubtful whether it can be done effectively before Christmas. The dealers get so busy that you can't depend on them to take old jackets off stock and put new jackets on during the holiday season. It may be that we'll get much better results if our boys take out the new jackets on their first trip after Christmas. I'll see how they feel about it. At any rate we'll get the jacket design made and the plates done as fast as possible with good workmanship. Then we'll be ready to shoot.

Following your suggestion, we'll chuck the Parthenon picture. But if you want to cut down the ego element, why substitute the portrait? Better give Miss Phillips promptly the picture you want to use instead of the one left out. You understand, I'm sure, that it won't be feasible to change the illustrations until we print again.

I am not sure that you have the right idea about the advertising. The theory we've built up by a lot of experiments and long experience is that it's better to pound away and pound away with a lot of little ads than it is to use a full page or half-pages, once in a while. But I'll go into this carefully when I get to New York.

Your offer to share the expense is characteristically generous, and I appreciate it fully. Please be sure that all I say is for your best interest, and the books', and ours. We're partners, you bet, and we'll work with and for one another. I know your interest in the house; I understand it, and am grateful for it. You know, for your part, that we're as anxious as you to keep both books going, and build up GLORIOUS ADVENTURE to a glorious height. But we must both be careful to use the coolest possible judgment in any changes we make in the book, the jacket, the advertising, etc. If we have made mistakes, we don't want to make more, as we certainly shall if we allow ourselves to be railroaded into this change and that because of the casual criticisms of our friends and enemies! This is no time to take any steps that won't lead in the right direction; otherwise they'll do actual harm.

The last figures I had howes [*sic*] that we had spent the full amount of the advertising allowance you gave us for THE ROYAL ROAD. I'll check up again and make sure.

It will be mighty nice if you'll call up Evelyn when you get to Pittsfield. Mrs. Chambers was awfully sorry not to see you. She hasn't been very well, and is going to the hospital this afternoon to have a spur removed from her nose. I am waiting anxiously for word about Baker's operation this morning. I'm afraid that at best he'll be out of commission for some time, but we shall carry on somehow and no[t] allow any slow down.

About the jacket blurbs, don't you think it might be better to put on the front flap quotes from the many fine reviews of G.A. and on the back the copy, as you've amended it, that was originally on this front flap? This would omit altogether the general personality business to which you are sensitive.

Yours ever,
[D. Laurance Chambers]

* * *

The company cultivated booksellers as a matter of policy, and Halliburton's frequent store and lecture appearances were an important part of the promotion of his books. Halliburton complained to Bobbs-Merrill about impostors on the bookstore circuit; he forwarded as evidence this letter from a Spokane admirer.

Mary E. Dwight to Halliburton, 11 January 1929

Dear Mr Halliburton,

Probably you have ten-thousand imitators. I just met number nine-thousand-nine-hundred and ninety-nine.

He so cleverly insinuated that he was you and so artifully [*sic*] tried to keep me from guessing he was you incognito, that he aroused my curosity [*sic*] enough for me to take the liberty to write to you and ask.

I met him during the months of February, March and April and again in August of last year. I will be so glad to learn where you were during that time.

Before I met him the only article I had read about you was printed in the American Magazine several years ago.

When I arrived at my home last September, I immediately went to the public library and "looked you up"–The American Magazine was all I could get so I re-read it with great interest but the article was not satisfying. I placed my name on the waiting lists for "The Glorious Adventure" and "The Royal Road to Romance". This week I was able to get one, of the several number, of editions of "The Royal Road to

Romance". Many of the romances your imitator had already told me and elaborated upon.

Your imitator also looks like you and is a striking likeness of you in all the pictures of you in both your books and the American Magazine article.

Nobody seems to be able to enlighten me and I am still wondering if I met Richard Halliburton incognito or just a "clever devil". I can't decide. I doubt if you would be quite so adrent [*sic*] but I can't tell, of course, nor you either.

It is needless to say that I am reading your books with a great deal of interest and that any news of you is very absorbing.

Aside from any personal reason I find "The Royal Road to Romance" charming literature and think you are a unique and glamourous personality who, if I have not already met, I will be most happy to sometime.

I hope you will pardon me for taking the liberty to write to you.

It will make me very happy if you will care to answer but do not let me presume upon your good nature.

Wishing you success and happiness and the fullfillment of your dearest wishes, I am,

Very sincerely,
Mary E. Dwight.

* * *

"Lafe" was Charles D. LaFollette, an assistant to Chambers. Frederic G. Melcher edited Publishers' Weekly. *The writer of the letter is unidentified.*

MRH to Halliburton, 24 January 1929

Dear Dick:

Thank you for your letter about the doity dopes who are impersonating you. Lafe has done a letter for the trade and I've written to Mr. Melcher of Publishers' Weekly, which both ought to squelch this business in practically no time. I hope you wrote to poor little Miss Dwight of Spokane and set her little heart at rest.

It's a lousy trick, and will no doubt be stopped. I hope these birds haven't been cashing any checks. It'd be just too bad if one of 'em would get caught–it'd be plain durance vile for him, thassall.

Yrs,
[MRH]

* * *

Chambers wrote Halliburton concerning The Flying Carpet *(1932). Mina Kersey was on his Indianapolis staff. In the end, he allowed the offending passage about headhunters to remain.*

Chambers to Halliburton, 8 October 1932

Dear Dick:–

The copy for Chapter 33 arrived this morning. Miss Kersey has taken it to Crawfordsville by automobile in the effort to get it set, proof-read, plated and shipped with the rest of the plates today.

It carries the adventure and excitement right up almost to the last word. These Borneo chapters are all most interesting, but I am afraid your critics are going to think that the ending of Chapter 32 is pretty sentimental. They will, I fear, gag on the statement that "Heads or no heads, they are far wiser, perhaps far more nearly arrived at the ultimate goodness of life, than ourselves." Will they be inclined to accept the idea that head-hunting is an arrival at the ultimate goodness of life?

Faithfully yours,
[D. Laurance Chambers]

* * *

Reader's Report

Anne Johnston Ross submitted the following undated report on the manuscript that was published as Richard Halliburton's Book of Marvels: The Occident *(1937).*

RICHARD HALLIBURTON'S BOOK OF MARVELS

Richard Halliburton has been loved and admired by boys and girls ever since he first showed them his Royal Road; it is not to be supposed that they will not appreciate the compliment he pays them in addressing a book exclusively to their eyes. Any one who has ever seen him in a crowd of youngsters, the patience and kindness with which he answers questions, autographs bits of paper, and has seen their shining eyes as they look and listen with all their hearts–any one who has seen this must be charmed by such a relationship. It is natural, it is right, it is very pleasing that he should now turn to the most delighted and delightful of all his audiences and write a book that is frankly for boys and girls alone. Be it said, however, that boys and girls will not be his only readers; like all the best children's books it will draw the eyes also of their elder brothers and sisters, their fathers and mothers.

This Book of Marvels is a book describing and picturing the great wonders of the world. The first fourteen chapters deal with the two great new bridges of San Francisco–the biggest in the world–, Yosemite, the Grand Canyon, Boulder Dam, Niagara, New York, the Washington Monument, Fort Jefferson, Popocatepetl, Chichen-Itza, Christophe's castle in Haiti, the Panama Canal, Macchu Picchu, and Iguazu Falls. These are all

Flier for Halliburton's 1932 book (courtesy of The Lilly Library, Indiana University, Bloomington, Indiana)

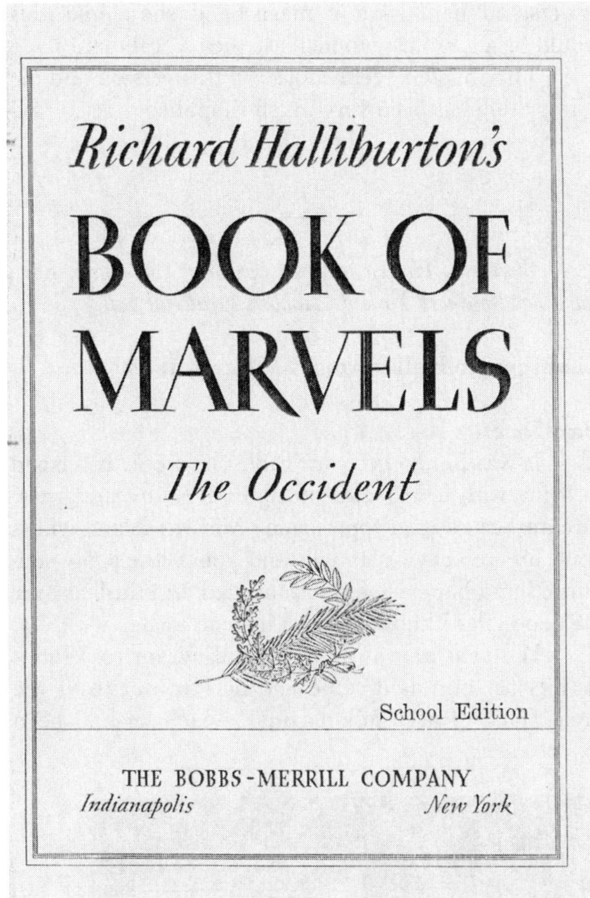

Title page for Halliburton's first book for young readers, published in 1937 (Thomas Cooper Library, University of South Carolina)

graphically described in the author's w.k. enthusiastic, eager style that sweeps the reader up mountains and through rapids, over great cities and through jungles. Of course half the book must be lost without the photographs, for evidently and properly this is intended to be a picture book, references are frequently made to the illustrations, and much must be more clear when they are to be seen. The use and importance of photographs as illustrations in books for young people, especially books that are informative as well as entertaining, is being more and more emphasized, which of course adds to the timeliness of the present volume. But one of the nicest features does not need photographs to expand or emphasize–this is the multitude of little stories the author tells about the places to which he takes us. Mr. Halliburton has always been a delightful story teller, and his tales of the cannon that didn't fire for President Grant, the explorers of the Grand Canyon, the Seven Cities (even an old yarn like this one can read again with pleasure in his fresh exhilerating [*sic*] style), the Virgins of the Sun, Dr. Mudd, and all the rest, are always lively and to the point, sometimes dramatic, or tender. Boys will dote on the statistics given on the San Francisco bridges, girls will take them in their stride, for they are never tiresome, and will enjoy as much as the boys the description of the actual building, will sigh over the "holiday for death" and laugh over the guns that didn't go off. There is some information that is new to most of us and a great deal that we have known and forgotten, there are old familiar corners of the world and new ones, there are reminders of some of the author's old adventures, and these, I think, are not over-emphasized, but kept properly in their places.

The subjects for description seem to me well chosen with perhaps two exceptions. One is the Washington Monument. The chapter that is called by this name has actually very little to say of the Monument and that little reeks too heavily with sweetness and light and love of country. Perhaps Washington (the Monument included) is one of the world's wonders (I am certainly not qualified to judge) but if so the chapter should be headed Washington, or the reader is confused. If it is the Monument rather than the city that is to be described–why, let it be described, let us hear its height, let us see the city from its top, etc., etc. But I don't feel, myself, convinced by this chapter that it deserves inclusion in the book at all. I should be more interested in a chapter about a lot of famous towers–the Leaning Tower of Pisa, the Eiffel Tower, the Monument, and heaps of others that no doubt would occur at once to the author. Then there is Fort Jefferson. Is it really a marvel or an oddity? It certainly strikes me, from the description, as the latter. It cost a great deal of money and served little purpose when it was finished, but was it wonderful for any other reason?

The author's swift, easy style has long recommended itself to youngpeople [*sic*], but one small criticism occurs to me. I do wish he would strike out some of the wonderfuls and marvelouses, I wish that the tour on which he takes us might be a tour, a voyage, what you will, but not a wonder-tour. The wonders that are here described will be even more striking if they are described with a little more restraint.

Anne Ross

* * *

Related Letters

The author of this memo regarding Richard Halliburton's Book of Marvels: The Occident *is unidentified. By this time Chambers was company president as well as trade-department editor. Jessica Brown Mannon was an associate editor.*

Jerry to Chambers, 16 February 1937

Jessica said that in the revision Halliburton has made the sentences shorter and clearer, that the manuscript is now calculated to appeal to children from 8 to 14. She thinks that any child of 8 would like it and even younger. She read some of it to her little niece who is about 6 years old and she liked it and begged her not to stop reading.

She says the whole thing is now definitely a juvenile whereas before it was directed to children, but was more like the author's other books. In her opinion it is well done and exactly what we want. It might not appeal as much to older children as it would have in its previous form, some of it might seem a little babyish to 14-year olds, but, to set a more specific age limit within the general one, she thinks it would be meat for children from 9 to 12.

The vocabulary is within the range of experience of most children and words are given so that children would get the meaning whether they were familiar with it or not. Such words as "cataract" and "stupendous" might not be known to the child at first, but they will understand here what it means and she thinks this would be a good way to increase their vocabularies.

The chapters seem shorter in this version and the whole thing has been very much simplified.

Jerry

* * *

Walter J. Hurley managed the New York office. Rosemary was Rosemary York of Chambers's editorial staff.

Chambers to Halliburton, 23 March 1939

Dear Dick:

It was fine to get your cable last week. It seemed to bring with it the spirit of high adventure and I picture the Sea Dragon approaching Midway Island with a good breeze bellying its sails and you at the prow sunburned and happy. I get both excited and thrilled over the good tales I know you will have to tell.

We sent a copy of your radiogram to Walter Hurley as soon as it came and he sent out to us the great stack of accumulated mail which he had been

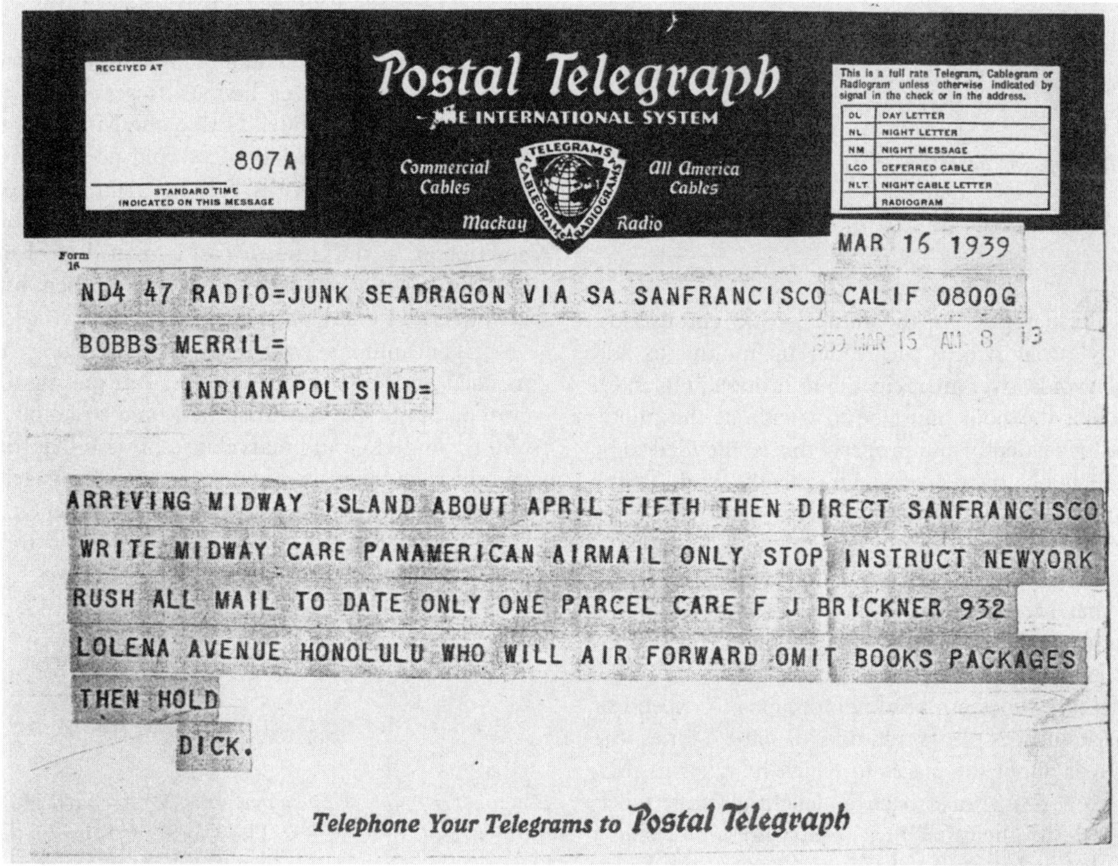

Postal Telegraph
THE INTERNATIONAL SYSTEM
Commercial Cables · All America Cables · Mackay Radio

RECEIVED AT 807A
STANDARD TIME INDICATED ON THIS MESSAGE

This is a full rate Telegram, Cablegram or Radiogram unless otherwise indicated by signal in the check or in the address.

DL	DAY LETTER
NL	NIGHT LETTER
NM	NIGHT MESSAGE
LCO	DEFERRED CABLE
NLT	NIGHT CABLE LETTER
	RADIOGRAM

MAR 16 1939

Form 16

ND4 47 RADIO=JUNK SEADRAGON VIA SA SANFRANCISCO CALIF 0800G

BOBBS MERRIL=

INDIANAPOLISIND=

ARRIVING MIDWAY ISLAND ABOUT APRIL FIFTH THEN DIRECT SANFRANCISCO WRITE MIDWAY CARE PANAMERICAN AIRMAIL ONLY STOP INSTRUCT NEWYORK RUSH ALL MAIL TO DATE ONLY ONE PARCEL CARE F J BRICKNER 932 LOLENA AVENUE HONOLULU WHO WILL AIR FORWARD OMIT BOOKS PACKAGES THEN HOLD

DICK.

Telephone Your Telegrams to Postal Telegraph

Halliburton's last communication with Bobbs-Merrill (courtesy of The Lilly Library, Indiana University, Bloomington, Indiana)

holding. We also had quite a bit for you here. Jessica and Rosemary sorted out the obvious advertisements and circulars which would be of no interest to you now and have held them here. They also removed the newspaper clippings from their heavy envelopes in order to reduce the bulk of the package. The one parcel was then sent by first class mail to Mr. F. J. Brickner, 932 Lolena Avenue, Honolulu with an accompanying letter saying that we were forwarding the package to him at your request with the understanding that he would send it on by air to you at Midway.

Since you are coming straight on from Midway without stopping at Honolulu, you should make good time and save considerable distance. But I'll be looking for a letter from Midway. I'm starved for a full account of all your experiences!

Everyone here joins me in sending you love and best wishes.

Affectionately yours,
[D. Laurance Chambers]

* * *

Bobbs-Merrill Press Release

FOR IMMEDIATE RELEASE September 30, 1947

Bobbs-Merrill's publication on September 19 of THE FAMOUS ADVENTURES OF RICHARD HALLIBURTON, an omnibus including THE FLYING CARPET, SEVEN LEAGUE BOOTS, and the adventures from HIS STORY OF HIS LIFE'S ADVENTURES, calls to attention the perennial public interest in the glamourous travel stories. Since Bobbs-Merrill in 1925 published the first Halliburton book, 1,923,555 copies of his books have been sold in various editions all over the world. THE ROYAL ROAD TO ROMANCE leads the list of sales for any single title. Although Halliburton died in 1939 when his Chinese junk foundered in mid-Pacific, his publishers still receive letters addressed to him and his parents have received more than 350 poems about their son, sent from enthusiastic lovers of adventure from all over the world.

Lost at Sea

When contact with Halliburton was lost, Chambers sent a telegram to Wesley Halliburton, his father, in Memphis.

Chambers to Wesley Halliburton, 31 March 1939

WE ARE THINKING OF YOU AND MRS. HALLIBURTON IN THESE ANXIOUS HOURS OF WAITING BUT WE HAVE ALL CONFIDENCE IN RICHARD'S ABILITY TO RIDE ABOVE THE FORCES OF NATURE.

D. L. Chambers

Alice Tisdale Hobart (1882–1967)

The wife of a Standard Oil executive, Alice Tisdale Hobart lived for two decades in China. Her observations on city and country, and the revolution under way, were published in several essays and three books before she turned to writing novels. Her most popular book was her first for Bobbs-Merrill, Oil for the Lamps of China *(1933), which was compared favorably at the time with Pearl S. Buck's* The Good Earth *(1931).* Oil for the Lamps of China *was filmed twice, the first time starring Pat O'Brien (1935). Not until* The Cup and the Sword, *published in 1942, was a Hobart novel set entirely in America. Her next,* The Peacock Sheds His Tail *(1945), was based on her two years in Mexico. Hobart is usually cited for being the first writer to bring into fiction the Western business community in China and for being successful at the business of writing. Some four million of her books had been sold by the time of her death.*

BOBBS-MERRILL BOOKS BY HOBART: *Oil for the Lamps of China* (Indianapolis: Bobbs-Merrill, 1933; London: Cassell, 1934);

River Supreme (Indianapolis: Bobbs-Merrill, 1934; London: Cassell, 1934); **first edition,** *Pidgin Cargo* (New York & London: Century, 1929);

Yang and Yin: A Novel of an American Doctor in China (Indianapolis: Bobbs-Merrill, 1936; London: Cassell, 1937);

Their Own Country (Indianapolis: Bobbs-Merrill, 1940; London: Cassell, 1940);

The Cup and the Sword (Indianapolis: Bobbs-Merrill, 1942; London: Cassell, 1943);

The Peacock Sheds His Tail (Indianapolis: Bobbs-Merrill, 1945; London: Cassell, 1946);

The Cleft Rock (Indianapolis: Bobbs-Merrill, 1948; London: Cassell, 1950);

The Serpent-Wreathed Staff (Indianapolis: Bobbs-Merrill, 1951; London: Cassell, 1953);

The Innocent Dreamers (Indianapolis: Bobbs-Merrill, 1963; London: Cassell, 1964).

Alice Tisdale Hobart (from Stanley J. Kunitz and Howard Haycraft, eds., Twentieth Century Authors, *1942; Thomas Cooper Library, University of South Carolina)*

Related Letters

Hewitt H. Howland had been company vice president D. Laurance Chambers's predecessor as chief editor of the trade department. He was subsequently a literary agent and part-time editor for Bobbs-Merrill.

Alice Tisdale Hobart to D. Laurance Chambers, 12 March 1933

My dear Mr. Chambers:

On the eve of my entrance into the Bobbs Merrill family of authors I should like to express to you my pleasure in the association and my appreciation of the strong hand of cooperation and intelligent interest you have reached out to me. Your letter has given me a sense of belonging such I [*sic*] have never felt in any other publishing house. That you have accorded me so honorable a place among yourselves I deeply appreciate.

I am sorry that the length of the book has seemed a problem to you and that the dramatic "line" seems by your readers held too much at a level. I want you to know that I will do all in my power to cooperate with Mr Howland in the cutting. I have the greatest respect for Mr. Howland's literary judgement and shall weigh carefully any and all suggestions he makes.

Not with any intention of defending my position but only with the desire to bring us into complete understanding I should like you to know that the length and the dramatic "line" held to a level were not accidental results. It was so that I concieved [*sic*] of the story. My previous novel, a man's struggle with the great impersonal force of the Yangtse River I wrote with swift dramatic accents. But this struggle of a man with the great impersonal force of modern business seemed to me could not be thus written. There was the danger of seeming to manipulate the the [*sic*] material to my own ends if I gave free reign [*sic*] to the highly dramatic quality of Big Business in its exploitation of the individual. I wanted to avoid anything that could be interpreted as a dramatic gesture. I felt the story must creep forward with the slow movement of life itself, without the exaggeration that is inevitable in the dramatic heightening of material. Only so would the story carry the conviction of reality. I have a feeling that much of the impressiveness that seems to be a quality of the book–and which you felt–lies in this treatment.

Please do not think I am saying all this in order to stubbornly defend each and every scene in the book. I do believe that cutting will add to the artistry of the book as well as to its sales value but I wanted to take you behind the scenes, so to speak, in my mind so that you might know the spirit in which the book was written.

I do not wish in any way to be a trouble to you but if at any time I can aid in the furtherance of the book through my knowledge of China, or in giving you data on my previous work, or put you in touch with groups of people whom I know will be interested in the book, I hope you will feel free to call upon me.

Again may I express my appreciation of your letter.

Most Sincerely
Alice Tisdale Hobart

* * *

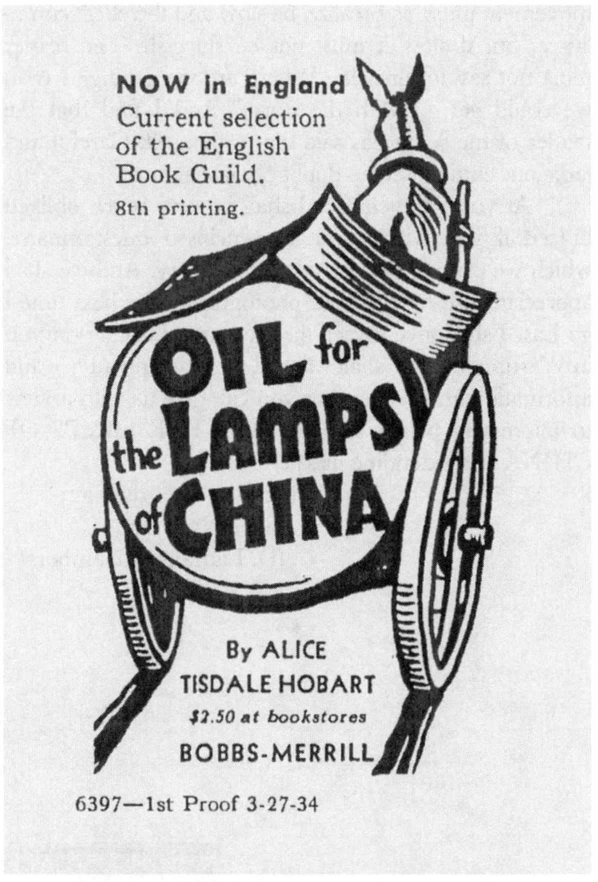

Proof of an advertisement for Hobart's best-known book, her first with Bobbs-Merrill, published in 1933 (courtesy of The Lilly Library, Indiana University, Bloomington, Indiana)

Chambers to Hobart, 17 March 1933

My dear Mrs. Hobart:–

My devoted thanks for your very gracious letter of the 12th, which Mr. Howland has forwarded to me, with the signed copy of the contract for OIL FOR THE LAMPS OF CHINA. I know that everyone in our force shares my happiness that we are to publish this book and even more, as we hope, that we are to become your permanent publishers; for we like to think in terms of the author and the author's whole career, and not in terms of a single book–notable as this book is. We shall endeavor to the best of our ability to give you good service and to justify your loyalty.

I must record my gratitude for your gracious consideration of the suggestions offered for possible improvement of the script. Of course on the literary side we have no right to speak with authority. Our experience ought perhaps to be of some help from the commercial. I should like to think so. Your comment helps to clarify my own thinking about the difficulty. Very likely recurring climaxes would impair the impressiveness of the work. The movement must, as I realize, be slow and the effect cumulative; but if slow it must not be sluggish. The reader must not say to himself: "Where are we getting? I wish we could get on with the story." And I find that the reader of the script has said that to himself. Careful and judicious cutting will no doubt obviate all this.

At your convenience I shall be very much obliged indeed if you will fill out the enclosed questionnaire, which we can use later on in our publicity. And we shall appreciate also having your photograph. The next time I go East I shall give myself the pleasure of calling on you in Washington. We shall want all the help and advice and information and suggestions you can give us with a view to interesting people in OIL FOR THE LAMPS OF CHINA and extending its sale.

With kindest regards, I am
Sincerely yours,
[D. Laurance Chambers]

* * *

Reader's Report

Jessica Brown Mannon reported to Chambers on Hobart's The Cup and the Sword *in a memo dated 1 April 1942. Chambers was now president as well as trade-department editor in chief.*

I've finished Mrs. Hobart's novel. It is perfectly swell. She's written it with a master hand and I have only the most minor criticisms to make.

Perhaps the most important concerns the difficulty I had in keeping the names straight. The book is the chronicle of Jean Philippe Rambeau's family–California Winemakers. All the important characters are quickly established and easily identified except for their last names. They all, of course, belong to the Rambeau family, but which were Fairons and which were Rambeaus, never was quite clear. I finally figured out that two of Philippe's daughters married brothers by the name of Fairon. The Fairons were Francis and Ronald.

Design study for Hobart's 1933 novel (courtesy of The Lilly Library, Indiana University, Bloomington, Indiana)

Yet once I thought Andre was a Fairon and his wife Charlotte was a Rambeau. Later I decided that Charlotte was not either. So Andre must have been a Rambeau. I don't have the manuscript now and can't go back and recheck.

At any rate it is important to make it clear at the right time that Elizabeth is marrying a Fairon and not a Rambeau; that John, Monica and Charles are Rambeaus, not Fairons, etc.

It maybe [*sic*] that the typist made an error that caused my confusion. I think the names should be checked carefully throughout.

The other general criticism concerns the time. The years were not always quite clear. There is one particular place where I have questioned the time on the margin of the manuscript. It concerns John and his Black Brocade grapes. This is on page 478. There are one or two other things I have questioned on the margin for your attention.

The chief weakness in the story as I see it, concerns Elizabeth. She has played the star role up to the time of her marriage. That is carried off rather hurriedly and then she disappears from the scene for quite a while. I could wish that a little more time could have been given to her decision to pick Andrew as a means of escape. It wouldn't take much–perhaps only a paragraph–to prepare the reader for her action. Then it seems that there should be a short scene with Elizabeth after she runs off with Andrew in which she writes the letter to her grandfather that Martha intercepts. I think this would make an easier transition. And it would make clearer that the grandfather really was right in accusing Martha of having broken Elizabeth. Her marriage did make her selfish and untrue to the best in her nature. It is years before she develops into a real person.

It occurs to me that the best way to keep the people in the family straight, would be for Lon to tell Elizabeth when he ships her off to Martha, the names of all his brothers and sisters. Then when she meets them at the family dinner, the reader could catch on a little quicker. They all come in too much of a rush as it is, and I never did get a chance to go back and check them up. Consequently I never was sure who was a Fairon and who a Rambeau.

Except for these small matters, the book is ready for the printer, in my estimation. It is a much better, more interesting, more readable and fascinating novel than THEIR OWN COUNTRY. At all times the

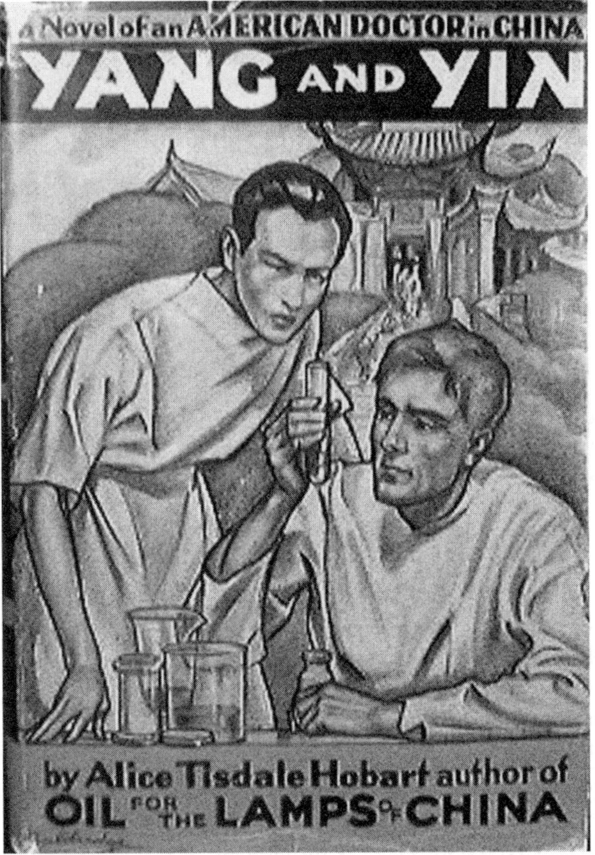

Dust jackets for Hobart's first and third (1936) Bobbs-Merrill novels (Michael Manz/Babylon Revisited; Jonathan Nelson Booksellers)

reader is much concerned about what happens to the characters in the book. There was no time that I wanted to put it down. And as usual, Mrs. Hobart has shown her amazing ability to describe a business and make it fascinating. I was at all times absorbed in her descriptions of the vineyards, the winery, et cetera. That alone would make the book worthwhile. But in old Philippe Rambeau, in Martha, in John, in Elizabeth, she has created people of unusual personalities, very distinct, quite complex and very much alive.

It is extremely difficult to manage so many threads of story and keep the book unified. But Mrs. Hobart has done this. I remember that in THEIR OWN COUNTRY the book at times creaked under its mechanical construction. I do not find this true in THE SWORD AND THE CUP. It seems to grow as naturally as old Philippe's vineyards. I never felt that she was preaching propaganda. There is a consciousness of social problems, but they make the reading all the more interesting–they do not interfere or annoy. I have a feeling that for the first time, perhaps, the author writes without any personal animosity. As a result the book is much more delectable. (Incidentally, the winemakers ought to pay Mrs. Hobart a commission. She has raised a terrible thirst in this reader.)

Jessica Mannon

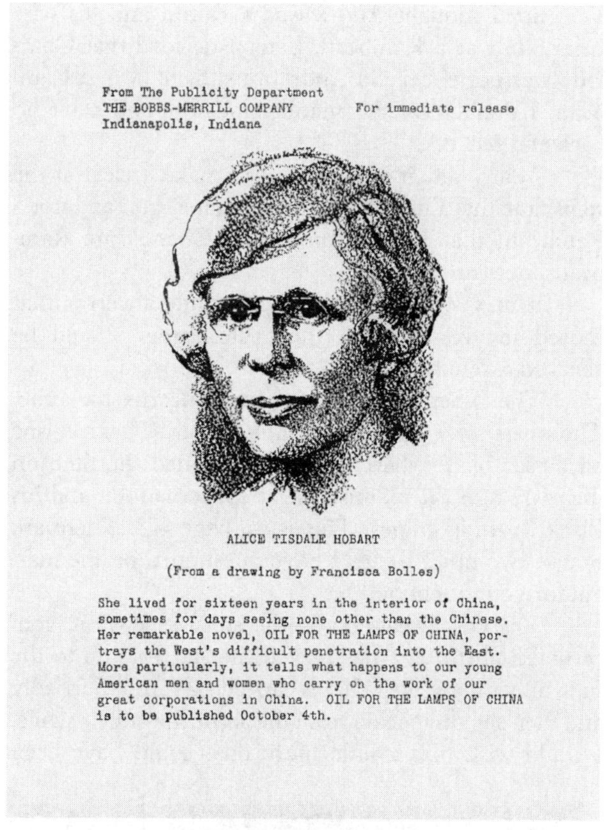

From The Publicity Department
THE BOBBS-MERRILL COMPANY For immediate release
Indianapolis, Indiana

ALICE TISDALE HOBART

(From a drawing by Francisca Bolles)

She lived for sixteen years in the interior of China, sometimes for days seeing none other than the Chinese. Her remarkable novel, OIL FOR THE LAMPS OF CHINA, portrays the West's difficult penetration into the East. More particularly, it tells what happens to our young American men and women who carry on the work of our great corporations in China. OIL FOR THE LAMPS OF CHINA is to be published October 4th.

Publicity release promoting Oil for the Lamps of China *(courtesy of The Lilly Library, Indiana University, Bloomington, Indiana)*

* * *

Related Letters

H. A. Caddow was secretary-manager of the Wine Institute, the association of California winegrowers, in San Francisco. At the bottom of the letter is the notation "8-29-42–Copies of this letter sent to the salesmen.–MH."

H. A. Caddow to Chambers, 22 August 1942

Dear Mr. Chambers:

I, as well as members of my staff, have just read the advance copy of "The Cup and the Sword" by Alice Tisdale Hobart, and I am writing to congratulate you upon the publication of this great book.

In all of the ages-old history of wine, no writer has ever discovered and given the world the rich human story of the wine grower's world, his life, dreams, strivings, and ideals, until Alice Hobart wrote this great story. She has brought to the printed page for the first time the romantic and adventurous lives of those who produce "the blood of the grape." Especially, she has translated the spiritual significance of wine and has woven it into a truly thrilling story.

While she has, with evident care, avoided certain historical details that would embarrass certain organizations, individuals and their families within the grape and wine industry, it is easy to see in her fictional handling of certain sensational occurrences that she did a splendid job of research into the history of California wine growing before she wrote the book. Her story will undoubtedly capture the public imagination, but it will also be tremendously interesting to all who have any familiarity with wine and with the wine industry.

The Wine Institute, which is the association of California wine growers, will enthusiastically approve "The Cup and the Sword," and our organization will help to tell the reading public about this book, so that the largest possible number of people may have the opportunity to enjoy it.

Congratulations to The Bobbs-Merrill Company, as well as to Mrs. Hobart, and may "The Cup and the Sword" quickly become one of the greatest of best-sellers.

Very truly yours,
WINE INSTITUTE
H. A. Caddow
Secretary-Manager

* * *

Annie Laurie Williams was a literary agent specializing in movie rights; she handled those for the 1939 adaptation of Margaret Mitchell's Gone with the Wind *(1936). Hobart's* The Cup and the Sword *was made into the movie* This Earth is Mine *(1959).*

Chambers to Caddow, 29 August 1942

Dear Mr. Caddow:–

Many thanks for your fine letter of the 22nd which I find on my desk on my return today from a short business trip. My associates and I are most grateful to you and the members of your staff for your appreciation of The Cup and the Sword by Alice Tisdale Hobart and for all you are doing to help us extend its sale and distribution.

Nothing could be finer than to have your active support, including the releases from your Publicity Department and the assistance of the thirty-nine men in your Dealer Service Department operating in thirty states and encouraging the work of the bookseller. We are pleased, too, that you have suggested to certain wine retailers who occasionally offer books about wine for sale that they display The Cup and the Sword.

Your sincere words of praise for Mrs. Hobart's novel should be of real assistance to Miss Annie Laurie Williams in her effort to sell the motion picture rights.

I am sure that it is quite unnecessary for me to mention it and I mention it simply to be on the safe side: one should be careful not to let it appear to anyone that the writing of The Cup and the Sword was inspired by the Wine Institute, for both booksellers and newspapers are very wary of an inspired book and very quick to suspect advertising. One must bend over backwards as I am sure you realize. Emphasis may be placed on the fact that Mrs. Hobart in her own search for literary material happened upon this material so rich, so dramatic and so spiritual in its significance, entirely by her own motion.

With kindest regards, I am
Sincerely yours,
[D. Laurance Chambers]

Dust jacket for Hobart's 1948 novel (Frugal Books)

Emerson Hough (1857–1923)

See also the Hough entries in *DLB 9: American Novelists, 1910–1945* and *DLB 212: Twentieth-Century American Western Writers, Second Series.*

Emerson Hough produced literature of many kinds, along with journalism and polemics. A sportsman and conservationist, he wrote authentically about the American West, starting with The Story of the Cowboy *(1897), which Theodore Roosevelt publicly admired. While Hough's fiction about the frontier was romantic (though less so than dime novels), his nonfiction treated it more realistically. He was intensely patriotic, to the point of being a nativist, and he found commercial success when he turned to historical fiction of the kind Bobbs-Merrill was promoting early in the twentieth century. Beginning with* The Mississippi Bubble *(1902), his formula was to use actual historical events as the basis for melodrama. His racial and political views were controversial but did not hinder his overall success. Bobbs-Merrill's promotion made Hough wealthy, and yet he left the firm in a dispute over royalties. With D. Appleton and Company he published his famous* The Covered Wagon *(1922) and lived long enough to see the 1923 movie adaptation.*

Emerson Hough (courtesy of Special Collections, University of Iowa Libraries)

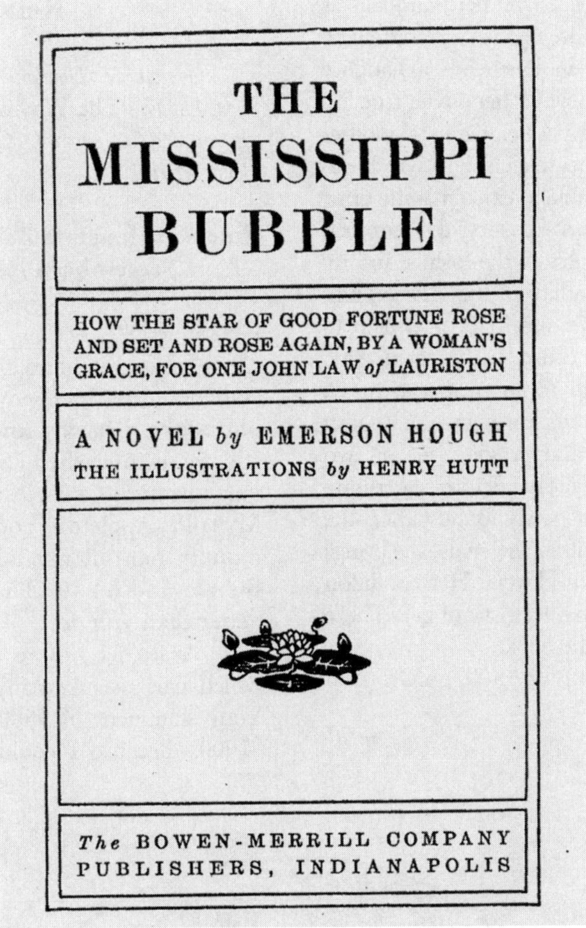
THE MISSISSIPPI BUBBLE

HOW THE STAR OF GOOD FORTUNE ROSE AND SET AND ROSE AGAIN, BY A WOMAN'S GRACE, FOR ONE JOHN LAW *of* LAURISTON

A NOVEL *by* EMERSON HOUGH
THE ILLUSTRATIONS *by* HENRY HUTT

The BOWEN-MERRILL COMPANY
PUBLISHERS, INDIANAPOLIS

Title page of Hough's first historical novel for the firm, published in 1902 (O'Neill Library, Boston College)

BOWEN-MERRILL/BOBBS-MERRILL BOOKS BY HOUGH: *The Mississippi Bubble: How the Star of Good Fortune Rose and Set and Rose Again, by a Woman's Grace, for One John Law of Lauriston* (Indianapolis: Bowen-Merrill, 1902; London: Methuen, 1903);

The Way to the West and the Lives of Three Early Americans: Boone–Crockett–Carson (Indianapolis: Bobbs-Merrill, 1903; London: Hodder & Stoughton, 1925);

The Law of the Land: Of Miss Lady, Whom It Involved in Mystery, and of John Eddring, Gentleman of the South, Who Read Its Deeper Meaning (Indianapolis: Bobbs-Merrill, 1904);

The King of Gee-Whiz; or, The Enchanted Banjo, by Hough and Wilbur D. Nesbit, illustrated by Oscar E. Cesare (Indianapolis: Bobbs-Merrill, 1906);

54-40 or Fight (Indianapolis: Bobbs-Merrill, 1909; London: Hodder & Stoughton, 1924);

The Purchase Price; or, The Cause of Compromise (Indianapolis: Bobbs-Merrill, 1910; London: Hodder & Stoughton, 1925);

The Singing Mouse Stories (revised and enlarged, Indianapolis: Bobbs-Merrill, 1910; **first edition,** New York: Forest & Stream, 1895);

John Rawn, Prominent Citizen (Indianapolis: Bobbs-Merrill, 1912);

The Lady and the Pirate: Being the Plain Tale of a Diligent Pirate and a Fair Captive (Indianapolis: Bobbs-Merrill, 1913).

Review: *54-40 or Fight* (1909)

Although the reader might be interested in the historical part of Emerson Hough's novel, he will probably be more interested in following the fortunes of the woman in the case. He will know from the very beginning that Calhoun will get what he wants of the beautiful, mysterious Baroness who is supposed to be the friend of England and who is known to have caused jealousy in the heart of the wife of the Mexican Minister at Washington. The man who tells the story of how America won her boundary as far as British Columbia and Oregon is Secretary Calhoun's right-hand man. He is in love with a haughty Southern girl who refuses to believe her lover true on account of a small white satin slipper belonging to another woman which is found in his possession, and which circumstance the young man is unable to explain at the time. Calhoun is persistent, and so is his secretary; the Baroness is charmed by the old-time chivalry of the former and by the perfect "innocence" and gentility of the latter. Their persistence and American daring and vigor also help to win the Austrian lady to their cause. In her own way, which is good, although peculiar to an American mind, she gets for America what she wants, throwing the English Ambassador's proposals down and proving one or two other foreign representatives traitors. Before she disappears from Washington with her newly found father–the hero intimates that he knows whither she went–she brings about a reconciliation between the lovers. Her condition for adjusting their quarrel was characteristic of her. There are several color illustrations in the book.

–*New York Times,* 12 June 1909, pp. 375–376

* * *

Related Letters

Hewitt H. Howland was chief editor in the trade department. Hough's The Way of a Man *had been published by Outing in 1907. John J. Curtis ran the New York office of Bobbs-Merrill.*

Emerson Hough to Bobbs-Merrill, 4 September 1909

Gentlemen:–

I have at hand, reforwarded from Paris, your statement of sales of my books, June 30 last. As to the old books, I hardly know what to say, except that I still retain uncashed, your last check $1.85, which I value rather as a curiosity than as a commercial asset. My old Appleton books have paid me far more money than all my books with you, excepting the Bubble and 54-40. They seem to keep up their list better than you do.

As to 54-40, we are all gratified at its success, which was useful to myself and perhaps to you also. Your statement of $6600., shows net profit to me of $1600., because I could have serialized the book for

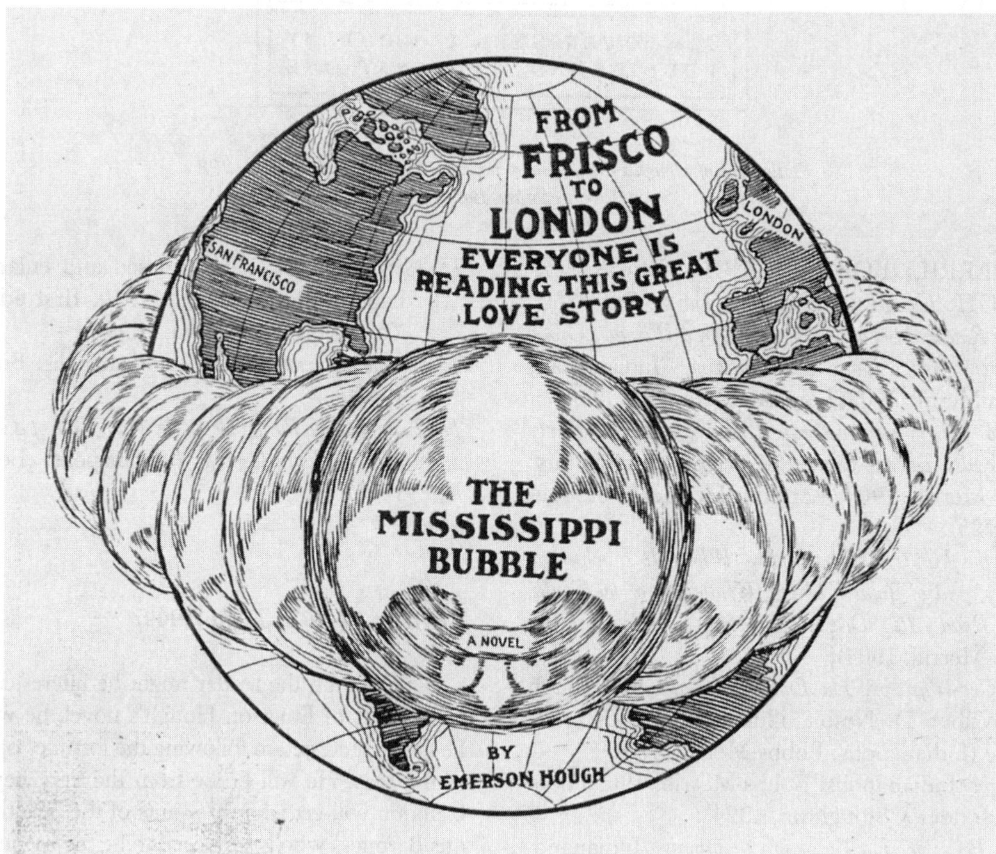

Advertisement for Hough's historical novel (courtesy of The Lilly Library, Indiana University, Bloomington, Indiana)

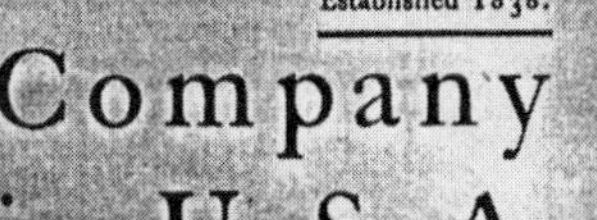

Established 1838.

The Bowen-Merrill Company
Publishers, *Indianapolis*, U. S. A.

William C. Bobbs, *President*. Charles W. Merrill, *Treasurer*. John J. Curtis, *Secretary*.

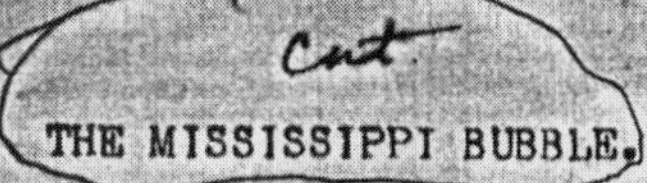

Cut

THE MISSISSIPPI BUBBLE.

"Mr. Hough has constructed a romance more than ingenious. It is clever, fascinating, thrilling. And if it is sometimes theatrical, it is never more so than was the actual, brilliant career of historic John Law upon which it is founded."- N. Y. World.

IN FRANCE AND AMERICA.

"The exquisite descriptions in "The Mississippi Bubble" of the American Wilderness,-the glittering picture of dissolute, spendthrift, money-gorged Paris are triumphs of literary art."- Toledo Blade.

A RARELY BEAUTIFUL LOVE STORY.

"As a love story it is rarely and beautifully told. John Law, as drawn in this novel, is a great character, cool, debonair, audacious, he is an Admirable Crichton in his personality, and a Napoleon in his far-reaching wisdom."- Chicago American.

Draft of a promotional piece for Hough's 1902 novel (courtesy of The Lilly Library, Indiana University, Bloomington, Indiana)

Original olive-green cloth binding of Hough's novel; one of the many later bindings, in maroon cloth (courtesy of The Lilly Library, Indiana University, Bloomington, Indiana)

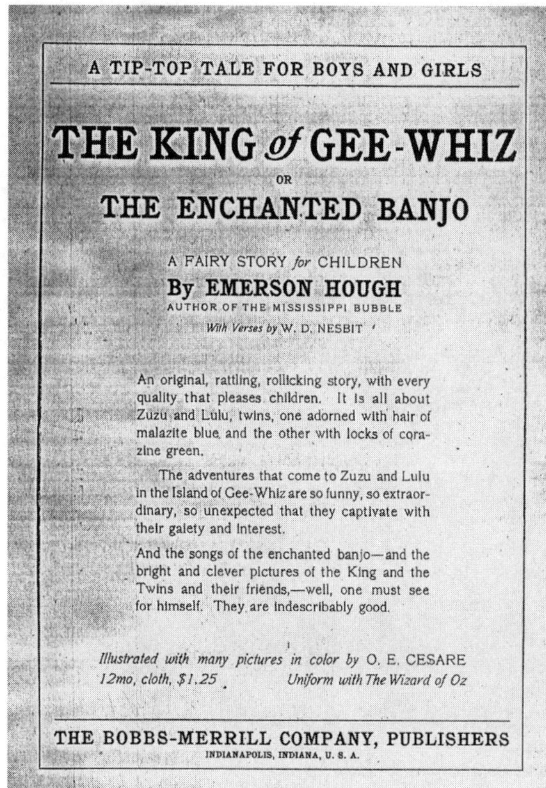

Flier for Hough's 1906 children's book (courtesy of The Lilly Library, Indiana University, Bloomington, Indiana)

$5000. Also, I could have had an advance of $5000. cash at the end of serialization, this from another firm. These matters do not make me waver in my judgment in coming to you, although they confirm my judgment that I ought to have serialized the book. A best seller ought to make one more money than this in one way or another.

Mr. Howland says he will explain anything I do not understand in this statement. There are two items I do not understand–sales at 7-1/2c royalty. I have had no arrangement or understanding at least, warranting any division of royalties in that way at this stage of the game. I wish you would explain this, agreeable to Mr. Howland's suggestion.

I enclose you [*sic*] copy of the attorneys of the Outing Co. letter. I fear you got on the ground too late to be of service to us. I hope however you will ask Mr Curtiss [*sic*] to look into this matter of "The Way of a Man," find out who bought it and under what terms. I think we can stop the publication on the face of my contract which, as I have stated before, leaves the right to purchase in author's hands in case of failure to publish on the part of publishers. I shall be very much obliged to hear from you in this matter.

Yours very truly,
E. Hough

* * *

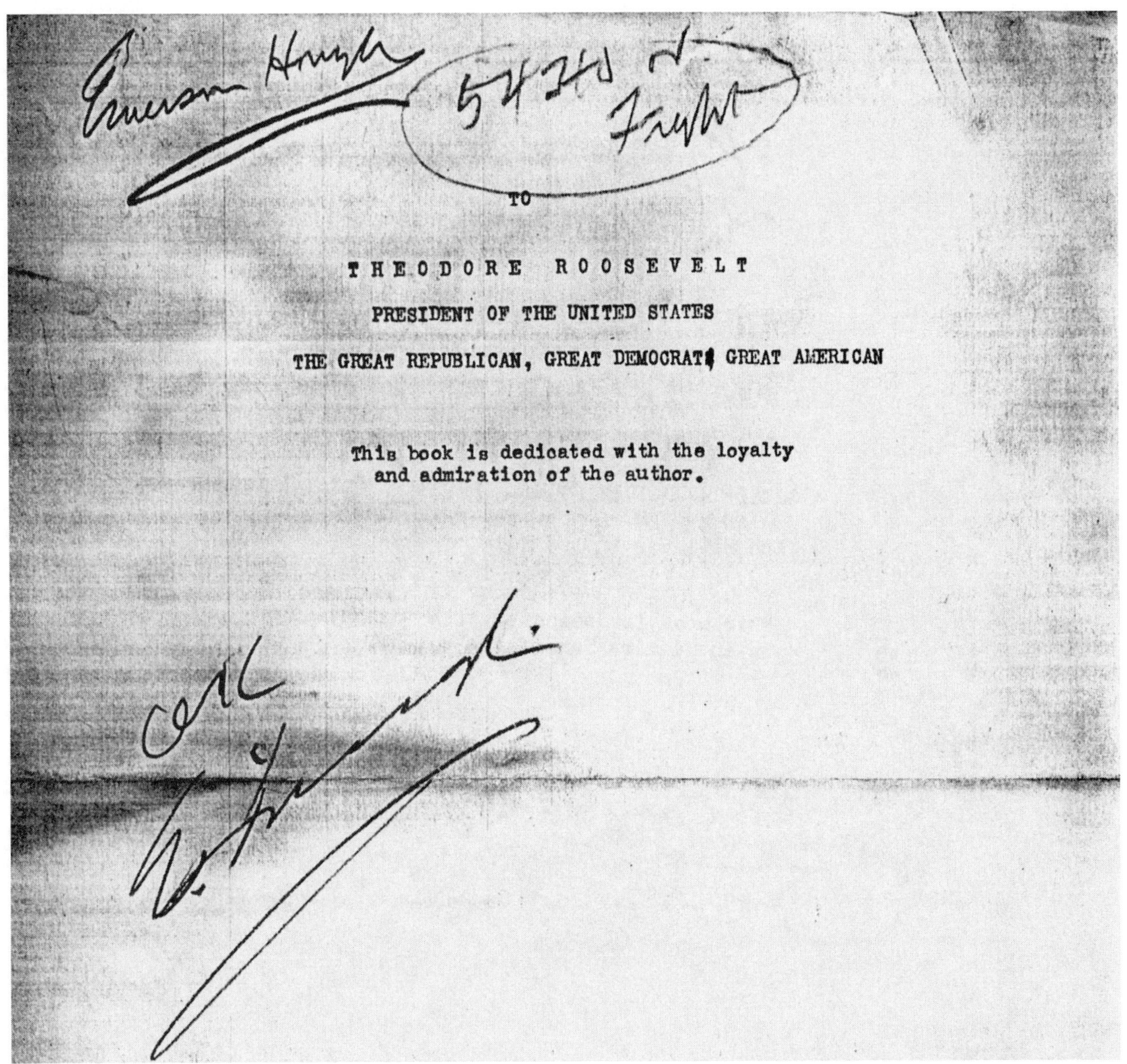
Emerson Hough

54–40 or Fight

TO

THEODORE ROOSEVELT

PRESIDENT OF THE UNITED STATES

THE GREAT REPUBLICAN, GREAT DEMOCRAT GREAT AMERICAN

This book is dedicated with the loyalty and admiration of the author.

Three trial dedication pages for 54-40 or Fight *(1909), annotated by Hough. The final version was "TO* | Theodore Roosevelt | *PRESIDENT OF THE UNITED STATES* | *AND FIRM BELIEVER IN THE RULE OF THE PEOPLE* | *THIS BOOK IS DEDICATED* | *WITH THE LOYALTY AND ADMIRATION* | *OF THE AUTHOR" (courtesy of The Lilly Library, Indiana University, Bloomington, Indiana).*

Hewitt H. Howland to Hough, 11 September 1909

My dear Mr. Hough:

In reply to your letter regarding copyright, we find that the receipt for the American copyright of "The King of Gee Whiz" and the English certificate for "54–40 or Fight" have never been sent you. They got into our files by mistake. Let us know if this completes your records. We cannot make a transcript of the other certificates as you suggest for they are, or at least they should be, in your possession.

In answer to your inquiry as to the seven and one-half cent royalty as shown on your report for the Canadian and Australian editions, this is caused by the fact that in these countries the book retails at seventy-five cents and ten percent on this amount is seven and one half cents.

We have written Mr. Curtis again with regard to "The Way of a Man" and shall advise you as soon as we hear from him. We regret that we did not get in earlier on this Outing sale but the matter was taken up immediately on receipt of information by this department.

Very sincerely yours,
[Hewitt H. Howland]

* * *

#1

54-40

TO

T H E O D O R E   R O O S E V E L T

PRESIDENT OF THE UNITED STATES

GREAT REPUBLICAN, GREAT DEMOCRAT, GREAT AMERICAN

And Believer in the Rule of the People

This book is dedicated with the loyalty and admiration of the author.

The President might not think the real meaning of all this perfectly apparent. E. Hough.

Hough left the manuscript of The Lady and the Pirate *(1913) with Bobbs-Merrill and went on vacation. He returned to find it published in a cheap edition with many errors, without a contract. This mishap was the result of a complicated dispute over his previous book. Hough wrote company president William C. Bobbs about this matter.*

Hough to William C. Bobbs, 5 September 1913

Dear Mr. Bobbs:

Yes, I admit a feeling of mild surprise, and consider it warranted, over the publication of my book without contract and contrary to all my advices to you. Two things ought to be attended to as soon as you can get around to it, better if you or someone of the house should be here; one is the correction of the plates–the proofreading is very bad–and the other is the mere formality of a contract between us so that we shall know where we stand.

In regard to the latter, I presume you printed the book because you knew I would no more squeeze you with the advantage on my side than without. I thought over the matter a long time while I was in the North, and had concluded not to print this book over my own name at all, but to give it to you, Harper's or Brown over the name "Henry Richmond Coyle". I have had very good contracts offered me on that basis. But I certainly do not wish to be unpleasant, for I am feeling very calm and normal at last; and I only write to suggest that we get together at your first convenience;

Yours very sincerely,
E. Hough

[Handwritten on verso, probably a draft for a telegram by Bobbs:]

#2

TO

THEODORE ROOSEVELT

PRESIDENT OF THE UNITED STATES

This book is dedicated with the loyalty and admiration of the author.

Simple & beyond any criticism, but it doesn't say quite all the author feels like saying!

E. Hough

Congratulations for your good health and fine spirits. Send on your corrections to Indpolis at once and I will run up to see you just as soon as I get back home
<u>Day Letter</u>

* * *

Bobbs wrote William A. Tilden, president of the Fort Dearborn National Bank in Chicago, informing him of Hough's legal action against Bobbs-Merrill. Ultimately the dispute was settled out of court, and the stipulations included paying Hough $1,500 and granting him the movie rights to his books.

Bobbs to William A. Tilden, 27 December 1913

Dear Mr. Tilden:–

Yesterday we had a letter from A. C. McClurg & Co. informing us that their account with us had been attached by Emerson Hough and we had a telegram from Emerson Hough which read:

"Merry Christmas. Sued you today."

The differences between Hough and us involve $2500.00 which we owe him and $1900.00 which he owes us. Neither party is disputing the amount of the indebtedness and the only question involved is either the payment or the security of our $1900.00.

For the last eight months Hough has been in very bad condition of body and mind. In fact he has been a source of serious concern to his friends and associates.

I had a talk with him about this matter two months ago and at that time urged him very strongly to put the whole question in the hands of his attorney for adjustment. This he subsequently did and since that time we have had two letters from the lawyers asking us to send a representative to Chicago to talk the matter over, to each of which we promptly replied that all the records in the case were here and we hoped that a member of the firm would come down here to go through the matter. There was no suggestion in either of their letters of this course of action and I am wondering if you can give me some line on the attorneys. The firm is Beach & Beach and their office is 1501 Ashland Block, Chicago.

I have written to Ogden McClurg suggesting that perhaps instead of sending our attorneys to Chicago with the matter it would better be looked after by their attorneys inasmuch as they were made a member in the attachment. To that letter I suppose I will hear on Monday.

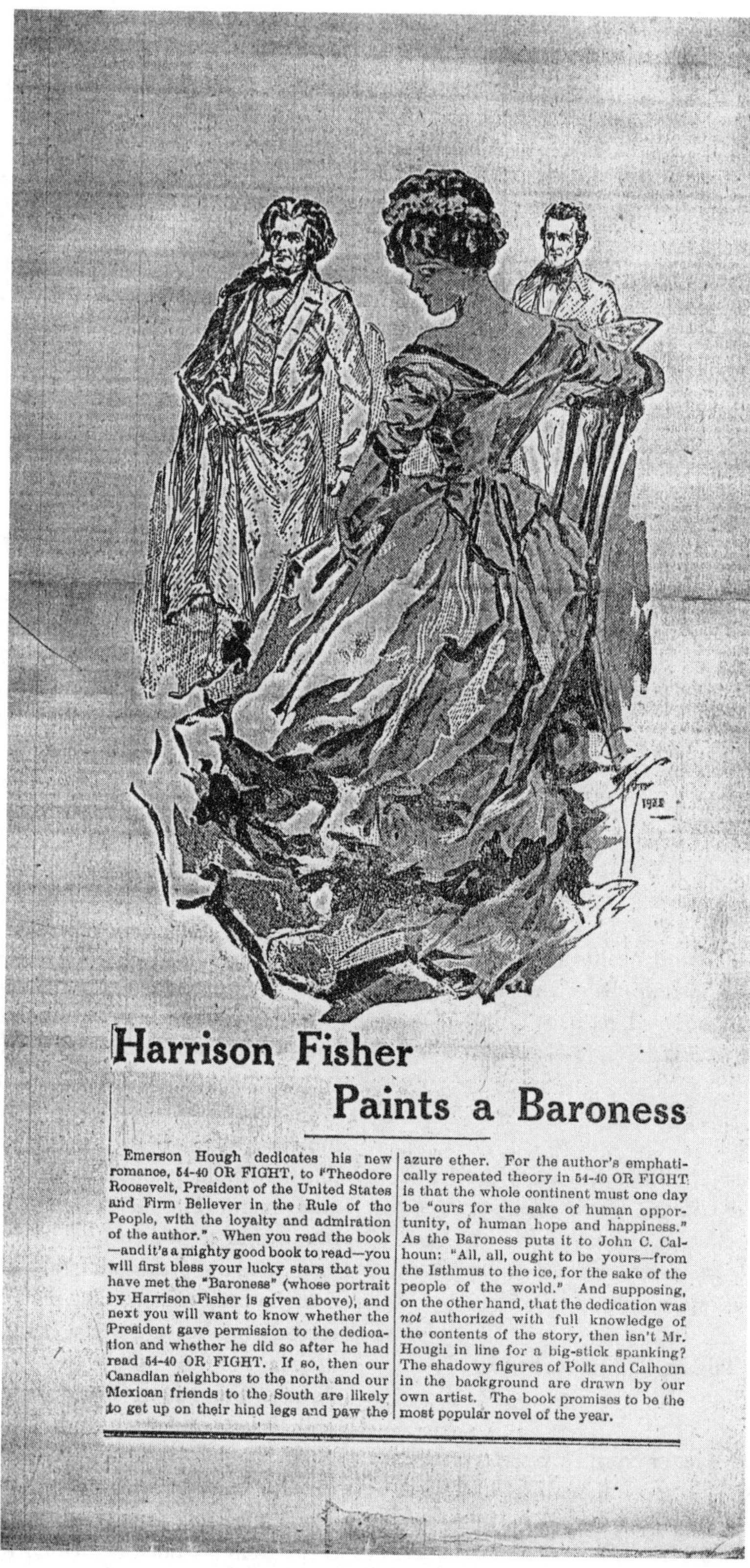

Harrison Fisher Paints a Baroness

Emerson Hough dedicates his new romance, 54-40 OR FIGHT, to "Theodore Roosevelt, President of the United States and Firm Believer in the Rule of the People, with the loyalty and admiration of the author." When you read the book—and it's a mighty good book to read—you will first bless your lucky stars that you have met the "Baroness" (whose portrait by Harrison Fisher is given above), and next you will want to know whether the President gave permission to the dedication and whether he did so after he had read 54-40 OR FIGHT. If so, then our Canadian neighbors to the north and our Mexican friends to the South are likely to get up on their hind legs and paw the azure ether. For the author's emphatically repeated theory in 54-40 OR FIGHT is that the whole continent must one day be "ours for the sake of human opportunity, of human hope and happiness." As the Baroness puts it to John C. Calhoun: "All, all, ought to be yours—from the Isthmus to the ice, for the sake of the people of the world." And supposing, on the other hand, that the dedication was *not* authorized with full knowledge of the contents of the story, then isn't Mr. Hough in line for a big-stick spanking? The shadowy figures of Polk and Calhoun in the background are drawn by our own artist. The book promises to be the most popular novel of the year.

Advertisement for Hough's 54-40 or Fight, *which provided a showcase for John J. Curtis's promotional techniques (courtesy of The Lilly Library, Indiana University, Bloomington, Indiana)*

THE AUTHOR OF 54-40 OR FIGHT.

Emerson Hough was born in Iowa. His people were Southerners and the family a very old one, dating back to 1683. He was a bookish boy, yet fond of the out-of-doors. After graduation from the State University of Iowa, he read law in the office of H. S. Winslow for a year or less and was admitted to the bar at Newton. Then he went to White Oaks, N. M.,—just why it would be hard to tell, for White Oaks is the last place in the world for anybody to select to practice law in. In a year or so, Mr. Hough and the other lawyers got the town all tied up, and most of them walked back to the States. More than twenty years later Mr. and Mrs. Hough went down that way to see the boys he used to know. They were still there and still hopeful. They think they are going to have a railroad any century now, although no railroad can get up that canyon any more than a church steeple.

While Mr. Hough was in New Mexico and doing five finger exercises in his law practice, he began to write for the old *American Field*. Then his father failed in business, and it was up to Emerson to hustle for the family. He tried to break into newspaper work at Des Moines, Sandusky and Chicago, but did not land anywhere until about 1888, when he took charge of the Western office of *Forest and Stream*, a position which he held for fifteen years. During that period he went hunting and fishing pretty much all over America.

In 1895 he printed his first little book, *The Singing Mouse* stories. It attracted little attention. *The Story of the Cowboy*, published in 1897, fared better. Theodore Roosevelt, not then President, wrote Mr. Hough a most glowing letter about it. Under this encouragement, he sat up and began to notice things, to the extent of writing *The Girl at the Half-Way House*. It was hard work to do these books, as he was obliged to write after midnight and to solicit advertising the next day. Not until the appearance of *The Mississippi Bubble*, in 1902, did success really come his way, but then, indeed, it came his way in large and elegant quantities.

Mr. Hough's favorite sports are grizzly-bear hunting, quail-hunting and trout-fishing—to which must be added a passion for old mahogany.

The Bobbs-Merrill Company.
February, 1909.

LITERARY NOTE.

Emerson Hough, the author of *54-40 or Fight*, has little time for the "fake" atmosphere with which many modern writers endeavor to attract the public. In a recent discussion of "wild West faking" in literature, Mr. Hough says:

"It is a singular fact, not capable of any geographical or philosophical explanation so far as I know, that the best wild West writers live in Brooklyn, New York, and that most of the prominent wild West artists reside in Lyme, Conn. I don't know why this is. Neither, for that matter, should one file any objection to this, because genius has no law. In the old days we were as apt to get pure Canadian maple syrup from Ohio as anywhere else. The only reservation existing in my mind is purely a legal one. It seems to me that there is a question of reasonable doubt under the pure food law whether these stories and fiction ought not to be labeled '99.5 per cent pure East.'

"I recall one picture by a celebrated artist of the East who does Western things. It depicts a 'Cowboy at Rest.' He is lying on his stomach in the sun, his chin in his hands. His horse stands near by with the reins thrown over the horn of the saddle. Now, a cowboy in the daytime, well filled with beans and canned tomatoes, would not lie thus. He would pull the reins down over the horse's head and let them hang, elsewise his cowhorse would depart. I recall yet another picture of a faithful cow-puncher who, with his trusty rifle, defends himself from behind his dead horse, which he uses as a fortress. The dead horse is about four feet and a half through sidewise—excellent for a fortress, but a trifle wide for a thin-flanked cowhorse. It would be useless to point out any detail like this to any earnest artist of to-day. Worse than useless would it be to suggest that a cow-puncher is the laziest created thing; for in art he must do perpetual 'stunts' of 'action.'"

The Bobbs-Merrill Company.
February, 1909.

Advertisements for 54-40 or Fight *of the kind defining the general audience to which the novel was directed (courtesy of The Lilly Library, Indiana University, Bloomington, Indiana)*

In the mea[n]time if you can give me some information about this firm I will be very grateful and glad of course to take care of any expense involved in making the inquiry.

Yours very truly,
[William C. Bobbs]

* * *

Hough to Bobbs-Merrill, 15 January 1920

Gentlemen:

I appreciate very much your sending to me the manuscripts, clippings, etc., duly at hand with your favor of January 8th. I had no idea where these things were when, a while ago, I was looking up my stuff for moving picture purposes, and with the general intention of getting it all together. For a long time I was very ill and I doubt if even now I have picked up all the lost threads. It is possible that I can use some of this stuff somewhere.

I regret that you have not found it desirable to answer the letters of Beach & Beach, and Appletons, looking to the purchase of plates of my books. Why can't we strike up some sort of a trade in regard to these things? The titles are not making you any money and never will make you any money, and an investment on which there are no dividends practically means lost capital. While I don't know that we could take on all of these at once, it would be the intention to take them all, if you like, as fast as possible. That would release just that much more capital for you. It probably would not mean very much money for me, but as I know I shall not be hanging around very many years longer–in all likelihood not more than six or eight years at the outside–I am trying to get my little estate in such shape that Mrs. Hough can get as much use as possible out of my life work. Whatever may be your feelings in regard to myself, I don't believe that you really have any animosity against Mrs. Hough. This little transaction might be of some possible benefit to her later on–it probably would not be of any very immediate benefit.

Working along as best I can, I am making more money now than I ever did, and adding something to my little estate from year to year. Thus far I have been able to carry a heavy life insurance for Mrs. Hough, almost $100,000.00. But I want to get my list of books together the best I can, so that a concerted action regarding them may possibly bring her in an occasional dollar or so in royalty after I have cashed in. My lawyers and publishers simply are trying to be my friends in this matter. So let us see if we can make some sort of an arrangement for a transfer of property which is worthless to you, and which may be of possible worth to Mrs. Hough later on. Then we can clean up and go on our way rejoicing. After all, that is probably the best way to do.

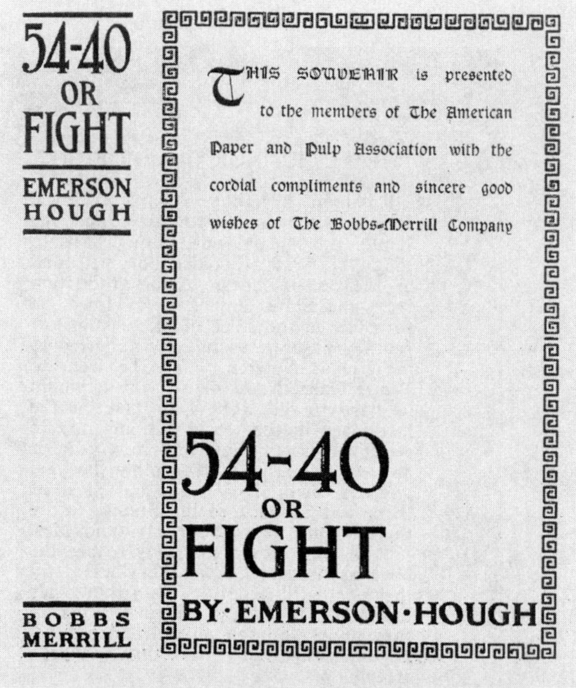

Special dust jacket for a particular audience, the modern beneficiaries of President James K. Polk's commitment to keep the Oregon border at 54 degrees, 40 minutes (courtesy of The Lilly Library, Indiana University, Bloomington, Indiana)

If you will take up the matter with either of my representatives, preferably Appletons, I shall be very much obliged.

Yours sincerely,
Emerson Hough

* * *

Bobbs to Howland, 19 January 1920

Yes indeed there is something very pathetic in this letter. It is pathetic for any man to stand behind his wife and use her either for the purpose of protection or appeal and in this case the plea is as unnecessary as it is futile, for the sooner we can get all trace of Hough out of the establishment, the happier we will all be.

Mr. Curtis has already taken up with Appleton's the question of their taking over the list but they will have to find some means of taking everything we have, or nothing.

The answer to Hough is, I think, that negotiations have already been instituted between Mr. Curtis and the Appleton's.

W. C. Bobbs

Kin Hubbard (1868–1930)

See also the Hubbard entry in *DLB 11: American Humorists, 1800–1950.*

Frank McKinney "Kin" Hubbard was an Ohio-born Indiana humorist of the cracker-barrel school. His observations were syndicated daily across the country for the twenty years before his death. They were delivered in the words of the rube philosopher Abe Martin, whom he also drew in some eight thousand sketches. Typically, Abe is shown loafing in a country setting, sometimes with neighbors as broadly drawn as he. Abe's sayings were collected every year and published either privately or commercially. The first (private) printing of Hubbard's first book in 1906 sold one thousand copies in three days. He became accustomed to selling these yearly compilations for $1.50 each. His income later on was much increased by the widespread newspaper syndication of his writings. Hubbard's wit was highly praised by his contemporaries, including Will Rogers, and many of the sayings are still funny. Not all of Abe's humorous and commonsense observations, however, lived beyond their time.

BOBBS-MERRILL BOOKS BY HUBBARD: *Abe Martin of Brown County, Indiana,* introduction by Meredith Nicholson, tribute by James Whitcomb Riley (Indianapolis: Bobbs-Merrill, 1907; **first edition,** Indianapolis: Privately printed, 1906);

Abe Martin's Almanack [for 1908] (Indianapolis: Bobbs-Merrill, 1907);

Short Furrows (Indianapolis: Bobbs-Merrill, 1911);

Kin Hubbard (Bruccoli Clark Layman Archives)

Abe Martin, Hoss Sense and Nonsense, foreword by Franklin P. Adams (Indianapolis: Bobbs-Merrill, 1926);

Abe Martin's Barbed Wire (Indianapolis: Bobbs-Merrill, 1928);

Abe Martin's Town Pump (Indianapolis: Bobbs-Merrill, 1929);

Abe Martin's Broadcast, Kin Hubbard Announcing (Indianapolis: Bobbs-Merrill, 1930).

Related Letters

Despite the language of this memo to vice president and trade-department editor D. Laurance Chambers from his assistant, Charles D. LaFollette, Bobbs-Merrill had already published three of Hubbard's books by this time.

Charles D. LaFollette to D. Laurance Chambers, 10 June 1926

Had a talk with Kin Hubbard this afternoon. His negotiations with Simon and Schuster have about reached a definite point. The only thing that prevents a mutual understanding, at the present, is a disagreement of the amount of the royalty. Mr. Hubbard says that they are making him an offer which he considers the same kind of an offer made to anyone with a new book, and I am of the opinion that it is 10%.

At the close of our conversation he wanted me to write you and tell you the three points on which we desired information. These three points are;

The book he wants to sell for $1.50. He can have the material ready by July 1st, and wants a fall book made of it [*Inserted:* "To come out by Dec 1st"], and he wants a royalty of 15% straight.

His negotiations with Simon and Schuster are for a publication of the sort of thing he has always done, that is an annual resumé, which is being polished up, and some new material added. He is of the opinion that he cannot write any other book. He is interested very much in the mechanical make-up. I do not believe anything definite has been done about this point, by Simon and Schuster.

The best-years sales he has ever had is 5,000 copies. Out of this amount 3500 was in Indiana. He seems to feel that Indianapolis could be depended upon to take two or three thousand. I don't believe his last book did this well, because he did not get it out until December 23rd.

He wants to make his decision fairly soon, as to the publisher, and he is going to wait in his negotiations with Simon and Schuster until you have my letter and have given me your ideas. He told me that he would rather we would have the book instead of Simon and Schuster, because of our convenience to him, and he said in closing, "I had virtually closed with Simon and Schuster, but I am perfectly willing to listen to reason, and had rather Bobbs-Merrill Company do the job."

Personally I would like very much to see us have him on our list. Of course you know much better than I do, in respect to sales, but I do not believe we would have any difficulty in matching his best record, which is really quite an achievement, when you consider it was done entirely without a sales organization. He gets orders unsolicited from Seattle, Los Angeles, Tulsa and other book dealers, for sometimes as high as 25 copies. It seems to me that the 138 cities in which his material is syndicated, would be receptive markets, and to me "Abe Martin" will live as lustily as Samuel Pickwick.

Don't think for a minute that Kin got me under the influence of stimulants and got me to write this letter! This is my own and unbiased opinion.

Lafe

* * *

Chambers responded to LaFollette from the New York office. In the statement of his philosophy concerning royalties and advertising, Chambers refers to books by John Erskine and Bruce Barton published by Bobbs-Merrill the year before and now best-sellers.

Chambers to LaFollette, 12 June 1926

Dear Lafe,–

Glad to hear about your negotiations with Kin Hubbard. Of course we want him and we must get together with him. But he's got the wrong slant on royalty. It isn't the rate that counts. It is the total amount of money earned the author. At 15% the margin for advg is so greatly reduced that it would be impossible to put on the kind of general campaign that would establish him over the country. His sales have been predominantly local. Authors whose names and popularity are so well founded in the book trade that their books sell with little advg, are entitled to the 15%; but Kin is not yet in that class.

Explain this to him and see how he reacts. He probably doesn't understand. Tell him Helen of Troy is on a straight 10% and Man Nobody Knows 10% to 25th–the two best sellers of the year.

Continue the negotiations and don't let him get off the hook–till I get back.

The essential thing is to get an attractive format. Send me one of his books–I think there's one on my desk–and samples of others if he, or the local booksellers, have 'em.

DLC

* * *

O. O. McIntyre was a syndicated columnist and story writer. Ray Long was an anthologist and editor of Cosmopolitan. *George Ade was a Bobbs-Merrill author.*

LaFollette to Chambers, 16 June 1926

Had a great time with Kin Hubbard. Simon and Schuster had made him another offer since my first conversation with him. After we had been talking awhile he read it to me. They said that if he would send the manuscript to them they would consider possibility of giving him a scaled discount. They made the point that on a book of this kind, it is customary to allow 10%, a practice which they believed is followed by Harpers, Scribners, and Bobbs-Merrill. They were anxious to close on a 10% basis, and apparently were equally as anxious to consider possibility of giving more if necessary.

I used the ammunition you gave me; we talked of "Tom" Hubbard, who graduates from Culver, and Charlie and William Taylor of the Boston Globe, of Kin's trial cruise on the Leviathan, Wabash College, and other subjects, equally pertinent! and finally he said, he guessed he would let us have it.

He is interested mightily in the format. We talked a bit about having one page in front which will give the cast of characters. He also said he had an idea of writing your friend, O. O. McIntyre, and Ray Long, George Ade, and two or three others for paragraphs to put on the jacket. My contribution was a suggestion that we should use Riley's poem on Abe Martin as a frontispiece. He would like to see a book about 175 pages long, and he is not sure that the book he put out is the right size.

We also discussed titles a bit. I had one idea and he had another. My title was "From Genius Clean to Base Ball." His title was "The Joker on Facts." It seems to me the the [*sic*] name of Abe Martin ought to be in any title we have because this character is so much better known than the author. Kin is putting in some extra licks on the book, and has taken quite a bit of pride in it, apparently more than usual because he

Dust jacket and a promotional postcard for Hubbard's 1926 book (courtesy of The Lilly Library, Indiana University, Bloomington, Indiana)

feels somewhat relieved of the freedom of manufacturing worries. He said he would have the manuscript to us about July 1st.

It pleases me mightily to have him on our list. I think he's got the stuff. As a matter of fact there isn't anybody that you could have sent me after that could have given me any more pleasure to sign up.

Do let me know what you want done about the contract.

Lafe

* * *

The title finally settled upon was Abe Martin, Hoss Sense and Nonsense *(1926). Tubman K. Hedrick's* Orientations of Ho-Hen *was published by Bobbs-Merrill in 1921. F.P.A. was Franklin P. Adams, who wrote the witty syndicated column "The Conning Tower" and agreed to supply a foreword to Hubbard's book.*

LaFollette to Chambers, 21 June 1926

Another session with Kin Hubbard, and the title, "Abe Martin, Two A Day" hit him as he said, right between the eyes. He made two other suggestions, neither of which he liked so well, "Back Country Folks" and "Brown County Folks".

I am enclosing a drawing which is for the jacket if you approve. He likes it. He wants to use, and I think, he is assuming, that there will be several cuts in the book, of old pictures which he has used. There is no doubt that they will relieve the monotony you spoke of this morning.

He also likes an uncut book, and he spoke as though he would like to have a book that the pages came flush to the edges of the cover.

He mentioned Old English type, but I told him that I thought it was inconsistent with the contents.

He liked the ORIENTATIONS OF HO-HEN as a dummy. He said he would not object at all to a paper cover board binding.

He is writing F. P. A. to do him a foreward [*sic*]. I shall do the blurb tomorrow if possible.

He showed me a very gracious letter from Schuster, in reply to the announcement that he had signed with us.

Lafe

Marquis James (1891–1955)

Marquis James's training as an historian was not academic. It began with his mother's teaching him to read from history texts on the Oklahoma prairie, where the family had moved from Missouri. He graduated from high school and thereafter was mostly self-taught. During his career as a newspaperman, he wrote fiction on the side. After service in World War I, James contributed colorful but well-researched historical items to The American Legion Monthly. *Similar accounts were solicited by* The New Yorker, *but he did not yet receive scholarly recognition. Then his* The Raven: A Biography of Sam Houston *(1929) won the 1930 Pulitzer Prize in biography and sold one hundred thousand copies in ten years. His work on Andrew Jackson was similarly honored in the next decade. As a biographer James was something of a throwback, focusing novelistically on characters and not avoiding moralism. Later he also drew upon the business world for biographies and histories.*

BOBBS-MERRILL BOOKS BY JAMES: *The Raven: A Biography of Sam Houston* (Indianapolis: Bobbs-Merrill, 1929; London: Hutchinson, 1929);

Six Feet Six, the Heroic Story of Sam Houston, by James and Bessie Rowland James, illustrated by Lowell Balcom (Indianapolis: Bobbs-Merrill, 1931);

Andrew Jackson, the Border Captain (Indianapolis: Bobbs-Merrill, 1933);

The Courageous Heart: A Life of Andrew Jackson for Young Readers, by James and Bessie Rowland James, illustrated by Balcom (Indianapolis: Bobbs-Merrill, 1934);

They Had Their Hour (Indianapolis: Bobbs-Merrill, 1934);

Andrew Jackson: Portrait of a President (Indianapolis: Bobbs-Merrill, 1937);

The Life of Andrew Jackson, Complete in One Volume (Indianapolis: Bobbs-Merrill, 1938)–comprises *Andrew Jackson, the Border Captain* and *Andrew Jackson: Portrait of a President;*

Mr. Garner of Texas (Indianapolis: Bobbs-Merrill, 1939);

Alfred I. DuPont, the Family Rebel (Indianapolis: Bobbs-Merrill, 1941);

Biography of a Business, 1792–1942: Insurance Company of North America (Indianapolis: Bobbs-Merrill, 1942).

Marquis James (from Stanley J. Kunitz and Howard Haycraft, eds., Twentieth Century Authors, *1942; Thomas Cooper Library, University of South Carolina)*

Related Letters

Anne Johnston (later Anne Johnston Ross), editor and assistant to company vice president D. Laurance Chambers, wrote James to thank him for sending biographical information. Johnston's undated response was typed below on the same sheet of paper.

Anne Johnston to Marquis James, 14 June 1929

Dear Mr. James:

Thanks very much indeed for your portrait and questionnaire which have come to my desk as Mr. Chambers is out of town. Both are just awfully nice and exactly what we wanted. Very impressive too. I just can't believe that we really and truly have an author related to the original Jesse James, not to mention Frank. It's wonderful.

Sincerely yours,
Anne Johnston

* * *

ANALYSIS OF MR. JAMES' SUGGESTIONS FOR
PROMOTION OF THE RAVEN.

Promotion

For Salesmen:

March 2nd -- anniversary of signing of the Declaration of Independence of the Texas Republic generally observed throughout the state. Speeches and exercises in schools. THE RAVEN reenacts the scene of the original signing -- strange and exciting circumstances. SHOULD BE CALLED TO THE ATTENTION OF PUBLIC SCHOOLS. The material is histórically valuable. STATE, DISTRICT and COUNTY HISTORICAL ASSOCIATIONS, Women's Clubs and DAUGHTERS OF THE TEXAS REPUBLIC. These organizations have to do with arranging programs, and might be able to assist in bringing the book to public notice.

April 21st -- San Jacinto Day, the anniversary of the battle. The account in THE RAVEN is recognized as the clearest, most accurate and most picturesque. THIS IS A LARGE CELEBRATION AND THE BOOK SHOULD COME INTO THE PICTURE. GET AFTER DEALERS WITH THIS.

Should the prize-winning essay contest go through, the salesmen can help stir up the dealers about it.

Direct Mail;

Daughters of the Texas Republic (or Revolution) are a live and active organization. Membership should be circularized.

Circularize Daughters of the Confederacy in Texas, Tennessee, Oklahoma, Arkansas and Alabama.

Circularize membership of Texas, Tennessee, Oklahoma, Arkansas and Alabama Historical Societies.

Nacagdoches, Texas; Marion, Alabama; Maryville, Gallátin and Lebanon, Tennessee. also Lexington, Tennessee, are brought into national notice in THE RAVEN. Mr. James suggests that signs in the windows of book dealers in these paces might pay for themselves.

Southern Societies in Chicago, San Francisco, and possibly Los Angeles may be circularized. This will have to be looked up.

Texas, Oklahoma, Arkansas, Alabama and Tennessee small towns. Have them paste of display a copy of their own hom paper review in the window, tie it up with a review or reviews from some of the large city papers, and have a sign saying "WE HAVE THIS GREAT BOOK!" or something to that effect. Make the dealer see that this is a chance to capitalize on local publicity, and that the use of the revew will be better than a paid advertisement for him.

Miscellaneous:

Mr. Clarence Wharton, Esperson Bldg., Houston is a very wealthy lawyer with one of the finest private libraries in Texas. He has offered to help us in every way possible.

Major Ingham Roberts, President of the Harris County Historical Society, will do the same.

Promotional ideas for James's The Raven: A Biography of Sam Houston, *published in 1929 (courtesy of The Lilly Library, Indiana University, Bloomington, Indiana)*

James to Johnston, undated

Dear Miss Johnston,

Think I'd better add, to be filed with the record, an impairing p.s. on the Jesse business. I'm not his first cousin. We are simply authentically members of a common tribe of Jameses that originated in Va and is now scattered, pretty thickly in some parts, through Tenn., Ky., southern Ohio and out to Missouri–a common track of post-Revolution migration. The tribe is large, though few, like Jesse have attained distinction in life. Without some parenthetical allusion to this fact I shouldn't like to be singled out to the exclusion of others equally deserving as connected with the James of such salient renown. A few years back I declined to consider a biography of Jesse James, which I'd really like to do, simply for family reasons.

Marquis James

N.B. Just run onto another picture, taken some yrs back, which may be better.

MJ

* * *

James received a letter of thanks from Sam Houston's grandson Franklin Williams, of the Houston office of the Mercantile Insurance Company of America. Emil Ludwig was a biographer.

Franklin Williams to James, 1 November 1929

My dear Mr. James:–

I wish to acknowledge receipt today of the copy of "The Raven" which I shall prize very highly, not only on account of the contents which are by far the best delineation of the character of Houston I have seen, but because the volume was presented to me by your good self.

Several members of the family have finished reading it at this time and all seemed to be satisfied with your treatment of the subject and think that you have endeavored to be fair to all concerned. I am sorry that it was necessary to make some of the other characters appear to a disadvantage but history should be true or else not written. [*Marginal note:* "The writer is a grandson of Gen. Houston"]

As Houston said–"If my character cannot stand the shock, let me lose it." The records speak for themselves and his enemies must abide by the outcome tho I am no

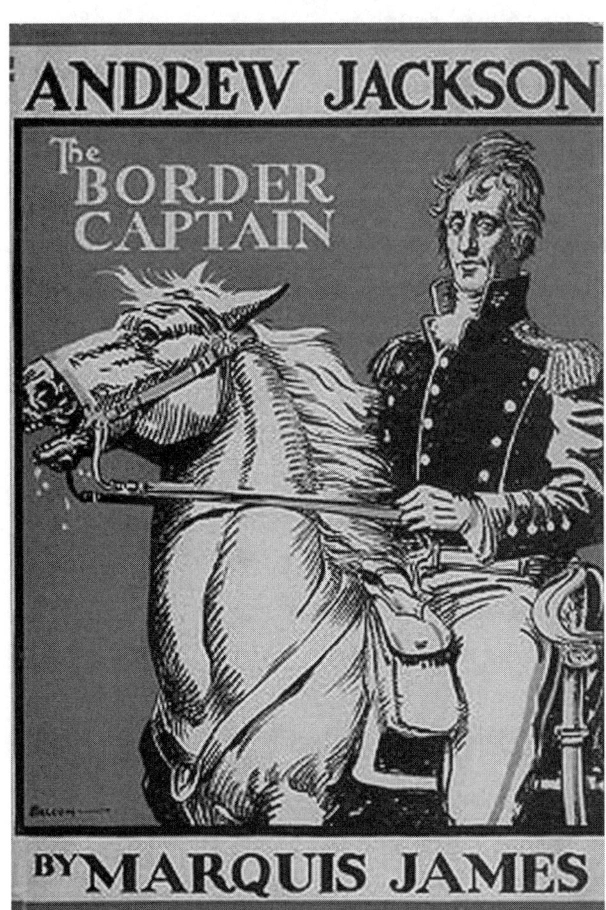

Dust jackets for James's 1933 Andrew Jackson biography and for the 1938 republication of that book with the second part of the Jackson biography, originally published in 1937 (Between the Covers Rare Books; Woodshed Books)

THE BOBBS-MERRILL COMPANY
From the Publicity Department

WINNER OF PULITZER PRIZE FOR BIOGRAPHY IS "MARKEY" JAMES

A cry of despair from the West Coast in the person of Joseph Henry Jackson, literary editor of the San Francisco Argonaut and radio book reviewer, requests the pronunciation of Marquis James' first name. Mr. James is the winner of the Pulitzer Prize for Biography for his life of "Sam Houston, entitled "The Raven". Mr. Jackson's request follows:

"I've heard that Alec and Evelyn Waugh
Fail to answer to Woff or Woo;
I've a limber lip and a jimber jaw
For names like Strachey and Capek too;
Good old favorites, Cabell, Proust,
Hans Heinz Ewers, Cleugh, Dimnet,--
I can say 'em till chickens go to roost,
Or cows come home,--all night, all day;
But this prize biographer, Marquis James,
That's the fellow who puzzles me;
(These Anglo-Franco-god-knows-names!)
Please, it is 'Markwis' or 'Markee?'"

The Bobbs-Merrill Company hastens to make reply:

The Pulitzer Prize biographee
Was not inscribed by the man, 'Mar-kwee;'
Incline thine ear and mark this:
The James first name is not called 'Mar-kwis'.
The Christian name--now, hark 'ee, hark 'ee--
Of THE RAVEN winner is just plain 'Markey.'
L'Envoi
This game of names is getting larky,
But the name of James is simply 'Markey.'

A few days after the Pulitzer Prize Committee announced the awards, Mr. James was called to his old home in Enid, Oklahoma, where his aged mother is ill. It was through his mother's love of history that Mr. James acquired his own interest in America's history, and later, his desire to delve into biography of American heroes. Marquis James' first newspaper job came from the Enid Weekly Events. He collected "personal items" for the local paper, at the tender age of thirteen, and composed 'poems' which, oddly enough, got printed in the paper. Once he wrote a satire on several of the leading town characters, and, it is regrettable to relate, he was fired from his job.

P. S. Some time later he won a Pulitzer Prize!

Humorous press release in the wake of James's 1930 Pulitzer Prize for The Raven. *The author of the Bobbs-Merrill poem may have been D. Laurance Chambers, a dabbler in light verse (courtesy of The Lilly Library, Indiana University, Bloomington, Indiana).*

hand to rattle dry bones and deplore the necessity for bringing out things that reflect on the ancesters [*sic*] of good men, some of whom are my friends.

Old Burnett to my mind was a "Whited sepulcher" and a sublime ass and I think his bible thumbing was a smoke screen to hide his nefarious doings. No man would do as he did from pure jealousy. I am glad that you have been kind to some of them.

I am informed by a Mrs. Donnellan of this City that she has written to your publishers that one of the pictures in the Raven is an infringement on her copy-right. She wished me to assist her in the matter but I assured her that she was mistaken. We had given you all of the pictures, especially the one she claimed and would assuredly back you up in the matter.

You can assure the publishers that they need not worry about any trouble from this source. This lady claims that her husband painted the picture of Houston in the blanket with hat and cane which was taken by Fredericks gallery in New York (see first picture in book) and that she had same copy-righted but I have proof that my mother sent to Fredericks in New York over forty years ago and had him send her a dozen copies of the picture which they had taken years before.

I can also prove that Mr. Donnellan could not paint a portrait as good as this one as there are several in Houston which are jokes. I will be glad to assist you should she endeavor to give you trouble.

On yesterday I sent you a copy of the Gargoyle, a weekly magazine of this City which had an article about the book by the editor. Hope it reached you all right. Will be glad to hear from you when you have time to drop a line and would like to know how the Raven went over generally.

Let me again assure you of my appreciation of your kindness in sending me the copy and and [*sic*] tell you that you that you [*sic*] have exceeded my hopes in the manner which you handled the subject. I dont [*sic*] think Ludwig could have done better.

Sincerely your friend,
Franklin Williams

Ring Lardner (1885–1933)

See also the Lardner entries in *DLB 11: American Humorists, 1800–1950; DLB 25: American Newspaper Journalists, 1901–1925; DLB 86: American Short-Story Writers, 1910–1945, First Series;* and *DLB 171: Twentieth-Century American Sportswriters.*

Ringgold Wilmer "Ring" Lardner was the greatest humorist ever published by Bobbs-Merrill, and the company lost him just as he reached his peak. He first made his mark as a sports reporter and as author of the column "In the Wake of the News" for the Chicago Tribune. *In 1914 he wrote, for* The Saturday Evening Post, *the first of his famous baseball tales. (Eventually his short stories commanded as much as $4,500 each.) Unlike many other writers who borrowed the common speech and are now unreadable, Lardner, like Mark Twain, found a way to transmute the vernacular into a fluid literary dialect. He also populated his stories with satirical types that are still recognizable, whether in the sports world or in the middle class at large. In 1924 he moved on to greater fame and more money with Scribners, publishers of his friend F. Scott Fitzgerald. But even for Scribners and the great editor Max Perkins, Lardner never wrote a novel, a limitation that did not bother his admiring contemporaries. It has, however, kept him from being placed in the first rank of American authors.*

BOBBS-MERRILL BOOKS BY LARDNER: *Gullible's Travels, Etc.* (Indianapolis: Bobbs-Merrill, 1917; London: Chatto & Windus, 1926);
My Four Weeks in France (Indianapolis: Bobbs-Merrill, 1918);
Treat 'Em Rough: Letters from Jack the Kaiser Killer (Indianapolis: Bobbs-Merrill, 1918);
Own Your Own Home (Indianapolis: Bobbs-Merrill, 1919);
The Real Dope (Indianapolis: Bobbs-Merrill, 1919);
The Young Immigrunts (Indianapolis: Bobbs-Merrill, 1920);
Symptoms of Being 35 (Indianapolis: Bobbs-Merrill, 1921);
The Big Town (Indianapolis: Bobbs-Merrill, 1921).

Ring Lardner

Related Letters

A truly unself-conscious artist, Lardner kept no copies of his stories once he had submitted them to magazines. This trait posed problems when Bobbs-Merrill (and later Scribners) tried to create collections of his work, as the following telegram indicates.

Ring Lardner to Bobbs-Merrill, 29 November 1916

I HAVE NO COPIES OF STORIES ASK POST FOR THEM
RING W LARDNER

* * *

Hewitt H. Howland was trade-department editor in chief. Artie was perhaps Lardner's close friend Arthur Jacks.

Lardner to Hewitt H. Howland, 4 December 1916

Dear Mr. Howland:–

I have no copy of "Three Without, Doubled," but I sent the proof back to the Post about ten days ago, so if you don't want to wait for it to come out, I think you will have no trouble getting it from them.

Have seen Artie but once since you were [*sic*]. He was in good voice, but I, being on the wagon, was not.

Sincerely,
Ring. W. Lardner

* * *

Reader's Report

The following is an unsigned report on Gullible's Travels, Etc. *(1917).*

GULLIBLE'S TRAVELS, Etc.

The people with a capital, or the American People with two capitals are the stock in trade of the politician, the psychologist and the humourist and the subject continues to grow in their hands. The present writer unites two of these functions although he might disclaim any title save that of entertainer. He specializes on a certain, well defined, not overworked, stratum of Chicago life–the people who live in a four room flat, play rum by preference, go to the movies, adore Charlie Chaplin and prefer the Sunday comic supplement to most other reading

Bulletin No. 1

WE WAS playin' rummy over to Hatch's, and Hatch must of fell in a bed of four-leaf clovers on his way home the night before, because he plays rummy like he does everything else; but this night I refer to you couldn't beat him, and besides him havin' all the luck my Missus played like she'd been bought off, so when we come to settle up we was plain seven and a half out. You know who paid it. So Hatch says:

"They must be some game you can play."

from

Gullible's Travels

By Ring W. Lardner

Promotional card for Lardner's first Bobbs-Merrill book, published in 1917 (from Matthew J. Bruccoli and Richard Layman, Ring W. Lardner: A Descriptive Bibliography, *1976)*

matter. The social ambitions of this husband and wife,–for they flourish,–their understanding of Grand Opera, their journey to Palm Beach, their efforts to play auction bridge, are effectively sandwiched between a week-end trip to St. Jo, friendly games of bummy with some neighbors, visits from a Hoosier sister-in-law, calls from her suitor, all against the background of flat life, corner drugstores, and cheap restaurants.

To comment on the entire fidelity to truth, on the exact realism, on the glaring cheapness of life as thus lived, may be superfluous since the stories aim to amuse, not to make any serious contribution. Yet posterity could perfectly reconstruct this aspect of our society just from those tales alone. The easy money yet the constant talk in dollars and cents, the absolute democracy of the would-be social climbers, their naive ignorance, their refreshing freedom of speech, the intense yet innocent vulgarity, the absence of any moral uplift, or cultural outlook and the inexhaustible, irresistible fun, could only all be true of Americans of this class, of this class in Chicago and perhaps of those two special people in Chicago. This criticism may be all besides the mark for this last reason, that this husband and wife are individuals before being types. The repartee, the slang, the local allusions, the home life are all secondary to the narrator and his Missus themselves. One wishes that the author had given us a handle to use, but as no proper names ever appear, one must fall back on the old designation of the hero and heroine which are appropriate enough, since this couple always take the center of the stage.

Five stories complete the MSS. and one only wishes they were ten, not because of undue brevity but because of hunger for more and still more of the same kind. If the Grand Opera stories are funny, the Palm Beach journey is funnier and the St. Jo trip and the auction bridge game deserves adjectives all to themselves.

When the two couples go to the Auditorium on their rum winnings, Mr. Hatch has no more evening clothes than a kewpie and wears the same old bay pants he'd word [*sic*] the day he got mad at his kind and christened him Kenneth. However this does not matter since it would take a steeple-jack to reach their seats. The plot is told over into Chi slang and the words was either throwed together by the stage carpenter, or else took down by a stenographer outdoors during a drizzle. The Janesville, garage, yards, Halsted street rendering of Carmen, the singer who moans in the chimney or he who misses in the downstairs radiators, enter into this entensely [*sic*] local criticism. The next story deals with the Opera which the hero calls three kings and a pair and here enters Mr. Bishop who claims to be a millionaire scenario writer, who really is an extra at the movies, whose dimensions all run perpendicular, who didn't have no latitude. If his collar slipped over his shoulders, he could have stepped out of it. Mr. — cannot make any deal with the ticket agent because one of the party is a little skinny fellow and the other a refuge [*sic*] from Wabash, "We aint running no Hoosier Welfare League", so they pay full price and dissect and describe the love of the three kings after the same pattern as the Carmen criticism. Bess wears a creation built like the Cottage Grove Avenue cars, enter in front. Carmen was a human refrigerator compared to the leading lady in this show. There are so many stabbings in Grand Opera that the State's Attorney must have been on the jump all the while in them days. Mr. — is hungry but as he has only 35 cents, offering his stomach 17 1/2 cents worth of food would be just about like sending one blank cartridge to the Russian Army.

The social microbe in its work, the two read the society column, quit attending picture shows because of the class of people and make so many excuses of being tired, going to bed, etc., to the Hatches that they must have thought he and the Missus has got jobs as telephone linemen. The prices, the loneliness, the Afromobiles, the chance acquaintances, the continual dancing with his own wife–there aint no man who could do this as much as I have and live without liquid stimulants, show Palm Beach in a dreary light that is as amusing as it must be true.

The story called "The [W]ater Cure" shows the pair very tired of Bessie's hanger on and the working out of a plot to sicken them of each other. The boat trip, the babies, the mothers all named Jennie,–all perfect cubes, all fond of apples, all in need of a dentist; the sea sickness of the millionaire truck drivers[,] the wealthy Creek shoe shiners, the heiresses from the lace department, who have made an outlay on cracker jack and peanuts that is a total loss; the marriage licenses that you can get any any [*sic*] delicatessen shop, the street car conductors all authorized to perform the ceremony; the Hawaian [*sic*] native melodies composed by a Hungarian waiter who was too proud to fight are as funny as they are effectual. Bess and her suitor get acquainted and that ends the love affair.

Last of all is the auction bridge club, the breaks of Mr – and Missus, the vulgar slams at the meager dinner and the rage of the woman who loses the prize because of inexpert doubling of no trumps. Perhaps one must know the game fully to appreciate this fun, if he does not, he will ask nothing better.

The stories bear re-reading–in fact this has been the second perusal–without any loss of entertainment. Good fun is so scarce, especially when wedded to faultless realism, that this MSS ought to be considered a find by the G.P.

* * *

Related Letters

Howland sent the following day letter to Lardner urging haste with the corrected proofs for Gullible's Travels, Etc.

Howland to Lardner, 5 January 1917

Cant you return your corrected proofs by mail today Our plan is to publish the book this month.
H. H. Howland.

* * *

The "book department" was that of the Chicago Tribune. *F.P.A. was Franklin P. Adams, author of the syndicated column "The Conning Tower." Bert Leston Taylor ("B.L.T.") wrote the column "A Line o' Type or Two." Grantland Rice was a well-known sportswriter.*

Lardner to Howland, 2 March 1917

Dear Mr. Howland:–

I apologize for not having answered your letter before. Inasmuch as I had resolved that February was going to be my last liquid month for some time, I was busy preparing for the dry spell.

The book is, I think, very attractive and ought to be a go on its appearance alone. Our book department last Sunday said it had been one of the six best sellers in Chicago last week, but perhaps our book critic was using her imagination and merely wanted to help me out.

I haven't sent a copy to F.P.A., but will do so; also will hand one to B.L.T., our own column conductor, who is widely read in these and other parts. Or No. I'm afraid I haven't another one to spare and will ask you to send him one. Just B.L.T., care of the Chicago Tribune, will reach him.

I enclose a brief letter to dealers, as you requested.

Others to whom you might, to our mutual profit, send copies, are Grantland Rice of the New York Tribune, and the sporting editors of some of the larger metropolitan papers.

Sincerely,
Ring W Lardner

* * *

Howland to Lardner, 14 March 1918

My dear Lardner:

I have labored over the title and brought forth the following which has made a great hit here:

<u>The World Series</u>
<u>Allies vs Huns</u>

What do you think of it? We feel we can do some business on this title and should like to use it if it is agreeable to you. There has been so much of the Over Here and Over There stuff that it would be well to avoid it if we can. Send me back word by return mail so that we may get busy.

As ever yours,
[Hewitt H. Howland]

* * *

Lardner to Howland, 19 March 1918

Dear Mr. Howland:–

I don't believe the "world's series" title fits very well. There is no baseball in the book, nor any war as far as that is concerned, and people thinking I was going to treat the war in a baseball way might be disappointed. Can I have a day or two more to think it over?

Sincerely,
Ring W. Lardner

* * *

Howland to Lardner, 20 March 1918

My dear Mr. Lardner:

I think yourobjection [*sic*] to <u>The World Series</u> as title is well taken, but would that objection hold if we called the book simply <u>Allies vs Huns</u>? We are ready to close on this if it is agreeable to you. I will be glad if you will telegraph me at our expense as lack of title is holding up work on the pages.

Faithfully yours,
[Hewitt H. Howland]

* * *

James W. Gerard's My Four Years in Germany *had been published the previous year.*

Lardner to Howland, 25 March 1918

Dear Mr. Howland:–

I was out of town for a couple of days and didn't get your letter till this morning.

I have been trying hard to think of a title, but can't seem to get one that would hit anybody "right in the eye." Would "My Four Weeks in France"–a sort of parody on Mr. Gerard's "My Four Years in Germany"–be any good? The "Allies vs. Huns" one doesn't seem to get me. If I have an inspiration I will wire you. However, you are the best judge and if you think any of the ones we have discussed will do, I have no objection to your going ahead with it.

Sincerely,
Ring W. Lardner

* * *

In the Wake of the News

• By RING W. LARDNER

WELL!

CHARACTERS.

A Husband.
His Wife.

[The living room of their apartment. Flusday evening.]

Husband—Well——

Wife—Well——

Husband (after a pause, looking at his watch)—Well, it's half past seven.

Wife (after a pause)—Well, dearie——

Husband (after a pause)—Well, I s'pose we'd better see a show.

Wife—Why, they're closed up.

Husband—Well, a picture, then.

Wife—Why, they're closed, too.

Husband—Hell! Well, do you feel like dancing?

Wife—Why, dearie, it's barred.

* *

Husband—Well, we can go over to the Pink Garden and see the cabaret.

Wife—No, we can't, dearie. They're called off.

Husband—Hell! (after a pause) Well——

Wife (after a pause)—Well, I s'pose we might go to bed.

Husband (looks at his watch)—At eight o'clock?

Wife (after a pause)—Well, we'll have to talk, then.

Husband—What about?

Wife—Well——.

Husband—There isn't anything.

* *

Wife—Well, we can quarrel.

Husband—Not without a drink or a dance. (He looks round the room; appears startled and points at the bookcase.) What's that?

Wife—Why, it looks like a bookcase!

Husband—It is! And there are books in it! We can read!

Wife—Can you?

Husband—Why, yes. Anyway I could pick it up again in a minute.

Wife—I believe I could, too.

Husband—Well, let's!

Wife (excitedly)—But wait till I get a dustcloth!

Copyright The Chicago Tribune.

You'll Never Need a Dust Cloth on Your Stock of—

My Four Weeks in France By RING W. LARDNER	Treat 'Em Rough By RING W. LARDNER

THE next thing to do is to laugh. The world is about to be made safe for everybody. The terrible Turk is already a terrible mess, and the horrible Hun will soon be only a horrible example. Peace is smiling, so why shouldn't we

LAUGH WITH LARDNER

We can't get printers and binders to make these books fast enough to keep them in stock. Don't wait till you're out before ordering. The demand will be great from now on and the situation is not going to improve. These are facts. We are not trying to talk an order out of you, but here's an order card, just the same.

THE BOBBS-MERRILL COMPANY

INDIANAPOLIS PUBLISHERS NEW YORK

Advertisement for Lardner's two 1918 books on World War I, reprinting one of his columns (courtesy of The Lilly Library, Indiana University, Bloomington, Indiana)

Pictorial binding for Lardner's 1919 story collection (from Matthew J. Bruccoli and Richard Layman, Ring W. Lardner: A Descriptive Bibliography, *1976)*

Lardner to Howland, 5 May 1919

Dear Mr. Howland:–

I was in St. Louis two weeks ago and spent last week recovering; else I would have answered your letter before. I wrote a series of short stories about building a home three or four years ago. The series was printed in the Red Book and I don't know whether or not it could be obtained now; nor whether it would be worth printing.

I saw by the paper that you and Mrs. Howland were here last week, but my telephone told me nothing to that effect. Next time home, you are supposed to call up.

Sincerely,
R. W. Lardner

* * *

Lardner covered the heavyweight championship fight between Jess Willard and Jack Dempsey, which took place in Toledo on 4 July 1919. The illustrator Howland mentions was Fontaine Fox.

Howland to Lardner, 30 June 1919

Dear Lardner:

On the off-chance that all your time won't be taken up with the Big Fellow, as you have nicknamed him, I am writing you this letter. Speed is important or I'd not attempt to break in on your visits to the training quarters. Here's what I have on my mind:

To make a book out of four stories, the first to be the title story:

Own Your Own Home

the others, in the order in which they fall, are:

Welcome to our City
The Last Laugh
Uncivil War

If you don't remember them I'll tell you they are letters by Fred A Gross addressed to Brother Charles and have to do with the Gross family's attempt to build a house and establish themselves socially in a suburb. The stories are closely connected, the same characters appearing in all of them, and

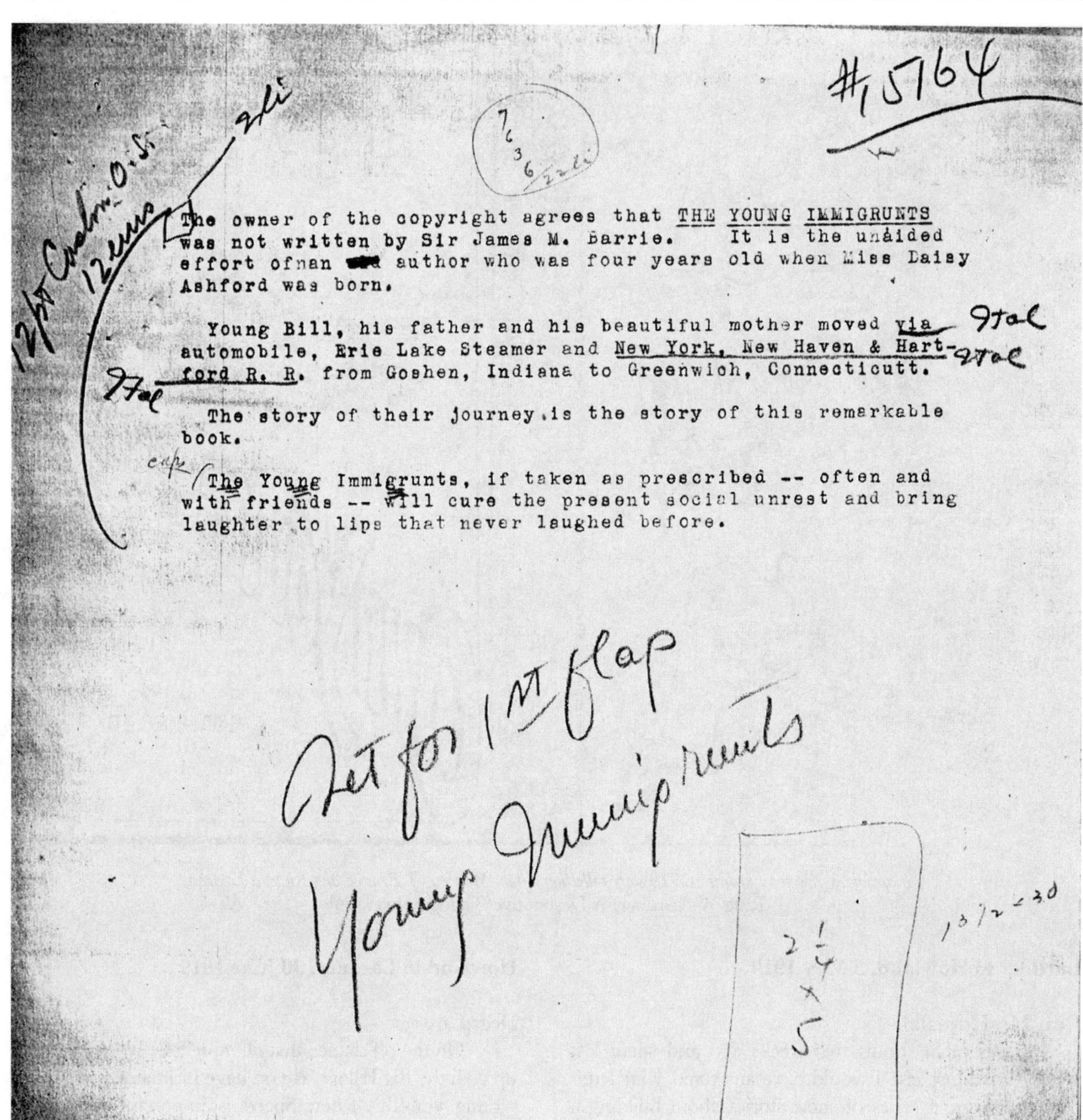

#15764

The owner of the copyright agrees that THE YOUNG IMMIGRUNTS was not written by Sir James M. Barrie. It is the unaided effort of an author who was four years old when Miss Daisy Ashford was born.

Young Bill, his father and his beautiful mother moved via automobile, Erie Lake Steamer and New York, New Haven & Hartford R. R. from Goshen, Indiana to Greenwich, Connecticutt.

The story of their journey is the story of this remarkable book.

The Young Immigrunts, if taken as prescribed -- often and with friends -- will cure the present social unrest and bring laughter to lips that never laughed before.

Copy for a dust-jacket flap of Lardner's 1920 collection The Young Immigrunts *(courtesy of The Lilly Library, Indiana University, Bloomington, Indiana)*

they come to a fairly well defined stopping place. Also for your better understanding I will add that they are darned good. Of course, the title has become the real estate man's slogan and as such is a peach, and should be used while the Own Your Own Home campaign is going strong.

The illustrations by Fox are wonders! I have written The Red Book people a preliminary letter and have their reply asking what the reproduction rights would be worth to us. I offered them one hundred and fifty dollars for said rights, subject to our going through with the job. Of course I wouldn't commit myself until I had your approval of the scheme. If you give it, we'll try to show you some fast foot work, so we can get the little book out for early fall distribution. We believe it has a good chance of a big sale, and are anxious to get busy. It's easier to telegraph than to write a letter, also less expensive if you send the message collect. A word to the wise.

Yours ever,
[Hewitt H. Howland]

* * *

Illustration of the putative author of The Young Immigrunts *(courtesy of The Lilly Library, Indiana University, Bloomington, Indiana)*

Lardner sent Howland a telegram expressing his approval of the plan for publication of Own Your Own Home *(1919).*

Lardner to Howland, 3 July 1919

ITS ALL RIGHT WITH ME
RING LARDNER

* * *

Lardner to Howland, 14 March 1921

Dear Mr. Howland:–

I suppose I ought to keep copies of my stuff, but I never have, so I guess the Post will have to be called on to provide you with the five that would go into "The Big Town". The titles are "Quick Returns", "Beautiful Katie", "The Battle of Long Island", "Only One" and "The Comic", the last named not yet published. May Preston did the pictures for all of them and don't you think it would be a good idea to have her illustrations in the book?

Sincerely,
Ring W. Lardner

* * *

Howland to Lardner, 18 March 1921

Dear Ring:

I find in our files here copies of The Post containing the four Big Town stories already printed. So we are all set as far as they go. We'll have to wait till The Comic appears, but I imagine that it won't be long.

Yes, I am for the May Wilson Preston illustrations and will take the thing up with the Post when the proper time comes.

Suppose the check reached you all right. Am going to do, along with The Big Town, John McCutcheon's The Restless Age and Sam Blythe's Keeping Fit at Fifty, so you won't be in bad company. You know how that would distress you.

Yours,
[Hewitt H. Howland]

* * *

Lardner to Howland, 11 April 1921

Dear Mr. Howland:–

I haven't heard when the Post is going to publish "The Comic," the last story in The Big Town series, but presume it will be in two or three weeks.

I enclose the contracts, which I haven't signed on account of Clause No. 2, providing that I offer the next two books to Bobbs-Merrill. If this clause is in every con-

Design study for the 1921 collection that was Lardner's final Bobbs-Merrill publication (courtesy of The Lilly Library, Indiana University, Bloomington, Indiana)

tract I sign, it means that I sign with Bobbs-Merrill not only for life, but also for two books afterwards, and while I have no fault to find with Bobbs-Merrill's treatment of me and see no immediate prospect of switching to another company, where would I be at if Doran or Appleton or some one else should go crazy and offer me a million for book rights to some future set of stories?

Can you have this clause removed?

Sincerely,
Ring W. Lardner

* * *

Howland to Lardner, 14 April 1921

Dear Ring Lardner:

Sure I can remove it. Should never have been there, for we know you'll always give us a chance even if Doran or Appleton should go crazy. Am sorry to have put you to the trouble.

Yours ever,
[Hewitt H. Howland]

* * *

The George H. Doran Company published Lardner's Say It with Oil: A Few Remarks about Wives *with Nina Wilcox Putnam's* Say It with Bricks: A Few Remarks about Husbands *in a back-to-back edition in 1923. Scribners handled all of Lardner's books thereafter. The Doran edition combining Irvin S. Cobb's* Oh, Well, You Know How Women Are! *with Mary Roberts Rinehart's* Isn't That Just Like a Man! *was published in 1920.*

Lardner to Howland, 12 June 1922

Dear Hewitt:–

I received notice in February that a royalty on the "35" story, amounting to $293.66, would reach me in May. It hasn't arrived, so will you please nudge the bookkeeper?

Nina Wilcox Putnam and I have written one of those double stunts, like the one Irvin Cobb and Mrs. Rinehart wrote on men and women; ours will appear in the November American and Doran wants to make a book of it. Mrs. Putnam, as you doubtless know, is signed up with Doran, so I told them it was all right with me, though I was going to tell you about it first. Between you and me, I don't think the book will set the world afire, but it may help toward the mortgage.

Sincerely,
Ring W. Lardner

Harold MacGrath (1871–1932)

Harold MacGrath was a newspaper reporter before he was twenty, and his literary career began when an editor set him to writing a humorous column. He then took to fiction, publishing his first novel, Arms and the Woman, *with Doubleday and McClure in 1899. His works were usually considered entertainments; few found in them much genuine realism or intellectual depth. He was, however, popular enough for Bobbs-Merrill to publish nineteen of his books in fifteen years, and four of them were top-ten best-sellers.* The Man on the Box *(1904) was made into a successful 1905 play, and MacGrath's contributions to the cinema included work on the famous serial* The Perils of Pauline *(1914). His earnings enabled him to become a world traveler. He was serious about his work and could turn out seven thousand words a day in his prime, but he admitted that his novels were "fairy-tales for grownups." Editor Hewitt H. Howland more charitably referred to such works as "romantic-historic novels," whose vogue more or less corresponded to the span of MacGrath's career with the firm. In fact, the unsolicited manuscript of* The Puppet Crown *(1901) arrived because of Bobbs-Merrill's prior success with Charles Major's* When Knighthood Was in Flower *(1898) and its successors.*

Harold MacGrath (from Stanley J. Kunitz and Howard Haycraft, eds., Twentieth Century Authors, *1942; Thomas Cooper Library, University of South Carolina)*

BOWEN-MERRILL/BOBBS-MERRILL BOOKS BY MACGRATH: *The Puppet Crown* (Indianapolis: Bowen-Merrill, 1901; London: Methuen, 1902);

The Grey Cloak (Indianapolis: Bobbs-Merrill, 1903; London: Ward, Lock, 1904);

The Man on the Box (Indianapolis: Bobbs-Merrill, 1904; London: Hodder & Stoughton, 1914);

Enchantment (Indianapolis: Bobbs-Merrill, 1905);

Hearts and Masks (Indianapolis: Bobbs-Merrill, 1905);

The Princess Elopes (Indianapolis: Bobbs-Merrill, 1905);

Half a Rogue (Indianapolis: Bobbs-Merrill, 1906; London: Gay & Bird, 1907);

The Best Man (Indianapolis: Bobbs-Merrill, 1907);

The Enchanted Hat (Indianapolis: Bobbs-Merrill, 1908);

The Lure of the Mask (Indianapolis: Bobbs-Merrill, 1908; London: Stead's, 1909);

The Goose Girl (Indianapolis: Bobbs-Merrill, 1909);

A Splendid Hazard (Indianapolis: Bobbs-Merrill, 1910; London: Ward, Lock, 1910);

The Carpet from Bagdad (Indianapolis: Bobbs-Merrill, 1911);

The Place of Honeymoons (Indianapolis: Bobbs-Merrill, 1912);

Deuces Wild (Indianapolis: Bobbs-Merrill, 1913);

Parrot & Co. (Indianapolis: Bobbs-Merrill, 1913);

The Adventures of Kathlyn (Indianapolis: Bobbs-Merrill, 1914);

Pidgin Island (Indianapolis: Bobbs-Merrill, 1914);

The Voice in the Fog (Indianapolis: Bobbs-Merrill, 1915).

Review: *Hearts and Masks* (1905)

Harold MacGrath's name on the title page of a book is synonymous with adventures of the heart. The title of his new book, "Hearts and Masks," (Indianapolis: Bobbs, Merrill & Co.) gives a fair idea of what the contents might be. It is a book to be read in a half hour, but it contains adventure enough to last a lifetime.

Mr. Dicky Cornstalk starts an evening, which later fairly seethes with excitement, innocently enough at Moquin's. He meets there a charming lady, and in the

An example of John J. Curtis's innovative advertising: a two-page spread in Publishers' Weekly *(1 June 1901) for a single work, MacGrath's first company publication*

Dust-jacket art by Harrison Fisher for MacGrath's 1908 novel. In an undated memo, Curtis claimed that this was the first "illuminated jacket, printed in two or four colors with the titles of the novels embossed in gold on the side and backbone." Compare, however, the dust jacket for Frederic S. Isham's The Strollers *(1902) on p. 44 (courtesy of Michael Manz/Babylon Revisited).*

spirit of friendly bonhomie exchanges some pleasant words with her, all the time noting the color of her hair, which was like ripe corn silk, and the shape of her mouth, which was arched like a bow. Later, in a spirit of recklessness, he determines to be an uninvited guest at a masquerade dance given by a fashionable hunt club. It was not as if he was an ordinary interloper, since the price of entrance was $10 and the card of admission an ordinary playing card of a certain style back. Besides, he was well acquainted with Teddy Hamilton, the M. F. H. of the club, and might have been a member himself had he chose. It was easy enough, however, for the adventurous Richard to secure another card–it hardly mattered what the back was like–so having cut with himself and drawn the ten of hearts, he went gayly to the ball.

The ten of hearts proved both a lucky and an unlucky draw. There were other uninvited guests at the dance; indeed, a number of them, and mysteriously enough, all held the ten of hearts–the story deals mainly with these–but in the end, after some lively escapades, all turns out well, with no blood shed, save only the shattered arm of a most deserving villain.

–"At a Masked Ball," *New York Times,* 9 December 1905, p. 885

* * *

Related Letters

MacGrath wired treasurer Charles W. Merrill about overdue royalties.

Harold MacGrath to Charles W. Merrill, 13 (?) October 1914

MY ROYALTIES WERE DUE OCT FIRST THEIR NONARRIVAL MEANS LOSS OF ELEVEN DOLLARS INTEREST ADD THE ELEVEN DOLLARS TO MY DRAFT AND SEND AT ONCE

HAROLD MCGRATH [*sic*]

* * *

MacGrath to Merrill, 17 October 1914

DRAFT RECEIVED AMOUNT IS SIX DOLLARS LESS THAN ROYALTY REPORT INTEREST AS [*sic*] NOT INCLUDED.

HAROLD MCGRATH

* * *

Flier for one of MacGrath's two 1913 books (courtesy of The Lilly Library, Indiana University, Bloomington, Indiana)

Merrill to MacGrath, 17 October 1914

My dear Mr. MacGrath:–

Your telegram has just come in. I am sorry there was any lack of understanding about the $6.00 charge. Here is a statement which shows the items. If there is any question about the correctness of this, write and we will of course adjust it.

I believe I already explained that the war troubles and the general financial slump prevented our taking care of royalties quite as early as usual.

With my very best wishes, I remain

Yours very truly,
[Charles W. Merrill]

* * *

D. Laurance Chambers wrote company president William C. Bobbs about a visit from MacGrath's lawyer.

D. Laurance Chambers to William C. Bobbs, 21 October 1914

Dear Mr. Bobbs,–

Mr. MacGrath's attorney, Mr. Thomas Hogan, and his "brother", H. MacGrath Faulder, arrived today to examine our motion picture contracts, 2¢ royalty on Canadian editions, etc., etc.!

Yours
DLC

* * *

Hewitt H. Howland was editor of the trade department. It is uncertain which of Judge Learned Hand's decisions is referred to; 1912 was the year when Congress gave copyright protection to movies. Lasky was the founder in 1913 of Jesse L. Lasky Feature Play Company (later Paramount Pictures); its first director was Cecil B. DeMille. Carl Bernhardt handled the dramatic rights in the New York office. Baker and Castle is unidentified.

Chambers to Bobbs, 21 October 1914

My dear Mr. Bobbs,–

The MacGrath situation looks critical and very ugly, close to a break, if the break has not already been made. I have just found from Mr. Merrill that when the MacGrath royalties were paid October 10 th Mac wrote and later wired us that we must pay him ten days' interest which he had figured out amounted to $11 00. Can you beat it?

Some days ago came a letter from a firm of Syracuse lawyers (Hogan, Byrne & Byrne, acting for Mr. MacG.) asking in a general way for a full statement of our position relative to the motion picture rights of MacGrath books; which had been sold; how much we had received, etc. I sent the letter into Hewitt, who held it without comment and, I find, without answer.

Today arrived Mr. Thomas Hogan and MacG's adopted brother, H. MacGrath Faulder. Just what they were after, I don't know. Faulder no doubt expected to kick the roof off the establishment; and he'll doubtless go home mad because he accomplished little or nothing. Hogan is a gentleman. I'm sorry he didn't come alone. Faulder is an impossible pup. He said some things hard to stomach and neither Hewitt nor I took them with a smile.

They wanted to see our mot. pic. contracts and I showed them everything. They asked for copies of them and I said as a matter of formality I'd have to get the approval of our Board before I could furnish them. (Guess I'd better send 'em on, hadn't I?)

Faulder exhibited much bad blood over:

① Popular Editions. Quoted you as having said to MacGrath that when we paid him 2½¢ we were giving him half of what we got. He asks to have the Voice in the Fog contract rate on pop. edn. increased to 6¢. We said in reply that we could not make any change in a contract without your approval and would submit the question. (Hewitt tells me it's a short book and we'd not be likely to sell a pop. edn.)

② Motion Pictures. Said that after repeatedly assuring MacG. that we would do nothing without consulting him we went ahead and made contracts. There's something in this. I promised we'd be good hereafter, but maintained that he had exaggerated our failure to consult.

Hogan proposes, in view of the fact that Judge Hand's decision has rendered the status of mot. pic. rights doubtful on books copyrighted since Feb 1912, that we cede to MacGrath whatever photoplay rights we may have in such books of his, to wit:

Parrot & Co. Place of Honeymoons
Pidgin Island

Let me have your judgment. They ask also for a copy of our contract with H. MacG. for A Splendid Hazard. I don't think there ever was one. We'll look into that tomorrow.

They kick about a payment of one cent a copy on certain Canadian Editions. This is probably some pop. edn. matter. I'll investigate. They could give no dates or quantities.

They insist that on Puppet Crown motion pictures we must pay H MacG. 80% of receipts–not 50%. That is in accord with the original contract. I'm sure a 50%–50% understanding was reached later but may have difficulty showing documentary evidence.

This Puppet Crown matter has bearing on Lasky request to have royalties reduced from 10% to 5%. Don't let Bernhardt take any action on that without first

You made BIG MONEY with the Picture; Now make BIG MONEY with the BOOK!

ESTABLISHED 1838

THE BOBBS-MERRILL COMPANY
PUBLISHERS ··· INDIANAPOLIS

HERE'S A CHANCE TO CAPITALIZE ALL OVER AGAIN THE ADVERTISING AND PUBLICITY YOU GAVE THE GREAT MOVIE FEATURE—

The ADVENTURES OF KATHLYN

NOW READY IN BOOK FORM

SELL THE BOOK AT YOUR TICKET WINDOW AND IN YOUR THEATER—LARGE DISCOUNT—ENORMOUS PROFIT—UNUSUAL OPPORTUNITY

The first chance of the kind ever given the motion picture theater owner, this is an opportunity you can not afford to overlook. You can actually make money on advertising and publicity that otherwise would be as dead as Hector.

THE ADVENTURES OF KATHLYN, by Harold MacGrath, rewritten from the serial version which appeared in the newspapers simultaneously with the production of the pictures, is now ready in book form. The volume is specially prepared for sale in the motion picture theaters. It contains *sixteen* full-page illustrations reproduced from scenes in the picture play. The cover is of specially embossed paper with full-color portrait of MISS KATHLYN WILLIAMS, the STAR of the photo-play cast, by Neysa McMein.

Nine out of every ten people who saw the Kathlyn Pictures in your theater will want to read the finished version of the story as it appears in the book. It's the biggest chance to coin money with a side-line ever offered you.

To Moving Picture Theaters Handling KATHLYN in Book Form, We Will Furnish, Without Charge

(1) A beautiful advertising slide, in colors, showing a portrait of Kathlyn Williams.

(2) A placard for your lobby reading: "Patrons of this theater desiring to secure THE ADVENTURES OF KATHLYN in book form, can obtain copies at the box office."

Fill in and mail us at once the card attached on back and we will send you full particulars by return mail, together with a sample copy of the book for your inspection.

If you are not interested, prompt information to that effect is of equal importance to us, and in either event we ask you to advise us immediately that we may be at once in a position to move in a matter which requires the utmost promptness.

Address The Bobbs-Merrill Company, University Square, Indianapolis, Indiana

Advertisement for an early movie tie-in edition (1914) of a MacGrath story (courtesy of The Lilly Library, Indiana University, Bloomington, Indiana)

hearing from me. I told Hogan to ask MacG. what he would like to have us do.

Yours

DLC

Two other things:

① Perhaps we'd better put up to MacG. the terms of any agreement we may reach with Baker & Castle on mot. pic. rights Goose Girl.

② Get Ger [?] to tell you what he knows about Faulder,–ask for the trained nurse story.

* * *

John L. Lockwood was the company attorney.

Chambers to Bobbs, 21 October 1914

Dear Mr. Bobbs,

I suppose some adjustment will have to be made with Baker & Castle on The Goose Girl mot. pic. They've written C.B. about it. All the documents are in Lockwood's hands. Our copy of the contract with H. MacG. has the dram. clause marked out; but his copy, as D accidentally discovered today, has it in.

Lockwood may think we ought to go halvers with B. & C. but I believe they'd be satisfied with 1/3 if shown that no use would be made of their production.

DLC

* * *

Howland to Bobbs, 21 October 1914

My Dear Will

Thomas Hogan and young MacGrath–the adopted–paid us an unexpected visit today. Hogan is a lawyer and a friend of the family. He is square and honest but rather stupid, a dangerous combination. Just what they hoped to find out I wasn't able to determine, but the dramatic, motion picture and pop. ed. phases of the business seemed uppermost in their minds. Their ignorance is monumental and I think they took most of it away with them. They asked me about royalties on Popular Canadian Editions, about which I knew nothing. They asked about royalties on American popular ed. and I refered [*sic*] them to their contracts calling for 5% on the selling price, and explained the absence of a pop. ed. provision in the earlier contracts. They professed to be under the impression that we had told them that we were giving them half that we received for plate rights. I told them that doubtless agents and other publishers trying to get MacGrath's books had advised them that they should get half, but that we always operated on a percentage business. They discussed old contracts, talked to the whole question of the reasonableness of our terms,–popular edition, secondary serial etc. They want us to give them a statement, in the form of a letter, that in paying them 1¢ a copy on Canadian Popular Editions we are paying them half that we recieve [*sic*]. To this I replied that these sales were made by our N. Y. office and that the facts would have to come from them. To other questions I told them that I was only the Editor! The blanket agreement that MacG. gave us granting dramatic or moving picture rights on such of his books not already covered by contract, was absurdly misconstrued by Hogan. He thought MacGrath was giving us dramatic rights on books that we ourselves had not published. He also tried to substantiate a claim that the cancelation of that agreement vitiated any sales or contracts that we might have made under it, or as a result of it. Of course I wouldn't stand for this and he finally dropped it. The talk ran all over the place and on almost every phase of the publishing business. I took them to lunch and then the Brat made some statement that I wouldn't stand for and I said so with some show of heat. Again in Lawrence's office he said that when I left Syracuse the last time after showing the Kathlyn samples that they all felt when I left that they were "going to be done." I blew out of the water at this and told him that I didn't propose to have him say this kind of thing to–My temper entirely disappeared, I'm afraid. I felt like telling him to get out of the office and take the whole MacGrath outfit with him. He was as insulting as a Brat can be. When L. made a statement he turned on him and asked in peremptory [?] tones if he'd "please put that in writing and sign his name to it." I told L. in the boy's presence to do nothing of the kind. L. has a list of these troubles which he is submiting [*sic*] in detail. My letter is to give you the atmosphere. Hogan before the day was over undoubtedly felt that we were trying and wanting to do the fair thing, he also felt that he hadn't gotten very far and that the Brat would have been better left at home. Alone we could have handled Hogan–the Brat wants to make trouble–he wants the motion picture rights to work on himself–he'd like to upset the apple cart. It hasn't been a pleasant day and I don't know what the result will be, but we had to discuss the matter and we discussed it as it seemed best to us at the time. Excuse this long written letter but my stenographer has gone for the night. I think I'll go get a drink–possibly two.

Yours

HHH

Talbot Mundy (1879–1940)

Talbot Mundy, born William Lancaster Gribbon in London, became an American citizen in 1917. He wandered the world, admitting to a special fascination with the occult, which he took seriously. He also took seriously Germany's colonial exploitation of Africa and wrote of it in The Ivory Trail *(1919). What he gathered in exotic places he put into his fiction, which included about 150 stories for magazines. These tales were as well known as his popular novels; from 1911 on,* Adventure *magazine published more than a hundred of them. Mundy's best-known work remains the first he published with Bobbs-Merrill,* King–of the Khyber Rifles *(1916). John Ford filmed it as* The Black Watch *in 1929, and it was adapted for the screen again in 1953, as* King of the Khyber Rifles, *starring Tyrone Power.*

BOBBS-MERRILL BOOKS BY MUNDY: *King–of the Khyber Rifles* (Indianapolis: Bobbs-Merrill, 1916); republished as *King, of the Khyber Rifles* (London: Constable, 1917);

The Winds of the World (Indianapolis: Bobbs-Merrill, 1917; **first edition,** London: Cassell, 1916);

Hira Singh: When India Came to Fight in Flanders (Indianapolis: Bobbs-Merrill, 1918); republished as *Hira Singh's Tale* (London: Cassell, 1918);

The Ivory Trail (Indianapolis: Bobbs-Merrill, 1919; London: Constable, 1920);

The Eye of Zeitoon (Indianapolis: Bobbs-Merrill, 1920; London: Hutchinson, 1920);

Told in the East (Indianapolis: Bobbs-Merrill, 1920);

Guns of the Gods: A Story of Yasmini's Youth (Indianapolis: Bobbs-Merrill, 1921; London: Hutchinson, 1921);

Her Reputation (Indianapolis: Bobbs-Merrill, 1923); republished as *The Bubble Reputation* (London: Hutchinson, 1923);

The Nine Unknown (Indianapolis: Bobbs-Merrill, 1924; London: Hutchinson, 1924);

Talbot Mundy (from Stanley J. Kunitz and Howard Haycraft, eds., Twentieth Century Authors, *1942; Thomas Cooper Library, University of South Carolina)*

Om: The Secret of the Ahbor Valley (Indianapolis: Bobbs-Merrill, 1924; London: Hutchinson, 1924);

The Devil's Guard (Indianapolis: Bobbs-Merrill, 1926); republished as *Ramsden* (London: Hutchinson, 1926);

Cock o' the North (Indianapolis: Bobbs-Merrill, 1929); republished as *Gup Bahadur* (London: Hutchinson, 1929);

Queen Cleopatra (Indianapolis: Bobbs-Merrill, 1929; London: Hutchinson, 1929);

Black Light (Indianapolis: Bobbs-Merrill, 1930; London: Hutchinson, 1930).

Related Letters

Mundy's biographical questionnaire is reproduced in facsimile in the DLB Yearbook, 1985, *pp. 37–39; M. A. Cleland's report for* King–of the Khyber Rifles *in the* DLB Yearbook, 1990, *pp. 145–146. Paul Reynolds was a literary agent.*

Talbot Mundy to Bobbs-Merrill, 24 June 1916

Gentlemen,

Absence from home prevented my getting your letter of June 6th until yesterday. At once, however, on my return I put the matter in hand, and the photos you ask for are being rushed to you today. I hope they are such as you require. The photo is a copy of a drawing by Walter Lyman Stone.

I was glad to learn from Paul Reynolds that you have accepted my book "The Winds of the World", and I agree with Reynolds that your decision to publish it after "King, of the Khyber Rifles" is a wise one. Here is hoping both books will satisfy all of us concerned.

By the time that "The Winds of the World" shall have run its course I hope to have another, better book for you.

Faithfully yours,
Talbot Mundy

* * *

Hewitt H. Howland was chief editor of the trade department at this time.

D. Laurance Chambers to Mundy, 27 June 1916

My dear Mr. Mundy:–

Your very good letter of the 24th arrives during Mr. Howland's absence from the city and so comes into my hands. The photographs have been received in excellent condition and will serve our purpose very well indeed.

We are glad that you agree with the wisdom of postponing the publication of THE WINDS OF THE WORLD until after the publication of KING, OF THE KHYBER RIFLES, and we are delighted that you are already planning a story to follow THE WINDS OF THE WORLD. You will have to "go some" to beat KING.

Don't you want to interview yourself and send me the interview in connection with the publicity for KING? I shall be very grateful. Please make the interview include a short sketch of your life.

Faithfully yours,
[D. Laurance Chambers]

* * *

Mundy to Chambers, 7 July 1916

My dear Mr Chambers,

In answer to your kind letter of the 27th of June,–my objection to being interviewed is that a man who is earnestly thinking–(that is to say, a man who will not voice thoughts at second or third hand if he can help it)–must of necessity make statements during an interview that he will likely enough retract in a year's time, or sooner. Thought is progressive.

It does not matter where I live, or what I do with my spare time, or how many hours a day I work, or what I did in former years. The point is, Of what am I thinking now, and how earnestly? And my book is the answer to that. I cannot answer the question better than I have done in my book. If I could answer it better I would have written a better book.

I have reached the conclusion at present that an author's business is to appreciate. I have no time to read or write things deprecatory. Depreciation and pessimism may be some other body's business, perhaps, but they positively are not mine. It has become habit with me to look for and appreciate other men's good effort, and I know no better way of appreciation than to make a book about what I find.

In KING OF THE KHYBER RIFLES we find King faced with a problem that looks titanic; and in the course of the story Patience and silent Method carry King through to a triumphant conclusion. I faced him with that problem for two reasons: (1) that the situation was perfectly possible, and (2) because I have met men in various places of the world not at all unlike Athelstan King, who silently convinced me that there is no problem too big for them; their utter absence of personal greed and their entire loyalty to first principles can conquer anything but a greater honesty, which if met with would be on their side.

A to me most interesting point about King's service is that it is the business of his kind to forestall trouble, unlike the old order of secret servants whose trade was to make it.

To appreciate other men's effort requires too much thought to permit great interest in one's own affairs. The public often mistakes the thought expressed in a book for true glimpses of the author's private life; whereas of course until said author leaves off doing exciting things–things that excite his brain or his nerves, as distinguished from things that appeal to his heart–he has no time to appreciate properly the things that are worth putting in a book. There is nothing truer than that "As a man thinketh in his heart, so is he."

For instance, I have hunted elephants–hunted them for the ivory. But I can assure you that hunting them lent me no aid to writing books. I remember one bull elephant alone who so terrified me before I shot him that I could not have written about anything sensibly for a long time afterwards. And to suppose that while a man squints down his rifle at a charging pachyderm his thoughts are worth ink and paper is to suppose the ridiculous. One has to forget the material horror of the thing, and the sordid motive that led to it, before becoming receptive enough of ideas to merit an audience. Besides, the sheer hard labor, danger, and adventure of hunting elephants are so terrific as to preclude consideration of any problems but one's own.

So I don't see that it makes any difference that I have fought savages now and then, under orders from His Britannic Majesty. I have also watched more than one dog-fight, and have taken part in efforts to drag the dogs apart. I lay no claim to distinction on that account, and claim no merit. I have shot lions (more than fifty of them), and was once chased by a policeman for a mile, because I bathed in a forbidden place without a suit on–to the vast edification of a crowd that included ladies, none of whom would have seen me but for the policeman. I am inclined to think that the "cop" was more dangerous than the lions, at least to my self respect; certainly had he caught me the result would have been longer drawn out and harder to live down; but I could run faster than he, and when you get right down to hard tacks I am a practical fellow after all.

It would probably be useless for me to deny having been in India; there are whole pages in KING OF THE KHYBER RIFLES that are proof I have been there, and that I kept eyes and ears open. I saw plague there, and cholera (having something to do with both), and I shot some tigers–all of them things that prevented me from giving proper attention to matters of real importance, with which I might have filled many books had I had more sense. But we all miss opportunities, and the world is full of those that the other fellows missed, so we need not worry.

I was born in London, England, and educated at Rugby, which accounts for some of my virtues. There is no accounting for defects.

Since coming to America I have married an American lady who is a far better painter of pictures than I ever dare hope to be writer of stories. I claim that is proof of sound good sense, and of ability to recognize a good thing when I see it. I live in Norway, Maine, partly because I like the climate, and partly because the people in the village make no attempt to take me seriously. The worst conceivable thing that can happen to a writer of books is to be taken seriously in private life. After he has written twenty or thirty books perhaps it does not matter, but I have only written three.

For the future–I earnestly believe that the world is hesitating on the threshold of the most wonderful renaissance it has ever seen–of virtue, of art, of understanding, and of everything that matters. I believe we are all going to laugh at what has gone before–good-naturedly, of course, as becomes men of understanding; and I hope, as I surely shall strive, to be somebody in the swim.

So I should be sorry to burden myself with an unnecessary yoke by stating in advance what my next book is to be about. It is not agreeable to have to eat one's words, yet a prophesy [*sic*] of one's own making is an intolerable limitation that can not be allowed to stand. I rather think I know what the problem of the next book is; I am sure I know the hero's name, and I think I know the title. I am quite sure I like the hero, and he and I are going many a long walk together before he sees the printed page–not in the dust in an auto, but on foot, where brooks run under green trees, or where in winter the breeze comes clean and cold and sweet from the White Mountains. One can get familiar with a character under those conditions.

There is no knowing how long it will take me to write the book. Once I could write a longish novelette from Saturday to Monday, and sell it on Tuesday morning; but the sins of one's youth prove nothing except the kindness of editors and the patience of the public. I have reformed quite a lot since then.

Oh yes, and I am thirty-six and a month or so. There's plenty of time ahead.

Faithfully yours,
Talbot Mundy

* * *

Sketch for an illustration in Mundy's King–of the Khyber Rifles, *published in 1916 (courtesy of The Lilly Library, Indiana University, Bloomington, Indiana)*

Chambers to Mundy, 11 July 1916

Dear Mr. Mundy:–

Your extremely interesting letter of the 7th has been read with the keenest interest. I am most heartily obliged to you for interviewing yourself, in the face of your objections to being interviewed. All that you have written me will be very helpful in the work on KING, OF THE KHYBER RIFLES. I read the manuscript with such interest and so much appreciation that it is going to be a great satisfaction to me to do everything I possibly can to extend the sale and distribution and I am grateful for your help to that end.

Mr. Howland will be interested, as we all are, in what you say about the next book. We count ourselves your pardners now in your literary future and are eager to make it realize its splendid possibilities.

With kind regards, believe me
Sincerely yours,
[D. Laurance Chambers]

* * *

Hewitt H. Howland to Mundy, 17 February 1917

My dear Mr. Mundy:

Our people feel that it might be better not to publish The Winds of the World this spring but hold it off until fall. We are still hammering away at King of the Khyber Rifles with some results. They are not large but enough to show the book has life and if we keep the track clear we may get it going big. As your decision affects the make-up of our latest spring announcement, now ready to go to the press, won't you wire me your judgment?

With kind regards, as ever,
Sincerely yours,
[Hewitt H. Howland]

* * *

Mundy to Howland, 19 February 1917

TAKE WHICHEVER COURSE APPEARS TO YOU BUSINESSLIKE AND WISE
TALBOT MUNDAY [*sic*]

Dust jacket for Mundy's 1929 novel of the Indian-Afghan war (courtesy of Michael Manz/Babylon Revisited)

Robert Nathan (1894–1985)

See also the Nathan entry in *DLB 9: American Novelists, 1910–1945.*

Many authors complained to Bobbs-Merrill about the royalties paid them and the company's promotion of their books. In Robert Nathan's case such matters were particularly urgent because, after brief work with an advertising agency and the New York University School of Journalism, he never again held a nonwriting job. He wrote more than forty novels and more than a dozen volumes of poetry, drama, and essays, in addition to writing screenplays for M-G-M in the 1940s. The novels, particularly those published during his brief association with Bobbs-Merrill, have been characterized as satirical fantasies, owing much to the inspiration of Cervantes, Jonathan Swift, and Anatole France. Nathan moved from Robert M. McBride and Company to Bobbs-Merrill and then to Alfred A. Knopf for the next forty years.

BOBBS-MERRILL BOOKS BY NATHAN: *The Woodcutter's House* (Indianapolis: Bobbs-Merrill, 1927; London: Mathews & Marrot, 1932);
The Bishop's Wife (Indianapolis: Bobbs-Merrill, 1928; London: Gollancz, 1928);
A Cedar Box (Indianapolis: Bobbs-Merrill, 1929);
There Is Another Heaven (Indianapolis: Bobbs-Merrill, 1929);
The Orchid (Indianapolis: Bobbs-Merrill, 1931; London: Mathews & Marrot, 1932).

Robert Nathan (Bruccoli Clark Layman Archives)

Related Letters

At the time of this letter, D. Laurance Chambers was vice president and trade-department editor in chief. Grace Zaring Stone was a Bobbs-Merrill writer whose novel The Almond Tree *was published in 1931.*

Robert Nathan to D. Laurance Chambers, 18 February 1932

Dear Laurence [*sic*],

There's no case to be surprised. I know that you have an option on my next book; but do you actually want to go on publishing me? We're not a very successful partnership.

Nor does it please me to hear that you do three times as well for Mrs. Stone as you do for me–or to realize that McBride today sells more of my old titles than you do.

I'm tired of getting the best reviews in the country, and selling the fewest books. My sales ought to reach ten thousand copies; and I shan't publish unless they do. If you really want my next book–just begun–you can certainly have it–but I shall ask for some very definite assurances that a reasonably able organization will see to it that my sale is not unreasonably small.

Sincerely
Bob

* * *

Inscribed half-title page of Nathan's 1928 novel (courtesy of the Boston Public Library)

George Shively and Max Aley were in the New York office.

Chambers to Nathan, 19 February 1932

Dear Bob:–

Thank you for your letter received today. It reveals a mental attitude which calls for free and full discussion hardly possible to correspondence. I suggest that you talk things over with George Shively and Max Aley.

You throw all the burden of responsibility on the publisher. I wish I could flatter myself that a publisher is so powerful. It doesn't seem to work that way. At any rate the bookseller's [*sic*] appear to think that the author is the more important and responsible end of the partnership.

Of course it has occurred to you that if McBride is selling more of your old titles than we are, it may be due to the fact that we loaded them up with more at the start.

Of course we want to carry on with you, but our success will depend on what you give us to publish.

I suppose the Grosset & Dunlap organization is generally regarded as the best merchandising bunch in the publishing business. You might compare what they have done with THE BISHOP'S WIFE with what we did.

Sincerely yours,
[D. Laurance Chambers]

* * *

Nathan to Chambers, 24 February 1932

Dear Lawrence [*sic*],

Perhaps you're right; perhaps, as you say, my books are so unsaleable that you can't sell them.

But surely, that is all the more reason not to publish them.

Sincerely
Robert Nathan

* * *

Chambers to Nathan, 25 February 1932

Dear Bob:–

Thanks for your letter received today.

The only point I was trying, in my awkward fashion, to make, is that there is a difference in the selling quality of an author's books, something apart from literary quality, and something beyond the publisher's control. We did well with The Bishop's Wife for example; we did not so well with There Is Another Heaven. I don't believe–at least I find no evidence–that less intelligence went to our handling of the latter than the former. Get what I'm driving at?

Julia smiled. But her thoughts were small and sharp, like needles stitching in her heart. Yes, she thought, you are very grown up, my darling. You are not a baby any more. You can do things for yourself, think out things for yourself. The little hands which fumbled for life, already point in not-to-be-disobeyed commands. Soon you will not need me at all, not even to take care of you in the Mall. You will turn to some one else. Will he leave you heartsick, too, for the beauty you hoped to find, for the love you meant to give?

And what will I do then? What will happen to me when you do not need me any longer? Shall I sit down in a corner like an old woman? But what have I to remember? Only . . . only the great love I wanted to give some one who was too busy—and too ashamed. . . .

32

THIS *is part of a page from a forthcoming novel. There is only one author in America who could have written it. Guess correctly his or her name and we shall send you an advance copy with our compliments. Just write the name of the author you think it is, on the other side of this sheet, add your name and address and we will do the rest.*

Cordially,

THE BOBBS-MERRILL COMPANY

Indianapolis, Indiana

Promotional piece for The Bishop's Wife *(courtesy of The Lilly Library, Indiana University, Bloomington, Indiana)*

I want you to be fair to us because the figures show we've been generous with you, honest and devoted in our efforts.

Have you talked things over with Max and George?

Sincerely yours,
[D. Laurance Chambers]

* * *

By the date of the following letter Chambers had become president of the company.

Nathan to Chambers, 24 May 1937

Dear Lawrence [*sic*],

Thanks for the contracts and copyrights. I'm sorry we never did better together–financially, that is; personally, we did as well as anyone could. I feel like making a little funeral oration.

Best of luck to you–

Cordially
Bob Nathan

* * *

Chambers to Nathan, 26 May 1937

Dear Bob:–

Thank you for your letter of the 24th. I have shed a very sincere tear over the loss of your name and your books from our list.

All good luck to you.

Faithfully yours,
[D. Laurance Chambers]

THE BISHOP'S WIFE

really? . . . What a wonder, what a wonder.

But Juliet paid no attention to this look with which she was familiar. "I'm more grown up than him," she said. "He's only a little child."

Julia smiled across at Potter's nurse. But her thoughts were small and sharp, like needles stitching in her heart. Yes, she thought, you are very grown up, my darling. You are not a baby any more. You can do things for yourself, think out things for yourself. The little hands which fumbled for life, already point in not-to-be-disobeyed commands. And Potter obeys them, with his mouth open. Soon you will not need me at all, not even to take care of you in the Mall. You will turn to some one else. Will he leave you heartsick, too, for the beauty you hoped to find, for the love you meant to give?

And what will I do then? What will happen

31

THE BISHOP'S WIFE

to me when you do not need me any longer? Shall I sit down in a corner like an old woman? But what have I to remember? Only . . . only the great love I wanted to give some one who was too busy—and too ashamed . . .

"Bother," said Juliet; "I've broke my chalk."

And she looked hopefully at Potter.

"No," said Potter.

"Give me your chalk, Potter," said Juliet, holding out her hand, "and then we can both play."

"I won't," said Potter.

Juliet looked at her mother, as one woman to another. "He won't," she said simply. And she added, as though that explained everything,

"He's only a little child."

It made no difference to Potter. Squatting on his heels, he began to draw uncertain

32

Pages from Nathan's 1928 novel showing the published version of the text selection used earlier for the promotional item reproduced on the preceding page (Boston Public Library)

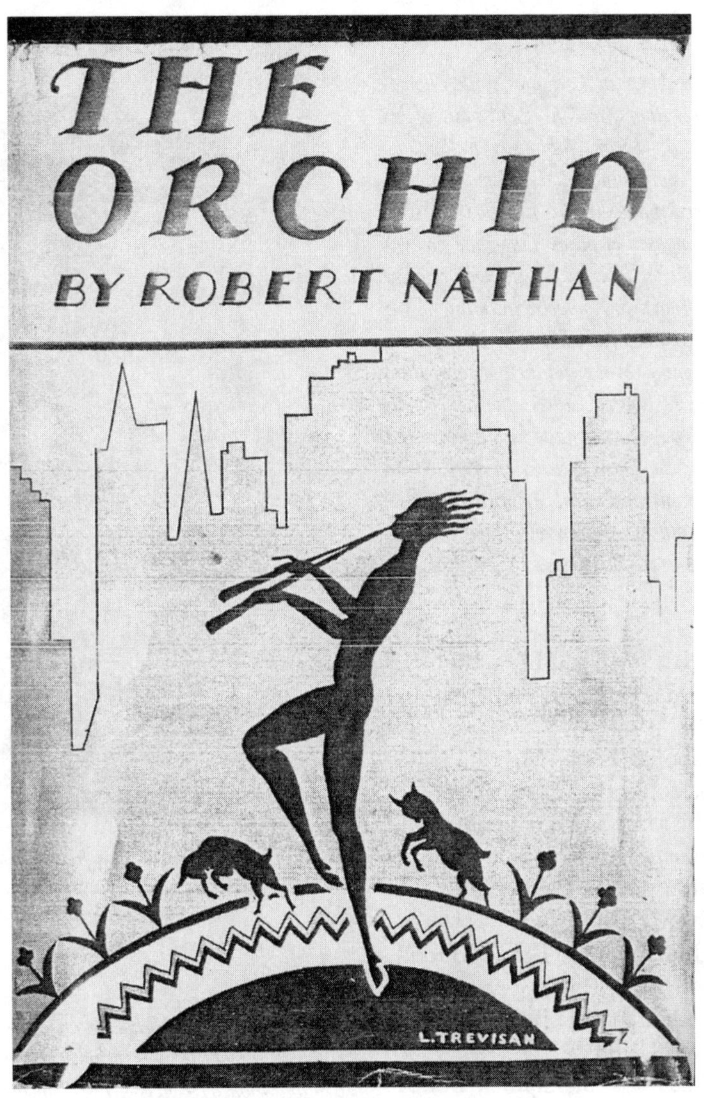

Dust jacket for Nathan's last Bobbs-Merrill novel, published in 1931 (Thomas Cooper Library, University of South Carolina)

Meredith Nicholson (1866–1947)

Meredith Nicholson was born in Crawfordsville, hometown of many notable Indiana authors, and he spent most of his life in Indianapolis. Known as the Dean of Hoosier Letters, he was proud of his native state and found in it the material for much of his work. Bowen-Merrill published his first book, Short Flights *(1890), which was composed of poems that gave no sign of his considerable success as a writer later on. In the new century Bobbs-Merrill published Nicholson's first novels, including* The House of a Thousand Candles *(1905), a mystery set in Indiana instead of the customary exotic haunts. More than 250,000 copies were sold in the United States; the novel was also translated into several languages and made into a play and two movies. Broad-minded as he was, Nicholson refused to indulge in the satire of small towns and rural America that produced great realistic writing in others, and he celebrated the values he associated with the life he knew in Indiana. Things always turned out well in his novels.*

BOWEN-MERRILL/BOBBS-MERRILL BOOKS BY NICHOLSON: *Short Flights* (Indianapolis: Bowen-Merrill, 1890);
The Main Chance (Indianapolis: Bobbs-Merrill, 1903; London: Ward, Lock, 1904);
Zelda Dameron (Indianapolis: Bobbs-Merrill, 1904);
The House of a Thousand Candles (Indianapolis: Bobbs-Merrill, 1905; London: Gay & Bird, 1906);
Poems (Indianapolis: Bobbs-Merrill, 1906);
The Port of Missing Men (Indianapolis: Bobbs-Merrill, 1907; London: Gay & Bird, 1907);
Rosalind at Red Gate (Indianapolis: Bobbs-Merrill, 1907; London: Everett, 1908);
The Little Brown Jug at Kildare (Indianapolis: Bobbs-Merrill, 1908);
Style and the Man (Indianapolis: Bobbs-Merrill, 1911);
The Cavalier of Tennessee (Indianapolis: Bobbs-Merrill, 1928);
Old Familiar Faces (Indianapolis: Bobbs-Merrill, 1929).

Meredith Nicholson (from Stanley J. Kunitz and Howard Haycraft, eds., Twentieth Century Authors, *1942; Thomas Cooper Library, University of South Carolina)*

The Genesis of *Short Flights*

Many of the claims in the 1923 pamphlet The Hoosier House *need to be weighed against other sources. The company lore contained in the Nicholson anecdote is typical of the folksy way in which the house liked to present the gradual beginnings of literary publication by Bowen-Merrill in the wake of Merrill and Meigs's success with James Whitcomb Riley (who had several titles on the list by 1890). Nicholson's biographical questionnaire is reproduced in facsimile in the* DLB Yearbook, 1985, *pp. 34–36.*

In possession of a list containing one whole title still The Bowen Merrill Company did not realize that it had put on its publishing trousers, or, as Riley often said, "its literary overalls," though there was something stirring in the young minds of the concern, even if they were not wholly conscious of it themselves.

Meredith Nicholson at this time was writing verse, and as indication of this subconscious tendency toward publishing, it is told how Bobbs sought the young poet out and together nightly over a jug of milk read, discarded, selected and finally collected enough poems for a small volume which, when the local booksellers published it, was christened *Short Flights.*

–*The Hoosier House* (Indianapolis: Bobbs-Merrill, 1923), p. 9

* * *

Review: *The House of a Thousand Candles*

The anonymous reviewer in The New York Times *mistakenly refers to the author as "Nicholas Meredith."*

Here is a story bristling with adventure. Mr. Nicholas Meredith calls his novel, "The House of a Thousand Candles," (Bobbs, Merrill & Co.,) which is a very picturesque title, although, after all, the thousand candles are not absolutely essential to the story other than to add a sort of flickering weirdness to the tale. An old gentleman, rather eccentric and reputed to be immensely rich, dies in Vermont attended only by a faithful servant. His fortune, save a bewildering estate in Indiana, has mysteriously disappeared. The house is large and unfinished and of a rambling style of architecture, which includes subterranean passages and strange uncanny crypts and tunnels. The old gentleman was something of a student of architecture, and his keen regret was that his lusty young grandson preferred tiger shooting in the jungle to building poems in stone and granite at home. Being fond of the young man, nevertheless, the old gentleman so worded his will that young John Glenarm was to remain for a year a resident of the house of a thousand candles with the view to cutting him off from convivial companionship, and so, from sheer force of "nothing else to do," turning the young man's mind toward completing the house. Also, it was expressly stated in the will that should young John quit Indiana for any reason at all, he forfeited his claims to the estate, and the property passed on to one Marian Devereaux; or in the event of a marriage between the said John and Marian the property was to be disposed of still otherwise.

There is, of course, a villain in the story, smooth tongued, but black hearted, and again, of course, the villain is in love with Marian and John scorns Marian, but falls desperately in love with a delightful creature who calls herself Olivia, but who is an impostor inasmuch as she is only Olivia's friend and Marian herself.

There is shooting in the story, and even some slugging, but John has a stanch friend or two, and Marian is not idle rooting for the right person. The secret passages and strange doings are quite as bewildering as the author intends them to be, and when finally the dead returns to life and the old gentleman himself steps out of the fireplace and confronts all the dramatis personnae [*sic*] it is quite to be expected, and the cheerful reader accepts it all and asks no questions.

–"Adventure in Indiana," *New York Times,* 16 December 1905, p. 905

* * *

Related Letters

Hewitt H. Howland was trade-department editor in chief at the time of this letter.

Hewitt H. Howland to Nicholson, 22 January 1915

My dear Meredith:

It has occurred to us that possibly you might care to take over the plates of <u>Short Flights</u>. If so, we will deliver them to you, lock, stock and barrel, in exchange for fifty of Professor Wilson's silver dollars. If the suggestion doesn't

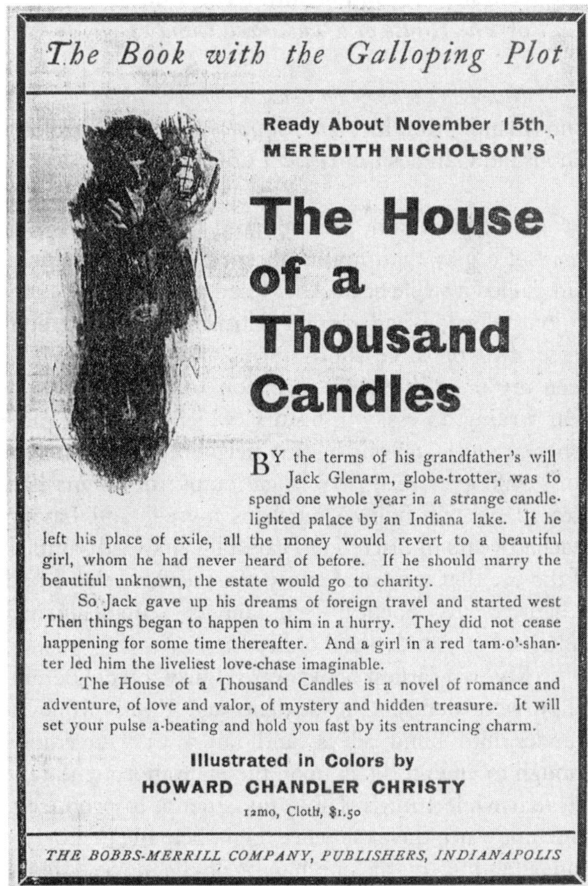

Flier for Nicholson's first best-seller, published in 1905 (courtesy of The Lilly Library, Indiana University, Bloomington, Indiana)

appeal to you on this snowy morning, when the shorter the flight the better, please don't hesitate to say so.

As ever yours,
[Hewitt H. Howland]

* * *

Nicholson to Howland, 27 January 1915

My dear Hewitt:–

I am deeply moved but not "touched" by your favor of January 22, offering to sell me the plates of "Short Flights" for fifty dollars. I have a strong feeling that the sooner those immortal lyrics are thrown into the melting pot the better it will be for American song.

Therefore, I respectfully decline your offer, without relief from valuation or appraisement laws.

Yours always,
Meredith Nicholson

* * *

The Genesis, Promotion, and Reception of *The House of a Thousand Candles*

Nicholson's apology for romance appeared anonymously in The Atlantic Monthly. *The illustrator for* The House of a Thousand Candles *was Howard Chandler Christy.*

That my name has adorned best-selling lists is more of a joke than my harshest critics can imagine. I had dallied a while at the law; I had given ten full years to journalism; I had written criticism, and not a little verse; two or three short stories of the slightest had been my only adventure in fiction, and I had spent a year writing an essay in history, which, from the publisher's reports, no one but my neighbor and my neighbor's wife ever read. My frugal output of poems had pleased no one half so much as myself; and having reached years of discretion I carefully analyzed samples of the ore that remained in my bins, decided that I had exhausted my poetical vein, and thereupon turned rather soberly to the field of fiction. [. . .]

My two earliest books were clearly too deliberate. They were deficient in incident, and I was prone to wander into blind alleys, and not always ingenious enough to emerge again upon the main thoroughfare. I felt that while I might fail in my attempt to produce a romantic yarn, the experience might help me to a better understanding of the mechanics of the novel,–that I might gain directness, movement, and ease.

For my third venture, I hit upon a device that took strong hold upon my imagination. The idea of laying a trap for the reader tickled me; and when once I had written the first chapter and outlined the last, I yielded myself to the story and bade it run its own course. I was never more honestly astonished in my life than to find my half-dozen characters taking matters in their own hands, and leaving me the merest spectator and reporter. I had made notes for the story, but in looking them over to-day, I find that I made practically no use of them. I never expect to experience again the delight of the winter I spent over that tale. The sight of white paper had no terrors for me. The hero, constantly cornered, had always in his pocket the key to his successive dilemmas; the heroine, misunderstood and misjudged, was struck at proper intervals by the spot-light that revealed her charm and reëstablished faith in her honorable motives. No other girl in my little gallery of heroines exerts upon me the spell of that young lady, who, on the day I began the story, as I waited for the ink to thaw in my work-shop, passed under my window, by one of those kindly orderings of providence that keep alive the superstition of inspiration in the hearts of all fiction-writers. She never came my way again,–but she need not! She was the bright particular star of my stage,–its *dea ex machina.* She is of the sisterhood of radiant goddesses who are visible from any window, even though its prospect be only a commonplace city street. Always, and everywhere, the essential woman for any tale is passing by with grave mien, if the tale be sober; with upturned chin and a saucy twinkle in the eye, if such be the seeker's need! [. . .]

When I had finished my story, I still had a few incidents and scenes in my ink-pot; but I could not for the life of me get the curtain up, once it was down. My little drama had put itself together as tight as wax, and even when I had written an additional incident that pleased me particularly, I could find no place to thrust it in. I was interested chiefly in amusing myself, and I never troubled myself in the least as to whether any one else would care for the story. I was astonished by its sale, which exceeded a quarter of a million copies in this country; it has been translated into French, Italian, German, Danish, Swedish, and Norwegian. I have heard of it all the way from Tokyo to Teheran. It was dramatized, and an actor of distinction appeared in the stage version; and stock companies have lately presented the play in Boston and San Francisco. It was subsequently serialized by newspapers, and later appeared in "patent" supplements. The title was paraphrased by advertisers, several of whom continue to pay me this flattering tribute.

I have speculated a good deal as to the success of this book. The title had, no doubt, much to do with it; clever advertising helped it further; the cover was a lure to the eye. The name of a popular illustra-

ROYALTY REPORT

FROM

The Bobbs-Merrill Company

INDIANAPOLIS

House of 1000 Candles

TITLE OF BOOK	Bound Copies on Hand Last Report	Copies Bound Since Last Report	Copies Exempt from Royalty	Bound Copies on Hand This Day	Totals	Subject to Royalty	Rate	AMOUNT
		62000			62000			
Dec. 1905			1918	10772	12690	49310	.15	7396.50
		2000			2000			
Canadian						2000	07½	150.00
		1000			1000			
Australian						1000	07½	75.00
								7621.50
June 30. 1906								
	10772	39194			49966			
			531	10567	11097	38869	.15	5830.35
		2306			2306			
Premium Ed						2306	02½	57.65
		3000			3000			
Canadian						3000	07½	225.00
		500			500			
Australian						500	07½	37.50
								6150.50

Five pages of royalty reports for The House of a Thousand Candles, *1905–1913 (courtesy of The Lilly Library, Indiana University, Bloomington, Indiana)*

ROYALTY REPORT

FROM

The Bobbs-Merrill Company

INDIANAPOLIS

TITLE OF BOOK	Bound Copies on Hand Last Report	Copies Bound Since Last Report	Copies Exempt from Royalty	Bound Copies on Hand This Day	Totals	Subject to Royalty	Rate	AMOUNT
	10567	5511			16078			
The June 30. 1906			151	5183	5334	10744	15	1611.60
		750			750			
English Ed						750	07½	56.25
		500			500			
Canadian						500	07½	37.50
Edition		5000			5000			
Ladies Home Journal						5000	07½	375.00
		489			489			
Premium Ed						489	02½	12.23
								2092.58
June 30. 1907								
	5183				5183			
1332 rebate / 3947 cost			4822	1365	6187	1004	15	
100000 Popular Ed							02½	2500.00
1000 " " Canadian							.01	100.00
								2600.00

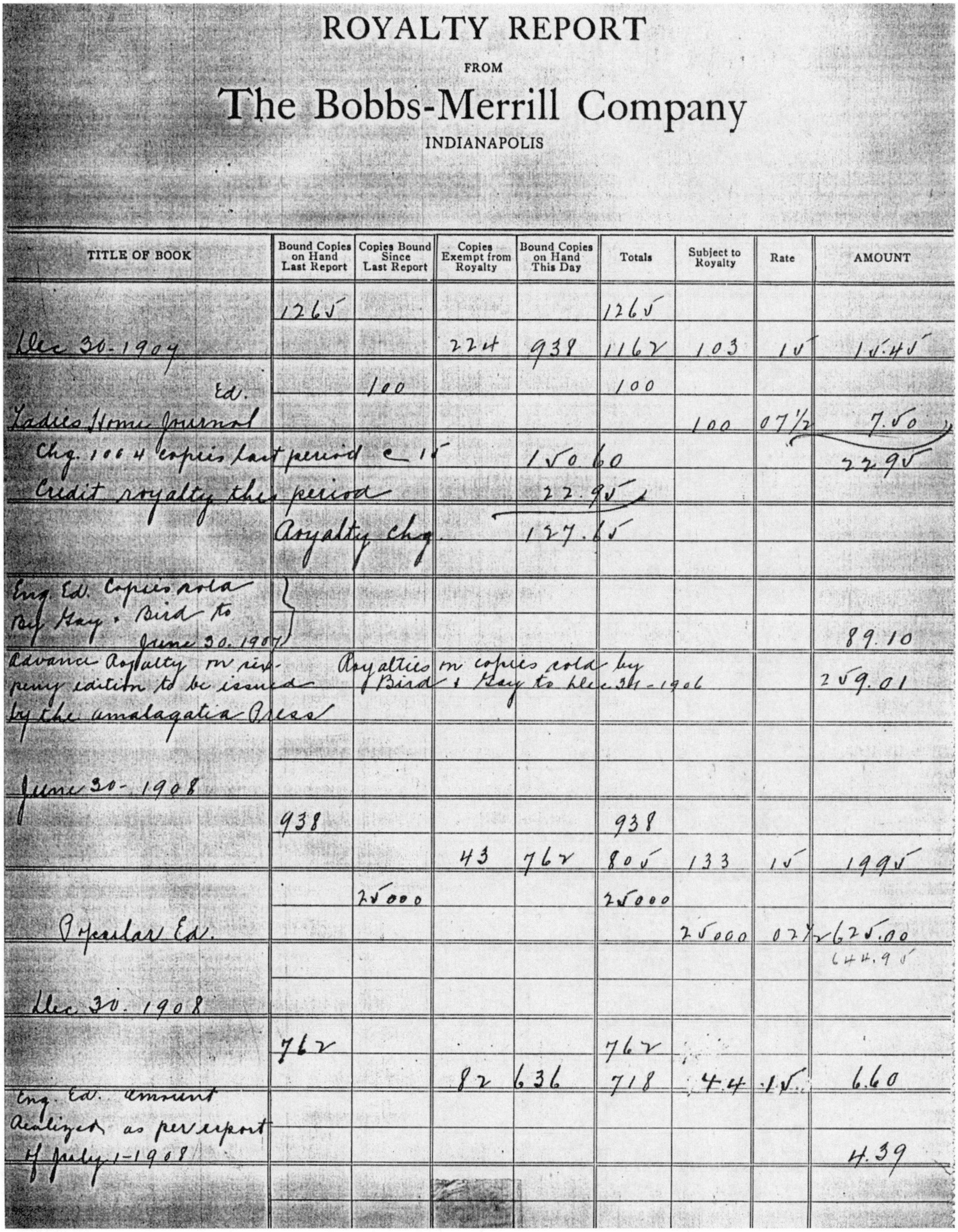

ROYALTY REPORT

FROM

The Bobbs-Merrill Company

INDIANAPOLIS

TITLE OF BOOK	Bound Copies on Hand Last Report	Copies Bound Since Last Report	Copies Exempt from Royalty	Bound Copies on Hand This Day	Totals	Subject to Royalty	Rate	AMOUNT
	1265				1265			
Dec 30-1907			224	938	1162	103	15	15.45
Ed.		100			100			
Ladies Home Journal						100	07½	7.50
Chg. 1004 copies last period @ 15				150.60				22.95
Credit royalty this period				22.95				
	Royalty Chg.			127.65				
Eng. Ed. Copies sold by Gay & Bird to June 30. 1907								89.10
Advance royalty on sixpenny edition to be issued by the Amalgamated Press	Royalties on copies sold by Bird & Gay to Dec. 31-1906							259.01
June 30-1908								
	938				938			
			43	762	805	133	15	1995
		25000			25000			
Popular Ed.						25000	07½	625.00 644.95
Dec 30. 1908								
	762				762			
			82	636	718	44	15	6.60
Eng. Ed. amount realized as per report of July 1-1908								4.39

ROYALTY REPORT

FROM

The Bobbs-Merrill Company

INDIANAPOLIS

TITLE OF BOOK	Bound Copies on Hand Last Report	Copies Bound Since Last Report	Copies Exempt from Royalty	Bound Copies on Hand This Day	Totals	Subject to Royalty	Rate	AMOUNT
	636				636			
June 30. 1909			30	591	621	15	.15	2.25
		81			81			
Dec. 30. 1909			4.	11	15	66	15	9.90
	11	293			304			
June 30. 1910			210	23	233	71	15	10.65
		25,000			25,000			
Pop Edition						25,000	02½	625.00
	23	42			65			
Dec 30 1910			15	32	47	18	15	2.70
	32	30			62			
June 30. 1911			16	23	39	23	15	3.45
		25000			25000			
Popular Ed.						25,000	02½	625.00
	23	65			88			
Dec 31. 1911			31	37	68	20	.15	300
Eng. Rights								104.30
Eng. Rights								2.41
	37	11			48			
June 30. 1912				33	33	15	15	2.25
Eng. Rights								20.99

ROYALTY REPORT

FROM

The Bobbs-Merrill Company

INDIANAPOLIS

TITLE OF BOOK	Bound Copies on Hand Last Report	Copies Bound Since Last Report	Copies Exempt from Royalty	Bound Copies on Hand This Day	Totals	Subject to Royalty	Rate	AMOUNT
	33	47			80			
Dec 31-1912			35	18	53	27	15	4.05
English Roy.								26.56
Spanish Rights								10.89
August 1-1913						24	15	3.60
German Right								16.44
Eng. Royalty								25.37
February 2-1913						7	15	105
			Total Roy paid					20,840.84

D²

COPYRIGHT OFFICE
OF THE UNITED STATES OF AMERICA

LIBRARY OF CONGRESS, WASHINGTON

CERTIFICATE OF COPYRIGHT REGISTRATION

THIS IS TO CERTIFY, in conformity with section 55 of the Act to Amend and Consolidate the Acts respecting Copyright, approved March 4, 1909, as amended by the Act approved March 2, 1913, that ONE copy of the DRAMATIC COMPOSITION named herein, not reproduced in copies for sale, has been deposited in this Office under the provisions of the Act of 1909, and that registration of a claim to copyright for the first term of twenty-eight years has been duly made in the name of the claimant

George Middleton,
158 Waverly Place, New York, N.Y.

title, The House of a Thousand Candles. Play in 4 acts. By George Middleton, of United States. Founded on the novel by Meredith Nicholson.

one copy received March 24, *19*15; *registration made as Class D, XXc., No.* 40154.

[SEAL]

W. L. Brown
Register of Copyrights

Copyright certificate for the 1915 stage adaptation of The House of a Thousand Candles *(courtesy of The Lilly Library, Indiana University, Bloomington, Indiana)*

tor may have helped, but it is certain that his pictures did not! I think I am safe in saying that the book received no helpful reviews in any newspapers of the first class, and I may add that I am skeptical as to the value of favorable notices in stimulating the sale of such books. Serious novels are undoubtedly helped by favorable reviews; stories of the kind I describe depend primarily upon persistent and ingenious advertising, in which a single striking line from the *Gem City Evening Gazette* is just as valuable as the opinion of the most scholarly review. Nor am I unmindful of the publisher's labors and risks,–the courage, confidence, and genius essential to a successful campaign with a book from a new hand, with no prestige of established reputation to command instant recognition. The self-selling book may become a "best-seller;" it may appear mysteriously, a "dark horse" in the eternal battle of the books; but miracles are as rare in the book trade as in other lines of commerce. The man behind the counter is another important factor. The retail dealer, when he finds the publisher supporting him with advertising, can do much to prolong a sale. A publisher of long experience in promoting large sales has told me that advertising is valuable chiefly for its moral effect on the retailer, who, feeling that the publisher is strongly backing a book, bends his own energies toward keeping it alive. [. . .]

Pleasant it is, I must confess, to hear your wares cried by the train-boy; to bend a sympathetic ear to his recital of your merits, as he appraises them; and to watch him beguile your fellow travelers with the promise of felicity contained between the covers of the book which you yourself have devised, pondered, and committed to paper. The train-boy's ideas of the essentials of entertaining fiction are radically unacademic, but he is apt in hitting off the commercial requirements. A good book, one of the guild told me, should always

Flier for a Nicholson best-seller, published in 1907 (courtesy of The Lilly Library, Indiana University, Bloomington, Indiana)

begin with "talking." He was particularly contemptuous of novels that open upon landscape and moonlight,–these, in the bright lexicon of his youthful experience, are well-nigh unsalable. And he was equally scornful of the unhappy ending. The sale of a book that did not, as he put it, "come out right," that is, with the merry jingle of wedding-bells, was no less than a fraud upon the purchaser. Sitting in the secret confessional afforded by these pages, a cloaked and masked figure, I frankly admit that, on one well-remembered occasion, dating back three or four years, my vanity was gorged by the sight of many copies of my latest offering in the hands of my fellow travelers, as I sped from Washington to New York. A poster, announcing my new tale, greeted me at the station as I took flight; four copies of my book were within comfortable range of my eye in the chair-car. Before the train started, I was given every opportunity to add my own book to my impedimenta.

The sensation awakened by the sight of utter strangers taking up your story, tasting it warily, clinging to it if it be to their liking, or dropping it wearily or contemptuously if it fail to please, is one of the most interesting of the experiences of popular authorship. On the journey mentioned, one man slept sweetly through what I judged to be the most intense passage in the book; others paid me the tribute of absorbed attention. On the ferry-boat at Jersey City, several copies of the book were interposed between seemingly enchanted readers and the towers and citadels of the metropolis. No one, I am sure, will deny to such a poor worm as I the petty joys of popular recognition. To see one's tale on many counters, to hear one's name and titles recited on boats and trains, to find in mid-ocean that your works go with you down to the sea in ships, to see the familiar cover smiling welcome on the table of an obscure foreign inn,–surely the most grudging critic would not deprive a writer of these rewards and delights. [. . .]

–"Confessions of a 'Best Seller,'" *Atlantic Monthly,* 104 (November 1909): 577–580, 583–584

Howard W. Odum (1884–1954)

Howard W. Odum published a remarkable trilogy of novels with Bobbs-Merrill. Known as the Black Ulysses novels, they center on a black character and use African American dialect, although Odum was white. His first doctorate was in psychology; the thesis dealt with folk songs of black migrant workers. His second, from Columbia University, was in sociology, and the dissertation was published as Social and Mental Traits of the Negro *(1910). It was the beginning of Odum's career as an applied social scientist, anchored at the University of North Carolina at Chapel Hill. He continued studying and writing about black people and was considered a Southern progressive whose social planning aimed to improve the lot of everyone in his region. Fellow North Carolinian Gerald Johnson, a journalist and author, praised Odum for his "ability to spend a long life fighting for righteousness without any touch of the moral arrogance that is the besetting sin of most crusades." Johnson's friend H. L. Mencken, an influential critic, thought highly of the Black Ulysses novels and supplied blurbs for their jackets.*

BOBBS-MERRILL BOOKS BY ODUM: *Rainbow Round My Shoulder: The Blue Trail of Black Ulysses* (Indianapolis: Bobbs-Merrill, 1928);

Wings on My Feet: Black Ulysses at the Wars (Indianapolis: Bobbs-Merrill, 1929);

Cold Blue Moon: Black Ulysses Afar Off (Indianapolis: Bobbs-Merrill, 1931).

Howard W. Odum (American Sociological Association)

Related Letters

The readers' reports for Rainbow Round My Shoulder *(1928) that company vice president and trade-department editor D. Laurance Chambers enclosed with this letter are no longer in the file. Uncle Remus was the black narrator of tales by Joel Chandler Harris.*

D. Laurance Chambers to Howard W. Odum, 15 April 1927

My dear Dr. Odum:

Here are reports from two of our readers. I felt much the same way about it as reader A when I read the first seven chapters you sent us, though I found it less interesting than he; and changed my opinion very much as he did when chapters IX and XI were read.

It strikes me as quite too kaleidoscopic–so shifting and scattering as to lose depth and personality and interest. Instead of knowing more about Black Ulysses as the chapters unroll, you seem to know less. That is to say, he has a sharper definition of pity and reality in chapters III and IV than he has later.

Report B was written by a sensitive and cultivated woman, who I was sure would not like the book (or any negro book). I gave her the manuscript to see how emphatic the devil's advocate would be. She's emphatic all right, unreasonably so. But she's right about some things, I think. The first paragraph of Chapter I is an example, and she's right that this chapter should be made a Foreword.

But frankly I'm disturbed about the criticism of the interest, for a third reader (a woman again, this time of more catholic taste) was just as emphatic in asserting lack of interest. She was plainly bored. I'm going to try it on some more–for I assume you have a duplicate copy of the manuscript and do not need our copy back.

It seems to me that to get a readable and fascinating book is going to require more art, more refashioning of the material. I am still of the opinion that this material, which you have so painstakingly gathered, is quite wonderful. But it must be worked up, out of the composite, so as to make a distinct and living personality, some one we can understand and pity and even love, perhaps, and laugh and cry over. It is a case of selection and grouping and legitimate coloring and heightening.

Keep your eye on Black Ulysses and be not diverted to whole chapters of other character sketches.

Less importantly: since it is all in dialect, every care should be taken to make it mechanically easy for the reader. More frequent paragraphing will help–a new paragraph with each shift in the sense.

There seems no reason to spell a word in dialect form when the dialect pronunciation does not differ noticeably from the normal English pronunciation. Why "wus" and not "was"? Why "recon" and not "reckon"?

When Black Ulysses quotes some one, why not use quotation marks?

When a word or phrase not intelligible to the ordinary reader is first used, why not explain it in a footnote?

The persistent dialect becomes wearing. I'm not sure but that you should speak in propria persona at the beginning of each chapter, after all. Maybe more of a framework is needed. Even Uncle Remus found need of one.

I'll send on more reactions as we get them.

Take your time. Don't hurry with this book. It is altogether too important to get it right. And I'm satisfied it can't be done right in a rush.

Faithfully yours,
[D. Laurance Chambers]

* * *

Bobbs-Merrill had published Julia Peterkin's Black April *in March 1927. She wrote of the Gullahs of coastal South Carolina.*

Odum to Chambers, 19 April 1927

My dear Mr. Chambers:

I sent you a day letter yesterday suggesting that you do not submit these chapters to any other critics until we shall have revised them and added the complete story. You will recall that not one of them has been checked over even for minor details of dialect and that they were submitted only as an approach to the form and contents of this book. I certainly should not approve of any one of those chapters myself and the subject for jacket and other details were sent simply for your consideration.

In the first place we are certainly agreed that the book must have as much art as is possible to get into it.

And we must be agreed that the question of interest shall be taken care of.

It is manifest that a book of this sort cannot be unduly hurried, although I agree with you that we ought to rush the complete first draft of the crude rich materials just as soon as possible.

I had already written you about the dialect. We must remember that about half of the dialect will be eliminated and that it shall remain as far removed from Mrs. Peterkin's type of story and Negro as possible.

We must remember that whether the dialect seems simple or not that most of this mixed speech was taken down exactly as spoken.

We must remember that Black Ulysses is "A Big Buck of a Negro" from whom most ladies would run.

The story is for the most part as told and almost unbelievably so.

There will be more sensitive people who feel that the facts are not worth presenting and that the vulgar realism of it all is below the literary level. Nevertheless Black Ulysses is a remarkable folk character of the ages. Whether we shall present him as a study in sociology or whether we can have a maximum amount of art in it remains to be seen.

What we must avoid is picturing him as most people who know nothing about him would want us to picture him. The Negro is the subject of pathetic and ridiculous misrepresentation and certainly you and I would not put our signature to a portraiture which a great many sensitive and cultured ladies would dictate.

I am not sure whether we want to weep over Black Ulysses or not. Probably not. The worth and even vividness of the picture must depend upon its accuracy. And Ulysses is unreasonably stupid and kaleidoscopic, shifting and scattering.

Probably 8,000 words of dialect would drive any of us wild. We must fix this up.

If only I can paint Ulysses and his civilization accurately I should be unreasonably happy.

I am really much encouraged by the criticisms and, while I know we are a great way off from the finished book, I believe it can be done. My suggestion is that I send to you as soon as possible two or three copies of the revised manuscript with at least the first twenty chapters.

You will find one group really very enthusiastic about the crudeness of the material with perhaps another group very sensitive. Your reader rather missed the point about "Blue Jim and the Black Buzzard". The value and vividness of this are found in its very crudeness and its meaning as a perfect picture of the Negro's mind. The same is true of "What Became of Jim".

This leads me to suspect that I shall probably have to go back to the original plan of introducing the chapters, interpreting some of the background and atmosphere and explaining some of the terms. If I can do this I can also break into some of the chapters with some discussions upon which I shall like very much to enter briefly.

And we cannot describe Black Ulysses without describing a great deal of his environment and fellow sufferers. The material and the pictures are too rich to lose.

In other words suppose you await further copy from me. I shall send you the whole manuscript in the present form with dialect and sentences much revised, or I shall send you certain chapters in which I utilize the combination of my story and Ulysses' story as originally planned.

But please don't get discouraged yet. And I gladly give up my "wondorobocian" adjective. This was the product of two hours' attempt to give an accurate objective combining the African [*sic*] tribe background as opposed to the Greek Elegance. That is, Ulysses is an African and not a Gre[e]k wanderer. But I must remember that I am not writing for anthropologists and sociologists.

I shall be very happy indeed to throw away all of chapter one and send you one that is not a mongrel combination of anthropology, sociology and comparative Greek literature!

Very cordially yours,
Howard W. Odum

* * *

Herschel Brickell's name does not appear on the jacket of Cold Blue Moon *(1931). Mencken is quoted on the rear flap: "What a trilogy! It will be read for many years." Walter J. Hurley managed the New York office.*

Chambers to Odum, 10 January 1931

Dear Dr. Odum:

Thank you for your letter of the seventh. I am awfully glad you like the copy for the jacket. I think myself it would be a great mistake to leave out Herschel Brickell's name, for he is known to the public as a critic and I think only a few will realize that he is connected with Henry Holt and one of your publishers. The personnel of a publishing office isn't as well known as the writers of books.

I'm afraid we can be sure if we approach Mencken that he'll turn his thumb down on the use of a quotation from his letter. On the other hand, if you'd write him, I think he'd find it hard to refuse. We'd like to use not only what he said about the trilogy on the flap, but much more important, we'd like to have him say something particularly about COLD BLUE MOON which we can use on a band around the jacket. You remember what he said of RAINBOW: "The story of Black Ulysses is an epic in the grand manner and one of the most eloquent ever produced in America. Walt Whitman would have wallowed in it, and I suspect that Mark Twain would

(Continued from front flap)

Through the veil of Black Ulysses' mystic interpretations slowly looms the clear picture of life in this great southern house; its family, its loves, its quarrels, its pleasures, its sorrows—and from that picture in turn emerges the similitude of the Old South itself as it was.

Here is a book extraordinary in both matter and method.

COLD BLUE MOON

is the third book Dr. Odum has written about Black Ulysses. H. L. Mencken exclaims: "What a trilogy! It will be read for many years." Those who meet the wanderer for the first time in *Cold Blue Moon* may want to hear of his other experiences in

RAINBOW ROUND MY SHOULDER

The most remarkable document of negro life that has come out of the present interest in the race.—*New York Evening Post.*

A clod, a cog in the great machine, a handful of black dust, soon to return to dust. But in him, more, perhaps, than in the hero of epic cycles, we perceive the Wanderlust working its spell, working its curse.—*New York Times.*

WINGS ON MY FEET

It defies classification. It is beautiful as the Rhapsody in Blue is beautiful. It has tune, form and rhythm. It is rugged with the virility of warriors. It has tragedy, pathos and humor. One feels that this simple tale of a common soldier, in its indefinite rhythm, comes nearer to expressing the enlisted man's reaction than any other has yet done.—*Boston Transcript.*

By GRACE ZARING STONE
THE BITTER TEA OF GENERAL YEN

Subtle and beautifully done story of an ambitious military leader and an American girl. The best novel of East and West thus far written.—ELSIE MCCORMICK in *N. Y. World.*

By JANET AYER FAIRBANK
THE LIONS' DEN

We shall offer no protest if the Pulitzer Prize for fiction goes to Janet Fairbank's *The Lions' Den.* In the literal sense of the word, it is a fine book.—HOWARD VINCENT O'BRIEN in *Chicago Daily News.*

By INEZ HAYNES IRWIN
FAMILY CIRCLE

This rich, vivid and unconventional novel deals with the fortunes and personalities of a cultured American family from 1900 to the present day.

By ADELINE ATWATER
THE MARRIAGE OF DON QUIXOTE

A charmingly individual story of a quixotic Don whose philosophy of a life without ambition opens him to strange and interesting tests, not the least of which is his marriage.

By C. E. SCOGGINS
THE HOUSE OF DARKNESS
A Novel of Two Worlds

The story of five modern Americans trapped in the Maya jungle—a story of courage and cowardice, love and hate, and of a big blond man who played a god.

By WILLSON WHITMAN
CONTRADANCE
A Puritan's Progress in New Orleans

The flavor of New Orleans in the early days creeps into the story through countless hints and appeals to the senses. There is not a false note in the entire book.—*New York Times.*

Dust jacket for the final novel (1931) in the Black Ulysses trilogy, with a blurb by H. L. Mencken on the back flap (Collection of Richard J. Schrader)

have been deeply stirred by it too." If you could get him to say something like that about COLD BLUE MOON, it would be a tremendous selling boost! We shall hold off until you have had a chance to hear from him.

We shall be very careful about the corrections incidated [*sic*] on the last page.

So much opposition developed in the salesmen's conference to the jacket drawing that we have asked Mr. Hurley to get up an entirely new jacket. We suggested to him that he get a picture of Big House Hall in the moonlight. Our new Southern representative, who is a Southerner himself, thought it advisable to emphasize the house element.

Do by all means stop off and see us on one of your trips to or from Chicago. We should certainly talk over your writing future and your plans, and develop some sort of program. Be sure to let me know when you expect to come, for as you know I too make frequent trips to New York and if I should miss you were [*sic*] I should want to be sure of seeing you there.

With kindest regard, believe me

Faithfully yours,
[D. Laurance Chambers]

* * *

Odum to Chambers, 12 January 1931

Dear Mr. Chambers:

Why not just quote the Mencken Epic stuff about Rainbow as applying to Black Ulysses and let it go at that? I am reasonably sure he won't agree for me to send in something because he is pretty stubborn in keeping to his rules. Why not just use that, even on band if needed?

I return page proof in this letter simply to save time. Something important is left out, nearly a whole page. I am sure they will check it up but wish you would let me see the revised page proof if convenient. [*marginal note:* "find this one page thing [?] send him today"]

Also they have been a little careless in spacings between paragraphs; we have indicated this in several places.

I had a long talk with the new Southern representative. He certainly knows the South and I hope he can get through their prejudices enough to land this book.

Here's wishing the best of luck for it. I like the new idea about the big house in shadows but also like the present jacket unless the other is done well. I saw them in New York yesterday. [*marginal note:* "Hurley"]

It will probably be some time before I'll have time to discuss future plans but hope to do so some time.

Cordially yours
Howard W. Odum

Julia Peterkin (1880–1961)

See also the Peterkin entry in *DLB 9: American Novelists, 1910–1945.*

Julia Peterkin came to Bobbs-Merrill after publishing Green Thursday *(1924) with Alfred A. Knopf. The book consisted of sketches based on her personal knowledge of plantation life, and the race of the author was a matter of speculation for reviewers. Peterkin drew upon the same material for Bobbs-Merrill, who loudly ended all speculation about her (white) race. Her output was slight but well received at the time, particularly for the depiction of the Gullahs who lived in coastal South Carolina. So strikingly did she portray them that* Scarlet Sister Mary *(1928) won the 1929 Pulitzer Prize in fiction and eventually sold a million copies. Critics recognized that Peterkin had gone well beyond the conventional stereotypes of black people in earlier Southern writing. Her reputation later suffered from charges that she presented blacks as primitive and implicitly inferior. A reassessment is under way, helped by Susan Millar Williams's 1997 biography,* A Devil and a Good Woman, Too: The Lives of Julia Peterkin. *After* Bright Skin *(1932) Peterkin's fiction career effectively ended.*

BOBBS-MERRILL BOOKS BY PETERKIN: *Black April* (Indianapolis: Bobbs-Merrill, 1927; London: Nash & Grayson, 1927);

Scarlet Sister Mary (Indianapolis: Bobbs-Merrill, 1928; London: Gollancz, 1929);

Bright Skin (Indianapolis: Bobbs-Merrill, 1932; London: Gollancz, 1932).

Julia Peterkin (from Susan Millar Williams, A Devil and a Good Woman, Too: The Lives of Julia Peterkin, *1997; Thomas Cooper Library, University of South Carolina)*

Related Letters

Peterkin came to Bobbs-Merrill because she felt that Knopf had not sufficiently promoted Green Thursday. *The "kind Fate" that guided her to Bobbs-Merrill was Max Aley of the New York office, following Knopf's rejection of her next novel, which had the working title "On a Plantation." Trade-department editor and vice president D. Laurance Chambers persuaded her to change the title to* Black April *(1927). Anne Johnston was an editorial assistant with Bobbs-Merrill.*

Julia Peterkin to Anne Johnston, before 24 March 1927

Dear Miss Johnstone [*sic*]:

Somehow, I cannot take it all in! Mr. Knopf had convinced me that my stuff would never sell; that to advertise it would be a foolish waste of money.

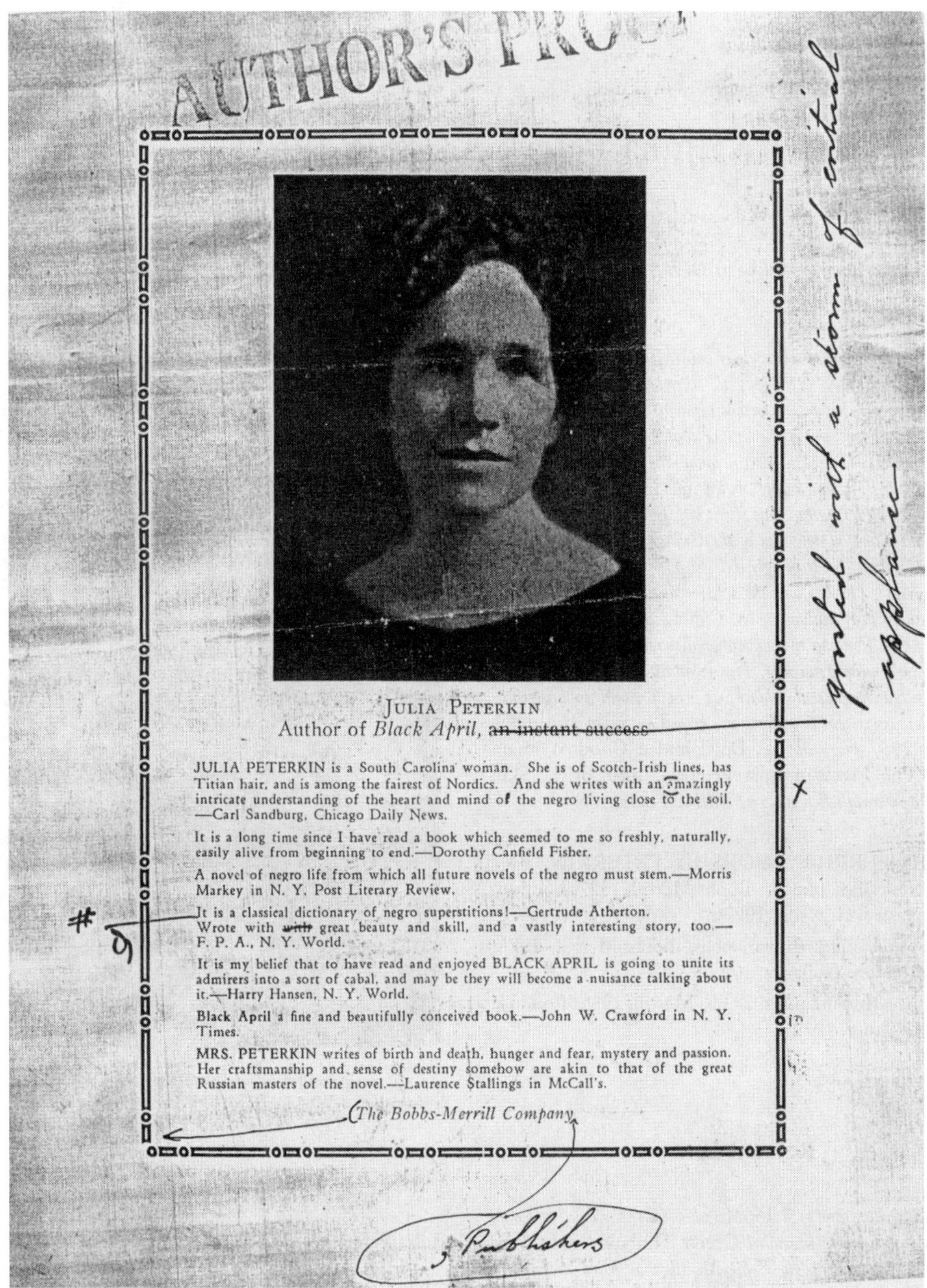

AUTHOR'S PRO

JULIA PETERKIN
Author of *Black April,* ~~an instant success~~

JULIA PETERKIN is a South Carolina woman. She is of Scotch-Irish lines, has Titian hair, and is among the fairest of Nordics. And she writes with an amazingly intricate understanding of the heart and mind of the negro living close to the soil. —Carl Sandburg, Chicago Daily News.

It is a long time since I have read a book which seemed to me so freshly, naturally, easily alive from beginning to end.—Dorothy Canfield Fisher.

A novel of negro life from which all future novels of the negro must stem.—Morris Markey in N. Y. Post Literary Review.

It is a classical dictionary of negro superstitions!—Gertrude Atherton.
Wrote with ~~with~~ great beauty and skill, and a vastly interesting story, too.—F. P. A., N. Y. World.

It is my belief that to have read and enjoyed BLACK APRIL is going to unite its admirers into a sort of cabal, and may be they will become a nuisance talking about it.—Harry Hansen, N. Y. World.

Black April a fine and beautifully conceived book.—John W. Crawford in N. Y. Times.

MRS. PETERKIN writes of birth and death, hunger and fear, mystery and passion. Her craftsmanship and sense of destiny somehow are akin to that of the great Russian masters of the novel.—Laurence Stallings in McCall's.

The Bobbs-Merrill Company

Author's proof of a publicity piece created to promote Black April, *published in 1927 (courtesy of The Lilly Library, Indiana University, Bloomington, Indiana)*

I was bitterly discouraged. You've no idea how much so. Now, I walk on air! Let the S.C. ladies gnash their sharp white teeth as much as they like! Let the heathen rage! Somebody does believe in me!

I'm deeply, humbly, grateful to you people and to the kind Fate that guided me to you.

Truly,
Julia Peterkin

I'm keen to know what the Negroes think.

* * *

Peterkin wired Johnston to protest the choice of advertising outlets for Black April. *Mary Rose is unidentified.*

Peterkin to Johnston, 4 September 1927

AM UNHAPPY OVER ADVERTISING STOP I THINK DAILY NEWYORK WORLD WASTES MONEY STOP MY AUDIENCE READS AMERICAN MERCURY NEW MASSES NEW REPUBLIC NATION OPPORTUNITY STOP THEY ARE SOPHISTICATED AND RADICAL STOP YOU AND MARY ROSE TALK THIS OVER AND PUT BLACK APRIL ACROSS STOP YOU TWO CAN.

JULIA PETERKIN.

* * *

Chambers was misinformed: Scarlet Sister Mary *did win the 1929 Pulitzer Prize in fiction.*

Chambers to Peterkin, 15 March 1929

Dear Julia Peterkin:

This is a sad day for us, for we have just heard–in absolute confidence, you understand–that the Pulitzer Prize is to be awarded to John Rathbone Oliver for his novel, VICTIM AND VICTOR; of which, as far as I can find out, no one has ever heard. It's a blow, for our hopes ran high. Dr. Richard Burton of the Committee was enthusiastically for SCARLET SISTER MARY. Some time ago he wrote me this, and immediately we got to work to try and help him win over the other two judges. We made up portfolios of the beautiful things that have been said of BLACK APRIL and SISTER MARY by the most distinguished critics in America and sent one to each member of the committee. We pulled, I confess, every wire we could find. How on earth they could consider any other book this year in the same class with yours is beyond me!

Dr. Burton writes me now: "In sending in my report I stated that several books, one in special, SCARLET SISTER MARY, stood very high with the jury. (Privately let me add that had the Peterkin story not been exclusively of negro life it would have got the prize! Such is human nature, such the difficulties involved in literary judgments). As art and treatment of life, however, ignoring the kind of life, Mrs. Peterkin's work is a masterpiece and in my judgment the years will emphasize that fact. Her novels already published make her as promising a candidate for a coming Pulitzer contest as the country contains."

A foolish quibble that, as to the life with which it deals, when one considers some of the other Pulitzer Prize winners. But let it go. With another novel, the Committee will have to recognize you–not to do so would be to make themselves ridiculous, as indeed I find their present decision.

Devotedly yours,
[D. Laurance Chambers]

* * *

Given the subject matter of Scarlet Sister Mary, *it was not well received in all Southern quarters. It was banned in Gaffney, South Carolina (and also, inevitably, in Boston).*

Chambers to Southern buyers, 15 May 1929

To Southern Dealers:

In the award of the Pulitzer Prize for the best American novel to Mrs. Julia Peterkin, for her SCAR-

Dust jacket with a wraparound band to celebrate Bobbs-Merrill's first Pulitzer Prize, which Peterkin's 1928 novel won in 1929 (courtesy of The Lilly Library, Indiana University, Bloomington, Indiana)

LET SISTER MARY, this signal recognition of literary merit has for the first time, we believe, been given a Southern novelist.

During the past few years interest in the literature of the South has notably increased all over the world. Southern books and Southern authors have brought this interest about not only by the fascination of their subjects but also by the brilliance of their treatment.

We congratulate ourselves anew on being the publishers of so distinguished a novel as SCARLET SISTER MARY, and are sure that you rejoice with us in the recognition that has been accorded Mrs. Peterkin.

Cordially,
[D. Laurance Chambers]

* * *

Sales of Scarlet Sister Mary *jumped in the wake of the announcement of the Pulitzer Prize. Seventy-six thousand copies were printed by the end of 1929.*

Bobbs-Merrill to the country's 250 foremost book buyers, 18 May 1929

To the Trade:

SCARLET SISTER MARY'S new honor has produced a tremendous sales response. Orders received last Monday completely exhausted our stock. Five presses were immediately put into action and two large editions will be completed today.

Mats of the enclosed advertisement are on hand, and we shall be happy to advertise with you on a fifty-fifty basis.

If this is feasible, will you please notify us of the expense involved so that we may make allowance for it in our budget?

We shall be grateful for the opportunity of advertising with you in order to take full advantage of the sales possibilities of the new Pulitzer Prize novel.

Cordially,
THE BOBBS-MERRILL COMPANY

* * *

Bobbs-Merrill press release, March 1932

JULIA PETERKIN STARS IN PLAY

Julia Peterkin, creator of the Pulitzer prize-winning Scarlet Sister Mary, added new laurels to her name last week.

After over two weeks of strenuous rehearsals, lasting about ten hours a day, she played title role in Ibsen's Hedda Gabler before the Columbia, S.C., Stage Society.

For three nights and at one matinee the play was presented.

Following the performances Mrs. Peterkin returned to her plantation to await the publication of her new novel BRIGHT SKIN, the proofs of which she corrected during the first week of rehearsals.

* * *

Chambers wrote Peterkin enclosing a letter from a Newberry, South Carolina, man who offered to organize promotions for her books. Peterkin was attending the Bread Loaf Conference in Vermont at this time.

Chambers to Peterkin, 20 August 1935

Dear Julia:–

One Hal Kohn, of Newberry, S. C., wrote us that he had a great idea for promoting the sale of your books. I wrote and asked him for details and he sends me the letter of which I inclose a copy. I send it to you thinking you will find it amusing, and possibly there is here some root idea that may be helpful when your next book comes out.

I hope you are having an awfully nice time in Vermont.

Faithfully yours,
[D. Laurance Chambers]

* * *

Hal Kohn to Bobbs-Merrill, 10 August 1935

Gentlemen:–

Thank you for your letter 8th. In answering I do not wish to appear too commercial, but I have

"Selling to Beat the Band"

Chambers wired Peterkin at her home, Lang Syne Plantation in Fort Motte, South Carolina, with news of the success of her prize-winning novel.

Chambers to Peterkin, 24 May 1929

CHECK GOING FORWARD TODAY SPECIAL DELIVERY DELIGHTED TO SEND IT SCARLET SISTER MARY IS SELLING TO BEAT THE BAND

D L CHAMBERS

BOBBS-MERRILL BOOK NEWS

January Indianapolis 1932

ARTHUR STRINGER

Author of

THE MUD LARK

In 1931 the "wife ship" was leaving England, carrying its cargo of young girls. Joan Alicia Eustis, daughter of an Earl, was among them, bound for Canada and a husband she had never seen.

Arthur Stringer returns to the wheat fields and the prairies of the North, to the subtle study of a woman's struggle against terrific odds.

A Mud Lark, as you know, is a horse that runs best on a heavy track. It was the name Joan rather liked to think she deserved. This is the story of her great adventure, and how she finds a happy marriage only in an understanding of the fundamentals of life.

Since the first great success of *The Prairie Wife* many people refuse to believe that Arthur Stringer is not a pen name. No man, they say, could know and write so vividly of the inner secrets of a woman's soul. It may be unbelievable, but it's true! For we know that Arthur Stringer is a man and that in *The Mud Lark* he even surpasses the insight and understanding of *The Prairie Wife.*

EARLY SPRING PUBLICATIONS

(In the Order in Which They Will Be Issued)

THE MUD LARK by Arthur Stringer
GOOD TIMES by Ethel Hueston
WHITE PANTS WILLIE by Elmer Davis
THE MASTER OF CHAOS by Irving Bacheller
The A. B. C.'s of the OFFICIAL SYSTEM of CONTRACT BRIDGE by Kay Coffin
THE STRETCH-BERRY SMILE by Dorothy Scarborough
FIRST FIDDLE by Margaret Weymouth Jackson
OLD GARDENS *in and about* PHILADELPHIA by John T. Faris
GEORGE WASHINGTON—COUNTRY GENTLEMAN (New Edition) by Paul Leland Haworth
HE UPSET THE WORLD by Bruce Barton

Having just completed our own economic survey, we offer this report, condensed and in three parts.

You may give it to your children or great Aunt Ella with perfect equanimity—it has been censored. As a matter of fact the censor is in a huff—there was nothing for him to do. We have no cause for swear words this spring.

Part I

A short list (decided before any one else began making surveys) but a sweet one! Authors whom you know, who know how to repeat—and have they done it! And a few new authors that even Mr. Cheney would not forgive us if we passed up.

Part II

Clothes don't make the man (agreed) but when you've real material why not dress it up? What's inside is the important thing, but that's checked off in a big way—and now wait until you see the books!

Part III

But even the finest book is only a book until it is read. That's the reason for this little paper. We hope the material contained herein will be of interest and use—above all (since expectation is part of the pleasure) we hope that it will add to your personal awareness of what's coming.

ELMER DAVIS

Author of

WHITE PANTS WILLIE

The author of *I'll Show You the Town, The Keys of the City,* and *Friends of Mr. Sweeney* had a whale of a good time when he wrote *White Pants Willie.*

White Pants Willie is gratefully dedicated to Scheherezade, who invented such good plots that she kept the Sultan from brooding over the depression, and from executing her sentence, for a thousand and one nights.

White Pants Willie too is a life-saver, a gloom-killer, a smile-bringer. It is a Florida Nights' Entertainment—the Florida of the winter of 1923-24, fabled Land of Promise. Then the production of oil and speculations in stocks and real estate, were enterprises by which money could be made! Then young people generally felt that the natural consequence of falling in love was getting married and often married with the intention and expectation of making it stick! Then God was in His heaven, Cal Coolidge in the White House, and the devil chained up in the bottomless pit, not to be let loose for a thousand years!

Coming BRIGHT SKIN

by JULIA PETERKIN

Copy of a publicity newsletter marked for inclusion in Peterkin's file (courtesy of The Lilly Library, Indiana University, Bloomington, Indiana)

done so many free things for the public that my business has suffered, so much so that I ask a modest promotional fee for such ideas, the value of which is left to the beneficiary.

My idea, in connection with the Peterkin plan, is to have a big rally at her birthplace, some 40 miles above here, between Laurens and Greenville. At this rally we would have the service clubs, from about 10 neighboring cities, and as many other folks as possible, to meet there, along with Mrs. Peterkin and her Father, a Sumter Rotarian. The newspapers in Greenville would go strong for this (I have talked with city editor) and I believe that we could get national publicity.

At this meeting we should unveil a suitable marker and on the main state highway, which runs near the home, should be another marker, or sign, and another thought was to hang signs every few hundred yards, both directions, from her old home, each sign to bear the name of one of her books. The cost of signs is to be borne by firm or firms deriving benefit from such boosting. These signs and markers can be made in S.C. or sent here. I could get sketches and estimates easily.

A barbecue or picnic or just a big meeting would attract a great throng. It might be made into a very literary affair, in fact it offers many, many angles.

The writer feels that he is fitted to promote this but if the idea appeals to you and you wish to work it out yourself then you are welcome to the thought.

Very truly,
Hal Kohn

P. S. A literary tea could easily be arranged at either Greenville or Laurens. The idea offers many, many opportunities for due recognition for Mrs. Peterkin and publicity for her past, present and future books.

* * *

Katharine Hepburn photographing Peterkin, her grandson, and servant (South Caroliniana Library)

Peterkin had returned to her South Carolina home by the time of her reply to Chambers.

Peterkin to Chambers, 4 (?) September 1935

Dear Laurance,

Please, for God's sake, keep this Mr. Kohn from starting this business of marking my birth-place etc. I simply could not bear it. I want to get down to work and who could work with such a thing hanging over them. I'll run away and never be heard of again if they persist in this foolishness. So please, please stop it.

Truly,
Julia

* * *

Editorial assistant Jessica Brown Mannon replied in Chambers's stead.

Jessica Brown Mannon to Peterkin, 5 September 1935

Dear Mrs. Peterkin:

Mr. Chambers is away on a little vacation and in his absence I am happy to acknowledge your note and to assure you that Mr. Kohn has been called off and you need not have a minute's discomfort over his proposal of marking your birthplace! Mr. Chambers would be distressed to know that you had been worried by Mr. Kohn's letter. He merely thought you would be entertained by it. We'll never put on any promotion scheme that does not have your wholehearted approval! We all hope so much that the work on the new book will progress satisfactorily. You can't imagine how interested everyone of us is in it. Only last week the man in charge of our shipping room asked me when we would have another book from you. He is such a hard-boiled character and so scornful of the average novel, that I considered his inquiry a great tribute.

With warmest regards, believe me

Sincerely yours,
[Jessica Mannon]

Herbert Quick (1861–1925)

Herbert Quick overcame infantile paralysis to become a farmer, teacher, and lawyer in his native Iowa, later moving to West Virginia. At the beginning of the twentieth century he took up writing in a serious way, and Bobbs-Merrill published his first successful novel, Double Trouble *(1906). Eventually giving up the law, he edited magazines and wrote books of various kinds, including Progressive political treatises such as* On Board the Good Ship Earth *(1913). Quick's best work as a regional novelist was the Iowa trilogy of* Vandemark's Folly *(1922),* The Hawkeye *(1923), and* The Invisible Woman *(1924). He wrote them at a time when the nation's westward movement was the most popular subject for historical novels, and his aim was to explore the pioneer time in a generous spirit. His 1925 autobiography is only partial, but the career and crusades of the hero of* The Hawkeye *are thought to mirror Quick's own.*

Herbert Quick (from Stanley J. Kunitz and Howard Haycraft, eds., Twentieth Century Authors, *1942; Thomas Cooper Library, University of South Carolina)*

BOBBS-MERRILL BOOKS BY QUICK: *Double Trouble; or, Every Hero His Own Villain* (Indianapolis: Bobbs-Merrill, 1906);

Aladdin & Co.: A Romance of Yankee Magic (Indianapolis: Bobbs-Merrill, 1907; **first edition,** New York: Holt, 1904);

The Broken Lance (Indianapolis: Bobbs-Merrill, 1907);

Virginia of the Air Lanes (Indianapolis: Bobbs-Merrill, 1909);

Yellowstone Nights (Indianapolis: Bobbs-Merrill, 1911);

On Board the Good Ship Earth: A Survey of World Problems (Indianapolis: Bobbs-Merrill, 1913);

The Brown Mouse (Indianapolis: Bobbs-Merrill, 1915);

The Fairview Idea: A Story of the New Rural Life (Indianapolis: Bobbs-Merrill, 1919);

From War to Peace: A Plea for a Definite Policy of Reconstruction (Indianapolis: Bobbs-Merrill, 1919);

Vandemark's Folly (Indianapolis: Bobbs-Merrill, 1922);

The Hawkeye (Indianapolis: Bobbs-Merrill, 1923);

The Invisible Woman (Indianapolis: Bobbs-Merrill, 1924);

The Real Trouble with Farmers (Indianapolis: Bobbs-Merrill, 1924);

There Came Two Women: A Drama in Four Acts (Indianapolis: Bobbs-Merrill, 1924);

One Man's Life: An Autobiography (Indianapolis: Bobbs-Merrill, 1925);

We Have Changed All That, by Quick and Elena S. MacMahon (Indianapolis: Bobbs-Merrill, 1928).

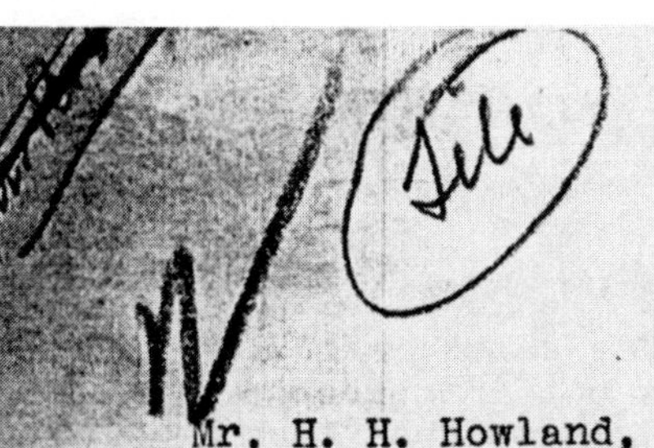

HERBERT QUICK
COOLFONT
BERKELEY SPRINGS, W. VA.

December 5th, 1921

Mr. H. H. Howland,

Indianapolis, Ind.

Dear Hewitt:

I am very greatly obliged to you for the careful examination you have given the VANDEMARK proofs, and the editorial work you have done on them. The first half of the story was copied by my secretary, when I had one, and the latter half was done by me. The final copying gave me the chance to make some changes in form and should be better in this respcet than the first, but probably will not be found better. Every time one goes over a manuscript changes suggest themselves, if for no other reason than the change of mood. Your markings call attentions to things on which there is a probability of difference of oipnion and give me the opportunity to weigh and accept or reject them, or even to adopt an entirely new device for doing what you think should be done. I have carefully considered them all, though from Galley......to 65 I did not have your work to aid me.

All this matter has been gone over time and again in the past years, and has been often rewritten. Save for verbal defects and some things which escape the eye inevitably almost, everything you call in question has a reason for existence and has been considered. In the first place the type of man represented in the narrator must be established in the mind of the reader. This is essential, for what is said as well as the manner of saying it is all given color and even substance by his lifelong environment and the changes therein. The story is not only a narration of what one man saw taking place, but of what he did not see, and of his thoughts and his philosophy.

Many of the passages in which the text is open to the objection of tautology arise from the type of vocabulary circumstances place in his possession. You probably did not note that when he begins to discuss some subjects he has a considerable scientific vocabulary. This comes from reading done on such subjects as stockbreeding and agriculture in his later years. When dealing with ordinary topics he uses short words and common ones---common except where he falls into locutions which are preserved, and which in his day were still more numerously preserved, in the speech of the country people--like "blowth", referring to the mass of bloom of the flowers. These words are not only good, but classic English, are in the main self-explanatory, and harmonize with the character of the man. I myself have been from childhood intimately acquainted with them.

Four-page letter from Quick to chief editor Hewitt H. Howland. At this time D. Laurance Chambers was company vice president and a trade-department editor (courtesy of The Lilly Library, Indiana University, Bloomington, Indiana).

HERBERT QUICK
COOLFONT
BERKELEY SPRINGS, W. VA.
-2-

Yet, these repetitions, while in only a few cases really tautological, should be cured if the cure does not introduce elements of discord, and I have made many changes to cure them. I call your attention to the fact, however, that your markings indicate an extreme and I almost might say a morbid sensitives- to repetitions of even such common words as "by" and the like.

The placing of the prespositional phrase, or the adverb or adjective at the close or nearer the beginning of the sentence is a convention for which very often nothing can be said one way or the other except that common usage tends a certain way. This of course does not apply where the sense becomes obscured. Take this: "I enquired for letters at the post-office in Buffalo, Syracuse, Albany and Tempe at every chance, but finally gave up in deapsir". You suggest placing the words "at every chance" at the beginning of the sentence. Almost any schoolmaster would agree with you, I think. Basically, however, it is no improvement. It makes the meaning no clearer. It is more conventional. And it is less what Vandemark would have written. In other cases your corrections would change the sense. Where I say that Rucker sat "dazedly" I do not mean "dazed". I mean that he sat in a dazed manner.

The Vandemark Township History thought is far too deeply interwoven into hundreds of passages to allow of its being eliminated, and I do not believe in its elimination. For one thing it is a principal device in establishing the type of man. But I am willing to have some of it eliminated and to transfer the rest to an introduction. As you go over the proofs you will see that a good deal of it goes out.

The introduction should be signed "J. T. Vandemark".

You will find that there is scarcely any place where you have suggested a change that has not been altered in one way or another.

Now I come to something which you did not suggest and which I submit for consideration. Chambers suggested in one of his letters that the chapters are long and look rather solid. So I have indicated at many places a breaking up of the long paragraphs. I did not begin this until I had got perhaps a third of the way through the first 64 galleys, and if you think it an improvement I hope you will treat the earlier chapters in the same way. But the innovation which I developed in thinking of what Chambers wrote has led to the breaking up of the chapters into from 2 to 6 sections, numbered, and each provided with a subhead.

Now it sometimes seems to me that there is a sacrifice of dignity in this, and that it is not a thing which JakeV andemark would have resorted to; but there may be no merit in this objection. My judgment on the whole is that the sections and subheads should be adopted. I do not number the first section of each

[December 5th, 1921]

HERBERT QUICK
COOLFONT
BERKELEY SPRINGS, W. VA.

-3-

chapter, but when the need for a division occure I simply insert it with the number "2". Numbering the first section introduces a complexity ~~in the sections between~~ in the matter of heads and subheads coming together.

When I think of Les Miserables I am in less perplexity as to the loss of poise arising from these sections and subheads; as that great work is in five volumes, each with its title; each volume is broken up into several separately-named books, and each book into numerous ~~...~~ chapters with heads. It is true that Victor Hugo was not using the autobiographical style, which, my instinct tells me, makes a difference. Perhaps not much difference, however. As Dickens remarks in one of his prefaces, the autobiographical style has its limitations, but if its advantages ~~did not outweigh the~~ had not outweighed them he would not have clung to it. Two of the great classics which oscur to me are in this style--David Copperfield and Lorna Doone. So also of Tristram Shandy, if it can be said to have any definable style at all. And in the way of later popular favprites I remember Joseph Vance and Eben Holden. The latter, if it could have been finished as well as it was begun would have taken its place among the masterpieces, but it failed in the latter half. Robinson Crusoe could not have been the wonder it is in any other style. I think I have the same reason for adopting it that De Foe and Blackmore had--the interpenetration of an environment with a personality. I feel sure that some of the things which seem defects will prove benefits. Nobody can tell a priori what will interest people. The successful editor, for instance, is never the man who can say unerringly, "This will be of interest to the reader". The great editor is the man with the instincts of the reader who says, "I will print this because it interests me". If his personality and mind are such that what interests him attracts the public, he is a good editor. If not he had better turn his attention to something else. This will explain some of my markings.

When I got your proofs I began ~~marking~~ work on the proofs you had marked. Soon I transferred my attentions to the other proofs, as you intended me to do. Please therefore disregard all markings on your proofs, and let the others be your guide. I wish I could see a proof of the Introduction as soon as possible. You will note that in some parts I have cut the proofs up pretty badly, and I shall want to go over the final revise as it cannot be free from palpable errors as I send it in. I am sending the proofs back by express so as to be sure of delivery. I have worked like a dog on these for a week and went to bed every night quite tired out.

[December 6th, 1921]

HERBERT QUICK
COOLFONT
BERKELEY SPRINGS, W. VA.
-4-

I hope you can find tdme to go over the rest of the proofs. The fact that I have been over this MS so often is in itself a bar to good proof reading. I know almost every sentence by heart, and this makes be blind to errors which in any other MS I should be likely to càtch. Thakk you!

Yours sincerely,

Herbert Quick

Reader's Report

A. A. Spruance submitted this report (circa 1923) on The Hawkeye.

The Hawkeye
A reader's report

Although the elder McConkeys "wagoned" from New York state into the virgin Iowa lands, they came after Jake Vandemark of "Vandemark's Folly", and their son, Fremont, the hero of The Hawkeye, was, as the title indicates, native born. Here, as in the preceding novel, the State itself, its up-building, its mistakes and its opportunities, the phases of its growth, might almost be called the chief actor in the narrative, were not young Fremont so wholly a part of the rich acres, the budding communities, that what concerns the one must concern the other. The two can not be divorced.

The bookish boy who clothes every homespun experience in the garb of romance, seems a white blackbird among his kindred, but the author proves his insight into human nature by showing the strong family affection that never loosens between the McConkeys. From those first hard pioneering winters when the children must eat bran bread–a blot never erased from their escutcheon–; through years of viciss[i]tudes when the farmers slip deeper and deeper into debt while tilling the richest soil in the world, until the concluding times of plenty, young Fremont is one with his people, teaches, ploughs, thrashes,–does whatever his hand finds to do,–sure of his mother's understanding heart. That mother, and, through her, the pioneer mothers, receives some beautiful words praise [*sic*], for she keeps abreast mentally with her son, she shows in her own person the capacity of the submerged for development. The uncouth boy with his mania for the printed page finds food even in the old copies of the New York Ledger, and the author pays a tribute to these early editors who "every week served high intrepidity and generous enthusiasm, piping hot" to the starved minds. It may have been a false world, says the author, but it was <u>another</u> world, and the American people owe a debt of idealism to these forgotten pages. How Fremont learns to read better things, as they come his way, how he takes part in the politics of the times, and learns distasteful lessons of corruption in office, how he loves and marries, studies law, finds his place as an editor, are all part of the book–an absorbing part, but less in historic importance than "the building of a democracy based on ponderous production, and deprived of the sea as a highway". A mighty subject for the novelist's pen, a momentous epoch, but one made fascinating, even simple, by the author's sympathy and sincerity. In every natural aspect, whether it be "the swales enamelled with flowers, and flooded with verdure, the brooks hidden under drooping grasses and paved with the braided glories of shining pebbles, the air vibrant with the call of wild fowl and the

Dust-jacket art by N. C. Wyeth for the first book in the trilogy of Iowa novels, published in 1922 (courtesy of Michael Manz/Babylon Revisited)

song birds of the prairies"; or the kingly sport of shooting the ruffled grouse, or prairie chickens; or the homelier tasks of thrashing or husking, or tending the herds; or the spearing of fish on Sunday night, "a fearful sin, as bad as playing cards"; the poet sees, and the philosopher reflects.

The salt of humor is sprinkled everywhere, the signs that precede Fremont's birth, the midwife's comments, or Aunt Zuby to whom "an unexpected wedding was like the turning-up of buried treasure", or Fremont's agony at the lack of nightshirts and detachable cuffs, or the racy speech of the country-side that "Fremont's got more in his head than a fine tooth comb will take out", or Kate's confession that "We ain't the property kind. It runs in some families like consumption", or the author's comment that shoes seemed to cramp Fremont's style,–the reader is never allowed to feel dull, for this humor wearies no more than that of George Eliot, both coming from the soil.

To call this book a novel seems almost an injustice–for it is a novel, and so much more. It might be the record of one man's life, were it not again, so much more. If the Bushyagers are the villains, if they are horse thieves and possible murderers, whose sins culminate in the lynching of the two prisoners, and the death of Bent from his wound, they may divide the honors with that likable, outspoken rascal, Roswell Upright, who steals the county's money so openly, and is proud of it. But both here and there, the author's sympathy never fails. The death of Bent Bushyager, his persistent love for his old schoolmate, Fremont, has true pathos, for he is only "the neglected child of society" with much of good hidden among his misdeeds. As Fremont grows so grows his Iowa world, and the strange drama of self-government has many scenes. The reader shares, for it is all so tremendously real, the writer's love for his people, his sorrow for their sins and their mistakes, his joy in their progress and achievements. It is the drama

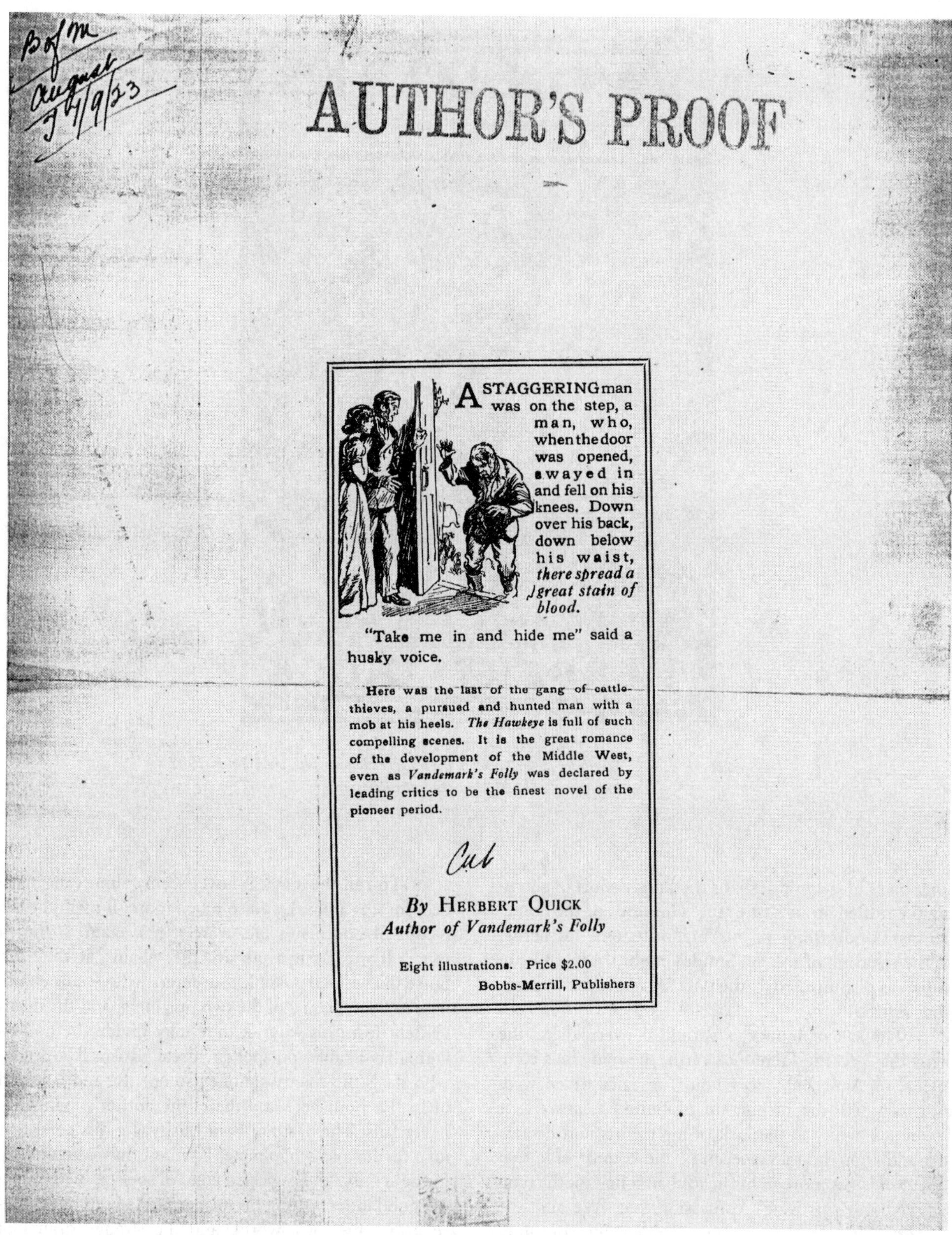
AUTHOR'S PROOF

A STAGGERING man was on the step, a man, who, when the door was opened, swayed in and fell on his knees. Down over his back, down below his waist, *there spread a great stain of blood.*

"Take me in and hide me" said a husky voice.

Here was the last of the gang of cattle-thieves, a pursued and hunted man with a mob at his heels. *The Hawkeye* is full of such compelling scenes. It is the great romance of the development of the Middle West, even as *Vandemark's Folly* was declared by leading critics to be the finest novel of the pioneer period.

By HERBERT QUICK
Author of Vandemark's Folly

Eight illustrations. Price $2.00

Bobbs-Merrill, Publishers

Proof of an advertisement for The Hawkeye, *published in 1923 (courtesy of The Lilly Library, Indiana University, Bloomington, Indiana)*

of community life that Mr. Quick gives us, of its sharp rivalries and eager ambitions, its racy personalities; the renewal of old friendships with the Gowdys, and Shooklesons, and Vandemarks; the idylls of nature, of first love, of the passion of manhood, of the fruition of worthy ambition, of the hardships and the joys of domestic life, and the darker hues of the rural slums. Long as the narrative is, no reader will wish it shorter, for these are chapters in an unwritten history, cross sections of throbbing life, scenes in a great national and social drama, and all interpreted with poetry and humor and pathos and unfaltering truthfulness, for the author is a part of that which he portrays. He, himself, has sprung from this rich soil, and one wonders if the name of Fremont is not merely a pseudonym for that of the author, himself. Such tenderness, such sympathy, such a wealth of veracious detail, must surely have come from life at first-hand.

The book needs not to borrow from the success of "Vandemark's Folly", for it stands splendid and alone, but the friends of the former will welcome these later chapters of another typical[l]y American novel.

A. A. Spruance *[crossed out]*

* * *

Related Letter

Frederic F. Van de Water was a novelist, historian, journalist, and critic. Diedrich Knickerbocker was a famous character of Washington Irving. Peter Stuyvesant was a Dutch colonial governor in America during the seventeenth century. The Puk Wudjie is from Native American folklore. Quick's Double Trouble *was only modestly successful, selling about eighteen thousand copies in its first year and not much thereafter. Ralph Hale, later a publisher, is mentioned in D. Laurance Chambers's memoirs (see Appendix). Boris Aronow is unidentified.*

Herbert Quick to Frederic F. Van de Water, 28 April 1924

Dear Mr. Vande Water:

My publishers have referred to me your letter to them of the 21st. Of course the facts as to my career are interesting to me. My modesty is such that I wonder if they can be to any large body of the public. However, here goes!

Whether or not my literary bent was inherited is a question. I think it is; but there is nothing in my ancestry to prove it. I believe I inherited from my mother the psychic elements which made me a writer. She, however, was one of a line of pioneer women who may be traced back to the beginning of America. Many of our young people have this psychic list to letters, but they lack determination. My determination, such as I have, I may inherit from my Dutch ancestors.

I am fifteen sixteenths Dutch. On my father's side we trace back through Quicks, Denises and Winfeldts or Winfields, and on my mother's through families like those of Krum, Vandemark, and Rapalje. If we had enough of the record, it might even go to the Van de Waters–but I shall make more modest claims. When the British had a garrison in New York a certain Dutch girl named Hannah Koms married a British soldier named John Coleman. He was Irish. The people who follow those things up now have promoted him to the rank of an officer; but he may have been a camp-follower for all I know. He had his leg shot off by a cannon ball in the attack on Havana–I forget which war this was in–and his posthumous son John Coleman was the grandfather some degrees removed of my mother, whose name was Margaret Coleman. Sometimes I think Coleman was a prepotent strain, for while there was little of this Irish blood in my mother, she was a good deal of an Irish woman. She never went to school, for she was born in the forest, at least more than two or three months, but she was the best-read member of our family; and [s]he had a weakness which caused her to weep over great things in poetry or prose. She was psychically a poet.

Father was a typical Dutchman. You can find him in the pages of Knickerbocker.

I come of a race of humble pioneers. We are of the Rondout Valley Dutch, who refused to go on up the Hudson into the domains of the Patroons, but filed off by the left flank and went up the Rondout Valley, and over the divide into New Jersey, and across the Delaware into Pennsylvania. I suppose that celebrated or notorious Indian Fighter Tom Quick was one of us. We plunged into the forest away back before the Revolution, and kept ahead of civilization until it overtook us in Iowa, where I was born. This occurrence took place in 1861. Our halting places were in the Rondout Valley, in the Lake Region of New York, in western New York, in the Connecticut Reserve of Ohio, in the lumber regions of Michigan, in Wisconsin, and in Iowa. Forest life is not one in which literary abilities are likely to manifest themselves. But the artistic nature goes on. I know nothing at all of our ancestry in Holland.

Some of the genealogy sharps have decided that one of our ancestors–through Hannah Koms I suspect–was a member of the royal family of Holland, and was private Secretary of old Pieter Stuyvesant. I have made myself obnoxious by suggesting, (1), that any member of any great family who would consent to work under old Piet must have had mighty strong reasons for leaving Holland,

and (2) that Holland then had no royal family. I have made no headway however, with this theory.

My own position is that nobody can have a better ancestry than just plain Dutch, with a dash of Irish and a little New England Yankee, carried down through a race of plain working pioneers.

I am a very uncultured person, never having been to school save in the district schools of Iowa. I wanted to go to college, but one thing and another stood in the way. Times were pretty hard. I taught school for a long time, and did pretty well, but suddenly realized that I had no degree, and could not expect to get good positions as an educator. So I studied law, teaching school at the same time. Then I practiced law for nearly twenty years in Sioux City, Iowa, and accumulated a family. I married Ella Corey of Syracuse, thus going back to the old Lake Country for my wife. She was a singer, and one of the graduates of Syracuse University. I carry my college degrees in my wife's name. I carry most of my virtues in the same way.

After I decided that I would not be President of the United States right off, anyhow, I always looked upon myself as a potential writer. While practicing law I was always getting ready to write. I cannot remember when things which I saw and experienced did not appeal to me as the stuff of writings. I read and studied a lot; but as for writing, I kept putting it off, save for literary essays, orations and the like. Finally I wrote a child's book which was accepted by a New York publisher. I planned a series in which I meant to make the Puk Wudjie the Great American Fairy. Prior to this I had published a poem in The Century. It was a good poem, too. The fairy book was published in 1901 when I was 40 years old. So, you see, I started late. But then, you must remember, I am Dutch. Who was that ancestor of Diedrick Knickerbocker who spent so many years preparing to build the church? I think he was an ancestor of mine, too.

I remember when I was not twenty, planning this series of Iowa novels upon which I have been engaged for the past few years. I have changed the plan somewhat since then, but I told the whole plan to Ralph Hale in the park in Indianapolis at least twenty years ago.

I have had no struggles in the ordinary sense. In some ways, I have had excellent luck. For instance, when I was twenty months old, I was stricken–I believe that is the word–with infantile paralysis. This gave me bad feet and legs, and robbed me of the robustness necessary for farm work. So I went over into things which did not call for good feet and legs. I was polyomyelitised into the educational field, thence into law, and finally into literature. Again, in 1919, after I had been in official life in Washington for some years, I resigned to devote myself to literature. But I am the worst hound pup you ever saw for following off false trails. There are so darned many things I like to do that I feel sure I should have neglected my Iowa novels, had it not been for a great piece of luck. I followed off a trail into Siberia as the head of a commission of the American Red Cross to close up their Far Eastern work–and there I had a fearful hemorrhage from an intestinal ulcer. Everybody said I'd die, and I didn't mind if I did; but strange to say, I didn't. I got home, was carved, and recovered just enough to enable me to write, and not enough to allow me to follow off any rabbit tracks. This is the ideal condition for me.

Dust jacket for Quick's 1924 novel (courtesy of Michael Manz/Babylon Revisited)

Sometimes I should have starved if I had depended on my fiction; but I could always write special articles, do editorial work and the like. After I published my first really successful novel–"Double Trouble" away back in 1906; I locked my law office door on the outside, and became a writer by profession. This was at the early age–for a Dutchman–of 45. All my good friends said, "Poor old Quick! The old simpleton will starve surely now! And he had a fairly good law practice!" Well, on form, they were right; but I always got along. When the fiction failed, I took up editorial work. To be sure, I might have written better fiction if I had devoted my whole time to it; but I couldn't do that. I had to live. So, you see, I have no story of either inherited literary bent, or early struggles, or adversity to tell. I have been lucky. If there is anything more you want to know, please let me hear from you. I remember that corking review you wrote of THE HAWKEYE. Well, I am just finishing far the best novel I ever wrote. It is the baby, you know.

Yours sincerely,
[Herbert Quick]

P. S. NO. 2 [*sic*]:

You want anecdotes; but I haven't any in mind relating to literary work. There is one, however, for which my Russian friend Boris Aronow is the authority, which might pass; but I don't know.

When I was so ill in Siberia in 1819 [*sic*], I lay in the Red Cross barracks in Vladivostok in a bunk from which I could look without turning my eyes, out across Vladivostok harbor to a beautiful rounded hill over the bay. I was in pretty bad shape. I had told Boris that I wanted a certain friend of mine to finish Vandemark's Folly in case of need, and otherwise said all there seemed to be to say. Boris and the rest were doing all they could to keep me on earth, but with one's heart missing on all the cylinders but one for lack of circulating medium, and the blood drawn down by hemorrhage to a hemoglobin content of 17 and a red-cell count of only 1,300,000, one lacks vivacity in most cases.

Boris heard a whisper and a movement as if I wanted to speak to him. He stooped to catch the words of wisdom.

"Boris", said I, "when I die, bury me on that hill over there. Build over the spot a big monument. Make it of hay . . . so that other American jackasses who come over here can have the chance to rally round my tomb and have a good time."

Boris tells this. I don't remember it. But he is quite incapable of having invented it. In fact, I think he was a little shocked at it; and it was a month after I began to mend before he told it.

The moral is uncertain; but I think it shows a philanthropic disposition, anyhow.

I am sending you a copy of a new book I have written. In it I play my role of economist, and sociologist. It may interest you–and then again, it may not.

Yours,
H. Q.

Ayn Rand (1905–1982)

See also the Rand entries in *DLB 227: American Novelists Since World War II, Sixth Series* and *DLB 279: American Philosophers, 1950–2000.*

Ayn Rand (born Alysia Zinovievna Rosenbaum in St. Petersburg, Russia) was dissatisfied with Macmillan over the handling of her first book, We the Living *(1936), and she could not find an American publisher for the novella* Anthem *(1938).* The Fountainhead *(1943) was then rejected by twelve publishers. She was drawn to Bobbs-Merrill because of its conservative reputation, and New York editor Archibald Ogden famously put his job on the line in writing to President D. Laurance Chambers: "If this is not the book for you, then I am not the editor for you." (The readers' reports by Ogden and three others are reproduced in facsimile in the* DLB Yearbook, 1990, *pp. 151–169.)* The Fountainhead *was not at first well promoted by the company, but word of mouth produced massive sales, which reached four hundred thousand copies by 1948. Rand wrote the screenplay for the 1949 movie version, which starred Gary Cooper and Patricia Neal.* A Letter from Ayn Rand *(1945) is a sixteen-page brochure that was mailed in answer to reader inquiries. She took her final novel,* Atlas Shrugged *(1957), to Random House after her release from Bobbs-Merrill, who published* Philosophy: Who Needs It *posthumously in 1982.*

BOBBS-MERRILL BOOKS BY RAND: *The Fountainhead* (Indianapolis: Bobbs-Merrill, 1943; London: Cassell, 1947);

A Letter from Ayn Rand, Author of The Fountainhead (Indianapolis: Bobbs-Merrill, 1945);

Philosophy: Who Needs It, edited by Leonard Peikoff (Indianapolis & New York: Bobbs-Merrill, 1982).

Ayn Rand in a photograph inscribed to Nick O'Connor, her brother-in-law (from "The Papers of Ayn Rand," Fine Books & Manuscripts, *sale catalogue, Butterfield, Butterfield & Dunning, p. 2, lot 5852)*

Reader's Report

The following is an unsigned reader's report (circa 1957) on Atlas Shrugged.

General Notes on
ATLAS SHRUGGED
By Ayn Rand

If we can make a deal we can live with for this book, I suppose we shall want to publish it. It is too long, and the endless repetition of some essay ideas (3 or 4) hurt it, but it still reads with an eery story interest. It is in many ways an awful book, will probably be attacked and kidded by many reviewers, but it might sell in the general order of The Fountainhead.

It is a gamble in many ways. Almost twice as long as the previous book, it will be very expensive to manufacture. The author may demand a lot. We won't be able to hold down the advance, and if the book does not go, we'll have to eat a lot of returns. There are other factors in the gamble but these are the quickest.

The book is about half novel and about half endlessly repeated bits of essay about the ultimate consequences of cooperative effort and welfare state philosophies–very lamentable consequences. Miss Rand evidently believes the reading public is so moronic it can't understand her unless she beats in each idea with ten thousand repeated blows, often repeated in the same words. This reiteration of the essay ideas is both boring and irritating, if the two can go together. Both the novel and the essay would be much more effective if the essay was vastly cut.

The unset time has bothered all readers. It doesn't need a date, but some clear-cut relation to the present (a decade, a generation, a century from now?) would orient the reader. It could be done by a reference back to 1956 or 1957 tucked in early–maybe the date an old building or bridge was constructed would do the trick.

This is a satire on the present put in the future, just as Lilliput represents England but is stated to be an island elsewhere, or just as 1984 is not now but discusses the tendencies Orwell saw in now. Most readers are willing to accept this future world of the book providing it consistently miantains *[sic]* its own rationale. In the future as now the same facts about metal, etc. obtain. I don't see, for instance, how an alloy of copper and steel can be as light as magnesium or aluminum. (Incidentally, the world of the book uses much copper and iron when it can be had, but references are made to magnesium and aluminum. Were they forgotten even by Rearden?) Yet Rearden Metal is said to be very light and very strong.

★ *Bobbs-Merrill Books* ★

FICTION		*GENERAL*	
By C. M. Sublette and Harry Harrison Kroll PERILOUS JOURNEY	$2.75	*By Lt. Col. Walter L. J. Bayler* LAST MAN OFF WAKE ISLAND	$2.75
By Hiram Haydn BY NATURE FREE	$2.75	*By Robert J. Casey* TORPEDO JUNCTION	$3.50
By Rhoda Truax GREEN IS THE GOLDEN TREE	$2.50	*By Channing Pollock* HARVEST OF MY YEARS	$3.50
By John Shirley Hurst THEN GILDED DUST	$2.00	*By Lloyd Wendt and Herman Kogan* LORDS OF THE LEVEE	$3.00
By Robert Greenwood THE SQUAD GOES OUT	$2.50	*By Bell Irvin Wiley* THE LIFE OF JOHNNY REB	$3.75
By Michael Hardt A STRANGER AND AFRAID	$2.50	*By M. B. Palmer* WE FIGHT WITH MERCHANT SHIPS	$2.75
By Lange Lewis JULIET DIES TWICE	$2.00	*By William Adams Simonds* HENRY FORD	$3.50
By Jefferson Farjeon MURDER AT A POLICE STATION	$2.00	*By Robert P. Parsons* TRAIL TO LIGHT	$3.00

THE BOBBS-MERRILL COMPANY
Indianapolis & New York

Back of dust jacket for The Fountainhead, *published in 1943 (from Vincent L. Perinn,* Ayn Rand: First Descriptive Bibliography, *1990)*

I have a note on the destruction of Wisconsin and the Starnes plant there on page 540 and following. In something like four years jungle takes over to the extent that a former filling station is unrecognizable woods. Not only people but nature is accelerating the disintegration. I can't believe it either as part of real life or as part of the story. The latter is the important thing. It wouldn't matter whether it might actually happen if I could believe it might happen in the story.

It is also hard to find the adversary to the producers. I suppose it is government. But government is made to appear very puny as well as very vague. There are many references to the Legislature but very few to Congress. What's happened? We are never told. Nobody in government is as big as a pigmy. Or part of the enemy may be people like Orren Boyle, Jim Taggart and the various magazine writers, educators and philosophers. Jim is spoken of as quite a conspirator. But every time we see him he is pretty scared and talks obvious non-

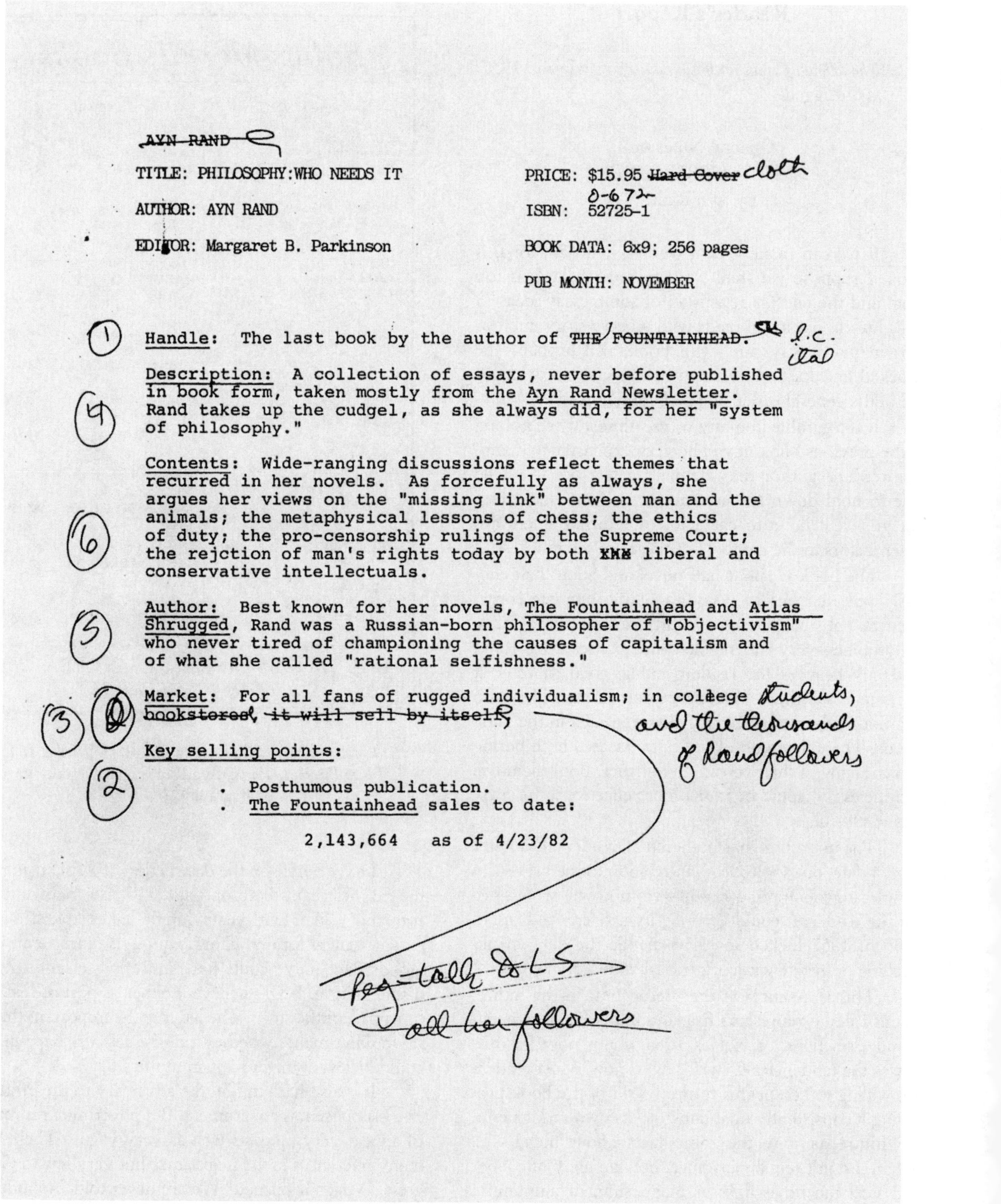

~~AYN RAND~~

TITLE: PHILOSOPHY:WHO NEEDS IT

PRICE: $15.95 ~~Hard Cover~~ cloth

AUTHOR: AYN RAND

ISBN: 0-672-52725-1

EDITOR: Margaret B. Parkinson

BOOK DATA: 6x9; 256 pages

PUB MONTH: NOVEMBER

(1) Handle: The last book by the author of ~~THE FOUNTAINHEAD.~~

(4) Description: A collection of essays, never before published in book form, taken mostly from the Ayn Rand Newsletter. Rand takes up the cudgel, as she always did, for her "system of philosophy."

(6) Contents: Wide-ranging discussions reflect themes that recurred in her novels. As forcefully as always, she argues her views on the "missing link" between man and the animals; the metaphysical lessons of chess; the ethics of duty; the pro-censorship rulings of the Supreme Court; the rejction of man's rights today by both ~~XMX~~ liberal and conservative intellectuals.

(5) Author: Best known for her novels, The Fountainhead and Atlas Shrugged, Rand was a Russian-born philosopher of "objectivism" who never tired of championing the causes of capitalism and of what she called "rational selfishness."

(3) Market: For all fans of rugged individualism; in college students, and the thousands of Rand followers ~~bookstores, it will sell by itself.~~

Key selling points:

(2)

- Posthumous publication.
- The Fountainhead sales to date:

  2,143,664 as of 4/23/82

~~all her followers~~

Draft of publicity release for Philosophy: Who Needs It, *the collection of Rand's essays published posthumously in 1982 (courtesy of The Lilly Library, Indiana University, Bloomington, Indiana)*

sense. He doesn't seem a smart plotter; he seems a coward and a fool. If Miss Rand means (and she may) that the producers beat themselves and consequently very puny opponents can seem to score victory after victory over them–she does say the producers beat themselves but does not say that even the weakest and most silly, cowardly antagonists are too strong for them. If this is true, the producers are fairly silly too, but to let them appear so would be damaging to Miss Rand's thesis.

The reader wonders about Miss Rand's mechanical and scientific knowledge. She never describes or analyzes a piece of machinery. She has emotions about its clean lines, its spare, functional efficiency, perhaps its compactness. She admires people who understand maintenance of machinery–much as a woman with a balky car admires the filling station man who adjusts her carburetor or unsticks her automatic choke, not knowing what he has done but crediting him with a good kind of witchcraft. She likes the colors of a steel mill and almost always speaks of the red glow at night. She gets a certain stimulation of the rush of heat and light when a furnace is tapped. A big factory's apparently orderly maze of shafts, pipes etc. appeals to her as big, powerful, under the control of a master hand, and this gives her a boot. She never explains how it functions, never goes into specific detail. How is static electricity made to give up its power with smooth continuousness instead of releasing it instantaneously as in lightning. Nobody asks. People just goggle at the Motor and admire the use of a Single Equation.

The reader seeking to make contemporary applications of the Emperor-size fable wonders, too, where she would put the businessmen whose greed, ambition and selfishness (qualities Galt is proud to claim) cause them to adulterate food with harmful chemicals, or to sponsor worthless battery additives (see the 1953 fight between the Bureau of Standards, a cooperative, bureaucratic organization, vs. the manufacturer, a producer, and the Secretary of Commerce, in private life a manufacturer and producer. The insistence on honest value in this real-life instance is the direct reverse of Miss Rand's contention.) Are these businessmen both producers and looters? The careful preservation of black and white values in the story doesn't carry over very well into life. Somewhere shouldn't Miss Rand allow for the businessman whose greed and selfishness does not make him turn out lean, spare, beautifully efficient products but cheap adulterations looking like honest goods? He exists. Much governmental regulation came into being because he exists and exploits the unwary.

Again on the score of credibility: How about the Taggart Board of Directors? DuPont controls General Motors with about 22% of the stock. Dagny owns close to half of Taggart Transcontinental. Yet she sits helpless while the relatively non-owning Board of Directors bumble into decisions she can't abide and she does nothing with her stock ownership to block them. How come? Is there some unexplained change in the organization of corporations that gives one director one vote regardless of stock ownership?

In the personal stories characters get lost for a time. For instance after Hank and Dagny take their vacation together in Wisconsin, she gets interested in tracing the inventor of the Motor and forgets Hank. He is clear out from 583 until somewhat after 700. I thought for a time everybody had just got tired of Hank and dropped him forever. He more or less disappears several times thereafter. Francisco likewise is in and out. I thought he was gone for a while but he turned up again. These loose ends and gaps seem to result from too much concentration on the essay material and too little attention to the novel.

James Whitcomb Riley (1849–1916)

James Whitcomb Riley put the company on the literary map and was the firm's Hoosier author par excellence. Millions heard in his voice the perfect evocation of life at that time and place. His first home was a log house on the old National Road, and nearby were forests, creeks, swimming holes, and a congenial community. As a boy Riley read the standard contemporaries (many now classics) and became a skilled performer of drama and music. His poetry began appearing in newspapers in the 1870s; his first book, "The Old Swimmin'-Hole," and 'Leven More Poems, *was published in 1883. Riley also took to the lecture circuit and widened his audience with much-admired recitations of his verse, more than half of which was in dialect. Bowen-Merrill and Bobbs-Merrill published his thousand poems in several original collections and recyclings over the years, as a result of which he was one of the first American poets to become rich. He was honored by many colleges and by praise from such contemporaries as James Russell Lowell, Mark Twain, and Rudyard Kipling. There are no written contracts with Riley in the company files, and few personal documents of any kind. When it was time to publish, he would just walk from his home to the office for a chat.*

Titles listed are those with significant first-book-appearance content; where the actual year of publication differs from the stated year, this difference is indicated.

James Whitcomb Riley (courtesy of the Indiana State Library)

SELECTED MERRILL, MEIGS; BOWEN-MERRILL; AND BOBBS-MERRILL BOOKS BY RILEY: *"The Old Swimmin'-Hole," and 'Leven More Poems* (Indianapolis: Merrill, Meigs, 1883; **first edition,** Indianapolis: Privately printed, 1883); enlarged as *"The Old Swimmin'-Hole," and 'Leven More Poems: Neghborly [sic] Poems on Friendship, Grief, and Farm-Life* (Indianapolis: Bowen-Merrill, 1891);

The Boss Girl, A Christmas Story, and Other Sketches (Indianapolis: Bowen-Merrill, 1886 [i.e., 1885]);

Afterwhiles (Indianapolis: Bowen-Merrill, 1888 [i.e., 1887]);

Old-Fashioned Roses (Indianapolis: Bowen-Merrill, 1889 [i.e., 1888]; London : Longmans, 1888);

Pipes o' Pan at Zekesbury (Indianapolis: Bowen-Merrill, 1889 [i.e., 1888]);

Rhymes of Childhood (Indianapolis: Bowen-Merrill, 1891 [i.e., 1890]);

The Flying Islands of the Night (Indianapolis: Bowen-Merrill, 1892 [i.e., 1891]);

Green Fields and Running Brooks (Indianapolis: Bowen-Merrill, 1893 [i.e., 1892]);

Armazindy (Indianapolis: Bowen-Merrill, 1894);

A Child-World (Indianapolis: Bowen-Merrill, 1896; London: Longmans, 1896);

Home-Folks (Indianapolis: Bowen-Merrill, 1900);

An Old Sweetheart of Mine (Indianapolis: Bowen-Merrill, 1902);

His Pa's Romance (Indianapolis: Bobbs-Merrill, 1903);

Out to Old Aunt Mary's (Indianapolis: Bobbs-Merrill, 1904);

A Defective Santa Claus (Indianapolis: Bobbs-Merrill, 1904);

Morning (Indianapolis: Bobbs-Merrill, 1907);

The Boys of the Old Glee Club (Indianapolis: Bobbs-Merrill, 1907);

The Riley Baby Book (Indianapolis: Bobbs-Merrill, 1913);

James Whitcomb Riley's Complete Works, memorial edition, 10 volumes, edited by Edmund H. Eitel (Indianapolis: Bobbs-Merrill, 1916);

Letters of James Whitcomb Riley, edited by William Lyon Phelps (Indianapolis: Bobbs-Merrill, 1930).

Riley Centennial

Guernsey Van Riper Jr., an editor at Bobbs-Merrill, wrote this article on the centennial of Riley's birth.

At its outset Governor Schricker of Indiana proclaimed 1949 the James Whitcomb Riley Centennial Year, and called on all the people to give it due observance. Beginning in January there have been all sorts of Riley doings, in an astonishing variety, from Lake Michigan to the Ohio River. In February the Indiana Society of Chicago put on a great show. The celebration culminated on the birthday, October seventh. At the poet's birthplace, Greenfield, a 77-foot tower, erected on the courthouse lawn, was hung with flowers sent by school children from over the state. At Indianapolis the Governor unveiled at the Riley Memorial Hospital a huge slab of engraved limestone, cornerstone for a new research wing. This new unit for scientific investigation is to be built by a million-dollar fund which has been contributed by Hoosiers. Could there be a more perfect tribute to the children's poet than the children's hospital which bears his name?

At the Lockerbie Street home on the birthday four hundred school children as usual brought their birthday flowers and this time performed a pageant composed for the Centennial. There were memorial services at the classic tomb in Crown Hill cemetery, amid a great throng of young and old. In the newspapers and on the radio there were reminiscences of the Riley times and tributes to the Hoosier poet. At colleges, secondary and grammar schools throughout Indiana, even between halves of football games, the best-loved poems were read or recited on this day and throughout a week in which nearly every citizen of the state and indeed of the Middle West paused to recall the pleasure Riley brought and still brings.

The Centennial serves to recall a unique publishing history. It seems likely that no other poet ever had such a varied presentation of his works. The story commences with the now rare and prized "The Old Swimmin'-Hole, and 'Leven More Poems." This first volume, issued in July, 1883, listed authorship by "Benj. F. Johnson, of Boone" but carried below it in brackets [James Whitcomb Riley]. Thereafter Riley used his own name only. The book bore the imprint of George C. Hitt & Co. George Hitt was a newspaperman, Riley's lifelong friend. The "Co." was Riley himself. A thousand copies were printed.

BOBBS-MERRILL AND RILEY STARTED ASSOCIATION IN 1883

The Bobbs-Merrill Company (then Merrill, Meigs & Company) brought out a second edition of "The Old Swimmin'-Hole" in the fall of 1883, and this began the close association of the author with the publishing house which continued till his death. "The Boss Girl" appeared in 1886. Then followed basically the so-called "original" volumes as they came from Riley's pen, starting with "Afterwhiles" in 1887 and ending with "Fugitive Pieces" in 1914, which constituted the "Greenfield" set for the trade and the "Homestead" edition by subscription. Two of these sixteen volumes

MRS. HEWITT H. HOWLAND
117 EAST 77TH STREET
NEW YORK CITY

O what a joy to meet
The bookish little man
As he strolls down the street,
Musing o'er many a plan
And plot of Song's conceit.—
Smoking his pipes o' Pan—
Aye, punning puns as neat
Almost as Shakespeare can.
O what a joy to meet
The bookish little man
As he strolls down the street,
Accompanying his feet
As only poets scan.

J. W. R.

To Hewitt Hanson Howland from
his old litry friend
James Whitcomb Riley
March 5, 1904

Poem written by Riley to editor Hewitt H. Howland (courtesy of The Lilly Library, Indiana University, Bloomington, Indiana)

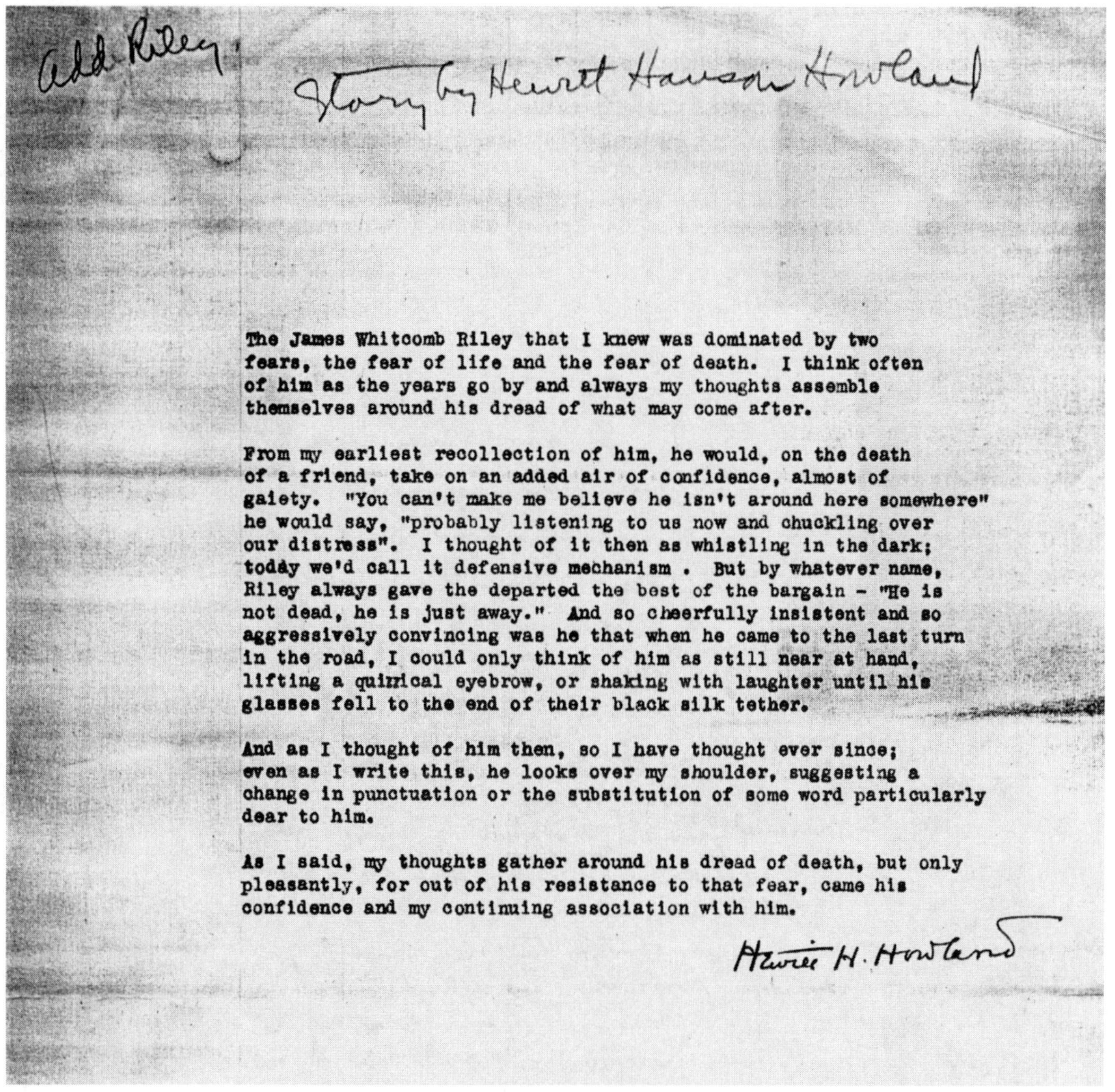

add Riley

Story by Hewitt Hanson Howland

The James Whitcomb Riley that I knew was dominated by two fears, the fear of life and the fear of death. I think often of him as the years go by and always my thoughts assemble themselves around his dread of what may come after.

From my earliest recollection of him, he would, on the death of a friend, take on an added air of confidence, almost of gaiety. "You can't make me believe he isn't around here somewhere" he would say, "probably listening to us now and chuckling over our distress". I thought of it then as whistling in the dark; today we'd call it defensive mechanism . But by whatever name, Riley always gave the departed the best of the bargain - "He is not dead, he is just away." And so cheerfully insistent and so aggressively convincing was he that when he came to the last turn in the road, I could only think of him as still near at hand, lifting a quizzical eyebrow, or shaking with laughter until his glasses fell to the end of their black silk tether.

And as I thought of him then, so I have thought ever since; even as I write this, he looks over my shoulder, suggesting a change in punctuation or the substitution of some word particularly dear to him.

As I said, my thoughts gather around his dread of death, but only pleasantly, for out of his resistance to that fear, came his confidence and my continuing association with him.

Hewitt H. Howland

Undated tribute to Riley by Howland (courtesy of The Lilly Library, Indiana University, Bloomington, Indiana)

were issued by the Century Company and one by Scribners, but were later taken over by Bobbs-Merrill. All were points of departure for many illustrated collections by different categories for poems published individually. William C. Bobbs, the president of the company, kept the staff working overtime to evolve ideas for Riley books.

HOWARD CHANDLER CHRISTY ILLUSTRATED MANY RILEY BOOKS

Howard Chandler Christy was one of the illustrators whose name became closely linked with Riley's. There were five exceedingly popular "Christy-Riley" books, of which "An Old Sweetheart of Mine" was the crowning success. (A limited, large-paper edition of "An Old Sweetheart" became a collector's item.) How quaintly old-fashioned and Gibson-girlish those Christy pictures look now, but in 1902 and for many years after, this was the perfect gift book from Benedick to Beatrice or from Darby to Joan. We remember once making an elaborate compilation to determine the word-rate revenue to the author from "An Old Sweetheart" and demonstrating to our satisfaction that no other one poem in English, or in fact any other language, was ever so well rewarded.

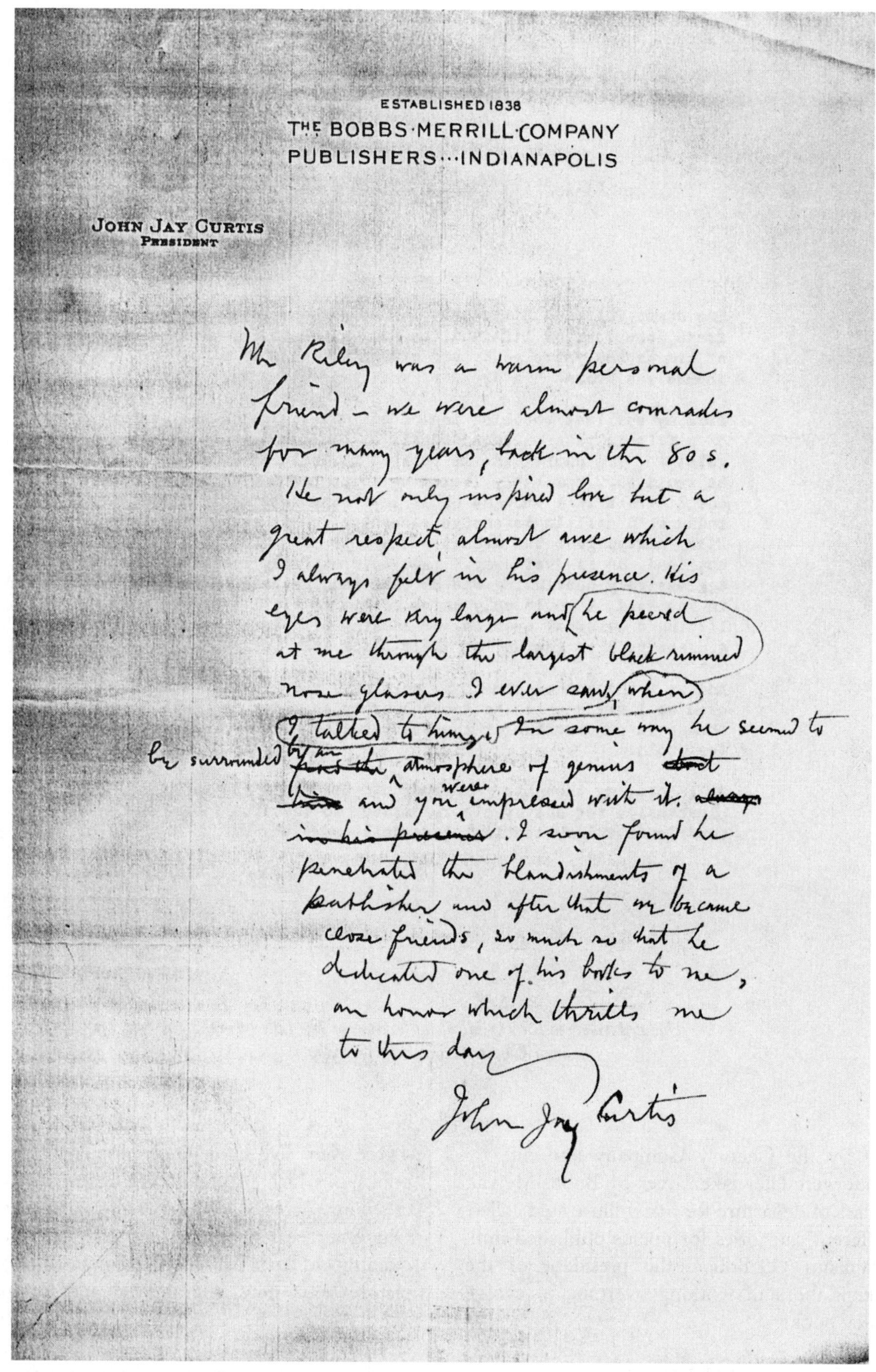

ESTABLISHED 1838
THE BOBBS-MERRILL COMPANY
PUBLISHERS ... INDIANAPOLIS

JOHN JAY CURTIS
PRESIDENT

Mr Riley was a warm personal friend – we were almost comrades for many years, back in the 80s. He not only inspired love but a great respect, almost awe which I always felt in his presence. His eyes were very large and he peered at me through the largest black rimmed nose glasses I ever saw, when I talked to him. In some way he seemed to be surrounded by an atmosphere of genius and you were impressed with it. I soon found he penetrated the blandishments of a publisher and after that we became close friends, so much so that he dedicated one of his books to me, an honor which thrills me to this day

John Jay Curtis

Undated tribute to Riley by John J. Curtis, president of the company from 1926 to 1931 (courtesy of The Lilly Library, Indiana University, Bloomington, Indiana)

At that, the seven "Deer Creek" or Vawter-Riley volumes in the original Bobbs-Merrill and the Grosset and Dunlap reprints far outsold the Christy books, with "Riley Child Rhymes" at the head of the list. Also born in Greenfield, like Riley, Will Vawter, gentle soul, was recognized as the ideally sympathetic illustrator for the Hoosier poet. Riley and Vawter formed a mutual admiration society.

When the original plates for the books were entirely worn out by many printings, Vawter (his skill had improved with the years) made an entirely new set of drawings, hundreds and hundreds of them.

MORE THAN 90 RILEY TITLES ON BOBBS-MERRILL TRADE LIST

First and last there were more than ninety Riley titles on the Bobbs-Merrill trade list. Subscription sets were issued by Scribners, Harper and Colliers, under arrangement with Bobbs-Merrill. Editions on Bible paper picked up the reader demand for pocket editions.

We asked our accountants to tell us how many Riley books have been sold. They were well toward the three-million mark when they reported, with chagrin, that the record of sales before 1893 was no longer in existence.

RILEY DID NOT MAKE WRITTEN AGREEMENTS

Yet all this variegated publishing (it ranged from a complete set edited by the poet's nephew, Edmund H. Eitel, down to a "Riley Baby Book") was accomplished without a single written agreement. Riley had a congenital aversion to signing a legal document. It was as much an idiosyncrasy as his umbrella or his lack of a bump of locality. After his death the only thing we could find in our files was his indorsement on a subscription contract we had made with Scribners–"This has my approval." Yet so wisely and prudently did his brother-in-law, Henry Eitel, vice-president of the Indiana National Bank, manage his business affairs with William C. Bobbs and John J. Curtis that there was never a serious quarrel or disagreement. Has there been another case like this in the history of author-publisher relations? [. . .]

–"The James Whitcomb Riley Centennial Year Celebrated in Indiana," *Publishers' Weekly,* 156 (26 November 1949): 2201–2203

Mary Roberts Rinehart (1876–1958)

On the basis of the rank of each book in the monthly lists, Irving H. Hart in "The One Hundred Leading Authors of Best Sellers in Fiction from 1895 to 1944" (1946) calculated that Mary Roberts Rinehart was "the leading author of best sellers in fiction" within that fifty-year span. Rinehart's early career, beginning with poems, stories, and finally mystery novels, competed with the duties of a doctor's wife, but later her husband became her business manager. She published a previously serialized novel, The Circular Staircase, *with Bobbs-Merrill in 1908, and in the next year caught on with* The Saturday Evening Post, *where her first "Tish" short story appeared. The Tish novels began with* The Amazing Adventures of Letitia Carberry *(1911). Despite Rinehart's great early success, in 1913 the number of returns exceeded the number of sales for her books. She took her next novel to Houghton Mifflin, and in 1921 Bobbs-Merrill sold her backlist to the George H. Doran Company. No Rinehart correspondence remains in the Bobbs-Merrill archives.*

BOBBS-MERRILL BOOKS BY RINEHART: *The Circular Staircase* (Indianapolis: Bobbs-Merrill, 1908; London: Cassell, 1909);

The Man in Lower Ten (Indianapolis: Bobbs-Merrill, 1909; London: Cassell, 1909);

When a Man Marries (Indianapolis: Bobbs-Merrill, 1909; London: Hodder & Stoughton, 1920);

The Window at the White Cat (Indianapolis: Bobbs-Merrill, 1910; London: Eveleigh Nash, 1911);

The Amazing Adventures of Letitia Carberry (Indianapolis: Bobbs-Merrill, 1911; London: Hodder & Stoughton, 1919);

Where There's a Will (Indianapolis: Bobbs-Merrill, 1912);

The Case of Jennie Brice (Indianapolis: Bobbs-Merrill, 1913; London: Hodder & Stoughton, 1919).

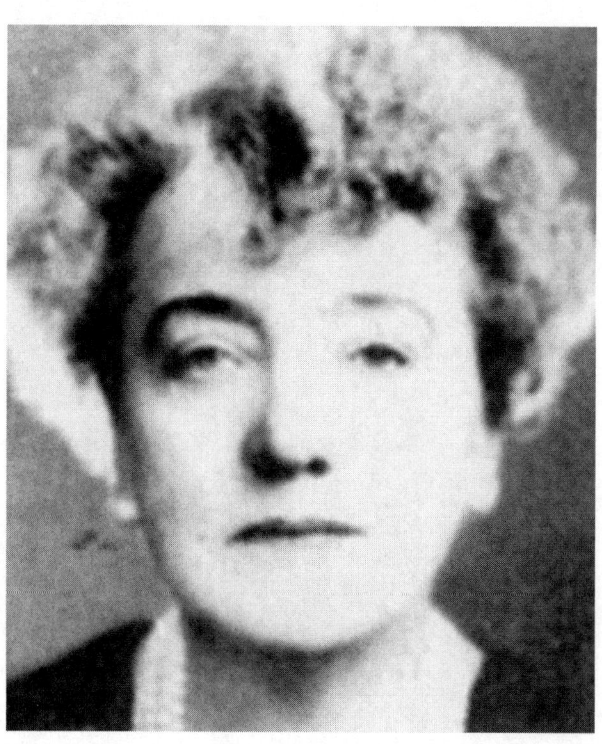

Mary Roberts Rinehart (from Stanley J. Kunitz and Howard Haycraft, eds., Twentieth Century Authors, *1942; Thomas Cooper Library, University of South Carolina)*

Autobiography

Rinehart's My Story *(1931) was originally serialized in* Good Housekeeping *(1930–1931). She helped subsidize Farrar and Rinehart as a business for her three sons, who were born between 1897 and 1902. John J. Curtis ran Bobbs-Merrill's New York office.* The Bat *was a dramatization of* The Circular Staircase *that ran for 878 performances in 1920. Anna Katharine Green's work for Bobbs-Merrill included the first book to have only the Bobbs-Merrill imprint,* The Filigree Ball *(1903).*

From nineteen, when I was married, to twenty-seven when the youngest boy at last seemed to be over his troubles, I deliberately suppressed the desire to write. For one reason, I was not very well. In the intervals between babies I had had two abdominal operations; and six months after Ted, the last baby, had arrived, we almost lost him with whooping cough and convulsions. I have the record in my own hand of those convulsions, a hundred and ten of them, and as I read them now I am once again in the nursery in that old rocking chair, holding him in my arms, with a bottle of chloroform at my elbow and a desperate prayer in my heart.

His father and I took care of him. There was a trained nurse, but he was our child. Now and then solemn processions of other medical men came in, shook their heads and went away. We faced them down. He would live. He must live.

One night they sent me to bed, to waken me soon and call me to the nursery. Ted was lying on the bed, not moving, and my husband put his arms around me.

"I'm afraid it's over, darling."

But it was not over. He lived and began to thrive, only to drink carbolic acid one day a year or so later, and again almost to escape us. Sitting by the bed for days, one or the other of us, with the intubation set ready and that loud stertorous breathing which might at any moment cease. Who could write? Who wanted to write? All that mattered was the family, to keep it together, to hold it intact.

Our nerves went a bit in those days. One day a big brute of a dog jumped on our collie, and a man driving a milk wagon ran over them deliberately. He left the collie paralyzed, to be chloroformed later in agony of spirit, and my husband chased that wagon for three blocks and almost killed the man. But we had assumed a certain philosophy. When Stanley, the eldest boy, fell over the banisters and broke his arm, I did not go into hysterics. When they came down with childish diseases I kept my head. There came a day, however, when that same eldest boy went down with diphtheria, and I took it from him. When that convalescence was over I had begun to write.

Cover of Rinehart's 1908 novel, a key book in the development of the American mystery (courtesy of The Lilly Library, Indiana University, Bloomington, Indiana)

Strange that, since I remember so much that is irrelevant, I cannot recall the name of that young nurse who cared for me, and who showed me where a magazine was advertising for verse.

"Why not try it?" she said. "It might amuse you."

And try it I did, the two "poems" being carefully fumigated according to the best hospital method before they were put in the mail. They were accepted, and I received twenty-two dollars for them. The incredible had happened. I was writing.

Not stories, of course. Only verse. I wrote reams of it. It was very bad verse indeed, but now and then one would be taken at ten dollars, twelve dollars. When I was well again I wrote a book of poems for children, and made the second visit of my life to New York to hunt a publisher. I could take only one day away from the children, my mother taking my place at home; my mother, who now lived alone in a queer new thing called "a flat." For Olive was married.

At high noon one day I had sat in the old church once more and watched my sister walk up the aisle; the same aisle where I had gone, on Uncle John's arm, to be married. Now I was a mother, and beside me in the expectant hush my small Stanley's voice rang out:

"Mother, will there be ice cream?"

So Olive was married, and soon I was to take that book of poems to New York to hunt a publisher. All day I walked about, seeing one after another, wearing blisters on my feet, and receiving real attention from only one man, Mr. Curtis of the Bobbs-Merrill Company. He did not take my poems, but he was friendly; and it was to his firm by sheer accident that I later sent my first real book; this time to be accepted. [. . .]

I had learned, through lack of time, to sit down at my desk, pick up my pen and go to work. But every now and then I had to go back to the hospital, and it was while another operation was pending that I wrote my first long story, *The Man in Lower Ten.* I had had no confidence in my ability to sustain interest for any length of time, and no desire whatever to write a book. A book was for real writers. As a matter of fact, the carbon copy of *The Man in Lower Ten* lay in my desk for two years after serialization before the fact that it had book possibility was brought home to me. Lay with my second serial, *The Circular Staircase,* accumulating the ever-penetrating smoke and dirt of Pittsburgh, and only by chance being brought into the open at all.

It was Bob Davis of *Munsey's,* for whom I had been doing considerable writing, who asked me to try my hand at a long story. I would not have done it, I think, had I been well and active; but at that time I was obliged to spend most of my time in a chair, and so it was written, in a series of notebooks held in my lap. [. . .]

The Circular Staircase, although my second serial, was my first book. I liked mystery, and it was easy for me. It has always been comparatively simple, although a logical crime story requires more concentration than any other type of writing, bar none. A crime novel is a novel, and requires the technique of the novel. In addition, however, it must have the involved consistent plot, the ability to tell as much as possible, and yet to conceal certain essential facts. It can never afford to depend on its thrills, although after the success of *The Bat* I was to see dozens of plays depending only on those, and throwing aside all consistency and all appeal to the intelligence in a mad rush for sensational and horrifying stage effects.

My health was improving now, I was cheerful again, my sense of humor had returned. And strange to relate *The Circular Staircase* was intended to be a semi-satire on the usual pompous self-important crime story. When later on as a book it was taken seriously and the reviews began to come in, I was almost overwhelmed. [. . .]

I went back to short stories, to a serial now and then. I had published three serials now in minor magazines, receiving, I think, four hundred dollars each. There was more time, for now the children were going to school. One day Uncle John came from Cincinnati to visit us, and asked to read something I had written. I looked about, and found in my desk the battered old carbon copy of *The Circular Staircase,* and gave it to him. He read it all day, and I was greatly pleased when he hurried through lunch to get back to it. When he had finished he came to me.

"That's a book, Mary. You ought to have it published."

"It isn't good enough for a book."

"Certainly it is," he said stubbornly. "I've read a lot of worse books."

The idea rather amused my husband. His literary standards were high, and while he had regarded my writing leniently, it was also with a certain indulgence. Some time in those years, too, I had happened on a sentence in Stevenson's *Virginibus Puerisque:* "Certainly, never if I could help it would I marry a woman who wrote," and that had impressed me. My writing, while open enough, was not to come between my husband and myself. I was rather timid when I mentioned the book then, but he said that it would do no harm to try.

The next day I took those tattered pages to a bindery, where they agreed to cut off the soiled edges and to bind the manuscript in a flexible cover. They would even put the title in gilt letters on that cover, and all for the sum of three dollars. When it came back dressed up beyond recognition I picked a publisher by the simple method of taking a story by Anna Katherine [*sic*] Green from the book case, noted the name Bobbs-Merrill of Indianapolis, and sent it off.

I had very little hope. [. . .]

I still went to market three times a week, and it is entirely characteristic that over the butcher's telephone, set out among various cuts of meat, I listened while my husband read me the publisher's letter which accepted my first book.

"My dear Mrs. Rinehart: I have read *The Circular Staircase,* not only with pleasure but with thrills and shivers."

Thrills and shivers! What did he know of thrills and shivers, that man back in Indianapolis?

THE PULLMAN COMPANY
TICKET AGENTS OFFICE DIAGRAM

CAR Ontario LINE Penna
Train No. 27 Leave 12[01] A.M.
From Pittsburg
To Washington
Date Sept 9th 1908

AGENT'S STAMP

UPPERS	LOWERS
1 The	Mr. Jones 1
2 Man	Mr. Carnegie 2
3 in	Mr. Weldin 3
4 Lower	Mrs. Boggs 4
5 Ten	Miss West 5
6 by	Mrs. Curtis 6
7 Mary	Mr. Sullivan 7
8 Roberts	Mr. HotchKiss 8
9 Rinehart	Mr. Blakeley 9
10 author	Mr. Harrington 10
11 of	Mrs. Conway 11
12 The	Mrs. Horne 12
13 Circular	Miss Frick 13
14 Staircase	Mr. Davis 14

A SOFA DRAWING ROOM U L

12-03 FORM No. 3

NOTE:—BRACKETED SECTIONS ARE OPPOSITES. SECTIONS ARE NUMBERED FROM MEN'S TOILET

Advertisement for Rinehart's The Man in Lower Ten *(1909) in the shape of a Pullman ticket. Mr. Harrington's name is in red (courtesy of The Lilly Library, Indiana University, Bloomington, Indiana).*

The thrills and shivers were mine, bending over that gory meatstand. They would publish the book, without cost to me, illustrate it, do everything. And the editor wanted to come on and talk about other books. Other books, and I had two ready for him; two books and a million ideas! I would write forever and ever, write books, write dozens of books.

I wired him to come on. My husband was interested but still rather amused, and I baked a cake that afternoon. A cake of mother's baking meant a party to the boys. I beat eggs and whipped icing and sang, and we had ice cream and cake for dinner that night. [. . .]

The editor came; Hewitt Howland, now editor of the Century Company and later to marry Manie Cobb, Irvin Cobb's sister. Whether the curtains and the valance impressed him I do not know, but the two other manuscripts apparently did. He sat in the living room all day, with dogs and children around him, and he read the two stories and accepted them. I was to publish, not one book but three. In the evening we gathered around the piano, and I played and we all sang. The collie too always howled at those times, and I daresay that in a long experience Mr. Howland can remember no more domestic evening than that, nor any more unliterary atmosphere.

Three books meant a reprieve. My husband was earning abundantly, but I had fallen into the way of spending my own money, as well as his. We had more servants, the children were going to expensive schools. Doctor Rinehart did not entirely approve. He wanted to support his family, and he did. But as my earning power increased so my standard of living rose.

–*My Story* (New York: Farrar & Rinehart, 1931), pp. 82–83, 91, 92, 94, 95, 96

* * *

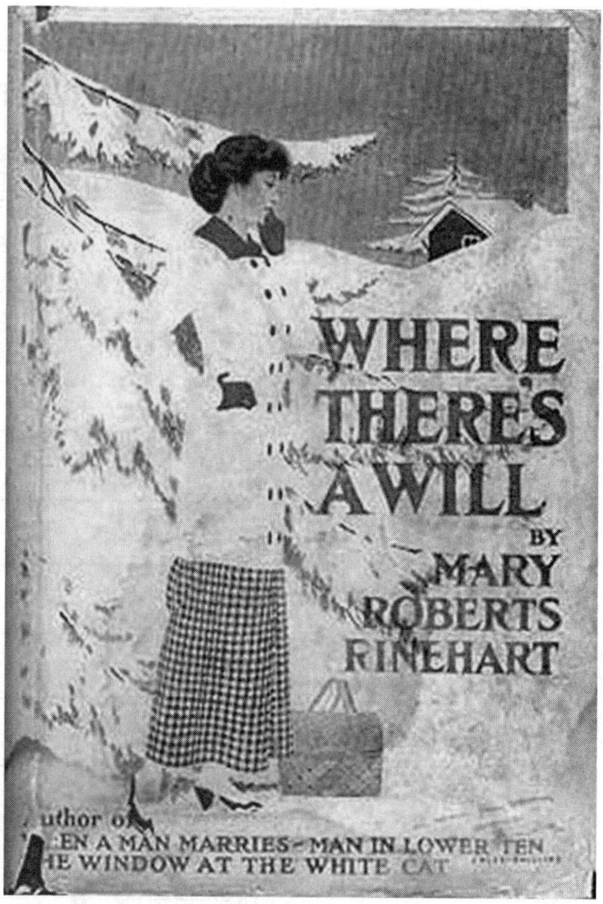

Dust jacket for Rinehart's 1912 novel (Between the Covers Rare Books, Merchantville, N.J.)

Review: *The Circular Staircase*

In "The Circular Staircase" (Bobbs-Merrill) Mary Roberts Rhinehart [*sic*] has given the jading reading public a tale of mystery with a new piquancy. It might be possible, though it would be difficult, to contrive a more involved network of circumstances and a [*sic*] create a more hopeless mystification. But it would not bc possible to invent a more pleasantly diverting character than the lady (it would be a pleasure to call her young, but she confesses to gray hairs) who is at the centre of the mystery and who herself narrates it. Written in any old style, "The Circular Staircase" would be the sort of thing people sit up nights to finish; written in the delightfully humorous vein which makes it stand out so much above the ordinary detective story, it is bound to be, with more than usual deserts, a popular success.

It is all about an old house with an unsuspected secret chamber, a bank President who loots his own institution in order to hoard the spoil where he can feel it his own; a doctor who buries a pauper's corpse for the body of the bank President; an unruly son; two Nemesi in the forms of women; a matter of three or four murders; two unhappy love affairs and one tragic one; an automobile and a freight car, and a gentlemanly detective who ought to have married the lady who was no longer young–and who will do so yet if an entertaining author will be so good as to write another book.

–"Entertaining Mystery," *New York Times,* 22 August 1908, p. 460

Hallie Erminie Rives (1876–1956)

Hallie Erminie Rives's first novel defended lynching; her second explored a woman's sexual awakening. The third, published with Bowen-Merrill in 1902, though less controversial, was nonetheless sensationally promoted. Like much of her remaining work for the company, Hearts Courageous *took advantage of the popular taste for historical romance. It was turned into a play and a movie, with future cowboy star William S. Hart acting the part of Patrick Henry in both. Rives spent much of her adult life abroad as the wife of diplomat Post Wheeler. His first mission was to Japan, where she set* The Kingdom of Slender Swords *(1909). In* The Valiants of Virginia *(1912) she returned to the plantation society she knew from her youth in Kentucky (again with unfortunate racialist attitudes). Both of these novels, as well as* Satan Sanderson *(1907), were best-sellers.*

BOWEN-MERRILL/BOBBS-MERRILL BOOKS BY RIVES: *Hearts Courageous* (Indianapolis: Bowen-Merrill, 1902; London: B. F. Stevens & Brown, 1902);

The Castaway: Three Great Men Ruined in One Year–A King, a Cad, and a Castaway (Indianapolis: Bobbs-Merrill, 1904);

Tales from Dickens, illustrated by Reginald B. Birch (Indianapolis: Bobbs-Merrill, 1905);

Satan Sanderson (Indianapolis: Bobbs-Merrill, 1907; London: Hutchinson, 1908);

The Kingdom of Slender Swords (Indianapolis: Bobbs-Merrill, 1910; **first edition,** London: Everett, 1909);

The Valiants of Virginia (Indianapolis: Bobbs-Merrill, 1912; London: Mills & Boon, 1913).

Related Letters

Hewitt H. Howland was trade-department editor, and company vice president John J. Curtis was in charge of the New York office at the time of this letter, which included a note from Curtis. William C. Bobbs was the president and Charles W. Merrill the treasurer.

Hallie Erminie Rives to Hewitt H. Howland, 23 November 1911

Dear Mr. Howland:

After my pea-green days on the sea I am just emerging into the white lights.

Hallie Erminie Rives (from Post Wheeler and Hallie Erminie Rives, Dome of Many-Coloured Glass, *1955; Francis Marion University Library)*

I have been away from Ocean Grove three days with Post's parents away up state, so if you have sent a letter to me it is hung up somewhere between lines. I am very anxious to see you and am in America for only four weeks more. Wire me when you get this, in care of Mr. Curtis, what would be the best time to come to New York to see us. I go to Washington to-morrow night for two or three days, and then to Virginia for Thanksgiving. Of course Post will want to see you too and he is not going with me to Washington and Virginia.

Now just give me a chance at knowing what is the best time that we can meet in New York after Thanksgiving day. If you can come to Washington to see me on Monday and stay in the East until after Thanksgiving day so that Wheeler and you and I can have a talk also, why come along the sooner the better, because I want to see you so much that I can stand seeing you twice, but if you cannot stay until after Thanksgiving day for the New York conference for the three of us, you had, perhaps, better try to make the visit just after Thanksgiving day.

I see that SATAN SANDERSON was in Indianapolis last night and to-night, so I sent a congratulatory telegram to the hero. I am anxious to see it before I leave the country.

Give my best regards to Mr. Bobbs and Mr. Merrill. Can't you all come on for the celebration.

Please bring on the last statement, which you will recall I have not seen.

Yours very sincerely,
Hallie Rives Wheeler

HHH

Mrs Wheeler says there is a possibility of having her new novel for Jan. pub. if we have to have it & if you see her at an early date.

JJC

* * *

William C. Bobbs to Charles W. Merrill, 4 February 1912

Dear Charles:

After a week of about the hardest work it has ever been my joy and pride to devote to the publishing business the old Rives contract of Aug 1908 under which we owed her $12,000–, for nothing, the first of Feby has been adjusted so that it will not cost the house any money at all and will not require the present payment of any cash beyond what we owe her on our books with the possible exception of $500– which I may have to give her before the final contracts are signed. And in addition to this we will have the contract for her next book with no advancement–over the $500–until her MSS is received and accepted. If you don't think this is a fairly good job ask Howland.

I am counting on giving her an Irving check for the $500–, if need be and you would better wire me Monday if there is objection to this from bank a/c standpoint. The $2500– due her on our books is for the popular edition of Slender Swords. Please send to me here on Monday a check payable to her for this amount and I will turn it over to her when she has returned the letter of credit we gave her broker.

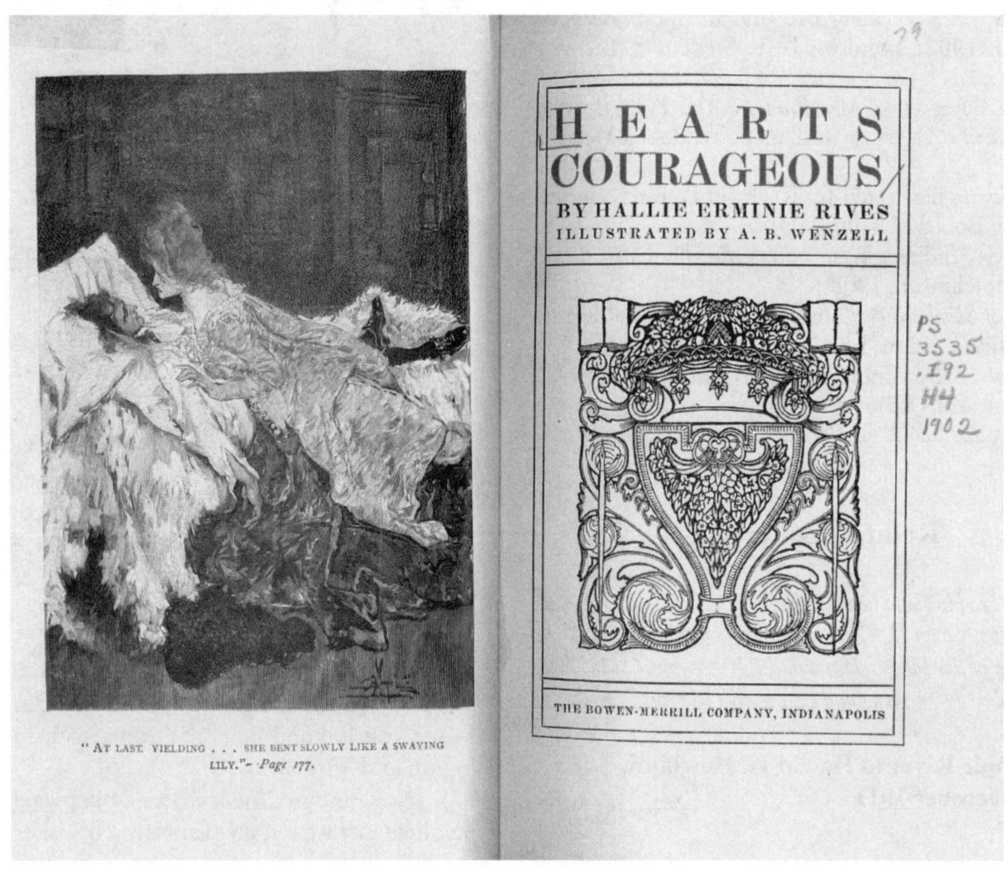

Frontispiece and title page for Rives's first novel with the company, published in 1902 (Thomas Cooper Library, University of South Carolina)

Established 1838

The Bowen-Merrill Company
Publishers, *Indianapolis*, U. S. A.

NEW YORK OFFICE, 131 TRIBUNE BUILDING, PARK ROW

WILLIAM C. BOBBS, *President*. CHARLES W. MERRILL, *Treasurer*. JOHN J. CURTIS, *Secretary*

NEW YORK OFFICE, TEMPLE COURT, 5 BEEKMAN STREET

New York, Nov. 24, 1902

Gentlemen:

The enclosed clippings from the New York Journal and New York Press show the reports of the booksellers of Greater New York as to the popularity of recent novels.

It is very gratifying to see that "Hearts Courageous" heads both of the lists, which is proof positive that Miss Rives' novel is the best selling book in New York, and probably indicates that it is the best selling novel in the United States.

Outside of the literary merits of the story, the beautiful cover adds greatly to the attractiveness of this novel as a holiday book. We hope to have your liberal orders before it is too late for the holiday trade.

Very truly yours,

THE BOWEN-MERRILL COMPANY.

AN INSTANT SUCCESS

Promotional form letter from the New York office for Rives's Hearts Courageous *(courtesy of The Lilly Library, Indiana University, Bloomington, Indiana)*

I sent you on Wednesday a note of hers for $3900– and asked that she should have a check for an amount named–about $130–. So far she has not had the check and I have not heard whether you got the note. Her check may have gone astray or not forwarded to her. But I should like to know whether her account is balanced Jan 1st as I figured it would be. When her matters are all straightened out everything will take care of itself excepting the note. That covers amounts advanced her about which Wheeler does not know. First the $2 th on the Satan Sanderson serial, then an increase juggled from time to cover that–I don't know how we can arrange payments on that–but at least we have it so that these subterranean advances are stopped–and I will do the best I can to arrange for payments on the note. Please be sure to send the $2500– check to me on Monday.

Sincerely Yours

Bobbs

* * *

Merrill to John J. Curtis, 11 April 1912

ACCOUNTS–WHEELER

Dear Mr. Curtis:–

Here is a check for Five Hundred Dollars made payable to the account of Hallie Erminie Rives Wheeler. Won't you please deposit it to her credit in the Corner Exchange Bank.

She has been pestering Mr. Bobbs for six or eight hundred dollars to help furnish her new home in Rome, and this is the result of a compromise. Mr. Bobbs has wired her that we will stand for her future troubles up to $500.00, no more.

Yours very truly,

[Charles W. Merrill]

* * *

Frontispiece and title page for Rives's 1904 novel (Thomas Cooper Library, University of South Carolina)

Established 1838 Number 0323

The Bobbs-Merrill Company

Publishers

Indianapolis, U.S.A. Dec. 20, 1911

In Account with SATAN SANDERSON -- Dramatic Rights

WEEK ENDING DEC. 9th, 1911

Indianapolis	Dec. 4	134.30
"	4	122.00
"	5	118.80
"	5	221.30
"	6	117.70
		200.40
		109.65
		241.85
		114.75
		185.85
		184.85
		336.15
		2087.60

CHARGE E. D. STAIR

Royalty at 5% of $2087.60 104.38

CREDIT KIRK B. ALEXANDER

1/3 of $104.38 34.79

CREDIT MISS MARBURY

COM. at 10% of $69.59 6.96 41.75

$ 62.63

CREDIT HALLIE ERMINIE RIVES

50% of $62.63 $ 31.31

Royalty statement for the dramatic rights to Rives's 1907 novel Satan Sanderson *(courtesy of The Lilly Library, Indiana University, Bloomington, Indiana)*

D. Laurance Chambers was vice president and trade-department editor at the time of this letter from Rives, then in Paris. Curtis Brown was a London literary agent.

Rives to D. Laurance Chambers, 29 November 1928

Dear Mr. Chambers:

This is written with reference to my novel "The Castaway," published by your firm twenty-four years ago.

In 1911, as no dramatization had been secured up to that time, my husband asked the firm whether you would return to us the dramatic rights, which had been given you by the contract, as we wished to do it ourselves in play form. Verbally this was agreed to by Mr. Bobbs, but the only written record I have of it is in a letter to my husband written by Mr. Howland, dated January 31, 1912, which says:

> "With regard to the dramatic rights of 'The Castaway,' we are willing to give them, and almost anything else, to you if you will in return persuade Mrs. Wheeler to finish her new story, but you will no doubt mention this to Mr. Bobbs along with whatever else may be on your mind."

We spoke to Mr. Bobbs, as I say, about it and he replied that whatever Mr. Howland said "went" with him. The m.s. of the new story ("Valiants of Va") was duly finished and delivered, and we rested on the agreement and set to work on the dramatization of "The Castaway." We had no suggestion that the reversion was not quite understood between us till an account, rendered us in January 1915, showed an item of $75 credited to "Picture Rights, Castaway."

For several years (we were in the Far East during the next few years) we tried vainly to discover the status of this transaction, but the Bobbs-Merrill has never given us any information. We have taken it for granted that you could not have made any contract that did not call for a production within a maximum time, and so far as we have been able to discover, the film was never made. You will remember, no doubt, your own correspondence with Mr. Curtis Brown about the matter, copies of which he sent me. Mr. Bobbs' letter to me of December 1, 1924, said the affair was in your hands and that you were trying to rebuy the rights. Later you told me the New York office had no record of the sale and you could not tell me to whom it had been sold, but that when you went to Indianapolis you would let me know about it. This is nearly three years ago and I have never heard from you.

It seems likely that the company that made the payment to the Bobbs-Merrill of $150 went out of business long ago and without producing the film or making any arrangement for its production. We have made wide inquiries through the movie companies and no trace of its production can be found. We infer, therefore, that whatever rights the purchaser company may have acquired have been lost through failure to produce. And if this is the case we wish to avail ourselves of the rights which it is our understanding were so long ago returned to us by the Bobbs-Merrill.

We have now interested a company in "The Castaway"; they are considering making it into a talking-film and I have cabled my friend Mr. John Golden of the John Golden Theatre, 202 W. 58th Street, asking him to negotiate with them for me. I don't want to override any rights of anyone else, but it is a very long time since the novel was published and I don't want to lose my chance to make something out of it.

I have cabled Mr. Golden also, asking him if he will talk to someone of your company, so that we may know exactly your point of view–whether you sold the film rights in 1914 without any clause providing for a production, and in that case consider that you no longer possess any rights in it–or whether (in case you count the rights reverted to you through non-production of the film) you will now honour the agreement that gave the dramatic rights to me, as indicated in Mr. Howland's letter above-quoted.

I thing [*sic*] we should know exactly where we stand in this.

I am sending a copy of this letter to Mr. Golden.

With best regards to you, believe me
Hallie Erminie Rives Wheeler

P.S.

We expect to be back in New York early in the New Year.

H.E.R.W.

* * *

Chambers to Rives, 17 December 1928

Dear Mrs. Wheeler:–

Your letter of November 29th is received.

THE CASTAWAY was one of the books about which we wrote you on January 14, 1926, as follows:

"The motion picture rights of some of your novels that were sold some years ago were sold outright and, we are advised, are not subject to cancellation because of nonproduction. The purchaser is at liberty to resell the rights. A production may help the sale of the book in a photoplay edition, and we are always

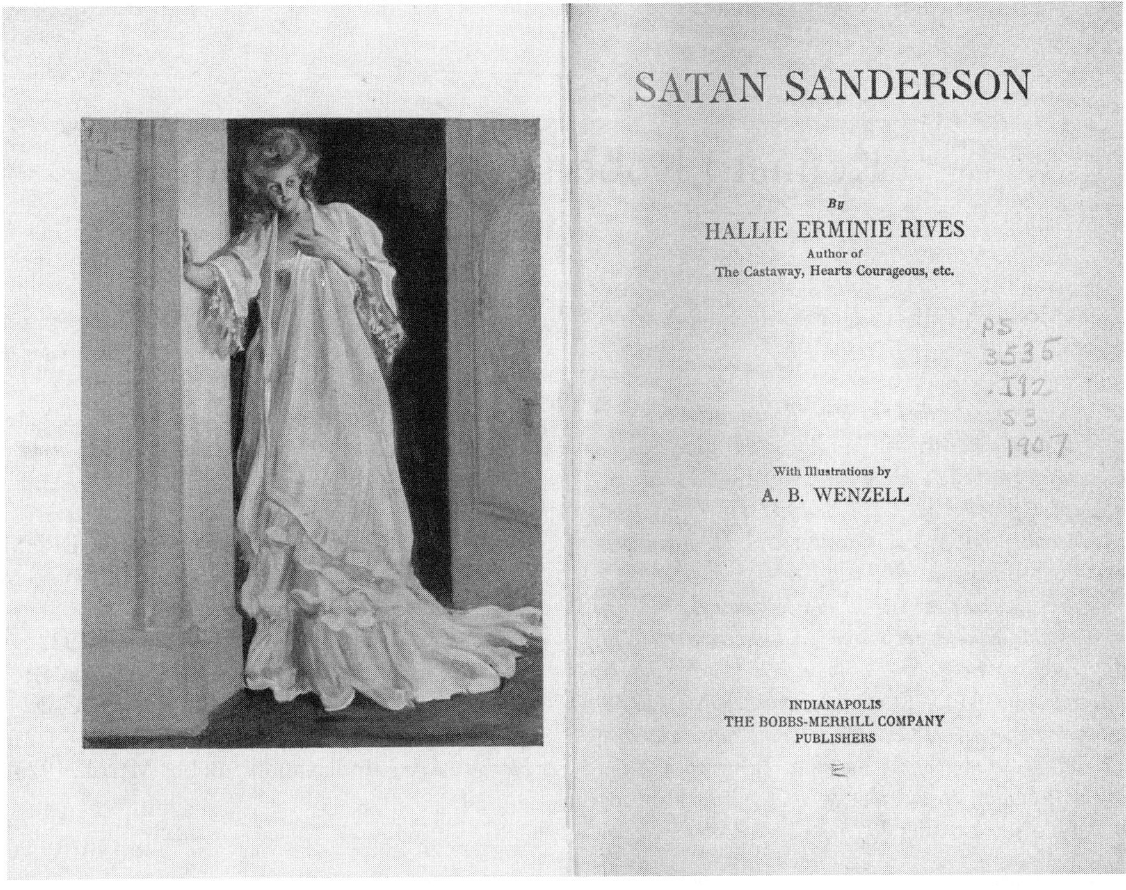

SATAN SANDERSON

By

HALLIE ERMINIE RIVES

Author of

The Castaway, Hearts Courageous, etc.

With Illustrations by

A. B. WENZELL

INDIANAPOLIS

THE BOBBS-MERRILL COMPANY

PUBLISHERS

Frontispiece and title page for Rives's 1907 novel (Thomas Cooper Library, University of South Carolina)

eager to do all that we can to promote and pave the way for production."

Before, therefore, we could sell the talking picture rights it would be necessary to buy back the movie rights from Colonel W. N. Selig, who bought them, and who is very much alive at the Selig Zoo, 3800 Mission Road, Los Angeles, California.

If Mr. Golden inquires of us we shall be glad to refer him to Colonel Selig, but we have not heard from Mr. Golden as yet.

Mr. Curtis is here and sends his kindest regards to Mr. Wheeler. I shall hope to see you in New York on your return early in the New Year.

Cordially yours,
[D. Laurance Chambers]

Kenneth Roberts (1885–1957)

See also the Roberts entry in *DLB 9: American Novelists, 1910–1945.*

A month before he died, Kenneth Roberts won a special Pulitzer Prize for the contributions he made to literature with his historical novels. The best known of these, Northwest Passage, *was published by Doubleday, Doran in 1937. His earlier work for Bobbs-Merrill, however, was of another kind. He began writing for the* Boston Post *in 1909 and then contributed pieces to humor magazines. Next came more than two hundred articles he wrote as a roving reporter, in Europe and America, for* The Saturday Evening Post. *Some of these were collected into his Bobbs-Merrill books.* Why Europe Leaves Home *(1922) presented such a low view of Central Europeans that it was credited with causing passage of the Restricted Immigration Act of 1924. The topicality of the Florida books–*Sun Hunting *(1922) and* Florida Loafing *1925)–was owed to the current real-estate boom.* Black Magic *(1924) had good words for Benito Mussolini and fascism, views that Roberts later recanted. The great Hoosier novelist Booth Tarkington was his friend and collaborator. Tarkington was also friendly with the Bobbs-Merrill editors, and a recommendation from him about a young author carried great weight.*

BOBBS-MERRILL BOOKS BY ROBERTS: *Why Europe Leaves Home* (Indianapolis: Bobbs-Merrill, 1922; London: Unwin, 1922);
Sun Hunting (Indianapolis: Bobbs-Merrill, 1922);
Black Magic (Indianapolis: Bobbs-Merrill, 1924);
Concentrated New England: A Sketch of Calvin Coolidge (Indianapolis: Bobbs-Merrill, 1924);
Florida Loafing (Indianapolis: Bobbs-Merrill, 1925).

Kenneth Roberts (Bruccoli Clark Layman Archives)

Related Letters

Hewitt H. Howland was trade-department editor.

Hewitt H. Howland to Roberts, 6 August 1921

My dear Mr. Roberts:

Without straining your psychic powers I suspect you'll be wise to the promptings of this letter before you have finished its opening paragraph.

I read a manuscript on salesmanship the other day in which the author proudly delivered himself of the discovery that every human action has back of it an impelling desire.

Back of the action involved in the composition of this letter is the desire to see your name on a Bobbs-Merrill title page. The salesmanship author seems to have been on to his job, doesn't he? I don't want to step on the toes of any of my fellow book-makers–the old wheeze about theives [*sic*] and their honor holds good here–but if you are free to consider us as possible publishers, I hope you'll be willing, as well.

What I have read that you have written, plus what Booth Tarkington has said, must be my excuse and apology for this intrusion. We do want you with us.

Cordially yours,
[Hewitt H. Howland]

* * *

William Harlowe Briggs was a playwright and editor at Harper and Brothers.

Roberts to Howland, 9 August 1921

Dear Mr. Howland:–

Thanks very much for your letter of the 6th.

The foundation of the world, they say, is put together with brass tacks; so we might as well examine them.

I have no fiction and probably wont [*sic*] have for some months.

Dust jacket for Roberts's 1922 collection of articles first published in The Saturday Evening Post *(courtesy of The Lilly Library, Indiana University, Bloomington, Indiana)*

I have a series of articles which ought to make a salable book, but which lack a connecting thread. Most of them have run in the POST during the past few months, and a few of them are still to run in the POST. I spoke of these articles to Mr. Briggs of Harpers; and he said that the lack of connection in them would probably militate against their being made into a book. So I didn't send them to him, and he has never seen them.

I'll tell you about them; and if you see a possibility in them, I'll send them to you. If you don't, then we will have saved lots of time, and you will have been spared the labor of reading them.

Two of the articles are on immigration to America from northeastern Europe: two are on the prohibition movement in England and Scotland: two are on European aviation–airplane and dirigible: two are on the fate of the titled Russians who have swarmed into western Europe and are living from hand to mouth: one is on Paris styles; and one is the only accurate report ever written on Monte Carlo. The total is about 120,000 words, since each chapter averages from 12,000 to 15,000 words.

The reason that I think they will make a salable book is this:

This country is intensely interested in immigration. Each of a series of five immigration articles brought me scores of letters from people of influence. Permanent immigration legislation will be passed at the end of another year, and it will be preceded by a noisy campaign. There's some good hot stuff in the two immigration articles that I want included, and you can get boosts from such people as Madison Grant, author of THE PASSING OF THE GREAT RACE, Lothrop Stoddard, author of THE RISING TIDE OF COLOR and Prof. R. DeCourcy Ward of Harvard.

The Russian refugee articles show the finish of the old nobility of Russia–princes working as cooks, princesses waiting on table, admirals and generals acting as door-porters and janitors, and so on. Women seem to eat that stuff alive.

The prohibition articles would sell a good many copies abroad, especially in Scotland, where the prohibition fight starts all over again next year. The Scotch get themselves all worked up over the matter.

After the first of the aviation articles ran in the POST, I had letters from the heads of all the different airplane companies in America assuring me that the article had done more for aviation in this country than anything ever written. I think that that would probably give you an advertising toe-hold.

All of the articles are more or less humorous. I don't know what title to give the collection:–maybe WHY EUROPE LEAVES HOME.

That, I think, about covers the situation.

Very sincerely yours,
Kenneth L. Roberts

* * *

Vice president and associate trade-department editor D. Laurance Chambers wrote a brief note to Howland expressing his approval of Roberts's proposal, and Howland then wrote to Roberts on the same date.

Howland to Roberts, 11 August 1921

My dear Mr. Roberts:

If you had a miscellaneous lot of short stories, I'd be inclined to agree with Mr. Briggs, but with your articles I can't see the necessity for a connecting thread. I have read some of the articles and know just how interesting they are. The idea of putting them into a volume appeals to me as being mighty well worth while doing and I shall be glad if you will send them to me so that I may propose the plan more intelligently to my associates. Your suggested title–*Why Europe Leaves Home* is most attractive.

With many thanks and kind regards, I am,

Cordially yours,
[Hewitt H. Howland]

* * *

Howland to Roberts, 2 September 1921

My dear Mr. Roberts:

You have given the most satisfactory as well as the most entertaining explanation [of] Why Europe Leaves Home and we shall be proud and glad to transform the manuscript into a volume that shall at least approach the contents in beauty and charm. In other words we accept with pleasure. As to terms of contract, time of publication, style of manufacture and other details, I should likc to dcfcr their consideration until I come to see you at Kennebunk some time, subject to your convenience, the latter part of this month. It gives me the greatest pleasure to write this letter and to sign myself, with congratulations and good wishes,

Cordially yours,
[Hewitt H. Howland]

* * *

KENNETH L. ROBERTS
KENNEBUNK BEACH
MAINE

September 5th. [1921]

My dear Mr. Howland:-

Your letter was welcome news; and I am particularly glad that you will come down and pay us a visit. The Tarkingtons live only a mile and a half from us. We can't offer you as many luxuries as they can; but our front door is only fifty yards from the first tee, we have a number of pre-war drinks left, and we will guarantee you a partridge dinner. Mrs. Roberts says to bring Mrs. Howland; and don't forget your golf clubs. We will have the links practically to ourselves.

As to time, set your own. I shall be here all through the month; and you will be made welcome on whatever date you may select. Name it, and I'll have the partridges ready.

Very sincerely yours,

Kenneth L. Roberts

Roberts's reply to editor Hewitt H. Howland's 2 September 1921 letter informally committing the firm to the publication of the nonfiction collection that appeared the following year as Why Europe Leaves Home *(courtesy of The Lilly Library, Indiana University, Bloomington, Indiana)*

Review: *Why Europe Leaves Home*

Keenly observant, vividly and breezily written, often humorous and always sound, this book is as important to present-day Americans as notice of approaching hurricane to the captain of a ship at sea; indeed, it is more important, for whereas the captain cannot still the waves by writing to his Congressman, the foundering of the United States in a sea of South and Central European immigration may be prevented if we, the passengers and crew, have but the energy to tack a "No Admittance" sign upon the bowsprit.

That, in effect, is what Mr. Roberts has to tell us as the result of his observations during the last two years in Europe, and he tells it so convincingly, with such richness of color and anecdotal detail, that sane and disinterested readers will, I believe, find it impossible to disagree with him. Objections to Mr. Roberts's book will, to readjust the metaphor, be heard only in the steerage of our luxurious national craft, and from persons more concerned with getting their friends aboard than with maintaining a certain standard of desirability in the ship's company. It is claimed by Mr. Roberts's publishers that an article of his, first published in The Saturday Evening Post and here presented in revised and enlarged form, did more than anything else to impel Congress to rush through emergency immigration legislation, and, further, that the conclusions drawn in Chapter IV. of "Why Europe Leaves Home" form the basis for a permanent law now under consideration. May the day soon come when this book, having served its purpose, will sink to unimportance!

In emphasizing the importance of "Why Europe Leaves Home," I do not, however, wish to alarm those potential readers who regard important books as being as dry as a guest room inkwell. Mr. Roberts's tale of his interview with King Constantine of Greece is the most wickedly humorous thing of the kind I have seen since the late John Reed's interview with William Jennings Bryan was published a good many years ago in Collier's Weekly. Though one feels throughout this book the underlying intensity of the author, Mr. Roberts's manner is anything but heavy. Just when you think he has become so wrapped up in his message as to forget the requirements of a large American audience, he surprises you by turning a back somersault. [. . .]

It is the opinion of the author if more immigrants continue to pour in and we fail as we have been failing to assimilate them the United States will develop large numbers of separate racial groups as distinct as those of Czechoslovakia, "where various people lie around in undigested lumps," or else that America will be populated by a mongrel race entirely different from the present American people.

He cites the ruin of Greece and Rome by immigration, and warns that history repeats.

Races cannot be cross-bred without mongrelization [he writes] any more than breeds of dogs can be cross-bred without mongrelization. The American Nation was founded and developed by the Nordic race, but if a few more million members of the Alpine, Mediterranean and Semitic races are poured among us the result must inevitably be a hybrid race of people as worthless and futile as the good-for-nothing mongrels of Central America and Southeastern Europe.

I strongly urge Americans whose children are to live in the United States to read Mr. Roberts's "Why Europe Leaves Home." It ought at the present time to have the right of way over any other book I know.

–Julian Street, "Why Europe Leaves Home," *New York Times Book Review,* 30 July 1922, p. 17

Irma S. Rombauer (1877–1962)

and

Marion Rombauer Becker (1903–1976)

Irma S. Rombauer's The Joy of Cooking *was Bobbs-Merrill's most successful trade publication. The book was privately published in 1931 and had its first Bobbs-Merrill edition in 1936. Rombauer's daughter, Marion Rombauer Becker, provided illustrations for the early editions and helped with the compilation of recipes. She was first listed as co-author in 1951. In* Stand Facing the Stove: The Story of the Women Who Gave America *The Joy of Cooking (1996) Anne Mendelson recounts the publishing history of Rombauer's book, which included titanic clashes between the authors and Bobbs-Merrill staff members. (Among other things, the firm printed the 1962 edition without a contract.)* The Joy of Cooking *went through*

Marion Rombauer Becker and Irma S. Rombauer (© Bettman/CORBIS)

many printings in six editions while the company existed and, with later revisions, remains in print. It may well be America's favorite cookbook, its humor and anecdotes complementing the wide-ranging, clearly presented recipes. Becker brought greater formality to the work, along with her interests in such things as health foods and organic gardening. On her own she produced Little Acorn: The Story Behind *The Joy of Cooking,* 1931–1966 *(1966), a brief and uncontentious account of the history of her mother's book, and* Wild Wealth *(1971), a collaborative work on gardening with wild plants.*

BOBBS-MERRILL BOOKS BY ROMBAUER AND BECKER: *The Joy of Cooking,* by Rombauer (Indianapolis: Bobbs-Merrill, 1936; London: Dent, 1945; **first edition,** St. Louis: Privately printed, 1931);

Streamlined Cooking: New and Delightful Recipes for Canned, Packaged and Frosted Foods and Rapid Recipes for Fresh Foods, by Rombauer (Indianapolis: Bobbs-Merrill, 1939);

A Cookbook for Girls and Boys (Indianapolis: Bobbs-Merrill, 1946);

Little Acorn: The Story Behind The Joy of Cooking, 1931–1966, by Becker (Indianapolis: Bobbs-Merrill, 1966); republished as *Little Acorn: Joy of Cooking, the First Fifty Years, 1931–1981,* afterword by Ethan Becker and Mark Becker (Indianapolis: Bobbs-Merrill, 1981);

Wild Wealth, by Becker, Paul Bigelow Sears, and Frances Jones Poetker, illustrated by Janice Rebert Forberg (Indianapolis: Bobbs-Merrill, 1971).

Related Letters

Vice president and trade-department editor D. Laurance Chambers met Rombauer at an Indianapolis dinner party in 1932. He politely agreed to look at a revision of her 1931 cookbook and handed the matter over to associate editor Jessica Brown Mannon. She secured three readers, one of whose reports along with Mannon's comments appear in facsimile in the DLB Yearbook, 1990, *pp. 147–150. After the initial rejection of the book, details are sketchy, but following two more revisions it was accepted in 1935.*

D. Laurance Chambers to Irma Rombauer, 23 February 1933

Dear Mrs. Rombauer:

After studying your cookbook and the additional new manuscript with the greatest of care, we have regretfully come to the conclusion that it would be a mistake for us to attempt to take over its publication now. It is a most humiliating confession to make, but we feel that you yourself have done well with the book and that we would only disappoint you with our efforts.

The new manner of arranging the recipes found much favor with our readers, especially with those who were less experienced cooks. And all of them, after trying out a few recipes, agreed that the arrangement was a convenience and help. I had hoped that with this selling point in our favor, we could see our way clear toward undertaking the new edition, for there is no question about the quality of the recipes themselves. But the true fact of the matter is that the book trade is in such a low state that we could not get any wider distribution for THE JOY OF COOKING than you are doing without our help.

It is a disappointment to us all that we cannot have the book on our fall list and I return the manuscript with our most cordial thanks for your courtesy and patience, and my sincere personal regards.

Cordially yours,
[D. Laurance Chambers]

* * *

Mannon learned to cook by testing Rombauer's recipes in her kitchen. Mina Kersey was on the editorial staff.

Rombauer to Jessica Brown Mannon, 9 December 1935

Dear Mrs. Mannon

In the first place, do not hesitate to send me any criticism whatever. I shall welcome it if it is constructive and promp[t]ly reject it if it is not, but at no time will there be a trace of personal feeling about it. You, Mr. Chambers, Mrs. Kersey and I are all working toward as good a cookbook as we can produce. Let's hope it will be a great success. I have asked a number of people of discernment about the comments. All asked that they be retained. As for cutting the book, let me know about that when you send the proof. I cannot well cut anything from the first two volumes of the manuscript, but may be able to do so from then on if necessary.

As to the servings given, they are sometimes determined by the ingredients used, as in the case of the chicken soufflé. That is the amount to be made with an average stewing chicken, but usually the servings have been calculated after the recipe has been written–that makes for their irregularity. In soups and sauces it is possible to reckon them in cups. On the whole they are based on a family of four but as appetites vary it is hard to determine just what constitutes a serving. Many peo[p]le have expressed them selves as pleased with the comparatively small amounts of ingredients called for.

It might have been wise to have tried to make them all for the same number of persons, but it seems to me that any intelligent person can increase or decrease the recipes with ease. Throughout the book I give instructions (how to divide one egg, how to guard against over-seasoning when doubling a recipe, etc.) Every attempt has been made to guide and assist the novice.

The book buyer at Marshall Field told me voluntarily that he liked my "approach to my subject" because it was easy and I made it inviting. (This was two years ago. I wish I knew his name for I could then ask for a written recommendation).

A number of such letters are on their way to Mr. Chambers. How many are needed? I have asked eight or ten people to send one and all expressed themselves as glad to do it.

My photographic proofs have come but unfortunately they are impossible, so mournful that no one would connect so dejected a countenance with anything joyful! I must try again. Perhaps I was too tired after my Indianapolis rush.

This is not a good letter. I have been in town all day winding up my Christmas purchases and other affairs so as to be ready for work on the proof when it comes.

Please forgive me, but I like to answer your communications at once, and am not waiting in this instance until I am rested. With greetings to you.

Yours,
Irma S. Rombauer

* * *

Rombauer to Mina Kersey, 16 December 1935

Dear Miss Kersey

Having consulted several French menus and the professor of French at the university I regret to say that I

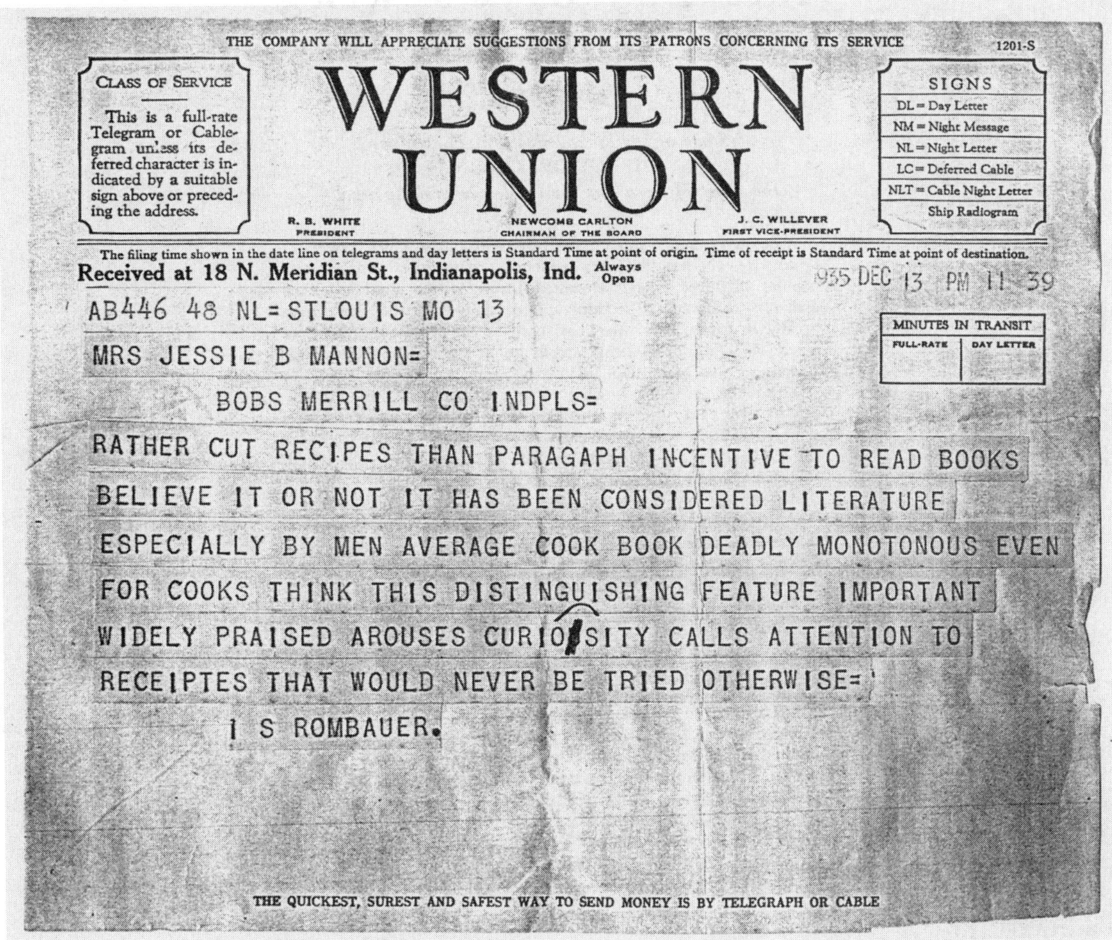

THE COMPANY WILL APPRECIATE SUGGESTIONS FROM ITS PATRONS CONCERNING ITS SERVICE 1201-S

CLASS OF SERVICE
This is a full-rate Telegram or Cablegram unless its deferred character is indicated by a suitable sign above or preceding the address.

WESTERN UNION

R. B. WHITE PRESIDENT — NEWCOMB CARLTON CHAIRMAN OF THE BOARD — J. C. WILLEVER FIRST VICE-PRESIDENT

SIGNS
DL = Day Letter
NM = Night Message
NL = Night Letter
LC = Deferred Cable
NLT = Cable Night Letter
Ship Radiogram

The filing time shown in the date line on telegrams and day letters is Standard Time at point of origin. Time of receipt is Standard Time at point of destination.

Received at 18 N. Meridian St., Indianapolis, Ind. Always Open 1935 DEC 13 PM 11 39

MINUTES IN TRANSIT — FULL-RATE — DAY LETTER

AB446 48 NL=STLOUIS MO 13
MRS JESSIE B MANNON=
BOBS MERRILL CO INDPLS=
RATHER CUT RECIPES THAN PARAGAPH INCENTIVE TO READ BOOKS
BELIEVE IT OR NOT IT HAS BEEN CONSIDERED LITERATURE
ESPECIALLY BY MEN AVERAGE COOK BOOK DEADLY MONOTONOUS EVEN
FOR COOKS THINK THIS DISTINGUISHING FEATURE IMPORTANT
WIDELY PRAISED AROUSES CURIOSITY CALLS ATTENTION TO
RECEIPTES THAT WOULD NEVER BE TRIED OTHERWISE=
I S ROMBAUER.

THE QUICKEST, SUREST AND SAFEST WAY TO SEND MONEY IS BY TELEGRAPH OR CABLE

Rombauer's 13 December 1935 reply to suggestions by editor Jessica Brown Mannon (courtesy of The Lilly Library, Indiana University, Bloomington, Indiana)

am right. Hors d'oeuvre have no final s. They will have to come out. Too bad, but I do want my French right.

Yours sincerely
Irma S. Rombauer

* * *

Chambers became president of the company in 1935. Keller is unidentified.

Chambers to Rombauer, 31 December 1935

Dear Mrs. Rombauer:–

Thank you for your letter of the 30th. I note that you report some confusion as to type. Every detail of the type arrangement was discussed with you when you were in Indianapolis and if the printer has failed to follow instructions it is his mistake and he must stand the expense of correction.

You will understand that my estimate of the total cost of original composition and of the 15% allowance was only approximate. The printer's actual figures when the work is done will have to govern.

I do not understand what you mean by "our errors". We are publishers, not printers. Any errors made by the printer are carefully marked by us and he is expected to correct them at his own expense.

I would expect you to exercise the same care in indicating corrections as you would if the entire amount

The Joy of Cooking

By IRMA S. ROMBAUER

Some of the Special Features That Make
THE JOY OF COOKING
the Most Modern and Desirable General Cookbook

A new convenient and wonderfully clear and succinct *method of writing recipes* has been worked out. It has proved immediately popular wherever it has been tested. Instead of the usual list of ingredients followed by a paragraph of directions, the ingredients become a part of the directions, each at the right point without repetition, and yet by being set in bold type they stand out for assembling. No other standard cookbook has this feature.

This is the only book which gives, in addition to the time for baking, *the size of the pan* in which cakes are to be baked. Yet this is a most important point in successful cake-baking. The best recipes are not failure-proof unless the size of the pan to be used be stated. Mrs. Rombauer has been the first to offer this service.

An entirely *new method of cooking meat* sponsored by certain modern packers, is given, in addition to the standard method. It is simple, time-saving, economical and has outstanding results.

Rules for using an electric mixer, which every modern housewife owns or expects to own, are scattered throughout the book.

A great many recipes in this book draw attention to *the use of left-over food.* Charts of suggestions are given. This is a feature that no other cookbook has given sufficient attention and it solves an ever-present problem confronting the careful manager.

The book contains a chapter on the making of alcoholic *cocktails,* a chapter on the correct serving of *wines.*

For the convenience of the efficiency housekeeper there are a number of *uncooked desserts,* listed separately.

Through a long foreign residence, the author is well acquainted with *foreign foods.* Many of these have been Americanized to suit the purposes of our table.

640 *pages,* 8vo (6" x 9"), *fully indexed and cross-referenced, every copy guaranteed*

Advertising copy for the first Bobbs-Merrill edition of Rombauer's cookbook, published in 1936 (courtesy of The Lilly Library, Indiana University, Bloomington, Indiana)

were to be charged to you. It is the publishers' expectation that the author will do all his correcting in the copy before the copy is delivered to him. The leeway of 15% which the publishers assume is not by any means intended to encourage an author to make corrections to the full amount of that limit, or anything like it.

There is no occasion for you to keep track of printer's errors. We do that.

Mr. Keller insists that he cannot be mistaken about his consulting you with reference both to setting the titles flush with the margins and following them immediately with the number of servings.

To change them now involves far more correction than you seem to think. We know from our own careful checking of all the material now in type.

Sincerely yours,
[D. Laurance Chambers]

* * *

Mannon to Rombauer, 2 January 1936

Dear Mrs. Rombauer:

Thank you for your letter of yesterday which I am acknowledging as Mr. Chambers has gone on to New York for the salesmen's semi-annual conference.

We are going ahead with the composition of THE JOY OF COOKING keeping the titles flush with the margin, but putting the servings on a separate line underneath. They will also be flush with the margin.

The sample pulled pages that Mr. Chambers sent you had not been proof read and that accounts for the errors you found. The printer, of course, pays for all his errors.

I have consulted Miss Kersey and she thinks that you should continue to make such improvements in the galleys as you feel are necessary. I know you will watch the expense. Miss Kersey says that the corrections you have made on the returned galleys have not been exces-

The Joy of Cooking

IRMA S. ROMBAUER

A Compilation of Reliable Recipes with a Casual Culinary Chat

Illustrations

MARION ROMBAUER

THE JOY OF COOKING

by

IRMA S. ROMBAUER

A Compilation of Reliable Recipes with a Casual Culinary Chat

Illustrations by

MARION ROMBAUER BECKER

THE BOBBS-MERRILL COMPANY
Publishers
INDIANAPOLIS NEW YORK

Title pages for the privately printed 1931 edition and the first Bobbs-Merrill edition of Rombauer's cookbook, which became the company's all-time best-selling trade book (courtesy of The Lilly Library, Indiana University, Bloomington, Indiana)

sive. Of course we hope you will not find many instances where alterations are necessary.

Today I ordered an electric range for the home my husband and I are building and I hope to talk to the cabinet maker about the arrangement for the kitchen this weekend. I keep thinking of you and wishing you were here so that I could bother you for advice! It is all a great thrill to me since I've never had a kitchen of my own before and I dream about all the lovely things I'll cook from your book once we are settled there! (Then I'll write you the most gorgeous testimonial you've had yet.) On the noon mail I sent a special delivery letter to New York about THE JOY OF COOKING for Mr. Chambers to read to the salesmen and in that I tried to express my enthusiasm for the book. But it is hard to put into written words the warmth of feeling that a woman has for her home and cooking, after all, is a large part of a woman's home life, whether she does it herself or merely supervises it. You've caught the spirit in your book and that is why I think it is the greatest cook book ever written.

I'm wishing you all joy and success in 1936.

Cordially yours,
[Jessica Mannon]

* * *

The friends Rombauer mentions in the following letter were Mazie Whyte (later Hartrich) and Laura Corbitt.

Rombauer to Mannon, 27 April 1936

Dear Mrs. Mannon

Today as Miss Whyte, an intimate friend (Mrs. Corbitt) and I were having lunch in my house the cook-book arrived.

Nothing could have been nicer. We have come together so frequently to discuss the manuscript and the details of its publication, and now we have had the pleasure of a pre-view together and all to ourselves.

Thank you so much for your many kindnesses.

I am very happy about the book. I like its appearance, its fine, clearly typed index and its good print. These are just a few of its good points. You have made a good job of it and I shall find more to say shortly.

At present I am writing in haste so that this will reach you to-morrow.

I appreciate all you have done in the past months.

Yours gratefully,
Irma S. R.

* * *

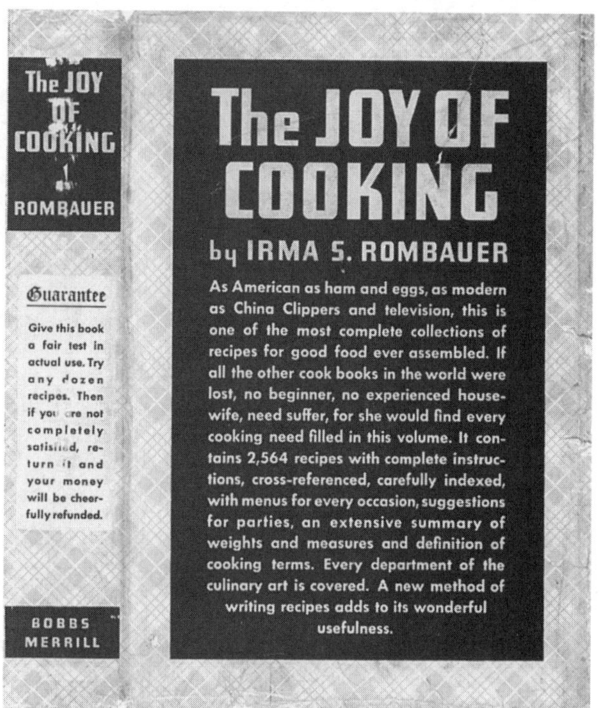

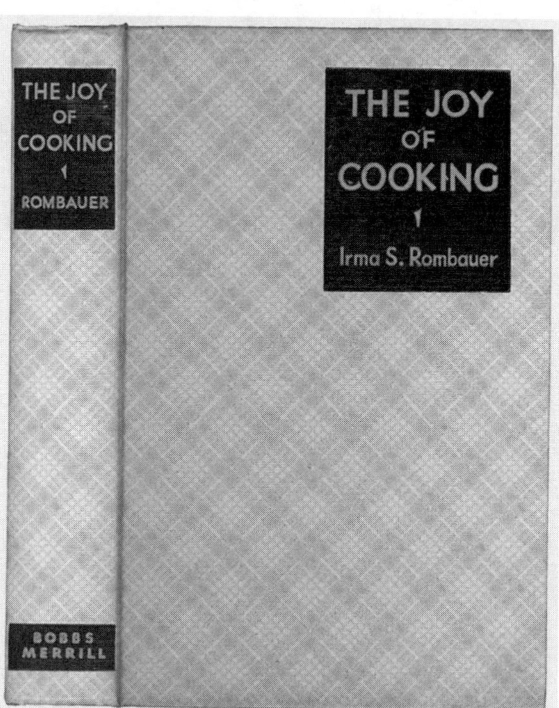

Dust jacket and binding of the first Bobbs-Merrill edition of Rombauer's cookbook (courtesy of The Lilly Library, Indiana University, Bloomington, Indiana)

Bobbs-Merrill staffer Jean Shrawder sent out a promotional letter for Rombauer's Streamlined Cooking *(1939).*

Jean Shrawder to program managers, 28 April 1939

Dear Program Manager;

We are soon [t]o publish a very unusual sort of cook book, written by the author of the famous JOY OF COOKING. The new book, STREAMLINED COOKING, is written expressly for the modern woman and concerns itself almost entirely with canned and packaged foods. The style of the book will be delightfully informal; the recipes will carry a money-back guarantee covering any failure.

Naturally, we are anxious to publicize STREAMLINED COOKING in every possible way, and are endeavoring to reach the American woman by newspaper, magazine and radio.

No doubt your station has at least one culinary expert who broadcasts commercial or sustaining programs locally on cooking. We would like very much to bring STREAMLINED COOKING to the attention of these experts in some way–send them a book if they are sufficiently interested in it–and would appreciate it a lot if you would tell us whether or not you have such a person on your staff, and how many programs on cookery she broadcasts. The enclosed envelope is for your answer. Thank you for your trouble.

Very sincerely,

[Jean Shrawder]

THE BOBBS MERRILL COMPANY

Zola Helen Ross (1912–1989)

Zola Helen Ross was born in Iowa and lived in the Northwest. She taught creative writing at the University of Washington and adult education in Kirkland, Washington. Her first three books for Bobbs-Merrill were mysteries (published under the name Z. H. Ross); the rest were westerns, for which she is best known. Generally, they feature strong women who, after many perils, manage to move from the wrong to the right man and also find their own strengths. With Lucile Saunders McDonald, Ross wrote several juvenile novels as well. She was cofounder of the Pacific Northwest Writers Association. In 2003 their annual literary contest became known as the Zola Awards, in honor of a writer and instructor "whose students went on to publish hundreds of novels."

BOBBS-MERRILL BOOKS BY ROSS: *Three Down Vulnerable: A Beau and Pogy Murder Mystery* (Indianapolis: Bobbs-Merrill, 1946);

Overdue for Death (Indianapolis: Bobbs-Merrill, 1947);

One Corpse Missing: A Beau and Pogy Murder Mystery (Indianapolis: Bobbs-Merrill, 1948);

Bonanza Queen: A Novel of the Comstock Lode (Indianapolis: Bobbs-Merrill, 1949; London: P. Huston, 1951);

Tonopah Lady (Indianapolis: Bobbs-Merrill, 1950);

Reno Crescent (Indianapolis: Bobbs-Merrill, 1951);

The Green Land (Indianapolis: Bobbs-Merrill, 1952);

Zola Helen Ross (courtesy of Ron Miazga and Sharyn Bolton)

THREE DOWN VULNERABLE

In the dark mountains of Nevada lies Lost Canyon Camp, a collection of thirteen shacks that a philanthropist has turned over for the use of actors out of work. Nobody ever thought of its being used except in summer. But when Beau Smith and Pogy Rogers, Reno private detectives, drive up through a winter snowstorm in answer to an SOS call from Calla Larkin they find nine actors hugging the stoves in the ramshackle cabins, uneasy, nervous and distrustful of one another, but apparently waiting for something—just what not even Calla Larkin wants to say.

Beau and Pogy are city people, at home where there are lights and traffic. The crouching mountains make them feel trapped in the canyon. The slippery, snow-choked road, the wind blowing more snow out of the low, thick clouds depress them and make them eager for the drinks Calla serves.

If the actors are waiting for something, they don't have long to wait. In the early evening, when Beau gets more wood for the stove in Calla's cabin he finds a body stuffed into the wood box. The curtain is up on a grim drama in the camp, but the cast is not yet complete. Beau bucks through the snow to the nearest town and brings back Sheriff Green and his deputy. Then the driving storm seals off the camp.

Now there are thirteen, of whom one is dead. Four of them are manhunters. One of them is a

(Continued on back flap)

(Continued from front flap)

murderer. The other seven are possible victims. Like Beau and Pogy, they are city people, out of place and uncomfortable in the canyon camp.

They resist being protected. They have to go for wood. They have to go to the camp's only well for water. They visit one another in search of drinks or just for company. Like perverse sheep they insist on putting themselves in jeopardy in spite of all the Sheriff's efforts to keep them out of danger. They are strangely vulnerable. They lay themselves wide open to the killer. Though they are second-rate actors, they are good enough at concealing their thoughts to make Green complain that he can't tell when they are lying. And they all have something to conceal.

Little by little, under Green's bludgeoning and Pogy's sharp questions, they let out bits of truth. Pieced together with Pogy's shrewd guesses, they begin to take form for her. She divines the killer's danger, the reason why he must kill. Meanwhile he has struck again. She knows his need but she does not know his face. When he strikes a third time she resolves on a bluff and takes a long chance.

Z. H. Ross builds a spine-chilling atmosphere out of the howling wind, the relentless snow, the mountains crouching over the bleak shacks in the remote canyon. Against the darkness the bright dialogue, the brisk characters of Beau and Pogy and the well-defined personalities of the actors make a contrast easy to take. Pogy Rogers and Beau Smith are a pair of sleuths that will be heard from again—with pleasure.

MAY 25 1946

Copy for the dust jacket of Ross's first Bobbs-Merrill novel, published in 1946 (courtesy of The Lilly Library, Indiana University, Bloomington, Indiana)

Cassy Scandal (Indianapolis: Bobbs-Merrill, 1954; London: A. Redman, 1956);

The Golden Witch (Indianapolis: Bobbs-Merrill, 1955; London: A. Redman, 1956);

A Land to Tame (Indianapolis: Bobbs-Merrill, 1956; London: A. Redman, 1957);

Spokane Saga: A Novel of a Rebuilding of a City Destroyed (Indianapolis: Bobbs-Merrill, 1957; London: A. Redman, 1959).

Reader's Report

Mary Kaye Platt submitted the following report (circa 1947) on the manuscript that was published as Overdue for Death *(1947).*

NO POCKETS IN A SHROUD
(Revised)
by
Zola Helen Ross

This is a darn good revision. The author has not only clarified the plot by eradicating all the main flaws, but has intensified her style, thereby strengthening the entire manuscript.

The code has been handled pretty adeptly. The author has made its existence plausible by emphasizing it as the quixotic notion of a quixotic mind. As it stands now, the simple code is easily cracked by the police. From there on in, it's Penny's baby and, with her special knowledge, she eventually interprets its meaning. It is so much simpler and cleaner this way and the author has done it with such ease that I have to keep pinching myself as a reminder that there was once a problem.

The traced phone call I objected to before is out of the revision at no loss to the manuscript.

Jamie's character as a whole remains unchanged. But, by building up his ineptitude in affairs of the heart and by underplaying his business acumen, the author has turned his duplicity into simplicity. He is both a stronger and a more believable character now and, strangely, this both reduces and emphasizes the possibility of his being the murderer. He is both harder to guess and more plausible for the part.

The thing that pleases me most about the revision is the minimization of the heroine's purposeful efforts to walk into unseen blows on the head. The first one is completely revised. It is now a quite accidental meeting with danger instead of an aforethought one. The other one is still headed for knowingly, but the heroine takes the precaution of protection in the form of Gus, the cab-driver. As this scene furnishes the climax, it is necessary that it be dramatic. So necessary that the climax would be anticlimax handled any other way.

This is really a very tight job of revising. The plot remains unchanged, but there's nothing makeshift about it. It's amazing how a few words changed here and a paragraph left out there can make a fuzzy manuscript a whole neat piece.

I don't think any more revision is necessary, though a blue pencil line every now and then won't hurt it.

To my own surprise, I liked this better on second reading.

Mary Kaye Platt

Dust jacket for Ross's 1950 novel (The Bookworm, Oroville, Cal.)

* * *

Related Letter

Ross responded at length to a reader's request for advice on performing research.

Zola Helen Ross to Miss Throckmorton, 27 December 1949

Dear Miss Throckmorton:

Thanks for your letter of December 19th. Frankly, it horrifies me, but I'll do my best. The trouble is that I never have any wild experiences with research. I just spend hours and days and weeks ploughing through old newspapers–I went through Tonopah and Goldfield papers for the space of about seven years each and through Reno ones for about the same length of time. Nevada folks were most cooperative–after they found out I wasn't bent on writing a divorce novel. A writer in Nevada after divorce material is about as popular as an avowed Communist at a Republican rally. But if you're writing about boom towns, they're wonderful to you. Edward Castagna, of the Washoe County Library, was most helpful. (Incidentally, he reviewed BONANZA QUEEN for the Reno and Virginia City papers.) Doctor Jeanne Eliazabeth [*sic*] Weir, of the Nevada State Historical Society, was also invaluable. Professor Semanza of the University of Nevada helped me a great deal, too. And scores of other folks really gave me helping hands on all sides. After folks got over the notion I was in Reno for "the cure", everything went smoothly.

Of course, I had a very warm feeling for Nevada in general and boom towns in particular. I had spent a lot of time when I was younger, listening to my father pursue his favorite hobby–collecting tales about Virginia City, Tonopah, Goldfield and other mining camps that rose, boomed, and died. Tonopah, of course, wasn't really dead as the others were, and, to me, that made it more exciting.

I suppose Judith Southard, my lead character, was born when I listened to my father and another man argue years ago about following in your ancestor's footsteps. My father said, "At eighteen, you're sure you'll correct all your ancestors' mistakes, and the first step is to divorce yourself from anything they ever did. At thirty, you usually find yourself fitting your feet into the prints of one ancestor or another." Judith had that notion at eighteen, and I tried to write a book about whether or not she could divorce herself as she wanted to do.

About the only thing I can think of to say about research is that research on any subject leaves you with a lot of hanging threads on which you want to do more research. Detective business. You find out something about Tonopah and it leads to questions about Goldfield, Bullfrog, etc.

Looking back over this, Miss Throckmorton, I doubt very much if any of this is any good at all to you. Maybe if you'd ask me some specific questions, I might do better. As it [is] now, all I can say is that I think for research you must have a very partisan, warm feeling for your subject; you have to resign yourself to reading reams to acquire a paragraph worth a hoot to you; then you have to watch that the petticoat of your research doesn't show through your story and make the machinery creak. I had the first–I love stock companies, show folks; I read the reams; about the petticoat, I still don't know.

If you think of anything special, let me know. Best wishes for a fine holiday season.

Sincerely yours,
Helen Ross

P. S. One facet of my research was a bit unusual. When I did research in Nevada last summer, the cooks, waiters, bartenders took that time to go on strike. Now while you can do research without bartenders, it is rough doing it on an empty stomach. However, I had a bit of Nevada luck. A woman who kept divorce candidates was "fresh out of the last one and the other one wouldn't be around for a spell". So she kept me and fed me beautifully while most of the hotel and rooming house people were driving miles to acquire food other than coffee and doughnuts. Temporarily, I had a fellow feeling for the folks who had trouble getting supplies into Tonopah, before and during the epidemic.

Limitation page for the special edition of Ross's 1956 novel (courtesy of The Lilly Library, Indiana University, Bloomington, Indiana)

Arthur Stringer (1874–1950)

See also the Stringer entry in *DLB 92: Canadian Writers, 1890–1920.*

Arthur Stringer may well have had more titles on the Bobbs-Merrill list than anyone else except James Whitcomb Riley. The company was the American (and sometimes sole) publisher of works by this prolific native of Ontario. His first book for the firm was the beginning of the trilogy for which Canadians best remember him: The Prairie Wife *(1915), which was followed by* The Prairie Mother *(1920) and* The Prairie Child *(1922). In a writing career that began with the* Montreal Herald, *Stringer published more than forty novels and fifteen books of poetry. He also contributed work regularly to magazines and wrote for the stage and screen. (He even contributed to the famous 1914 silent-movie serial* The Perils of Pauline.*) Stringer became adept at turning out popular novels with sentimental themes, but in the Prairie trilogy he showed that he could rise above romance formulas. His last book for Bobbs-Merrill was nonfiction, a 1948 biography of Rupert Brooke based on materials gathered by Richard Halliburton. Stringer moved to New Jersey in 1921 and became an American citizen in 1937.*

Arthur Stringer (Bruccoli Clark Layman Archives)

BOBBS-MERRILL BOOKS BY STRINGER: *The Prairie Wife* (Indianapolis: Bobbs-Merrill, 1915; London: Hodder & Stoughton, 1921);

The Door of Dread: A Secret Service Romance (Indianapolis: Bobbs-Merrill, 1916; London: Amalgamated Press, 1935);

The House of Intrigue (Indianapolis: Bobbs-Merrill, 1918);

The Man Who Couldn't Sleep (Indianapolis: Bobbs-Merrill, 1919);

The Prairie Mother (Indianapolis: Bobbs-Merrill, 1920; London: Hodder & Stoughton, 1920);

Twin Tales: Are All Men Alike? and The Lost Titian (Indianapolis: Bobbs-Merrill, 1921);

The Prairie Child (Indianapolis: Bobbs-Merrill, 1922; London: Hodder & Stoughton, 1923);

The Diamond Thieves (Indianapolis: Bobbs-Merrill, 1923; London: Hodder & Stoughton, 1925);

Empty Hands (Indianapolis: Bobbs-Merrill, 1924; London: Hodder & Stoughton, 1924);

Power (Indianapolis: Bobbs-Merrill, 1925);

In Bad With Sinbad (Indianapolis: Bobbs-Merrill, 1926);

White Hands (Indianapolis: Bobbs-Merrill, 1927);

The Wolf Woman (Indianapolis: Bobbs-Merrill, 1928; London: Stanley Paul, 1929);

A Woman at Dusk, and Other Poems (Indianapolis: Bobbs-Merrill, 1928);

Cristina and I (Indianapolis: Bobbs-Merrill, 1929);

The Woman Who Couldn't Die (Indianapolis: Bobbs-Merrill, 1929);

A Lady Quite Lost (Indianapolis: Bobbs-Merrill, 1931; London: Stanley Paul, 1931);

The Mud Lark (Indianapolis: Bobbs-Merrill, 1932; London: Readers Library, 1932);

Dark Soil (Indianapolis: Bobbs-Merrill, 1933);

Marriage by Capture (Indianapolis: Bobbs-Merrill, 1933; London: Methuen, 1934);

Man Lost (Indianapolis: Bobbs-Merrill, 1934);
The Wife Traders: A Tale of the North (Indianapolis: Bobbs-Merrill, 1936);
Heather of the High Hand: A Novel of the North (Indianapolis: Bobbs-Merrill, 1937);
The Lamp in the Valley: A Novel of Alaska (Indianapolis: Bobbs-Merrill, 1938);
The Old Woman Remembers, and Other Irish Poems (Indianapolis: Bobbs-Merrill, 1938);
The Cleverest Woman in the World, and Other One-Act Plays (Indianapolis: Bobbs-Merrill, 1939);
The Dark Wing (Indianapolis: Bobbs-Merrill, 1939);
The Ghost Plane: A Novel of the North (Indianapolis: Bobbs-Merrill, 1940);
The King Who Loved Old Clothes, and Other Irish Poems (Indianapolis: Bobbs-Merrill, 1941);
Intruders in Eden (Indianapolis: Bobbs-Merrill, 1942);
Shadowed Victory (Indianapolis: Bobbs-Merrill, 1943; London: Hodder & Stoughton, 1944);
Star in a Mist (Indianapolis: Bobbs-Merrill, 1943);
The Devastator (Indianapolis: Bobbs-Merrill, 1944);
Red Wine of Youth: A Life of Rupert Brooke (Indianapolis: Bobbs-Merrill, 1948).

Related Letters

Paul R. Reynolds was a literary agent. Hewitt H. Howland was trade-department editor in chief, and John J. Curtis managed the New York office.

Paul R. Reynolds to Hewitt H. Howland, 18 March 1915

Dear Mr. Howland:

As I have told Mr. Curtis, Mr. Stringer is willing to accept your offer of five hundred dollars ($500.00) on a ten per cent royalty for "The Prairie Wife". He wishes, however, to reserve his dramatic rights. Mr. Curtis spoke to me about your having the first offer of the next book, and I told him that I thought Mr. Stringer would agree to this. He also said he would like to have Mr. Stringer do the additional work on the manuscript at once, and I am writing Stringer to this effect.

Will you kindly confirm this arrangement?

Yours sincerely,
Paul R. Reynolds

* * *

I stooped over the trap-door and lifted it up "Get down there quick!" Page 109 The Prairie Wife.

THE
PRAIRIE WIFE

By
ARTHUR STRINGER

INDIANAPOLIS
THE BOBBS-MERRILL COMPANY
PUBLISHERS

Frontispiece and title page for the first novel in Stringer's Prairie trilogy, published in 1915 (Thomas Cooper Library, University of South Carolina)

The Bernhardt in question was Carl Bernhardt.

Howland to Reynolds, 20 March 1915

My dear Mr. Reynolds:

Your letter of the eighteenth with regard to the Prairie Wife has just been received. I am glad we are going to be able to publish this story, though its serialization in The Saturday Evening Post gives me a good deal of uneasiness. The addition of ten thousand words isn't going to remove this handicap by any means. The readers of The Post got the substance out of [the] story as it appeared there and they are going to be very loathe to pay real money for additional embroidery. Under all the circumstances, I feel Mr. Stringer should be willing to put the dramatic rights in our hands. I believe if you will have a talk with Mr. Bernhardt at the New York office, who is in charge of our dramatic affairs, that you will feel disposed to urge Mr. Stringer to sign our uniform contract. I am writing Mr. Curtis to-day who, having initiated the negotiations, will have to close them, and I very much hope you will be able to get together on terms mutually agreeable.

Very sincerely yours,
[Hewitt H. Howland]

* * *

Copy of a telegram.

John J. Curtis to Howland, 22 March 1915

If agreeable send contract here for Stringer stating that additional manuscript must be acceptable. He has already negotiated dramatic rights. Better see if you can't get Stringer to come to Indianapolis or go and see him and get the dramatic rights away from him. His address is Cedar Springs, Ontario.

J. J. CURTIS

* * *

Reynolds to Howland, 21 April 1915

Dear Mr. Howland:–

I am enclosing contract in duplicate for "The Prairie Wife" signed by Mr. Stringer. You will note changes in clauses one, two and five which have been initialled by Mr. Stringer. If these are satisfactory to you will you kindly initial each of these clauses before returning the one copy of the contract to me for Mr. Stringer?

Under separate cover I am sending you the revised copy of "The Prairie Wife". Mr. Stringer has added more than the ten thousand words you suggested. If the manuscript is now satisfactory will you kindly add a line to the contract or write me a letter stating that the manuscript as revised is approved and accepted by you?

It has been impossible for Mr. Stringer to preserve a second copy of the alterations so he would like to have the manuscript kept as safely as possible.

Very truly yours,
Paul R. Reynolds

* * *

"According to gunter" means "quite correct" and refers to the distinguished Renaissance English mathematician Edmund Gunter.

Reynolds to Howland, 3 September 1919

Dear Howland:

I have a new story by Arthur Stringer which I sold serially to Hearst's Magazine and which is running there now. I wish you would let me know how you feel

That gink
called Alexander Pope
was a poor guesser.
The proper study of
mankind is woman!
The
PRAIRIE
WIFE
The Prairie Wife
By Arthur Stringer
Illustrated in Full Color
By H. T. Dunn, $1.25 Net
The Bobbs-Merrill Company
Publishers, Indianapolis

Promotional item quoting from the first novel in the Prairie trilogy (courtesy of The Lilly Library, Indiana University, Bloomington, Indiana)

about Stringer. He is not very well satisfied. He thinks he ought to get a larger advance. I have had applications from one or two houses here in New York for this book. I don't want if I can help it to do anything which you think is not according to gunter but on the other hand, I am here to satisfy the author. Write me frankly how you feel.

This book could not come out till next year but I would like to be arranging for it at once.

Yours sincerely
Paul R. Reynolds

* * *

At the top of the following letter is a note from Howland to Bobbs-Merrill president William C. Bobbs dated 8 September: "Think you have the other letter."

Reynolds to Howland, 6 September 1919

Dear Howland:

I shall have shortly another book in hand called "The Prairie Mother" which is a sequel to "The Prairie Wife". I have already sold this story serially to the Pictorial Review. I could sell you both books if we could make a satisfactory arrangement. If you would pay me an advance of fifteen hundred dollars on each book I think that would be satisfactory.

This supplements my letter written to you about the other story which is running in Hearst's.

Yours faithfully
Paul R. Reynolds & Arthur Stringer
[in Reynolds's hand]

* * *

William C. Bobbs to Howland, 10 September 1919

Notwithstanding the record on the last three books the house is for Springer [*sic*] and we want to keep him. But a jump from 750 to 1500 per takes some Spring.
Perhaps the ans is to ask to see the MSS.

WCB

* * *

Howland to Reynolds, 11 September 1919

Dear Reynolds:

We are, all of us, strong for Stringer and feeling as we do we want him to stay with us and we want to satisfy him if we possibly can. I haven't read any of the new story running in Hearst's because I would much rather take it as a whole in manuscript form. Can't you send it on to me? I am delighted to hear that he has written The Prairie Mother. We ought to do big things with it. I take it from your letter that this manuscript isn't quite ready. Please don't think of letting him go anywhere else.

Faithfully yours,
[Hewitt H. Howland]

* * *

The A. L. Burt Company and Grosset and Dunlap were reprint houses. Arthur T. Vance edited the Pictorial Review.

Arthur Stringer to Howland, 13 September 1919

My Dear Mr. Howland:–

I have just finished revising, for prospective book-publication, the script of "The Prairie Mother", a sequel to "The Prairie Wife", which will appear serially in the February (1920), March, April, and May numbers of The Pictorial Review. This novel, I understand, Mr. Paul Reynolds will very shortly be sending on to you, along with "This Light Must Live", which will complete serialization in the March or April (1920) issues of "Hearst's Magazine". The latter script, indeed, may already be in your hands. I should like to place the two books with the same publisher. The publisher of "The Prairie Mother", I need scarcely add, should be the publisher of "The Prairie Wife", or vice versa if you prefer it. I think I have two popular successes in these stories, especially so with "This Light Must Live", though there's no use enumerating the signs which point that way. If you don't agree with me, of course, your house is not the house to handle the book. And I don't wish in any way to infringe on Mr. Reynolds['s] prerogatives or duties, but I'm writing to you directly to point out that there has been one phase of my last two novels which has been disappointing to me, and that is the Canadian end of the business. I know personally Mr. George McLeod, who takes over your books in Canada, and he is a very charming gentleman. But I think that my contention that he is deficient in 'pep' (or altogether too much preoccupied with his more lucrative Burt and D & G [*sic*] reprint business) is evidenced by the fact that although I am a Canadian with a so-called Canadian following, "The Man Who Couldn't Sleep" hasn't received a single review from any newspaper, magazine, or weekly in this Dominion of Canada. When I wrote to Mr. McLeod on this matter, he replied explaining that your house had overlooked sending copies of the novel for review-distribution, though he had sent out three copies to three Toronto papers, on his own hook. And there the matter was, apparently, permitted to rest. The possibilities of the Canadian market, of course, are not large, though the neglect of the home field is a factor in discontent, and I've been wondering just how closely your Canadian editions–or shipments–are tied up with McLeod, and, should we come to terms, if it's possible for me to withold [*sic*] the Canadian edition and take it to a Toronto publisher I had reason to expect to be more aggressive in the matter.

It will be still some time before I can learn your decision on the two books I mention, which go to you first, I believe, because of an earlier contract–and perhaps, when I'm in New York in October, I may have the good fortune to see you personally, which is much more satisfactory in any such discussion. I might add, in the meantime, that next year I intend doing "The Prairie Child" for Vance of The Pictorial, which will, of course, exalt me to the beatitudes of the trilogists!

With every good wish,
Very sincerely,
Arthur Stringer

* * *

The "something more" was perhaps alcohol, soon to be prohibited by the Volstead Act.

Howland to Stringer, 16 September 1919

My dear Mr. Stringer:

I was glad to get your good letter of the 13th, confirming word already received from Reynolds. We are enthusiastic over the prospect of The Prairie Mother and I am eager to read This Light Must Live. I haven't indulged myself in a word of it as it has appeared in the magazine because I much prefer to take my fiction in unbroken doses. Because you are enthusiastic–modestly so, of course–I am pretty certain to be also. I flatter myself we are not so far apart in taste and judgment.

I am glad you wrote us about the Canadian situation. What was done there is as great a disappointment to us as it is to you. Before we make any radical change, wouldn't you do well to advise us. Can't you give us the name of the right man over there? If you feel disposed to do this, I assure you we shall negotiate with him for your next book and confer with you before closing. Mr. McLeod's statement about the distribution of editorial copies in Canada is an eye-opener to me. I will write our New York office about it and get the facts and if possible, place the responsibility. It looks now as if I will be in New York in October when we can get together for a powwow and possibly something more although the law seems to be against it. Will you get in touch with me through our New York office.

The news that you are about to become a trilogist delights me greatly. There is nothing like doing the whole Prairie family, once you get started. This sounds flippant, but it isn't so intended. With all good wishes, as ever,

Faithfully yours,
[Hewitt H. Howland]

Design study for the second volume in the Prairie trilogy, published in 1920 (courtesy of The Lilly Library, Indiana University, Bloomington, Indiana)

SHADOWED VICTORY
AND OTHER ~~WAR~~ POEMS OF THE WAR
by
Arthur Stringer

This new collection of poems by Arthur Stringer is an interesting recording of the emotional effect of modern war upon a writer skilled in expressing in fresh and colorful words the age-old themes of life and fiction.

Shadowed Victory, the long narrative poem which dominates the book, is essentially a novel, told in the poetic form of smooth-flowing free verse -- a form that accentuates and reflects the emotional content of the narrative. It is, simply, the story of four young people whose destinies are suddenly reshaped by war. The story, concentrated and sharpened by the limitations of the verse, is simple in outline, yet it points up the more definitely the complexity of the emotions involved. This is an outline of its plot:

Clyde Barlow, the central figure, is a young farmer on the prairies of western Canada. He loves his land and his work, perhaps more passionately because they are bound up with his aspirations of success and his dreams of Lynn Lansdale, the girl he hopes someday to marry. When the second World War comes to Canada, Clyde can do nothing but remain on the farm and continue his work, since it is essential to the war effort, and his acres cannot be left to the care of his ailing old father. Soon after war is declared his father, who had settled the land, dies, leaving it as a precious heritage to Clyde. But the young man longs to enlist and fight, and he feels a sharp stab of jealousy when his friend Hugh Bidwell comes to say good-bye before he leaves for training in England. And Clyde's jealousy is intensified when Lynn tells him she has promised to drive Hugh to his train. He guesses what Hugh, who also loves the girl, will ask of her on this last night, and he knows that Lynn is too generous to deny Hugh. As he had unhappily foreseen, Lynn does yield herself to Hugh, and when she confesses to Clyde, his faith in her is destroyed.

While he bitterly tries to forget her by absorbing himself in his hard work, Lynn leaves Canada to join the WAACS in England. Clyde desperately works his farm alone, until one day a strong young blonde woman appears at his house and asks to work in his

Unsigned reader's report for Shadowed Victory, *published in 1943 (courtesy of The Lilly Library, Indiana University, Bloomington, Indiana)*

fields. She is Freya Earling, a Norwegian refugee whose parents had died in Canada, leaving her homeless now. She cares nothing for public opinion of her reputation, and is glad to work in Clyde's house and fields, in return for shelter. But as time goes on Clyde becomes more and more physically aware of her, and at last declares his feeling for her. After this revelation Freya insists that they cannot continue to live alone on the farm, and Clyde reluctantly asks her to marry him.

On their wedding night, however, Clyde is aroused by Lynn Lansdale's mother, bringing tragic news. Hugh, who had joined a Canadian unit of the Commandos, had taken part in the Dieppe raid. He had come through the raid unscathed, but on the boat returning to England he had been stabbed by a maddened German prisoner, and died at once. And Lynn, who had been sent to drive an ambulance to meet the wounded veterans, was the victim of an air raid. She has been blinded by flying shrapnel from the bomb that struck her ambulance.

When Lynn comes home to Canada she sends for Clyde, who goes unwillingly to see her. He knows she is still the woman he really loves, though fate has forced them apart and sentenced him to a life and marriage that will never satisfy his dreams and aspirations. His conquest of his land is, he realizes, a "shadowed victory" -- shadowed as his country victory, achieved at a bloody price.

* * *

This story is made more vivid and contemporary by its close relation to events of the war. The protagonists of Mr. Stringer's poem are simple and ordinary young people who meet tragedy through the dreadful agency of world-wide war. The elements of their story have been recorded before, in all generations in wartorn countries, but Mr. Stringe takes the opportunity to place them poignantly today against a simple and beautiful background of the great western prairies of the new world.

The narrative form in which the author has chosen to tell his story gives his verse-novel some particular advantages. In the short lyrics which precede each chapter he is able to set the emotional tone of the following lines. In the more sensuous medium of poetry he can suggest more forcefully and significantly the color and atmosphere and peac of Canada and an isolated little Devon town, and, in striking contrast, the bloody horror

3

of the Dieppe raid.

In simplifying his story to the demands of verse Mr. Stringer has achieved an emphasis and concentration on his characters that outline them more firmly against their poetic background than prose might have done. The tragic simplicity and timelessness of their story is brought out clearly in the lines of verse. Shadowed Victory is emphatically a story of today -- and yet its elements, the basic conflict of love and duty, are of ageless importance. Mr. Stringer's readers will find in this short but touching verse-novel a fresh and modern version of an ancient theme, told with his particular delicacy, in a new and thoroughly effective manner. His free verse, smooth and effortless, is perhaps the most appropriate means he could take of making his novel different and memorable.

The book is rounded out with twenty-[illegible] war poems that suggest various aspects of World War II. Shadowed Victory was inspired by the heroic Canadian participation in the war, but the short lyrics are wholly American, in both subject and feeling. Two, for instance, were inspired by the plane spotter's night watch along our seacoasts; others commemorate our Memorial Day services. Some are poetic reminders of the part we are playing in the Pacific theater of war, while "A Ghost Walks Valley Forge" recalls our war history. The variety of subjects Mr. Stringer has crystallized in poetry suggests, in fact, the many-faceted existence of modern war. Like the long narrative poem, these short lyrics show the poet's deep sensitivity to color and natural beauty, and his awareness of the poignancy often inherent in everyday details, but the brief poems are perhaps more purely emotional and personal in effect. All in all, the poems of this collection constitute the expression of a sensitive observer of the wartorn world today.

Cid Ricketts Sumner (1890–1970)

Bertha "Cid" Ricketts was born in Brookhaven, Mississippi. In 1915 she married James B. Sumner, who shared the 1946 Nobel Prize in chemistry several years after the couple's 1930 divorce. Of her many works of fiction and nonfiction, Sumner is best remembered for three Bobbs-Merrill publications that were turned into movies: Quality *(1946), adapted as* Pinky *(1949);* Tammy Out of Time *(1948), adapted as* Tammy and the Bachelor *(1957); and* Tammy, Tell Me True *(1959), filmed in 1961.* Pinky *was one of Hollywood's earliest attempts at an interracial theme. Produced by Darryl F. Zanuck and directed by Elia Kazan, the movie starred Jeanne Crain, Ethel Barrymore, and Ethel Waters, all of whom received Oscar nominations.*

BOBBS-MERRILL BOOKS BY SUMNER: *Quality* (Indianapolis: Bobbs-Merrill, 1946);

Tammy Out of Time (Indianapolis: Bobbs-Merrill, 1948; London: Macdonald, 1950);

But the Morning Will Come (Indianapolis: Bobbs-Merrill, 1949; London: Macdonald, 1951);

Sudden Glory (Indianapolis: Bobbs-Merrill, 1951; London: Macdonald, 1953);

The Hornbeam Tree (Indianapolis: Bobbs-Merrill, 1953; London: Macdonald, 1955);

Tammy, Tell Me True (Indianapolis: Bobbs-Merrill, 1959);

Saddle Your Dreams (Indianapolis: Bobbs-Merrill, 1964).

Cid Ricketts Sumner (courtesy of Special Collections Department, J. Willard Marriott Library, University of Utah)

Reader's Report

Lillian Smith's Strange Fruit *(1944), mentioned in this report, centers on the affair between a mulatto girl and a white boy.*

QUALITY
by Cid Ricketts Sumner

This is a very interesting novel, based on the old tragedy of the educated and sensitive mind in the dark skin. Extremely well written, it evokes the beauty of the Mississippi countryside with unusually beautiful language. From the first paragraph the reader is struck with the lovely power of descriptive writing and the unusual sensitivity, the clear concrete images.

It is the story of a girl born, it would seem, to tragedy, of mixed ancestry, nice looking, and so fair she seems to belong to the white race. Sent to New England tobe [*sic*] educated as a nurse, she almost comes to believe herself white, but the shadow is on her. When she falls in love with a white man, she is so far tempted to go on that she set the wedding day. But she ran from him, back to Mississippi and her old grandmother. The story opens with a poignant picture of the girl on the station platform of the little town, facing the two doors [of] the station, one for colored one for white.

Here sunk in her personal misery, she gradually comes to feel something of the needs of her race. In her experiences in this most intolerant of states, we meet typical characters of both races. Aunt Dicey, Pinky's grandmother is the old time faithful retainer, wise with a native wisdom and with age. Jake, the rising young colored property owner, is at once bitter and servile. He has listened to the agitators, and agreed with them that now, in war time, is the time for the race to make its gains toward equality. But he has learned the worst of their shibboleths, and has not learned how to manage his own affairs or his woman, Rozelia, who is another type, the razor toting, elemental, savage woman. He brings to Pinky another typical man, Arch Naughton, a Chicago newspaperman, colored, and a professional agitator, bitter and frustrated, hoping for violence, and provoking it as the only way to help the injustices among his people. Last of all is the colored doctor, who comes from Pinkey's old school to work among his own people, who hopes to set an example of tolerance and improved helath [*sic*] and outlook, and in that way help his people to a better life.

Among the white people, there are, too, typical figures, the bigoted station master, who changes his attitude when he realised that it is a colored girl who has just arrived, Miss Em, the last chatelaine of the "Big House" where Dicey has worked all her life, arrogant, family proud, but wise and understanding of the people for whom her own people have been responsible. Dying, she makes the act of atonement which almost wrecks Pinky's new attitude to life,–she leaves the "Big House" and all it's [*sic*] valuable antiques to Pinky, whose appearance proves that she belongs to Miss Em's white family. Miss Em's cousin, whose washing Dicey does, is the worst type of Southern white, powerful and unscrupulous, she will stop at nothing. It is ridiculous to her that Miss Em could have wanted to leave her possessions to one of "the inferior race" "not the ones the Constitution was talking about" hence Pinky must have caused the will to be written. She contests it with every distortion of facts that she can find. On her side she has public opinion, especially of the ignorant white population, who assemble in the court at the hearing not to see justice done, but to threaten Pinky if she seems likely to inherit by law.

There are white police, of this type, and a storekkeper [*sic*], common in small Southern towns, but there are also two or three enlightened white people there. The judge, who sees the problem whole, his daughter, who was a pupil of Miss Em's, the other judge who hears the case, and is swayed in his decision by the use Pinky means to make of the "Big House" rather than by abstract justice, but at least has the courage to make it.

The colored doctor has come to make plans with Pinkey, and incidentally to restore her hope in the future, when the house is burned. "It is in the way you take what you can't help that counts" Dotcor [*sic*] Canaday tells Pinkey, and they go ahead with their plans for a hospital for their people, on the land, with the cabins, and with what was saved from the fire. They are to be helped by the white community, too. "Do them good to be ashamed, sometimes" said Aunt Dicey.

It is a pleasant book, in spite of the inescapable look at the problem of the two races, and the tragedy of the futility of any immediate answer. It is hopeful, and while it does not dodge the problem it leaves the reader the feeling that it can, one day, be solved by both races using what they can of good will and courage. If anything, it is a little too sweet in its easy solutions. It will probably make students of race relations who are all for immediate removal of bans and injustices simply froth at the mouth, with its advocacy of long, tedious methods of building up racial equality. With the thesis that "Quality" is what counts in black or white. And it will probably irritate many "professional" southerners (many of whom live in the North) who think the least said in public, the less they need to think about the problem. Or who agree with Mrs. Worley that the colored race "was meant to be hewers of wood and drawers of water". It is a timely book, and well worth publishing.

There is one thing, however, that seems to me all wrong. The courtroom episode. I had noticed, all through the book, a tendency in Pinkey to think in long words, and abstract phrases. Some people do this, and probably well educated colored people do, perhaps in defense against the simplicity of their beginnings. I think it would be well to check her words, and conscious thoughts. It is all right when she is a nurse, she should think like a nurse, but in the stress of emotion, it seems to me she, or anyone else, white or dark, would think in simple terms. And in her situation, where she is trying to help Arch, who has made trouble, and is being threatened by the "poor Whites" in the courtroom, she would not only be simple in her language, she would if only in hypocrisy, be what the whites wanted her to be, supplicant, servile, demure or humble. But still clear and strong. She would not "withdraw all claim to the property" and talk about "legislating integrity." She might say "I give it up. A colored girl can't claim it against a white woman,–not here,–not now. I didn't want it for myself,–to live like that. I wanted to make it into a hospital for my people." Something like that, and surely not the forensic speech, the calm reasoning the author gives her.

Similarly, when she sees the men leaving the courtroom, and the deputies not barring the way, to "get" Arch, she would not rise and withdraw her claim. She would leap to her feet and cry "Stop" or something dramatic. The author has not only been misled by her own eloquence to put Pinkey out of character, she has failed to extract the drama inherent in the situation and in the girl's nature. And this grandiloquence should be watched. Most of the time it is not present, but now and then it appears. In this one scene, it makes the whole thing flat. I think more might be made of the threat of violence, in a few instances. It is a very real horror, especially to those who have no recourse against it, and who have not grown up with it on the fringes of their consciousness.

With these few criticisms, I find the book very good, beautifully written, with tenderness, sympathy and an honest attempt at a solution of the problem it states so well. If it rouses discussion, so much the better, both for the problem and for the sale of the book. It is not another "Strange Fruit", it is hardly as passionate and deeply involved as that. But it is a book which may find more readers, since it is more impersonal, more equal in distributing blame and obligation, more reasonable in its solution.

H. Mellett

* * *

Related Letters

Lucius Lamar Jr., Georgia representative of Bobbs-Merrill's educational department, wrote Lowe Berger of the same department thanking him for a copy of Quality. *At the time of this letter D. Laurance Chambers was trade-department editor as well as president of the firm.*

Lucius Lamar Jr. to Lowe Berger, 6 July 1946

Dear Lowe:

Again, thanks very much to you & Mr. Chambers for the book Quality. Have received & read it with a great deal of interest.

Mrs. Sumner tells her story as skillfully as did Lillian Smith in Strange Fruit. She puts her finger on problems as accurately as did Richard Wright in Black Boy. To my way of thinking, however, she surpasses both these authors because she offers some answers which can well be taken to heart by both black & white.

As I understand the deep South, and I think I do, Mrs. Sumner's story moves so easily and naturally that I found myself predicting every major episode in her book. As an example–the burning of Miss Em's house. In the South I know, that was so inevitable the book would not have made sense if Mrs. Sumner had omitted it.

I believe Quality is easily the best B-M trade book I have read and if it doesn't stay high on best seller lists for a long time I'll be surprised.

Regards,

Lucius Lamar Jr.

* * *

Howard W. Odum was a well-known social scientist at the University of North Carolina. He also published a trilogy of novels with Bobbs-Merrill that dealt with black life; Odum was white.

Howard W. Odum to D. Laurance Chambers, 7 August 1946

Dear Mr. Chambers:

I hardly know what to write about QUALITY. I will, therefore, write you this personal letter and we shall see then subsequently whether there is anything we can quote.

Naturally I wish everybody could read the book. Particularly Southerners. Particularly Northerners. This book has more realism in a few pages than most of the others have in volumes. This author really understands cultural conditioning and psychology. She shows a greater understanding of the culture and traditions than most of the anthropologists. The book is well written. It does have suspense and one wants to read it through before putting it down.

Now, the reason I can't commend the book is two-fold. From the viewpoint of the new Negro and of genuine folk culture, I can't approve of a book which ends up still giving sanction to the term "Aunty" and the assumption that the white Doctor and Judge are to be commended for having genuine respect for these Negroes of such fine quality. (You understand, of course, that this is a very accurate and true picture that she is presenting.) On the other hand, there is no implication that the people who burned the house will be punished. Here again this is a very accurate and extraordinarily realistic picture.

I shall like your reaction to this letter and if you wish to write out something that you would like to quote from me and send it to me, taken from this version, I suspect we could arrange it. We are just caught up in the midst of a situation which, as the book shows, has no solution and many solutions. You are to be highly commended for putting out so good a book which is not seeking mere destruction.

Cordially yours,
HWO

* * *

Chambers to Odum, 12 August 1946

My dear Dr. Odum:

Many thanks for your letter of the 7th. I am ever so grateful to you for reading QUALITY and writing me about it at a time when I know you are so busy.

I am not at all a sociologist and I am not clear that I quite understand your dilemma. Has not Mrs.

Dust jackets for Sumner's 1949 and 1953 novels (Between the Covers Rare Books, Merchantville, N.J.; Stray Dog Books, Newton Falls, Ohio)

Sumner been realistic and left the reader to make his own assumptions and draw his own conclusions from a faithful picture of conditions? If so, is her work to be condemned for that? Is not the use of the term "Aunty" realistic? Has the author commended the white doctor and the judge for their respect of the quality Negroes, or does the reader feel that they should be commended because of the state of local white opinion and pressure? Would the white Mississippians who burn a house in such circumstances be punished?

Is not your quarrel therefore rather with facts as they are than with the novel?

Might we quote you to this effect:

"Naturally I wish everybody could read Quality. Particularly Southerners. Particularly Northerners. This book has more realism in a few pages than most of the others have in volumes. This author really understands cultural conditioning and psychology. She shows a greater understanding of the culture and traditions than most of the anthropologists. The book is well written. It does have suspense and one wants to read it through before putting it down.

"Of course I cannot commend from the viewpoint of the new Negro and of genuine folk culture any sanction of the term "Aunty" or any assumption which the reader may draw that the white doctor and judge are to be commended for having genuine respect for these Negroes of such fine quality, or the implication that the people who burned the house will not be punished."

With kindest regards, I am

Gratefully yours,

[D. Laurance Chambers]

Henry Kitchell Webster (1875–1932)

Henry Kitchell Webster was one of those writers who seemed to produce work mechanically. In his prime he dictated thrillers at the rate of twenty thousand words per week. He began by collaborating on several projects with Samuel Merwin (later a Bobbs-Merrill author), including three novels celebrating captains of industry. On his own Webster cranked out many stories for such well-paying magazines as The Saturday Evening Post. *His debut with Bobbs-Merrill was* The Real Adventure *(1916), a best-seller. Webster died in 1932 before finishing* The Alleged Great-Aunt; *the mystery novel was completed by the sisters Janet Ayer Fairbank and Margaret Ayer Barnes, friends of the Webster family, and published in 1935. They called it "an experiment in imitative writing," claiming in the preface that they were leaving as their own little mystery the point where their writing began.*

Henry Kitchell Webster (from Stanley J. Kunitz and Howard Haycraft, eds., Twentieth Century Authors, *1942; Thomas Cooper Library, University of South Carolina)*

BOBBS-MERRILL BOOKS BY WEBSTER: *The Real Adventure* (Indianapolis: Bobbs-Merrill, 1916; London: Constable, 1917);

The Painted Scene, and Other Stories of the Theater (Indianapolis: Bobbs-Merrill, 1916; London: Constable, 1917);

The Thoroughbred (Indianapolis: Bobbs-Merrill, 1917);

An American Family: A Novel of To-Day (Indianapolis: Bobbs-Merrill, 1918);

Mary Wollaston (Indianapolis: Bobbs-Merrill, 1920; London: E. Nash & Grayson, 1922);

Real Life, Into Which Miss Leda Swan of Hollywood Makes an Adventurous Excursion (Indianapolis: Bobbs-Merrill, 1921);

Joseph Greer and His Daughter (Indianapolis: Bobbs-Merrill, 1922; E. Nash, 1923);

The Other Story, and Other Stories (Indianapolis: Bobbs-Merrill, 1923);

The Innocents (Indianapolis: Bobbs-Merrill, 1924; E. Nash & Grayson, 1925);

The Corbin Necklace (Indianapolis: Bobbs-Merrill, 1926); republished as *The Mystery of the Corbin Necklace* (London: J. Hamilton, 1929);

The Beginners (Indianapolis: Bobbs-Merrill, 1927);

Philopena (Indianapolis: Bobbs-Merrill, 1927; E. Nash & Grayson, 1927);

The Clock Strikes Two (Indianapolis: Bobbs-Merrill, 1928);

The Quartz Eye: A Mystery in Ultra Violet (Indianapolis: Bobbs-Merrill, 1928; London: Hodder & Stoughton, 1929);

The Sealed Trunk (Indianapolis: Bobbs-Merrill, 1929; London: Stanley Paul, 1929);

The Man with the Scarred Hand (Indianapolis: Bobbs-Merrill, 1931);

Who Is the Next? (Indianapolis: Bobbs-Merrill, 1931);

The Alleged Great-Aunt, by Webster, Janet Ayer Fairbank, and Margaret Ayer Barnes (Indianapolis: Bobbs-Merrill, 1935; London: Stanley Paul, 1935).

Related Letters

Hewitt H. Howland was editor in chief of Bobbs-Merrill's trade department. Joseph H. Sears was president of D. Appleton and Company at the time of this letter, and Rutger B. Jewett was editorial head.

Henry Kitchell Webster to Hewitt H. Howland, 8 May 1915

Dear Howland:–

I caught myself saying to you last Wednesday, that I thought it highly improbable that any conversation with Sears or Jewett could convince me that the thing for me to do was to go on publishing with them. I turned the matter over in my mind for the next twenty-four hours, and decided that I could not conceive of any outcome to the conversation that would so convince me and that if that was so, it would be foolish to go on for months keeping matters in suspense for a talk that could only have one outcome.

Yesterday I wrote to Sears stating that I had come to a definite decision to make a change in my publishing arrangements. I said that, while I might be wrong in thinking that another publisher could do better by my books, I could not convince myself that this was so, except by trying.

Consequently, I now feel as free as if I had had a talk with them, to talk business with you.

Is it altogether too late to get out my theatre stories under the title of The Painted Scene, for a Fall book? I know it would be too late to get out a book that you were going to make a big campaign with. I shall follow your judgment unquestioningly in this matter, but I would like to take it up with you.

It seems rather a pity that I couldn't have made up my mind a week sooner, in which case we could have put in our time together to more definite advantage.

I am inclosing the little article on How Samuel Merwin Works, which I hope is what you and The Bookman want.

Yours most sincerely,
Henry K Webster

* * *

Webster to Howland, 15 May 1915

Dear Howland:–

The manuscripts making up the volume that I call The Painted Scene, came back from Appleton's last night, and I have forwarded them to you. When you read them, would you mind beginning at the beginning as you would with a novel manuscript, and reading on through in order? They have a definite order and progress, and I think they'll be more effective that way.

In the envelop with my contract, I found a little memorandum of yours, which I inclose herewith.

The Real Adventure continues to go very well and I hope a month from today, to have widened materially, the gap between me and the printer, which is still uncomfortably narrow.

Yours most sincerely,
Henry K Webster

* * *

The Hattons are unidentified. William C. Bobbs was president of the company at this time. "Bat" was a slang term meaning "spree."

Howland to Webster, 17 May 1915

My dear Webster:

Thank you for your letter of the eleventh and the memorandum regarding the Hattons. The Painted Scene hasn't yet reached me but when it does, I will give it immediate attention and shall read the stories straight through in the order in which you have them arranged. I am glad The Great Adventure comes on at such a good gait. You will feel easier in your mind when you get a couple of jumps between yourself and the typesetter.

Are you entirely satisfied with the present title? I only question it because it is our habit to challenge every title on the chance that somewhere there may be a better one. Has "Adventure" been used too often?–The Beautiful Adventure, The Great Adventure. Is there danger of the word conveying a wrong impression of the character of the story to the man who sees it on the book's cover for the first time? Does "Adventure", to most people, mean some active physical experience? If the story appears in a magazine as The Real Adventure, that rather definitely commits us to the use of the same title, doesn't it? Let me know how you feel about this.

I have been pretty busy since I got home or I should have written you before this to tell you how pleased our people are over ha[v]ing you in the family. Mr. Bobbs is delighted and approved, without question, the paragraphs we wrote into the contract. Don't forget you are coming down to see us the first time The Great Adventure goes stale on you and you feel the need of a bat.

Very sincerely yours,
[Hewitt H. Howland]

* * *

Webster to Howland, 22 May 1915

Dear Howland:–

I'm glad to hear that The Painted Scene has arrived safely and I shall await, with much interest, to learn what you think of it. Thanks very much for your assurance that Mr. Bobbs is pleased over our agreement, and that he approves the modifications we made

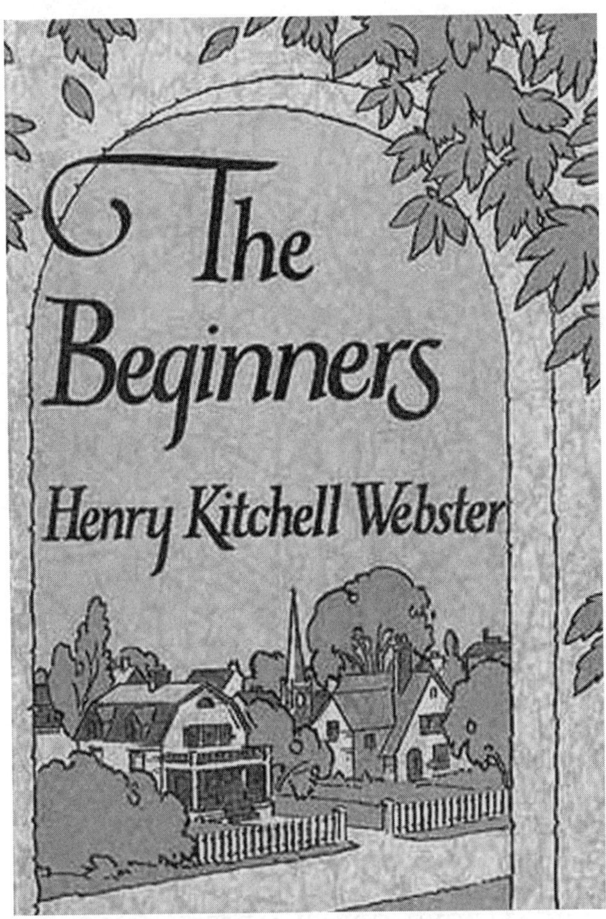

Dust jacket for Webster's 1927 novel about a middle-aged man who embarks on a new life (Between the Covers Rare Books, Merchantville, N.J.)

in it. You may be sure I'll get down to Indianapolis as soon as I can.

Regarding the title, I admit that the word Adventure is badly frayed for titular purposes. For that matter, the word Real is too. But The Real Adventure is, to my ear, a rather fresh sounding title. I'll admit I'd have preferred The Great Adventure, if Arnold Bennett hadn't got ahead of me. There may be another better title somewhere that nobody has anticipated. But I feel rather strongly, the thing you intimate; namely, that the acceptance of the title and the use of it in the magazine commits us to it. Not irretrievably of course, but, in the absence of any really compelling reason to the contrary, definitely.

The first installment of it is now out in Everybody's. That's my view of the case. If yours differs from it, let me know.

Henry K Webster

* * *

Howland to Webster, 27 May 1915

My dear Webster:

We were glad to get your telegram this morning, saying that you would come to the race Saturday. It is an excellent idea to avail yourself of the Monon Special. That obviates the necessity of landing at the crowded Union station and the difficulty of finding Bobbs there. When you get to the Speedway grounds, you will have to buy a general admission ticket, then go to Grandstand A, hunt up an usher and have him find Mr. Bobbs for you. His box, in grandstand A, of course, is No. 004 Row B. This ought not to present any great difficulties but I believe I would put this letter in my pocket if I were in your place to show any officious official. I tried to get you on the telephone to-day but all I wanted to say is in this letter.

I am sorry that you are coming at a time when I shan't be able to see you but am hop[e]ful that, having broken the ice, you will be willing to come soon again. I know you will enjoy the day and only wish I could be with you.

As ever yours,
[Hewitt H. Howland]

* * *

Ida Tarbell was a leader of the "muckrakers."

Howland to Webster, 14 June 1915

My dear Webster:

Enclosed is a clipping from a local paper that I thought might interest you. Doubtless Miss Tarbell's article will have more to do with the business than with Ford himself.

There is, in our judgment, not [*sic*] doubt about the desirability of publishing The Painted Scene; the only question is when. The more we study the situation, the more firmly are we convinced that The Real Adventure should have a clear field. That book should be the first book of H. K. W.'s that The B-M Company offers to the trade. We called our head salesman in off of the road and told him we were proposing to publish your theatrical stories this fall and the novel next spring. He begged us with tears in his eyes not to do it. He had read the first instalment in Everybody's and is strong for it. He insisted that no matter how carefully we handled The Painted Scene, it would unavoidably deprive us of a certain kind of punch when we came to The Real Adventure. But we believe that, at the right time, we can do better with it than you expect.

I am afraid you will experience some disappointment in reading this letter but, at the same time, I know we both want the same thing, and that is to make a real noise and a real success with The Real Adventure.

As ever yours,
[Hewitt H. Howland]

* * *

Webster never wrote the Henry Ford biography for Bobbs-Merrill.

Webster to Howland, 17 June 1915

Dear Howland:–

Essentially, of course, I'm not disappointed about your decision to defer The Painted Scene until after the publication of The Real Adventure, because I agree with you absolutely, that if there is even a chance that the short stories published first would hurt the novel, we shouldn't run that chance. And I am pleased with the intimation in your letter that you liked The Painted Scene somewhat better than you expected to, and regard it as a better publishing proposition than the run of volumes of short stories.

I'm working very hard on the novel, and though I'm not progressing with it at any meteoric speed, my confidence in it grows steadily. I have delivered, I think, in a convincing way, the scenes where Rose leaves her husband and where she begins work in the chorus; which are, I believe, the trickiest part of the job. I have still got difficulties ahead, of course, but they don't look so serious as these I have surmounted.

I'm mighty glad your head salesman likes the way the thing begins in the magazine, and I hope Mr. Bobbs likes it too.

Regarding the Ford biography: I don't think Miss Tarbell's magazine article will interfere with it. I sha'n't give the thing a thought, of course, until the novel is fully completed, nor, until then, can I be finally sure that I want to undertake it. But my idea is that the few weeks after the completion of the novel, when I won't be able to write any fiction anyway, can be spent agreeably enough, getting the material ready for the job. If the material is interesting, and I fancy it will be, the actual writing of forty or fifty thousand words shouldn't take long. I don't think it should run over fifty, and I think forty might do.

I did have a bully time in Indianapolis and I am anxious to go back sometime when I can come up to the office and have a visit with you.

There's a chance of my going to New York next month for a few days, and if I do, I'll try to stop off on my way there or back.

Do give us a chance, the next time you are in Chicago, to have you out in Evanston.

Yours most sincerely,
Henry K Webster

* * *

D. Laurance Chambers was company vice president and chief trade-department editor at the time of this letter. Paul R. Reynolds was a literary agent.

D. Laurance Chambers to Paul R. Reynolds, 28 May 1934

Dear Mr. Reynolds:

Have you any news for me about THE ALLEGED GREAT AUNT, the story by Henry Kitchell Webster, Mrs. Barnes and Mrs. Fairbank?

Cordially yours,
[D. Laurance Chambers]

* * *

Chambers to Reynolds, 18 June 1934

Dear Mr. Reynolds:

Although we have not yet seen any part of the manuscript, I am happy to send you a contract for THE ALLEGED GREAT AUNT drawn in accordance with the terms I mentioned when I was in your office. If you find it all right will you please send it on to Mrs. Webster. I enclose a copy for your files. This agreement follows precisely the form of our contracts with Harry except as to the royalty rise to 20% after 5,000. We know of no way to publish profitably at 20%, but profit is not the element of consideration in this matter. If the contact is not drawn properly under the terms of Harry's will you can let me know.

What is the latest news about the serial rights?

With kindest regards, I am

Sincerely yours,
[D. Laurance Chambers]

* * *

Reynolds to Chambers, 20 June 1934

Dear Mr. Chambers:

Thank you for the contracts for the book rights of THE ALLEGED GREAT-AUNT. I am expecting that Mrs. Barnes will turn up as I understood she was going to be in New York this week and as all my relations to this manuscript have been through her I think I will speak to her about the matter before I send the con-

And then indeed, but very faint and far away, she could hear the slow, deliberate ticking of a great clock. It was getting louder too, gradually, unhurriedly, louder and louder, nearer and nearer——

The grip on her wrist tightened. Something else was going to happen. The panic-stricken old man knew and was waiting——

Mr. Webster has recaptured the secret of delicious terror in this novel of today. He was never before so clever in the invention of a gripping plot. You are one with the masterly blind old man, and the young girl and her lover, hedged about with fear. You are frightened, *and you love it.*

New Mystery Novel by

Henry Kitchell Webster

The Clock Strikes Two

Read it and creep!

$2.00 all stores Bobbs-Merrill

P3—1-20-28—7032

Flier for one of Webster's thrillers, published in 1928 (courtesy of The Lilly Library, Indiana University, Bloomington, Indiana)

THE *Alleged* GREAT-AUNT

Begun by HENRY KITCHELL WEBSTER
Finished by JANET AYER FAIRBANK and MARGARET AYER BARNES

To be published in May

When that beloved author, Henry Kitchell Webster, died, he had begun a new novel. He felt it was one of the most engaging of his conceptions in that field where he was so much the master—the "love-mystery story." He had "planted" his characters, he had brought them to Stanwix Falls, New York, the complication was beginning to develop at the home of old Lily DeLong, once a triumphant diva, once the toast of two continents, the "*alleged* great-aunt" of young Gilbert Meade, the Big Moment in the life of Gilbert's uncle,—but he left no outline, no scenario to indicate how it was to progress, how be solved.

Two of Mr. Webster's closest friends were those well-known novelists, the Ayer sisters—Janet Ayer Fairbank and Margaret Ayer Barnes. They read that beginning; they were excited by it; and they were struck by the idea that together they would like to finish this tale of mystery in tribute to one who had ever been an inspiration to his writing friends.

But they had achieved distinction in serious novels of the social drama. Neither had written a mystery story. They must learn how it is done, for this must remain Harry Webster's book, they must impersonate him, identify themselves with his style and method.

How delightful is the result of this three-way association, the reader will be quick to perceive. *The* Alleged *Great-Aunt* is deliciously deserving of such distinguished authorship. The identification is so complete that one forgets the multiple hand and is conscious only that this is a grand Webster story, so smoothly and swiftly it unfolds.

The Alleged *Great-Aunt* is amusing, charming, with just the right touch of whimsy. And it is engrossing—thrillingly so! Mystery readers, lovers of fun, lovers of romance—all gentle readers, in short—will recommend it to one another with the warmest, most enthusiastic pleasure.

308 pages, 12mo, $2.00

Flier for the 1935 book that was completed by friends of Webster's family after his death in 1932 (courtesy of The Lilly Library, Indiana University, Bloomington, Indiana)

tracts on to Mrs. Webster. Of course I will let you know as soon as I have sold the serial rights.

Yours sincerely,
Paul R. Reynolds

* * *

Reynolds to Chambers, 28 July 1934

Dear Mr. Chambers:

I am just back from a three weeks vacation. My son spoke to me about the contracts that you sent me for THE ALLEGED GREAT-AUNT, the story started by Webster and finished by Mrs. Barnes and Mrs. Fairbank. I spoke to Mrs. Barnes before I went off on my vacation, when she was here in New York, and she said she thought we had better hold the contracts up until the matter about the serial rights was settled, and I therefore did that. I should have written you to this effect, and I am sorry I didn't. I'll write to Mrs. Barnes now about the matter and see if we cannot have the contracts signed and the matter settled.

Yours sincerely,
Paul R. Reynolds

* * *

Reynolds to Chambers, 27 October 1934

Dear Mr. Chambers:

Thank you for your letter of October 25th. I am very sorry that you should have to wait so long in publishing THE ALLEGED GREAT-AUNT. We sold it to the Herald Tribune for more than $5,000 so that as our object was to get as much money as possible for Mrs. Webster we were glad to make this serial sale. The Herald Tribune people said that as they hoped to syndicate the story over the country they would have to have this amount of time. I am very sorry that it cannot be published earlier.

Mrs. Barnes writes me that she is sending you a copy of the story. I hope despite the delay in publication that it may have a good sale.

Yours sincerely,
Paul R. Reynolds.

* * *

Chambers to Reynolds, 29 October 1934

Dear Mr. Reynolds:–

Thank you for your letter of the 27th. In the circumstances we are very glad indeed to accommodate our plans for the publication of THE ALLEGED GREAT-AUNT in book form to the requirements of the serial situation, and will accordingly schedule it for May 1st. We could not, however, agree to its publication in a single issue of any paper as this would have to be regarded as an invasion of the volume publication rights.

Sincerely yours,
[D. Laurance Chambers]

Bobbs-Merrill published The Alleged Great-Aunt *on 10 May 1935.*

Brand Whitlock (1869–1934)

See also the Whitlock entry in *DLB 12: American Realists and Naturalists.*

Successful as both a writer and a Progressive politician, Brand Whitlock wrote realistic (but not naturalistic) novels in the manner of his friend William Dean Howells. He began as a reporter for a Chicago paper in 1890, became an ally of reform politician John Peter Altgeld, and studied law. Whitlock came back to his native Ohio and practiced law in Toledo, all the while trying to establish himself as a writer. After The 13th District *(1902), his well-regarded study of grassroots politics, was rejected by Harper and Brothers, he turned it over to Bobbs-Merrill, where editor Hewitt H. Howland became his mentor. The company promoted it in typically flamboyant fashion by sending a copy to each member of the U.S. House of Representatives. Whitlock's next two novels for the firm, also on political themes, had actually been written before* The 13th District *and then revised on the basis of what he had learned. Whitlock was elected mayor of Toledo in 1904 and was reelected four times.* The Turn of the Balance *(1907) was published in the midst of his attempts at reform in the city; it is based upon the ills he found there. The last of his books published originally by Bobbs-Merrill were collections of short stories. Whitlock became minister to Belgium just before World War I began in 1914 and served there with great distinction. Afterward, he eventually broke with his friends at Bobbs-Merrill and went on to publish with D. Appleton and Company.*

Brand Whitlock (photograph by Pirie MacDonald; Bruccoli Clark Layman Archives)

BOWEN-MERRILL/BOBBS-MERRILL BOOKS BY WHITLOCK: *The 13th District: A Story of a Candidate* (Indianapolis: Bowen-Merrill, 1902; London: B. F. Stevens & Brown, 1902);
Her Infinite Variety (Indianapolis: Bobbs-Merrill, 1904; London, 1904);
The Happy Average (Indianapolis: Bobbs-Merrill, 1904);
The Turn of the Balance (Indianapolis: Bobbs-Merrill, 1907; London: Alston Rivers, 1907);
The Gold Brick (Indianapolis: Bobbs-Merrill, 1910);
The Fall Guy (Indianapolis: Bobbs-Merrill, 1912).

Review: *The Turn of the Balance*

Brand Whitlock, in his new novel, "The Turn of the Balance," (Bobbs-Merrill Company, Indianapolis,) has written a book worthy of even more attention than it is likely to receive. For the commonplaces of the ordinary love story he has substituted human interest of wide variety, but all more or less closely involved with the commission or punishment of crimes. The leading male characters of the story are a Prosecuting Attorney–a young man of cold-blooded disposition, who is seeking to make a reputation that will give him high office in the community; a young lawyer with generous heart and humane ideals, who naturally comes to the assistance of the under dog, and whom the under dog as naturally trusts; Archie Koerner, who has seen service in the Philippines, and who, having returned home, falls into the criminal society of which he becomes a member; his father, the old man Koerner,

Drawings by Howard Chandler Christy for Whitlock's Her Infinite Variety, *published in 1904 (courtesy of The Lilly Library, Indiana University, Bloomington, Indiana)*

who has worked thirty-five years for the railroad only to lose his leg in an accident and to be cheated by the law of his just damages, and a number of criminals. The leading female characters are Elizabeth Warner, who sympathizes with the poverty-stricken Koerners, and has an interest in life not common among people of her class, and Gusta, the pretty sister of Archie, whose fate and beauty finally bring her to the street.

The story is not contrived like a machine; it resembles the progress of events in real life. It is not artificial, and its main hold on the reader is its obvious sincerity. In the hands of most authors this material would have resulted in a melodramatic product of the deepest dye. In the hands of Mr. Whitlock, who writes without forcing himself and with able simplicity, even the most horrible succession of catastrophes becomes convincing. The story is an arraignment of the law as it is administered at present in our free country–not an insensate condemnation of the law, but a plea for more generous human sympathy. [. . .]

"The Turn of the Balance" contains many revelations of our own city life. It is fascinating to read and worth reading. All of its many characters in all classes of society are aptly and convincingly sketched. It moves with precision and to a definite purpose. Gordon Marriott, the young lawyer who makes the long and futile fight for the downtrodden characters of the narrative, is far from being the conventional hero, and never is to be charged with heroics. He does what he can as a practical and honorable man–and does not know when he is beaten. The wealthy girl whom he marries, the young woman who has seen beyond the limited range of her own society, is his worthy companion.

–"Brand Whitlock's Novel," *New York Times*, 23 March 1907, p. 170

* * *

Related Letters

The revised edition of The Turn of the Balance *was not published until 1924. William C. Bobbs was president of the company at the time of this letter, which Whitlock sent from the American embassy in Brussels, Belgium.*

Brand Whitlock to Hewitt H. Howland, 10 March 1920

Dear Hewitt:

I am delighted with the thought of a new edition of "The Turn of the Balance." I am greatly flattered by the suggestion and quite willing to do anything you say in connection with it. I think probably before it comes out I ought to look it over and change a word or two, here and there, and so I wish you would send me a copy of it, that I may do this; an unbound copy, if you have one, would be better.

As to the preface, I am willing to adopt any suggestion you may make. I don't know who is the person to write the preface. Why not create an innovation and let the publisher write it?

A most extraordinary thing happened while I was home in the autumn that I am sure will interest you. You remember Curley, who figures so largely in "The Turn of the Balance." Well, when we were with the King and royal party going west, we stopped one evening at about six o'clock at Gary, Indiana, where the train was switched on to the Chicago, Milwaukee & St. Paul. The operation took about half an hour, and while it was in progress I was sitting in the stateroom, when suddenly there came a knock at the door, and, upon opening it, whom should I see, of all persons in the world, but Curley, standing there! I wondered what on earth could have happened. You can imagine the speculations that went flitting through my mind. But there he was, indubitably, very well dressed, very fit, smiling as ever, and the one gold tooth showing, and this is what he said:

"Oh, don't be alarmed. It is nothing. Everything is all right." And he turned back the lapel of his coat and showed me a detective's badge. Then he said: "I have been waiting for this day for six years. I have been wanting to tell you that I have reformed and that I have been leading a decent life ever since, and that it is all due to your influence on me and belief in me." This was so flattering that I asked him to sit down and tell me about it, and he did.

Some six years ago, determining on reform, he had succeeded in getting a position with the New York Central Railway as a detective or railway policeman of some sort. He had told them all about his past; everything, as he said, was open and above board, and they knew all. "And I have been successful," he said, "and the greatest honour that ever befell me in my life was when I was chosen to guard Their Majesties from Boston to Chicago." He said, "I saw you at Boston and at Buffalo and at Cleveland and at Toledo, and at every place we stopped, but I saw to it that you did not see me, for I did not want to show myself until I had discharged this mission faithfully and brought them safely to Chicago. I have done that, and now my duty is performed and I leave the train."

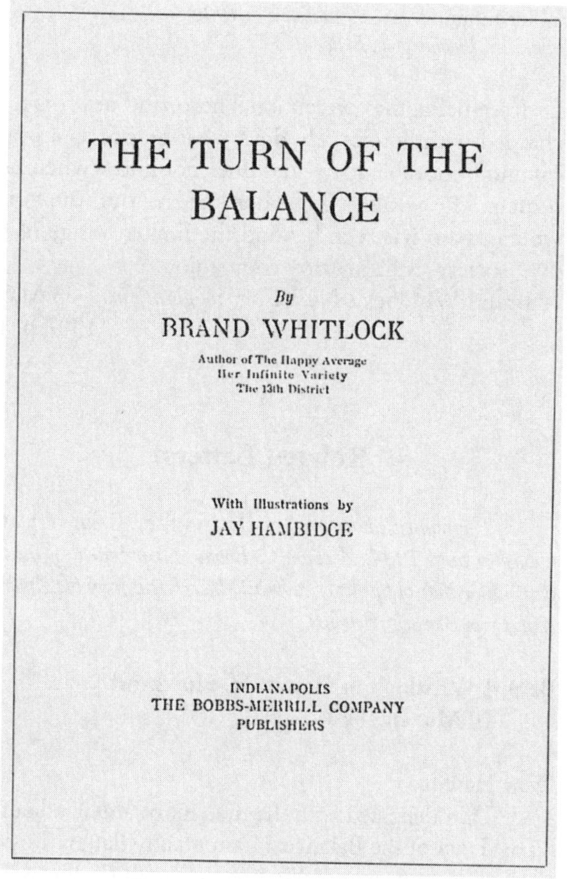
THE TURN OF THE BALANCE

By

BRAND WHITLOCK

Author of The Happy Average
Her Infinite Variety
The 13th District

With Illustrations by
JAY HAMBIDGE

INDIANAPOLIS
THE BOBBS-MERRILL COMPANY
PUBLISHERS

Title page and "advance limited edition" dust jacket for Whitlock's most ambitious novel (1907), based on his observations as mayor of Toledo, Ohio (Thomas Cooper Library, University of South Carolina; courtesy of The Lilly Library, Indiana University, Bloomington, Indiana)

We sat and chatted a long time, and you can believe that the incident made me feel very happy, and yet very humble, too. I had, of course, never given him a word of preaching in my life; but he insists that his reformation is all due to me. Well, well, wonders never cease, do they?

This story, of course, is between us, for I should not like to have it get out and be given any sort of publicity. It would not help Curley or anybody. He has a wife and a child, whom he told me they are rearing as well as they know how, and they are very happy in their home.

And now as to the Walt Whitman:

I should have written you long ago in answer to your inquiry about the progress of the Life of Whitman, but I have been encumbered with a multitude of little businesses, and so have fallen far behind in my personal correspondence.

I feel somewhat chagrined every time I think of the Whitman book, for it has been so long since I promised to write it. For years I could lay the blame of the delay on the war, but now that the war is over that excuse avails me no more, even if the peace is almost as bad as the war and does not afford me that opportunity of leisure from which, as Ecclesiasticus, or someone as wise, said, "the wisdom of the scribe cometh." I began the book a good while ago and have a pile of manuscript that would not be discreditable to my industry if it were in any final form, but I haven't been able to give it that form. I encounter, too, difficulties when I try to put my thought and judgment of him in final form. I could have written a most enthusiastic book about him a decade or more ago, but since then I have grown older, if not wiser. I do not mean to imply any recantation of my belief in the central and moving spirit of his work; but I can not escape the feeling that he would do better in an anthology than in a complete collection of his own works. But if one were to put such a heresy down on paper, all the free verse writers and radicals would be in high dudgeon and would at once get out bell, book and candle and excommunicate one for recreance.

As you grow older do you find yourself sound on the subject of "vers libre," or, like me, have you a sneaking, unworthy feeling that some of it is rather disappointing and lacking in the true poetic spirit? Do you think that the rather pale emotions of the free verse writers constitute poetry merely because they have them set up in lines that have not been justified, as the old time printers used to say? Old Walt has a lot to answer for; he made the writing of poetry seem too easy; that's why they are so enthusiastic about him; he made poetry seem easy to them and encouraged an unfortunate fluency on their part. Of course it isn't as easy as it seems; poetry isn't poetry because it is in free verse, any more than poetry is poetry because it is in classic or conventional form, but they don't know that. Whitman himself found it too easy at times, and everything that a poet, even a great poet, writes is not poetry simply because he puts it down on paper.

And then I begin to have serious doubts as to whether there is, or ever will be, any such thing as democratic art, as Whitman and others preach. Indeed, we shall be lucky if the rising tide of democracy does not swamp art along with a great many other things that are, after all, in their nature, unfortunately, and perhaps unjustly, the possession of an elite. All great poets have been more or less democratic in their aspirations and feelings, as it is natural and proper for a great poet to be; but most of them have been read and admired and praised by the aristocrats more than by the democrats. I hope that it is no cynical asperity, or any indication of a lack of respect for the people, to say that in general their appreciation of art is not apt to be very highly cultivated. What the people like, in all times and in all countries, is what they get at the cinema. Whitman himself was never a poet of the people in the sense of being popular. The people have never read him and never will; they know little about him and care less, and even if they were to give themselves the trouble to read him they wouldn't know what it was about, or like it. Our dear old Riley was much more a poet of the people than ever Whitman was, though he never made any pretence of the sort. He expressed them in many ways better than Whitman ever did and was more widely read than Whitman ever will be. Of course, in the subjective and intellectual sense he was not as great, but in the lyrical sense, and in the human sense, he was more of a poet. The defect in Whitman was that he was a preacher of democracy, and it is precisely when he was most consciously the democrat that he was least the poet. He had a thesis that he felt called upon to develop and exemplify, and thus he was frequently using his art as a means of propaganda. When he was in the glow and passion of the true poetic fervour, as when he wrote the exquisite threnody about Lincoln and all those beautiful poems that Lincoln and the war inspired, he was a great poet. When propaganda comes in at the door art flies out of the window; and thus, much that Whitman wrote leaves one unmoved, and on a spring morning the lines that come spontaneously to one's mind, out of one's own youth, recalling one's own land, are apt to be some homely lines of Riley's that breathe the odours o[f] farmyard and orchard, and the old-fashioned, mid-western life. I wish that I could think that it was there still as it was when I was a boy, and that nothing, not even democracy or democratic poets, could change it or make it other than it was!

All this makes the job difficult, especially as one of his charges to us was that he must be taken as a whole and nothing left out,–it's as bad as the curse of the scriptures that is called down upon him who takes one jot or tittle away from them; and to be a true Whitmanite one must be a believer in his verbal inspiration and in the inerrancy of the text of the D. McKay edition. However, I'll do the best I can.

How are you coming on in these parlous times? Are you ever able to get a drink to warm the cockles of your heart? And has the literary centre moved from Indiana yet? Give my remembrances to Will Bobbs and all the rest, make my compliment to your wife, and write me a long letter.

Ever devotedly yours,
Brand Whitlock

* * *

D. Laurance Chambers was vice president and an editor at the time of this letter.

Whitlock to Howland, 20 November 1923

Dear Huwett [*sic*]:

I sent you some time ago the revised copy of the "Turn of the Balance". I trust that it has reached you safely. I intended writing at the time, but I have been frightfully busy and kept putting it off. I went over the book many times and read it, I think, entirely through from cover to cover in all five times. It was a curious experience; the first feeling I had to overcome was a desire to re-write the whole thing. If I had it to do now, I should write it in a different way, but of course I had to decide, and wisely too, that the thing is done and must stand for good or ill as it is. I therefore only made a few corrections, cutting out some opinions that time has softened and turning a phrase here and there a little differently, but respecting the whole. What irritates me most in it is that I "go bad" as Henry James used to say, with too many characters, but after all that was the style in those days and there is nothing to be done about it now. I am sure of one thing: that if I were to write it today, I could not recapture the youthful enthusiasm and energy which is worth more than everything else in a book, and though time, as I say, has softened many of my opinions, and though I have lapsed into a kind of middle-aged conservatism, the book has truth in it, a terrible truth, so that I am glad you are going to bring out another edition. Chambers wrote me that you wished an introduction or preface of some sort, and I shall write one and send it you shortly. [*Marginal note regarding the James quotation:* "What Henry James said, and what I dictated was: 'Go behind.' But perhaps my stenographer who is a French woman, and so writing in another language has come nearer the truth than I intended she should do."]

We have decided to linger over here yet a little longer and to pass the Winter months at Cannes; I have crossed the North Atlantic too many times in Winter ever to wish to do it again if I can avoid it; but I hope to see you in the Spring.

With ever kind regards, I am

Your devoted friend,
Brand Whitlock

P.S. Pray pardon the appearance of this letter. Were I to have her write it over, she like the linotype printer in correcting proof, would only make two errors grow where one grew before.

* * *

Whitlock to Howland, 1 September 1924

Dear Hewitt,

I find in my papers an old letter from a poor devil in the penitentiary at Leavenworth asking me for a copy of "The Turn of the Balance."

As the book was out of print I could not send it to him but now that there is a new edition, will you please send him one and charge it to my account.

This book is popular among the criminal classes at any rate and I have misgivings when I think of the expense I shall be put to by the increased demand that the new edition will occasion!

Ever devotedly yours,
Brand Whitlock

Dust jacket for Whitlock's 1910 story collection (courtesy of The Lilly Library, Indiana University, Bloomington, Indiana)

Other Bobbs-Merrill Authors, 1960–1985

Imamu Amiri Baraka (1934–)

See also the Baraka entries in *DLB 5: American Poets Since World War II; DLB 7: Twentieth-Century American Dramatists; DLB 16: The Beats: Literary Bohemians in Postwar America;* and *DLB 38: Afro-American Writers After 1955: Dramatists and Prose Writers.*

By the time he published with Bobbs-Merrill, Imamu Amiri Baraka (LeRoi Jones until 1968) was already a prominent figure in the revolutionary black-theater movement, owing to such plays as Dutchman *(1964). Also a poet and essayist, Baraka's literary roots were in both Greenwich Village and Harlem. Toward the end of the 1960s his work was growing more radical in its advocacy on behalf of black Americans.*

BOBBS-MERRILL BOOKS BY BARAKA: *Black Magic: Sabotage, Target Study, Black Art: Collected Poetry, 1961–1967* (Indianapolis: Bobbs-Merrill, 1969; London: Calder & Boyars, 1971);

Four Black Revolutionary Plays: All Praises to the Black Man (Indianapolis: Bobbs-Merrill, 1969; London: Calder & Boyars, 1971);

In Our Terribleness (Some Elements and Meaning in Black Style) (Indianapolis: Bobbs-Merrill, 1970).

Imamu Amiri Baraka (from Baraka, Transbluesency, *1995; Richland County Public Library)*

Colette (photograph by George Platt Lynes; from the dust jacket of Robert Phelps, ed., The Collected Stories of Colette, *1983; Richland County Public Library)*

Colette (1873–1954)

See also the Colette entry in *DLB 65: French Novelists, 1900–1930.*

Bobbs-Merrill's posthumous translations of works by Colette (born Sidonie Gabrielle Colette) were drawn from various periods in her long working life. Her fiction often marks stages in that life under aliases, such as the Claudine of Retreat From Love *(1974; originally* La Retraite sentimentale, *1904).* The Evening Star: Recollections *(1973; originally* L'Etoile Vesper, *1946), written after the end of Colette's career as a novelist, was a "souvenir" of wartime Paris, based on her celebrated "virtuosity of the memory."*

BOBBS-MERRILL BOOKS BY COLETTE: *Places,* translated by David Le Vay (Indianapolis: Bobbs-Merrill, 1971; **first edition,** London: Owen, 1970);

Journey for Myself: Selfish Memories, translated by Le Vay (Indianapolis: Bobbs-Merrill, 1972; **first edition,** London: Owen, 1971);

The Other Woman, translated by Margaret Crosland (Indianapolis: Bobbs-Merrill, 1972; **first edition,** London: Owen, 1971);

The Thousand and One Mornings, translated by Crosland and Le Vay (Indianapolis: Bobbs-Merrill, 1973; **first edition,** London: Owen, 1973);

The Evening Star: Recollections, translated by Le Vay (Indianapolis: Bobbs-Merrill, 1974; **first edition,** London: Owen, 1973);

Duo and Le Toutounier: Two Novels, translated by Crosland (Indianapolis: Bobbs-Merrill, 1974; London: Owen, 1976);

Retreat from Love, translated by Crosland (Indianapolis: Bobbs-Merrill, 1974; **first edition,** London: Owen, 1974).

Dean R. Koontz (1945–)

Four of the five novels that Dean Ray Koontz wrote under the pen name Brian Coffey were published by Bobbs-Merrill. Beginning in 1972, Koontz moved away from science fiction and toward suspense fiction, a genre in which he was to establish himself as a best-selling author. During his apprenticeship he learned enough about storytelling to win both popularity and critical acclaim.

BOBBS-MERRILL BOOKS BY KOONTZ: *Blood Risk,* as Brian Coffey (Indianapolis: Bobbs-Merrill, 1973; London: Barker, 1974);

Surrounded, as Coffey (Indianapolis: Bobbs-Merrill, 1974; London: Barker, 1975);

The Wall of Masks, as Coffey (Indianapolis: Bobbs-Merrill, 1975);

Dean R. Koontz (photograph by Jerry Bauer, from the dust jacket of Koontz, Intensity, *1995; Richland County Public Library)*

The Face of Fear: A Novel of Suspense, as Coffey (Indianapolis: Bobbs-Merrill, 1977); as K. R. Dwyer (London: Davies, 1978).

Joel Oppenheimer (1930–1988)

See also the Oppenheimer entries in *DLB 5: American Poets Since World War II* and *DLB 193: American Poets Since World War II, Sixth Series.*

Considered a product of both the Black Mountain poetry movement and the New York literary scene and showing the influence of E. E. Cummings and William Carlos Williams, Joel Oppenheimer wrote about personal interactions at all levels of society. Works such as In Time *(1969) and* On Occasion *(1973) demonstrate his proficiency at composing occasional poetry, while* The Woman Poems *(1975) has a serial structure reminiscent of what Oppenheimer encountered in the works of Black Mountain poet Charles Olson.*

BOBBS-MERRILL BOOKS BY OPPENHEIMER: *In Time: Poems 1962–1968* (Indianapolis: Bobbs-Merrill, 1969);

On Occasion: Some Births, Deaths, Weddings, Birthdays, Holidays, and Other Events (Indianapolis: Bobbs-Merrill, 1973);

The Wrong Season (Indianapolis: Bobbs-Merrill, 1973);

The Woman Poems (Indianapolis: Bobbs-Merrill, 1975).

Joel Oppenheimer (Bruccoli Clark Layman Archives)

Sam Shepard (photograph by Bruce Weber, from back cover of Shepard, A Lie of the Mind, *1986; Richland County Public Library)*

Sam Shepard (1943–)

See also the Shepard entries in *DLB 7: Twentieth-Century American Dramatists* and *DLB 212: Twentieth-Century American Western Writers, Second Series.*

The first four separate publications of Sam Shepard (born Samuel Shepard Rogers) were by Bobbs-Merrill, and they included a representative sample of the many plays he had written since 1964. These works established Shepard as the most important contributor to the Off-Broadway movement, and his achievement between 1964 and 1970 was recognized by six Obie Awards for playwriting.

BOBBS-MERRILL BOOKS BY SHEPARD: *Five Plays: Chicago, Icarus's Mother, Red Cross, Fourteen Hundred Thousand, Melodrama Play* (Indianapolis: Bobbs-Merrill, 1967; London: Faber, 1969);

La Turista: A Play in Two Acts (Indianapolis: Bobbs-Merrill, 1968; London: Faber, 1969);

Operation Sidewinder: A Play in Two Acts (Indianapolis: Bobbs-Merrill, 1970);

The Unseen Hand and Other Plays (Indianapolis: Bobbs-Merrill, 1972).

Robert Silverberg (photograph by Susanne Lee Houfek, from dust jacket of Silverberg, Lord of Darkness, *1983; Richland County Public Library)*

Robert Silverberg (1935–)

See also the Silverberg entry in *DLB 8: Twentieth-Century American Science-Fiction Writers.*

Robert Silverberg's prolific career has established him as a classic science-fiction author. Most of his work for Bobbs-Merrill, however, came at a time when he was dissatisfied with the artistic and monetary rewards of that genre and had turned to nonfiction as well. Shadrach in the Furnace *(1976) is speculative fiction of the kind that made Silverberg famous, a story ably told and with a philosophical dimension.*

BOBBS-MERRILL BOOKS BY SILVERBERG: *Kublai Khan, Lord of Xanadu,* as Walker Chapman (Indianapolis: Bobbs-Merrill, 1966);

The Golden Dream: Seekers of El Dorado, as Chapman (Indianapolis: Bobbs-Merrill, 1967); abridged as *The Search for El Dorado,* as Chapman (Indianapolis: Bobbs-Merrill, 1967);

The Longest Voyage: Circumnavigators in the Age of Discovery (Indianapolis: Bobbs-Merrill, 1972);

Shadrach in the Furnace (New York: Bobbs-Merrill, 1976; London: Gollancz, 1977).

OTHER: *Antarctic Conquest: The Great Explorers in Their Own Words,* edited, with an introduction, by Silverberg, as Walker Chapman (Indianapolis: Bobbs-Merrill, 1965).

Audrey Thomas (1935–)

See also the Thomas entry in *DLB 60: Canadian Writers Since 1960, Second Series.*

Bobbs-Merrill published the first four books of Audrey Callahan Thomas. Her fiction is largely autobiographical, drawing on her experiences in Upper New York State, Africa, and Canada, where she settled in 1959. Because of Thomas's narrative inventiveness, her works are considered experimental. Songs My Mother Taught Me *(1973), the last of her Bobbs-Merrill books, is actually a revision of a novel written earlier in her career.*

BOBBS-MERRIL BOOKS BY THOMAS: *Ten Green Bottles: Short Stories* (Indianapolis: Bobbs-Merrill, 1967);

Mrs. Blood (Indianapolis: Bobbs-Merrill, 1970);

Audrey Thomas (photograph by Bill Schermbrucker; from dust jacket of Thomas, The Wild Blue Yonder, *1990; Richland County Public Library)*

Munchmeyer, and Prospero on the Island (Indianapolis: Bobbs-Merrill, 1971);
Songs My Mother Taught Me (Indianapolis: Bobbs-Merrill, 1973).

Jack Vance (1916–)

See also the Vance entry in *DLB 8: Twentieth-Century American Science-Fiction Writers.*

John Holbrook "Jack" Vance has published many works of science fiction, fantasy, and mystery. By the time he entered the Bobbs-Merrill list his awards included the Edgar Allan Poe, the Hugo, and the Nebula. Vance's first three titles for the company were mysteries. The Gray Prince *(1974) is part of an open series set thirty thousand years in the future and is marked by the didactic strain of his later fiction.*

Jack Vance (copyright MC Valeda; from John Clute, Science Fiction: The Illustrated Encyclopedia, *1995; Bruccoli Clark Layman Archives)*

BOBBS-MERRILL BOOKS BY VANCE: *The Fox Valley Murders,* as John Holbrook Vance (Indianapolis: Bobbs-Merrill, 1966; London: Hale, 1967);
The Pleasant Grove Murders (Indianapolis: Bobbs-Merrill, 1967; London: Hale, 1968);
The Deadly Isles (Indianapolis: Bobbs-Merrill, 1969; London: Hale, 1970);
The Gray Prince (Indianapolis: Bobbs-Merrill, 1974; London: Coronet, 1976).

Appendix

The Autobiography of D. Laurance Chambers

Appendix: The Autobiography of D. Laurance Chambers

Apart from two stray leaves, D. Laurance Chambers's brief and unfinished reminiscences are in the possession of his granddaughter Diana Leslie and consist of two batches. The first, reproduced by kind permission of Mrs. Leslie, is covered by a slip marked "Autobiography." The sheets are handwritten, apart from a 1904 lease and two citations for honorary degrees. They are not in order but are composed of several blocks of memories that are here rearranged chronologically. Otherwise, the text is quoted verbatim. Editorial insertions are indicated by braces (< >) because Chambers uses brackets in the text. The sheet dealing with the 1904 rental is marked "9-7-56"; those for his 1929 illness and the Kin Hubbard/Meredith Nicholson anecdote, "12-26-55"; those on Chambers's 1940 reunion down to the lament about bridge, "6-1-56" and "6-2-56." The second batch, not included here, includes documents pertaining to the attempt to get Princeton University to grant him an honorary degree.

Two handwritten leaves, headed "5-7-56," are in the "Writings" file in the Bobbs-Merrill archives at The Lilly Library. This group of anecdotes (from Allen Johnson's book to Laurel Tarkington's death) has been kept intact and is inserted among the rest in the proper chronological position.

Chambers's correspondence with Henry Van Dyke (at Princeton) reveals that the dispute over Poems of Tennyson *(1903), which they co-edited, had to do with his getting his name on the cover of the book and on all publishers' announcements. Chambers was the son-in-law of Thomas Taggart, owner of the French Lick Springs Hotel and an important Democratic politician. Among other things, Taggart was mayor of Indianapolis three times and a U.S. senator in 1916, filling an unexpired term. A glossary added at the end expands upon some of the other persons and titles Chambers mentions. J. Kent Calder assisted in editing the memoir.*

Autobiography

I was born on a snowy Sunday morning. Mother used to say that they thought of naming me January.

Of vacations in my childhood I recall one with some Clayton cousins on a farm after I'd had "inflammation of the bowels"–I suppose appendicitis; and one at Rock Enon Springs in the mountains of northern Virginia. It was some distance from the railroad to the resort hotel, which was covered by stagecoach. Father enlivened the trip by giving the rebel yell at intervals. He made a great hit with the ladies by his psychic demonstrations. One would be sent from the room. The others would then tell him what they wanted her to do. She would be called in, he would put his hands very lightly on her shoulders, and after a few false starts she would do as mentioned–pick a handkerchief off a chair, or whatever. This was at the time of Oscar Wilde's visit to America and there was an Oscar Wilde craze. Ted went to a hotel party with a sunflower in his buttonhole. As for me, I was miserable because I once used dirty or cross words. Mother made me so ashamed that they hung on my conscience for a long time. Halfway up a mountain, or high hill, one day I met up with a rattlesnake coming out of an opening in the rocks. Some men arrived in a hurry to my rescue and killed the rattler.

I must have been about ten years old when Ted and I spent a vacation at Deer Park on the B. & O. in West Virginia. Ted had got up to the finals in a tennis tournament when we were summoned home because May had typhoid fever & was out of her head. We boys were put up in the Rudolph Kauffmann house on 16th Street. May's hair was cut off.

Beginning with the second grade and skipping one grade (I think the third) I went through to the eighth in Washington. Mary Macartney had taught me <?> my letters on the third floor at home. I can remember the names of some of my teachers–Ella Macartney whose brother John married my aunt Laura; they were parents of Kate and James; Ella later married Dr. Lane, superintendent of Central High School); Miss Archer <Maher?>; Miss McGill–and some of the boys and girls–Aubry Lanston whose father invented the Lanston Linotype and whom I thoroughly despised; Guy Merean; Quirof Harlow–his father & uncle went through the alphabet giving their children unique names; they had got down to Quirof and Rolvix in my time; Emily Eckfeldt; Olive Schreiner–famous name; Constance Adams; Esther Bartlett who had an eye for the boys–when she married money in Pittsburgh there was a scandal because her bridal bouquet got caught in the best man's stud. She was called "the Violet Bride." She dropped me for a boy in long pants.

I went first to the Denison School Building on S Street between 13th and 14th and then to the Barrett Building at the corner of Q and 14th.

Of the neighborhood boys I recall especially Ned Brady, a little older than I, who lived next door; the Barringers, Laurence and John–Laurence became an official of General Electric–and the Curtises. William Elroy Curtis was Washington correspondent of the Chicago Daily News, where his story appeared daily for years over his byline in the first column on the front page. George, my age, had heart disease, evidenced by blue lips. His funeral was the first, I think, that I ever attended. Elroy was a classmate at Princeton and the last person to call me "Tim." How that nickname started among the boys on Q Street I can't imagine. We played games in the street–Prisoner's Base, etc.–and wherever there was a vacant lot. I can recall brushes with the Burnett boys–sons of Frances Hodgson Burnett. Lionel was a good sort, but Vivian–such names!–who was the original of Little Lord Fauntleroy–was a perfect pest. I detested manual training, in which I had to take a course in the Franklin School downtown.

After grade school I went to the Columbian Preparatory School, which was on H Street near 14th. It was a small school and one got, if one wanted it, a thorough training from the five or six teachers–Jackson, Burke (?), Alden, Hodgkins, Chichester (?)–nothing inspired, but thorough.

When I graduated from Columbian Prep I got a lot of medals–Evey had them for a long time on her dining-room wall–because the competition wasn't stiff. Best fellow in the school was Stanton C. Peeble, whose father came from Indpls and was Judge of the Court of Claims. Stanton became a well-known Washington lawyer.

I might have gone to college in 1895 but I wouldn't be seventeen till the next January and I was thought (wisely enough) too young. That fall Ted and I took a trip to the Pacific Coast, traveling on passes which Father got because he represented the Huntington railroad in Washington. I was miserably sick at Salt Lake City on the way out for a couple of days. In San Francisco we were quite feted by Mr. Mills <?> of the Southern Pacific. At San Bernardino, a girl who had taken a fancy to Ted, showered fruit on us. We got to Mariposa at night after an all-day ride through dust in a stagecoach. There was a cavalry detachment there. They put us on great cavalry horses and galloped us into the Yosemite Valley. I recall the giant redwoods, Sutro Park in San Francisco, Del Monte and the marvelous drive along the coast at Monterey, the new college at Palo Alto (Stanford), the raw town of <*illegible*>. We came east on the Southern Pacific across the desert to New Orleans, of which I can picture in memory only the cemeteries with graves above ground; and then to Atlanta where there was a world's fair or something of the sort. Of that no trace remains in my mind. What stands out is getting into a sleeper at night–it had been shut up all day–and being eaten alive by mosquitoes. The only other comparable encounter in my experience was when I visited the birthplace of Grover Cleveland at Caldwell, New Jersey. But mosquitoes were pretty bad in Washington, and very bad at Cape May and Spring Lake, New Jersey, where we spent several summer vacations.

At Princeton I was a greasy grind, an objectionable character. Having got all first groups the first term, I set sail to keep up this record, a form of egotism which I now despise, all the more because I accomplished it. This accomplishment was not due to my exceptional intelligence but to the development of a parrotlike memory–an unintelligent matter. There were subjects about which I understood little, like Billy Magee's courses in Mechanics and Physics, but in an exam, if I could spot about where in the textbook the answer to a question began and ended, I could spin it off almost word for word. I had to be careful

Bliss Perry (Bruccoli Clark Layman Archives)

lest my dumbness would show itself in my covering too much ground–overanswering the question.

Courses at Princeton that I remember with gratitude were: Freshman English Composition with Bliss Perry (he introduced me to the English novel; I read Middlemarch, The Return of the Native, The Ordeal of Richard Feverel and one other–what?); and seminars with him in Senior year in the dramas of Byron and Shelley; and in Browning; a Sophomore course with George M. Harper in French literature, and a seminar course some time with Livy Westcott in which I read J. Caesar's Civil Wars and Cicero's letters. <*In margin:* "Also one with Thomas Marc Parrott on Shakespeare".> Westcott's freshman course in Livy was stuffy. Since he was called Livy, his assistant was called "Titi" Smith. (Titi Livi on the back of the text book.) I read Tacitus with excitement and became proficient enough to read Plautus and Terence without translating–a play in an evening. With Westcott and his good-looking wife I grew very friendly, often dining at his house on Sundays. Squirt Daniels was a distant relative; he was kind but I didn't take to Economics.

Math always came hard though I admired the steel-like precision of Harry Fine's mind. The math. tutor in Freshman year was called "Bull" Hinton. He was an Englishman and he must have been smart for he invented a baseball gun which was used to save pitchers' arms. But his pay could have been only a pittance. He wore a long blue coat which came halfway down to his knees. He would go to the blackboard and cover it with figures. Then he'd say, "No; that isn't right," erase them with his hands and wipe his hands on the back of his coat. While his back was turned the boys would let fly with erasers all over the room.

On Sundays I can recall seeing Bull and Mrs. Hinton walk to church on Nassau Street, followed by five or six children all dressed alike, as from a charity institution.

A Greek course in Demosthenes and Aeschylus given by Sister Orris was awful. Amid the clamor of the bored students he would say plaintively, "Bear with me, gentlemen." In a little box which he kept in his room over a store on Nassau Street he had what he claimed were bones of Agamemnon. The current quip was that they couldn't be anyone else's bones, so they must be Agamemnon's. But he had a fine Italian painting or two.

When I was an undergraduate at Princeton I took all the pre-Law courses I could get. It was Father's idea and mine that after graduation I should study law at Columbian (now George Washington) University Law School and read in the office of Darlington & Somebody, a leading firm. Besides Woodrow Wilson's wonderful lecture courses on Constitutional Government and Jurisprudence, I took his English Common Law, which was as dull as dishwater, for he dictated every word and every word we had to write down. Livy Westcott gave a course in Roman Law, which was much more interesting. My examination paper pleased him; he said I was entitled to several days rest afterward.

I regret that I did not take Winans course in the Odyssey at Princeton. The men who did felt an enthusiasm for Homer. All I read was the first four or five books of the Iliad. I never had enough Greek to get a real feel for the language, only an unsatisfied taste. Harper's course in Shakespeare must have been interesting, and Paul van Dyke on the Renaissance quaintly refreshing. I did get some sense of English poetry and French prose literature, but I think the taste for English literature must have been largely on my own, except for what Bliss Perry gave me. John Finley came to Princeton from Knox College, where he had been president, or professor of Politics. His first lecture created a campus sensation; the second was not quite so good; then his material began to peter out. Perry left Princeton for Harvard and later became editor of the Atlantic Monthly. Finley became Editor of the New York Times. I used to run across him in New York (he was a great walker; tramped all over the Holy Land). He always knew me, though I hadn't taken his course, and sometimes we'd walk along together and chat.

I left Princeton knowing nothing about music or art. History, which in my later years has taken so much of my reading time, was most indifferently taught. The prof., whose name I can't remember–Coney, or something like that–had an impediment in his speech. Children in freshman and sophomore years of high school have far better courses in the range of world history, far better written and illustrated texts, than could be enjoyed in my time at college.

When I was graduated I didn't know what I wanted to do or was good for, if anything, but it was quite clear to me that I didn't want to be a lawyer. Father was greatly disappointed. Winning the Charles Scribner Fellowship in English inclined me to English studies. I thought a little of teaching and there was a vague sort of opportunity at Wells College, but they were indifferent about it and so was I.

In the year after graduation I became secretary to Henry van Dyke, Professor of English Poetry. I knew no system of shorthand but invented my own and wrote his letters out in long hand. (I do not recall having to rewrite any but suppose I did.) I worked with him on a selection of Poems of Tennyson in Ginn's Atheneum Series. He did the introduction and I the notes. When proofs came along without my name on the title page I got sore. Henry had the Ginn editor write me a letter of severe reprimand. But my name went on the title page in smaller letters than Henry's. I do not recall my emolument–no royalties.

Bobbs-Merrill in the fall of 1902, or rather I think the spring of 1903, asked him to read the manuscript of a novel about the Exodus, by Elizabeth Miller, called The

POEMS OF TENNYSON

EDITED BY

HENRY VAN DYKE

AND

D. LAURANCE CHAMBERS, A.M.

ASSISTANT IN ENGLISH, PRINCETON UNIVERSITY

GINN AND COMPANY

BOSTON · NEW YORK · CHICAGO · LONDON
ATLANTA · DALLAS · COLUMBUS · SAN FRANCISCO

Henry Van Dyke (from Thomas B. Reed, ed., Modern Eloquence, *1900); title page for the 1903 book over which Van Dyke quarreled with his assistant (Thomas Cooper Library, University of South Carolina)*

Yoke. He said he was too busy, but he had an assistant who might. I reported at length on The Yoke, and after that they sent me at intervals one or two other scripts. The work seemed down my alley. I asked if they had an opening. No; but they'd keep me in mind. My correspondence, I think, was with Jacobs, not Howland.

Armed with letters of introduction from van Dyke, I went up to New York and interviewed Messrs. Charles and Arthur Scribner, and old Mr. Scott at the Century Co. They used almost identical words: "Young man, if you want to make money, don't go into the publishing business."

Through Henry's influence I got a job in the summer of 1903 with the Curtis Publishing Company in Philadelphia as assistant to the managing editor of the Ladies' Home Journal, a Mr. Alexander who had been a real estate broker in Boston. It was a hot summer, awfully hot in the room I rented in some Main Line suburb, a place I think called Avalon. And I was bored with the idea of working on a woman's paper, which seemed very effeminate. I couldn't make out what the job called for. Maybe it had been invented to please van Dyke, whose popularity with the ladies was great. All I can now recall doing was to write tags to go at the end of stories or articles.

After three weeks I got a wire from Indianapolis in August asking, if I was still interested in a job, would I come out for an interview? I took it to Alexander for advice. He said, "Chambers, the Editor-in-Chief [Mr. Edward Bok] is the kind of man who is liable to come in any morning and fire the lot of us, including me. Go west, young man." When I talked with Mr. Bok he spoke of the quiet homes of Indianapolis, on Meridian and Delaware Streets, each with a little land around it, and thought I'd like the place.

My interview with W. C. Bobbs in Indpls resulted in his offering me a job as his secretary, which I was happy to accept. I went home for a couple of weeks and then returned to start work in September 1903.

The first book I got for Bobbs-Merrill was At the Big House (1904), by Anne Virginia Culbertson, whom I had known in Zanesville. They were good stories in the manner of Uncle Remus. Most of these Negro tales seem to have had an Indian origin. Now the unhistorically minded Negrophiles rant and rave at thick dialect. At the Big House was followed by Banjo Talks, a collection of rhymes, not so good. Neither book did much.

But the next book I secured was Knights of the Silver Shield and Other Stories by my Columbian Prep teacher, Raymond Macdonald Alden. It was soon retitled Why the Chimes Rang and Other Stories, still in print and still selling well after more than fifty years. Nothing like a hardy perennial to give satisfaction in juvenile publishing.

. . . .

Carl McCulloch was the literary doctor. Riley, Tarkington, Nicholson were among his patients, and all owed much to him.

For four months October 1, 1904 to February 1, 1905, Norman & Colin Macbeth, Ralph Hale and I lived together in a house on Meridian St., the block where the Scottish Rite Cathedral now stands. We had a cook-housekeeper. Norman Macbeth, romantic figure with a background of life in India, became engaged to Lucia Holliday but was paying a lot of attention to Eleanor Lemcke. He & Colin were in the Atlas Engine Works. Later Norman married Lucia, went to live in Los Angeles, where after many years they were divorced and Lucia returned to Indpls. Colin went back to England and in time became manager of the Dunlop Tire Co. Hale I had known at my three weeks on the Ladies' Home Journal. I got him a job as assistant Trade Editor for B. M. He brought his bride Margaret here; she had a neurotic fear of the outdoors, especially of dogs. They stuck about for a while and then went back to Boston, where Ralph was for a time American agent for the Medici Prints and later founded the publishing house of Hays, Cushman & Flint.

While on a visit to this country in the 40s Colin got this lease from Hale and sent it to me. *<The lease, signed by all parties on 30 June 1904, is included with the memoirs.>*

Allen Johnson was well along with a book on The Principles of Historical Evidence. I'd like to have it to refer to. <*In margin next to this paragraph:* "1924.">

Sir Harry Johnston worked on a novel to be called Relations and on a history of the colonial relations of the white peoples. I had Aley, in England for us, go see Sir Harry.

Mary Converse working for us in editorial department, very young, pretty, sensitive, she married soon and went to live in a New York suburb.

Arthur Stringer<'s> selection of the ten most entertaining books (this was for something called the Year-Round Bookselling Plan):

1. Tess
2. The Egoist
3. Vanity Fair
4. The Golden Treasury
5. Spring Floods (Turgenev)
6. Huckleberry Finn
7. Hamlet
8. Browning's Dramatic Lyrics
9. Keats' Poems
10. Anthon's Classical Dictionary

On Oct 20 <*In margin:* "1923.">, Stringer wrote me: "There'd be a great publicity stunt in having Joe Dunn have some skeptical couple take off their clothes and go into the woods and see how long they could survive–as that chap Knowles did up in Maine about twelve years ago and had the world on tiptoe when he came out.

This led to the most outrageous publicity stunt with which I ever had aught to do. A young man and a girl were induced to go up empty-handed into the Pocono Hills. It made the front pages in New York and elsewhere. But I'm afraid it didn't sell so many Empty Hands! <*In margin next to this paragraph:* "1923">

I went to see Edward Lucas White, the author of El Supremo and Andivius Hedulio on Sept 22 in Baltimore, where he taught in a Latin school. Later he submitted to us a novel called Aithre about Helen of Troy, but we were not taken with it as we were later with Erskine's Private Life, though he too had Helen and Menelaus and the rest talking English and not the preposterous jargon used by most writers of romances with classical settings and characters. <*In margin next to this paragraph:* "1223 Mt. Royal Ave.">

It was I who suggested to Brand Whitlock that he revise The Turn of the Balance for a new edition.

I called Albert Edward Wiggam of Vernon, Indiana, "Prince." He was a great friend of Glenn Frank, whom Howland succeeded as editor of the Century, which he had pretty well ruined, when Frank became President of the University of Wisconsin, where he served without distinction.

Laurel Tarkington died on April 13, 1923. "A merciful end to a sad little journey in the world," Howland wrote Harry Webster.

After the purchase of the Bobbs stock and the public sale of stock I was exhausted. In New York on a business trip in July I was taken ill while lunching with Tim Coward at the Vanderbilt and said I'd have to get out of there quick. Tim took me to the Duane and called his doctor (? Coffin) who arrived late in the afternoon. He sent me to St. Luke's Hospital, where they gave me various tests and massages without finding the root of the trouble. A Dr. Goodman, on the hospital staff and junior partner of Teddy Roosevelt's physician Dr. <*lacuna*>, came in for a look at me one Sunday morning. He said, "Were the palms of your hands dry when you caved in at the Vanderbilt?"

I said, "That's funny. They were. I noticed it. What made you think of that."

He said, "Tomorrow you have a metabolism test."

The test proved that I was a hyperthyroid case. I was given thyroid extract and ordered to take a long rest without thought of business.

A great depression had settled on me, "alone in the big season." The family came on and was I glad to see them. We went to the Grand Central to take the train for Hyannisport. Ralph Waldo Trine and his wife showed up at the station and he insisted on engaging me in prolonged talk. Standing and weak, I did not feel in tune with the Infinite.

At Hyannisport the depression hung on. I sat for hours in the sun, as per doctors' orders, on the terrace by the garden back of the cottage, and occasionally with little on would lie in the little fenced-in sty <?> on top of the Taggarts' big white house where I could look up and see nothing but the white clouds racing by the blue sky. Suddenly, after seven weeks, I felt better. I'm well now, I said, and went back to work in September. <*Lower portion trimmed from this sheet.*>

<*On a half sheet:*> Kin Hubbard was with Will Fortune and Meredith Nicholson on the trip to New Orleans when they stopped off at Nashville on the way home and laid a wreath on the tomb of James K. Polk at two o'clock of a Sunday morning after a party at Evelyn Norton's florist shop.

Among Abe Martin's sayings two linger in my mind:

"Fawn Lippincott is confined to the house with a swollen chiffonier."

[During the Prohibition Era] "Tilford Moots was awakened last night by burglars singing in the cellar." <*End half sheet.*>

The favorite poems of Princeton 1900 at graduation were (1) Tennyson; (2) Longfellow; (3) Shakespeare; (4) Kipling; (5) Riley and Milton tied. In 1939 they were (1) Kipling; (2) Browning; (3) Shakespeare; (4) Keats. Exclamation points.

My biography for the 40th reunion was written by Karl Burr of Columbus, Ohio with assistance from David and possibly from Will Thompson, with whom he had worked on some important law cases (? Bell Telephone). It is flattering enough to be an obituary. Nice if it were true! The facts per se are correct.

"Anyone recalling Laurance Chambers' winning of various undergraduate prizes for honors in oratory, literature, essays and debate–he was also Latin Salutatorian and Class Orator at Commencement–will not be surprized to learn that his life's work, started so signally during college years, has run true to form thereafter. Indeed, not satisfied with his A.B. degree, he was Charles Scribner Fellow at Princeton during 1900 and 1901, received his Master's Degree there and rubbed shoulders during the period with such literati as Dr. Henry van Dyke, for whom he was secretary, and others without number.

"In 1903 he joined the well-known firm of Bobbs-Merrill Company, publishers, with headquarters at Indpls, and while his career there could not exactly be styled 'From Printer's Devil to President,' he nevertheless did progress through the various departments of that very interesting and successful company until his election as President in 1935, followed by his election to the position of Chairman of the Board two years later. Thus, when this sketch is published, he will be rounding out 37 years of continuous service with that company.

"Under his direction the company has published books for Mrs. Woodrow Wilson (My Memoirs, published in March 1939); former Vice-President Marshall; former Secretary of State Lansing; Admiral Hugh Rodman; André Lardieu; Premier Nitti and former Foreign Minister Sforza, both of Italy; Viscount Samuel; Ramsay MacDonald; Lord David Cecil; Senators Beveridge, Tydings and Watson; Congressman Bruce Barton, et al., et al.,–an impressive list. Princeton authors for whom he has published books include George McLean Harper, Richard Halliburton, Benedict Thielen, Heath Bowman, David Cushman Coyle and many others.

"So much for his business, and now for its by-products. He is a member of the Council of the Princeton University Press, a former Vice-President and Director of the National Association of Book Publishers, a life member of the American Historical Ass'n, and a member of such clubs as the Players of New York, the Woodstock Club of Indpls (now ex), the Indpls Athletic Club, the Contemporary Club (now ex) and the Dramatic Club of Indpls, the latter founded by Booth Tarkington some fifty years ago.

"In 1932 Laurance was commissioned to write a history of the state, together with inscriptions to accompany the murals by Thomas Hart Benton depicting the social and industrial development of Indiana for its exhibition at the Chicago World's Fair. In 1937 he received the honorary degree of Litt.D. from Wabash College. It is too bad that space will not permit the insertion of the entire citation on that occasion, but by way of example, one sentence goes thus: 'You have encouraged young writers to persevere in their work and inspired young and old to strive for the attainment of their ideals.' Enough said.

"On the lighter side he is the very modest owner of a remarkably fine collection of postage stamps, fairly wallows in Civil War history and its battlefields, reads manuscripts and galley proofs with the same avidity that the ordinary mortal eats peanuts, plays a sound game of bridge, writes a bit of blithesome verse, and, as someone has said of him, 'still shuffles around a tennis court but will not run for a fast one.' Although insisting that he is tone-deaf, he is a Trustee of the First Baptist Church and Chairman of its Music Committee. Politically, he is a Carter Glass Democrat, and for some unknown reason is a Colonel on the staff of the Governor of Tennessee, of all things.

"In the matter of Princeton connections, his brother is a member of the Class of '90, his son a member of '34, son-in-law '37, and nephew '39.

"As might be expected, Laurance and his very charming lady live in a delightful house, filled with books and lovely old things. Their dinners recall the days of long ago when dining was an art, and there is a constant succession of interesting visitors who still find pleasure in the equally outmoded art of polite conversation. In these parlous times, when sanity, conversation and sound judgment are at such a premium, may Laurance and his kind not altogether perish from the earth.

"K. E. B."

In contrast with this Epicurean and rather smug picture read the account of Bob Carter's noble self-sacrificing life and death in the same volume.

Notes on the above after 16 years:

The Wabash citation (attached) hit on what still has given me the greatest pleasure in publishing–the encouragement of authors. Whether the results were good, bad or indifferent, I was always in a glow at the first firing and often kept puffing and blowing for a long while. This citation was much more to the point and better written than the Indiana University one (LL.D.–date?). It was Joe Daniels who suggested the idea to Wabash and I strongly believe he composed the citation. It came at a time when he was in love with Evelyn and her papa got letters after his name as a means of ingratiation. I never had the slightest notion who proposed the Indiana University adoption.

Bridge, which I always enjoyed though I was never a "book" player, never an expert, has become too much for me–I can't keep track of the cards–one of the minor humiliations of senility.

Wabash Citation 1937

David Laurance Chambers, graduate of Princeton University, now resident of the city of Indianapolis, we welcome you into the fellowship of Wabash men as you join the group whom the college has delighted to honor. Your scholarly capacities and interests have given to you an ever increasing skill and competence in the field of literature. Your conscientious and painstaking work as author, editor, and publisher, has been a strong factor in the literary taste of Indiana by giving to others wider acquaintance, broader interest, deeper appreciation and keener enjoyment, not only in the world of letters but also in the finer aspects of human relations and human conduct. You have encouraged young writers to persevere in their work and inspired young and old to strive for the attainment of their ideals. Because of your notable achievements within the realm of your activities and by virtue of the authority vested in me by the Board of Trustees I confer upon you the honorary degree of Doctor of Literature.

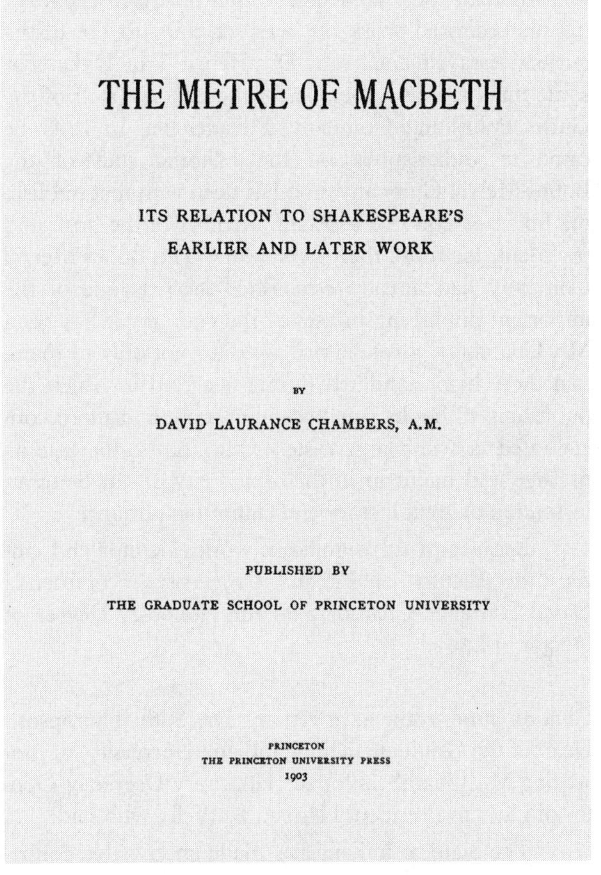
THE METRE OF MACBETH

ITS RELATION TO SHAKESPEARE'S EARLIER AND LATER WORK

BY

DAVID LAURANCE CHAMBERS, A.M.

PUBLISHED BY

THE GRADUATE SCHOOL OF PRINCETON UNIVERSITY

PRINCETON
THE PRINCETON UNIVERSITY PRESS
1903

Title page for Chambers's M.A. thesis as a Charles Scribner Fellow (courtesy of Diana Leslie)

<Indiana University Citation 1948>

Mr. President:

David Laurance Chambers was born in Washington, D.C., and received his university education in Princeton, where he took the degree Master of Arts in 1901. For his first editorial work, he was secretary to the distinguished essayist and poet, Dr. Henry Van Dyke. For some time he was a member of the editorial staff of the Curtis Publishing Company, Philadelphia. In 1903 he came to Indianapolis on the editorial staff of the Bobbs-Merrill Company, and has been with that publishing house as editorial assistant, member of the firm, and president, for more than forty years. The Bobbs-Merrill Company had already established itself as one of the important publishing houses of the country. It has been Mr. Chambers' great service as editor not only to maintain these high standards during a period in which the publishing of books was becoming more and more concentrated in a few large eastern cities, but to increase its prestige and maintain in the capital city of our State an institution of great literary and cultural importance.

Because of this significant work as editor and citizen, the Faculty of Indiana University recommends David Laurance Chambers for the Honorary Degree of Doctor of Laws.

- - - - - - - - - - - - -

Citation June 13th, as given by Dr. Stith Thompson, Dean of the Graduate School, Indiana University, in presenting Mr. Chambers for the Honorary Degree of Doctor of Laws to President Herman B. Wells, who said:

The State of Indiana has made an enviable contribution to the world of letters. This is one of its proudest achievements. David Laurance Chambers, you have done much to sustain our Hoosier literary tradition. In grateful appreciation of this and of your distinguished career as publisher, the University of your State is happy to have the privilege of conferring upon you the degree, Doctor of Laws, with all the rights and privileges thereto appertaining.

Glossary

Alexander: William V. Alexander.

Aley, Maxwell: literary adviser in Bobbs-Merrill's New York office.

Anthon: Charles Anthon.

Banjo Talks: *published in 1905.*

Bobbs stock: the public sale was in June 1929.

Burnett, Frances Hodgson: author best known for Little Lord Fauntleroy *(Scribners, 1886).*

Burr, Karl: wrote Chambers's biography for the 1900 Quadrigesimal Record.

Carter, Robert: a missionary doctor in the Philippines; he died in 1919.

Coney: John H. Coney.

Converse, Mary: unidentified.

Coward, Tim: Thomas R. Coward, the publisher.

Daniels, Squirt: Winthrop M. Daniels.

David: Chambers's son, David Laurance Jr.

Dunn, J. (Joseph) Allen: a Bobbs-Merrill novelist.

Empty Hands: *1924 book by Arthur Stringer.*

Evey: Chambers's daughter, Evelyn.

Fine, Harry: Henry B. Fine.

Finley: John H. Finley.

Fortune, Will: an Indianapolis businessman.

"Harper's course in Shakespeare" was more likely taught by James O. Murray or Bliss Perry.

Hays, Cushman & Flint: "Hays" should be "Hale."

Hinton, Bull: Charles H. Hinton.

Jacobs: unidentified.

Johnson, Allen: author of The Historian and Historical Evidence *(Scribners, 1926).*

Johnston, Sir Harry: author of Relations *(Chatto & Windus, 1925) and* The Backward Peoples and Our Relations with Them *(Oxford University Press, 1920).*

Knights of the Silver Shield and Other Stories: *published in 1906.*

Knowles, Joseph: author of Alone in the Wilderness *(Small, Maynard, 1913).*

Lanston Linotype: invented by Tolbert Lanston.

Magee, Billy: William F. Magie.

May: Chambers's sister.

Norton, Evelyn: unidentified.

Orris, Sister: S. Stanhope Orris.

Schreiner, Olive: the author of that name was famous for The Story of an African Farm *(Chapman & Hall, 1883).*

Scott: Frank H. Scott.

Smith, Titi: Charles S. Smith.

Tarkington, Laurel Louisa Fletcher: first wife of Booth Tarkington, whom she divorced in 1911.

Ted: Chambers's brother, Tilston F.

Trine, Ralph Waldo: author of In Tune With the Infinite *(Crowell, 1897).*

Webster, Harry: Henry Kitchell Webster.

Westcott, Livy: John H. Westcott.

White, Edward Lucas: E. P. Dutton published El Supremo *(1916) and* Andivius Hedulio *(1921); George H. Doran published "Aithre" as* Helen *in 1925, the same year as John Erskine's* The Private Life of Helen of Troy.

Why the Chimes Rang and Other Stories: *published in 1908.*

Wiggam, Albert Edward: author of several Bobbs-Merrill books, including The New Decalogue of Science *(1923).*

Winans: Samuel R. Winans.

Yoke, The: *published in 1904.*

The Bobbs-Merrill Archives

Housed at The Lilly Library, the "Bobbs-Merrill MSS" are open, free of charge, to all visitors with legitimate research interests. Inquiries should be addressed to the Manuscripts Department, The Lilly Library, Indiana University, Bloomington, IN 47405. A brief description is available on-line at the library's website.

Donation of Howard W. Sams (1964)

A mimeographed "Complete Back List of Adult Titles from Bobbs-Merrill" extends to 1961. Under each author is an alphabetical list of titles, with years of contract or publication and of sale to foreign publishers or reprint houses, together with book clubs, paperback publishers, appearances in magazines and newspapers, and motion-picture and dramatic rights. A separate list covers "Children's Titles." The other records are in boxes or ledgers as follows:

Author files (material is generally fullest from about 1903 to 1960)	198 boxes
Readers' reports (for books never published)	9 boxes
Childhood of Famous Americans series	1 box
Complete Books of the Outdoors series	1 box
Law Series (correspondence)	1 box
Business Correspondence 1907–1959, including The College Book Exchange, The FTC, Reid vs. Bobbs-Merrill (1950s), etc. (actually begins 1885)	2 boxes
Bobbs-Merrill Chronological Correspondence 1900–1959 (actually begins 1909)	2 boxes
Writings (miscellaneous, regarding the company)	1 box
Printed (miscellaneous)	2 boxes
Book Store Accounts, including W. K. Stewart & Co. correspondence, etc. (1909–1958)	2 boxes
Salesmen (correspondence 1925–1957)	1 box
Unidentified Fragments, etc.	1 box
Record of Education Publications (1913–1917)	1 volume
Royalties (1898–1939)	43 volumes
Juvenile Promotions	3 boxes
Bobbs-Merrill/Curtis Brown (London literary agent)	6 boxes
Minutes of Stockholders Meetings (1885–1947)	1 volume
Minutes of Board of Directors Meetings (1913–1935)	3 volumes
General Ledgers (1893–1902, 1908–1909, 1914–1915; financial)	3 volumes
Author Ledgers (1909–1918)	2 volumes
Newspaper Story Purchases (1902–1924, arranged by state)	1 box
Drama and Production Rights (1902–1922)	1 box
Miscellaneous Letters (1908–1940)	1 box
Dramatic Ledger (1911)	1 volume
Record of Publications (1896–1906)	1 volume
Dramatic and Syndicate Sales (1918)	1 volume
Business Records (loose leaves)	1 folder

Donation of Macmillan and Company (1993)

Some of the records that had passed to Macmillan after the dissolution of Bobbs-Merrill in 1985 were donated to The Lilly Library by Charles Scribner III. They comprise twenty-two boxes of author files extending to that year. The twenty-first box has a few miscellaneous business records, and the twenty-second contains only children's writers. There is a finding list of the authors. Most of the major literary figures still active in 1985 are not among those in the archives.

A Representative Author File: Jane Harvey Houlson

This author was chosen at random. Because she published only once with Bobbs-Merrill (*Blue Blaze: Danger and Delight in Strange Islands of Honduras,* 1934), her file is simpler than most, containing just three folders:

"Biographical material": questionnaire (the form Houlson filled in with a typewriter and a mimeographed copy), photographs, brochure for a lecture tour, "Very brief synopsis of idea for an address" (two-page carbon copy), and a batch of clippings.

"Correspondence and royalties, 1933–38": sixty-five pieces of the former, eleven of the latter.

"Reader's report, pro[motional]. mat[erial].": eight-page reader's report by J. E. Armstrong on *Blue Blaze,* sketch of title design, sheet of calculations, "Suggested Titles," proof of dust-jacket flaps, two carbon drafts of same, author's copy of suggested dust-jacket blurb, five pages of advertising copy and mimeograph of same, carbon of quotation from *Vanity Fair* review, and a checklist of newspapers.

Author files from the Sams donation typically contain one or more of the following, in addition to items of the kind listed above: trial and final dust jackets, original artwork for illustrations, interoffice memos, book designs, store displays, illustrated advertising copy, mailers, and movie tie-ins. They do not, however, contain manuscripts, which were customarily disposed of as the author wished. Not every *Bowen*-Merrill author is represented in these files, and author correspondence is generally spotty until the 1910s.

Bibliography

This list does not include works cited as documentary texts or the standard biographical dictionaries used without citation for the author entries.

Bruccoli, Matthew J., and Richard Layman. *Ring W. Lardner: A Descriptive Bibliography.* Pittsburgh: University of Pittsburgh Press, 1976.

Cady, Edwin H., ed. "Studies in the Bobbs-Merrill Papers." *Indiana University Bookman,* no. 8 (March 1967).

Calder, J. Kent. "Ordeal and Renewal: David Laurance Chambers, Hiram Haydn, and *Lie Down in Darkness.*" *Journal of Scholarly Publishing,* 27 (1996): 171–182.

Crunden, Robert M. *A Hero in Spite of Himself: Brand Whitlock in Art, Politics, & War.* New York: Knopf, 1969.

Fitzpatrick, Vincent. *Gerald W. Johnson: From Southern Liberal to National Conscience.* Baton Rouge: Louisiana State University Press, 2002.

Hackett, Alice Payne, and James Henry Burke. *80 Years of Best Sellers, 1895–1975.* New York: R. R. Bowker, 1977.

Hart, Irving H. "The One Hundred Leading Authors of Best Sellers in Fiction from 1895 to 1944." *Publishers' Weekly,* 149 (19 January 1946): 285–290.

Holloway, W. R. *Indianapolis: A Historical and Statistical Sketch of the Railroad City.* Indianapolis: Indianapolis Journal Print, 1870.

Kautz, John. "A Literary Friendship." The Lilly Library, Indiana University, ca. 1967.

Madison, Charles A. *Book Publishing in America.* New York: McGraw-Hill, 1966.

Mauck, Virginia L., and James W. Hipp. "The Bobbs-Merrill Archive at the Lilly Library, Indiana University." In *Dictionary of Literary Biography Yearbook,* 1990. Detroit: Bruccoli Clark Layman/Gale, 1991.

Mendelson, Anne. *Stand Facing the Stove: The Story of the Women Who Gave America The Joy of Cooking.* New York: Holt, 1996.

Merrill, Catharine. *Catharine Merrill, Life and Letters,* edited by Katharine Merrill Graydon. Greenfield, Ind.: Mitchell, 1934.

Murray, Timothy D. "The Bobbs-Merrill Company." In *American Literary Publishing Houses, 1900–1980: Trade and Paperback,* edited by Peter Dzwonkoski. Dictionary of Literary Biography, volume 46. Detroit: Bruccoli Clark Layman/Gale, 1986.

Murray. "Bowen-Merrill Company." In *American Literary Publishing Houses, 1638–1899,* edited by Dzwonkoski. Dictionary of Literary Biography, volume 49. Detroit: Bruccoli Clark Layman/Gale, 1986.

O'Bar, Jack W. "A History of the Bobbs-Merrill Company, 1850–1940; With a Postlude through the Early 1960s." Dissertation, Indiana University, 1975. Published in part as "The Old Merrill Bookstore: Its Indianapolis Background and History and Its Relationship to the Bobbs-Merrill Company," *Journal of Library History,* 20 (Fall 1985): 408–426; and "The Origins and History of the Bobbs-Merrill Company," *Occasional Papers [University of Illinois Graduate School of Library and Information Science],* no. 172 (December 1985).

Perinn, Vincent L. *Ayn Rand: First Descriptive Bibliography.* Rockville, Md.: Quill & Brush, 1990.

Russo, Anthony J., and Dorothy R. Russo. *A Bibliography of James Whitcomb Riley.* Indianapolis: Indiana Historical Society, 1944.

Russo, Dorothy R. *A Bibliography of George Ade, 1866–1944.* Indianapolis: Indiana Historical Society, 1947.

Russo, Dorothy R., and Thelma L. Sullivan. *Bibliographical Studies of Seven Authors of Crawfordsville, Indiana: Lew and Susan Wallace, Maurice and Will Thompson, Mary Hannah and Caroline Virginia Krout, and Meredith Nicholson.* Indianapolis: Indiana Historical Society, 1952.

Stewart, Lotys Benning. "They Achieve: Minds and Hands of Indianapolis Women at Work for Others, (No. 3) Jessica Brown Mannon." *Indianapolis Star,* 30 March 1941, p. 4.

Stillson, Blanche, and Dorothy R. Russo. *Abe Martin–Kin Hubbard: A Study of a Character and His Creator Intended Primarily as a Check List of the Abe Martin Books.* Indianapolis: Hoosier Bookshop, 1939.

Tebbell, John. *A History of Book Publishing in the United States,* 4 volumes. New York: R. R. Bowker, 1972–1981.

Tucker, Glenn. "Laurance Chambers: The Man Who Knew Books–and Their Writers." *Indianapolis Star Magazine,* 20 April 1975, pp. 26, 28–31.

Vonnegut, Theodore Franklin. *Indianapolis Booksellers and Their Literary Background, 1822–1860, and a Glimpse of the "Old Book" Trade of Indianapolis.* Greenfield, Ind.: Mitchell, 1926.

Weber, Olga S., and Stephen J. Calvert. *Literary and Library Prizes,* tenth edition. New York: Bowker, 1980.

Williams, Susan Millar. *A Devil and a Good Woman, Too: The Lives of Julia Peterkin.* Athens: University of Georgia Press, 1997.

Cumulative Index

Dictionary of Literary Biography, Volumes 1-291
Dictionary of Literary Biography Yearbook, 1980-2002
Dictionary of Literary Biography Documentary Series, Volumes 1-19
Concise Dictionary of American Literary Biography, Volumes 1-7
Concise Dictionary of British Literary Biography, Volumes 1-8
Concise Dictionary of World Literary Biography, Volumes 1-4

Cumulative Index

DLB before number: *Dictionary of Literary Biography,* Volumes 1-291
Y before number: *Dictionary of Literary Biography Yearbook,* 1980-2002
DS before number: *Dictionary of Literary Biography Documentary Series,* Volumes 1-19
CDALB before number: *Concise Dictionary of American Literary Biography,* Volumes 1-7
CDBLB before number: *Concise Dictionary of British Literary Biography,* Volumes 1-8
CDWLB before number: *Concise Dictionary of World Literary Biography,* Volumes 1-4

A

B

D

E

F

G

H

J

L

M

N

O

Q

S

T

U

V

W

ISBN 0-7876-6828-1
90000
9 780787 668280